D0015354

THE HISTORY OF ISRAEL

THE HISTORY OF ISRAEL

BY

MARTIN NOTH
Professor of Old Testament
University of Bonn

HARPER & BROTHERS
PUBLISHERS · NEW YORK

TRANSLATED FROM THE SECOND EDITION
OF 'GESCHICHTE ISRAELS'
BY STANLEY GODMAN

MADE IN GREAT BRITAIN
PRINTED BY R. & R. CLARK LTD EDINBURGH

CONTENTS

ABBREVIATIONS

AASOR	= Annual of the American Schools of Oriental Research
AfO	= Archiv für Orientforschung
ANET	= Ancient Near Eastern Texts Relating to the Old Testament edited by J. B. Pritchard (1950)
AO	= Der Alte Orient. Gemeinverständliche Darstellungen herausgegeben von der Vorderasiatisch-Ägyptischen Gesellschaft
AOB²	= H. Gressmann, Altorientalische Bilder zum Alten Testament, 2. Aufl. 1927
AOT²	= H. Gressmann, Altorientalische Texte zum Alten Testament, 2. Aufl. 1926
BASOR	= Bulletin of the American Schools of Oriental Research
BBLAK	= Beiträge zur biblischen Landes- und Altertumskunde
BHK	= Biblia Hebraica ed. R. Kittel
BRL	= K. Galling, Biblisches Reallexikon (Handbuch zum Alten Testament, I, 1) 1937
BWANT	= Beiträge zur Wissenschaft vom Alten und Neuen Testament
BZAW	= Beihefte zur Zeitschrift für die alttestamentliche Wissenschaft
EA	= J. A. Knudtzon, Die El-Amarna-Tafeln (1915)
HAT	= Handbuch zum Alten Testament
IEJ	= Israel Exploration Journal
JBL	= Journal of Biblical Literature
JPOS	= Journal of the Palestine Oriental Society
MVA(e)G	= Mitteilungen der Vorderasiatisch(-Ägyptischen) Gesellschaft
NKZ	= Neue Kirchliche Zeitschrift
PJB	= Palästinajahrbuch
RB	= Revue Biblique
TGI	= K. Galling, Textbuch zur Geschichte Israels (1950)
ThLZ	= Theologische Literaturzeitung
WAT	= M. Noth, Die Welt des Alten Testaments (² 1953)
WO	= Die Welt des Orients. Wissenschaftliche Beiträge zur Kunde des Morgenlandes
WZKM	= Wiener Zeitschrift für die Kunde des Morgenlandes
ZAW	= Zeitschrift für die alttestamentliche Wissenschaft
ZDMG	= Zeitschrift der Deutschen Morgenländischen Gesellschaft
ZDPV	= Zeitschrift des Deutschen Palästina-Vereins

INTRODUCTION

1. *'Israel'*

THE question what 'Israel', the subject of a 'History of Israel', actually was, is not so simple and obvious as not to require a few words of explanation at the very outset: and although the evidence on which the answer to the question is based will emerge only in the course of our presentation of the 'History of Israel', the very fact that the problem exists at all must be made clear and a provisional answer given that will enable us to define the object of our enquiry and the magnitude of our task.

All the information at our disposal serves to establish that 'Israel' was a historical reality with its own historical period, during which it was intimately involved in the multifarious life of the surrounding world. It can therefore be adequately understood only by historical research. It has to be remembered, however, that knowledge of the sequence of events which constitute the history of Israel within a definite period of time and of their relationship with one another and with the oriental history of the same era, which was so surpassingly rich in personalities and events, is only to some extent readily available since it has come down to us directly, whilst, as in every other sphere of history, where the evidence is more indirect, the never-ending concatenation of cause and effect must be reconstructed intuitively. In a history of 'Israel' the whole field has to be explored with the utmost thoroughness from every possible angle and by all the methods open to historical scholarship, precisely because 'Israel' is without question a historical reality.

The authenticity of that reality is not affected by the circumstance that in its history we also meet an element beyond the range of human understanding, things that cannot be ascribed to known causes and effects. An element of the inexplicable is in fact present in *all* human history and is bound to be present not merely because it is not even remotely possible to embrace the whole profusion of cause and effect even in the historical present, let alone in the past, and least of all the remote past, but above all because history is not merely a constant repetition of complicated concatenations of cause and effect if we believe that God is really active in history not simply as a πρῶτον κινοῦν but as the ever present Lord working within the superficial interplay of cause and effect[1]. Inevitably, therefore, there is an element of mystery, of the 'unhistorical', in all human history which makes its presence felt on the frontiers of all historical knowledge.

The history of 'Israel' is no exception to this general rule, yet in spite of, or possibly just because of, this it remains authentic history. It would, however, be too easy to assign all the obscure events in the history of 'Israel' to this 'unhistorical' sphere, possibly on the basis of some preconception of the true nature of 'Israel', since deeper historical insight and new possibilities of comparison with events in other areas of world history may easily throw light on what is at first apparently incomprehensible; and the historian's task is to be always seeking for possible comparisons and explanations, though he must also never forget the presence of the element of the 'unhistorical'.

The study of the history of the Orient, which has been proceeding for over a century now with such undreamt of success and with so many unexpected discoveries to its credit, has brilliantly illuminated the background of the history of 'Israel'; it has revealed how closely involved the history of 'Israel' was in the varied life and historical movements of the ancient Orient and it has supplied us with abundant material with which to compare events in the history of 'Israel', so that it is no longer possible to expound the history of 'Israel' as a whole or in detail without a knowledge of the history of the ancient Orient. There is hardly any event in the history of 'Israel' that is not clearly related to this ancient Oriental background, the roots of which do not have to be sought in the tumultuous history of the ancient Orient and for which parallels cannot be found in Israel's Oriental environment. These multifarious connections have illuminated the historical reality of 'Israel' with the utmost clarity and have taught us to understand better the historical tradition of the Old Testament in its far-reaching context and reality. They have often opened up surprising possibilities of comparison and sent us back to study the historical information of the Old Testament with renewed seriousness.

Yet in spite of all these historical connections and possibilities for comparison, 'Israel' still appears a stranger in the world of its own time, a stranger wearing the garments and behaving in the

[1] Cf. Karl Barth, *Die kirchliche Dogmatik*, III, 1 (1945), pp. 84 ff.

manner of its age, yet separate from the world it lived in, not merely in the sense that every historical reality has its own individual character, and therefore an element of uniqueness, but rather that at the very centre of the history of 'Israel' we encounter phenomena for which there is no parallel at all elsewhere, not because the material for comparison has not yet come to light but because, so far as we know, such things have simply never happened elsewhere. To make this fact clear will be one of the tasks we shall have to face in our presentation of the history of 'Israel'.

From this point of view the question as to what Israel actually was becomes even more urgent. Apart from a more specialised and circumscribed use of the name which arose later in a closely defined historical situation and in circumstances with which we are quite familiar (cf. p. 183) the name 'Israel' is used in the Old Testament tradition only as a collective term for a group of twelve tribes which had a separate history of their own. The name first occurs in the Old Testament where, in the course of a personifying description of prehistorical Israel, the father of the twelve ancestors and *heroes eponymi* of the tribes is called 'Israel' (Gen. xxxii, 29) and after that the name is used for this person or as a collective term. There is not a trace of evidence as to how the group of the twelve tribes acquired it and whether it had had a previous history in the course of which certain changes of meaning led to this collective name. It is, in any case, idle to make conjectures for which there is no real foundation at all. Even the oldest, very early epigraphic occurrence of the name does not help us. It is found in a song of triumph for the Pharaoh Mernephta on a stele which was set up in this Pharaoh's mortuary temple in the Pharaonic necropolis in Thebes, and it is now in the Egyptian Museum in Cairo (the so-called 'Israel stele'[1]). In line 27, in connection with the conquest of some Palestinian cities, the Pharaoh is also extolled for destroying 'Israel'[2]. It is, however, impossible to say with any certainty what the 'Israel' referred to here actually was in the Palestine of *circa* 1225 B.C., whether it was already the 'Israel' of the twelve tribes in the form known to Old Testament tradition or some still older conformation which bore the name 'Israel' and then for some now obscure historical reason passed it on to the 'Israel' that we know.

[1] Translation of the text AOT[2], pp. 20-25; reproduction of the Stele, AOB[2], No. 109.

[2] The Egyptian explanatory sign placed behind it indicates that the name is that of a 'foreign people', whilst the other Palestinian names are provided with the explanatory sign denoting 'foreign land'.

Even if it could be established beyond doubt, the etymology of the name would scarcely be any help. All that we know for certain is that, structurally, the name conforms to a type which is fairly common among the oldest personal and tribal names known to us[1]; on the other hand, indisputable place-names of exactly the same structure are also found in Palestine[2], so it is impossible to form any definite conclusion about the original meaning of the name. Further than the data provided by the Old Testament tradition we cannot go, and must rest content with the fact that the earliest known connotation refers to the group of the twelve tribes. This group of tribes therefore forms the subject-matter of a 'History of Israel'.

The question that must now be asked is whether, without detriment to its special character, 'Israel' can, on the basis of its undoubted historical reality and connection with the history of the ancient Orient, be assigned to a particular category. Whenever a definite appellative term is used at all, 'Israel' is normally described as a nation in the Old Testament tradition, and thereby reckoned among the many nations of the ancient Orient[3]. It is a description that was bound to suggest itself. The tribes of Israel were bound together by a common language, though, admittedly, they shared it with numerous neighbours. It was one of the Canaanite dialects established in the civilisation of Syria-Palestine[4]. In the period before the taking of the land their forefathers had presumably spoken an ancient Aramaic tongue, in common with the other nomadic, land-seeking elements on the borders of Syria and Palestine. They were also bound together by living in the same restricted area. It is true that they never held it entirely for themselves and their dwellings never formed a completely self-contained unit: nevertheless they were united in one neighbourhood. Finally—and in the present context this is the most important point of all—they were bound together by a basically similar historical situation and hence by a common historical experience. It has to be admitted, however, that they did lack certain elements which are

[1] Further details about this in M. Noth, *Die israelitischen Personennamen* (1928), pp. 207 ff.

[2] Cf. the place-names Jezreel, Jabneel, Jirpeel and the names jš'p'r (No. 78) and j'ḳb'r (No. 102) which occur presumably as place-names in the Palestine List of the Pharaoh Thothmes III.

[3] The Old Testament words for 'people', 'am and gōj, were used in earlier times for both one's own people and for foreign peoples too; it was only later on that the plural of the latter became a special term for foreign peoples, 'heathen peoples'.

[4] For this language, or more precisely, for the later Judaean form of language in which the Old Testament was revised, the term 'Hebrew' has been used since New Testament times on the basis of a secondary meaning of the concept 'Hebrew'.

usually considered essential to the concept of a 'nation'. As far as we know, the tribes of Israel never acted for a longer time in history as a unit—apart from the quite temporary phase of the monarchy of Saul, which was, on their ground, obviously incapable of surviving for long. In the period before the rise of the monarchy on Palestinian soil we only find single tribes—evidently organised in the forms of tribal constitution current at the time—and, occasionally, small groups of tribes intervening actively in historical events. A combination of the tribes of Israel did not provide the foundation for the later political structures. When the State declined, the tribes continued to live as a subject race in various provinces of successive large imperia and their later varied destinies also failed to stir them into joint historical action. If, therefore, following the Old Testament, we apply the rather vague concept of 'nation' to Israel as, in spite of everything, the most appropriate label for the historical reality, it must be borne in mind that the term cannot be used here in exactly the same sense as it is used of other nations; it may even be better to discard it altogether and speak simply of 'Israel'.

What united the tribes of Israel and held them together—in other words, what constituted the real nature of this strange reality—can only emerge from a detailed presentation of its history. On the other hand, the fact that 'Israel' was a unique phenomenon in the midst of the other historical nations arises from a quite general consideration. Thoroughly misguided though it would certainly be to regard later Judaism and 'Israel' as one and the same, and to identify these two quite distinct historical phenomena, there is, nevertheless, a direct historical connection between them; and the historically unique element in Judaism must have been present in embryo in the 'Israel' from which it evolved. Recognition of this fact, however, must not tempt us to isolate 'Israel' from the historical world of the ancient Orient and disguise the reality of its total involvement in that world.

As will be shown in detail later on, the tribes which formed the greater whole of 'Israel' did not all combine together until the occupation of the land on the soil of Palestine and it is only from that point that the real 'History of Israel' can take its departure. It must be stated emphatically that Old Testament tradition does not recognise any earlier form of 'Israel' than this union of the twelve tribes domiciled in Palestine. What it reports of the events before the occupation of the land it also refers to this same 'Israel' which it recognises only in its later historical form. This 'Israel' comes on the scene almost abruptly as the descendant of the twelve *heroes eponymi* who, with their common father, are, once again, simply the personification of the historical situation after the occupation of the land. On the historical evolution of 'Israel' we have no sort of information, only traditions about events in prehistorical times, the contents of which are admittedly of decisive importance but, in their present form, presuppose the subsequent 'Israel' of history. We also have no information whatsoever about earlier forms of social organisation in which a 'primeval Israel' may have existed, to be replaced later by the 'Israel' of the twelve Palestinian tribes which did constitute a kind of nation; and even for pure surmise there is a complete lack of likely clues[1].

If the appropriate starting-point for a presentation of the 'history of Israel' is thereby established, it is not immediately clear to what point in time the existence of 'Israel' may be said to have continued and how far an exposition of its history must be extended. The destruction of political autonomy on the soil of 'Israel' which took place in the events of the years 733/721 B.C. and 587 B.C. no more signified the end of Israel than the development of political forms of organisation marked the beginning of its life: it merely meant the end of a particular period of its history; and only a false conception of the extent of the deportations which followed those events could lead anyone to conclude that the substance of the tribes of Israel was, generally speaking, dissolved and destroyed at that time and that the old 'Israel' really came to an end. In fact, the tribes and 'Israel' itself survived. To pursue the history of 'Israel' beyond the decline of its political autonomy is desirable not only on practical grounds and with reference to the historical background of the later and latest strata of Old Testament literature, but also for purely objective reasons. The historically significant decline of the ancient Orient which set in with the emergence of Alexander the Great and the incipient Hellenisation of the Orient were big with meaning for Israel too, but had no decisive effect on its situation; there is no reason to cut the thread of the history of 'Israel' at that point. The end of the historical existence of 'Israel' and the scattering of Jewry among the nations were brought about by events that took place in the Roman era. In this period we find the tribes of Israel once more domiciled in their own

[1] I have fundamental doubts about the validity of W. Caspari's attempt to discover a 'pre-national organisation' of the 'subsequent people of Israel' in *Die Gottesgemeinde vom Sinai und das nachmalige Volk Israel* (1922), in which he discusses M. Weber's *Das antike Judentum* (Gesammelte Aufsätze zur Religionssoziologie, III (1923)), though in itself his attempt is full of interest and remarkable detail.

land and conscious of their common inheritance[1]; at the same time, however, the process of inner and outer dissolution of which the unhappy and disastrous insurrections of A.D. 66–70 and 132–135 were the consummation, had already begun, and it is these revolts which may be said to have brought the history of 'Israel' to its close. Therefore they form the appropriate conclusion for a presentation of the history of 'Israel'.

What sprang from this decline of 'Israel' was the phenomenon which we usually call 'Judaism'. Admittedly, it had its roots in the history of 'Israel' and was related to developments which had emerged in the later period of the history of 'Israel' and it has always applied the name 'Israel' to itself; but as the centre of worship had been abolished and there was no homeland and therefore no chance of joint historical action it was in fact something substantially new, so that we do well to use the special term 'Judaism' rather than the old name 'Israel'. It is true, of course, that from the womb of 'Judaism' there has emerged in most recent times a new historical quantity named 'Israel' which has sought its homeland again in the ancient land of Israel under the auspices of the Zionist movement and established a new State of 'Israel'. In spite of the historical connections which undoubtedly exist this new 'Israel' is separated from the Israel of old not only by the long period of almost 2000 years but also by a long history full of vicissitudes and it has come into being in the midst of entirely different historical conditions. It would therefore be improper to extend our historical enquiry from the end of the 'Israel' of old to the 'Israel' of the present day.

2. *The Land of Israel*

From its beginning to its end, taking both terms in the sense we have just defined, the history of Israel took place in a narrowly confined space, in a land which may, for the period in question, be appropriately described as the 'land of Israel', to use an expression that occurs once in the Old Testament (1 Sam. xiii, 19). An authentic and original name for this land as a whole has not come down to us from Old Testament times[2], and presumably none such ever existed; since as a natural phenomenon it was never a homogeneous, self-contained entity and was never occupied by a

[1] Josephus still combines the Israelite tribes in the land under the joint term 'the people' (τὸ ἔθνος).

[2] More precise details on this in WAT, pp. 42 ff.

homogeneous population nor did any political development ever take place in an area substantially identical with its territory. So the expression 'the land of Israel' may serve as a somewhat flexible description of the area within which the Israelite tribes had their dwellings. This region is constituted by the southern third of the extensive mountain country between the eastern border of the Mediterranean and the Syrian desert, which is divided into a western and eastern half by a deep valley which traverses it longitudinally. To the north the land of Israel extended approximately as far as the southern extremities of the high mountains of Lebanon and Anti-Lebanon, and to the south as far as the transition from agricultural land to the steppe and desert of the so-called Sinaitic peninsula, roughly on the latitude of the southern extremity of the Dead Sea.

It is usual to call the land of Israel 'Palestine', a name that arose in early Christian literature to describe the setting of the Bible story, following the official language of the period; when, after the various Jewish insurrections, the provincial name of Judaea which had been used hitherto and was now no longer suitable, had to be avoided, the earlier name of Palestine ('Land of Philistines')[1] was chosen to describe the Roman province which more or less coincided with the land of Israel, though, to begin with, the term had been applied to a more limited area; and ever since then this name has remained in use, officially and unofficially, in the Christian church and its basic connotation has remained unaltered, though the lines of demarcation have wavered slightly from time to time.

As a real and authentic history the history of Israel was always profoundly conditioned by the conditions of the soil on which it took place. A knowledge of the geography of Palestine is therefore one of the preconditions for a proper understanding of the history of Israel; and an exposition of the history of Israel must be preceded by a brief survey of the basic characteristics of the land itself[2].

The heart of the country is formed by a chain of limestone mountains, the strata of which were originally horizontal but, owing to various tectonic incidents on the eastern border of the Mediterranean, they disintegrated. Whilst, therefore, the original tableland character of the country is still apparent in the eastern

[1] More precise details in M. Noth, ZDPV, 62 (1939), pp. 125-144.

[2] We cannot offer even the outlines of a real geography of Palestine here. Cf., above all, H. Guthe, *Palaestina* (Monographien zur Erdkunde, 21) ([2] 1927), and also H. Guthe, *Bibelatlas* ([2] 1926), and G. E. Wright and F. V. Filson, *The Westminster Historical Atlas to the Bible* (1945). In WAT, pp. 1-82, may be found a discussion on the natural and historical geography of Palestine, which will not be repeated here.

part, in the western part, on the side bordering the Syrian desert, the limestone plateau has decomposed into a confusion of soils. The powerful inroad of the valley which traverses the whole land from north to south and continues further at each end, is particularly striking. On its soil the bed of the Jordan meanders along, having risen at the northern extremity of the land at the foot of the Anti-Lebanon: it flows into the Dead Sea which covers the soil of the deep valley on the southern frontier. It is therefore usually called the Jordan Valley and the whole country is divided into the land east and west of the Jordan. The plateau east of the Jordan, most of which survives, and into whose borders the beds of numerous rivers and rivulets have sawn their way, is confronted on the other side of the Jordan Valley by the mountains west of the Jordan which have broken through in many places and which are separated from the Mediterranean coast by a maritime plain. Thus, within its narrow confines, the land embraces the greatest possible differences and contrasts of landscape and climate and conditions of life varied greatly in the different parts of the country.

Life was different on the—roughly 600-800 m. high—fertile plains in the southern and northern part of the land east of the Jordan, which gradually pass into the steppe and desert as the rainfall decreases, from life in the mountainous central part of the land east of the Jordan which is wooded even today; and it was different again on the hot, desert-like soil of the ravine-like Jordan Valley, in which water, issuing at various points at the foot of the steep mountains, has produced oases with luxuriant vegetation, from life on the airy heights of the mountains; and life was different on the broad, fertile plain of Jezreel which interrupts the mountains west of the Jordan, and which is drained into the Mediterranean by the Kison which constantly carries water in its lower course, from life on the heights west of the Jordan which are intersected by streams that are dry in summer; and different again on the less hilly, milder middle sections of the mountains west of the Jordan and north and south of the plain of Jezreel, which are interspersed with pleasant plains of varying sizes, from life in the more precipitous, intensely rugged, rather barren parts of the mountains further to the north and south which are very inaccessible; and different again on the western sides of the mountains west and east of the Jordan which are well soaked with winter rain, from life on the often desert-like eastern slopes of the land west of the Jordan with its low rainfall; and different again on the warm, productive maritime plain with its relatively high humidity, which is separated from the coast by an almost uninterrupted line of dunes, from life on the wooded ridge of Carmel which cuts through them and projects into the sea; different again on the southern declivity of the mountains west of the Jordan, with their meagre pastures and poor soils, from life in the adjacent desert to the south in which shepherds and flocks depend on the few available springs. It is not surprising that this land was able to contribute little to a uniform settlement by a uniform population or to combine its existing inhabitants into a unity. The parts of the country where conditions were more favourable, above all, the maritime plain and the plain of Jezreel, the oases of the Jordan Valley and also the high plains of the northern and southern lands east of the Jordan, were inevitably the most inviting from the point of view of permanent settlement and cultivation; and the poorer hilly districts only attracted settlers when the other parts of the country were already well and truly occupied and newcomers had to make do with more modest dwellings. Thus the very nature of the land led, from the very outset, to a great lack of uniformity in the settlement. It was not especially favourable either to the subsequent amalgamation of the whole of its inhabitants. The different conditions in the various parts of the country led to differences in the way of life of the people and this tended to estrange them from one another. And the mountains which traverse the land, which are everywhere furrowed by deep, precipitous valleys, made communications difficult; more or less unrestricted communications were possible only in the great plains, whilst in the mountains conditions promoted small isolated groups.

Nevertheless, in very important matters all the inhabitants did share certain presuppositions, including, above all, the climatic conditions. Palestine shares the subtropical climate of the Mediterranean world and the particular consequences which this climate has in the limestone mountain regions of that world. This climate is characterised by the alternation of a winter rain period and a rainless summer. The winter rain does not fall generally throughout the country: it falls rather in isolated, brief, violent downpours, often separated by whole days which produce torrents of often dangerous ferocity in the mountain valleys not merely in the periods of the early rain (above all in October), of the main rain (mostly in January) and the late rain (roughly in April), but also within these periods. Since, moreover, the calcareous soil is very porous and real forests are almost entirely lacking and have probably been lacking from the earliest historical times—what is usually described as 'forest' here really represents merely a rather low-lying underwood—the land dries up to an extraordinary degree in the summer months; the springs—which are in any case far from numerous in the mountainous parts of the country and only limited in number even on the plains at the foot of the mountains—flow more sparsely and to some extent they dry up completely, and only a few valleys, above all in the plains and especially in the vicinity of the Mediterranean coast, still contain water.

Only the Jordan which is fed by the underground reservoir of the high mountains on the northern border of Palestine, constantly carries an abundance of water to the Dead Sea; but this watercourse which meanders through the desert region of the deep Jordan Valley, has little practical significance for life in the land.

The water supply has always been the most vital problem of all for the inhabitants of Palestine. In contrast to the great river oases, Egypt and Babylon, in which the great floods regularly inundate the land and the river water can constantly be made available for the use of human beings and animals, Palestine and the whole of Syria is dependent on rain for the needs of plants, animals and human beings. If the rain comes too meagrely at the times when it is due or fails to come altogether, it means a great catastrophe for the whole life of the country. And whilst the vegetation of the annual non-wood-forming plants is limited to the months of winter rain, human beings and animals can only live permanently where even in the summer something of the blessing of the previous winter's rain is still available, that is to say, where springs are fed by an underground water supply all the year round, or where the winter's rain has been collected in adequate quantities in so-called cisterns. This latter invention, which had already been made when the Israelite tribes settled in the land[1], made permanent settlement possible even in those areas where the springs were insufficient or where it was not at any rate possible to gain access to a subterranean supply of water by boring ground water wells. Admittedly, the cistern water was not equal to the 'living water' of the springs; and in some districts, as in parts of the eastern slopes of the mountains west of the Jordan, there is such a meagre rainfall that it is not even enough to fill the cisterns, and in such places it is impossible for men and animals to settle permanently.

Thus the water situation had a decisive influence on the distribution of the human settlements in the land and on the life and economy of the people in the different parts of the country. Every

[1] Cf. W. F. Albright in *Studies in the History of Culture* (1942), p. 33.

spring of water inevitably attracted people to settle in its immediate vicinity; and as springs rise above all at the foot of mountains the borders of the plains were colonised particularly early on and particularly densely. Wherever springs and ground water wells were sparse and unproductive, where there was no space for an accumulation of people, small, unassuming, easily satisfied flocks of cattle, sheep and goats were able at any rate to live with their shepherds; from the very beginning the eastern side of the mountains west of the Jordan and the borders of the land on the east and south sides have been grazing country for small flocks of sheep, goats and pigs.

The peculiarities of the climate have always had a basic influence on the seasons of human life and work[1]. It is easy to understand why the new vegetation in the autumn which resulted from the increasing dew and early rain was considered the beginning of a new year. For the indigenous, agricultural population there followed the season of ploughing, sowing and—once the rainy period had ended—of harvesting and the celebration of the ancient traditional religious festivals of the beginning and end of the harvest, the feast of unleavened bread and the feast of harvest (Exod. xxiii, 15, 16); and in high summer and autumn there followed the ripening of the tree fruits, especially the grapes, figs and olives and the joyful season of their harvesting, and finally the 'feast of ingathering' (Exod. xxiii, 16). But for the owner of a small flock of sheep, goats and pigs the year's events included a regular migration, the so-called change of pasture[2]; whilst the rainy period in the winter offered their flocks adequate opportunities for grazing even in areas of steppe and desert, in the dry summer they were forced to take them to the climatically more favourable agricultural land, where they found sufficient fodder in the fields that had been harvested, just as today the Arab tribes still have their definite winter and summer pastures[3].

All this meant that there was continual intercourse between the agricultural countryside and the neighbouring steppe and desert country; and it is one of the historically significant characteristics of the geography of Palestine that the land is enclosed by natural conditions on some sides and open on others. On the whole of its western side Palestine is bordered by the Mediterranean, which

[1] For a wealth of details on this subject see G. Dalman, *Arbeit und Sitte in Palaestina*, especially Vol. I, i, 2 (1928): Jahreslauf und Tageslauf.

[2] Cf. most recently L. Rost, ZDPV, 66 (1943), pp. 205 ff.

[3] Cf. M. v. Oppenheim, *Die Beduinen*, I (1939), II (1943), III (1952).

means that its coast is very long in relation to its total area. Yet, in spite of that, it has no very positive relationship to the sea, and on the whole its inhabitants have taken little interest in seafaring and maritime trade. In contrast to the adjacent Phoenician coast to the north at the foot of Mount Lebanon and with its old and famous Phoenician sea-ports and commercial cities, the coast of Palestine, which is accompanied by a straight line of low-lying dunes, is almost entirely lacking in natural harbours which might have tempted the inhabitants to go in for seafaring and might have attracted foreign sailors. From time immemorial the Egyptians traded by coastal routes with the more distant Phoenician cities, but hardly at all with Palestine, in spite of the fact that it was so much nearer to Egypt. The straight line of the flat coast is only relieved by rocks which jut out to sea and by cliffs which tower up from the sea at a few places, and even at these points there were no really practicable natural harbours, at yāfa, the Old Testament Japho, ḳēṣārye, the later Herodian-Roman Caesarea on Sea, ʿatlīt, the Castellum Peregrinorum of the crusaders. The straight line of the coast is only interrupted by Mount Carmel, and under its protection there arose a great bay, though the coast is still flat and sandy, and at the northern end of the bay there was an old coastal city which is called Akko in the Old Testament and which, apart from Japho, was the only settlement by the sea in ancient oriental times worth mentioning.

The fact that the land was shut off from the neighbouring sea explains why seafaring and sea-trading played no part at all in Israel and why, in spite of its proximity, the sea plays a purely marginal part in Israel's outlook on life and why it was possible for Israel to formulate a story of Creation which completely ignores the very existence of the sea[1]; and wherever the sea is mentioned in the Old Testament it hardly ever appears as a connecting link between different countries but as a menace on the edge of the inhabited earth, whose dangerous and uncanny power is broken only when it meets dry land[2]. On the northern side, too, the land of Palestine is shut off by a natural barrier. The high mountains of Lebanon and Anti-Lebanon hem the country in on this side; and the most northerly part of the land west of the Jordan, the Upper Galilean Mountains, which contains the highest elevations of the whole country[3], is already a far from accessible region. The

[1] Thus the Yahwistic narrative, Gen. ii, 4b ff. [2] Cf. *e.g.* Job xxxviii, 8-11.
[3] If the volcanic mountain of jebel ed-drūz far beyond in the east, which rises even higher, is not included in Palestine.

country also has no natural outlets to the north either along the coast on which the foothills between Akko and Tyrus come right down to the sea, offering an almost insuperable obstacle to the road leading to Phoenicia, or in the Jordan Valley whose corridor into the low land between Lebanon and Anti-Lebanon is also very difficult to pass. There is an outlet in the direction of Damascus only in a north-easterly direction on the eastern side of the Anti-Lebanon from the northern land east of the Jordan. On the other hand, however, Palestine is all the more open to the east and south, to the steppes and desert which form the frontier. The transition takes place quite gradually as the land moves away from the rain-bringing Mediterranean and rainfall decreases. There are hardly any difficult natural obstacles here to bar the way. On the border of the land east of the Jordan as on the southern border of the land west of the Jordan it is impossible to fix an exact frontier at all; and the area of human settlement has varied in these parts from time to time according to the extent to which artificial devices made it possible to settle in the marginal areas by fully exploiting the winter rainfall[1]: when husbandry was neglected these areas lapsed into desert again. It is therefore easy to realise that there was constant intercourse between the agricultural land and the neighbouring steppe and desert land on the east and south, since the inhabitants of the latter regions always had their eye on the coveted agricultural land and tried to gain a footing in it at every favourable opportunity. The change of pasture made many herdsmen with small flocks regularly seek out the summer pastures for their flocks in the agricultural land and this resulted in a constant to and fro between both sides of the frontier. This openness of the land to the east and south was of basic importance for its history in many ways. In addition to the constant infiltration of smaller groups, large-scale immigrations from these areas had a decisive influence on the history of Palestine. At the same time natural conditions brought Palestine in touch to some extent with the great long-distance trade routes in the ancient Orient. Like the greater unit of Syria as a whole it was a transit area and was therefore repeatedly involved in the intercourse and conflicts of the great powers of the ancient Orient. On Asiatic soil, after passing the northern part of the Sinaitic Peninsula, the route from Egypt to the Near East inevitably led first of all to the maritime plain of

[1] On the definition of the concepts steppe and desert and their distribution in the vicinity of Palestine cf. R. Gradmann, ZDPV, 57 (1934), pp. 161 ff. and especially Plan 1.

Palestine; and, as the coast road to Phoenicia on the northern border of the country was almost impracticable, the route across Palestine was often preferred: the plain of Jezreel being reached by passing along the back of Mount Carmel and then crossing the Jordan Valley south or north of the Sea of Tiberias and then making for Damascus in the land east of the Jordan, whence it was possible to reach the middle Euphrates by way of northern Syria or on caravan routes through the Syrian desert. The routes from southern Arabia to the Mediterranean area which were important for commercial traffic also touched the border of Palestine; the route passed either along the edge of the land east of the Jordan and then northwards towards Damascus or from the northern extremity of the gulf of el-ʿaḳaba to the south Palestinian coast; and thus Palestine also shared in the exchange of the products of the civilisation of the ancient Orient. The nature and situation of the land conferred on its inhabitants an extremely varied life with many different interests, enriched by all kinds of contacts with the outside world.

Palestine has never been a rich country and its inhabitants have always had to eat their bread 'in the sweat of their brow'. The land has never been able to feed a population of more than limited density. Even in the more favoured and fertile parts of the country the people have always had to slave on their fields and plantations to wrest a living from the soil, and vegetation of any luxuriance is found only in the few oases of the Jordan Valley. In the mountains, however, life was even harder if anything was to grow at all in the stony fields or, where even that was impossible, if the small flocks were to find enough food in the scanty pastures and watering-places. And even this meagre subsistence depended on sufficient well-distributed rain falling after the dry and hot summers. But this could never be relied on and there was inevitably always an anxious awareness of the fact that an absence or insufficiency of rain would bring drought and thirst and the catastrophic menace of a bad harvest and starvation. And, even if everything had grown satisfactorily, one of the recurrent plagues of locusts could always destroy the whole bounty of the land in no time and condemn men and beasts to starvation. In addition, the human settlements were constantly menaced by the earthquakes which are not unusual in this country.

Until even the most recent times men have led a very modest life in this country and it will always have been the same. As the inhabitants' livelihood depended on a combination of agriculture and small cattle breeding, varying according to local conditions, home-baked bread and a variety of milk products, with various seasonal fruits, represented the main foods. Meat eating was always exceptional and limited to certain special occasions and feast days —in the old days, religious festivals with animal sacrifices and sacrificial meals—special visits by guests who were entertained with typical Oriental generosity, and similar occasions; more frequent consumption of meat was regarded as the sign of an unusually luxurious life[1]. Probably a moderate consumption of wine was customary, varying according to the income of the individual, until Islam forbade its followers to drink it. Probably there was more wild game and beasts of prey than there is today. Apart from the Mediterranean coast, fishing was a rewarding occupation, above all on the Sea of Tiberias, whilst, owing to its strong mineral content, the largest inland lake in the country, the Dead Sea, makes organic life in and around it impossible. When in the Old Testament—especially in the deuteronomic-deuteronomistic literature—Palestine is praised as a 'good land' 'flowing with milk and honey', the reference is primarily to the contrast between the blessings of the agricultural land as such and the steppe and desert. 'Flowing with milk and honey' is moreover apparently a stereotyped term for a paradisean region, which was current in the ancient world and which was not coined with any special reference to Palestine at all, but was used by Israel to praise its own land in comparison with the immediately adjacent and accessible steppe and desert, not the more remote and unfamiliar river oasis lands of the ancient Orient. The reference to 'milk and honey' must therefore not be regarded as having arisen from specifically Palestinian conditions; the people that first adopted the expression in Israel certainly had in mind the fine pastures which existed in some parts and which increased the milk production of the small herds of cattle, and also the vineyards which supplied the grape honey (this was what they had in mind—not bee-honey)[2]. For the inhabitants of the steppes and deserts even the miserable agricultural soil of Palestine inevitably seemed an alluring and desirable object, and there was a time when the Israelite tribes had also seen the land in that light, when they were preparing to establish themselves there, and they rejoiced in its fruits, and learnt to value them again, especially when their sojourn in the land was threatened.

[1] Cf. *e.g.* Amos vi, 4b.

[2] More details in A. Bertholet, *Kulturgeschichte Israels* (1919), pp. 4 ff.

It is more curious that in Deut. viii, 9 Palestine is praised because its stones contain iron and because brass could be dug out of its hills. There is some exaggeration here. It is true that in the land east of the Jordan iron does occur at one or two places on the northern side of the Valley of Jabbok and it is possible that they were exploited in ancient times like the iron mine of mghāret warde not far from tulūl eḏ-aḏhab, the ancient Pnuel[1]. But these occurrences of iron can hardly have been of much importance and in general all necessary metals had to be obtained from abroad, from the wādi el-ʿaraba (between the Dead Sea and the Red Sea) and from the Lebanon region. The land did not have any other mineral wealth of importance[2]. Nevertheless it could be said that in contrast to the steppe and desert it did have at least something of that kind to offer to its inhabitants.

Palestine had no surplus products of any potential importance in the commerce of the ancient Orient. At the most it could only part with some of the produce of its fields and orchards in order to pay for urgently needed imports[3], perhaps it was also able to sell some of its flocks of small cattle. It was probably possible to meet the immediate need for foreign products—especially metals—in this way. But it can scarcely have been feasible to carry on any large-scale trade with Palestine's modest products. In this respect the country gave its inhabitants no chance of entering into active relations with the great world of the ancient Orient. Apart from its situation in the midst of important long-distance trade routes, its natural conditions were more calculated to isolate the people of Palestine from the greater world beyond the steppes and deserts, just as the nature of the land itself was more apt to separate the inhabitants from one another than to unite them.

3. *The Historical Situation in Palestine* circa *1200 B.C.*

When the Israelite tribes entered the land it could already look back on a long and eventful history which had given rise to a particular situation in regard to human settlement and civilisation, which was bound to be of direct and substantial importance for the

[1] Cf. C. Steuernagel, *Der ʿAdschlūn* (1927), p. 286.

[2] In ancient Oriental times the mineral treasures of the Dead Sea were hardly exploited at all; there is no evidence that such exploitation began before the Hellenistic period (cf. Hieronymus of Kardia in Diodorus Siculus, XIX, 98, 1–99, 3), and large-scale exploitation has only begun in the most recent times.

[3] According to 1 Kings v, 24 f. Solomon gave wheat and olive oil for King Hiram of Tyre's timber supplies.

early development of Israel. It must therefore be carefully examined; and we are in a position to describe it fairly concretely and accurately, since the tradition of the Old Testament is not our sole source of information about the conditions which confronted the Israelite tribes when they entered Palestine—thanks to some lucky finds, we possess a whole series of documents about the history of Syria and Palestine in the course of the second millennium B.C. and we also have at our disposal the results of the archaeological investigations, carried on intensively and successfully especially in the last thirty years, into the material remains which the various historical periods have left behind in Palestine[1].

The first of the documents which must be mentioned are the Egyptian so-called execration texts from the final period of the Egyptian 12th Dynasty *circa* 1800 B.C.[2] written on potsherds, which were used for a special magic rite[3]. In these texts all manner of enemies of Egypt and its royal house are enumerated, including some from the neighbouring Asiatic lands of Palestine and Phoenicia. In this connection we learn all kinds of names of princes and places. The way the rulers' names are formed provides some clue to the ethnic origins of those who bear them and sheds some light on the ethnic structure of the population and the place-names also shed a little, though not much, light on the nature of the settlement. The so-called Mari texts[4] are more or less contemporaneous—only slightly later; they represent the very extensive archives of the Kings of Mari, an old city on the middle Euphrates (the modern tell ḥarāri near abu ʿl-kemāl) and beside legal and economic texts they contain the wide-ranging political correspondence of the kings, with various information about contemporary Syria as well. They can, however, hardly be expected to contain any specific details about Palestine.[5]

[1] On the work and results of the archaeology of Palestine cf. WAT, pp. 83-143.

[2] On the division of Egyptian history into 'Dynasties' cf. WAT, pp. 195 ff. For full details on the most important phenomena of ancient Oriental history and the main concepts of the terminology which has become customary in the study of the ancient Orient, the reader may be referred, once and for all, to WAT, pp. 144-236.

[3] The texts have been published by K. Sethe in *Die Ächtung feindlicher Fürsten, Völker und Dinge auf altägyptischen Tongefässscherben des Mittleren Reiches* (Abh. d. Preuss. Ak. d. Wiss., 1926, phil.-hist. Kl., No. 5), and G. Posener, *Princes et pays d'Asie et de Nubie. Textes hiératiques sur des figurines d'envoûtement du Moyen-Empire* (1940). On the subject cf. A. Alt, ZDPV, 64 (1941), pp. 21 ff.

[4] In combination with a few other texts which have recently become known, the Mari texts have made possible a rectification of the chronology of the Land of the Two Rivers that used to be accepted. Cf. E. F. Weidner, AfO, 15 (1945–1951), pp. 85-105 and also a brief reference in WAT, p. 214.

[5] The Mari texts which were found from 1934/1935 onwards during the French excavations in Mari, have so far only been published in part in *Textes cunéiformes du*

The documents from the 14th century B.C. are more fruitful and come nearer in time to Israelite history. The so-called Amarna tablets must be considered first of all. They consist of barely four hundred clay tablets, the first of which were found *in situ* in 1887 and all of which come from an upper Egyptian hill ruin (tell) which is situated in the area now inhabited by the Bedouin tribe of el-ʿamārina. This hill ruin contains the remains of the newly established and soon-abandoned residence of the Pharaoh Amenophis IV (1377–1360 B.C.) and the Amarna tablets form a part of this Pharaoh's political archives that contained his predecessor's and his own foreign correspondence with the States of the Near East, and, above all, with the dependent minor rulers of Palestine and Syria from a period in which Palestine and Syria were, at any rate nominally, under Egyptian sovereignty. This correspondence is written in Babylonian script and language on the clay tablets in common use in the Land of the Two Rivers, as was apparently the custom at the time in international correspondence in the ancient Orient, and it offers a wealth of detailed information about political conditions, historical events of the time and life in Palestine and Syria. The Amarna tablets were the first document to reveal clearly the historical background of the beginnings of Israel in Palestine and they are still one of the direct sources for the history of Israel[1].

The so-called Ras-Schamra texts which have only been discovered quite recently also date from the same period as the Amarna tablets. They were found during the French excavations which, stimulated by a chance discovery made in 1929, were carried out until 1939 on a hill ruin on the North Syrian coast—opposite the outstretched finger of the island of Cyprus—and were resumed in 1949. In this hill ruin, now called rās esch-shamra, are buried the remains of the ancient city of Ugarit which we also know from the Amarna tablets and Egyptian texts. From 1930 onwards numerous clay tablets have been found here every year which display the well-known technique of cuneiform writing on clay tablets, but were written for the most part in a hitherto entirely unknown cuneiform alphabet of thirty characters which was deciphered surprisingly quickly. This is the first extensive

Musée du Louvre, Vol. XXII (1946), XXIII (1941), XXIV (1948), XXV (1951), V (1952). Provisional information about the contents of the political correspondence will be found in G. Dossin, *Syria*, 19 (1938), pp. 105-126, and in W. v. Soden, WO, I, 3 (1948), pp. 187-204.

[1] A transliteration and German translation of the Amarna tablets with explanatory notes will be found in J. A. Knudtzon, *Die El-Amarna-Tafeln* (Vorderasiatische Bibl. 2), 1915.

discovery of written documents in Syria-Palestine dating from pre-Hellenistic times. They contain numerous religious and mythological texts, great and small, and are the first and so far the only original documents on the religious history of Syria-Palestine in ancient oriental times, though some of them are very difficult to understand; they also contain governmental texts of great variety from the royal archives which contain little historical information, but, among other things, a wealth of personal names which shed light on the ethnic structure of the population. It is true that the rās esch-shamra is a good distance from the land of Israel and it is the setting of an old coastal town and port with a fine natural harbour (now called mīnet el-bēḍa, 'the white harbour') and to that extent the scene of a life quite different from life in Palestine. But nevertheless it was part of the greater entity of Syria-Palestine, which, in the period before the appearance of the Israelite tribes, had lived a richly varied but basically uniform life, and so the Ras-Shamra texts do help to illuminate the situation which the Israelite tribes found on their arrival in Palestine[1].

Apart from the groups of texts already mentioned, the Egyptian reports on the campaigns of the Pharaohs of the New Kingdom in Palestine and Syria also provide some material about pre-Israelite Palestine. For a time, these Pharaohs did in fact or at least in name enjoy sovereign rights over Palestine and Syria and between the 16th and 13th centuries B.C. the country saw the Egyptian kings or at any rate their armies on its soil time and again. So far as we know, Pharaoh Thothmes III was the first, in the first half of the 15th century, to have lists made of his campaigns and to have them displayed to his greater glory on the walls of the great Imperial temple of the god, Amon-Re, in Egyptian Thebes. One of them is the so-called 'Palestine List' of Thothmes III, which originally contained 117 Palestinian place-names and place-descriptions indicating where his troops were stationed on his first campaign in Palestine[2]. It is true that this list cannot, by its very

[1] Most of the Ras-Shamra texts have been published in the journal *Syria* from Volume 10 (1929) onwards. O. Eissfeldt, ZDMG, N.F. 21 (1942), pp. 507-539, reviewed the whole body of texts known up to that date. The grammar, transcriptions of the text and a glossary will be found in C. H. Gordon, *Ugaritic Handbook* (Analecta Orientalia, 25 [1947]). C. H. Gordon provides an English translation of the texts in *Ugaritic Literature* (Scripta Pontificii Instituti Biblici, 98 [1949]) and a selection will be found in ANET, pp. 129-155 (H. L. Ginsberg).

[2] Published in W. M. Müller, *Die Palästinaliste Thutmosis' III* (MVAG), 12, 1, 1907 and J. Simons, *Handbook for the Study of Egyptian Topographical Lists relating to Western Asia* (1937), No. 1; for detailed explanations cf. M. Noth, ZDPV, 61 (1938), pp. 26-65.

purpose and nature provide a survey of the settlements in Palestine at that time; but the names it mentions do testify to the existence of numerous places in Palestine.

Circa 1200 B.C., that is, about the time when the Israelite tribes settled in the land, a period of civilisation was drawing to its close in Palestine, the 'Bronze Age' which was now being superseded by the Iron Age. Though the knowledge and use of these metals (bronze and iron) may not be a very substantial or safe and clear criterion for demarcating the two ages, it is customary to use these conventional terms to describe the great periods of civilisation which can be classified archaeologically on the basis of their cultural inheritance. In particular, the kinds and forms of their pottery, the fragments and remains of which have survived in great quantities on all the sites of ancient settlements and have lasted thousands of years, and also the characteristics of their jewellery, of which only scanty relics have survived, and their methods of building houses and city walls, are typical of these periods of civilisation and their different parts. Excavations in Palestine have given us a fairly clear picture of the Bronze Age civilisation in that country, which evolved in various stages: an early Bronze Age in the third millennium B.C.; a middle Bronze Age in the first four centuries of the second millennium and a late Bronze Age between about 1550 and 1200 B.C. In this period, living in fixed settlements, in cities, developed intensely, and what knowledge we have of the civilisation of the Bronze Age is based on the manifestations of its urban culture. These cities were—and this remains true right up to the beginning of the Hellenistic period—in fact not really cities for living in but walled-in strongholds and storehouses of small size with a rather rambling jumble of small houses and an irregular mass of narrow lanes and, usually, one fair-sized square immediately inside the city gate which was the scene of public life. But the everyday life of the inhabitants took place mainly outside the city, in the fields and plantations, where it was no doubt the custom to spend the night in summer time and during the harvest. The number of permanent cities in the country gradually increased in the course of the Bronze Age. So far as we can infer from archaeological discoveries, new cities were founded in the middle Bronze Age and again in the late Bronze Age; and even if, occasionally, older settlements were abandoned to make way for these new cities, it still meant that the number of Bronze Age cities was constantly growing. This is in exact accordance with the fact that, according to Old Testament tradition, the Israelite tribes found

'Canaanites' dwelling in permanent cities when they occupied the land (cf., for example, Num. xiii, 28). The technique of walling-in, which was the prime concern in the building of these cities, also made constant progress in the Bronze Age. The middle Bronze Age already knew how to build imposing, escarped city walls in the so-called 'cyclopian' technique[1] (using huge stones without mortar), and the late Bronze Age took over these walls and the technique of building them.

These cities provided the preconditions for the rise and growth of a simple urban civilisation in so far as the urban concentration of population inevitably promoted the development of specialised occupations and the transmission of particular skills. It is true that the normal type of farmer and small cattle breeder predominated in the Bronze Age cities of Palestine; but as the local products of an already advanced pottery and metal work trade show, there were clearly professional trades and even arts and crafts in these cities, and these were usually the beginning of a commerce which consisted to begin with of barter and then, as trade widened and developed, money was introduced as the means of payment. Thus there is evidence that a simple money economy with different weights of metal as the means of payment was in force at any rate in the cities of the Late Bronze Age in Palestine[2].

This is also confirmed by the fact that in the Old Testament the name 'Canaanite', with which it was customary to describe the whole of the old non-Israelite and pre-Israelite population, whose ancestors had maintained the civilisation of the Bronze Age, occasionally assumed the special meaning of 'merchant' and 'trader' (Isa. xxiii, 8 and elsewhere)[3]. Archaeological discoveries show that commercial relationships and cultural exchanges in the urban civilisation of the Bronze Age extended far and wide on every side, as was only to be expected in Syria-Palestine, which was so markedly a land of transit. In the Bronze Age strata of the cities the Land of the Two Rivers and Egypt are represented by all kinds of imported articles of pottery and jewellery and to these purely imported goods there were added native imitations of foreign products in the arts and crafts. The welcome given to

[1] For more precise details on this technique see WAT, pp. 114 ff. and illustration 5A.

[2] Cf. K. Galling, BRL, 174 ff.

[3] The word 'Canaanite' was probably originally simply a term for 'purple manufacturers', 'purple traders', of whom there were many, especially in the coastal towns of Phoenicia, and from that specific meaning the name 'Canaan' developed into a more or less vague term for the country itself (cf. B. Maisler, BASOR, 102 [1946], pp. 7-12). The Old Testament can hardly have been familiar with the original meaning of the word, it only thinks of the term in its secondary sense as the description of a country or a people.

imports and cultural influences from the Mediterranean world is also characteristic of the late Bronze Age. These influences emanated particularly from the islands of Cyprus and Crete, and Palestine, which gave so little heed to the sea, probably shared in these imports through the intermediacy of the Phoenician coastal towns[1].

Literary sources from the second millennium have shed some light on the motley and changing mass of people who lived in this world and their movements[2], without giving us anything like a complete insight into the whole complicated situation. No doubt the various groups which settled in the land each brought their own traditions and cultural possessions with them, which were then absorbed into the greater whole of the civilisation of their new country. According to the evidence of archaeological discoveries this civilisation was in fact fairly homogeneous in the Bronze Age, not only in Palestine but throughout Syria, including Palestine. In spite of their different origins and character and the difficulty they found in combining into a great political unit, the inhabitants of the urban settlements all shared in this civilisation, the products of which were distributed by exchange and commerce over the whole land. The urban system of the Bronze Age in Syria-Palestine was a civilisation based on the soil which gradually developed and changed until it finally expired around 1200 B.C., though it is difficult to discern any definite causes for its decline and fall.

As far as our knowledge extends, *i.e.* from the early Bronze Age in the third millennium B.C., men of Semitic language formed the main mass of the population of the country. Departing from Old Testament usage, which describes the whole of the older population as 'Canaanites' regardless of their origins and language, but following on from that tradition, scholars usually describe the basic stock of the population, with its different Semitic dialects, as 'Canaanite'. The reference is not to the original inhabitants or to the earliest inhabitants of the country. The numerous old, and, to some extent very old, non-Semitic names prove that people of different origin had settled in the country previously. But we still know nothing for certain[3] about these people, and in any case they are of no significance as far as the history of Israel is concerned.

[1] P. Thomsen, *Palästina und seine Kultur in fünf Jahrtausenden*, 3rd edition (AO, 30 [1932], pp. 33-61), gives a short review of the Bronze Age in Palestine.

[2] More details will be found in M. Noth, ZDPV, 65 (1942), pp. 9-67 where the references for the following account will also be found.

[3] Periods of civilisation preceding even the Bronze Age have been proved to exist by archaeological discoveries, and these pre-Canaanite inhabitants probably belonged to these earlier ages. But the lack of any literary information precludes us from any more precise knowledge about this early period.

When the Israelite tribes arrived, however, they still found that the language spoken was the Semitic 'Canaanite', and, like many earlier immigrants, they and their relations adopted this language in place of the probably Aramaic dialect they had spoken previously. We know nothing about the period and the nature of the occupation of the land by the 'Canaanites' and their conflict with the inhabitants they found already living there. They established themselves in the older settlements and also founded new ones alongside them. They appear to have been the first to have occupied the Phoenician coastal centres with their natural harbours which later became so important: their names are in fact thoroughly Semitic[1]. The Phoenician section of the coast lay behind the mighty wall of Lebanon and was only opened up for settlement relatively late. The 'Canaanite' immigration must have been so tremendous that the older population was absorbed by it, and, from that time on, their language was spoken in the country, until it was displaced, very much later, at first partially, and then entirely, by Aramaic.

In the 19th/18th century B.C. a new, likewise Semitic, ruling class imposed itself on Syria-Palestine. According to the evidence of the typical personal names that occur in the Egyptian exsecration texts and the Mari texts they were elements of the stratum which about the same time seized the reins of government on the middle Euphrates and in the south of the Land of the Two Rivers and there established the 1st Dynasty of Babylon and the ancient Babylonian Empire. The historical significance of this movement for Syria-Palestine is not yet really clear nor has any appropriate name been found for this ruling class; they are often wrongly described as 'Amorites'.

The documents of the 14th century B.C. which bring us quite close to the beginning of the history of Israel, reveal a great alteration in the make-up of the population. Here, too, the number of personal names from this period known to us is remarkable. The new constituent which they reveal is a non-semitic element, particularly in the urban centres. It is clear that in the intervening period movements of population had changed the ethnic structure of the country. People with names which may, according to the tradition of cuneiform writing, be called 'Hurrian' appear in especially large numbers among these newcomers. According to cuneiforms sources these 'Hurri'[2] were also found at the same time

[1] Cf. M. Noth, WO, I, 1 (1947) pp. 21-28.

[2] This name still occurs in the Old Testament ('Horites') but without any concrete connotation.

in Mesopotamia, that is, in the region between the middle Euphrates and the Tigris, as well as east of the middle Tigris, and their language, which is neither Semitic nor Indo-Germanic, has been proved to be cognate with the language of the Urartians, the inhabitants of the Armenian mountains, who are known to us from the first half of the first millennium. According to this the Hurrians appear to have come from a north-easterly direction into the area of the ancient Orient and to Syria-Palestine, to have settled especially in Mesopotamia but to have spread also in great numbers to Syria-Palestine[1] as a new ruling class which seized possession above all of the cities. But simultaneously with the Hurrians other elements of non-Semitic origin also appeared, of Indo-Iranian descent, Indo-Germans from the region where the group of so-called Satem languages was spoken[2], few in numbers but perfectly identifiable from their names. They appear here and there in the Amarna tablets in Syria-Palestine among the minor rulers of the country, and there is also evidence that they ruled in Mesopotamia. There is evidence of all kinds of other personal names from the late Bronze Age in Syria-Palestine, which are difficult to interpret, obviously non-Semitic but difficult to classify more accurately. These names indicate, however, how heterogeneous the population was. Factually the Old Testament tradition is quite right when, alongside the all-embracing description of the whole of the pre-Israelite population of the urban civilisation of the Bronze Age[3], it very often enumerates, in varying combinations and sequences, a whole series of ethnic names, most of which mean nothing to us, to indicate the variety of the population which the Israelite tribes found when they occupied the land (Gen. x, 16-18; xv, 19-21 and elsewhere).

The influx of non-Semitic elements which imposed themselves on Syria-Palestine as a new ruling class must have taken place as part of a wider historical movement of which we have no direct information though we can see its after-effects. It is almost impossible not to connect this movement with events which took place in Egypt in the period in question, about which Egyptian sources of information are unfortunately scanty and far from coherent. Between the Egyptian Middle and New Kingdom Egypt

[1] On the rās esch-shamra some texts have even been found in the Hurrian language.

[2] Since the word for 'hundred' is characteristic, the Indo-Germanic languages are usually divided into the two big groups of *centum*—and *satem*—languages.

[3] The name 'Canaanite' is mostly used in this sense; but in certain parts of Old Testament literature the names 'Amorites' and 'Hittites' are used in the same sense. Cf. WAT, p. 67.

was subject from about the end of the 18th to the beginning of the 16th century to foreign rule which resulted from conquest by an enemy who came from the direction of the adjacent land of Palestine-Syria. The conquerors made themselves kings over Egypt and subjugated the land and its inhabitants. Their kings resided in the city of Awaris in the eastern delta of the Nile near the Egyptian-Asiatic frontier; and the very situation of this residence that indicates their kingdom included a part of the Near East, at any rate, Palestine-Syria, as well as Egypt. These kings proudly called themselves 'rulers of the foreign lands', *i.e.* in the Egyptian language officially used by them as Kings of Egypt, which later developed, in Greek transliteration, into the word Hyksos[1], which it is customary to use, rather inaccurately, as a general term for this whole historical phenomenon. When the first Pharaohs of the New Kingdom liberated Egypt from the rule of these conquerors, they expelled them to Palestine and after that they subjugated Palestine-Syria, evidently in order to take possession of the inheritance of the Hyksos kings.

It is hardly possible to avoid the conclusion that the rule of the Hyksos, which possibly extended as far as Mesopotamia[2], and certainly included Syria-Palestine and, finally, Egypt, was the result of a great migration which came from a north-easterly or easterly direction and introduced a powerful new ruling class into the ancient Orient and in connection with which these Hurrian and Indo-Iranian and possibly other foreign, non-Semitic elements came to Syria-Palestine which appear in such great numbers in the documents of the 14th century B.C. Such a powerful historical movement usually makes, however, not merely a contribution to the structure of the population, but changes the historical situation so that its effects extend beyond the period of its immediate influence. Thus the face of Syria-Palestine in the 14th century, with which we are comparatively familiar, was influenced in many ways by the preceding rule of the Hyksos, though it is difficult to define the influence at all concretely, since not only have we no direct information at all about the Hyksos period but we have so few details about conditions in Syria-Palestine before the Hyksos came that it is impossible to establish precisely what changes

[1] This word is well known from the extensive quotation preserved in Josephus, *Contra Apionem*, I, 14, § 75 ff. Niese about the Hyksos from the Αἰγυπτιακά of the late Egyptian priest Manetho, who gives a false explanation of the word Hyksos.

[2] In the course of driving out the Hyksos the Pharaohs thrust forward at various times right through Syria-Palestine to the Euphrates, *i.e.* as far as Mesopotamia, where we also find Hurrians and Indo-Iranians.

occurred in that period. It is nevertheless possible to make a few likely suppositions.

The first thing of general importance was that, as far as we can see, it was through the Hyksos that Syria-Palestine was drawn into immediate involvement in the great world of events in the ancient Orient. Up till then the Egyptians had been interested in the ore deposits in the Sinaitic Peninsula and in the commercial ports of Phoenicia and the timber of the forests of Lebanon; the powers of the Land of the Two Rivers had been interested in the timber in the Amanus mountains and in the possible access to the 'upper sea' (the Mediterranean) through Northern Syria and to Asia Minor with its rich ore deposits, but Syria-Palestine as a totality had meant little in the history of the ancient Orient. It was only when the Hyksos established themselves in the country, from which they finally conquered Egypt, that Syria-Palestine began to play its part as a bridge between the ancient civilisations on the Euphrates-Tigris and on the Nile, which was prescribed by its geographical position; and through the mediacy of Syria-Palestine there developed a lively intercourse between the two civilisations. If the Amarna tablets reveal intensive diplomatic relationships between the numerous States of the Near East and the Egyptian Pharaohs, that was probably an after-effect of the Hyksos rule, in which the Pharaohs continued to play the role of the former Hyksos kings. It is permissible to surmise in this connection that the use of Babylonian writing and language which was customary in the Amarna period in diplomatic intercourse and for which there is evidence in a more restricted sphere for the period of the Mari texts, was promoted and extended as far as Egypt, above all by the Hyksos who first traversed areas with an old tradition of cuneiform writing on their voyages in the ancient Orient; the fact that in Syria-Palestine in the late Bronze Age this method of writing was used not merely within the country itself[1] but also in correspondence with the Egyptian overlord, can hardly be explained except as the result of a standardisation of international correspondence which was imposed by force to begin with and then retained.

In addition, the Hyksos also introduced a new technique of war which resulted in a new social order in the ancient Orient. The Hyksos introduced the horse-driven war chariot into the ancient

[1] This is shown by the cuneiform tablets found on the tell ta'annek (cf. the examples AOT[2], p. 371), some letters of the rās esch-shamra, clay tablets from Alalah in northern Syria (the modern tell el-'aṭschane near Antiochia).

Orient evidently from the steppes of the Asian interior; and henceforth the kings and rulers of the ancient Orient used this aristocratic weapon of war. It is true that the horse had not been entirely unknown in the ancient Orient before this: but it only acquired importance and general diffusion in connection with the war chariot. As a riding animal for use in war it was gradually introduced into the ancient Orient only later on—towards the end of the 2nd millennium B.C.—as a result of incursions into the marginal areas of the north-east by horsemen, from the interior of Asia; and as a working animal it is still uncommon in this area even today. But the war chariot played an outstanding part in warfare in the ancient Orient from the days of the Hyksos. It is clear that it could not become a weapon to be used by every member of a people's army: it called not only for skill and practice but for a high social position and corresponding affluence[1]. Only knights were able to fight with chariots, and so the Hyksos ruling class presumably represented a kind of chivalry. The Hyksos knights established themselves as minor rulers and lieges of the Hyksos king in the many old cities and in those newly founded in the Middle Bronze Age in Syria-Palestine; and if we find such rulers in almost all the cities of Syria-Palestine in the Amarna period, describing themselves as 'men of the city' (as opposed to the Pharaoh)[2] and exercising considerable dominion, they were in fact identical with these Hyksos knights who went to war in chariots; and it is precisely among these men that we meet Hurrian and Indo-Iranian personal names alongside numerous local Semitic names. And whatever the social order may have been like in the Bronze Age cities before the appearance of the Hyksos rulers, from the Hyksos period onwards we have to reckon at any rate with a feudal order, *i.e.* with the opposite of a 'dominion' and a slave population which was presumably subject to taxation and compulsory service. Syria-Palestine, which was perhaps the heart of the Hyksos dominion and, unlike the civilised regions in Egypt and the Land of the Two Rivers, did not possess a political and social order with deep historical roots, provided a suitable soil for the growth of such a feudal order. But, once again, the Old Testament tradition is right when it makes the Israelite tribes fear the city-dwelling

[1] It was only later that the State provided the warrior with the necessary weapons and equipment; in early times the soldier had to be responsible for them himself.

[2] The word 'man' (amelu) which already describes the legal and social position of the 'free man' in the statute-book of the ancient Babylonian king Hammurabi, must be a technical term in the above context and may be translated perhaps by 'vassal'.

'Canaanites' with their 'chariots of iron' (Jos. xvii, 16; Judges i, 19; iv, 3)[1].

We have no direct knowledge of the Hyksos rule, but know of it only from its remains and after-effects. From 1580 B.C. onwards the inheritance of the Hyksos rule in Egypt itself and in Palestine-Syria was taken possession of by the Pharaohs of the 18th Dynasty who subjugated and repeatedly compelled to obedience Palestine-Syria as far as the Euphrates in numerous campaigns. On the whole they appear to have retained the system of government of the Hyksos, inasmuch as they based their sovereignty on the acknowledgment of feudal dependency on the part of the minor rulers who resided in the cities; and they appear to have, at any rate partly, left the old families of Hyksos rulers in their seats so far as they submitted to the new sovereign, as is indicated by the fact that the rulers still have to some extent Hurrian and Indo-Iranian names. They also maintained a few fortresses as strong points, with a very small number of garrisons; in some coastal towns they established supply depots to meet the needs of their campaigns; here and there they erected Egyptian temples and made over some landed properties, *i.e.* their shrines and priests, to Egyptian gods[2]. But on the whole they merely claimed the feudal loyalty of the many city rulers; and their loyalty could only be depended on so long as the Pharaohs displayed their superior power in repeated campaigns. When, towards the end of the 18th Dynasty, the Pharaohs Amenophis III (1413–1377 B.C.) and Amenophis IV (1377–1360 B.C.) no longer maintained these campaigns, Egyptian rule over Syria-Palestine dwindled rapidly. The Amarna Tablets, which derive from the period of these two Pharaohs, show Egyptian rule in a state of complete dissolution; only a few vassals, such as the ruler of the city of Gubla (Byblos, the modern Jebeil, north of Berut) which brisk commercial relationships had tied to Egypt from the earliest times, still remained loyal to Pharaoh, whilst most of the others acted as independent rulers and tried to extend their modest power as far as possible.

The most important Pharaohs of the 19th Dynasty, particularly Sethos I (1308–1290 B.C.) and also Ramses II (1290–1223 B.C.), restored Egyptian sovereignty again in Syria-Palestine, though not to the same extent as before; in the meantime, from their

[1] These chariots were naturally not made entirely of iron, but of wood. The above expression refers to the metal fittings.

[2] Cf. A. Alt, ZDPV, 67 (1944–1945), pp. 1 ff.; BBLAK, 68 (1946–1951), pp. 97 ff.

centre in Asia Minor the Hittites had acquired dominion over Northern Syria; in the Battle of Kadesh on the Orontes (the modern tell nebi mend) they were strong enough to thwart the Pharaoh's attempt to attack the Hittite sphere of influence and were therefore able to maintain their position throughout the northern half of Syria. On the basis of the *status quo* which thus came into being, a treaty between Ramses II and the Hittite King Hattusil was concluded in the 21st year of Ramses II[1]. The Pharaohs of the 19th Dynasty thereby established Egyptian sovereignty once again in Palestine. But *circa* 1200 B.C., with the final decline of the power of the Egyptian New Kingdom, the rule of the Pharaohs came to an end in Palestine, which was their closest neighbour, and henceforth they only maintained a theoretical claim to this land. The fragment of a stele of Ramses IV (*circa* 1150 B.C.) which was found during the excavations in Megiddo, is the last tangible evidence of Egyptian rule in Palestine, which had, by that time, disappeared to all intents and purposes. Henceforward the country was left to its own fate.

But the fact that the occupation of the land by the Israelite tribes was immediately preceded by the century-long Egyptian rule has supplied us with a wealth of Egyptian information about the situation in Palestine in the Late Bronze Age. The Amarna Tablets are the most fruitful group of documents in this connection. From them, and from the Palestine List of Thothmes III, we can obtain a very precise picture of the population if we combine this information with the discoveries of the archaeologists[2].

Those urban settlements in which the native Canaanite subject population lived under the knightly rulers, were situated, according to these archaeological discoveries, almost exclusively in the parts of the country most favoured by nature, *i.e.* above all in the plains. But they were packed tightly together and often only a few miles apart from one another. First and foremost the coastal plain south and north of the Carmel, with its relatively abundant water-supply and fertile alluvial soil, was crowded with these 'cities'. And the inner edge of this plain at the foot of the west Jordan hills, with its numerous springs, was most densely populated of all. But the

[1] Cf. G. Roeder, *Ägypter und Hethiter* (AO, 20 [1919]) and pp. 36 ff. for the text of the treaty. On the historical background of the Battle of Kadesh cf. J. Sturm, *Der Hettiterkrieg Ramses' II* (Beihefte zur 'Wiener Zeitschrift für die Kunde des Morgenlandes', 4. Heft [1939], pp. 1 ff.).

[2] On the following, cf. above all A. Alt, *Die Landnahme der Israeliten in Palästina* (Reformationsprogramm der Universität Leipzig, 1925); reprinted in *Kleine Schriften zur Geschichte des Volkes Israel*, I (1953), pp. 89-125.

settlements extended out into the plain as far as the line of dunes which ran parallel to the coast, whilst the almost harbourless coast itself only had very few settlements. In the great fertile plain of Jezreel which was easily accessible north of the Carmel from the coast through the Kishon Valley from the southern coastal plain and over the low hill country between the Carmel and the central Palestinian hills there was a close sequence of numerous cities along the south-west border. In its northern half between the sources of the Jordan and that broad western salient which is traversed by a watercourse (now called nahr jālūd) coming from the plain of Jezreel the Jordan Valley contained a series of settlements, whilst the desert-like southern half was only inhabited in the few oases north of the Dead Sea. East of the Jordan Valley on the further side of the wooded mountain there was the great fertile plain of the northern land east of the Jordan on both sides of the Yarmuk, the most northerly tributary of the Jordan, an area dense with urban settlements. The table land of the southern land east of the Jordan, on the other hand, an area equally well suited for agriculture, had been filled with cities in the Early Bronze Age, according to the archaeological evidence, but in the first phase of the Middle Bronze Age these settlements had been abandoned, for reasons unknown to us, so that at the time of the Egyptian rule, there was scarcely any urban life here at all. And not until approximately the 13th century B.C. were any new settlements initiated here. Curiously enough, in this area which was so far distant from the coast, some of the people who settled there had connections with Mediterranean civilisation[1]. Even in the Late Bronze Age the mountainous parts of Palestine were still only very sparsely populated. In the wooded central part of the land east of the Jordan on both sides of the Jabbok, a tributary of the Jordan, there was an almost complete lack of permanent settlements and there were only a few in the valley of the Jabbok itself. The same applies to the most northerly part of the mountains west of the Jordan north of the plain of Jezreel. The middle section of these mountains was occupied above all by the old city of Shechem, which it was possible to reach from the western maritime plain by a convenient valley on the western border of a plain sunk deep into the mountains. It is mentioned in an Egyptian inscription in a reference to the period of Sesotris III, one of the Pharaohs of the

[1] There is evidence for this in a stele found in el-bālū'a south of the Arnon which bears an inscription in Cretan linear writing B (cf. A. Alt, PJB, 36 [1940], pp. 34 ff.).

12th Dynasty in the 19th century B.C.[1], and appears in the Amarna Tablets as the seat of a ruler who was able to extend his sphere of influence in various directions because there were hardly any competitors in the vicinity of Shechem. Further south, in the mountains, it is striking that in spite of its uninviting situation on an inaccessible and not very productive part of the mountains the area around Jerusalem was filled with a series of cities. Jerusalem itself, which the Egyptian proscription texts prove to have been in existence at the beginning of the second millennium, was in the Amarna period the seat of a ruler who is represented in the Amarna archives by a series of letters to the Pharaoh. To the south it had some freedom of movement: at that time Bethlehem which was 8 kilometres away on this side was 'a city of the land of Jerusalem'[2], *i.e.* a place subject to the rule of Jerusalem, and we have no knowledge of any other Bronze Age city in the mountains to the south. But in the north, north-west and west, Jerusalem had various Bronze Age neighbours of whom we know not from literary tradition but from archaeological discoveries *in situ*: on the road leading to the north from Jerusalem there was, ten miles away, the town of Lus[3] (the modern bētīn), which had been inhabited since the Middle Bronze Age; to the north-west, about 9 kilometres away, there was the Bronze Age ed-jīb, and 12 kilometres west of Jerusalem there was the city of Kirjath-Jearim, which was known to the Old Testament. Here, then, the whole summit of the mountain between the 'desert of Judah' (which is what this uninhabited region was called later on in the Old Testament) sloping down to the Jordan Valley in the east and the western slope of the mountain was occupied by a fairly coherent group of city state territories, which prevented one another from extending their respective spheres of influence. In its out of the way position this group admittedly had no great historical significance; and it is therefore not surprising that the Egyptian sources of information say nothing about it, except for Jerusalem. The same is true of Hebron (el-khalīl) which is situated in the mountains 40 kilometres south of Jerusalem—a district as famous for its wealth of grapes in olden days as it still is today. To judge from Num. xiii, 22 Hebron already existed in the Bronze Age; and that is probably the case, though Hebron is not mentioned at all in the Egyptian sources, just because, as a Bronze Age city, its situation

[1] Cf. AOT[2], pp. 81 f.

[2] EA, 290, 15 f. (from a letter of the ruler Abdihipa of Jerusalem).

[3] This was the original name of the place which was later given the name of Bethel after the famous sanctuary which was situated on its eastern side.

was rather isolated[1]. So at the time of the Israelite occupation there were hardly any settlements in the mountains—only sporadic towns and groups of towns. Political and economic life took place in the plains and on the high plateaus where communications were comparatively favourable. After the cessation of Egyptian sovereignty there was a lack of political cohesion between the numerous, usually anything but extensive, city states. Their rulers, once liegemen of the Hyksos kings and then of the Pharaohs, now called themselves 'kings'; at any rate that is how the 'Canaanite' city rulers are described in the Old Testament even after the Amarna period. The relationships between these city kings were alternately friendly and hostile and innumerable conflicts took place; but about all that we now know practically nothing.

As in the Amarna period, a certain element afterwards played a part in the country which belonged neither to the ruling class nor to the old indigenous urban population. According to the Amarna tablets it performed military service, above all for the anti-Egyptian, disloyal city rulers. In the cuneiform writing of the Amarna tablets it is usually depicted by a verbal symbol consisting of the two syllables SA. GAZ; and this term only appears in phonetic syllabic script as Ḫabiru[2] in the writings of the city ruler of Abdihipa of Jerusalem. There can hardly be any doubt that this is the same word as the Old Testament word 'Hebrew'[3]. We are now familiar with such 'Hebrews' from the whole world of the ancient Orient—they usually had to undertake or perform services of various kinds. We know them from the ancient Babylonian Empire and the Mari texts[4], from the documents of the city of

[1] The case of the town of Debir which is mentioned in connection with Hebron in Jos. xv, 13-19=Judges i, 10-15, and also Jos. x, 36 ff.; xi, 21, which is said to have been previously called Kirjath-Sepher, remains open to doubt. It is certainly an error to assume that this Kirjath-Sepher was already mentioned in the Egyptian Pap. Anastasi, I, 22, 5 from the time of Ramses (cf. M. Noth, ZDPV, 60 [1937], p. 224, Note 2). But judging from the Old Testament references one is inclined to regard Debir as a Bronze Age city. If, following W. F. Albright, *The Archaeology of Palestine and the Bible* (1932), pp. 77 ff. and elsewhere, Debir is to be set on the tell bēt mirsim, then it would have been situated at the foot of the mountains 20 kilometres west-south-west of Hebron and would not fit into the above context. But if, following the statements made in the Old Testament, one prefers to seek for Debir much nearer to Hebron in the mountains (a proposal for the placing of Debir will be found in M. Noth, JPOS, 15 [1935], pp. 48 ff.) then Debir must also be presumed to have been a Bronze Age city in the most southerly part of the mountains west of the Jordan.

[2] The equating of SA. GAZ with Ḫabiru has now been established above all by the cuneiform texts from the capital of the Hittite Kingdom (the modern boghazköi).

[3] The rendering of SAG. GAZ by 'prm which has recently been attested in texts of the ras esch-shamra does not make the equating with the word 'Hebrew' impossible; cf. W. F. Albright, BASOR, 77 (1940), pp. 32 f. (against E. G. Kraeling, *ibid.* p. 32).

[4] *Textes cunéiformes du Louvre*, XXII (1941), No. 131, 13.

Nuzu in the land east of the Tigris of the 15th century B.C., from Hittite Asia Minor of approximately the 14th century B.C., from Syria-Palestine of the same period and, finally, in the form ʿpr from Egypt of the 19th and 20th Dynasty.[1] That it was the name of a people is out of the question, or that there was a people of Hebrews, especially since, wherever the personal names of such 'Hebrews' are mentioned, we find they are of quite different origin. It was more a particular term for a special legal and social position; and we occasionally find the word used in this way in the Books of the Law in the Old Testament (Exod. xxi, 2; Deut. xv, 12)[2]. People or groups of people with inferior legal rights and small financial means appear under the name 'Hebrews': they perform services where and as they are required. They did not belong or perhaps no longer belonged to the various strata of the old-established population but represented certain restless nomadic elements who had no roots in the soil. The sources to which we have access do not enable us to define their character exactly, and possibly their position varied according to time and place and historical circumstances. Even the meaning[3] and origin of the widespread term 'Hebrew' is still somewhat obscure. But the fact that it was widespread means that there is no reason to see any material connection between the Ḫabiru of the Amarna tablets and the Israelite tribes, and there is no mention in the Amarna tablets that they came from Syria-Palestine from the desert or that they had come recently.

About the time the Israelite tribes established themselves in Palestine, an important movement affected the city state territories from another direction. About 1200 B.C. there was an influx of land-seeking elements from the Mediterranean region by sea and land into the civilised areas of the ancient East. We are familiar with this movement from Egyptian sources, since the immigrants also attacked Egypt and the Pharaohs Mernephta and, above all, Ramses III had to ward off these 'maritime people' from their

[1] The material that has been known for a good time will be mostly found in A. Jirku, *Die Wanderungen der Hebräer im 3. und 2. Jahrtausend v. Chr.* (AO, 24, 2 [1924], pp. 13 ff.). The new material includes the occurrence of ʿpr on a stele of the Pharaoh Amenophis II (1448–1420 B.C.), l. 30 (A. M. Badawi, *Annales du Services des Antiquités de l'Égypte*, 42 [1943], pp. 1 ff.) found in Memphis, where 'Hebrews' occur among the prisoners of war brought in by the Pharaoh from Palestine-Syria. The ʿpr which are mentioned on a stele of the Pharaoh Sethos I (cf. AOB², No. 97) found in the Palestinian town Beth-Sean, establish the connection between the Egyptian ʿpr and the Ḫabiru of the Near East.

[2] But cf. also A. Jepsen, AfO, 15 (1945–1951), pp. 54 ff.

[3] A surmise on this point will be found in W. F. Albright, *The Biblical Period* (in L. Finkelstein, *The Jews* [1949]), p. 57, note 39.

land. They succeeded in doing so and they described their victories in word and picture[1].

This assault by the 'maritime people' was merely the tail-end of a comprehensive ethnic movement which came over the eastern Mediterranean world from the north and of which the so-called Dorian migration in Greece was a part. With their bag and baggage these immigrants apparently came along the coasts to some extent on ox-carts, and partly on ships from island to island or along the eastern border of the Mediterranean. They travelled through Asia Minor and attacked and destroyed the Kingdom of the Hittites. On the coast of Syria-Palestine they moved to the south. They also appear to have crossed from Greece and the Greek islands to the Libyan coast of North Africa and to have threatened Egypt from this side. But the final waves of the movement broke on the frontier of Egypt. The Egyptians had all kinds of names for the 'maritime peoples' who came into their purview, including prst and ṯkr which are important for us, since we know that the 'maritime people' who were called by these names settled in Palestine at this period. Prst is the Egyptian version of the name 'Philistine'; and in the report of the Egyptian official Wen-Amon we hear that around 1900 B.C. the ṯkr occupied one of the few Palestinian coastal towns, the town of Dor (the modern el-burj near et-ṭanṭūra) south of the Carmel salient[2].

The settlement of the Philistines in Palestine was big with consequences for the history of Israel. According to an Old Testament tradition the Philistines had occupied the southern part of the coastal plain of Palestine to the north as far as nahr el-ʿōja and lived there in five fairly small states each containing one town —in most cases the evidence suggests that they were ancient Bronze Age cities—as the seat of government. These cities were Gaza (modern ghazze), Askalon (modern ʿasḳalān), Ashdod (modern esdūd), Akkaron[3] (modern ʿāḳir) and Gath (situated the furthest inland on the coastal plain at a spot which has not yet been identified). In these states the Philistines lived as an, in all probability, fairly compact, warlike[4] ruling class, over the old

[1] The illustrations and inscriptions in the Palace of Ramses III in medinet habu (on the west side of Egyptian Thebes), are particularly relevant; cf. J. H. Breasted, *Ancient Records of Egypt*, IV (1906), pp. 59-82; AOB[2], No. 111, 112.

[2] A translation of this travel report will be found in AOT[2], pp. 71 ff. and TGI, pp. 36 ff.; the passage in question will be found at I, 8 f., *ibid.* p. 71 or p. 36.

[3] In the Old Testament this name was wrongly vocalised as 'Ekron'; the correct pronunciation can be deduced from the later Assyrian rendering Amkarruna.

[4] Compare the description of the arming of a Philistine hoplite in 1 Sam. xvii, 5-7, which is given with obvious admiration and awe.

Canaanite inhabitants of the region, under five rulers[1] who united in a common alliance, at any rate when military necessity demanded, which was led by one of the five rulers as the *primus inter pares*. When one remembers that *circa* 1200 B.C. the Pharaohs still maintained their claim to supremacy in Palestine and that as the part of the land nearest to Egypt this southern coastal plain had particularly close ties with Egypt by reason of its Egyptian administration and Egyptian temples it may easily be surmised that the occupation of the land by the Philistines in this area did not take place without the tacit or even explicit consent of the Pharaohs who thus kept the 'maritime people' out of Egypt itself by encouraging them to settle in neighbouring Palestine.[2] However much the Philistines developed a vigorously expansive military dominion in Palestine, so far as we know they never threatened Egypt again. The Philistines entered the world of Palestine as a foreign element. The Israelites liked to call them simply the 'uncircumcised' since they did not know and did not adopt the custom of circumcision which was evidently a very old tradition in Syria-Palestine as well as in Egypt and had probably been adopted by the earlier immigrants as well. According to Amos ix, 7, Jer. xlvii, 4 they had come from Caphtor, *i.e.* Crete. But they were not natives of Crete, not the upholders of the Minoan civilisation, whom the Egyptians described quite differently. It may be that Crete was the last stopping-place on their journey before they settled in Palestine. Their starting-point had certainly been far distant, and the few Philistine personal names known to us suggest the possibility of Illyrian descent[3]. As they probably settled in fairly large numbers in a single self-contained area in Palestine they were able to preserve their own characteristics and their native warlike vigour for several centuries until finally they too succumbed to the fate of every ruling class and were absorbed more and more by the native subject population.

The Philistines were, if not the greatest, certainly the most important 'maritime' element and the one best known to us, that appeared *circa* 1200 in Palestine, but they were not the only one. Further north, in the coastal plain of Palestine and apparently separate from the Philistines, the above-mentioned ṯkr settled in Dor and established an, at that time, probably small dominion.

[1] According to the Old Testament these Philistine rulers bore the specific title of *seranim*, possibly a Philistinian word, which has been presumed to be connected with the word τύραννος.

[2] Thus A. Alt, ZDPV, 67 (1944–1945), pp. 15 ff.

[3] Cf. G. Herbig, *Jahrb. d. Dtsch. Arch. Instituts*, 55 (1940), pp. 58 ff.; A. Jirku, WZKM, 49 (1943), pp. 13 f.

Such elements of 'maritime people' seem, however, to have penetrated into the coastal plain north of the Carmel and the plain of Jezreel. The King Sisera, whom we know from Judges iv and v, who resided in the region between the northern coastal plain and the plain of Jezreel, also appears to have an Illyrian name[1]; during excavations in ʿaffūle in the centre of the plain of Jezreel 'Philistine ceramics' were found[2] and on the site of the city of Beth-Sean (the modern tell el-ḥöṣn near bēsān) on the nahr jālūd (which flows from the plain of Jezreel to the Jordan Valley) the excavations have revealed remains dating from the beginning of the Iron Age, which provide evidence of specific contacts with the Mediterranean world[3]. As the information about the ṯkr in Dor is merely accidental and incidental, we may assume that the same ṯkr or other groups of 'maritime people' gained a foothold in other places in the immediate vicinity of Dor, or further afield. As regards this more remote area, it is doubtful whether the occupation of the land by these strangers also took place with the consent of the Egyptians, as was probably the case when the Philistines settled in Palestine, or whether it was simply a matter of unauthorised conquest by force of arms. Remembering, however, that the excavations have established that at any rate the city of Beth-Sean was a definite stronghold of Egyptian power and the site of Egyptian temples, one is bound to reckon with the possibility that in this area of central Palestine too Egyptian territory was made available by the Pharaohs to land-seeking groups of 'maritime people' after they had been repelled from Egypt. But even if they first gained a footing in Palestine by being assigned land by the Egyptians the 'maritime' elements did not rest content with their initial possessions but strove to consolidate their position. From a somewhat later period we know of the powerful expansionism of the Philistines and their successful attempt to obtain dominion over at any rate the whole of the land west of the Jordan, and we shall hardly be on the wrong track if we assume that this was merely the continuation and consummation of an urge to expand which had goaded them on in Palestine from the very beginning. And if the Sisera mentioned in Judges iv and v came from the 'maritime peoples', this warlike lord may also be regarded as typifying the development of the power of the 'maritime peoples' in Palestine. It follows that the appearance of these people may have introduced

[1] Cf. A. Alt, ZAW, N.F. 19 (1944), p. 78, note 3.

[2] Cf. M. Maisler, *Biblical Archaeologist*, 15 (1952), p. 22.

[3] Cf. AOB², No. 675 with 671 and No. 676 with No. 674. On this whole complex of problems cf. J. Hempel, PJB, 23 (1927), pp. 52-92.

more unrest and movement into the land than is immediately obvious from the historical tradition that has come down to us. For with the actual cessation of Egyptian rule in Palestine the Egyptian information about conditions and events in the land breaks off, and the maritime people left no historical tradition of their own in writing, or, at any rate, none has come down to us. As the events in question took place in areas with which the Israelite tribes had little to do at first, we cannot expect the Old Testament to contain any information on the subject. The 'maritime peoples', coming from the coast, entered the Canaanite city-state territories and settled in that region. And the old Canaanite city states on the plains of the land west of the Jordan were the first and, to begin with, the sole territories to be affected by the aggressive 'maritime peoples', and had to try to defend themselves against their dominance. This no doubt led, during the 12th and 11th centuries B.C., to much excitement on the coastal plain and the plain of Jezreel, the details of which are completely unknown to us and only scattered traces of which remain[1]. Since archaeological research has discovered for the period in question numerous traces of military actions, conquests and cremations in the ruins of the cities in the area covered by these plains, we are bound to seek for an explanation above all in conflicts which took place with the 'maritime peoples'.

The Israelite tribes entered into a land which in certain areas was crowded with cities which, owing to a stormy past, were inhabited by a far from uniform population, made up of the most diverse elements living in a highly differentiated society, and which, after the cessation of Egyptian rule and the emergence of the new ruling class of the 'maritime peoples', were moving into a period of tumultuous military conflicts with one another. At the same time, however, these cities had, from the Bronze Age onwards, been centres not merely of an advanced material civilisation but of a certain intellectual life which is bound to have been as varied as the character and origins of the population. We know very little about this and have at the most some information—above all from the Ras-Shamra texts—about the religious system in which the powers of growth and fertility played the dominant role. With the Babylonian writing and language, which was possibly introduced by the Hyksos for diplomatic correspondence but may have been familiar previously, Babylonian traditions and outlook had also gained a foothold; since even to learn and practise this difficult

[1] An example of this will be found in A. Alt, ZAW, N.F. 19 (1944), pp. 67-85.

mode of writing samples of Babylonian literature were needed which thereby became familiar.[1] All kinds of elements of Babylonian tradition and ideas which became known to the Israelites, according to the Old Testament, certainly reached them through the mediation of the Bronze Age cities. In the field of law, too, especially in the documentation of legal business, Babylonian influence predominated in Syria-Palestine.[2] On the other hand, the century-long Egyptian rule in Palestine, with the Egyptian institutions and Egyptian temples which it had introduced, was bound to influence the intellectual life of the towns. If Psalm 104 reveals unmistakably a knowledge of the Hymn to the Sun composed by the Pharaoh Amenophis IV, who called himself Echnaton[3], it was once again no doubt through the mediation of the Bronze Age cities that the Israelites acquired this knowledge. The world into which the Israelite tribes came possessed a very important intellectual tool and an important precondition for the transmission and diffusion of its intellectual life: namely, an alphabet. In fact, Syria-Palestine in the Late Bronze Age appears to have been the place where this supremely significant and infinitely momentous discovery of a purely phonetic script was developed for the first time. The older system of writing of the ancient East, the originally Sumerian cuneiform script (which spread over the whole Land of the Two Rivers and the neighbouring regions) and Egyptian hieroglyphs, were extremely complicated combinations of incipient word writing and phonetic syllabic writing developed from hundreds of characters which could be written and read only by a handful of specialists and by scribes, who thereby occupied not only extremely important and influential positions in political and economic life, but became the guardians and mediators of intellectual traditions. It was the invention of an alphabetical phonetic spelling which was able to make do with some twenty different characters that made the universal dissemination of the art of reading and writing possible, since it was now possible for anyone to learn. And this invention had been made in Syria-Palestine *circa* 1200 B.C., and the Israelite tribes were able to learn and adopt it at once.

The Ras-Shamra script, in which most of the Ras-Shamra texts are written, is an alphabetic script which uses the technique of Babylonian cuneiform writing and therefore presupposes a knowledge

[1] For example, a copy of the Babylonic Adapa myth has been found in the Amarna archives which had obviously been used for the training of scribes.

[2] Cf. A. Alt, WO, I, 2 (1947), pp. 78 ff.

[3] Translation of this Hymn to the Sun in AOT², pp. 15-18.

of this system. It was used in the 14th century B.C. in ancient Ugarit (the modern rās esch-shamra), but was not entirely unknown outside Ugarit in Syria-Palestine. Two small traces of it have actually been discovered in Palestine, namely a clay tablet from the Late Bronze Age Beth-Semes on the inner border of the southern coastal plain[1] and a bronze blade of a knife from the district east of Mount Thabor dating from approximately 1350–1250 B.C.[2]); both examples have the writing from right to left as on a clay tablet of the rās esch-shamra, whilst usually this writing was written in the opposite direction in Ugarit. This script does not, however, appear to have been very widespread or to have been used for very long, since it yielded to a probably even older and at any rate more serviceable application of the alphabetic principle which did not derive from Babylonic cuneiform, but linked up with Egyptian hieroglyphs, even in its technique: it was not impressed on to the soft clay of a clay tablet like cuneiform writing, but, except in the case of stone inscriptions, was written in some ink or other on potsherds or papyrus.

This writing, the mother of all the alphabetic scripts in use in the world today, is known to us above all from a series of stone inscriptions from Byblos, which probably date from the 10th century B.C.[3]. But it is evidently older than that and had various precursors in a number of alphabetic experiments which were carried out in the middle and Late Bronze Age, beginning with the so-called Sinaitic inscriptions from the region of the Egyptian mines of serābīṭ el-khādem on the Sinaitic Peninsula which have become famous, but still not been entirely satisfactorily elucidated[4].

As early as *circa* 1100 B.C. papyrus was being used with great zeal as writing material in Phoenicia; according to the report of Wen-Amon which we have already mentioned, the timber of Lebanon was paid for by the Egyptians in Byblos and elsewhere with 500 rolls of papyrus[5], and in Syria-Palestine these rolls of papyrus will scarcely have been used for writing Egyptian hieroglyphs but probably for writing in alphabetic script. *Circa* 1100 B.C.

[1] Cf. WAT, p. 168.

[2] Thus Yeivin, *Kedem* 2 (1945), pp. 32-41, after BASOR, 99 (1945), p. 21.

[3] Cf. WAT, pp. 168 f. Possibly the Ahirim inscription, though the oldest, only belongs to the 10th century.

[4] Cf. WAT, pp. 169 ff. W. F. Albright, BASOR, 110 (1948), pp. 6 ff. has substantially promoted the deciphering of the Sinaitic inscriptions; he places it in the 15th century B.C. A new fragmentary archaic inscription of the Late Bronze Age has been found on the tell es-sarem (south of Beth-Sean); cf. R. Brandstetter-Kallner, *Kedem*, 2 (1945), pp. 11 ff. according to BASOR, 99 (1945), p. 21.

[5] Cf. AOT[2], p. 75; TGI, p. 41 (II, 41).

the writing of this script may well have been quite common, and its development—attended by numerous very clumsy experiments—no doubt took place in Syria-Palestine as early as the Late Bronze Age. That it spread further in time and space than is explicitly attested by the documents that have been preserved, is only to be expected. The everyday writing material of cuneiform, the dried or even burnt clay tablet on which the characters were impressed, could in tolerably favourable circumstances survive for thousands of years comparatively easily. But the ink with which potsherds were inscribed in the alphabetic script could survive only very rarely; and though the precious papyrus which was used as writing material was durable in the rainless climate of Egypt, it could not last long in Syria-Palestine; and so the only evidence of the earliest use of this letter script that has survived consists of stone inscriptions; but in Syria-Palestine stone inscriptions were evidently always few and far between.

It is difficult to over-estimate what the possibility of the wide diffusion of the art of reading and writing meant for government, for trade and commerce, for the law and for intellectual and cultural life in general. In Syria-Palestine the Israelite tribes encountered a world which was no match for the ancient civilisation of Egypt and the Lower Euphrates-Tigris in respect of the originality of its cultural achievements but which led a richly varied life, fertilised from many sides, and which possessed in the invention and first application of the alphabetic script a cultural asset of its own which was of supreme importance and with which it made a decisive contribution to human civilisation.

4. *The Sources of the History of Israel*

History can only be described on the basis of literary traditions, which record events and specify persons and places. Even archaeological discoveries can only be understood and appreciated in relation to information from literary sources. A description of the development of ancient cultures based merely on archaeology does not result in history but at the most pre-history. On the other hand, the investigation of the material remains of the periods under review often gives colour and life to the literary traditions and greatly assists our understanding of them. It is no longer feasible to describe the 'history of Israel' on the basis simply of the written records that have come down to us, ignoring the abundant and, to a very large extent well authenticated, results of Palestinian archaeology.

If we begin by enquiring about the origin of the information which enables us to establish the outward course of the history of Israel as a whole and in many of its details, we must refer, in the first place, to the Old Testament with its wealth of historical material, but also to a great mass of sources outside the Old Testament. In the Old Testament one must mention first of all the great historical work which comprises the books of Deuteronomy, Joshua, Judges, Samuel, Kings, which we call 'deuteronomistic'[1] by reason of its language and spirit and which offers the very first exposition of the 'history of Israel' up to the events of the year 587 B.C. The author of this traditional work passed on numerous sources from different periods, of different extent and different origin and nature, partly *in extenso*, partly in extracts, and developed the whole work from these sources[2]. He thereby conveyed to posterity a mass of valuable traditional material and without his work we should know very little about the earlier phases of the history of Israel. For the other great historical work in the Old Testament, the 'chronistic' work[3], made use of the deuteronomistic work as the only, or at least the principal, source for these earlier stages, in so far as it dealt with them at all, and only added new material for the period following 587 B.C. derived from a few other sources. For the history of Israel right into the 5th century B.C. our main source of information is therefore the Old Testament, which offers a great deal of historical material even outside the two above mentioned historical works.

A more difficult question in this connection is in what sense the Pentateuch can be called a historical work. There can be no doubt that it sets out to relate events that have happened and that it contains a good deal of material relating to historical traditions. On the other hand, however, it is certain that it did not originate and was not planned, at any rate from the outset, as a historical work at all, but has its source in the successive coalescences of sacred traditions which are based on particular historical events[4]. It is a great collective work which conveys historical information but was not designed and drafted as a coherent historical narrative. The question as to how far it may be drawn on in an exposition of

[1] It will be indicated by the abbreviation Deut.

[2] Cf. for further details M. Noth, *Überlieferungsgeschichtliche Studien*, I (Schriften der Königsberg. Gel. Ges., geisteswiss. Kl. XVIII, 2 (1943)), p. 3-110.

[3] Abbreviation: Chr.; on this matter cf. M. Noth, *loc. cit.* pp. 110-180.

[4] Further details in M. Noth, *Überlieferungsgeschichte des Pentateuch* (1948).

the course of the history of Israel is therefore especially problematical: it can only be used with many provisos. The close and constant connection of the history of Israel with the history of the ancient oriental world means that many of the historical documents of the ancient Orient—above all, royal inscriptions and other official records—are immediately, or at any rate indirectly, relevant to the history of Israel. Apart from all kinds of sporadic information from Egyptian sources, the inscriptions of the New Assyrian kings are the main source for the earlier period. To some degree these kings intervened in Israelite history with sudden decisiveness. Unfortunately the neo-Babylonian and Persian kings of whom the same is true, left behind only slight historical information in their inscriptions[1].

Where the real historical tradition of the Old Testament comes to an end, there is, to begin with, a painful gap in the sources of the history of Israel. It is only when we reach the second and third quarter of the 2nd century B.C. that a detailed historical tradition becomes available once more in the two books of Maccabees which have come down to us in the framework of the Hellenistic form of the Old Testament, that is, the Greek Septuagint. It is true that they also present some problems, above all concerning the relation of the two books of Maccabees to one another, but they do contain so much concrete historical information that the period they describe is one of the best known in the history of Israel. For the subsequent period the Jewish historian Josephus is the main source[2], with his large-scale work on the history of Israel composed under the Emperor Domitian, for the first half of which he depended almost entirely on the Old Testament tradition, including the books of the Maccabees; but in the end he began to write on the basis of trustworthy historical sources of his own and thereby himself became a historical source. From about the 1st century B.C. onwards Josephus's historical information becomes increasingly detailed and complete, so that he becomes our main source for the history of Israel up to the year A.D. 73[3].

For this later period too we still have numerous isolated reports

[1] The most important of these records will be found in translation in ANET and AOT², where, admittedly, the sections with the historical texts are rather scanty. The historical tradition of the Egyptians will be found in translation in J. H. Breasted, *Ancient Records of Egypt*, I-V (1906–1907), that of the Assyrians in D. D. Luckenbill, *Ancient Records of Assyria and Babylonia*, I/II (1927). A good selection of texts will be found in TGI.

[2] Edition of the text: *Flavii Josephi opera recogn.* B. Niese, I-VI (1888–1895).

[3] On the insurrection of A.D. 66–73 cf. Josephus, *ἱστορία Ἰουδαϊκοῦ πολέμου πρὸς Ῥωμαίους*, with a historical introduction that starts at the time of the Maccabeans.

referring directly or indirectly to the history of Israel, mainly deriving from the Graeco-Roman world. They are found, above all, in works concerning the history of the Hellenistic States and the Roman Empire, in which the history of Israel was now most intimately involved. Unfortunately these sources are rather scanty.

The study of historical sources cannot and must not be confined to the collecting and arranging of the relevant information. In certain circumstances the task of interpreting the relative usefulness and significance of the sources is even more important. This applies particularly to the history of Israel, and especially to its earlier stages, for which official records are few, and even those that do exist only represent a limited selection of which the underlying principle has to be discerned before they can be utilised. For the greater part, however, the Old Testament contains popular historical traditions especially concerning the early history of Israel, which were transmitted by word of mouth to begin with and not written down until later. They are usually the only information which we have regarding certain events and processes so that there is no chance of checking their accuracy. In such cases it is absolutely necessary to investigate the source of these records, to ask what occasioned them, why they were made and made in this form, what they are intended to connote and what they are capable of signifying historically. And this question must be applied to each single tradition. Even the purpose and nature of the beginnings of real historiography, which go back to a fairly early period in the age of David and Solomon and the productions of which have come down to us, in so far as they were included in his great collective work by the deuteronomist, must be investigated before their value can be assessed objectively. It would certainly be wrong to regard as authoritative only the traditional material which happens to have been preserved, and not raise questions and problems which this material can perhaps help us to answer merely incidentally. From the facts which it records it may be possible to draw cautious inferences about other matters beyond its immediate interest and concern.

The differences of opinion which still persist, especially regarding the beginnings and earliest periods of Israel's history, are based very largely on uncertainties involved in the utilisation of the popular traditions of the Old Testament. This is not surprising, however, since the examination of the origins, motives and development of this tradition has not yet been undertaken at all systematically, much less led to positive results. There is still much to be done in this field. It is not enough, in considering the popular nature of this tradition, to dispute the historical credibility of certain passages according to our own discretion and to stick to the rest as the 'historical nucleus' and incorporate it in the history of Israel or, alternatively, to assess the historical credibility on the basis of the approximate age of the various traditions. What is important is rather to grasp as precisely as possible the historical assumptions behind these traditions and then to assess as objectively as possible what they can contribute to our knowledge of the outward course of the history of Israel, and what they cannot contribute. The same applies, however, to the literary historical narratives and to the later more comprehensive historical works, and the traditional materials incorporated in them. Only when we have grasped the circumstances under which they arose and what they are driving at, can we answer the vital question as to how they arrived at their particular selection from the wealth of events and why they presented it in the particular way they did. Only when we have answered that can we discern the subjects on which they can be expected to supply information and the weight which may be attached to what they say and to what they suppress. It must be clear from the outset that it is absolutely necessary to ask these questions and to answer them as far as possible[1], but also that the answers cannot be given with mathematical clarity and certainty, since many unknown factors are involved and the answers must be arrived at by taking all the circumstances into account and reaching a synthesis as intelligently as possible. An exposition of history based on this kind of approach may be called 'subjective', even though it is committed to a conscientious interpretation of the sources. In this sense, however, every exposition of history is inevitably 'subjective' even if it is imagined to be 'objective', since the fact is that the available traditions shed a purely accidental light on the course of events as a whole and can only be evaluated within the framework of a specific approach to the material. But, by doing justice to all the available information, such a 'subjective' approach will be convincing and therefore justified.

Historical synthesis is indispensable even in the interpretation and utilisation of archaeological findings, that is, the entirely visible, concrete, verifiable remains of past history. In this case too it is a matter of constantly fitting the isolated details into historical

[1] Anyone who does not ask these questions misjudges the situation and inevitably gives tacit answers, only these answers will not be considered and well founded, and will therefore not withstand closer examination.

contexts which have first to be reconstructed. Admittedly, the sober consideration of all the probabilities and improbabilities is a specially urgent necessity in this field. One has to be very clear what the results of archaeological work can prove and what they cannot prove. For more than a century now the excavators' spades have brought to light from the soil of the Near East the material which has made possible a mass of surprisingly many-sided and accurate information on the great and rich world of the ancient Orient and its stirring history. When one asks, however, what this modern knowledge is primarily based on, the answer must inevitably be the innumerable written documents which have come to light as a direct or indirect result of the excavations. What knowledge of any real accuracy and historical substance of the ancient Orient should we possess if we had all the material remains excepting the literary relics in the widest sense of the word? Inasmuch as even the latter have in the main become available as the result of archaeological work this has acquired a position of absolutely prime importance for historical knowledge, including knowledge of the history of Israel. It is true that in the narrower sphere of Israel itself, in Syria-Palestine, discoveries of written memorials are rare surprises. And that is no mere accident. In contrast to the great river oases of the lower Land of the Two Rivers and of Egypt, the hilly and heterogeneous land of Syria-Palestine did not develop great political organisations and there was therefore little occasion for inscribed stone memorials or large buildings with inscriptions. But whilst it was possible for writings of an everyday character to survive in the Land of the Two Rivers in the form of clay tablets inscribed with quoins and also on inscribed sheets of papyrus in the completely dry climate of Egypt, it was not possible in Syria-Palestine where only the clay tablets of the Late Bronze Age, inscribed with cuneiform characters, were able to survive for centuries, whereas the papyrus perished entirely owing to the winter rain and even the writing on potsherds only survived under unusually favourable conditions. For the most part, therefore, the written documents of the Iron Age failed to survive at all.

As far as the Israelite age is concerned, Syrian-Palestinian archaeology is therefore almost wholly silent; and it is clear that under these circumstances the historical interpretation of archaeological discoveries is particularly difficult. The understandable enthusiasm with which, to begin with, unusually intensive excavations were carried out in Palestine, from purely Biblical motives, with the aim of finding positive and indisputable traces of Israelite history, has in many cases led to the drawing of hasty parallels between the discoveries and known events of history, which have turned out to be untenable; and although Syrian-Palestinian archaeology has long since developed from an auxiliary discipline of Biblical studies into an independent science with methods of its own and aims evolving from its own work[1], it has still not entirely overcome the improper search for direct Biblical connections. To look for its significance in the wrong direction is to make unfair demands on Palestinian archaeology and to overlook the really positive contribution it can make to our historical knowledge. In general, it must not be expected to yield positive evidence concerning particular historical events and processes, except when it leads to the happy discovery of written documents. But it can certainly shed a far-reaching light on the presuppositions and conditions of life and the changes they underwent in the course of time, and it can thereby reveal the background against which the historical personalities acted and the historical events took place; and in so far as these phenomena and movements are always closely related to that background, it makes a substantial contribution to our insight into the historical process. Thus an account of the history of Israel which does not refer constantly to the results of Syrian-Palestinian archaeology, is indefensible now that this source of information has become accessible. It has had the greatest possible and most enduring influence on our total conception of the history of Israel, by revealing through innumerable details the world in which this history ran its course and it has thereby enabled us to achieve a fresh and vivid understanding of the reality behind the historical events which have been transmitted by the literary tradition. It is true that in the nature of things it is only rarely that archaeological evidence is forthcoming to prove that a particular event actually took place and that it happened as described in the written records; since the fact that an event can be shown to have been possible is no proof that it actually occurred, and the archaeological illumination of the general situation in any particular period does not in any way enable us to dispense with the close study of the traditional information. On the other hand, however,

[1] Their results have been expertly and thoroughly collated with a wealth of illustrations, in C. Watzinger, *Denkmäler Palästinas. Eine Einführung in die Archäologie des Heiligen Landes*, I/II (1933–1935), and more briefly but still very reliably in P. Thomsen, *Palästina und seine Kultur in fünf Jahrtausenden nach den neuesten Ausgrabungen und Forschungen dargestellt*, 3rd ed. (AO, Vol. 30) and in W. F. Albright, *The Archaeology of Palestine* (1951). W. F. Albright, *From the Stone Age to Christianity*, 2nd ed. 1946, offers a comprehensive evaluation of the results of the archaeological work, especially for the inner continuity and progress of Israelite history.

information that has stood the test of time can usually be understood more precisely and concretely, and therefore more positively and comprehensively, and appreciated and visualised more vividly in the setting of a particular period when illuminated by the material remains, than would be the case without them; and at the same time, a picture which has only been drawn with single strokes in the literary records can often be supplemented and rounded off by the archaeological discoveries. Thus the history of Israel has gained substantially in colour and plasticity as a result of Syrian-Palestinian archaeology.

Everything we have said so far concerns the outward course of the history of Israel and the question of the available sources. Everything that can make any contribution, direct, or indirect, is to be welcomed wholeheartedly. But the fundamental meaning of the history of Israel cannot be inferred from the innumerable sporadic assertions that occur in the sources or from the course of the actual history itself; *the* source of information on this subject is simply the witness of the Old Testament which explains the fact that the history of Israel is, like all human history, mysterious and ambiguous when judged merely from the outside, by declaring outright that God, the Lord of the whole world, here used a people as his instrument so that in it 'shall all families of the earth be blessed' (Gen. xii, 3). That this testimony exists, is in the first place a historical fact, which is itself part of the history of Israel; and it would be unscientific to disregard this truly singular fact. This self-testimony makes the history of Israel not merely unique, as every national history on earth is unique and unrepeatable, but utterly unique in character among the histories of the nations. That this self-testimony is valid can no longer be proved. The outward history of Israel can be described as a coherent whole without deeper questionings even if this self-testimony is ignored; and the question as to the basis and meaning of many phenomena can be left alone as unanswerable: world history is, after all, full of such unanswerable questions. But to ignore this question as to the deeper meaning of Israel's history is to leave out of account a certain fact —the fact that the main traditional source of information in the history of Israel, beside which all other sources are purely supplementary, is indissolubly bound up with this testimony. The Old Testament relates the history of Israel in such detail simply for the sake of this testimony. And this fact must be taken seriously. The Old Testament is not merely a treasury of traditional historical information but, on a higher plane, *the* real source for the history of Israel besides which all other sources must be regarded as secondary, in so far as it not only gives a coherent account of the external course of this history over a fairly long period, but also utters the decisive word towards an understanding of this history[1].

[1] From the wealth of previous books on the subject we propose to mention here only those which can still claim more than purely historical interest, which means that it is not necessary to include anything published before the opening up of the ancient Orient and its utilisation for the history of Israel. In the first place reference must be made to the work by R. Kittel which first appeared in 1888–1892 as *Geschichte der Hebräer* and from the 2nd edition onwards (Vol. I, 1912, Vol. II, 1909) as *Geschichte des Volkes Israel* and who made unflinching use of the new discoveries and knowledge of the ancient Orient. In the final revised edition ($I^{5, 6}$, 1923; II^{6}, 1925) it can still be considered a standard work. The first two volumes which dealt with the history up to 587 B.C. were followed much later by a third volume in two parts (1927–1929) which extends to the end of the Persian period. Admittedly, no one would now begin the history of Israel with a description of the whole primeval and early age Palestine (against II^{6}, p. xi), since nowadays a history of Palestine is already a problem on its own and different from a history of Israel, and the cultural history of Palestine can only be treated, at any rate in its wider context, with that of Syria; but the incorporation of Israel in the greater entity of the world around it, which Kittel clearly discerned as his task, will always be a necessity for any historian of Israel. A more concise work is E. Sellin's *Geschichte des israelitisch-jüdischen Volkes*, I (1924), II (1932) which—with all kinds of original and not always tenable theses—extends to the period of Alexander the Great, since the third volume which was to have brought the history of Israel to its appropriate conclusion in the first two centuries A.D. was no longer written. On the basis of an intimate knowledge of its setting, the history of Israel to the period of Ezra and Nehemiah was written in an independent and stimulating way by E. Auerbach under the title *Wüste und Gelobtes Land*, I (1932), II (1936), in which the author brings out the influence of the neighbouring desert on the course of Palestinian and therefore Israelite history. There are other more detailed expositions of the subject by T. H. Robinson and W. E. Oesterley, *A History of Israel*, I/II (1932) and A. Lods, *Israël des origines au milieu du VIIIe siècle* (1930) and *Les Prophètes et le début du judaïsme* (1935). For the final period of the history of Israel there is now the comprehensive work of F.-M. Abel, *Histoire de la Palestine depuis la conquête d'Alexandre jusqu'à l'invasion arabe*, I/II (1952); for the last phase of the history of Israel the very detailed treatment of E. Schürer, *Geschichte des jüdischen Volkes im Zeitalter Jesu Christi*, I ($^{3, 4}$ 1901), II (^{4} 1907), III (^{4} 1909) is still of basic importance: it starts with the Maccabean period and extends to A.D. 135. A. Schlatter, *Geschichte Israels von Alexander dem Grossen bis Hadrian* (^{3} 1925) provides an easily understood account, based on penetrating independent study of the sources, of the concluding section of the history of Israel with special regard to religious and intellectual life. Among the smaller textbooks we may note H. Guthe, *Geschichte des Volkes Israel* (^{3} 1914), extending to A.D. 135, still useful, though in many respects out of date, and A. Jirku, *Geschichte des Volkes Israel* (1931) which only goes as far as 587 B.C. W. F. Albright, *The Biblical Period*, deals with the history of Israel précis-fashion, including the Persian period, and the subsequent period is dealt with similarly by E. Bickerman in *The Historical Foundations of Postbiblical Judaism* (both of these in the collective work L. Finkelstein, *The Jews; their History, Culture and Religion* [1949]). A. Alt, *Kleine Schriften zur Geschichte des Volkes Israel*, I/II (1953) contains numerous separate studies of basic importance on problems of the history of Israel.

of Israel besides which, all other sources must be regarded as secondary, in so far as it not only gives a coherent account of the external course of the history over a fairly long period, but also affords the decisive [illegible] towards an understanding of this history.

[illegible]

PART ONE

ISRAEL AS THE CONFEDERACY OF THE TWELVE TRIBES

CHAPTER I

THE ORIGINS OF THE TRIBES OF ISRAEL

5. *The Homes of the Tribes in Palestine*

'ISRAEL', which, according to Old Testament tradition, was an association of twelve separate tribes, cannot be really grasped as a historical totality until it becomes a reality living on the soil of Palestine. Naturally, the Old Testament tradition is unquestionably right in regarding the tribes not as indigenous to Palestine but as having entered and gained a footing there from the wilderness and steppe at a definite point in time. Even if the event had not been recorded in so many words it would be possible to infer that it had taken place from the location of the areas occupied by the tribes in Palestine and from their mode of living and dwelling there. It goes without saying that the tribes had a history of their own before they entered Palestine and in the Old Testament certain tribal traditions from that early period have been preserved which are undoubtedly genuine. We shall deal with them later on in greater detail. On the other hand, these traditions were first given their definitive form within an Israel that was already united in Palestine and they were conditioned by its point of view. Together with the historical events on which they are based they made a contribution of basic importance to the self-consciousness and faith of Israel when it was living in Palestine, but, at the same time, in their existing form they are based on presuppositions which did not exist until the tribes had already settled on Palestinian soil. Above all, as will be seen in a moment, the fusion of the tribes into the totality of 'Israel' only became a final and enduring reality in Palestine; and the individual tribes only became consolidated into permanent historical realities in the process of their occupation of the land. Traditions are part of the Israel that we know in Palestine and in this connection we must regard them as a historical fact of fundamental significance with their roots in the early history of Israel. On the other hand, the history of Israel, in the strict sense of the history of a more or less definable reality, only begins on the soil of Palestine.

To define this reality with precision it is necessary first of all to establish the order and sequence of the tribes of Israel and the areas which they inhabited. This can be done by using all the various data which are scattered about the fragments of narrative tradition, as preserved above all within the framework of the great collective work of the deuteronomist and, to some extent, in the Pentateuch which evolved on Palestinian soil. A few traditions which deal specifically with individual tribes are the most important source of all. At a subsequent date a comprehensive description of the tribal geography was admitted into the deuteronomist writings (Jos. xiii, 19 (21)) incorporating an old list of the borders of the tribal areas, which probably derives from the period before political organisation took shape and which states the various dwelling-places of the individual tribes in the form of an enumeration of the permanent boundary marks; it is true that it does not simply reproduce the tribal properties at a particular historical date but describes the areas to which the individual tribes laid claim, in accordance with the theory that the *whole* land of Palestine was to belong to the united tribes of Israel. Obviously, however, the territories actually inhabited by the tribes form the basis of the list[1]; to eliminate the purely theoretical elements we are not reduced to mere surmise and supposition, for in Judges i, 21, 27-35 we have a list the basis of which also derives from the pre-political era and which, at least as far as the tribes of central and northern Palestine are concerned, briefly states which Canaanite city-state territories they were in fact unable to occupy, although here too the supposition is that they were really entitled to them[2]. In addition there are one or two further traditions which, whilst they do not deal with the geography of the tribes, do contain some information about the substance and way of life of the tribes of Israel. In Num. xxvi, 4b β-51 we have a list of the families belonging to the tribes which is presumably fairly old, although it is impossible to give it a precise date[3]; and in Gen. xlix, 1b-27/28 and Deut. xxxiii, 6-25 we find collections of

[1] Cf. above all A. Alt, *Das System der Stammesgrenzen im Buche Josua* (Sellin-Festschrift [1927], pp. 13-24=*Kleine Schriften zur Geschichte des Volkes Israel*, I [1953], pp. 193-202), and also M. Noth, ZDPV, 58 (1935), pp. 185 ff.

[2] It is found in a conglomerate of supplements to the deuteronomistic work and it is uncertain how it got there. In its present form it presupposes the later incorporation of these city-state territories in the State of David and Solomon.

[3] This list was subsequently used to compile a later and apocryphal list of the numerical strengths of the single Israelite tribes as applicable at the time of the exodus from Egypt; and for this purpose Moses undertook a census of the people, and the whole episode was inserted as an afterthought into the Pentateuch narrative which had already been compiled: cf. M. Noth, *Das System der zwölf Stämme Israels* (1930), pp. 122 ff.

brief aphorisms about the individual tribes which were later inserted in the Pentateuch narrative in the form of 'Jacob's blessing' and 'Moses' blessing'; such sayings had probably been in circulation among the tribes for a long time; they arose from a desire either to praise or good-humouredly to chaff the other tribes; they were compiled unsystematically and derive from various, no longer precisely definable, periods.

The description of the behaviour of the various tribes of central and northern Palestine contained in the Song of Deborah (Judges v, 2-30) is based possibly not so much on the single event commemorated in that place as on the way the tribes habitually acted.

The tribes of Israel fall into a number of geographically correlated groups. As far as one can see, the tribe of Judah always played the leading part among the tribes of southern Palestine. It inhabited the southern part of the mountains west of Jordan, south of Jerusalem, and its area extended southwards almost as far as the city of Hebron. Bethlehem, at the Amarna period, 'a city of the land of Jerusalem'[1], was its centre. It is now impossible to say how this city, which was probably only temporarily subject to the rule of Jerusalem and had been a small seat of government, came into the possession of the tribe of Judah. To the north the territory of Judah was bordered by the city-state of Jerusalem and the territories of the other city-states in its vicinity; to the east the 'wilderness of Judaea', sloping down to the Dead Sea, formed a natural boundary. The few oasis settlements on the west bank of the Dead Sea may also have been inhabited by Judaeans. As far as these borders are concerned, the descriptions contained in Jos. xv, 1-12 correspond to the facts, but, for reasons which we shall discuss later, southwards and westwards they greatly extended the frontiers of Judah. In fact the mountains south of Judah were inhabited by other tribes, which will be mentioned directly, and even the city of Hebron belonged to one of them and not to the tribe of Judah. In the west, however, the southern part of the Palestinian coastal plain was in the hands of the initially powerful Philistines, who had subjugated the old Canaanite city-states formerly situated there; the only room for new settlements was in the hill country between the mountains proper and the plain, in which there were comparatively few city-states. This was the only direction in which the sturdy tribe of Judah could expand; and in time Judaean families did in fact advance into this hill country and apparently entered into normally peaceful relationships with the

[1] Cf. p. 32 above.

Canaanites already residing in some of the cities there[1]. The name Judah (יהודה) is not related to any well-known type of Semitic personal name and can hardly have been a personal name originally: in any case it cannot be explained philologically as a compound of the name for God (יהוה). On the other hand, we have evidence of a number of similarly constructed place-names[2] and the probability is that it was originally used in the phrase 'mountains of Judah' (הר יהודה) to describe part of a mountainous district south of Jerusalem[3] and in the phrase 'wilderness of Judah' (מדבר יהודה) to describe the area sloping down to the Dead Sea, to the east of the mountains[4]. It is probable that the families who settled in this area called themselves later the 'people of Judah', 'Judaeans' (בני יהודה), and thus became the 'tribe of Judah'.

From various scattered references in the Old Testament we know that a few more tribes or families resided south of these Judaeans in the most southerly part of the mountains. Hebron (in the area of the modern el-chalīl) which was probably already a Canaanite city, was in possession of the *Calebites* who belonged to the kindred of the Kenezites[5], other parts of which were represented among the Edomites[6]. The traditions behind Num. xiii, 14 and Deut. i, 22-45 and Jos. xiv, 6a Bb-15 are an attempt to explain how it came about that Hebron, a city of blessing and importance, was assigned to Caleb, the *heros eponymus* of the Calebites; they therefore presuppose the possession of Hebron by the Calebites. How far the area of the Calebites extended it is no longer possible to say with any certainty. According to 1 Sam. xxv, 1-3 a Calebite was living in Maon, which was about 15 kilometres south of Hebron (the modern tell ma ʿīn), and, according to 1 Sam. xxx, 14 the tribe of Caleb had a share in the Negeb, the somewhat indeterminate region of steppe south of the mountains west of the Jordan. The area occupied by the Calebites appears to have extended southwards from Hebron.

[1] This follows above all from Gen. xxxviii where incidents from the history of the tribes appear in an indistinguishable mixture with other narrative elements (cf. M. Noth, *Überlieferungsgeschichte des Pentateuch*, pp. 162 f.) and also from the geographical list of the settlements which is contained in 1 Chron. ii, 4 (cf. M. Noth, ZDPV, 55 [1932], pp. 97-124). On the incident itself cf. M. Noth, PJB, 30 (1934), pp. 31-47.

[2] From the old Testament we know the city names יגבהה and יראלה; on the other hand, the place name יהוד (Jos. xix, 45) is difficult to separate etymologically from the name יהודה.

[3] Cf. Jos. xi, 21 and especially Jos. xx, 7; xxi, 11, where Hebron, which was not inhabited by Judaeans at all, is described as situated on the הר יהודה; cf. further 2 Chron. xxvii, 4.

[4] Judges i, 16; Psalm lxiii, 1.

[5] In Num. xxxii, 12; Jos. xiv, 6, 14 Caleb is called a 'Kenezite'; cf. also Jos. xv, 17; Judges i, 13; iii, 9.

[6] Cf. Gen. xxxvi, 11, 42.

The *Othnielites* were another Kenezite tribe: according to Jos. xv, 15-19 = Judges i, 11-15 they owned the city of Debir, which is said formerly to have been called Kirjath-Sepher. Unfortunately its situation is not known for certain[1]. But in all probability it lay south-west of Hebron, presumably on the heights of the mountains west of Jordan. We have no information at all as to how far the land of the Othnielites extended in this area.

The most southerly part of the mountains was also inhabited by the *Kenites* whose *heros eponymus* Cain appears in Gen. iv, 1-16. If it is correct that in Jos. xv, 56-57, the words זנוח הקין belong together[2] and are to be translated by 'Zanoah of the Kenites', then the Kenites lived south-east of Hebron; for in Jos. xv, 55-57 this Zanoah is mentioned along with a number of other places in this district. In any case we may take it that the Kenites lived somewhere in the southern part of the mountains west of Jordan, since in 1 Sam. xxx, 29 'the cities of the Kenites' are referred to in connection with other well-known places in the southern part of the mountains. They had, too, a share in the Negeb; in 1 Sam. xxvii, 10 there is a reference to the 'Negeb of the Kenites'. The Kenites do not appear to have become completely domiciled until relatively late and possibly only a part of the tribe settled permanently. In Judges iv, 11-17; v, 24 we hear of a Kenite nomad pitching his tent somewhere or other in Galilee. It is true that, according to Judges iv, 11, he had 'severed himself from the Kenites', but probably there was quite a number of such 'severed' Kenites. On the other hand, according to 1 Sam. xv, 6, in Saul's time the Kenites still regarded themselves as belonging to the nomadic kindred of the Amalekites. Perhaps, therefore, only a section of the Kenites established themselves in a small area south-east of Hebron near the border[3] between the cultivated land and the steppe, whilst other sections maintained their nomadic way of life in the steppe and wilderness and in isolated cases even in the midst of settled civilisations[4].

Finally, we know very little about the *Jerahmeelites* who must also be mentioned in this connection. In 1 Sam. xxx, 29 'the cities of the Jerahmeelites' are mentioned beside 'the cities of the

[1] Cf. above (p. 33, note 1).

[2] Thus, according to the Septuagint.

[3] The fairly late information contained in 1 Sam. xv, 6 might originate in the fact of the juxtaposition of nomadic *and* established Kenites. According to Judges i, 16 (text. em.) it was especially the Kenite clan of בני־חבב that settled in Palestine.

[4] The name of the tribe might indicate that it was an association of desert smiths (cf. Arabic ḳain = 'smith'); but the Kenites who had settled were certainly farmers like the other inhabitants.

Kenites' and in 1 Sam. xxvii, 10 the 'Negeb of the Jerahmeelites' is referred to alongside the 'Negeb of the Kenites', in a later list Jerahmeel appears as the brother of Caleb (1 Chron. ii, 9-42). Although it is impossible to determine their territory very accurately we must also place the Jerahmeelites in the most southerly part of the mountains[1].

The tribe of *Simeon* evidently dwelt entirely in the far south; we know little about it, for in the list of the tribal boundaries in Jos. xiii ff. it is not mentioned at all, and in the historical tradition of the Old Testament it plays no part whatsoever. Only in the fragmentary narratives of unknown origin dealing with the occupation of land by Israelite tribes, contained in Judges i, 1 ff., which were subsequently taken into the Deuteronomist collection of writings, does the tribe appear (Judges i, 3) alongside Judah, and in Judges i, 17 we are informed, in the only concrete statement we have about it at all, that the tribe took possession of the city of Hormah, formerly called Zepthath (the modern tell el-mushāsh east of bīr es-sebaʿ = Beersheba); and the fact that the Simeonites resided in this southerly frontier area caused a late redactor to assign the most southerly district of Judah (Jos. xv, 21-32) at any rate partly to the tribe of Simeon (Jos. xix, 2-8). In the system of tribal frontiers Simeon's area was simply made a part of the totality of Judah (cf. also Jos. xix, 1-9); and in the narrative in Judges i, 1 ff. Simeon also appears entirely in the shadow of Judah. It seems, therefore, that the tribe of Simeon, living as it did entirely on the periphery of the Israelite territories, was in no position to play an independent role in the historical period known to us. Its name was almost certainly originally a personal name (cf. Ezra x, 31); it was therefore named after one of its ancestors.

The most important tribes historically were those of Central Palestine. First among them was the 'house of Joseph'. This term, which has a very original and ancient ring about it[2], gives special prominence to the significance of 'Joseph' within the totality of the tribes of Israel and appears to indicate that in reality more than a single tribe was concerned. It has its counterpart in the expression,

[1] Of the names of these tribes Othniel and especially Jerahmeel are evidently personal names, that is, names of real or fictive ancestors of these tribes. On the name of the Kenites cf. the previous note. There is still some doubt about the name Caleb, which apparently means 'dog' (in an archaic form of the word) and may be a personal name with this meaning; on the other hand, animal names might also be originally tribal names, if not on the basis of an old system of totemism, at any rate in connection with certain tribal tokens or the like.

[2] It occurs in fairly old contexts in Jos. xvii, 17; Judges i, 23, 35; 2 Sam. xix, 21; 1 Kings xi, 28 and also in Jos. xviii, 5; Amos v, 6; Ob. xviii; Zech. x, 6.

'the house of Judah', and the latter is used precisely when not merely the actual tribe of Judah but the whole group of south Palestinian tribes is concerned, which were united under the name of 'Judah' and then combined in a State of their own called 'Judah'[1]. In fact the 'house of Joseph' was a particularly large association of families holding the whole of the central part of the mountains west of Jordan and thereby possessing a more extensive area than any of the other tribes. If this part of the mountains, particularly in the northern half, was relatively intensely wooded, so that clearings had to be made before it was available for settlement[2], this was hardly less true of the mountainous areas in the south and north of the country where more numerous tribes lived side by side. According to the description of the frontier in Jos. xvi, 1-3, to the south the 'house of Joseph' occupied the West Jordan as far as the latitude of the city of Bethel[3] (the modern bētīn) and including this city; in the north—an exact description of the northern border of the tribe of Joseph is not given in the book of Joshua—its area extended as far as the southern boundary of the great plain of Jezreel, which interrupts the course of the mountains west of Jordan. To the east, the slopes leading to the Jordan Valley were probably very sparsely inhabited and in the valley itself there were no settlements west of the Jordan worth mentioning at all in this period. The coastal plain in the west, however, was and remained in the hands of ancient city-states, as far as it was capable of being inhabited at all (cf. Judges i, 29).

On the soil of Palestine the great association of the 'house of Joseph' (obviously originally a personal name) was in fact divided into two tribes, Manasseh and Ephraim[4], of which Ephraim was the greater and the more important. In Jos. xvi, 5-8 the territory of Ephraim is specially marked off within the greater totality of the possessions of the house of Joseph. According to this description Ephraim was the southerly neighbour of Manasseh and its territory extended northwards from Bethel in the south almost as far as the city of Shechem (the modern tell balāṭa east of the city of nāblus) which itself fell to the area occupied by Manasseh.

[1] Cf. above all 2 Sam. ii, 4, 7, 10, 11, also 1 Kings xii, 21, 23. The expression 'house of Israel' was probably modelled on the expression 'house of Judah' as a result of the juxtaposition of the states of Israel and Judah; thus 2 Sam. xii, 8; 1 Kings xii, 21 and elsewhere (not yet 2 Sam. ii, 10 and v, 3 cf. with ii, 4). 'Israel' was from the very outset not a tribal name at all, but a comprehensive total description.

[2] Cf. Jos. xvii, 18. [3] Cf. above p. 32.

[4] It was originally the custom to name the two names in this order and it was only later that the habit arose of putting Ephraim first because of its importance; cf. Gen. xlviii, 1-20.

The name 'Ephraim' is obviously not a personal name, but the name of a place, as is already indicated by its ending, which often occurs in the names of places and countries. According to 2 Sam. xviii, 6 there was in the country east of Jordan a 'wood of Ephraim' which was probably named after a particular district: it certainly has nothing to do with the Ephraim west of Jordan. The latter presumably appears in its original connotation in the term 'Mount Ephraim' (הר אפרים) which often occurs in the Old Testament. This term usually denotes the whole of the great central part of the mountains west of Jordan—beyond the land of the tribe of Ephraim[1]. But it may be that this is a later extension of the original meaning, which may have been restricted to quite a small area. According to 2 Sam. xiii, 23 the sanctuary of Baal-hazor, which is usually placed, probably correctly, on the mountain summit now known as el-ʿaṣūr a bare 10 kilometres north-east of Bethel, was situated 'beside[2] Ephraim'; and here 'Ephraim' most likely denotes a village[3]. But again, it is questionable whether in this case 'Ephraim' was in fact originally a place name and not rather the 'Mount Ephraim', that is, a closely confined mountainous district in which a village which developed there was given the name of Ephraim[4]. However that may be, it at any rate seems to be certain that as a local name Ephraim originally had its real home in the extreme south-east part of what later became known, in a wider sense, as 'Mount Ephraim' and that it arose in the extreme south-east part of the area inhabited by the tribe of Ephraim. The tribal name of Ephraim would then appear to have come about by families which settled in this area being called 'Ephraimites' (בני אפרים), just as the families which settled on 'Mount Judah' acquired the name of 'Judaeans' (בני יהודה). Thereafter kindred families further away to the west and north-west were probably included in the designation 'Ephraim', when a tribe was constituted in this area, and, with the name of Ephraim, that of 'Mount Ephraim' was also extended, until in the end it stretched far beyond the territory colonised by the tribe of Ephraim.

Quite early on, the vigorous tribe of Ephraim was no longer

[1] This clear above all in 1 Kings iv, 8; Jos. xx, 7; xxi, 21. Other old references to the expression 'Mount Ephraim' will be found in Jos. xvii, 15; Judges vii, 24; 1 Sam. i, 1.

[2] On the striking use of the preposition עם cf. Gen. xxxv, 4.

[3] This place Ephraim may have been situated on the ruined site of khirbet el merjame near sāmje; cf. W. F. Albright, JPOS, 3 (1923), pp. 36 ff. and AASOR, 4 (1924), pp. 127 ff. and also A. Alt, PJB, 24 (1928), pp. 35 ff.

[4] The change of meaning of this name may be compared with that of the name Gilead; on the latter cf. M. Noth, PJB, 37 (1941), pp. 59 ff.

satisfied with the territory west of the Jordan which could only offer limited scope for expansion, since to the north and south other tribes of Israel were settled and, to the west, Canaanite city-state territories blocked the way to the coastal plain[1]. And so Ephraimite families went over the Jordan Valley into the central part of the country east of Jordan. Here, on both sides of the Jabbok (the modern nahr ez-zerḳa), was a well-wooded mountain country which had hardly been opened up at all. Admittedly it was not particularly inviting country, but it did offer scope to a land-seeking tribe not afraid of the hard labour of clearing the forest. Coming from their dwellings west of Jordan the Ephraimites reached the district south of the Jabbok which was the original home of Gilead, a name which still survives in the place-names of the district. The people that settled there called themselves 'Gileadites' (גלעדי) or 'people of Gilead' (אנשי גלעד)[2] and the 'Gilead' mentioned in the Song of Deborah (Judges v, 17) is a reference to them. That they were of Ephraimite descent we learn from Judges xii, 4 where it is stated that in the course of a violent and dangerous quarrel they were contemptuously called 'fugitives of Ephraim' by their fellow-tribesmen from the land west of Jordan. They initiated the settlement of the area in the centre of the land east of Jordan. Admittedly, their territory was not all at large and scarcely capable of further extension, since any expansion worth mentioning was prevented by the deep incision of the Jabbok valley to the north and by the neighbouring Ammonites to the east and south-east.

The other tribe which established itself within the frame-work of the 'house of Joseph' as Ephraim's northern neighbour, seems to have had a rather complicated history. The Song of Deborah, one of the oldest documents in the Old Testament, mentions (Judges v, 14) *Machir* as well as Ephraim and the strangely tortuous formulation of Jos. xvii, 1 seems to suggest that the old system of tribal borders described in Jos. xiii-xix also assigned to Machir the remnant of Joseph's territory that remained after the territory of Ephraim had been subtracted[3]. But the tribe of Machir —or at any rate the main part of it—then migrated to the land east of Jordan, where it is usually located in Old Testament tradition; the people who remained in the land west of Jordan on the northern borders of Ephraim formed the tribe of *Manasseh*,

[1] Cf. Jos. xvii, 14-18.
[2] More details on this in M. Noth, PJB, 37 (1941), pp. 59 ff.
[3] Cf. also M. Noth, *Das Buch Josua* (² 1953).

which is clearly a personal name. Manasseh occupied the northern half of the central range of the west Jordan mountains from Shechem in the south. To the north its territory was still fairly intensely wooded and in the west, north and east it was encircled by the city-state territories in the coastal plain, in the plain of Jezreel and the Jordan Valley, which made expansion beyond the mountains impossible (cf. Judges i, 27-28). Machir, however, that is, the main constituent of the families which to begin with had been Ephraim's northern neighbours, had meanwhile migrated into the opposite section of the land east of Jordan, into the mountain country north of the Jabbok, where they had become the northern neighbours of the east Jordan Ephraimites. From the first constituent of east Jordan colonial territory south of the Jabbok the name Gilead was now extended to the area north of the Jabbok and thus Machir became the 'father of Gilead' as he is called in the Old Testament with almost monotonous regularity. (Jos. xvii, 1 and elsewhere). Numbers xxxii, 39-42 contains a few scanty notes about the process by which the land north of the Jabbok was occupied. This land was fairly extensive and was probably only sparsely populated in the more accessible areas. With advancing colonisation the name Gilead also travelled further on. The occupation reached a limit only where the arable land passed over into desert in the east and where the existence of numerous Canaanite city-states in the north-east and north in the area around the modern irbid made further expansion impossible. The greater importance of the west Jordan possessions compared with those east of Jordan was marked by the fact that 'Manasseh' rose to become the real tribal name and—without regard to the actual historical process—Machir was subordinated to Manasseh genealogically and made its son. (Num. xxvi, 29 and elsewhere.)

The southern neighbour of the house of Joseph and specifically of the tribe of Ephraim was *Benjamin*, a small tribe occupying a small territory north-east of the Jerusalem which still belonged to Canaan. Its borders are described very precisely in Jos. xviii, 11-20. According to this account, its lands included not only Jerusalem, which, according to Judges i, 21, Benjamin was unable to occupy, but also a group of Canaanite city-states north-west of Jerusalem which only subsequently entered into closer relationship with the tribe of Benjamin. The territory which the tribe of Benjamin actually inhabited was limited to part of the southern end of the Jordan Valley, west of the Jordan around the oasis of Jericho and as far as the adjacent western section of the land rising to the summit of the mountains where a few villages on the great road north to south across the mountains between Bethel and Jerusalem belonged to the Benjaminites. Most probably the name itself means 'he who lives in the south' and refers to the situation of the settlements within the framework of the central Palestinian group of tribes. If this is so, the tribe of Benjamin also acquired its name as a direct result of its occupation of the land[1].

Finally, the tribe of *Gad* which lived in the land east of Jordan and, alone among the tribes of Israel, probably made a permanent settlement there from the very beginning, has to be reckoned among the tribes of central Palestine. At any rate there is no reason to suppose that Gad, like part of the house of Joseph, only migrated later into the land east of Jordan from an original home west of Jordan. A description of the borders of Gad appears to be contained in the very complicated passage in Jos. xiii, 15 ff. where this tribe seems to have been assigned a strip of the mountain east of the Jordan from Arnon in the south (the modern sēl el-mōjib) as far as Jabbok and, in addition, the whole of the eastern half of the Jordan Valley. On the other hand, according to an older and more concrete tradition, it had established itself on the pasture land of the 'land of Yazer' (יעזר) (Num. xxxvii, 1). Admittedly, it has so far only been possible to define the position of the Yazer approximately; but this much is certain: the land 'of Yazer' must have been somewhere in the east Jordan mountains north-east of the northern end of the Dead Sea[2]. Gad therefore occupied only a small area, which was hemmed in on the east by the possessions of the neighbouring Ammonites and also provided little scope for expansion in the direction of the wooded mountain country to the north; whilst in the south-east the cities on the tableland north of the Arnon set a limit to peaceful expansion, so that the only outlet was southwards along the outer edge of the mountains on the eastern side of the Dead Sea, and the tribe of Gad did in fact gradually expand in that direction[3].

In the Old Testament references to tribal territories the tribe of *Reuben* is always mentioned in connection with Gad (Num. xxxii, 1 ff.; Jos. xiii, 15 ff.); but the details indicate that these references are not based on any clear-cut conception of a particular

[1] The tribe of Banu-jamina which is known from the Mari-texts (cf. W. v. Soden, WO, I, 3 [1948], is only connected with our Benjamin in name (it has the same meaning) but not in fact. [2] Details in M. Noth, ZAW, N.F. 19 (1944), pp. 30 ff.

[3] The name Gad is difficult to interpret; it may probably be regarded as originally a personal name (cf. M. Noth, *Geschichte und Altes Testament=Alt-Festschrift*, [1953], pp. 145 f.).

territory belonging to the tribe of Reuben but rather that the land of Gad was always divided, half of it being allotted to Reuben. The old inventory of the tribal borders does not seem to have contained anything about Reuben but only to have recognised the territory belonging to Gad in the land east of the Jordan. It is difficult to believe, however, that there was not some concrete reason for the later attempts to find a place for Reuben alongside Gad in the tribal geography. Probably there were families in the vicinity of Gad which called themselves Reubenites, though we know nothing for certain about their homes. Originally the tribe of Reuben resided, not in the land east of the Jordan, but somewhere or other west of the Jordan. The Song of Deborah still appears to connect Reuben with residences west of the Jordan (Judges v, 15b-16)[1]; and in other places too there are at least traces of former Reubenites west of the Jordan. According to Jos. xv, 6; xviii, 7 there was a village in the district on the lower edge of the mountains south of Jericho which was called 'stone of Bohan the son of Reuben'. This stone had originally been called 'thumb-stone', and the word 'thumb' had been mistaken for a personal name and its bearer for a Reubenite, evidently because Reubenites had once lived in the district in question—immediately opposite the territory of the tribe of Gad on the other side of the Jordan Valley. The formulation of this local name evidently took place at a time when the tribe of Reuben was no longer known in the borderlands of Judah and Benjamin, and all that survived was the memory of the earlier presence there of parts of the tribe. West of this 'thumb-stone' lay the plain of Achor (Jos. xv, 7) with the pile of stones on which was based the tradition of Joshua vii telling of Achan, of the family of Carmi (Jos. vii, 1-18), which is probably identical with the Reubenite family of Carmi. It is true that Achan and the family of Carmi are expressly assigned to the tribe of Judah in Jos. vii, 1-18, but the only point that arises from that is that Reubenites who resided in the vicinity of the tribe of Judah finally joined the latter tribe. The fact that the name Hezron occurs among the children of Reuben in Num. xxvi, 6 and was, according to Num. xxvi, 21, also the name of the subdivision of a Judaean family, can be explained in the same way. Consequently, as far as we can tell from Old Testament tradition, the tribe of Reuben had no real territory of its own. There are merely slight traces of an earlier presence of Reubenites from the district of the Judaean-

[1] The horizon is not extended to the land east of the Jordan until the following verse 17.

Benjaminite border on the eastern slopes of the mountains west of the Jordan and there is also the traditional view that Reuben lived with Gad exactly opposite in the land east of the Jordan. From this it may be inferred that the tribe of Reuben had once had its real territory somewhere in the land west of Jordan. All that tradition tells us for certain, however, is that disintegrated elements of the tribe finally retreated, apparently into the land east of the Jordan, to the very periphery of Israelite territory. Thus, the tribe of Reuben leads as shadowy an existence in the tribal geography as the tribe of Simeon which has been discussed above [1].

The north Palestinian tribes resided on the edge of the mountains which rise northwards from the plain of Jezreel to the highest eminences of Palestine and which we call the mountains of Galilee. The description of the borders contained in Jos. xix, 24-31 assigns an extensive territory to the tribe of Asher, including the northern part of the coastal plain and Carmel with its foreland. In fact, according to Judges i, 31, 32, the Asherites did not occupy the city territories in the plain, their actual possessions being limited to the western rim of the Lower Galilean mountains east of Akko and of the Canaanite towns situated in the plain around Akko. The little tribe of Asher, whose name could, but need not inevitably, be the name of a god[2], apparently had no necessity to expand eastwards and northwards into the almost empty lands in the interior of Lower and Upper Galilee; it was satisfied with the attractive hills and mountains above the plain of Akko. On the south-eastern edge of its territory on the western side of the great plain of sahl battof which is set deep in the mountains of Lower Galilee, Asher came into contact with its Israelite neighbour.

This neighbour was the tribe of *Zebulun*, whose borders are described fairly exactly in Jos. xix, 10-16. According to this account, the tribe resided in the mountains on the south edge of Lower Galilee between the plain of Jezreel in the south and sahl battof (which we have just mentioned) in the north, in the vicinity of the later city of Nazareth, the modern en-nāṣira. Zebulun was also a small tribe, and its territory not very extensive. In the west it bordered on the coastal plain north of Carmel, into whose city-state territories Zebulun found no access (Judges i, 30); in the south was the great plain of Jezreel, the soil of which was, and remained firmly, in possession of the Canaanite city-states. Zebulun does not appear to have needed the large-scale extension of its

[1] The meaning of the name Reuben is obscure.

[2] It would then be the male counterpart of the name of the female deity אשרה.

territory which could only have been effected by penetrating into the interior of Galilee. The name Zebulun cannot be explained for certain; it could originally have been a personal name[1].

In Deut. xxxiii, 18-19 Zebulun and Issachar are mentioned together, the main point being that they used to 'offer sacrifices of righteousness' together 'on a mountain'. The mountain referred to must be the Tabor, which towers up impressively like a dome in the north-eastern corner of the plain of Jezreel: the sanctuary on Tabor was a border sanctuary between Zebulun and Issachar in the south-eastern corner of Zebulun and the north-western corner of Issachar territory. From the reference to the territory of the tribe of Issachar in Jos. xix, 17-23 it may be gathered that Issachar occupied the southern spur of the Galilean mountains, which is bordered in the west by the plain of Jezreel, in the south by the broad valley of the nahr jālūd with the old Canaanite city of Beth-Sean (the modern tell el-ḥöṣn near bēsān) and in the east by the Jordan Valley. We shall discuss later in greater detail the special conditions under which Issachar had been able to gain a footing here[2]. They explain the tribe's curious name, which arose after its occupation of the land. Issachar means 'labourer' and the name was evidently first given to it as a nickname, in connection with the satirical line about Issachar which has come down to us in Genesis xlix, 15 in the blessing of Jacob, where Issachar's status is also referred to as that of a dependent labourer.

On Mount Tabor Zebulun and Issachar bordered on the tribe Naphtali whose territory, according to Jos. xix, 34, also reached as far as Mount Tabor and, according to Jos. xix, 32-39, lay along the eastern border of the Lower and Upper Galilean mountains. The fact that the territory of Naphtali is made to extend fairly deep into the interior of Galilee and as far as the territory of Asher is presumably merely due to the theory that the whole land was divided up among the tribes of Israel. The real centres of Naphtali will have been above the Sea of Tiberias and the adjacent part of the Jordan Valley. It is true that from that base Naphtali could, if necessary, have acquired further land to the west which was still wooded and uninhabited; but it is hardly to be supposed that the tribe made any extensive use of this possibility. The name Naphtali does not look much like a personal name and is altogether rather obscure; the point has at least to be considered whether it did not originally refer to a particular geographical region, in fact to the

[1] Cf. the personal name Zebul in Judges ix, 38 ff. as well as the Ugaritic zbl, which appears to be a particular honorary title.

[2] Cf. pp. 78 f.

'Mount Naphtali' mentioned in Jos. xx, 7[1], though, according to the existing tradition, the mountain is supposed to have acquired its name from the tribe. In fact the mountain may have given its name to the families that settled there, as happened in the case of Judah and Ephraim.

The tribe of *Dan* lived on the very periphery and in a rather isolated position, near the sources of the Jordan in the highest reach of the Jordan Valley. Its centre was the formerly Canaanite city of Laish (the modern tell el-ḳāḍi) mentioned in the Palestine list of Thutmoses III, which, according to Judges xviii, 27, the tribe had acquired by military conquest and to which it had given the new name of Dan (Judges xviii, 29) after its own name. The tribal name could originally have been a personal name[2]. A part of the section referring to Dan in the old inventory of the borders is probably contained in Num. xxxiv, 7-11, where its borders, as those of the most northerly tribe, are introduced to establish the northern frontier of the whole territory of Israel, just as in Num. xxxiv, 3-5 the southern frontier of Judah described in Joshua xv, 24 serves to determine the southern frontier of thé whole area. According to this, Dan had possessed not only the uppermost part of the Jordan Valley, but also part of the adjacent intensely wooded mountains to the east in the region now called jōlān; and this may in fact have been the case (cf. also Deut. xxxiii, 22), since the adjoining mountains westward were in the hands of the neighbouring tribe of Naphtali; in the north, however, the rather uninviting mountains of central Syria and, in the south, the marshes around the upper end of the Sea of Jordan were unsuitable for settlement, so that the opportunities for the tribe to expand lay in the east.

In this remote area Dan had found a home after a first attempt at occupation in quite another part of the country had failed. According to Judges i, 34-35, the Danites had first tried to gain a footing in the hill country between the mountains and the coastal

[1] According to this passage the place Kedesh (modern ḳedes) was specifically situated on the 'Mount Naphtali', which may therefore be sought north-west of the uppermost end of the Sea of Jordan, the lake that is now called hule. The Naphtalites will therefore have first gained a footing in this district. The same geographical connotation resides in thee xpression 'Kedesh-naphtali' (Judges iv, 6), in which 'Naphtali' may be the genitive of the region added to the place-name, as is certainly the case in the similarly compounded expression 'Jabesh-gilead' (1 Sam. xi, 1 and elsewhere) and probably in the expression 'Bethlehem-judah' (Judges xvii, 7 and elsewhere), in which 'Judah' also appears to have retained its original meaning as the name of a region.

[2] Cf. M. Noth, *Geschichte und Altes Testament = Alt-Festschrift* (1953), p. 146.

plain west of Jerusalem. But the earlier inhabitants[1] who ruled the country from their towns had not allowed the tribe of Dan to acquire the necessary land for settlement: an instructive example of the fact that the Israelite tribes found no room in the parts of the country which were already crowded with Canaanite cities and were usually not in a position and probably did not even attempt to make space for themselves by force of arms. So, according to Judges xviii, the tribe of Dan withdrew again from this area and, as the hitherto unoccupied land in the vicinity had meanwhile been taken over by other Israelite tribes, it made a permanent home for itself in the remote area in the far north, by way of exception, by occupying a small Canaanite city by force. Apparently it was thereby the last of the tribes of Israel to achieve a permanent settlement for itself.

6. *The Occupation of the Land by the Tribes of Israel*

When one looks at the whole range of the Israelite settlements in Palestine it is immediately obvious that the tribes of Israel entered those parts of the country that had only been inhabited sparsely or not at all in the Bronze Age[2]. They occupied the various parts of the mountains west of the Jordan as well as the central section of the highlands east of the Jordan whilst the plains on which nature had bestowed its blessings remained in the hands of the older Canaanite population which was concentrated in cities and alongside which the tribes now lived as a new element in the population. This fact in itself shows very clearly that the Israelite occupation did not ensue from a warlike encounter between the newcomers and the previous owners of the land. In the parts of the country occupied by the Israelites there were only a few scattered Canaanite settlements, though the tribes may have occupied some of these by military force sooner or later. But such minor military conquests did not involve any conflict with the main mass of the Canaanites, who did not inhabit the region occupied by the tribes of Israel; and where, in the mountains, there was a series of Canaanite cities

[1] In Judges i, 34, 35 they are called 'Amorites', the general name for the pre-Israelite population. According to the stories of the Danite Samson which took place in the same district (Judges xiii-xvi) the hostile neighbours were the Philistines, who had set up their dominion over the 'Amorites' in the southern coastal plain.

[2] Cf., in addition to A. Alt, *Die Landnahme der Israeliten in Palästina* (1925), especially pp. 31 ff., above all A. Alt, *Erwägungen über die Landnahme der Israeliten in Palästina* (PJB, 35 [1939], pp. 8-63 = *Kleine Schriften zur Geschichte des Volkes Israel*, I (1953), pp. 89-125 (especially pp. 121 ff.) and pp. 126-175.

in the neighbourhood, no large-scale conflict occurred either: on the contrary, the tribes did not advance any further than the immediate vicinity of these city territories. The special case of the tribe of Dan, with its unsuccessful attempt to gain a footing in the hill country on the inner edge of the coastal plain, may be regarded as an example of the way the tribes were incapable of venturing, and in fact did not venture at all, to challenge the firmly established cities of the Canaanites and their dreaded chariots of iron (cf. Jos. xvii, 16; Judges i, 19; iv, 3) to a large-scale military conflict.

It is clear that, to begin with, the occupation of the land by the tribes took place fairly quietly and peacefully on the whole and without seriously disturbing the great mass of the previous inhabitants. We may think of it as having proceeded rather in the way in which even today small cattle-breeding semi-nomads from the adjoining steppes and deserts pass over into a settled way of life in the cultivated countryside, the only difference being that at that time there was more uninhabited space available than there is today. Usually such semi-nomads make contact with agricultural land in the process of the so-called change of pasture: in the dry summer-time when their flocks of sheep and goats can no longer find enough fodder outside, they come by an explicit or tacit arrangement with the inhabitants into agricultural country where the fields have been harvested; and here their modest, easily satisfied flocks find fodder enough. But unlike the camel nomads of the desert with their proud contempt for a settled way of life, these peaceful semi-nomads always desire to continue living in the coveted agricultural countryside; and as soon as there is an opportunity, whether owing to gaps in the previous settlements or access to inhabitable but previously uninhabited districts, the day comes when they do not return to their winter pastures in the steppe and desert but settle down permanently in the agricultural countryside. The Israelites were land-hungry semi-nomads of that kind before their occupation of the land: they probably first set foot on the land in the process of changing pastures, and in the end they began to settle for good in the sparsely populated parts of the country and then extended their territory from their original domains as occasion offered, the whole process being carried through, to begin with, by peaceful means and without the use of force.

This means that the Israelitish occupation was a process that lasted for a good time, not merely in the sense that each individual tribe needed a certain time to occupy its own territory but also in the sense that the tribes did not all settle in the land at the same time. We know for certain that the tribe of Dan did not move into its final domains until after most or all the other tribes had already found their new homes. It may be that this was a unique case since this tribe had first tried to gain a footing in an area that was particularly unfavourable compared with the Canaanite cities; and we have no information to indicate that other tribes attained the ultimate possession of their territory only after unsuccessful attempts to establish themselves. But various details concerning the distribution of the tribal areas in Palestine show that the total occupation by the tribes of Israel was a complicated process which must have passed through several stages and covered a fairly long period of time.

In this connection the situation of the tribe of Reuben, which was discussed on pp. 63 f., and which always appears at the head of the list in the traditional enumeration of the tribes, is specially noteworthy. In the old tradition no special area was assigned to this tribe. If there were Reubenite families in the neighbourhood of the tribe of Gad, they had apparently only migrated later on to the land east of Jordan; in the opposite part of the land west of Jordan there were also a few traces of the former presence of Reubenites who had been absorbed to some extent by the tribe of Judah. We have evidence therefore only of the remnants of the former tribe of Reuben, which must have dwelt somewhere in the central part of the land west of Jordan. But in the period of which we have more exact knowledge, this area was fairly completely in the hands of other tribes in so far as it was available to the Israelites at all and was not occupied by Canaanite city-state territories, which were only able to take possession, or at any rate, full possession, of their territories after the tribe of Reuben had, for reasons unknown to us, with the exception of a few insignificant remnants, disappeared altogether. It follows that Reuben must have been established before the other tribes completed their occupation.

This inference is confirmed by an evidently quite similar situation in the tribes of Simeon and Levi, which usually follow Reuben in the traditional list of the tribes. The old tradition does not assign any particular district to Simeon either; and there is only a brief record of the fact that Simeonite clans lived in the extreme south of the land and were counted as part of the greater whole of 'Judah'. Tradition has nothing to relate, however, of the seats of the tribe of Levi and it is impossible to find any area where it could have dwelt in the same region as the other tribes[1]. But Simeon and Levi certainly once had their domiciles in Palestine since they are mentioned in the list of tribes; and the tradition of Gen. xxxiv originates in the fact that both tribes once lived in the vicinity of the formerly Canaanite city of Shechem. But it was there that the 'house of Joseph' resided later on, and, again, we have to conclude that the 'house of Joseph' was unable to occupy its new domiciles until after Simeon and Levi had departed, and that it entered Palestine later than those two tribes. In the reference to Simeon and Levi in Jacob's blessing both tribes are cursed to be 'scattered in Israel' (Gen. xlix, 5-7) on the traditional basis of Gen. xxxiv, and Reuben also receives a curse (Gen. xlix, 3-4). This refers to the later situation of these tribes and also indicates that the situation was not the same from the beginning. This being 'scattered' was the precondition, however, of the entry of other tribes into their domiciles in Palestine.

This also demonstrates that the prehistory of, and the occupation of, the land by the tribes of Israel were more involved than appears from the Old Testament tradition that was only evolved in a later age. This tradition proceeded from a situation in which the tribes were already living side by side in Palestine in an orderly way and had already accumulated some common historical experience. The assumption behind the tradition is that the events which led up to this situation were simultaneous and similar for all the tribes, in fact that Israel had been associated as a single unit in Palestine from the very beginning. Under the influence of a conception based on the development of large families and kinships it thinks of the tribes and the whole of Israel as having arisen by propagation and ramification from the family of a common ancestor and having formed a unity based on blood relationship from time immemorial and bound together by a common destiny. Thus the tribes were derived each from one ancestor who also gave his name to the tribe; and these ancestors appeared as brothers, as sons of a man called 'Israel' from whom the name of the whole derived[2]. It is quite true that in the building up of the tribes and also in their mutual connections the element of blood relationship did play an important part. But in addition to that there were usually particular

[1] It is clear from the fact that it is mentioned in the list of the other tribes and also from Gen. lxix, 5-7 that the tribe of Levi was a 'secular' tribe like the other tribes. In what relation the later Levite priesthood stood to it is a question on its own, which need not affect the above statement.

[2] The equating of the *heros eponymus* 'Israel' with the 'patriarch' Jacob occurs very early on in the Old Testament but is a secondary process in the historical tradition.

historical circumstances which led to the amalgamation of certain more or less related families into a tribe and to the association of a particular number of tribes into a tribal unit.

That the Old Testament took too simple a view of the events which led to the development of Israel as a totality is obvious from the fact, already mentioned, that the tribes of Israel did not all settle on the soil of Palestine at the same time but, judging from various statements in the tradition that has come down to us, their occupation of the land was divided into at least two distinct phases. The data are scanty and only incidental to the main stream of a tradition which was shaped by the conception of a common pre-history and a joint occupation of the land. We have to reckon with the possibility that the settlement of Israel in Palestine was an even more tempestuous and complicated process, but, owing to the lack of information, it is impossible to come to any firm conclusion one way or the other. But we know enough to infer that the individual tribes each had their own particular prehistory and that their mutual relationships were at best loose and fluid before they entered into a solid and lasting association one with another on the soil of Palestine under the collective name of Israel. Thinking again in terms of later conditions, the Old Testament tradition also simplified the facts by assuming that the individual tribes were firmly established as clear-cut entities from the very outset. Some of the Israelite tribes bear names that were originally place-names and derived from the areas in which the tribes in question settled[1]; in another case a tribe derived its name from the particular circumstances in which it had acquired its land[2]. These tribes cannot have been given their names until their arrival on the soil of Palestine, which means that they were not finally constituted until their arrival there. The families that were combined in these tribal units did not apparently bring a common tribal name with them which would have made the renaming which took place in Palestine unnecessary. It follows, therefore, that these tribes had not been self-contained units at all before their occupation of the land, but consisted of families which did not form themselves into tribes until they began living together in Palestine. The same may be assumed to apply to the tribes which adopted the name of their leading family, usually the personal name of an ancestor[3]. The Old

[1] Thus Judah, Ephraim, Benjamin and probably Naphtali too; cf. pp. 56 f., 60 f., 63, 67.

[2] This is true of Issachar; cf. pp. 76 f.

[3] Manasseh may be considered an example of this—the name is undoubtedly a personal name. Manasseh was presumably a Machiritic clan, which did not join in the migration into the land east of the Jordan and gave its name to all the parts of Machir

Testament tradition therefore not only goes beyond the facts by tracing the names of the tribes beyond the period of the occupation, but also by assuming that the tribes themselves had long existed as self-contained units. The process of the occupation must be reckoned to have lasted a long time, in the course of which the tribes were formed definitively, and that this process consisted of very many different movements of population which were geographically separate from one another.

It is true that the Old Testament records the conquest of the land of Palestine as the 'promised land' by the totality of the tribes of Israel, as a single, self-contained operation. What the old strata of the Pentateuch narrative amount to is in fact a description along those lines, though it is impossible to reconstruct it in detail as only its beginnings are preserved in Num. xxxii, 1 ff., and the continuation was dropped in the final editing of the Pentateuch. But it is possible to infer from Num. xxxii, 1 ff. that the united tribes set out for their subsequent domiciles, presumably all at the same time, from the southern part of the land east of Jordan. This accords in substance with the account of the possession of the land in the deuteronomistic narrative offered in Jos. i-xii on the basis of an old source which consisted of a sequence of single narratives. According to this account, the combined tribes conquered the land west of the Jordan by force of arms and took possession of it after crossing the lower Jordan, that is, approaching it from the southern part of the land east of Jordan. But on closer analysis the old basis of Jos. i-xii proves that the stories related in those chapters did not deal with Israel as a whole at all but—apart from the specifically Ephraimite tradition in Jos. x, 1 ff. and the specifically Galilean tradition in Jos. xi, 1 ff.—exclusively with the tribe of Benjamin. Geographically the whole thing takes place within the small territory of the tribe of Benjamin; the special tradition of the neighbouring tribe of Ephraim links up with this quite well, whereas the specific Galilean tradition stands completely on its own, quite unconnected geographically with what has gone before. But the Benjaminite tradition originally consisted of a series of aetiological narratives, which were collated on the assumption that the tribe of Benjamin entered into its territory around Jericho and the adjoining western part of the mountains from the east, over the lower Jordan[1]. This assumption represents the tribe of Benjamin's

that remained behind in the land west of the Jordan, and finally included under this name even the East Jordanites who had migrated (cf. p. 61 f.).

[1] More details in M. Noth, *Das Buch Josua* ([2] 1953), pp. 20 ff.

own living tradition about its occupation of the land; and we have here a concrete example of the fact that an individual tribe possessed its own special tradition concerning the way it came into possession of its land[1]. But what is true of the tribe of Benjamin will also be true of the other tribes; and if the tribes each had their own tradition in very early times, they will certainly each have moved into their subsequent territory in Palestine in their own special way. Almost all these special traditions of the tribes have been lost, however, because even in the Old Testament they were replaced by the conception of the joint conquest of Palestine by Israel as a whole, and only the Benjaminite narrative has been preserved because, for special reasons which we still have to discuss, it was specially suitable as a basis for the concrete version of the joint Israelite occupation of the land west of Jordan and was therefore developed and supplemented with this in mind; the Benjaminite foundation is still quite apparent, however. We must therefore attempt to throw some light on the complicated process of the occupation by considering the situation of the various tribal territories and a few scattered particulars in the Old Testament.

As far as the group of central Palestinian tribes is concerned we are on relatively safe ground. For Benjamin we have the foundation of the aetiological sequence of narratives in the first half of the Book of Joshua; and this accords so well in material matters with the situation of the tribe's domiciles that it is no doubt historically accurate. According to this account, the clans which formed the tribe of Benjamin made their way from the east or south-east through the southern part of the land east of the Jordan over the lower Jordan, established themselves in the territory belonging to the city of Jericho (the modern erīḥa)[2] and from there they climbed the west Jordan mountains up to the heights where the Canaanite cities north-west of Jerusalem put an end to their further advance to the west[3]. The 'house of Joseph' came from the

[1] It is no longer possible to say to what extent special tribal traditions lurk behind the narrative fragments in Judges i, 1 ff. In quite a different context we have a special tribal tradition in the traditional basis of Num. xiii, 14; cf. pp. 75 f.

[2] The question when Canaanite Jericho came to an end has not yet been completely elucidated archaeologically. Probably Benjamin did not find Jericho an established and fully inhabited city; cf. M. Noth, *loc. cit.* p. 21.

[3] It is wrong to conclude from Gen. xxxv, 16-20 that Benjamin only subsequently branched off from the 'house of Joseph' in Palestine and constituted itself as an independent tribe alongside Joseph. The conversion of narrative details of the 'patriarch'—stories into tribal history (Gen. xxxv, 16-20 draws attention to Rachel's grave)—is inadmissible. Benjamin originated in the first place on the soil of Palestine no more and no less than the other tribes; and we have a specific tradition concerning the manner of Benjamin's occupation of the land.

same direction; it evidently occupied the area in which it subsequently settled, from the south-east corner. Those clans which formed themselves into the tribe of Ephraim first gained a footing on 'Mount Ephraim', from which the tribe derived its name, and this 'Mount Ephraim' was presumably slightly north of the Benjaminite area above the lower Jordan Valley[1]. Since the 'house of Joseph' appears in the Old Testament tradition as a coherent unit of fair size, it is at least probable that not only the parts which joined to form the tribe of Ephraim but also the other parts of this unit came from the same direction, and then occupied the whole of the great central part of the west Jordan mountains without a break.

The territory of Gad lay north-east of the Dead Sea along the route on which all these elements advanced through the southern land east of the Jordan; it may therefore be assumed that the Gadite clans carried out their occupation of the land as part of the same migration. They remained in a small area east of the Jordan Valley, either because they found homes there straight away with which they were so delighted that they were able to save themselves the journey through the Jordan Valley[2], or because they found the west Jordan territories which were accessible from the southern land east of the Jordan already occupied and had to be content with the modest space available east of the Jordan Valley.

It is no accident that the Benjaminite tradition contained in Jos. i-xii was later used as the basis of the description of the combined Israelite conquest of the land west of the Jordan, since, independently of that tradition, the old strata of the Pentateuch narrative made the united forces of Israel advance to their occupation of Palestinian soil through the southern land east of Jordan. In time, therefore, the specific and historically accurate memories of the occupation of the land by the important central Palestinian tribes were imposed on all the tribes of Israel; when the conception of a common history of Israel existing even before the occupation of the land was developed in the light of later conditions, it was the specifically central Palestinian traditions which determined the picture of the total occupation of the land by Israel as a whole.

Before the tribes we have mentioned established themselves in the central part of Palestine, the tribes of Reuben, Simeon and Levi had (as we have discussed on p. 69 f.) settled somewhere in the

[1] Cf. p. 60 f. [2] The matter is described thus in Num. xxxii, 1 ff.

central territory west of Jordan, and had then, for reasons which are uncertain[1], migrated and dispersed and thereby made room for the tribes that came later. As we no longer know exactly where they settled to begin with, it is also impossible to describe the exact course of their occupation of the land. It is possible that they had entered the land by roughly the same route as the later tribes of central Palestine. In that case their starting-point will also have been somewhere in the steppes and deserts on the border of the southern land east of Jordan.

Matters were different with the south Palestinian tribes. For them we have, to begin with, a Calebite story which indicates that the tribe of Caleb entered its territory in Palestine from the south, that is, from the region of the so-called Negeb. The tradition on which the story contained in Num. xiii, xiv is based, and which sets out to explain how it came about that Caleb attained possession of the important city of Hebron, undoubtedly originally amounted to the fact that Caleb was assigned the city of Hebron along with its fertile surroundings as a reward for its courageous behaviour, without having first to join in the great detour through the southern land east of the Jordan. But the local starting-point of this narrative was the Negeb; it was from there that the thrust to the mountains in the north had been made which brought Caleb into possession of Hebron. The situation of the Calebite territory suggests that it is highly probable that this account of the journey of Caleb is historically accurate. By and large the most obvious assumption is that the tribes that had settled in the southernmost part of the west Jordan mountains had come from the adjoining semi-nomadic area to the south. In the case of Caleb there is the additional connection with a tribal unit which was also represented among the Edomites[2]; the home of this tribal unit of the Kenites can only have been in the Negeb, whence individual components had reached Edom over the wādi el-ʿaraba and others over the West Jordan mountains. The same applies to Othniel, whose relationship with Caleb and whose one-time membership of the tribal unit we have just mentioned also suggest that it originally came from the Negeb. The Kenites had also apparently come from the south, as far as they settled at all in the vicinity of Caleb and Othniel; since, according to 1 Sam. xv, 6, they had once belonged to the same tribal unit as the Amalekites, whose territory was somewhere in the northern part of the Sinai Peninsula. How much one

[1] According to Gen. xxxiv, military conflicts with the Canaanite city of Shechem appear to have been the cause for Simeon and Levi.

[2] Cf. p. 56.

has to reckon on unusual and unexpected tribal migrations is shown by the case of the tribe of Simeon which, although it resided in the extreme south in the region of Beersheba and therefore in the Negeb itself, had not come from this semi-nomadic area, at any rate not directly, but had migrated from the very heart of Palestine after it had become unable to maintain itself any longer in its original Palestinian settlements, had found a place on the extreme border of Israelite territory, like the tribe of Dan in the extreme north. It is permissible to assume that the southern part of the mountains west of Jordan was already occupied when the remnants of Simeon had to seek for new homes, so that it was only in the Negeb that they found a district suitable for permanent settlement.

It is also very difficult to establish anything for certain about how the tribe of Judah came into occupation of the land. From the south the cities of Hebron, and possibly Debir too, obstructed the access to its territory, and from the north city-states in the region of Jerusalem also made access difficult. The tribe of Judah established itself between these two regions. The situation of its territory suggests that it may either have moved in from the Negeb from a southerly direction or from the most southerly end of the Jordan Valley, and therefore, ultimately, from the east. The fact that, in the traditional enumeration of the twelve tribes of Israel, Judah appears in the leading group with Reuben, Simeon and Levi, suggests that it gained a footing in Palestine in the opening phase of the occupation; and as this oldest group of tribes appears to have settled predominantly in the central land west of the Jordan, we are probably entitled to assume that they came in over the lower Jordan from an easterly direction, and this may well have been true of Judah too. There is, however, a complete lack of concrete evidence to support this theory.

The course of events is least certain of all in the case of the Galilean tribes and the traditions that have come down to us about them are far and away the scantiest of all. It is highly probable that the ways by which the individual tribes in this group came into possession of their land in Palestine varied considerably. The only case about which we have more detailed information shows how complicated the prehistory of the occupation could be. We refer to the tribe of Dan, which ultimately found a place for itself in the far north near the sources of the Jordan after a vain attempt to gain a footing in quite a different place in Palestine. The situation was, again, quite different in the case of the tribes of Zebulun and

Issachar. After the organisation of the traditional twelve-tribe system, which we have still to discuss, these two tribes formed a special group on their own, with Reuben, Simeon, Levi and Judah, that is, with the tribes that had settled in the central land west of the Jordan in a very early stage of the occupation, and it is therefore probable that they had entered the land about the same time and in a similar fashion, and had been in more or less close touch with them. Of the Galilean tribes, their homes were nearest to the central part of the west Jordan mountains, only separated from it by the plain of Jezreel or the valley plain of nahr jālūd with its city-state territories. It cannot be proved with any certainty and need not necessarily be assumed that the tribe itself had resided there with those other tribes and had only subsequently been forced, for reasons unknown to us, to migrate from there to near-by southern Galilee[1]. But it may be considered probable that they had moved into their later dwelling-places from a southerly or south-easterly direction. The tribe of Naphtali, on the other hand, must have come through the northern land east of the Jordan from an easterly direction, particularly if it may be assumed to have first gained a footing on the 'Naphtali' mountains in the region of Kedes. It is almost impossible to say anything for sure as to how the tribe of Asher reached its territory.

In the Old Testament we have one or two striking statements from which we are able to gather something about the special conditions in which various of the Galilean tribes came into possession of their land in Palestine. In Jacob's blessing the tribe of Issachar is criticised and mocked because—as 'a strong ass couching down between two burdens'—it 'bowed its shoulder to bear' and 'became a servant unto tribute' for the sake of peace and quiet and a pleasant land (Gen. xlix, 14-15), and the name Issachar (labourer) is undoubtedly due to the same cause. If this statement was true, Issachar had acquired its territorial possessions at the price of its independence. What actually happened may be inferred from a few statements in the Amarna tablets, according to which the Canaanite city of Sunem (the modern sōlem) which was situated in the later Issacharite territory, was destroyed in the Amarna period and its soil had to be cultivated ('tilled') by forced labour on behalf of, and in the interests of, the then Egyptian sovereign and under the supervision and at the suggestion of the

[1] Since we do not know what special circumstances prevailed in this particular case, it is impossible to draw any positive conclusion regarding the earlier dwelling-places of Issachar from the fact that, according to Judges x, 1, 2, the Issacharite Tola lived and was buried in 'Shamir in Mount Ephraim' (exact position unknown).

Canaanite city governors[1]. The land-seeking clans apparently offered their services and were settled on the territory of the former city of Sunem and formed themselves into the tribe of 'Issachar' and from Sunem they finally occupied the adjoining mountain country to the east. Several other striking statements in the Old Testament about Israelite tribes can probably best be understood in the light of this fairly concrete situation. In the same blessing of Jacob it is said of Zebulun that it 'shall dwell at the haven of the sea' and 'shall be for an haven of ships'[2] (Gen. xlix, 13). Now the dwelling-places of this tribe that are known to us did not lie on the coast at all or even anywhere near it; and there is no reason to assume that Zebulun had lived by the sea at some previous time, since all the inhabitable places on the coast had been occupied long before the tribes of Israel appeared. It is more likely that this reference to Zebulun, which was probably intended as a criticism, means that the Zebulunites had to perform certain compulsory tasks, above all in the harbours of the northern coastal plain. And it is not difficult to surmise that the acceptance of this permanent obligation was the price the clans gathered at Zebulun had to pay in return for permission to settle in the lower Galilean mountains in the hinterland of the coastal plain. This supposition is confirmed by the fact that in Judges v, 17b Asher is also said to have 'continued on the sea shore', although in fact Asher no more lived on the coast than its neighbour Zebulun, but in the mountainous hinterland of the northern coastal plain. The remark may therefore be assumed to mean the same as the reference to Zebulun. Owing to their dependence on the neighbouring Canaanite cities much of the latter's wealth flowed into these tribes on the edge of the northern coastal plain and the plain of Jezreel. There are allusions to the good life in Asher in the blessing of Jacob and of Moses too (Gen. lxix, 20; Deut. xxxiii, 24); and in Deut. xxxiii, 19 Zebulun and Issachar are even said to 'suck of the abundance of the seas', which can only mean that they too gained indirectly from the commercial profits of the Canaanites. In Lower Galilee, therefore, the situation of the tribes was determined in a special way by the direct vicinity of the urban plains, and here the occupation of the land seems to have taken place under special conditions.

It is very curious that in Judges v, 17a the tribe of Dan is also

[1] The references and their precise explanation will be found in A. Alt, PJB, 20 (1924), pp. 34 ff.

[2] In the passage about the 'ships' the text is not quite in order and impossible to reconstruct with certainty. The final remark, that Zebulun's border 'shall be unto Zidon', appears to be a postscript.

said to have 'remained in ships' although its dwelling-place lay far away from the sea by the sources of the Jordan, a fact which is obviously taken for granted in the Song of Deborah, and in Judges xviii, 28 the city of Laish is explicitly stated to have been 'far from Zidon' But perhaps the latter remark is significant in so far as it does establish some connection between the territory of Dan and the city of Zidon (cf. also Judges xviii, 7) and the Mediterranean coast; and it looks as if at the time Zidon had sovereign rights in the uppermost reaches of the valley of the Jordan. The reference to Dan in Judges v, 17a can therefore probably be taken to mean that this tribe also had to buy its settlement by accepting a certain amount of compulsory labour service in South Phoenician seaports. Of all the Galilean tribes Naphtali is the only one which we do not find mentioned in this connection and that is probably no accident, since Naphtali owned the territory in the mountains west of the hule Lake and the Sea of Tiberias which was least favoured by nature. The Naphtalite families probably contented themselves with these modest dwelling-places and thereby preserved their independence.

Since the occupation of the land by the Israelite tribes was therefore a process which covered a long period of time and consisted of various, geographically distinct movements it is impossible to ascribe an exact date to the occupation as a whole. All one can do is to give an approximate *terminus a quo* and a *terminus ad quem*. Later on, the Old Testament tradition greatly simplified the process and concentrated it all into a single brief episode, so that as a source of direct information about the temporal duration and sequence of these movements it is quite unreliable; and we neither have nor can expect to have any historical information about these matters outside the Old Testament since, on the whole, the occupation took place more or less unobtrusively, away from the main scenes of the earlier history of Palestine, with no particularly striking events which might be expected to have attracted the attention of the ancient Oriental powers of the time and occasioned some kind of written record. The Amarna period may be considered the *terminus a quo*, but not because otherwise the process of the occupation of the land would be bound to have been mentioned in the political correspondence of the Amarna tablets[1]; the city governments of Palestine, from whose domain the Amarna tablets derive, were, in so far as they were concerned with Palestine at all,

[1] The Ḫabiru-Hebrews of the Amarna tablets are not to be identified with the Israelites. Cf. above, p. 33 f.

hardly affected to any degree by the Israelite occupation to begin with. But there are two points which suggest that in the Amarna period the Israelite tribes had not yet settled in the land. At that time Bethlehem was still 'a city of the land of Jerusalem'[1] and only later became the centre of the tribe of Judah; and at that period the destruction of the city of Sunem produced that gap in the Canaanite system of city-states in the vicinity of the Jezreel plain which was later occupied by the tribe of Issachar[2]. Judah and probably Issachar as well were part of the older group of Israelite tribes which were the first to settle in the land. On the other hand, in the case of Issachar, the external sequence of events suggests that this tribe moved into its territory not long after the end of the Amarna period. We must therefore place the beginnings of the Israelite occupation in the second half of the 14th century B.C. The final conclusion of the process will probably have taken place at least a hundred years before the accession of Saul. It is true that we have no trustworthy information at all regarding the temporal duration and sequence of the events recorded as having occurred on the soil of Palestine before the formation of the State of Israel. But the sequence of the 'Judges of Israel' in Judges x, 1-5; xii, 7-15[3], which belongs to this period, alone embraces sixty-eight years and it is not certain that the series is complete at either end. Judging from this the occupation had ended at the latest *circa* 1100 B.C.

These dates, especially the last, merely represent the extreme possibilities and they must not be assumed to mean that the occupation took two hundred years all told. That is unlikely. But the tradition being what it is, all we can do is cautiously to mark out the extreme limits of probability. Presumably the occupation took place within a considerably shorter period of time, in the course of a few decades; and the conditions prevailing in the tribe of Issachar, which we have already discussed, suggest that the process took place more in the first than the second half of the period, that is, approximately the 13th century B.C. But it must be remembered that this is nothing more than a likely supposition. In recent times attempts have been made to date the process or its individual elements more exactly on the basis of archaeological data. It is now possible to assign related strata of settlements on ancient sites which have been excavated, to a period of only a few decades, even without the aid of epigraphic discoveries, simply on the basis of the evidence of the material remains; and the idea inevitably suggests

[1] Cf. above, p. 32. [2] Cf. above, pp. 78 f.

[3] More details on this traditional element will be found below at pp. 101 f.

itself of relating the destruction of Palestinian cities, for which there is clear evidence within the period in question, to the appearance of the Israelites in Palestine and dating that appearance accordingly[1]. But so far there has been no absolutely certain evidence of this kind, and such evidence is in fact hardly likely to be found for the Israelite tribes did not acquire their living space by warlike conquest and the destruction of Canaanite cities[2] but usually settled in hitherto unoccupied parts of the country. These destructions were more probably due to the continual conflicts of the city governments among themselves, which are known to have occurred in the Amarna period, and, *circa* 1200 B.C., to the warlike emergence of the 'maritime peoples' in the regions of the city-states of Palestine. The Israelites established themselves chiefly in the settlements newly founded by themselves. If the beginnings of these settlements could be dated with archaeological accuracy, that would help to ascertain the date of the occupation. But that is scarcely possible. It is true that these new foundations at the beginning of the Iron Age had an enclosure erected with stones instead of the strong city walls of the Bronze Age Canaanite cities which have maintained the successive strata of the settlements intact for thousands of years. The old sites which date only from the Iron Age have usually disintegrated and their remains have been scattered in the course of time and have disappeared: all that has survived on the old sites are miscellaneous relics, usually without any ascertainable stratification. It must also be remembered that the civilisation of the Early Iron Age was very much more poverty-stricken than that of the preceding Bronze Age, and this fact makes it impossible to date the, for the most part scanty, remains at all accurately. It follows that the beginning of the Israelite settlement cannot be dated any more exactly and definitely from an archaeological point of view than from the evidence of the literary tradition. And there the matter must rest.

This occupation of the land was, however, part of a wider historical movement. At the same period land-seeking elements appeared everywhere on the borders of Syria and Palestine and, even beyond, in Mesopotamia between the upper reaches of the Euphrates and the Tigris and in the middle of the Euphrates, and they settled in large numbers especially in the Syrian interior and

[1] W. F. Albright has attempted this in numerous articles again and again.

[2] The conquest narratives in the first half of the Book of Joshua (cf. especially Jos. vi; viii; x, 28 ff.; xi, 10 ff.) originate in aetiological traditions which proceeded from the later events of the destruction of the sites in question (cf. M. Noth, *Das Buch Josua*, ([2] 1953).

in the adjacent area on both sides of the upper Euphrates and then established more or less permanent and, according to local conditions, more or less comprehensive political organisations. In the immediate vicinity of the Israelite tribes numerous clans settled as part of the same movement, in the southern part of the land east of the Jordan, which had hardly been inhabited at all for centuries, southwards towards the Gulf of el-ʿaḳaba, and here they established themselves as the peoples of the Ammonites, Moabites and Edomites[1] and apparently very early founded kingships. In Syria and Mesopotamia these elements were known by the collective name of Aramaeans, which occasionally occurs among the neighbouring Assyrians in central Assyrian royal inscriptions and then is also frequently mentioned in the Old Testament[2]. Therefore the great movement, of which the settlement of the Israelite tribes was part and which consisted of many different elements, took place during the transition from the Bronze to the Iron Age, proceeding from the Syrian-Arabian desert to the bordering agricultural lands: it is natural to call the movement the 'Aramaic migration' and it is perfectly in order to do so provided one remembers that it was not in fact a uniform and deliberately planned process. In the Old Testament itself the father of Israel is described as an 'Aramaean' in a solemn profession of faith (Deut. xxvi, 5); and the Israelites once spoke an ancient Aramaic dialect before they adopted 'the language of Canaan' (Isa. xix, 18) in the literal sense, the native Canaanite language, which was admittedly closely akin to their own ancient Aramaic. The Hebrew of the Old Testament still shows traces of the mixture of various dialects.

To take this view involves the rejection of a theory which is very old and has been revived in various forms and on different grounds right up to the most recent times: the theory that the prehistory of the Israelite tribes was bound up with the Hyksos movement[3]. Since it has been established that the Israelites cannot be simply identified with the conquering ruling class of the Hyksos, it has been thought that they came with the Hyksos migration from Mesopotamia, whence the Hyksos appear to have come and where, according to an Old Testament tradition, the forefathers of Israel had lived[4]. The numerous texts from the 15th century B.C. in which

[1] Further details on these peoples in WAT, pp. 68 ff.

[2] On the prehistory of the name Aramaean cf. A. Dupont-Sommer, Supplements to VT, I (1953), pp. 40 ff.

[3] Thus first of all Josephus, *Contra Apionem*, I, 14, § 75 ff. In modern times the opinion has been shared particularly by egyptologists.

[4] Cf. especially Gen. xxiv, 10 ff.; xxvii, 43 ff.; also Gen. xi, 10-32; xii, 5.

there are references to legal and social institutions such as are familiar from the Old Testament chronicles of the 'Patriarchs'[1], which have been found in the ancient city of Nuzu east of the Tigris (near the modern kerkūk) appear to support this theory. At that time Nuzu was a Hurrian city and still had connections with the Hurrian elements of the former Hyksos movement, and so the Israelites would have become familiar with these Hurrian elements through their connection with the Hyksos and introduced them into Palestine. But the arguments on which these suppositions are based are unsound. These institutions could have been introduced into Syria-Palestine by the Hyksos themselves and could have become known to the Israelites when they entered Palestine. But the tracing of Israel's ancestors to Mesopotamia is based on the accurate tradition of the Aramaic relationship[2], which was then specifically applied later on to the main Aramaic centre on both sides of the upper Euphrates. Against linking the Israelite occupation and the 'Aramaic migration' with the Hyksos movement there is, firstly, the fact that, to the best of our knowledge, the occupation took place much later than the appearance of the Hyksos and that the Aramaeans did not emerge as a migrant stratum until long after the period of the Hyksos; above all, there is the fact that the Israelite occupation took place in the very regions of Palestine which played no part at all in the Hyksos period and were not directly affected by the Hyksos rule at all and proceeded from directions which had nothing in common with the direction of the Hyksos movement. The Hyksos rule in Palestine extended to the city-state regions of the land; but it is clear that originally the Israelite tribes had no connection of any kind with that system of government, but only established a connection sooner or later according to local conditions.

[1] Cf. most recently C. H. Gordon, BASOR, 66 (1937), pp. 25 ff.; M. Burrows, JAOS, 57 (1937), pp. 259 ff.; R. de Vaux, RB, 56 (1949), pp. 22 ff.

[2] In its original form the tradition exists in the story of the relationship between Jacob and 'the Aramaean Laban' (cf. especially Gen. xxxi, 19 ff.).

CHAPTER II

THE CONFEDERATION OF THE TRIBES OF ISRAEL

7. *The Twelve-tribe System*

THE tradition that has come down to us refers to the Israelite tribes only as members of a greater whole. References to the dwelling-places, characteristics, particular destinies of individual tribes are based almost entirely on the assumption that they are members of a greater unit. This assumption is expressed in the well-defined tradition of the 'twelve tribes' which made up 'Israel'. This traditional element of the twelve-tribe system has come down to us in two forms which differ only on one point. In one form the tribe of Levi is included and Joseph appears as *one* tribe, whereas in the other form Levi is left out and Joseph's place is taken by Manasseh and Ephraim, the subdivisions of Joseph, which appear as independent tribes. The first form is found above all in the story of the birth of the ancestors of the tribes as sons of Jacob, in Gen. xxix, 31–xxx, 24 and also within the setting of Jacob's blessing in Gen. xlix, 1b-27, whilst the second form is found above all in the great list in Num. xxvi, 4bβ-51[1]. Since Levi had completely disappeared as a 'secular tribe' in the historical period of which we have more detailed knowledge, the form in which it is included must be considered the older of the two. Both forms share a quite definite grouping of the tribes which is expressed in Gen. xxix, 31 ff. in the derivation of their ancestors from different mothers and in Gen. xlix and Num. xxvi in the sequence in which they are enumerated. The older form begins with a group of six tribes which, following Gen. xxix, 31 ff., are usually called 'Leah tribes'. The tribes of Reuben, Simeon, Levi, Judah, Zebulun and Issachar[2]

[1] Further references and all details will be found in M. Noth, *Das System der zwölf Stämme Israels* (1930).

[2] The sequence Zebulun-Issachar appears in Gen. xlix and perhaps also in the oldest narrative stratum of Gen. xxix, 31 ff. whilst in the form of Gen. xxix, 31 ff. that has come down to us, and in Num. xxvi Zebulun follows Issachar.

are listed in a more or less established order. In the later form Gad takes the place of Levi, so that this form also opens with a group of six tribes. The 'Rachel tribes' form a further group, consisting of Joseph and Benjamin in the older and Manasseh, Ephraim, Benjamin in the later form. The rest of the tribes appear in a third group, which is the least stable in form. According to Gen. xlix Dan, Gad, Asher, Naphtali[1] belong to this group whilst in the later form represented by Num. xxvi Dan, Asher, Naphtali appear in this group.

To assess this traditional element of the twelve-tribe system objectively it must be remembered, on the one hand, that it obviously does not represent simply the organisation of Israel as given or naturally developed at a particular time, or, in view of the two forms, particular times. It in no way corresponds to the actual situation in the period of which we have more exact historical knowledge. It begins the sequence of tribes with the more or less forgotten tribes of Reuben, Simeon and Levi, and, on the other hand, the southern neighbours of Judah are missing, among which at any rate Caleb, with its possession of the city of Hebron, must have been at least as important as any of the Galilean tribes, all of which are listed as independent members, whilst the southern tribes—apart from the wholly peripheral Simeon—are to be regarded as included in Judah. But the system does not simply reproduce the situation of an earlier, historically uncertain period in which Reuben, Simeon and Levi were still playing their original roles and would therefore merit pride of place in the system, whilst the southern tribes had perhaps not yet settled in the land at all. This assumption is out of the question since the dispersion of Reuben, Simeon and Levi was the precondition of the occupation of the land by the 'Rachel tribes', which nevertheless do appear in the system. But one cannot ascribe the origin of the system to the period before the occupation since, on the whole, the tribes themselves did not become established entities until the occupation. It is therefore impossible to conceive of any period in which the actual situation of Israel corresponded exactly to the traditional system in either of its forms.

We must not, however, conclude that the system arose as a purely theoretical construction at a time when the tribes themselves were no longer playing any essential part historically and a

[1] This is the sequence in Gen. xlix. In Gen. xxix, 31 these tribes are again grouped differently; but probably this was due merely to the shaping of the narrative and is of no historical importance.

freely evolved organisation of ancient Israel into twelve parts was no longer hindered by historical reality. For, apart from the question whether such a period ever existed, the system undoubtedly links up with the fact of the existence if not of all yet of most of the tribes which are enumerated in it, and in such a way that the details cannot be explained in purely theoretical terms. It is impossible to explain either the choice of these particular twelve names or the fact that the system has come down to us in two different forms, though they actually differ only on one point, nor is it possible to explain the established sequence of names beginning with Reuben and Simeon, or the particular form of grouping, in which tribes living separately from one another appear together in the first and third of the above-mentioned groups, if the whole system is attributed to a more or less arbitrary compilation. Obviously extremely concrete historical presuppositions are involved and if, according to what has been said above, the system cannot be derived simply from the historical situation in particular periods, nevertheless it probably originated in a complicated historical process.

Admittedly, the system is so bound up with the very suspicious element of the apparently artificial number twelve, that that element must obviously be regarded as a quite essential constituent of the system, as is indicated above all by the fact that the number twelve was strictly adhered to in the transition from the earlier to the later form. This number twelve proves to be a historic factor shedding light on the origin and significance of the tribal system as a whole, for lists of twelve tribes—occasionally of six tribes too—also arose outside Israel and have come down to us. H. Ewald[1] was the first to point out that the Old Testament itself provides the handiest examples, since it contains in Gen. xxv, 13-16 a list of twelve Ishmaelite tribes and in Gen. xxxvi, 10-14 one of twelve Edomite tribes, whilst in Gen. xxxvi, 20-28 there is a list of Horitic tribes. The Israelite system of twelve tribes does not therefore by any means represent an isolated phenomenon and, for that reason, it cannot be attributed either to the chance circumstance of the co-existence of twelve brothers as ancestors of the tribes, or to an artificial dividing up of a greater unit; on the contrary, the number is the result of certain established organisations such as were customary in tribal societies which were still lacking settled political institutions. This is certainly true of all the examples known to us from the Old Testament. Admittedly these bare lists still say

[1] H. Ewald, *Geschichte des Volkes Israel*, I, 3rd ed. (1864), pp. 528 ff.

very little about the purpose of these organisations. The fact that similar associations of twelve tribes existed in ancient Greece and Italy is more helpful; and of these there are various traditional accounts which indicate that a common form of worship formed the centre and that the members of these associations used to meet for particular festivals at the central shrine, in fact that certain cults were sustained and administered[1] by such associations. There seem therefore to have been quite practical reasons for the fixed and constantly maintained number twelve (or six) inasmuch as the members of these associations had to assume responsibility for the upkeep of the common shrine and its worship in a monthly or bi-monthly rota. In Greece such a sacred society was called an amphictyony, a 'community of those who dwell around' (around a particular shrine); and this expression may serve as an appropriate technical term for this kind of association.

The sacred society of the Israelite tribes was in fact an 'ancient Israelite amphictyony'. The number twelve was part of the institution which had to be maintained even when changes took place in the system: it proves therefore to have been neither the mere result of the natural ramification of a human group nor the invention of a later period, but rather an essential element in the historical organisation of such a tribal society. The fact that the twelve-tribe system was part of a historically evolved and historically changing institution suffices to explain the traces of a complicated origin and development which are present in the system itself. The traditional precedence of the tribes of Reuben, Simeon (and Levi) can only have originated in a situation in which these tribes played an important part. That can only have been the case in a period in which the later central Palestinian tribes had not yet occupied their subsequent dwelling-places. These latter tribes belong to a different sub-group from the former. Reuben, Simeon (and Levi) lead the special group of the 'Leah tribes'; and the strictly maintained number six is a striking feature of this group. When, owing to the withdrawal of Levi[2], a gap arose in this group, the total number of twelve tribes was maintained not merely by dividing Joseph into Manasseh and Ephraim in the 'Rachel group' but also by transfer-

[1] Details and references in M. Noth, *loc. cit.* pp. 47 ff.

[2] It is impossible to ascertain the reasons for this omission, particularly as Reuben and Simeon, which had probably lost their old stock as much as Levi, continued to be counted, fictitiously, as tribes. Probably the elimination of Levi from the system is connected with the fact that, as is stated explicitly in the Old Testament tradition, people thought of the secular tribe of 'Levi' as having survived in the institution of the 'Levite priesthood'. Whether in fact there is a historical connection between the two or merely an identity of name, is another question.

ring Gad[1] to the position of Levi in the order of the list (cf. Num. xxvi) and thus the numerical continuity of the group of six tribes was preserved. The only reason for that must be that the number six of the first group was as vital a part of the institution as the number twelve was of the whole, that the group of six tribes had special functions within the life of the whole, which required its preservation in the greater whole. If one remembers, finally, that outside Israel six-tribe societies can be proved to have existed alongside numerous twelve-tribe societies, one must conclude that the 'Leah tribes', Reuben, Simeon, Levi, Judah, Zebulun and Issachar, had once formed a six-tribe society at a time when the first named of these tribes were still in full possession of their original possessions and Joseph and Benjamin had not yet completed their occupation, and that this six-tribe society was the forerunner and basis of the later twelve-tribe society. As far as we know, those six tribes were among the Israelite tribes which had settled in Palestine in a relatively early stage of the occupation. When after a violent upheaval of the hitherto existing conditions, of which we have only the most tenuous information, and which affected the tribes of Reuben, Simeon and Levi above all, and created a vacuum in the central part of the mountains west of the Jordan, new clans moved into the land and formed themselves into new tribes, the old six-tribe society was extended into a twelve-tribe society but so that the old six tribes, even though they now existed only in scattered remnants, not only continued to be reckoned as full partners but were given first place in the enumeration of the members of the system and were even preserved as a self-contained group within the whole, probably in consideration of the special rights and duties in the life of the extended society which still devolved upon them by reason of seniority.

Joseph and Benjamin were the chief newcomers. Whilst Benjamin was constituted with a probably small number of families as an independent tribe within a narrowly confined area and was always counted as an independent member in the system, the 'house of Joseph' represented an apparently very comprehensive association of families, which soon divided into two tribes when the occupation of the land began. The term 'house of Joseph' does not suggest a real tribal name, whilst, like the other tribes, when they became established in Palestine, Machir (Manasseh) and Ephraim appear to have formed themselves into fixed and self-contained tribes on

[1] It is impossible to know why Gad was incorporated secondarily in the group of six tribes.

the basis of dwelling together within a particular area. The question remains, where the name 'house of Joseph' came from. As it is not likely that two tribes subsequently joined together under a common name in Palestine, it must be assumed that the name 'house of Joseph' derives from the period before the occupation as a description of a fairly large association of tribes which finally settled in the central land west of the Jordan. They were received into the twelve-tribe system first of all only as a single member under the old common name, because there was only one place vacant for them within the framework of the established twelve, if the four tribes on the border—three Galilean and one east Jordan tribe—were to be incorporated simultaneously in the twelve-tribe society. We know nothing further at all about the prehistory of these four tribes, the time of their occupation of the land and the circumstances of their entry into the twelve-fold amphictyony.

Once the twelve-tribe society had been constituted on the model of the six-tribe society, the only change it underwent was caused by the withdrawal of Levi, which offered an opportunity for the tribes of Machir (Manasseh) and Ephraim to be incorporated into the system in place of the old entity of the 'house of Joseph'. Apart from that, no further change was made in the firmly established system, even when the tribes underwent various changes in the course of the process of history. This complicated development of the twelve-tribe system also explains why none of the forms that have come down to us reproduces the state of affairs prevailing at a particular time, since to some extent earlier organisations, to which the later elements were added, were always conserved within it. But all this merely shows that the system itself is a historical phenomenon related to a historical institution.

All these conclusions are based on a comparison between the traditional twelve-tribe system and other similar traditions outside Israel. The question is how far it is permissible to use this comparative material to complete the picture of the Israelite twelve-tribe system. The Greek amphictyonys, of which we have fairly extensive knowledge[1], offer the best example of a similar institution outside Israel. But one must be careful how one uses this material, particularly as it derives from a comparable, but different, historical setting; nevertheless if this material is capable of illuminating certain statements contained in the Old Testament tradition we should not disregard it.

[1] Cf. G. Busolt, *Griechische Staatskunde* (Handb. d. Klas. Altertumswiss. IV, I, 1), II (3 1926), revised by H. Swoboda, pp. 1280 ff.

Wherever we have any exact information at all about them, the important feature of the institutions of these tribal societies was always the central shrine. The same holds good of the Israelite society. In all probability the divine throne of the sacred ark[1] formed the centre of worship; the role which this chest played later on in the struggles of the Philistines, and under David and Solomon, makes it extremely likely that it had long held a position of central importance in the life of the tribes of Israel. We have no reliable information about its origin. Presumably it had originally been a travelling shrine of wandering clans[2]. Who brought it into Palestine and why it became the main shrine of the Israelite society is completely unknown, since all traces of ancient traditions concerning it have vanished. The question whether it played the central role from the very beginning even in the older society of the six tribes or was only later set up in the central place of worship as a particularly venerable relic, cannot be answered. But in this context the fact of primary importance is that, as far as can be inferred *a posteriori*, it was the common object of worship which united the society of the twelve tribes of Israel. Among the established tribes in Palestine the ark was no longer a real travelling shrine but, though it had as yet no permanent resting place[3], it was set up in one place for a more or less prolonged period and this place then formed the central place of worship, the geographical centre of the ancient Israelite amphictyony. It appears that, according to several traditions preserved in the Old Testament, the undoubtedly primeval tree shrine east of the city of Shechem in the middle of the mountains west of the Jordan (the modern tell balāṭa) was the centre of worship of the tribes of Israel; and that seems to have been the earliest state of affairs which it is still possible to discern. It seems reasonable to assume that even the old six-tribe society of the 'Leah tribes' which seem to have resided mainly in the central part of the mountains west of the Jordan, had its religious centre here and that the twelve-tribe society was in this case linking up with an older tradition. But that is merely a possibility. As far as the twelve-tribe society is concerned, however, we have, to begin with, the story of the 'diet of Shechem' in

[1] Num. x, 35 f. and Jer. iii, 16 f. suggest that it was highly probable that the Ark was originally conceived as the empty throne of the invisible God.

[2] Cf. especially the obviously old 'sayings of the Ark' in Num. x, 35 f. Their incorporation in the present context and also the remark about the Ark in Num. xiv, 14 probably point to the truth as does the late description in Exod. xxv, 10 ff.; xxxvii, 1 ff. which refers to the Ark as a portable sanctuary.

[3] Bearing this in mind, it is stated in 2 Sam. vii, 6 that the Ark had 'moved around' until the time of David.

Jos. xxiv, a special chapter which now exists in a deuteronomistic revised version as a later addition to the deuteronomistic history. According to this, Joshua gathered all the tribes of Israel to Shechem, to the holy place 'before God' and summoned them to decide whether they desired to serve the Lord Yahweh or another god, and after they had decided for Yahweh he made a covenant between God and the people and 'set them a statute and an ordinance in Shechem' and in witness thereof 'took a great stone and set it up there under an oak that was by the sanctuary of the Lord'. This tradition, or at any rate its transmission and preservation, certainly refers to a regular observance which took place before the sacred stone in the *Terebinth* (oak) shrine at Shechem and which evidently included a public profession of faith in Yahweh, an act of covenant-making and a proclamation of the statutes of the law. And the statement in the secondarily deuteronomistic passages Deut. xi, 29 ff.; xxvii, 1-26; Jos. viii, 30-35[1] according to which, immediately after their occupation of the land, the tribes of Israel set stones and an altar near Shechem and inscribed the 'Law (of Moses)' on the stones and spoke solemn blessings and cursings, must originate in the same ceremony. In these latter, fairly late passages, the traditional material may have been subsequently elaborated and reshaped; but that it refers to the same thing as Jos. xxiv is clear enough. According to this then, a ceremony was performed at probably regular intervals until comparatively late, which referred to a relationship to their God which was significant for the whole of the tribes of Israel. In addition, Yahweh appears to have been worshipped as the 'God of Israel' at this very shrine near Shechem (Gen. xxxiii; xx; Jos. viii, 30; xxiv, 2, 23[2]. All of which suggests that this shrine was once of central importance for the whole of Israelite society; and as religious observances have a habit of preserving with great persistence not only their actual form but also their association with a particular place, there is everything to be said for assuming that, even after the centre of worship had been transferred to other shrines, the old ceremony still continued to be observed near Shechem. This was taken for granted anyway in the passages of Old Testament tradition we have mentioned[3].

[1] These items are not uniform in word or content, but obviously all proceed from the same subject.

[2] Cf. C. Steuernagel, *Wellhausen-Festschrift* (BAZAW, 27 [1914]), pp. 329 ff.

[3] In them there is no mention of the Ark, apart from Jos. viii, 30 ff., which is probably the latest piece, which mentions the Ark only because of the part it plays in Jos. iii, 4, 6. These traditional fragments no longer recognise the sanctuary near Shechem as the central sanctuary, but merely as the place where customs are observed which had been maintained at the former site of the central sanctuary.

It follows that the shrine near Shechem was probably once the amphictyonic centre of the Israelite society of tribes; and that appears to be the earliest state of affairs it is possible to discern with any certainty. According to what was said above, the ark of Yahweh must have been set up on that spot at that time. Admittedly, there is no evidence that it was, but that is not surprising, since in the period of which we have direct historical records, the central shrine of the tribes, and therefore the ark, had already been shifted from Shechem, and on the old spot only certain traditional ceremonies had been preserved by dint of the usual stubbornness inherent in religious observances, which derived from the one-time importance of the shrine near Shechem.

It is much more difficult to answer the question whether it is possible to extract anything further from the old tradition in Jos. xxiv. Even though the transmission of this story is based on the regular repetition of the ceremonies described therein, nevertheless it recounts a unique event as the justification for these repeated observances; and its uniqueness is obvious above all from the part which the person of Joshua plays in it. The question is whether the person of Joshua is part of the basic substance of this traditional material. Now, since the Ephraimite Joshua[1]—apart from his doubtless secondary appearance in a few passages in the Pentateuch—did not originally appear in the originally Benjaminite aetiological narratives of the occupation of the land in Jos. ii-ix, and is no more firmly rooted in the probably equally Benjaminite narrative of the battle in Jos. x, 1 ff. than in the Galilean narrative of Jos. xi, 1 ff., the possibility must nevertheless be taken into account that, historically, Joshua derives from the context of Jos. xxiv. And that raises the question whether Joshua did not in fact play a part in the history of the twelve-tribe society. On the basis of Jos. xxiv, one can at least ask whether he was not the man who first gave the twelve-tribe society in Shechem its 'statute and ordinance' and therefore occupied a leading position in the establishment of this amphictyony. If this was the case, it would not be difficult to imagine that, as the founder of the statutes of the twelve-tribe society on Palestinian soil, he became the leader of the joint enterprise, once the idea of the unique event of an occupation of the land by Israel as a single unit had been formed. This supposition about the historical starting-point of the tradition concerning Joshua which is based on Jos. xxiv cannot, however, be established from the sources available to us and it is therefore simply a mere possibility.

[1] Joshua's burial place was shown in an Ephraimite place (Jos. xxiv, 30).

For reasons unknown to us the amphictyonic central shrine near Shechem was abandoned one day and shifted elsewhere. As it was only possible for it to play its role[1] by a friendly agreement with the city-state of Shechem on whose territory it was situated, perhaps a conflict with the Shechemites induced the tribes of Israel to shift it[2]. But possibly at this early period an occasional change of the central place of worship was provided for because the Ark was formerly a travelling shrine which it was not intended should become the object of a local cult after the manner of the Canaanites. At any rate the South Ephraimite shrine of Bethel (the modern burj bētin near bētīn) seems for a time to have taken over the role of the central shrine. This is suggested by the statement in Judges xx, 26 f. (cf. xx, 18; xxi, 2) according to which, at the time of the story contained in Judges xix f., the Ark stood in Bethel. As the Ark is not connected with Bethel anywhere else and it is not quite clear how such an assumption could have come about of its own accord[3], it may be taken for granted that the information is historically accurate. Its accuracy is also confirmed by the striking act of a pilgrimage from Shechem to Bethel, on which the story contained in Gen. xxxv, 1-7 is presumably founded.[4] According to this, certain preparatory actions were carried out in Shechem and then after the pilgrimage the real religious ceremonies were performed in Bethel. It looks as if a ceremony that had originally been self-contained was split up and only certain remnants were preserved at the original place of worship and that the main ceremony was transferred to another place. If one notes, moreover, that the 'putting away of the strange gods' which, according to Gen. xxxv, 2-4, was carried out in an actual ceremony at the shrine near Shechem, is textually unmistakably related to Jos. xxiv, 14–23, this pilgrimage from Shechem to Bethel was in fact occasioned by the transference of the amphictyonic central shrine from the one place to the other.

Then, sooner or later, Bethel itself was abandoned. For a time, the Ark appears to have found a home in the shrine of Gilgal in

[1] The city-state of Shechem had probably entered into friendly relationships with the tribe of Manasseh very early on and had been drawn into direct association with this tribe; cf. below, p. 146.

[2] We hear of such a conflict in Judges ix (cf. below pp. 152 f.). But another event of a similar nature which has not come down to us might equally well have been the reason for this transference of the central sanctuary.

[3] The meeting-place of the tribes in this story was Mizpeh (Judges xx, 1 ff.), and the only part that Bethel plays in it is as the site of the Ark.

[4] Cf. A. Alt, *In piam memoriam Alexander von Bulmerincq* (1938), pp. 218 ff. = *Kleine Schriften zur Geschichte des Volkes Israel*, I (1953), pp. 79 ff.

the urban region of Jericho which was occupied by Benjaminites. The part which the Ark plays in the basic substance of the narrative in Jos. iii, 4 concerning the passing of the Israelites over the Jordan, which undoubtedly originated in Gilgal, can hardly be taken to mean anything but that the Ark was one of the local appurtenances of Gilgal[1]. If, all the same, the Ark had no fixed abode before David, we may not be far wrong in assuming that the shrine of Gilgal also provided it with a home for a time. But we know nothing for certain. In Gilgal, too, and wherever else it may have stood, it did not remain permanently. At any rate, we find it finally in Shiloh (the modern khirbet sēlūn) in the midst of Ephraimite territory. Here the Ark even possessed a temple (1 Sam. iii, 3; cf. also Jer. vii, 14; xxvi, 9) which was probably not the case in Shechem and certainly not in Bethel and Gilgal. It is impossible to say why Shiloh was chosen. The terebinth near Shechem had been a centrally situated shrine which, seeing that it belonged to one of the few old Canaanite city-states in the mountains and in a region inhabited by the tribes, was undoubtedly of a venerable age when the Israelites appeared in the land. The same applies to Bethel; this shrine belonged to the city which had existed since the Middle Bronze Age[2] which had originally borne the name of Lus and was then called Bethel, after the shrine (the modern bētīn) had probably been, with Shechem, one of the most important ancient shrines in the central part of the mountains west of the Jordan, so that after Shechem had been abandoned, the idea of transferring the amphictyonic centre there inevitably suggested itself. Gilgal too was undoubtedly an ancient and probably much frequented shrine on the territory of the former city-state of Jericho. Shiloh, on the other hand, was a place of no particular importance in Mount Ephraim which was colonised by the Ephraimites[3] and then only acquired temporary importance because the Ark was set up in its shrine. We know too little about the events of that early period to be able to decide why the Ark was brought to Shiloh. It remained there until it finally fell into the hands of the Philistines who probably destroyed the city and shrine of Shiloh as well. In connection with the rising royal house the question of the central place of worship was considered completely afresh.

Israel was constituted as a historical entity in the form of an

[1] H.-J. Kraus, *Vetus Testamentum*, I (1951), pp. 184 f. has rightly drawn attention to this.

[2] This has been shown by the excavations on the site itself; cf. the preliminary reports by W. F. Albright, BASOR, 55 (1934), pp. 23 ff., 56 (1934), pp. 2 ff.

[3] Danish excavations have uncovered the old silo.

amphictyonic twelve-tribe society; this fact was of basic significance for the whole subsequent course of its history. Israel always thought of itself, at any rate, as a community of twelve tribes, and upheld the conception in spite of all later attacks on its validity. To the very end of Israel's history it never became a pure fiction, since there were always descendants of the old tribes to sustain the tradition. On the other hand, however, Israel's organisation into twelve tribes later tended to become part of a purely theoretical tradition, with no correspondence to the actual facts. To some extent this was the case from the very beginning, since even in the older twelve-tribe system members of the preceding six-tribe system were included though only scattered remnants of it survived. Probably the same thing happened later on with other tribes. Nevertheless, the system, of which the fixed number of twelve was part, continued to be maintained; and the system held together the surviving remnants of tribes under the traditional names.

Israel entered history in an outward form that was in no way unusual. The fact that similar amphictyonic twelve-tribe societies existed in the vicinity of Israel and beyond, in the ancient Mediterranean world, has enabled us properly to understand the Israelite twelve-tribe system. Israel formed itself into a twelve-tribe society in the process of a great movement of settlement which, in the form of an Aramaic migration, led many other elements from the wilderness into the agricultural land of Syria and Palestine (and the land of the twelve rivers) and within this great movement there is evidence of other twelve-tribe societies. Israel not only entered into a world with whose history its own was bound up in a great variety of ways from now on, but it achieved its destiny in association with larger historical movements. The special nature of Israel cannot therefore be sought merely in the events and organisations we have discussed, which include the gathering round a central shrine, an essential feature of the life of all these twelve-tribe societies. In Israel the central shrine no more excluded the use of other shrines than it did in other tribal societies; at these other shrines local communities and the families which made them up practised their local religions; it was at these shrines that the tribes met for themselves and traditional bands of pilgrims came together.

But for Israel as a whole only the worship at the central shrine was official, and it was here alone that the basic spiritual community of Israel was made manifest. The central shrine became a place of worship of particular significance for Israel; and the trend towards an even more far-reaching centralisation of religious observances, which was to play such an important part later on, existed in Israel from the very beginning. There was, however, nothing exceptional or peculiar about Israel's position in this matter: it simply followed a development shared by all twelve-tribe societies. The special feature about Israel's position was merely that the old pattern was preserved more widely than elsewhere even when historical conditions changed.

8. *The Institutions of the Confederation of the Twelve Tribes*

The Old Testament tradition provides us with almost no direct information about the life and functions of the Israelite twelve-tribe society, and it is only possible to a limited degree to draw indirect conclusions from various scattered data. But this is not surprising since it is not usual to record and transmit much about institutions which function in an orderly way and are therefore not particularly noteworthy. Usually they are not mentioned in documents until the stage of official record-making has begun and that stage was not reached in Israel until the rise of the monarchy. It is precisely because the constitution of the amphictyonic twelve-tribe society was so essential for Israel that it remained a continuous and therefore self-evident institution until the State was formed and the Old Testament therefore had little to report about it.

The common worship at the central shrine 'before Yahweh', that is, before the Ark as the place of God's presence (cf. Judges xx, 26 f.) was the visible expression of Israel's communal life. But we have no details about this worship. It may be assumed that it included regular offerings of sacrifices at particular times which were made in the name of the whole of Israel and the holding of pilgrims' festivals probably at least once a year. The old ordinance that 'three times in the year all thy males shall appear before the Lord God' (Exod. xxiii, 17; xxxiv, 23) can only refer to the local shrines throughout the country and to the three agricultural festivals which were celebrated at these shrines, as it would have been impracticable to carry it out at the central shrine. If, on the other hand, we hear in 1 Sam. i, 3 ff. that Elkanah, the father of Samuel, went with his family to Shiloh 'year by year' (verse 7) 'to worship and to sacrifice unto the Lord of Hosts' it may have been an annual amphictyonic festival at which all the tribes had to be represented officially, but to which many other Israelites came as well, especially if the central shrine was as accessible for them as it was for the Ephraimite Elkanah.

On the occasion of these festivals the tribes no doubt met to consult on questions of common interest, through their official representatives. It appears that these deputies were called נשׂיא and that this term may be taken to mean 'speaker', following the Hebrew expression נשׂאקול etc.[1] At any rate there are lists of twelve נשׂיאים in Num. i, 5-16; xiii, 4-15; xxxiv, 17-28, all of whom were members of one of the twelve tribes; and in Gen. xxv, 16 there is a reference to twelve נשׂיאים who evidently belonged to the Ishmaelite twelve-tribe system. As officials within the framework of a sacred institution these נשׂיאים were under the special protection of divine law, as is obvious from Exod. xxii, 27 where the cursing of a נשׂיא is forbidden, immediately following the prohibition to revile God himself. But we are not given any details about the office and tasks of the נשׂיא. Possibly, however, emphasis was not laid on the act of worship in the narrower sense in the Israelite twelve-tribe society. It is true that the institution of a permanent priesthood may have existed at the central shrine. In the temple of Shiloh, Eli and his sons officiated as priests before the Ark (1 Sam. i-iii) and when the Ark was marched off into the war against the Philistines it was accompanied by the sons of Eli (1 Sam. iv, 4-11[2]). To judge from this the office of priesthood before the Ark appears to have been hereditary. But we do not even know whether the priesthood at the amphictyonic central shrine was appointed by the tribes as a whole or whether it was the old local priesthood of Shiloh which undertook the care of the ark when the central shrine was transferred to Shiloh as the local priests of Shechem and Bethel and Gilgal are said to have done, and whether the נשׂאים of the tribes did not perform the necessary priestly functions at the great amphictyonic festivals. All that is quite uncertain and the scanty and scattered data of the Old Testament tradition leave various possibilities open. It is noteworthy that, at any rate in the case of Shechem, Bethel and Gilgal the amphictyonic central act of worship took place at ancient Canaanite shrines, even though Shechem, Bethel and Gilgal were in close touch with the tribes of Manasseh, Ephraim and Benjamin. Along with the holy places, no doubt much of the native Canaanite traditions and habits of worship also passed into the religious life of Israel. And that applies not

[1] Further references and details in M. Noth, *loc. cit.* pp. 151 ff.

[2] It is not expressly stated that the sons of Eli carried the Ark itself; only the presence of priests at the Ark was necessary; the actual carrying was probably performed by subordinate servants.

only to the numerous local shrines throughout the country but also to the official worship of the whole society, which took place before the ancient sacred terebinth of Shechem (cf. Gen. xii, 6), before the equally venerable stone of the 'Massebah' of Bethel (cf. Gen. xxviii, 18-22) and similar places. But all this merely accords with the fact that in Israel in the sphere of public worship the traditions of the new country were adopted to a very wide extent after the occupation: sacrifices were made in the manner native to the country[1], the agricultural festivals that were indigenous in Palestine were celebrated, the places that had been holy from time immemorial were venerated. This did not involve a change-over to Palestinian forms of worship, with its gods; but, in addition to all kinds of customs which Israel had brought with it from the wilderness, Israel did in fact widely adopt the religious framework which it found in Palestine and the traditional forms: it was only particular customs such as the cults of the Mother Goddess and the young vegetation god that were rejected as foreign and idolatrous. It follows that Israel's religious organisation was not in fact an expression of its own intrinsic character at all. It was entirely taken for granted that this sphere was part and parcel of its life and as a twelve-tribe society Israel, like other analogous societies, had its religious centre with pilgrims' festivals and sacrifices. But religious observances apparently were not regarded as of prime importance in Israel and it is scarcely an accident that, compared with other documents of religious history deriving from the world surrounding Israel[2], the Old Testament shows surprisingly little interest in purely devotional events and problems.

The scanty information which we have in the Old Testament about the religious ceremonies performed at the amphictyonic central shrine lays more stress on other things than the specifically devotional rites. In Jos. xxiv, there is no mention at all of sacrifices, but rather of a profession of faith in Yahweh and of making a covenant (though nothing is said about its outward form), and of the establishment of a 'statute and an ordinance' which were written 'in the book of the law of God', and, finally, there is mention of the setting up of a great stone 'under an oak tree that was by the sanctuary of the Lord'. And the late, only secondarily

[1] The thesis expressed in the title of the book by R. Dussaud, *Les Origines cananéennes du sacrifice israélite* (1921), has been entirely confirmed by the texts of Ugarit which were found later, with whose devotional terminology that of the Old Testament shows some points of contact.

[2] The texts of Ugarit must now be compared with their devotional-mythological contents.

deuteronomistic passages in Deut. xi, 29 f.; xxvii, 1 ff.; Jos. viii, 30 ff.; are similar; in these passages it is true that we read of the setting up of an altar and the offering of sacrifices (Deut. xxvii, 5-7; Jos. viii, 30-31), but above all of the writing of the 'words of the law' on great stones set up there (Deut. xxvii, 2-4, 8); Jos. viii, 32) and of a reading of the 'words of the law' (Jos. viii, 34-35), cf. Deut. xxvii, 9 f.) and of a solemn pronouncement of blessings and cursings which is no doubt connected with the 'words of the law' (Deut. xi, 29-30; xxvii, 11-13; cf. Jos. viii, 33 and also Deut. xxvii, 14-26). Admittedly, the deuteronomistic passages seem to combine various conceptions in a far from uniform and somewhat obscure manner and to contain a late and improbably authentic element in the reference to the writing of the words of the law on great stones. They cannot therefore be used as primary sources of information about the ceremonies at the central shrine, of which they clearly evince no direct knowledge; but they do seem to contain a very indirect reflection of these observances and one that is evidently in accord with Jos. xxiv, which states that the 'statute and ordinance', the 'words of the law' played a vital part in the tribal gatherings at the central shrine. They included blessings and cursings for the observance and infringement of the statutes of the law and the foundation of the validity of these statutes was the covenant between God and people which, according to Jos. xxiv, 25, was regularly renewed at the central shrine. We can obtain from all this an approximate picture of what Israel considered essential in the celebrations held at the solemn gatherings of the tribes, but we must be careful not to attempt to reconstruct the whole situation from the scanty and purely indirect information in the Old Testament. The passage in Deut. xxxi, 10-13 offers no more concrete evidence: it should probably be consulted in this connection, however, although it does not mention the location of the central shrine and is presumably already intended to refer to the Temple at Jerusalem. It is one of the secondary passages of the deuteronomistic history and contains the instruction that every seven years at the autumn festival, when 'all Israel is come to appear before the Lord thy God', the law shall be read 'before all Israel in their hearing'. It means especially the later deuteronomistic law, but seems to connect the instruction concerning the reading of the law at the end of every seven years with an old custom which had been observed, possibly from the very beginning, at the central shrine. If this be so, apart from the ceremonies which presumably took place once a year, a particularly solemn celebration took place every seven years at the central shrine in which the reading of the law played a leading part. From the very beginning, then, Israel's speciality did not consist in a particular and unique form of worship at the central shrine but in the fact that it was subject to a divine law which was recited at the tribal gatherings at regular intervals and to which Israel committed itself in constantly renewed acts of affirmation. This is consonant with the fact that the only all-Israel office explicitly mentioned in the oldest Old Testament tradition was not a priestly but a judicial office. In Judges x, 1-15; xii, 7-15 we have a list of so-called 'minor judges'. They are so described to distinguish them from the 'major judges' about whom detailed records exist in the 'Book of Judges' but who, from all accounts, were not judges at all but charismatic leaders of tribes in various warlike conflicts and were only incorporated in the list of 'judges' by the author of the deuteronomistic chronicle because one of them, Jephthah, was also represented in the list of the 'minor judges'[1]. In the old tradition the 'minor judges' were the sole judges of Israel, and, as a matter of fact and tradition, they alone were entitled to be called 'judges'. In the above-mentioned list they appear as the bearers of an office which was administered by *one* man; and the list mentioned six such judges, who filled the office of judge in an uninterrupted sequence. In each case only the name, descent and native place is briefly mentioned, then the duration of the tenure of office is recorded and finally the place of burial briefly stated; in some cases brief anecdotal remarks are also included[2]. Apart from these data this traditional material appears to be based on official records. This applies especially to the references to the years during which they 'judged' Israel. It deserves to be noted that we have here the only exact and obviously authentic chronological information (not merely in round figures) which the Old Testament contains for the period before the formation of the State. The fact that this information was recorded officially and transmitted to posterity can probably only be explained by the fact that in the earliest period of Israel's history dates were based on the period of the judges' years of office. If that is so, it follows that this was the central office in the Israelites' twelve-tribe society and that the law played a decisive role in this society[3].

Apart from the scanty details contained in the list, however, we

[1] On this literary process cf. M. Noth, *Überlieferungsgeschichtliche Studien*, I (1943), pp. 47 ff.

[2] Details in M. Noth, *Festschrift Alfred Bertholet* (1950), pp. 404 ff.

[3] If the cult had been all-important, dates could have been based on the years of the (high) priests of the central sanctuary, in so far as such existed.

have no further information about the position and functions of the judicial office. Were the judges who came from quite different tribes in an apparently irregular succession, elected by the tribes? Was the election made by the official representatives of the tribes, the נשׂיאים, on the occasion of one of the great federal gatherings at the central shrine? Or was the choice left to a divine decision which was obtained by drawing lots?[1] Various possibilities are conceivable, but we have no solid evidence of any kind. We can only surmise what the rights and duties of the office were. It is hardly likely that it included the administration of justice, for that lay in the hands of the eldest of the tribe (זקנים), whose custom it was to administer justice 'at the gate', *i.e.* in the passage-way of the city-gate and on the square in front of it, as the centre of the whole of public life, according to the traditional and, to begin with, purely oral statutes of the 'civil law'; or it lay in the hands of the priests at the country shrines, before whose sacred court certain cases were brought or who in cases where it was impossible to establish the facts were asked to secure a 'judgement of God'[2]. The 'judge of Israel' could be applied to at the most as a court of appeal, but it is doubtful whether an appeal against any sentence, once it had been passed, was considered admissible at all. It is far more likely that the central judicial office of Israel was related to the law that was valid in the whole of Israel, the divine law to which Israel was subject and which had to be regularly proclaimed anew, and that the 'judge' of Israel was the one who had to know and interpret it and give information about it, who had to see that it was observed and perhaps had himself to proclaim it in public and whose duty it was to apply it to new situations and thereby assume responsibility for its development and also constantly to instruct the tribes about the meaning and application of its individual clauses. From the little we know about the earlier age of Israel's history it is probably permissible to infer so much, and the existence of this office of judge testifies to the basic importance which was attached to the divine law in Israel.[3]

[1] This might be compared with the story of the drawing of lots to make Saul king in 1 Sam. x, 19b-21, though it is of late date (cf. also Jos. vii, 16-18); but at any rate it proves that the method was known in Israel.

[2] More details on this will be found in A. Bertholet, *Kulturgeschichte Israels* (1919), pp. 194 ff. and in L. Köhler, *Die hebräische Rechtsgemeinde* (Der hebräische Mensch [1953], pp. 143 ff.).

[3] Historical parallels are not required to confirm these conclusions drawn from Old Testament statements; but they are not unwelcome when they can be quoted, even if they are so far distant in time and place that no historical connection can be assumed to exist. A. Klostermann in *Der Pentateuch*, N.F. (1907), pp. 348 ff. has performed a useful service in studying closely the office of Icelandic 'law speaker' and using it to

The question suggests itself whether the numerous and comprehensive collections of legal ordinances which we have in the Old Testament do not contain the formulation of the oldest divine law of Israel. For even if it was handed down by word of mouth to begin with, in time it was probably set down in writing, and one would certainly expect it to have been incorporated in the Old Testament tradition. But we have no real chance of determining whether this in fact occurred, particularly as nothing is known for certain about its contents in any case. It is true that other tribal societies, like the Greek amphictyonies, had their 'amphictyonic law' which was binding on all their members; but on this point historical parallels are not very helpful, since it is highly probable that the divine law of Israel was something special and unique. The oldest traces of genuinely Israelite legal ordinances in the Old Testament may well be the original federal law of Israel[1] and the later books of the law as far as and including the so-called law of holiness in Lev. xvii-xxvi may be further developments of the early beginnings. But the early beginnings are found within the so-called Book of the Covenant in Exod. xxi-xxiii; and so the genuinely Israelite part of the Book of the Covenant, the religious and moral prohibitions in Exod. xxii, 17 ff.[2] have most right to be considered elements of the original divine law of Israel[3]. Their content cannot be summarised in a sentence; but it was their concern, as it was that of the Old Testament ordinances in general, to preserve Israel's relationship to God intact and to prevent its possible disturbance in all walks of life by the prohibition of unlawful acts[4].

Israel was subject to a divine law which required to be proved

explain the institution of the 'minor judges' (*loc. cit.* pp. 419 ff.) and the derivation of the form of the deuteronomic law from the interpretative recitation of the law. In spite of the detailed criticism of A. F. Puukko, in *Das Deuteronomium* (BWAT, 5 [1910]), pp. 175 ff., of the inferences drawn by Klostermann regarding the Deuteronomium, the latter's comparison of the Israelite institution with the Icelandic 'law speaker' has proved more and more to be relevant; cf., besides the reserved agreement of M. Weber, *Gesammelte Aufsätze zur Religionssoziologie*, III (1923), p. 93, above all A. Alt, *Die Ursprünge des israelitischen Rechts* (1934), pp. 31 ff. = *Kleine Schriften zur Geschichte des Volkes Israel*, I (1953), pp. 300 ff. on the judges of Israel and G. v. Rad, *Deuteronomium-Studien* (1947), pp. 7 ff. on the connection between Deuteronomium and the recitation of the law.

[1] Of the statutes which were formulated 'apodictically' or 'casuistically' (on this distinction cf. A. Alt, *loc. cit.* pp. 12 ff. and pp. 285 ff.) only the former are to be considered genuinely Israelite; they usually formulate prohibitions with the words 'thou shalt not . . .'.

[2] For the literary and textual analysis of the book of the Covenant and on the above description cf. A. Jepsen, *Untersuchungen zum Bundesbuch* (1927).

[3] The sentence must be formulated carefully since a self-contained corpus of legal statutes does not exist, at any rate in Exod. xxii, 17 ff.

[4] More details on this in M. Noth, *Die Gesetze im Pentateuch* (Schriften der Königsberger Gelehrten Gesellschaft, geisteswiss. Klasse, XVIII, 2 [1940]), pp. 40 ff.

and tested in all the situations of life and presupposed a strictly regulated relationship of Israel to its God. This divine law was proclaimed and interpreted to the tribes again and again at their assemblies and the central office of the 'judge of Israel' was carefully guarded; the rule of the divine law separated Israel from other peoples and the precondition of the divine law was the unique quality which determined the existence and nature of Israel[1].

The tribal society was not merely committed to this divine law but it was also bound to punish violations and could if necessary be summoned to enforce such punishment against any of its members, just as in other tribal societies, such as the Greek amphictyons, refractory members could be brought to heel by force. The punishment of transgressors took place in Israel 'to put the evil (or the evil one) from the midst of Israel' (as it is put in Deut. xiii, 6 and other places.) In order to cancel the transgression of the divine law the transgressor was 'rooted out of his people'—usually being stoned by the whole people—as though he had never belonged to this people. We hear of the violent punishment of a transgressor of the divine law in the only Old Testament tradition which shows the sacred tribal society as such in the period before the formation of the State, because it was evidently quite an unusual case which seemed worth recording for the benefit of posterity. According to the story contained in Judges xix, 20 which is certainly based on an old tradition and only appears to have been elaborated slightly for literary effect, there took place in the period in which 'there was no king in Israel' (xix, 1) in the Benjaminite city of Gibeah (the modern tell-el-fūl) a sexual offence against the wife of a Levite who had claimed hospitality in the city for a night. This meant that a נבלה בישראל had occurred (Judges xx, 10; cf. xix, 23)—a 'folly wrought in Israel'—this technical term apparently signified a violation of the divine law then in force in the tribal society, which was especially strict in sexual matters, in intentional contrast to the law of Canaan; and as the inhabitants of Gibeah had taken part in the crime *en masse* the Levite whose wife had been raped to death summoned the tribal society by dividing his wife into twelve pieces and sending one piece to each of the twelve tribes[2]

[1] The view of J. Wellhausen and his school that 'the law' was a late, post-prophetic phenomenon in Israel, is only correct to the extent that the legal sections contained in the Old Testament, which are very disparate, are on the whole fairly late. But as the formulation of the divine law the 'law' had its roots and its beginnings in the very earliest constitution of the Israelite association of the twelve tribes.

[2] On the prehistory of this method of raising an army cf. W. Wallis, ZAW, 64 (1952), pp. 57 ff.

accompanied by the formula that was probably specially provided for a case of this kind: 'Consider of it, take advice, and speak your minds' (Judges xix, 30 LXX). And the society of tribes came to this extraordinary assembly in Mizpeh (probably the modern tell en-naṣbe), almost certainly because Mizpeh was nearest to the scene of the crime, and decided to punish the deed as נבלה בישראל. But as the tribe of Benjamin, to which the city of Gibeah belonged, refused to hand over the guilty fellow-tribesmen of Gibeah (Judges xx, 13) and thereby declared its solidarity with the criminals, the other tribes waged a federal war against the tribe of Benjamin which ended in a defeat for the Benjaminites. And apparently that was considered the end of the matter: the crime had been dealt with. The case shows the importance that was attached to the observance of the statutes of the divine law in the twelve-tribe society. In the regular proclamation of these statutes, in the care that was taken to see that they were carried out, and in the punishment, if necessary by force of arms, of the transgressor, the life of the twelve-tribe society was expressed—apart from the common acts of worship at the central shrine. It does not appear from the tradition that has come down to us that the twelve-tribe society was a political and expansionistic military institution except in so far as a federation of twelve tribes inevitably implied a power complex anyway, even though the aggressive development of power was not one of its intrinsic tasks. In practice, at any rate, the waging of war against hostile neighbours was usually left to the individual tribes or, in certain cases, to a voluntary amalgamation of several tribes; and thus the individual tribes had in fact usually to depend on themselves for the maintenance and extension of their newly acquired possessions, and they waged the necessary struggles for themselves, on their own. They had their own political and military constitutions which were specially designed for the purpose. We know very little about the constitution of the individual tribes, but we must certainly assume that it it was not substantially different in Israel from what it was in the other elements which settled in Syria and Palestine in the process of the Aramaic migration, and that it was substantially the same in all the tribes of Israel. The most important points about the inner structure of the tribes may be gathered from Jos. vii, 16-18[1], according to which the tribes were made up of clans (משפחות[2]). Whilst the tribes—in

[1] This might be compared with 1 Sam. x, 20 f. where, however, one link in the chain is missing.

[2] Cf. also the great list in Num. xxvi, 4bβ-51, in which the משפחות of all the tribes of Israel are enumerated by name as its subdivisions.

the Old Testament the 'tribe' is called שבט or מטה, *i.e.* 'branch', 'staff', 'stick', following the same idea as the German 'Stamm'—contrary to the traditional idea, did not form themselves, until they reached Palestine as part of the historical process of the occupation of the land and settled there in a specific limited space—and were not simply held together by bonds of kinship, the clans may well have represented older associations which had existed before the occupation and which then stayed together in local communities in Palestine and preserved their old fellowship, for example, in certain definite acts of worship in which the clan as such took part[1]. Unfortunately it is no longer possible to ascertain the original meaning of the word משפחה but it is likely that basically the clan represented a union of blood-related groups and that it was the biggest unit still held together by ties of blood relationship[2]. The clans for their part consisted of a series of large families (בית or בית־אב), *i.e.* the descendants of common ancestors over about three or four generations who expressed their kinship not only in special acts of worship like the clans, but were probably held together by a common economy as well. The clarification of these relationships is made more difficult because in the Old Testament the terms are not always used precisely and consistently and because the actual situation, especially the subdivisions of the clans, was very often even more complicated owing to all kinds of secondary ramifications and amalgamations of which we have no information at all. On the whole, however, the picture which emerges from Jos. vii, 16-18 is probably a fairly accurate reflection of the usual state of affairs.

The organisation of the tribal militia which the tribes employed when they went to war corresponded to the structure of the tribes. The tribes waged their wars with the main body of their self-arming able-bodied, free men. The tribes had no real professional soldiery such as was represented by the ruling class in the Canaanite cities with their war-chariots. Only individual 'dedicated warriors', Nazarites, who like Samson, the embodiment of the original form of Nazaritism, submitted voluntarily to the law of sacred chastity by not cutting their hair and abstaining from the enervating gift of wine, and were then able to accomplish mighty deeds of warlike strength; leaders in battle driven by the spirit of

[1] Thus 1 Sam. xx, 29 presupposes that a clan like the Judaean clan to which David belonged was in the habit of observing its 'family sacrifice' (זבח משפחה) in its own place—in this case, it was Bethlehem—on which occasion the other scattered members of the clan also came together.

[2] Such a clan would correspond roughly to a Greek phratry or Roman gens.

God, like the majority of the so-called 'great judges' of the Book of Judges, were also well-known personalities. But they were not professional warriors who practised the art of war for its own sake, but charismatists capable of unusual achievements in time of war. But Israel's military strength was based on the tribal militias which marched to war on foot—without the aristocratic weapon of the horse-driven war-chariot. The men of a clan liable to serve in the militia formed a unit of their own in war and this was called a 'thousand'. The word 'thousand' (אלף) is occasionally used simply as a term for 'clan' when the 'thousands' of a tribe are mentioned in context where there is no reference to the militia (1 Sam. xxiii, 23; Mic. v, 1; also Judges vi, 15[1]); and, when it appears in some late passages of the Old Testament as an alternative for 'tribe', this is a secondary and improper use of the term. Naturally the clans differed greatly in strength; and 'thousand' is a traditional term, in which the number is in itself of no significance. Nevertheless, the use of the word 'thousand' for the military unit of a clan gives us at least an approximate idea of the number of men fit to bear arms within a clan. If 'fifties' occasionally appear as well as 'thousands' (1 Sam. viii, 12; cf. also 2 Kings i, 9 ff.)[1], possibly these were the units formed by the large families within the militia and they may indicate the approximate war strength of a large family[2].

The social order in Israel was patriarchal. There is no definite evidence of an older matriarchal order in Israel[3]. The large family was subject to the *patria potestas* of the grandfather as the head and this included the grown-up and married sons. But the larger units were led by councils of elders which administered justice, represented their association in negotiations and made other decisions. Here leadership was entirely by committee. Unfortunately we have no precise information about the structure of these councils. The heads of the constituent large, or at least the most important and respected large, families probably acted as elders

[1] According to a not improbable supposition of E. Meyer, in *Die Israeliten und ihre Nachbarstämme* (1906), p. 501, the word חֲמֻשִׁים (Exod. xiii, 18; Jos. i, 14; iv, 12; Judges vii, 11) really meant 'arranged in fifties', that is, organised on a war footing because the basic unit of the levies was the group of fifty; a different view is given by L. Koehler, *Lexicon*.

[2] 'Hundreds' occur in the Old Testament above all in mercenary contingents (that is, not in levies) (1 Sam. xxix, 2; 2 Sam. xviii, 1, 4; 2 Kings xi, 4, 19) and also in summary and not very reliable lists as for example Exod. xviii, 21. 'Hundreds' apparently played no part in the Israelite levy, probably because there was no corresponding element in the organisation of the tribes.

[3] But cf. A. Bertholet, *Kulturgeschichte Israels* (1919), pp. 83 ff.

of the tribes (זקנים). Since the clans lived together in local units in Palestine, the elders of a place (1 Sam. xi, 3; xvi, 4; 1 Kings xxi, 8; Deut. xix, 12 etc.) may be taken to have been the elders of the clans in question. But the institution of the elders of the tribe certainly goes back to the period before the occupation when the clans were still nomadic units, and it was introduced into Palestine with them; for such institutions are usually ancient and tend to be stubbornly preserved. The office of elder probably had its roots and real home in the clan. When the tribes established themselves permanently in Palestine councils of elders were also formed for the tribes; in the Old Testament we occasionally hear of the 'elders of the tribes' (Deut. xxxi, 28) as well as the elders of certain individual tribes (1 Sam. xxx, 26; 2 Sam. xix, 12; Hes. viii, 1; also Judges xi, 5), who led and represented the tribes. The institution was obviously transferred from the clans to the tribes. Unfortunately we are told nothing at all about the structure of the councils of the elders of the tribes. Perhaps they merely consisted of all the elders of the constituent clans. The Old Testament also makes repeated reference to the elders of Israel. But Israel as a whole was not a political organisation but rather a sacred amphictyonic association, whose members were represented by their נשׂיאים at the federal meetings; and it is not very likely that there existed a council of elders for the whole of Israel. The 'elders of Israel' were either the elders of many or all the single tribes, as in 2 Sam. iii, 17; v, 3; xvii, 4-15; 1 Kings viii, 1 who met together, or a secondary fiction which Israel as a total unit imagined as organised on the analogy of the clans and tribes.

CHAPTER III

THE TRADITIONS OF THE SACRED CONFEDERACY OF THE TWELVE TRIBES

9. *The Deliverance from Egypt*

OUTWARDLY Israel took the form of an amphictyonic society of twelve tribes similar to the societies that existed elsewhere in similar historical circumstances. In this sacred society it was subject to a divine law, the constant proclamation and observance of which was one of the most important, if not the most important, task of the society and its organs and institutions. This divine law was not unlike the amphictyonic law which prevailed in similar societies. But it was substantially more than a mere amphictyonic law. It was not concerned with the obligations of the individual members of the confederacy towards the central sanctuary or the relations of the members of the confederacy to one another and to foreign powers. It was concerned rather with Israel's relations to its God and was intended to safeguard the intactness of this relationship in every respect. In the law this relationship appears as a specific and unique commitment which is not derived merely from the simple process of gathering round a common central shrine. In Israel the situation was not, as appears to have been the case in the Greek and Italic societies of which we have more or less detailed information, that a number of tribes held together by the common observance of a rite, united round an age-old shrine, bound to one particular ancient and holy place. It is true that—at any rate to begin with—the local centre of the Israelite amphictyony was an ancient Canaanite shrine. But it was not the old Canaanite system of worship in use at this shrine that had brought and kept the tribes together; what happened was that Israel's own form of worship, with the shrine of the Ark, found a home for itself in an ancient Canaanite place of worship[1] but was not so bound up with this

[1] According to the ancient world it was impossible to declare or make any place at all a place of worship; it had to be hallowed by some event or other or be traditionally holy. Thus the central place of Israelite worship could only be established in some place that was already holy, *i.e.* in some Canaanite place.

place that it could not be shifted, if the occasion arose, to another place. This raises the question of the form of worship observed by the Israelite tribes and their special relationship to God.

The question is answered by certain traditions which were current among the Israelite tribes. They have come down to us in the great collective work of the Pentateuch, which, admittedly, only attained its ultimate form at a later date as the consummation of a long and complicated series of literary productions, though it has its source in an ancient stock of oral traditions which was developed quite early on and is rooted in a number of themes which had evidently been current among the Israelite tribes from the earliest times in connection with certain religious observances[1]. These themes are concerned with historical events which took place in the period before the occupation of the land, and concern certain encounters with the God whom the Israelites served in their central rites and to whose statutes they were subject: statutes intended to maintain the integrity of their relationship to this God. As far as we can trace them back any further at all, the traditions in question proceed from the existence of 'Israel' as an independent historical factor, in other words, from a fact which had no definitive existence until after the occupation of Palestine. The traditions exist, therefore, in the form in which they were cherished among the tribes which had settled in Palestine. They can only be understood historically as the traditions of the tribes united in Palestine concerning the crucial foundations of their faith. As such they were of fundamental importance. But we have to try to fit the historical information which they contain into historical contexts, even if by so doing we are ultimately bound to go back to the sphere of the historically inexplicable (cf. p. 3).

One of the original articles of Israel's faith was that it had once been 'brought out of Egypt' by its god Yahweh (cf. Num. xxiii, 22-24, 8; 2 Sam. vii, 23; 1 Sam. iv, 8; Judges vi, 13; and also Exod. xx, 2 and elsewhere); and the time when the Israelites were 'brought out of Egypt' by their god appears as the beginning of their relationship to God (2 Sam. vii, 6 and elsewhere). At the offering of the first fruits of the field in the sanctuary it was the custom to recite a religious formula the main theme of which was the 'bringing forth out of Egypt' (Deut. xxvi, 5-9). References to this 'bringing forth out of Egypt' appear in all kinds of places in

[1] On this point and what follows more details will be found in G. v. Rad, *Das formgeschichtliche Problem des Hexateuchs* (1938) and in M. Noth, *Überlieferungsgeschichte des Pentateuch* (1948).

the Old Testament tradition, sometimes in formulistic phrases, sometimes in more or less elaborate statements, and it forms a leading theme in the Pentateuch (Exod. i-xv). From all the more detailed references and especially from the relevant section in the Pentateuch it appears that 'bringing forth out of Egypt' connoted not merely the point of departure of the migration of the Israelite tribes but a mighty deed of the God of Israel: Israel had been enslaved in Egypt and was to be held there for good, but its God had wonderfully delivered it from bondage and saved it from the power of the Egyptians. There is no doubt that the concrete statement in this confession is based on a definite historical occurrence and it is not difficult to discern the circumstances in which it took place. After all, it was nothing unusual for Egypt to see all kinds of elements from the neighbouring Asiatic lands and primarily the Sinaitic desert appearing on the eastern border of the Delta. They came to Egypt in the first place owing to the lack of food caused by a deficiency of rain and they desired to be admitted, and were admitted, to the blessed land of the Nile which did not depend on rainfall. In the Papyrus Anastasi VI from the period of the Pharaoh Sethos II (*circa* 1205 B.C.) there is a report to his superior by an Egyptian frontier official from the eastern frontier of the Delta, in which it is stated, among other things, that on the frontier the transit of Bedouin tribes from Edom through the fortress of Merneptah in ṯkw[1] to the marshes of pr-, ʿtm[2] of Merneptah in ṯkw had been stopped (?) 'in order to keep them and their flocks in the possession of the king . . .'[3]. This statement in the official's report obviously did not refer to anything out of the way for Egypt. Such things often happened, no doubt; and the frontier official reported them to his superior as it was his duty to report on all important as well as unimportant incidents on the frontier. The 'Bedouin tribes of Edom' were probably groups of small cattle breeders with their flocks—no doubt quite small flocks—from the steppe beyond the Sinaitic desert[4], like the Israelite tribes before their occupation of Palestine; lack of food had persuaded them to

[1] The name of this Egyptian city appears in the Old Testament in the Hebraized form Sukkoth (probably the modern tell el-maskhūṭa in the Eastern part of the wādi ṭumēlāt).

[2] This is the Pithom which we know from the Old Testament (the modern tell er-reṭāble, about 10 km. west of the tell el-maskhūṭa in the wādi ṭumēlāt).

[3] Translation of the text in AOT², p. 97; TGI, pp. 34 f.

[4] Even if the reference in this text really is to the name 'Edom' which we know from the Old Testament, we can say nothing for certain about the origin of these Bedouin tribes, since we have no details about the specific meaning and connotation of the name Edom in the 13th century B.C.

try to 'preserve their life' in Egypt. They were admitted to Egyptian State territory in the wādi ṭumēlāt, which extends from the most easterly arm of the Nile eastwards to the modern 'Crocodile lake' (birket et-timsah) roughly in the middle of the Suez Canal, and represents a tract of cultivable land on the eastern border of the Egyptian Nile delta immediately adjacent to the Sinaitic desert. This wādi ṭumēlāt or a part of it seems to have had a name in ancient times which appears in the Old Testament in the form of 'Goshen'; and, according to Exod. viii, 18; ix, 26 it was in the 'land of Goshen' that the Israelites had resided in Egypt. The reference in the frontier official's report recalls, therefore, in almost every respect, what the Old Testament tradition says about the reasons for and the circumstances surrounding the Israelites' sojourn in Egypt; and the date of the incident mentioned in the report cannot be very far from what is reported in the Old Testament. I am not suggesting that the two incidents are identical, but rather that the frontier official's report shows that the Old Testament tradition refers to the kind of incident that was often taking place and illustrates the sort of motive which led the Israelites into Egypt.

These Israelites lived in Egypt in circumstances of which we have no details, as people with inferior rights who were usually called 'Hebrews'[1]; and the fact that the Old Testament often uses the word 'Hebrews' when referring to the Israelites in Egypt (Exod. i, 19; ii, 7, 11, 13; v, 3 and elsewhere) is entirely in accordance with the actual situation. The Egyptians were quite familiar with this foreign term which they transliterated as ʿpr. These ʿpr undertook or were compelled to undertake all kinds of service, and in Egypt all service was directly or indirectly for the State. This is mentioned in various Egyptian texts. Under Ramses II ʿpr people appear who 'haul stones for the great fortress of the city of Ramses, the beloved of Amon' and 'haul stones for the god Re, the Re of Ramses, the beloved of Amon, in the southern quarter of Memphis' —they were used as navvies in the building of cities and temples. Under Ramses III we hear of ʿpr people who had settled in the lower Egyptian city of Heliopolis; and under Ramses IV we come across ʿpr people among the workers in the quarries of wādi hammamat east of the Pharaonic city of Thebes[2]. Again, this is

[1] Cf. above, pp. 33 f.

[2] Cf. M. Chabas, *Mélanges égyptologiques*, I (1862), pp. 42 ff. German translation of the texts in H. J. Heyes, *Bibel und Ägypten*, I (1904), pp. 146 ff. and in A. Jirku, *Die Wanderungen der Hebräer im 3. und 2. Jahrtausend v. Chr.* (1924), pp. 24 f., TGI, pp. 30 f.

entirely in accordance with the tradition of the compulsory labour to which the Israelites were subjected in Egypt and, in particular, with the strikingly concrete information in Exod. i, 11 that the Israelites were used in the building of the cities of Pithom and Ramses in the eastern delta[1]. The point is not that the Egyptian texts refer specifically to the Israelites as 'Hebrews' but they do show that 'Hebrews' performing compulsory labour in Egypt were nothing unusual, and they therefore confirm in a most striking way the information about the fate of the Israelites in Egypt contained in the Old Testament.

Admittedly, all this merely forms the concrete background to the truth contained in the reference to the 'bringing forth out of Egypt'. The Israelites believed that it was the mighty hand of their God that had delivered them from the power of the Egyptians. Historically it is impossible to say much for certain about the circumstances surrounding this migration from Egypt. That the Israelites, who had probably gone to Egypt in the first place only under the pressure of dire distress and had been forced to submit to compulsory labour amid conditions of slavery, finally longed to recover their old freedom is understandable[2]. That the Egyptians—in a period of assiduous building activity, as under Ramses II, whose interests were concentrated on the eastern Delta—did not want to lose this labour force, is also understandable. The Israelites therefore tried to escape against the will of the Egyptians. In the Old Testament the story of the killing of the Egyptian first-born, and the story of the Egyptian plagues and the long negotiations with the Egyptians concerning the discharge of the Israelites which only bore fruit at the very end, was developed in conjunction with the historical explanation of the old traditional custom of the sacrifice of the Passover observed by the nomadic shepherds[3]. In Exod. xiv, 5a, however, a remnant of an earlier account has apparently been preserved, according to which the Israelites had

[1] On the situation of Pithom cf. above, p. 111, note 2. The city of (Per-)Ramses = 'house of Ramses' completed by Ramses II was probably on the site of, and around, the ancient city of Zoan (the modern ṣān el-ḥagar) about 50 km. north of Pithom, near the old mouth of one of the eastern arms of the Nile.

[2] This longing is particularly easy to understand if the immigration to Egypt had taken place not very long before and the memory of it was still alive. The computing of the sojourn in Egypt at 430 years in Exod. xii, 40 f. P (cf. the round figure of 400 years in the appendix, Gen. xv, 13b) is no doubt much too high. It is countered by the older reference to four generations in Gen. xv, 16 E which is more likely to be correct, though even that figure may be too high. We have nothing to work on for a more exact computation.

[3] More details on this will be found in M. Noth, *Überlieferungsgeschichte des Pentateuch* (1948), pp. 70 ff.

'fled' from Egypt without the knowledge of the Egyptians; and this account is more likely to be in accordance with the facts. It is true that it is no longer possible to discover any details regarding the circumstances of, and opportunities for, this flight. But there that great event took place which was always thought of first when Israel remembered the 'bringing forth out of Egypt' in its confession of faith. By the side of a sea which blocked their way in one direction and appeared to make escape impossible, the escaping Israelites were attacked by a detachment of Egyptian chariots[1]. This incident certainly occurred on the eastern border of the delta where the Israelites were bound to attempt to leave the sphere of direct Egyptian suzerainty. It is impossible to ascertain the locality of the incident more precisely and it would still be impossible even if we had exact information regarding the extent of the arms of the sea and the lakes in the modern Suez Canal area at the time in question. There is no reliable information about this in the Old Testament. It is true that in Exod. xiv, 2 there are some very precise references, and we may take it that they concern the district of what was called the Sirbonian Sea in Hellenistic and Roman times, *i.e.* the modern sebchat berdawil, the great lagoon which is about a day's journey east of the north-east corner of the delta[2], and it is quite possible that these references are accurate. But they are only contained in the late Priestly Code and probably represent a later effort to set the great, decisive event in a particular place in keeping with the traditional setting of the historical events. It is true that it is far and away the oldest such attempt known to us, but it was separated from the event itself by more than 500 years and was probably not based on an unbroken tradition, since the earlier strata of the Pentateuch narrative do not appear to refer to any such precisely defined place—at any rate, nothing of the kind has come down to us—but merely refer rather vaguely to a place 'on the sea'[3]. Inevitably, this 'sea' that exerted a decisive influence on

[1] That the Pharaoh himself was present is not even to be inferred with any certainty from the phrasing of Exod. xiv, 6 f. J (cf. verse 9a α) and Exod. xiv, 8 P (cf. verse 9a β P), and is historically out of the question in any case, since if he had been present we should hear about it in Egyptian sources on the well-known history of the Pharaohs of the New Kingdom, whereas the disaster that befell a group of Egyptian chariots was not so important for Egypt that we should expect it to have been recorded.

[2] For the details see M. Noth, *Der Schauplatz des Meerwunders* (Festschrift Otto Eissfeldt [1947], pp. 181 ff.).

[3] Outside the Pentateuch narrative (probably only at second-hand in some passages in the Pentateuch) this sea is specifically called the 'reedy sea' (provided ים־סוף really means that) (Jos. ii, 10; iv, 23 and elsewhere). If this should, as is the case in all the passages in the Old Testament which it is possible to interpret with certainty, refer to the gulf of el-'aḳaba, then we should have here a localisation deviating strikingly from

the course of events, must have lain in the vicinity of the modern Suez Canal, whether one takes Exod. xiv, 2 as referring to the lagoon of the sebchat berdawil or one of the lakes on the isthmus of Suez[1] which are now transversed by the Suez Canal, or, finally, following the example of the early Christian pilgrims, to the northern end of the gulf of Suez near the modern city of Suez (es-suwēs).

Our lack of knowledge about the local conditions contributes to the mystery of the incident. According to what is probably the earliest reference to the incident, contained in the short Hymn in Exod. xv, 21b, the essential feature was that Yahweh 'threw' the Egyptian chariots 'into the sea' with 'the horse and his rider'. The detachment of Egyptian chariots sank in the water owing to some unexpected disaster and the escaping Israelites were thereby suddenly liberated from supreme and apparently inescapable danger; they were convinced that God had openly intervened to help them in a mighty act and had set the seal on their escape from Egypt. Although they acknowledged that this divine miracle was fundamentally inexplicable and passed it on to posterity as such, attempts were naturally made later on to reconstruct the incident in greater detail—going beyond the description given in Exod. xv, 21b by imagining that a wonderful way of escape had been opened up for them through the 'sea' that barred their way and which engulfed the Egyptians when they went the same way. These attempts to reconstruct the incident probably include the simple account in Exod. xiv which makes the Lord 'cause the sea'—probably quite a shallow lake—'to go back by a strong east wind' (verse 21a), so that the Israelites were able to move on, whilst the Egyptians who had pursued them were driven into a state of utter panic by some mysterious divine action (verse 24b), and fled blindly into the sea that had returned meanwhile to its old place (verse 27a β). The phenomenon of the pillar of fire and cloud, which, to begin with, came protectingly between the Israelites and the Egyptians (verses 19b, 20) and through which the Lord 'looked

Exod. xiv, 2, which would show that an ancient and authentic local tradition about the miracle by the sea did not exist: it could not be historically accurate anyway, but could only be based on the second-hand association of the story of the deliverance out of Egypt with the story of the occupation of the land from the southern land east of the Jordan. It is, admittedly, not absolutely impossible that in this context the 'reedy sea' connoted the Gulf of es-suwēs or any other sheet of water on the eastern edge of the Nile delta.

[1] It is possible that in the 2nd millennium B.C. the Gulf of es-suwēs still had a shallow connection by water with the Bitter Lakes and even with the timsāḥ-lake, whilst further to the north the ballāḥ-lake was connected by water with the Mediterranean, so that there was only a relatively narrow isthmus between the timsāḥ-lake and the ballāḥ-lake.

unto the host of the Egyptians' (verse 24) to frighten and trouble them, already includes an element from a completely different context, namely, the Sinaitic tradition. Later on the incident was conceived even more impressively as is clear above all from the account of the Priestly Code in Exod. xiv, according to which 'the children of Israel went into the midst of the sea upon the dry ground; and the waters were a wall unto them on their right hand, and on their left' (verse 22), and closed in again over the pursuing Egyptians. All these are so many different ways of reconstructing the miracle of the deliverance, later rationalisations of the incident which are, admittedly, in the first place, simply an attempt to testify each in its own way to the great divine act of the 'bringing forth out of Egypt'. And in the last resort that was all that really mattered, though there was no authentic tradition about the actual course of events. There can be no doubt, however, that this was a real event; we can discern to some extent the conditions and circumstances which led to it and can fit it into a historical situation of which we have quite reasonable knowledge. The incident itself, which the Israelites experienced as an unexpected and mighty act of deliverance of their God, remains veiled from our sight.

One of the historical questions which the incident raises concerns the people who were involved in it. Hitherto they have been described as 'Israelites' in accordance with the tradition which was transmitted in the confederacy of the twelve tribes. But the 'Israel' of the twelve tribes only evolved on the soil of Palestine and there is no evidence that even the name 'Israel' existed before the entry into Palestine[1]. The traditions concerning prehistoric events were shaped from the point of view of the situation as it was in Palestine and these traditions referred to 'Israel' as if 'Israel' had already existed for a long time. Historically speaking, the 'bringing forth out of Egypt' cannot have referred to the later Israel whose ancestors had not shared any common history at all. The departure from Egypt and the deliverance which took place 'by the sea' do not suggest a great number of tribes but a numerically fairly small group which was in a position, because of its size, to 'flee' from Egypt. It is usual to think, therefore, of individual components of what later became Israel which had been in Egypt and may be considered the real transmitters of the tradition of the 'bringing forth out of Egypt'; the question is then asked, What group of tribes was actually involved? and the choice easily falls on the 'Rachel' group. But the reasons for this are not very sound. It is

[1] Cf. above, p. 3.

true that these important central Palestinian tribes were able to force the whole of Israel to acknowledge their special traditions but that is no compelling reason why they should have been involved in this incident 'by the sea'. The fact that Joseph and his brother Benjamin play such a large part in the account of the migration to Egypt is due not to historical reasons but to the way the tradition was passed on. The so-called story of Joseph is not based on a historical foundation at all, at least not in the sense of portraying the special destiny of a single tribe or group of tribes, personified in the figure of the ancestor. It is a fairly late element within the whole corpus of the Pentateuch tradition and conceived from the very outset from the point of view of Israel as a whole; it is not the story of Joseph but a story of 'Joseph and his brethren', and Joseph plays a special part in it, with Benjamin, only because it was moulded among the tribes of central Palestine, which resulted to some extent in the motif of the youngest son who is favoured by the father and therefore hated by his older brothers, since, according to the personification of the twelve-tribe system in Gen. xxix, 31–xxx, 24, Joseph and Benjamin were the youngest sons of Jacob. It is impossible to draw any historical inferences from the story of 'Joseph and his brethren'. Finally, the fact that in the Pentateuch the context leads from the deliverance out of Egypt to the occupation of the land from the southern land east of the Jordan and therefore to the manner in which the central Palestinian tribes occupied the land cannot be cited as evidence that events in Egypt specifically affected the 'Rachel' tribes. Like the interrelationship between the various themes in the Pentateuch, this connection between various events is secondary and there is a striking gap between the information about events in and around Egypt and the statements about the appearance of the Israelites in the southern land east of the Jordan, which shows that there is a lack of smooth continuity in the narrative. The reason is that the elaboration, for the purposes of the narrative, of the confession of faith in the divine bestowal of the land of Palestine, which led on from the development of the motif of the 'bringing forth out of Egypt', took place in the end among the central Palestinian tribes, and was based on their particular memories of the occupation of the land which were attached to the stories of the sojourn in Egypt as if they were the common property of Israel as a whole. The basis of the central Palestinian tradition is therefore the occupation of the land, not the sojourn in Egypt, much less a combination of the two themes.

In any case, however, it is wrong to ask which of the Israelite tribes were in Egypt since the tribes were only formed into permanent units when they arrived in Palestine. In some cases it can be proved, and it is probable in others also, that they were first given their names there too. The later tribes did not exist at all in Egypt. This makes the question as to who actually was in Egypt even more difficult to answer; we can only say that they were elements which became part of the tribes which were formed when the land was occupied. They were probably not absorbed by a single tribe, or even a single group of tribes, but by a whole series of them[1]. It may be surmised that those who migrated to Egypt had had a connection with the nomadic shepherds who sojourned on the borders of Palestine and had perhaps already been in touch with this land in the process of changing pastures, and that, in the course of time, they formed the tribes of Israel, and, after the deliverance out of Egypt, returned to this sphere again. We have no knowledge whatsoever as to how this came about, since the route taken by the Israelites on their departure from Egypt, which is presupposed rather than actually laid down in the Pentateuch, was based on the later combination of the various themes of the narrative and not on an original tradition. After crossing the Sinaitic desert, the elements which came from Egypt at any rate reached the territory of the clans living in the vicinity of Palestine who coveted this land. They were probably related to these clans and brought them the news of the divine miracle 'by the sea', which moved them so deeply that they passed the story on everywhere and transmitted it to their descendants as though it had happened to them all. In this way the confession of faith in the God who had manifested himself so gloriously by delivering them from the hand of the Egyptians became the common property of the whole of Israel and one of the foundations of the faith which lived in the institution of the sacred confederacy of the twelve tribes under the protection of the binding law of God.

Any attempt to fix the sojourn in Egypt chronologically can only be made on the basis of statements in the Old Testament. For Egypt the process of the arrival and departure of Asiatic neighbours was too frequent and repeated an occurrence, and even the

[1] Presumably only one of the different, chronologically separate phases of the Israelite occupation was concerned. To judge from the estimate of the time when the sojourn in Egypt took place, which we are about to discuss, it is probable that the old 'Leah'-tribes were already in Palestine (cf. above, p. 80) when these events occurred in and around Egypt, that the migrants who returned from Egypt were therefore absorbed by other groups of tribes.

disaster that befell a detachment of chariots on the eastern border of the delta too insignificant an incident for us to expect any information on the subject from Egyptian sources, which might establish the exact date of the event that had such a profound effect on Israel; for Palestine, the occupation of the land by nomadic shepherds in the course of the Aramaic migration was too long a process and too remote from the scenes of the previous history of the country for us to expect to find any information on its individual stages in Palestinian sources outside the Old Testament. It is true that the Old Testament does not contain any early, reliable information about the duration of the sojourn in Egypt, which was in fact probably quite short,[1] but it does contain a strikingly concrete item of information about the compulsory labour to which the Israelites were subjected in Egypt which it is possible to fix chronologically. According to Exod. i, 11, the Israelites were employed in the building of the cities of Pithom and Ramses in the eastern delta[2]. This takes us to the period of the Pharaoh Ramses II (1290–1223 B.C.). According to the evidence of discoveries made on the tell el-maskhūṭa, Ramses II began with the building of granaries in Pithom, and, above all, this Pharaoh is known to have developed the city of (Per-)Ramses as a delta residence and named it after himself. The reference to the two city names in Exod. i, 11 has every appearance of being based on first-hand information and it fits in so well with all we know from other sources about the sojourn in Egypt that it must be considered a reliable tradition. If this is so, the information has more weight than any dubious supposition regarding the historical circumstances and the date of the sojourn in Egypt[3]. Ramses II must therefore be regarded as the so-called 'Pharaoh of the oppression'. In view of this Pharaoh's long reign it is impossible to be very precise about the actual dates; one can hardly say more than that the sojourn in Egypt and the departure from that country took place during the 13th century. This does not fit in at all badly with the course of events in Palestine; at that time the occupation of the land was probably being carried out by the younger strata of the Israelite tribes, who were joined by the elements coming out of Egypt.

[1] Cf. above, p. 113, note 2.

[2] On the locality of the two cities cf. above, p. 111, note 2, and p. 113, note 1.

[3] This is also true of the late chronological constructions in the Old Testament itself, such as the chronological framework of the deuteronomist history, to which the chronological reference in 1 Kings vi, 1 belongs (on how this came about cf. M. Noth, *Überlieferungsgeschichtliche Studien*, I [1943], pp. 18 ff.).

10. *The Patriarchs*

One of the traditions that survived among the confederacy of the twelve tribes of Israel was that of the so-called Patriarchs. As in the similar case of the tradition regarding the deliverance out of Egypt, the background of the tradition was a historical manifestation from Israel's earliest history; but it acquired historical significance as an object of the faith in Israel. The essential and fundamental constituent of this tradition, as it appears in the Pentateuch as a whole, evidently lies in the divine promises regarding the possession of the land of Palestine and descendants that were bestowed on these patriarchs in repeated divine revelations in various holy places and which were ultimately fulfilled in the occupation of the land by the Israelite tribes, who constituted a numerous people. The occupation of the land was thus proved to be a work achieved under divine guidance which had long been envisaged and prepared. The tradition of the patriarchs was conceived and developed from this point of view in the Israelite confederacy of the twelve tribes. But it was connected with certain human figures which it refers to by name and of whose life it has all kinds of concrete details to record; and so the question arises as to what extent and in what respect the tradition was based on historical reality.

Evidently numerous local Palestinian traditions became attached to the personalities of the patriarchs which were not originally associated with them at all and which must be ignored if the question as to the nature of the patriarchs is to be answered; since it was only after the patriarchs had taken their place in tradition that they attracted local traditions[1]. They occupied this position as the recipients of divine promises—this was originally the specific nature of the whole phenomenon and its fundamental significance—and as the founders of systems of worship at the places hallowed by the divine promises and the encounter with God that these promises implied; these places were places of worship which continued to enjoy the high regard of the Israelite tribes for a long

[1] Among these second-hand local traditions will have to be reckoned the whole story of Sodom (Gen. xviii, 19), the aetiology of the substitution of the sacrifice of the son by that of the ram in the mountain sanctuary in 'the land of Moriah' (Gen. xx, 1-19), the stories of the well from the Negeb (Gen. xxi, 25 f., 30; xxvi, 14 ff.), the stories of Jacob and Esau which are native to the land of Gilead including the aetiology of the Israelite-Aramaic frontier on 'mount Gilead' (Gen. xxxi), the explanation of the name Mahanaim (Gen. xxxii, 1, 2 and 4 ff.), the story of the demon that appeared by night at the Jabbok ford near Peniel (Gen. xxxii, 23-32) and similar stories.

time: they included the tree sanctuary east of Shechem (Gen. xii, 6; xxxv, 2, 4); the holy place of Bethel (Gen. xii, 8; xiii, 3; xxviii, 11-22; xxxv, 1, 3, 5, 7); the sanctuary of Beer-sheba (Gen. xxi, 22 ff.; xxvi, 23 ff.; xlvi, 1-4); the sacred Terebinthe of Mamre in Hebron (Gen. xiii, 18; xviii, 1 ff.). All the basic elements of the authentic type of patriarchal narrative are to be found in summary form in the first passage of this kind in the Old Testament; in the statement regarding the appearance of Abraham at the 'oracle-giving Terebinthe' near Shechem which is given in Gen. xii, 6 f.: God 'appears' to Abraham, promises 'this land' to his descendants, and Abraham immediately builds an altar on the site for the 'Lord who appeared unto him'. The only point that needs to be added is that these 'descendants' (the 'seed' of Abraham) used to sacrifice on the altar on this hallowed spot 'to the God of their father Abraham'. It follows that knowledge of the patriarchs survived in connection with the sacred objects established by them (altars or massebahs)[1] at the holy places and that it was passed on by word of mouth, and that their names lived on in association with the deity ('God of Abraham' etc.), named after them and worshipped by their descendants.

This peculiar type of ancestor worship may be compared with similar phenomena of which there exists evidence on the borders of Palestine, though only from the Hellenistic-Roman period: the worship of *θεοὶ πατρῷοι*, *i.e.* ancestral gods who were invoked by their descendants because they had once appeared to their forefathers and been of assistance to them; this comparative material throws light on the basic element in the tradition of the patriarchs[2]. If, therefore, the figures of the patriarchs lived on among the Israelite tribes as the recipients of divine manifestations and the founders of systems of worship which continued to be practised by their descendants and with which their names remained associated, they were clearly men who had once lived as historical persons.

One of the special and evidently original elements in the Old Testament tradition of the patriarchs was the promise of descendants and the promise of the land of Palestine; the esteem in which

[1] Massebahs, upright stones, were among the usual contents of Canaanite shrines, originally intended as seats of the local deity, and later interpreted as memorial stones.

[2] We owe this important information to A. Alt, *Der Gott der Väter* (1929). The comparative material which Alt presents *in extenso* is to be found in Greek and Nabataean inscriptions, especially from the northern land east of the Jordan. Earlier interpretations of the figures of the patriarchs, both as personifications of tribes for which there is no real evidence, and the even less tenable mythological interpretation of them as originally deities, and the quite arbitrary interpretation of them as fairy-tale figures have thereby been exploded once and for all, so that there is now no need to discuss these interpretations.

the patriarchs were held as the recipients of this promise remained great precisely because this promise had ultimately been fulfilled. But the promise itself was bound up with the situation in which the clans which subsequently combined into 'Israel' sojourned on the borders of Palestine and were still merely at the stage of coveting the land and had at most made contact with Palestine through the summer pastures. The way of life of the patriarchs is described as essentially that of nomadic shepherds who have not yet really settled down, who live in tents and who are concerned above all with pastures and watering-places for their small herds of cattle. As historical personalities the patriarchs did not, if that description was correct, really belong to Palestine at all but only to its vicinity; the question is whether the divine manifestations which were vouchsafed to them occurred at sanctuaries in Palestine itself—when the change of pasture brought them into Palestine in the summer months, for example—or whether they did not usually take place somewhere outside Palestine in the steppe. It may be presumed that their descendants first established the worship of the 'god of the fathers' in Palestine after they had settled there and had seen the fulfilment of the promises made to their forefathers, and that they continued to practise this worship at the holy places in Palestine, and that it was only then that the tradition of the patriarchs assumed the form that the patriarchs had had all their encounters with the god at these same holy places. If that is so, then we have no evidence, beyond what has been said already, for making any definite historical assertions about the time and place, presuppositions and circumstances of the lives of the patriarchs as human beings. Even the original tradition of the patriarchs was not, however, much concerned with their human personalities, but rather with the divine promises that had been made to them.

Nevertheless it might be possible to find in the relatively familiar history of the ancient Orient in the 2nd millennium B.C. a situation in which the patriarchs might have appeared in the vicinity of Palestine as, in accordance with Old Testament tradition, the first heralds of the later Israel[1]. The Old Testament tradition itself suggests this possibility, since, in the story recorded in Gen. xiv, it shows Abraham acting within a far-flung context of ancient oriental history. But the story contained in Gen. xiv is so isolated

[1] Cf. the penetrating and thorough enquiries of R. de Vaux, *Les Patriarches hébreux et les découvertes modernes* (RB, 53 [1946], pp. 321-348; 55 [1948], pp. 321-347; 56 [1949], pp. 5-36).

within the whole tradition of the patriarchs that the question is whether it can be included among the authentic foundations of this tradition at all. In addition, the historical elucidation of Gen. xiv has attained no clear results in spite of much effort. It is true that kings of the ancient Orient appear in Gen. xiv with such concrete names and descriptions that they must be presumed to represent historical personalities; but it is so difficult to place the total content of the story in a definite historical period that one cannot help thinking that historical figures of the ancient oriental world were only later brought into a secondary relationship with one another. The relatively late chronological references in the Old Testament must be considered equally unreliable as evidence for fixing the period and classifying the patriarchs historically. On the other hand, there is a possible connection between the patriarchs and the elements which appeared in the 19th-18th centuries B.C. in the Land of the Two Rivers and in Syria-Palestine (see above, p. 24), the names of which have come down to us through the Egyptian execration texts (cf. above, p. 17). Since these names are strikingly similar to earlier Israelite personal names, it is not unlikely that there was at any rate a distant relation between these immigrants of the 19th-18th centuries and those who carried through the later 'Aramaic migration' (cf. above, p. 83)[1]. Now, if the Old Testament makes the patriarchs appear as the precursors of the clans which later combined to form 'Israel', it may be feasible to see their history within the framework of the migratory movement of the 19th-18th centuries, the more so as two of the three patriarchal names known to us, Isaac and Jacob, are typical of this stratum of immigrants. Against this assumption, however, there is the fact of the great distance of time, whilst the Old Testament brings the patriarchs very close to the historical events which had a fundamental effect on the life of what was later to become Israel. And it is unlikely that the tradition of the patriarchs could have entered the evolving tradition of the Pentateuch after an interval of more than 500 years. It is more likely that the historical figures of the patriarchs, however intangible, already belonged to the 'Aramaic migration'. It may be assumed that numerous 'patriarchs' were well known among the Israelite tribes. The fact that Abraham, Isaac and Jacob were particularly remembered was due to the peculiar evolution of the Pentateuch tradition. At an early stage this tradition was developed, to begin with, among the tribes of Central Palestine; and just as the theme of the occupation of the

[1] Cf. M. Noth, *Geschichte und Altes Testament=Alt-Festschrift* (1953), pp. 127 ff.

land was developed from their particular point of view, so the theme of the patriarchs was evolved from the point of view of the promise that was ultimately fulfilled in the occupation of the land by the Israelite tribes. But in the 'house of Joseph' Jacob figured as the recipient of the promise; according to the tradition, the figure of Joseph was associated with the sanctuaries of Shechem and Bethel and stories were associated with him which were native to the Josephite settlement east of the Jordan. In the course of the development of the Pentateuch tradition the figure of Joseph was, to begin with, the sole representative of the patriarchs[1] and, in spite of his originally belonging specifically to the 'house of Joseph', as a result of his association with the tradition of the occupation of the land, he acquired a significance for, and was acknowledged by, Israel as a whole. As the role of ancestor was part of the make-up of a 'patriarch' in the sense we have described, who had received divine promises for his descendants, Jacob logically became the Ancestor of the whole of Israel and the eponyms of the twelve tribes became his sons. Thus Jacob, who was well known among the clans of the 'house of Joseph' and whose name was handed down in connection with the worship of the 'God of Jacob' and whose memory survived in some of the sanctuaries in Palestine, finally assumed the role of Ancestor of the whole of Israel and in this role he became a figure of historic importance for the confederacy of the twelve tribes. The same kind of thing applies to Isaac and Abraham, who were added later on when the Pentateuch tradition was further developed among the southern tribes. They belong to the same type and only differ from Jacob in that stories about them circulated among the inhabitants of the Negeb. Their historical position has to be sought among the nomadic shepherds on the southern border of Palestine. It was here that the 'God of Isaac' and the 'God of Abraham' were worshipped on the basis of the divine manifestation which had occurred and the names of Isaac and Abraham were preserved in association with these forms of worship. When their worshippers settled down, all kinds of Palestinian traditions were connected with their names. Among the southern tribes they therefore became ancestors of Israel. When the Pentateuch tradition, which was first evolved in Central Palestine, was further developed by the southern tribes, they were given genealogical precedence over Jacob. Because their only real home

[1] The confessional formula in Deut. xxvi, 5-9 only mentions Jacob as patriarch (without referring to his name) and begins with the reference to his person the summary enumeration of the basic events in Israel's early history up to and including the occupation of the land.

was among the southern tribes, however, they apparently never acquired such universal significance among the Israelite tribes as the central Palestinian figure of Jacob. Outside the Pentateuch at least the names of Isaac and Abraham appear incomparably less frequently in the Old Testament than that of Jacob, which appears either as the name of the patriarch or as a poetic term for Israel in the most varied contexts as something obviously quite familiar.

The fact that the traditions of the patriarchs were originally limited to particular clans or tribes also suggests another probability that it is impossible to prove only because we do not know whether, owing to the peculiar development of the Pentateuch tradition, knowledge of 'patriarchs' who were known among other Israelite tribes may have been lost. To judge from the stories of the patriarchs which have come down to us, it might be supposed that the patriarchs and the worship of a *θεὸς πατρῷος* were the affair of the later stratum of Israelite tribes and not the earlier group of 'Leah' tribes. Jacob belonged to the 'house of Joseph' and Isaac and Abraham played a part in the tribes of the South Judean mountains and the Negeb. It is above all a striking fact that none of the patriarchs had any association with the 'Leah' tribe of Judah which was of such great historical importance; even the Terebinth shrine at Mamre in Hebron which was the scene of a relatively late complex of stories concerning Abraham, was not Judaic but Calebitic and the original tradition of Abraham, which, like that of Isaac, was native to the Negeb, did not extend further to the north at all[1]. The whole tradition of the patriarchs was therefore, like the tradition concerning the exodus from Egypt, presumably a later contribution to the stock of Israelite traditions, though it should be borne in mind that specifically Judaean traditions appear to be almost completely lacking in the Pentateuch, and the actual tribe of Judah evidently did not take part in the formation and development of the Pentateuch narrative[2]. However that may be, the tradition of the patriarchs as such became part of the tradition of Israel as whole, at least in the figure of Jacob, and through its connection with the tradition of the exodus from Egypt and the occupation of the land it acquired a significance as an article of faith among the Israelite confederacy of the twelve tribes which far exceeded the original significance of the systems of worship

[1] For this reason alone the idea which first appears in the 2nd Book of Chronicles iii, 1, that the 'mount Moriah' of Gen. xxii, 2 is identical with the Mountain of the Temple in Jerusalem and not situated much further to the south, is quite improbable.

[2] The Galilean tribes did not contribute anything to the Pentateuch tradition either.

inaugurated by the patriarchs as recipients of the promises. The promises made to the patriarchs had, it was inevitably thought, been fulfilled in the occupation of the land by the tribes which considered themselves the descendants of the patriarchs. Through the association of the patriarchs with the other traditions, however, the promises not only acquired a significance for Israel as a whole, but they also became the elements of an act of divine guidance in which the goal of the occupation of the land by a numerous people was not attained simply and suddenly, but by the roundabout way of the sojourn in Egypt and the miraculous deliverance from the hand of the Egyptians. Thus the entry of the tradition of the patriarchs into the faith of the Israelite confederacy of the twelve tribes made a substantial contribution to the development of the theological explanation of the divine action which had led Israel to its present position in history, a people of God in the land which its God had given to it[1].

11. *The Covenant of Sinai*

The tradition of Sinai was included in the Pentateuch material at a relatively late date, though before the earliest known version of the Pentateuch tradition and therefore probably still in the period when the tribes were living on their own, before the beginning of the formation of the State. It deals with the revelation of God which was bestowed on the Israelites on the holy mountain in the wilderness, which was followed by the self-commitment of the participants to the God who made himself known to them. An essential part of this Sinai tradition that was developed later on, however, was the story of the manifestation of God on the mountain amid terrifying natural phenomena which the people witnessed at the foot of the mountain (Exod. xix in various later literary versions) and of the establishment of a permanent relationship between God and the people in the form of a covenant similar to the agreements concluded between human partners (Exod. xxiv, 1-11; xxxiv, 1-28 which exists in several variants). This making of a covenant signified the submission of the people to the rule of the God who had appeared to them[2] and the acknowledgment of the

[1] Cf. G. v. Rad, *Verheissenes Land und Jahwes Land im Hexateuch* (ZDPV, 66 [1943], pp. 191-204).

[2] J. Begrich, ZAW, N.F. 19 (1944), pp. 1 ff. has tried to show that the Old Testament word for 'Covenant' connotes not so much a double-sided agreement between equal partners as a more or less one-sided order.

claim of this God to their exclusive worship even if the oldest tradition should not have known anything about written laws.

At any rate the commitment of the people to its God, who might now be described simply as 'the God of Israel', formed the real substance of the covenant-making in the Sinai tradition; of the various laws which were later gradually added to the story of Sinai, none can be traced back with any certainty to the original content of the tradition and most of them do not even go back to its earliest literary version.

There is no doubt that the Sinai tradition, the basic substance of which is quite isolated and unrelated to any previous event in the history of religion derived from an actual event. It must be admitted that the event is wrapped in mystery, and we are even in the dark about its historical background and context. This is mainly owing to the fact that, to begin with, the Sinai tradition was an independent tradition on its own sustained by a festival for the renewing of the covenant which was regularly observed by the Israelite tribes[1], and that it was only later that it was included among the themes of the Pentateuch as part of a wider context.

It is not even possible to say anything for certain about where the incident took place on which the tradition is based. The Pentateuch narrative and certain passages outside the Pentateuch refer to the mountain where God revealed himself as 'Sinai', whereas in the deuteronomic-deuteronomistic literature and in some passages which derive from this source the name 'Horeb' appears. The juxtaposition of these two names and their interrelationship is a complete mystery; only so much is clear that the name 'Sinai' is the older of the two in the tradition that has come down to us[2]. We therefore usually give preference to this name. Whereabout, then, is this 'Sinai'? Until the Byzantine period there is no evidence for the view that it is to be found in the mountainous southern part of the Sinaitic peninsula which is traditionally named after it, between the gulfs of es-suwēs and el-'aḳaba; whether we think specifically of the jebel mūsa ='mountain of Moses' (2244 m.) favoured by modern local tradition on account of its name or the jebel ḳāṭerīn ='mount Catharine' (2602 m.) with the Catharine Convent as the vehicle of the Byzantine-Christian tradition, or, finally—for reasons to be mentioned in a moment—of the jebel

[1] More details on this will be found in G. v. Rad, *Das formgeschichtliche Problem des Hexateuchs* (1938), pp. 11 ff.

[2] The occurrence of the name 'Horeb' in some passages in the Pentateuch narrative is probably entirely secondary; cf. M. Noth, *Überlieferungsgeschichtliche Studien*, I (1943), p. 29.

serbāl (2052 m.) which lies somewhat further to the west. The Byzantine tradition certainly links up with the fact that its 'Sinai' was already traditionally sacred in that period, and the very numerous Nabataean rock inscriptions which have been discovered, especially at the entrances to the massif of the jebel serbāl and which derive from Nabataean pilgrims, some of whom came long distances, prove that in the 2nd and 3rd centuries A.D. after the fall of the Nabataean State and after the abolition of the famous sanctuaries in the Nabataean capital of Petra, a mountain shrine in the southern part of the traditional Sinaitic peninsula had attracted Nabataean pilgrims[1]. This certainly presupposes that a pilgrims' shrine had already existed in the district for a long time, and since the sacredness of a place is usually preserved with great tenacity in spite of changes in the form of worship and religions and is more or less undisturbed by the comings and goings of different human groups and peoples, it may be assumed with great probability that in the district in question there had been a sacred mountain from time immemorial which may well have been the 'Sinai' of the ancient Israelite tradition.

It must be remembered, however, that the positive arguments in favour of this supposition are very weak. There is evidence only from the 6th century onwards of a tradition that the ancient holy mountain in the southern part of the 'Sinaitic' peninsula, which definitely existed, was identical with the 'Sinai' of the Old Testament. This means that, measured against the antiquity of the events which took place on 'Sinai', the tradition is very late, and may well be purely second-hand. There is nothing at all in favour of positing a route for the Israelites' journey in the wilderness which would suggest placing 'Sinai' in the so-called Sinaitic peninsula. In the first place, it is almost impossible to localise any of the place-names which appear in this connection with any degree of certainty. And then it is very doubtful whether the references to places in the various strata of the Pentateuch narrative are intended to suggest any particular route; even if that were the case, it would not be a primary source, since the Sinai theme was only included in the Pentateuch narrative at a relatively late date. General considerations are useless, however, in any attempt to locate Sinai, since we have no knowledge of the historical and geographical context to which the isolated Sinai tradition belongs. Presumably pilgrimages were made to holy Sinai and such pilgrimages can take their

[1] Cf. the treatment and utilisation of these inscriptions by B. Moritz in *Der Sinaikult in heidnischer Zeit* (Abh. d. Goett. Ges. d. Wiss., N.F. 16, 2), 1916.

participants a long way from their home, particularly when their district has no permanent population. The celebrated Sinai inscriptions from the district of the turquoise mines of serābīṭ el-khādem in the northern part of the mountains of the Sinai peninsula, to which the Egyptians had laid claim from the earliest times, were discovered by Flinders Petrie in 1905, but they must be completely excluded from the 'Sinai' problem, though they have occasionally been called in as evidence[1]. It is true that the inscriptions are written in a Canaanite alphabet and have become famous as the oldest known evidence of this type of script, and are, moreover, obviously written in a Canaanite dialect, but they have nothing at all to do with the Israelites. They derive from the 15th century B.C., that is, from a period when it is hardly possible that the Israelites were making pilgrimages to Sinai, and they were carried out by Canaanite mine-workers in the service of the Egyptians[2].

It is, admittedly, impossible to deny that Sinai may have been situated in the southern part of the traditional Sinaitic peninsula but it cannot be proved, and it is still possible that it lay elsewhere. In recent times it has often been suggested[3] that it may have lain in north-western Arabia east or south-east of the gulf of el-ʿaḳaba. One of the arguments used in support of this theory must be rejected straight away. It is suggested that Sinai must have lain in the district occupied by the Midianites, and that, according to the available information, the Midianites inhabited the eastern side of the gulf of el-ʿaḳaba, even though as nomads they often strayed far from their proper area. But there is no reference at all to the Midianites in the Sinai tradition; it is only in later connecting narratives such as Exod. iii, 1 ff., Num. x, 29 ff. that they appear in connection with Sinai owing to a second-hand and questionable identification of Sinai with the 'mountain of God' mentioned in Exod. xviii (where a meeting took place between Midianites and Israelites). Another argument, however, deserves serious consideration. A few details in the description of the circumstances that attended

[1] Cf. F. Petrie, *Researches in Sinai* (1906). In the meantime further expeditions have examined these inscriptions more closely and discovered new ones.

[2] On the dating, reading and interpretation of these inscriptions cf. latterly W. F. Albright, BASOR, 110 (1948), pp. 6 ff.

[3] The thesis that Sinai was located in the northern part of the Sinaitic peninsula (propounded among others by R. Kittel, *Geschichte des Volkes Israel*, I, 5/6 [1923], p. 346; A. Jirku, *Geschichte des Volkes Israel* [1931], p. 72) in the vicinity of the source of Kadesh Barnea (ʿēn ḳdēs) may be passed over since there is no evidence for its validity. The assumption that the Israelite tribes spent a long time in this area has no basis in the primary tradition of the Pentateuch (the statement in Deut. i, 46 is based on a secondary historical reconstruction) and the requirement that Sinai should be easily accessible overlooks the complications of events in Israel's early history.

the great revelation of God in Exod. xix suggest that Sinai was an active volcano, especially the statement that the whole of Sinai 'was altogether on a smoke, because the Lord descended upon it in fire; and the smoke thereof ascended as the smoke of a furnace, and the whole mount quaked greatly' (verse 18). There is also the strange phenomenon of the 'pillar of a cloud' and 'pillar of fire' which led them on their way (Exod. xiii, 21 f.) and which must have its source in the Sinai tradition. The significance of these very concrete details is not reduced by the fact that a variant in Exod. xix only appears to refer to 'thunders and lightnings and a thick cloud upon the mount' (verse 16). Now no active volcanoes have existed in the traditional Sinaitic peninsula in historical times but only on the other side of the gulf of el-ʿaḳaba in north-western Arabia in the area of the caravan route south-east of tebūk which leads to southern Arabia, about 200 kilometres south-east of el-ʿaḳaba. The considerable distance of this area from Palestine and its borders does not matter so much, since it is hardly likely in any case that Sinai was situated on the route of the migrant Israelites, and was not rather the goal of a pilgrimage for which even great distances were no decisive obstacle. On the other hand, it is just possible that among the tribes wandering about in southern and eastern Palestine volcanic manifestations which were well known in north-western Arabia were traditionally thought of as accompanying appearances of God, and that they were mentioned even when the theophany occurred in a place with no volcanoes. In favour of locating Sinai in north-western Arabia there is, finally, the point that Num. xxxiii, 1-49 appears to contain the list of halting-places on a journey to Sinai and that this route leads from Palestine via el-ʿaḳaba not, apparently, to the traditional Sinaitic peninsula but, presumably, to north-western Arabia[1]. To sum up, there are sound reasons for assuming that Sinai lay in the volcanic area of north-western Arabia, but these reasons are not unambiguous or adequate enough to prove the correctness of this assumption.

A few passages in the Old Testament outside the Pentateuch refer to Sinai in striking connection with the name Seir, which was applied pre-eminently to the mountainous country on the eastern side of the wādi el-ʿaraba between the Dead Sea and the gulf of el-ʿaḳaba. They refer to the coming of Yahweh from Sinai. This is quite clearly the case in Deut. xxxiii, 2: 'The Lord came from Sinai and rose up from Seir unto them'; and in Judges v, 4 too the 'going out of Seir' and 'marching out of the field of Edom'

[1] More details in M. Noth, *Der Wallfahrtsweg zum Sinai* (PJB, 36 [1940], pp. 5 ff.).

obviously refer to the God coming from Sinai, whether the explicit reference to the name Sinai in the following verse is original or not. On the other hand, in Deut. xxxiii, 2 there is also a reference to 'Mount Paran'[1], which is almost certainly identical with the modern jebel faran on the western side of the wādi el-ʿaraba, as well as to Seir[2]. It seems that these references to place-names are only very rough and ready, and one is probably right to assume that the direction from which Yahweh was expected to come from Sinai was indicated very vaguely from the point of view of Palestine. Nevertheless, the wording in Judges v, 4 suggests that the district of Seir really was the starting-point from which Yahweh came; and since any other localisation of Sinai is impossible, the two passages referred to would certainly suggest that the district of Seir should be borne in mind, though it is impossible exactly to define the scope of the term Seir even if these references to place-names have any objective validity at all.

The historical circumstances in which the pilgrimage to Sinai and the divine revelation on Sinai took place are just as doubtful as the place where the revelation occurred. The Pentateuch tradition refers simply to 'Israel' having been at Sinai. But the same thing applies here as in the case of the departure from Egypt and the deliverance 'by the sea'. Since the 'Israel' of the twelve tribes was not formed until the settlement on Palestinian soil and the individual tribes did not become established until then, the 'Israel' which was present on Sinai cannot have been the 'Israel' of the later period or a particular group of its tribes. All that can be said is that the divine revelation on Sinai was imparted to clans which later became incorporated in the tribes of Israel, though it is still impossible to say anything definite about their number and structure. What befell them affected the whole of the later tribes of Israel so powerfully that what took place on Sinai became a substantial and fundamental element in that common Israelite tradition which henceforth inspired Israel as a corporate unit. It is therefore probable that those who participated in the incident that took place on Sinai did not merely combine into one of the subsequent tribes of Israel but were rather incorporated in various tribes.

There remains the problem of the historical connection between the encounter on Sinai and the departure from Egypt. In the

[1] The naming of Meribat-Kadesh in Deut. xxxiii, 2 which has been obtained by textual conjecture is very uncertain; cf. Fr. M. Cross and D. N. Freedman, JBL, 67 (1948), p. 193.

[2] The 'Mount Paran' in a similar context in Hab. iii, 3.

Pentateuch narrative the two events follow on from one another smoothly and fairly directly, in fact the pillars of cloud and fire are made to appear to the Israelites departing from Egypt before the deliverance 'by the sea' (Exod. xiii, 21 f.). But the Sinai theme was not added to the others until much later, and the story of the departure and entry had been presented in a short didactic summary long before any mention was made of Sinai[1]. Meanwhile, the Sinai theme was transmitted independently within the framework of the festival of the making or renewal of the Covenant. In the oldest tradition there was evidently no connection between the two events, and it was only as the Pentateuch narrative developed that all the existing traditions concerning the prehistory of Israel were brought together and referred to 'Israel' as a whole and the story of Sinai was incorporated in the story of the departure from Egypt and the occupation of the land. If there was therefore no original traditional connection, it is just as unlikely that there was any historical connection. If, moreover, Israel did not yet exist at all as a uniform and permanent factor in this early period, it is quite unlikely that the same elements of what later became 'Israel' took part in the events in and around Egypt and also in the encounter on Sinai. But if they were two different groups, the incident that took place on Sinai becomes an even more completely isolated historical event, about the reality of which there can be no doubt, the historical framework of which is, however, completely beyond our ken. The one and only connection with historical facts known to us is that ancestors of what was later to become 'Israel' took part in it. This also means that it is impossible to assign a date to it and even impossible to fit it into any sequence of historical events or, above all, to define its relationship in time to the departure from Egypt. All one can do is to draw attention to the following circumstance. The deliverance from Egypt which took place 'by the sea' was so much to the fore in the Israelite tradition, as far as it is known to us, as the precondition of the occupation of the land, that one gets the impression that, as the divine action on which the very existence of Israel was based, it was a more lively and immediate memory than the divine appearance on Sinai, which was only transmitted within the framework of a regular religious observance. In view of this customary rite, the encounter on Sinai may be assigned to a comparatively early date and those who took part in it may be regarded as members of a fairly ancient stratum of what

[1] Cf. the compilations on the 'minor historical Credo' and its free variations in the devotional lyric in v. Rad, *loc. cit.* pp. 3 ff.

later became Israel, whilst the participants in the events which took place in and around Egypt belonged to later generations.

It is even more difficult to establish the content and nature of the event which took place on Sinai than it is to discern the outward circumstances and context. The only historical evidence available to us is the religious rite which bore repeated witness to the fact that God had appeared to the clans that came on pilgrimage to Sinai. But the actual incident extends into the realm of the historically inexplicable in the sense outlined above on page 3. This mysterious event and all that followed from it, the commitment of the people to the God who had appeared and their submission to his exclusive ('jealous') claim and will, took place in historically conditioned forms. If a pilgrimage to Sinai was the outward occasion, Sinai must already have been a sacred mountain to which pilgrimages were made and a place of worship. In fact this older form of worship on Sinai appears at least in one respect to have had a permanent influence on the faith of Israel; everything suggests that the divine name of Yahweh derives from the pre-Israelite worship on Sinai as the name of the deity who was worshipped on Sinai. This is suggested by the Pentateuch itself since the name Yahweh is imparted to Moses on his first visit to the subsequent site of the divine revelation (Exod. iii, 14 E.), though the narrative in which this occurs is admittedly comparatively late. Another point in support of this argument is the view, occasionally put forward in the Old Testament, that Sinai was the dwelling-place of Yahweh and that He always comes from Sinai (Judges v, 4 f.; Deut. xxxiii, 2 and also Hab. iii, 1) and that to find Him one must travel to the sacred mount of God in the desert (1 Kings xix, 8 ff)[1]. Indeed, if the supposition is correct that the curious expression זהסיני in Judges v, 5 is to be translated as 'the one from Sinai'[2], then, whether or not the words in the passage are part of the original text, Yahweh was here being called 'the (God) of Sinai' in a perfectly routine way. If this is a correct interpretation, we may imagine that the decisive revelation of God took place on this site in the name of this same Yahweh in the course of a pilgrimage to the holy mount of the Yahweh of Sinai amidst awe-inspiring, possibly volcanic, natural manifestations.

[1] The name 'Horeb' in 1 Kings xix, 8 is probably a (deuteronomistic) addition; according to what follows, the 'mount of God' at any rate means the place which is called Sinai in the Pentateuch narrative. On the possibility that, even apart from Elia, pilgrimages continued to take place for a long time to the holy mountain from Palestine, cf. M. Noth, PJB, 36 (1940), pp. 7 f.

[2] Thus W. F. Albright, JBL, 54 (1935), p. 204.

It has been generally assumed that Moses' historical work had its real centre on Sinai; whatever judgement may be passed on the content of the Moses tradition, that he was the leader of the people on Sinai, the interpreter of what took place there and the organiser of the divine community based on more or less firmly defined formulations of the divine will, seems to be more or less established. This view of Moses has its ultimate source in the deuteronomic-deuteronomistic literature of the Old Testament in which Moses' mediation on the holy mount is regarded as the decisive element in his work; and this is connected with the fact that of the events of prehistoric times of which it had knowledge it considered the theophany on the mountain and the legislation enacted there as the most important[1]. These events were singled out for special treatment. This led to Moses being thought of primarily as the legislator; and in the later literature of the Old Testament the name Moses appears above all in connection with the 'Law (book) of Moses'. The deuteronomic-deuteronomistic literature naturally refers back to the role which Moses played in the Pentateuch narrative; but in the latter the appearance of Moses on Sinai is merely one link in a long chain and Moses on Sinai is no more and no less the messenger of God and the spokesman of the people than in other events which took place between the departure from Egypt and the entry into the Promised Land. From his first appearance among the Israelites who were performing compulsory labour in Egypt right up to his death shortly before the entry into the Promised Land Moses is, from the point of view of the Pentateuch, the head of the wandering people who, though often attacked, is always confirmed anew by God.

It is this view of Moses, however, as offered by the oldest surviving tradition, which raises the historical problem of his personality. Since the Pentateuch narrative was compiled step by step from a series of originally independent themes, the regular appearance of Moses in most of these themes cannot be original but must be the result of later manipulation; and the inevitable question is to which theme or tradition Moses was originally attached and where we must look for his historical roots. The question is extraordinarily difficult to answer[2]. It is highly likely,

[1] The deuteronomic law, formulated as a speech by Moses, was naturally specially interested in this. In its train the deuteronomistic history begins in Deut. i, 1 ff. with the sojourn of 'Israel' in Horeb. The Priestly Code of the Pentateuch narrative concentrates its whole interest on the legislation on Sinai.

[2] Cf. the discussions in M. Noth, *Überlieferungsgeschichte des Pentateuch* (1948), p. 172 ff.

however, that it is possible to establish, negatively, that, according to the earliest tradition available to us, he was not especially firmly rooted in the Sinai theme, since nothing is said about him in that tradition apart from his general role as a leader[1]. His personality appears in very much more concrete and specific circumstances in other places in the Pentateuch. This suggests that Moses had no historical connection with the event which took place on Sinai[2]. Historically, it is therefore hardly justifiable to describe him as the organiser and legislator of Israel. The fact that it is impossible to name any specific human person who played an active or interpretative part on that occasion makes the event even more mysterious. Nevertheless, the core of the Sinai tradition was a historical occurrence, however vague the historical details may be. The same thing applies here as in the case of the deliverance 'by the sea'. We can analyse the traditions by which the sacred confederacy of the twelve tribes lived into their individual elements, and analyse the historical content of these elements, but we must state quite definitely that these traditions have come down to us only as parts of the greater Whole, that they are all related to the greater unit of 'Israel' and concerned with Yahweh as the 'God of Israel'. Within this great Whole the God who appeared on Sinai is, needless to say, the same as the God who showed his power in the deliverance 'by the sea'. And the basic elements of this great Whole existed at a very early date. It is true that the growth of the Pentateuch was a long process even in the stage of purely oral transmission which had probably already been very largely concluded before the beginning of the formation of the State, and the beginnings of which go back to the earliest period immediately following the occupation of the land by the tribes. But these beginnings already presuppose the existence of 'Israel' as a total unit and the unity of the traditions based on the faith in the 'God of Israel'. The gradually evolving narrative of the Pentateuch thus becomes important as a source of evidence for Israel's unity and consciousness of unity

[1] In view of his obviously Egyptian name one might look for his original role within the framework of the deliverance from Egypt, possibly as the messenger of God who announces the imminent action of God (cf. Exod. iii, 16-17a α). But perhaps the most concrete fact of all is the tradition of the tomb of Moses which was situated in a very definite spot. According to this, Moses would belong to the phase of the preparations for the occupation of the land by the tribes of central Palestine. More details about his specific role and significance will have been lost in the process of expanding his personality into one of relevance to Israel as a whole, so that it is impossible to say anything definite about it.

[2] To describe him as the 'founder of a religion', or even to speak of a 'Mosaic religion', is quite misleading and incompatible with the Moses tradition as it was developed later on.

immediately after the occupation of the land, and the gradually developing tradition of the Pentateuch, the religious content of which is quite without parallel, becomes a clear token of the particularity and qualitative uniqueness of Israel's position among the nations. At the same time, however, how the unit of 'Israel' came into being in the first place is a problem.

If the twelve tribes of Israel first met on the soil of Palestine, if it was various sections of this 'Israel' that had witnessed the deliverance from Egypt and the meeting with God on Sinai and the occupation of the land from the southern land east of the Jordan: if these events were unrelated in time or content[1] then the question is, how did it happen that 'Israel' felt itself so much a unified whole so soon after the occupation of the land that a framework of traditions came into being which was concerned with the common prehistory of 'Israel'? Clear though the facts themselves are, it is impossible to answer this question with any certainty, since the tradition does not take this process into account and does not say anything about it. Only conjectures are possible, but they must be made, since the question requires at least a feasible answer. And this answer must be based on the supposition that the unity of 'Israel' and its faith did not suddenly appear one fine day but grew by degrees from a nucleus on the soil of Palestine. If it were true that the Sinai tradition referred to an event of the fairly remote past, those who took part in the encounter with God on Sinai would have to be included among the earliest of those who later became 'Israel'[2], and, in the course of time, further groups will have joined with them and become associated with their extraordinary and momentous traditions. Among these people the encounter on Sinai would have meant that subjection to the will of God as formulated in a divine law was decisive and the significance of the divine law and a central judicature would both have their roots therein. When other elements in Palestine were added, which had taken part in the deliverance 'by the sea', the conviction would have at once impressed itself on their minds that the mighty God to whom they owed the deliverance out of Egypt could have been no other than the God who appeared on Sinai. And when

[1] There have been many modern attempts to establish some sort of connection between these happenings, without following the sequence of events transmitted in the Old Testament. In view of the circumstances of the tradition these attempts must inevitably remain questionable. From the most recent period we may mention Th. J. Meek, *Hebrew Origins* ([2]1950); H. H. Rowley, *From Joseph to Joshua* (The Schweich Lectures, 1948 [1950]).

[2] Anyone who is interested in hypotheses may think of elements which were absorbed by the older group of the so-called 'Leah'-tribes.

Israel formed itself into the sacred confederacy of the twelve tribes with the confession of faith in Yahweh as the God of Israel, the various traditions would have coalesced into the image of a coherent prehistory shared by the whole of 'Israel', though in such a way as to make the liberation from Egypt, combined with the promise to the Patriarchs, the main point of interest, as evidence of the mighty deeds of the God of Israel, whilst the old Sinai tradition remained on its own in the background to begin with. In the end, however, it was to be incorporated in the total corpus of the prehistoric traditions. The Sinai tradition would have contributed the name of Yahweh to the corpus of these traditions from the very beginning. It is clear that all this is a hypothesis which it is impossible to prove: it is merely an attempt to provide an answer to an inevitable question.

But what did its special position among the nations, based, according to its tradition, on a peculiar relationship to God, mean for 'Israel'? The earliest tradition says nothing on this point. But one of the earliest theological formulations of the old tradition, the Yahwistic narrative, conceives the history of Israel as part of a universal divine purpose for the blessing of humanity (Gen. xii, 1-3). One can at least wonder whether the Yahwist was not expressing something that was present in the faith of 'Israel' even before him and from the very first.

PART TWO

THE LIFE OF ANCIENT ISRAEL IN THE PALESTINIAN-SYRIAN WORLD

CHAPTER I

THE SELF-ASSERTION OF THE TRIBES IN PALESTINE

12. *Their Connections with the Earlier Inhabitants of the Land*

THE country in which the Israelite tribes settled was an inhabited land. In the Old Testament the people that had lived in the land in pre-Israelite times are usually called 'Canaanites' without regard to their ethnic differences, and we shall also use the term in that sense[1]. The Canaanite population was concentrated in the numerous permanently established cities which were, admittedly, not distributed evenly throughout the country but were most frequent in the plains favoured by nature, whilst there were only occasional cities in the more sterile and mountainous parts of the land. These cities, which were fortresses enclosed by a wall, with houses closely crammed together, with adjoining territory providing the necessary agricultural land, had already passed through their prime in the Bronze Age but they were still the heirs of a rich urban civilisation. The irregular distribution of these cities allowed the Israelites to gain a footing in the parts of the country which were only sparsely inhabited or not at all, which were still very largely wooded and still in need of clearing to be suitable for human settlement, without having to turn out the Canaanite inhabitants from their properties; and on the whole they did not expel them. The Canaanites remained in the land and, generally speaking, were able to continue unimpeded with their own way of life and with their possessions intact. But in the places of which they took possession the Israelite tribes frequently established new settlements, which they also called 'cities', and which were, like the Canaanite cities, enclosed by a wall in a situation as fortified as possible or at least not easily

[1] In addition to the description 'Canaanite' the terms 'Amorite' and 'Hittites' occur in the Old Testament with the same meaning. This use of the term 'Canaanite' does not throw any light on the etymology of the name Canaan which has not yet been completely explained (cf. above, p. 22, note 3) and its original reference to the area of the Phoenician coast, nor on the use of the term 'Canaanite' to describe a group of Semitic dialects native to Syria and Palestine which has become a convention in modern philology.

accessible, with densely packed dwellings in a confined space. Usually, however, they did not have such strong and carefully built walls as the Bronze Age cities. Their walls were much less resistant to the destructive influences of time, and the archaeological traces of the Israelites' Iron Age settlements have been obliterated more thoroughly and intensely than those of the earlier Bronze Age cities of the Canaanites. With the settlement in Palestine, the change over to agriculture as their main activity and the concentration of the population in 'cities' or places like cities, the Israelites' way of life approached that of the indigenous Canaanite population, which lived mainly in special parts of the country but was also represented here and there in the mountains occupied by the Israelites, and entered into neighbourly relations with them in many places. This led in time to the development of a particular kind of relationship between the two parties. We have only sporadic and more or less fortuitous information about this, but what we have shows that their mutual relations varied enormously according to time and place. On the whole, the Israelite tribes, who had come from quite different circumstances, regarded the Canaanite way of life as alien and it remained alien so long as the independent character of the Canaanites survived in the land. This is true at any rate of the period preceding the formation of the State in Israel and of the Israelite circles which deliberately maintained their old authentic traditions. In spite of their settlement in Palestine, the genuine urban culture, whose rich diversity was maintained even in the Iron Age, continued to be alien to the Israelites, who were used to simplicity and straightforwardness; what the essentially agricultural and cattle-rearing Israelites considered 'Canaanite', above all, was the interest in industry, commerce and profit-making which was rooted in their urban civilisation. In quite a late period they continued to describe the merchant and trader simply as a 'Canaanite' (Isa. xxiii, 8; Zeph. i, 11; Zech. xiv, 21; Prov. xxxi, 24; Job xl, 30 (=xli, 6 in the English Bible), thereby characterising this activity as something alien to their own character; in Hos. xii, 8 (=7 in the English Bible) there is a specific reference to the deceitful conduct of such 'Canaanites'[1]: 'He is a merchant, the balances of deceit are in his hand'. The Israelites, whose tribal organisation was based on the equal rights of all the free members of the tribe, regarded the social stratification in the Canaanite cities as alien to their own social outlook: a

[1] When Israelites take part in this behaviour, they turn themselves into 'Canaanites', which is probably the meaning of this difficult sentence in Hosea.

ruling, property-owning aristocracy on the one hand, with a feudal lord at the summit, who called himself a king or was at any rate usually called by that title in the Old Testament, and, on the other hand, a subject population devoted primarily to agricultural work. The military technique of chariot fighting as practised by the ruling classes was heartily disliked and feared by the Israelites. To begin with, the tribes which were accustomed to take the field with a militia of fighting men bearing their own weapons, felt thoroughly inferior to these contingents of iron chariots[1] and as a result they did not, generally speaking, undertake any warlike attacks on Canaanite cities (Jos. xvii, 16-18; Judges i, 19; iv, 3, 13) where the mode of fighting not only filled them with feelings of inferiority but inspired them with awe. Above all, however, it was the life and faith of the Canaanites that was alien to the Israelite tribes. They seemed to them to be morally inferior and degenerate, lustful and unprincipled. In the original form of Gen. ix, 20-27 'Canaan', the youngest son of Noah, the representative of the Canaanites, is described as shameless and perverse. The intention behind the story told in Gen. xxvi, 7-11[2] is to point out that anyone who comes near a Canaanite city must reckon with the possibility of his wife falling victim to the inhabitants' covetousness and himself, as the woman's husband, running the danger of being treacherously murdered. A girl who appears unprotected in the vicinity of a Canaanite may easily be raped by one of the inhabitants, possibly even by the son of the city king himself (cf. Gen. xxxiv, 1 f.). For the Israelite tribes, who were used to the strict discipline of a patriarchal society, all this moral laxity was contemptible and shocking. It was no doubt bound up to some extent with the special character of the Canaanite system of worship to which the Israelites, with their devotion to the demands of a stern deity, were particularly antagonistic. The cults which flourished among the Canaanites were the immemorial rites of the great fertility-bestowing mother-diety who was called Asthaarthe, and of a youthful deity who represented the annual blossoming and dying of plant life; these cults included the celebration of a 'holy marriage' at a holy place with female representatives of the deity and 'sacred' prostitution and the sacrifice of female chastity. There

[1] These contingents of chariots (רכב is used as a collective noun) consisted of war chariots, which were naturally not made entirely of iron but only provided with iron fittings. The chariots were made of wood and when the Israelites captured them they burnt them (Jos. xi, 6, 9 [the single chariot is called מרכבה]; cf. Ps. xlvi, 10 [=9 in the English Bible]).

[2] The transfer of this scene to Egypt in Gen. xii, 10-20 is a secondary tradition.

was also the cult of the multiform Baal, the fairly ancient Baal of heaven, and the numerous local Baals which were also givers of life and fertility and held sway in the sphere of sensual life. The Israelites were bound to reject all this, especially the worship of female deities. On the other hand, however, they had inevitably to establish certain relations with this Canaanite world. The change over to a settled and predominantly agricultural way of life based on the land involved an adaptation to the new conditions, a re-adjustment to the customs current among the previous inhabitants, since ideas and attitudes are intimately bound up with a people's whole way of life. I do not mean that certain circles among the Israelites succumbed to the danger of wholesale Canaanisation and simply became Canaanites even in the sphere of worship and members of the Canaanite population; naturally we have no information on this point but we must assume that a certain amount of assimilation occurred. The degree of assimilation will hardly have been on a large scale, however, and is therefore of no great historical significance. On the other hand, even the broad masses of the Israelites who remained fully aware of the differences separating them from the Canaanites inevitably adopted something of the Canaanite character and way of life. This also applies to the religious sphere which was necessarily closely connected with the whole way of life. The very fact that the Israelite tribes conducted their worship at the age-old shrines of the land led to the adoption of the native traditions. This is true of the central amphictyonic rite (cf. above p. 91 ff., 97 ff.) and even more of the numerous local rites observed by the tribes or clans that had now become local communities. The point is not that foreign gods were worshipped in these places, but the forms that were traditional in the land had a decisive influence on the Israelites' devotional rites. Thus, the great agricultural religious festivals were taken over (cf. above p. 97), which were closely connected with the seasons of the year in Palestine; and the whole system of sacrifice in general followed the ancient traditions of the country. Even though the specifically Canaanite rites of which we have spoken were excluded as essentially foreign, a far-reaching process of Canaanisation took place in the field of worship. The Israelite faith entered quite concretely into the world in which the Israelites were now living.

In daily life and work a strong approximation resulted quite automatically from the fairly similar outward conditions under which both peoples were now living; and while they were newcomers the Israelites no doubt learnt and adopted a good deal from the Canaanite inhabitants. It is therefore not surprising that in spite of all their mutual foreignness the Israelites' relations with their Canaanite neighbours were by no means entirely hostile. Sporadic information throws some light on the multiplicity of the various relationships which developed between Israelites and Canaanites in the course of time. The information available is nothing like sufficient to enable us to survey the whole field, but it does show what a variety of contacts was possible. So far as relationships were established at all, by reason of neighbourhood or communications, a peaceful *modus vivendi* was often found possible. One way was for one of the parties to enter more or less voluntarily into some form of dependence on the other. In the period of the occupation of the land the tribes of Issachar, Zebulun and Asser, which settled on the borders of the plain of Jezreel and the plain of Akko, apparently entered into a feudal relationship with the city governments in the plains, and probably received a share of the profits accruing from their rich estates in return for their services. They did not have to surrender their identity as members of the confederacy of Israel, and did not remain in this state of dependence permanently, but to begin with they did, nevertheless, enter into this one-sided relationship. The fact that the ancient city of Shechem, which lies in a rather isolated position in the mountains of Central Palestine, was admitted into the society of the tribe of Manasseh with the status of a Manassitic clan, forms a complement to this example: in the great list of clans in Num. xxvi which is arranged according to tribes, Shechem appears among the Manassitic clans (verse 31b) and hence within the organisation of the tribe of Manasseh as a minor member of the Israelite confederacy of the twelve tribes, and probably also as a participant in its divine worship, without abandoning the political and social structure of the old political order (see below p. 152 f. on Judges ix). We have no idea how this came about, and can only presume that the fact that Israelite clans had taken part in the worship at the shrine of Shechem from a early fairly period (cf. Jacob's association with this shrine), played a part, and that for a time Israel's central amphictyonic rite was performed there. Anyway, this attachment of Shechem to Manasseh must have taken place very early on, since it is taken for granted not only in the list in Num. xxvi which goes back to the pre-political period, but also in the story contained in Judges ix. In a similar way, the four Canaanite cities mentioned in Jos. ix, 17, which were situated in the mountains north-west of Jerusalem, appear as belonging to the tribe of Benjamin. The cities in question are Gibeon (not yet identified for certain), Chephirah (the modern khirbet kefīre), Beeroth (not yet identified precisely) and Kirjath-Jearim (dēr el-azhar near el-ḳerje). Their territories appear in the description of the frontiers for Benjamin (Jos. xviii, 11-20) which derives from the pre-political period, as part of Benjamin's tribal area[1]. On the other hand, however, their names do not appear in the list in Num. xxvi, so that we have to assume that they were not received into the society of the tribe of Benjamin until after this list had been compiled. Again, we know nothing as to how the annexation took place; in Jos. ix we have an aetiological narrative which takes for granted the fact that the four cities belong to Benjamin, and which undertakes to explain it. It amalgamates it, however, with the quite different fact that Gibeonites had to serve as 'hewers of wood and drawers of water' at the shrine of Gilgal near Jericho.

The facts mentioned so far indicate that in the parts of the land which were crowded with Canaanite cities, above all in the plains, the Canaanites had the upper hand to begin with, whereas in the mountains the Israelite tribes prevailed over the more scattered cities, even necessarily having recourse to arms. But in such a distinctly intermediary area as the hill country between the southern Palestinian mountains and the southern part of the maritime plain, what was apparently a fundamentally peaceful process of mutual assimilation ensued. It was here that the vigorous tribe of Judah was seeking to expand, and it found a chance to do so in this direction from its settlements in the mountains: the result was co-existence between Judaeans and Canaanites, with connubium and other friendly relationships. The stability of the Canaanite cities in this area does not seem to have been affected and the Judaeans only settled in intervening smaller settlements which they found when they arrived or which they established for themselves. This is clear from Gen. xxxviii. Admittedly, it is impossible in this passage to separate the element of tribal history, which is undoubtedly present, from the purely narrative element. Certainly the whole passage cannot be derived from tribal history. But the story of the birth of Shelah, who, according to Num. xxvi,

[1] This description of the frontier must be considered with reserve, since the system of describing the frontiers in the book of Joshua does not merely refer to the actual dwelling-places of the tribes in Palestine (cf. above, p. 53). Moreover, the later editor of the system included Kirjath-Jearim in Judah. But in connection with Jos. ix, 17 historical significance must obviously be attributed to the incorporation of the four city territories in the tribal area of Benjamin.

20, was the *heros eponymus* of a Jewish clan, is certainly a personification of a chapter of tribal history. According to Gen. xxxviii, 5, Shelah was born in Chezib (=Achzib, Jos. xv, 44). This was a small place in the hill country which is probably identical with the modern tell el-bēḍa[1]. According to Gen. xxxviii his father was Judah the tribal ancestor, whereas his mother was a Canaanite. His descendants, the Shelanites, who belonged to Judah, certainly settled in the region of Chezib[2].

It is true that the contacts between Israelites and Canaanites, so far as they occurred at all, were not entirely of a peaceful nature. Warlike encounters between them evidently occurred at a very early stage. The information we have is only sporadic and fortuitous but it gives us some idea of what may have happened, without allowing us to survey the encounters as a whole. Not surprisingly, we learn from Israelite sources only about the conflicts which ended in victory for the Israelites. No doubt the contrary also occurred. The fact that the Canaanite city rulers were able for the most part to maintain their properties is usually attributed to the fact that the tribes did not dare to attack them, but in isolated cases it may have been due to the fact that the cities were able to defend themselves against the encroachments of the Israelites by force of arms. Occasionally, the cities themselves probably attacked their unwanted and troublesome new neighbours, and they may have been successful in wresting this or that piece of their territory from them again. But such incidents will have been very few and far between. The Israelite tribes were also capable of warding off such attacks. We have an example in Jos. x, 1-15 in the story of the Battle of Gibeon. The core of the tradition is apparently that the 'kings of the Amorites that dwell in the mountains'[3] (verse 6) undertook an attack on the neighbouring Israelites—to judge from the site of the battle, the tribes in question may have been Benjamin and Ephraim —but were thoroughly routed[4]. Such incidents may occasionally

[1] This identification has been suggested by K. Elliger, ZDPV, 57 (1934), pp. 123 f.

[2] 1 Chron. ii and iv also contain a series of references which appear to indicate that the Judaeans interpolated themselves between the cities of the hill country; cf. M. Noth, ZDPV, 55 (1932), pp. 97 ff.

[3] The name 'Amorites' is used here in the same general sense as the name 'Canaanite'. The cities of these 'Amorite kings' were probably situated somewhere in the vicinity of Gibeon.

[4] The present connection between Jos. ix and Jos. x can hardly be an original element in the tradition. It might be asked whether the annexation by the tribe of Benjamin of the four cities mentioned in Jos. ix, 17 was not rather a result of the Battle of Gibeon and therefore at any rate indirectly a consequence of a warlike encounter: in other words not simply an act of peaceful agreement, as was assumed above on p. 146. On the analysis of the historical tradition of Jos. x cf. M. Noth, PJB, 33 (1937), pp. 22 ff.

have taken place at other times and places. There may have been plenty of such incidents, but it should be remembered that, on the whole, they were very limited in extent and significance. Above all, however, the Israelite tribes succeeded more than once in conquering individual Canaanite cities by force of arms and obtaining possession of their settlement and territory. According to the information available, the cities in question were in more or less isolated spots away from the great city-state territories. In Judges i, 10-15 = Jos. xv, 14-19 (cf. Jos. xiv, 12) there is a reference to the fact that the Calebites[1] had conquered the city of Hebron and the Othnielites, to whom they were related, had conquered the neighbouring city of Debir. They were, at any rate, subsequently in possession of these cities and the tradition which derives from this fact may be accurate in its reference to a conquest by force of arms. According to the note in Num. xiii, 22b, Hebron was already a Canaanite city; and the same may be true of Debir, though there is no positive archaeological[2] or literary[3] evidence on this point.

Farther to the north, according to Judges i, 22-26, the 'house of Joseph' conquered the city of Bethel which was situated right on the southern border of its settlement. Archaeological evidence shows that Bethel (the modern bētīn) was already a city in the Middle and Late Bronze Age. According to Judges i, 23b (cf. Gen. xxviii, 19b and elsewhere) this city had previously been called Lus, whilst the name Bethel probably belonged originally merely to the shrine that lies to the east of it (on the site of the modern burj bētīn), where Israelite clans had probably taken part in the worship from very early times: the name was probably only subsequently transferred to the city. It may be that the change of name was connected with the occupation by the 'house of Joseph'. In the land east of Jordan the tribe of Gad succeeded in conquering the city of Hesbon (the modern ḥesbān), which was directly adjacent to its territory, and ruled by the city king Sihon, as the old

[1] In Judges i, 10 the name 'Judah' may be assumed to have been originally 'Caleb' (as in Jos. xv, 14).

[2] The locating of Debir on the tell bēt mirsim (about 30 km. north-north-east of Beersaba), which is advocated above all by the eminently successful excavator of the tell bēt mirsim, W. F. Albright (cf. AASOR, 12 [1932]; 13 [1933]; 17 [1938]; 21/22 [1943]), is very questionable. To judge from the references in the Old Testament, one would prefer to look for it nearer to Hebron in the mountains.

[3] The assumption that Debir is called by its older name of Kirjath-Sepher (Jos. xv, 15 f.; Judges i, 11 f.) in the form of bt-tpr in the Egyptian *Pap. Anastasi*, I, 22, 5 from the period of Ramessides (about the 13th century B.C.) must be abandoned; bt-tpr was probably somewhere quite different. An older name, Kirjath-Arba, has also come down to us for Hebron (Jos. xiv, 15; xv, 13; Judges i, 10 and elsewhere). Were these two cities renamed after the above-mentioned conquest and resettlement? Cf. above, p. 33, note 1.

song of victory in Num. xxi, 27-30 informs us, to which the framework of a story was added in Num. xxi, 21-31. In the remote uppermost part of the Jordan Valley the city of Hazor (the modern tell wakkas), of whose existence in the Middle and Late Bronze Age there is documentary evidence in Egyptian sources and the Amarna tablets, was conquered and destroyed by Israelites, and probably by the neighbouring tribe of Naphtali, and its territory annexed. This proceeding forms the basis of the story contained in Jos. xi, 1-15. In the late Canaanite period the city of Laish (the modern tell el-ḳādi) which was situated near the sources of the Jordan, a fact which is confirmed by Egyptian sources—was, according to Judges xviii, 27 f. occupied and settled in by the land-seeking tribe of Dan, who called the city by their own name of Dan. It is true that the tribe of Dan thereby entered into some kind of dependence on the Phoenician coastal cities which apparently ruled over Laish and its territory[1]. In the Old Testament tradition all these conquests are directly related to the occupation of the land[2]. It should be remembered, however, that the occupation was a long process which certainly did not begin with the conquest of cities. On the contrary, the attacks on isolated Canaanite cities probably did not begin until the Israelite tribes had established themselves in their vicinity, and had gained a footing in uninhabited or only sparsely inhabited areas in Palestine. The occupation of Canaanite cities which were situated for the most part on the borders of Israelite territory, may be thought of at most as the very last stage in the process of occupation, if it is not in fact even better to think of it as a development and rounding off of the process of occupation, and a coming to terms with the earlier inhabitants after the real occupation was over[3].

We only hear once of a war of any importance waged by Israelite tribes against Canaanite cities within the city-state system proper, that is, in one of the plains; this is no mere accident, since such events were obviously quite exceptional. In the prose narrative of Judges iv and the song of victory in Judges v there is a reference to

[1] Cf. the striking reference to Zidon in connection with Laish in Judges xviii, 7, 28 and see above, pp. 79 f.

[2] The well-known stories of the conquest of the cities of Jericho (Jos. vi) and Ai (Jos. viii) have not been taken into consideration. They are in fact aetiological legends based on the fact that these cities were destroyed. But the destruction of these cities—as is certain in the case of Ai (the modern et-tell near dēr dubwān), and probable in that of Jericho (the modern tell es-sulṭān near erīha)—had taken place before the Israelites' occupation, so that the latter were able simply to take possession of the ruins and their territories.

[3] Cf. especially A. Alt, PJB, 35 (1939), pp. 14 ff. = *Kleine Schriften zur Geschichte des Volkes Israel*, I (1953), pp. 131 ff.

the famous victory which Israelite tribes obtained over the chariot armies of the King Sisera in the plain of Jezreel 'in Taanach by the waters of Megiddo' (Judges v, 19). We know little about the background of this victory[1]. Sisera was king in Haroseth (tell 'amr near el-ḥāriṯīje) at the north-western end of the plain of Jezreel. His name is possibly Illyrian[2] and if so, he may have been a member of the ruling class of the 'maritime peoples' (see above p. 37 f.). It may be that he exercised a kind of sovereignty over the cities in the plain of Jezreel which were occupied partly by 'Canaanites' and partly by 'maritime peoples', and perhaps in the plain of Akko too. According to the Old Testament tradition the conflict was started by the neighbouring tribes of Naphtali and Zebulun (Judges iv, 6, 10)[3]. There is no mention of the cause of the conflict and one can merely presume that the reaction was provoked by the state of dependence of the Galilean tribes on the borders of the plains on the cities in these plains (cf. above p. 78 f.). But the initiative was taken by the tribe of Naphtali which was in no such condition of dependence. Barak, a Naphtalite from Kedesh in Naphtali (the modern ḳedes) became the leader, inspired by a 'prophetess' called Deborah (Judges iv, 4). This is the first known example of Charismatic leadership among the Israelite tribes. A man is summoned to a particular undertaking by a messenger ('prophet') acting in the name of the God of Israel, a man with no official status of any kind. He embarks on this task and finds followers, as one called by God; and the war which is waged is a 'holy war'[4]. Barak's call was answered by his own tribe of Naphtali and the neighbouring tribe of Zebulun. From Kedesh where his followers were assembled, they proceeded to the holy mountain of Tabor in the north-eastern corner of the plain of Jezreel, and from there they sallied forth against the chariots of Sisera which had gathered meanwhile in the plain of Jezreel, and they achieved a complete victory over this dreaded enemy, which the Israelites could attribute only to the mighty aid of their God, in whose name Barak had entered the fight. Sisera himself was forced to flee on foot after the power of his chariots had been broken, and he was slain in the tent of a Kenite where he had sought refuge. The victors pursued and destroyed the enemy forces.

There is no reference to the results which flowed from this event.

[1] For conjectures on this point see A. Alt, ZAW, N.F. 19 (1944), pp. 72 ff.

[2] Thus A. Alt, ZAW, N.F. 19 (1944), p. 78, note 3.

[3] The Song of Victory in Judges v extended the circle of participants secondarily.

[4] Cf. G. v. Rad, *Deuteronomium-Studien* (1947), pp. 31 ff. and especially G. v. Rad, *Der heilige Krieg im alten Israel.*

It is not said, and it is therefore unlikely, that the Israelites proceeded to conquer and take possession of the cities in the plains either as a whole or one by one. The way they were later incorporated in the State of Israel (cf. below p. 163 f.) definitely suggests that they continued to exist as Canaanite cities. It may be assumed, however, that, though there is nothing to this effect in the tradition, the dependence of the Israelite tribes on the Canaanite cities now came to an end, if indeed it had lasted as long as this, and that at any rate these tribes henceforth enjoyed complete freedom just like the other tribes. But the most important result of the victory from the point of view of the Israelite tribes was undoubtedly the experience which they gained of being, with the help of their God, a match for and even superior to the might of the Canaanite chariots. This meant the disappearance of their feeling of insecurity and fear of the military technique and power of the earlier inhabitants of the land; and so it became possible for the tribes to attain a position of superiority over the Canaanite city state-system. At the same time, this victory proved that the God who, according to the traditions of the sacred confederacy of the twelve tribes, had intervened with his mighty aid in their early history and had led the tribes into the Promised Land, was still a living force in the present, and helping the tribes to hold the Promised Land against its previous inhabitants. All this was of fundamental importance beyond the immediate circle of the tribes that had taken a direct part in the fight. This is also shown by the song of victory in Judges v, the so-called Song of Deborah, which is one of the oldest passages in the Old Testament. It links up with the prehistoric traditions by speaking at the beginning of the coming of Yahweh from Sinai as an event of concern to all the Israelite tribes, excepting the remote and isolated tribes in the south. We have no evidence at all on which to assign a date to the victory over Sisera[1], even very roughly, but we shall not be far wrong if we assume that it presupposes the lapse of a certain time during which the tribes were settling down and securing and developing their properties. It may be assumed that this victory marked the end of the process of consolidation on the soil of Palestine and gave final definition to the Israelites' position in relation to the previous inhabitants. Admittedly, this relationship was full of latent tensions owing to the differences between

[1] As this victory does not appear to have had any direct and tangible effects on Canaanite cities, it is impossible to date it archaeologically—for example from the historical vicissitudes of the city of Megiddo (the modern tell el-mutesellim) which can be reconstructed from archaeological evidence; cf. especially A. Alt, ZAW, N.F. 19 (1944), pp. 67-85.

the character of the two peoples, and even when the relationship was firmly under control these tensions were bound to lead to greater or smaller conflicts.

We hear of such a conflict in the story of Abimelech, the 'son of Jerubbaal'[1] (Judges ix). This was an occurrence of a particular kind owing to the special relationship between the city of Shechem and the tribe of Manasseh, but it is of general significance inasmuch as it indicates how the differences between the political and social structure of the Israelites and Canaanites easily led to tension and conflict, even when a definite agreement between the two parties was in existence. The same cause will have led to friction in other places too, even when there is nothing recorded[2]. According to Judges ix the background of Abimelech's undertaking was the incorporation of the old Canaanite city of Shechem in the unit of the tribes of Manasseh (cf. above p. 36). This incorporation apparently embraced an Israelite-Canaanite connubium in this area. At this time the clan of Jerubbaal, which was living in the city of Ophrah, had the upper hand in Manasseh, and this predominance extended to the city-state of Shechem. An ambitious member of the clan, Abimelech, whose mother was a Shechemite, was able to exploit the dislike of the old Shechemite ruling aristocracy[3] for the predominance of the clan of Manasseh, and with their aid he succeeded in killing off most of the other male members of the clan of Jerubbaal. He thereupon had himself made king of Shechem by the aristocracy of the city: he was himself a Shechemite, at least on his mother's side. But he did not want to be merely a minor Canaanite city king in the old Canaanite style: with the aid of more or less pressure and force he extended his rule to the Manassite and Ephraimite clans living in the mountains around Shechem[4]. His

[1] The equation Jerubbaal = Gideon (Judges vii, 1; viii, 35; cf. vi, 25-32) is certainly secondary, though possibly fairly old; it is probably based on the fact that Gideon's home was also in Ophrah. But we probably owe to it the preservation of the story of Abimelech as an appendix to the stories of Gideon.

[2] The relationship of the tribe of Benjamin with the four Canaanite cities which were annexed to it (cf. above, p. 146) does not seem to have continued without difficulties. At least, we hear that the Benjaminite Saul as king later intervened with force in some of these cities; cf. 2 Sam. xxi, 1 ff. (Gideon) and 2 Sam. iv, 2, 3 (Beeroth).

[3] At that time Shechem was governed not by a city king but aristocratically—there is evidence to prove that Canaanite cities were occasionally governed in that way even in the Amarna period.

[4] Already in the Amarna period the city king Labaja of Shechem had extended his rule far over the mountains of Central Palestine (cf. A. Alt, *Die Landnahme der Israeliten in Palästina* [1925], pp. 18 ff. = *Kleine Schriften zur Geschichte des Volkes Israel*, I [1953], pp. 108 ff.). At this time, however, this area will hardly have been already occupied by Israelite tribes. Labaja therefore found a different situation from the one which existed at the time of Abimelech.

dominion thereby became a hybrid and inorganic structure and it was this that ruined him after a fairly short time. As he refused to be merely the city king of Shechem, but wanted to rule as far as possible over Israelite tribes as well, Abimelech moved his residence in due course from Shechem to Aruma (the modern el-ʿörme, about 10 kilometres south-east of Shechem in Ephraimite territory), and installed a 'Deputy' (פָּקִיד) in the city-state. The Shechemites, who had helped him to become king, took offence and charged him with disloyalty. They gathered in force to rebel against Abimelech. Thereupon Abimelech attacked the city—evidently with the mercenaries he had levied with the Shechemites' money—to exterminate the clan of Jerubbaal and to establish his rule, conquered and destroyed it. But he had thereby destroyed the basis of his own monarchy and this soon led to his destruction. He apparently still tried to extend his rule in one direction and another by conquests in Manassitic-Ephraimite territory. At least we find him finally occupied with an attack on the city of Thebez (the modern ṭūbāṣ, about 15 kilometres north-east of Shechem). In this attack he lost his life. His kingship, which was entirely his own personal achievement, then came to a rapid end.

The emergence of Abimelech was merely an episode. It apparently had no historical consequences[1]. One can hardly call this adventure of Abimelech a prelude to the subsequent formation of a State on the soil of Israel. After his death the relationship between Shechem and Manasseh will have reverted to the old arrangement. But the story of Abimelech is remarkable as evidence of the tensions existing between the Israelite and Canaanite systems, which he tried to turn to his own advantage, but which finally destroyed him. All the same, it is remarkable that in the tradition that has come down to us Abimelech was the first Israelite—though on his mother's side he was an Israelite-Canaanite half-caste—to call himself a 'king'.

13. *The Israelites' Altercations with their Neighbours*

On the eastern side the Israelite federation of tribes had a series of neighbours who had gone into Palestine from the desert and steppe, and settled there about the same time as the Israelite tribes, and in

[1] It is at least possible, but by no means certain, that the transfer of the amphictyonic central sanctuary from Shechem to Bethel was connected with the disturbances of the Abimelech period (cf. above, pp. 94 f.).

a similar way, as part of the same movement. They had settled in the, to some extent, favourable and fertile areas on the eastern border of Palestine, and had formed themselves into separate nations in the course of time, especially in the southern part of the land east of Jordan. They had attained the form of a State at a comparatively early date. We know almost nothing about the gradual process of their occupation of the land and their consolidation in the land, as there are no records. All that can be established archaeologically is that the southern part of the land east of Jordan, northwards right into the region of the Jabbok, had not been settled in permanently in the Middle and Late Bronze Age, and only began to be occupied with permanent settlements in the course of the 13th century[1]. To begin with there was no occasion for warlike conflicts with the peoples who were closely related to the Israelite tribes in character and each of whom had their own area. But the striving to extend their own territory, which is always characteristic of vigorous peoples, did occasionally lead to conflicts, and according to the traditions that have come down to us the initiative appears to have been taken by the eastern neighbours, whose living space was confined by the desert on the east, and who naturally tried to attack in the west. The Israelite tribes were therefore forced to defend their territory against these attacks.

In the southernmost land east of Jordan, south of the wādi el-ḥesa, which flows into the southern end of the Dead Sea, the Edomites had settled in the mountains east of the great inroad of the wadi el-ʿaraba. They had formed a State early on with, possibly, elected kings (cf. Gen. xxxvi, 31-39). Edom was situated in a remote spot with no direct frontier with the Israelites, so that there was no occasion for hostilities.

North of the wādi el-ḥesa, on the eastern side of the Dead Sea, was the region of the Moabites. Their land extended northwards as far as the Arnon (the modern sēl el-mōjib); but throughout their history they had aspired to acquire the fertile plain north of the Arnon, and at various times they did in fact possess various parts of this plain. Their only chance of extending their possessions was in a northerly direction beyond the Arnon; in this area they came into contact with the Israelite tribes. To begin with, the table land north of the Arnon appears to have been occupied in the course of the 13th century B.C. with all kinds of minor urban domains such as Hesbon, which the neighbouring Gadites were able to conquer in the end. It is impossible to say for certain who had founded these

[1] Cf. N. Glück, AASOR, 14 (1934) and 15 (1935).

cities, which also existed sporadically south of the Arnon[1], or who lived and ruled in them[2]. South of the Arnon they were absorbed at an early date by the incipient Moabite State, whilst north of the Arnon between Moab and Israel they were possibly able to maintain their independence somewhat longer. The Moabites formed a State of their own at a relatively early period and, like the Edomites, they had kings long before even the idea of a monarchy arose in Israel. It is true that we know nothing at all about how the State was developed in Moab, and it may be doubted whether a monarchy ruling over the whole country existed here from the very beginning. One has the impression that the Moabite kings whom we meet in the earliest period in the Old Testament were minor kings of whom there may, to begin with, have been several ruling simultaneously in Moab.

The earliest state of affairs which it is possible to discern is that the Moabites had advanced fairly far forward north of the Arnon —at least along the mountains which accompany the eastern border of the Dead Sea, assuming that the cities farther to the east, in the centre of the table land, were still independent at that time[3]. Between Hesbon (ḥesbān), and the northern end of the Dead Sea, there lay, in a promising spot on a terrace of the mountains east of Jordan, which rise up from the Jordan Valley on the site of the modern khirbet esh-shēkh jāyil, the mountain summit of Peor with the once-famous shrine of the Baal-Peor; Israelites—primarily members of the neighbouring tribe of Gad—and Moabites met at this shrine. It was apparently a frontier shrine, and at the time Moabites were living in the immediate vicinity. This situation is the background of the short narrative in Num. xxv, 1-5 and above all of the stories of Balaam in Num. xxii-xxiv[4]. The latter also show that the neighbourly relationships were not always friendly. It is true that there is no mention of warlike altercations with Balak, the 'king of the Moabites' in the stories of Balaam, and in the end the *status quo ante* between Israel and Moab remains unchanged, but they do presuppose that the two parties were enemies in spite of their joint participation in the cult of Baal-Peor. In this early

[1] According to the archaeological evidence an example of this is the ancient site of el-bālū ʿa.

[2] Cf. A. Alt, PJB, 36 (1940), pp. 29 ff., which deals particularly with the stele of el-bālū ʿa, which curiously enough, bears an inscription in *Cretan* linear script B.

[3] More details on the following will be found in M. Noth, ZAW, N.F. 19 (1944), pp. 17 ff.

[4] It is true that in the traditional context the stories of Balaam are transferred to the period of the occupation of the land, but originally they presupposed that the Israelites had already consolidated their territorial possessions.

period, however, the possessions of the Moabites even extended as far as the Jordan Valley west of Beth-Peor. Here lay the ערבות מואב on the east side of the Jordan opposite the ערבות ירחו on the other side; these refer to the parts in the Jordan Valley which belonged to Moab, or the city-state of Jericho. Now the term ערבות מואב only occurs in the latest stratum of the Pentateuch narrative; but it must have originated in a much earlier period, and only the early period dealt with here is feasible. The most southerly part of the Jordan Valley on the northern border of the Dead Sea, on the east side of the Jordan, had therefore at one time been the possession of the Moabites, at the very time when they were neighbours of the Gadites at the shrine of Baal-Peor. This extension of Moabite territory right down into the Valley of the Jordan is presupposed in the story of Ehud in Judges iii, 12-30. According to this the Moabites had even attacked on one occasion beyond the Jordan and occupied the territory of the former city-state of Jericho, and forced its Benjaminite owners to pay tribute to them, until in the end the Benjaminite Ehud succeeded in killing Eglon the 'king of Moab'[1] during the payment of tribute and, exploiting the confusion this caused among the Moabites, he destroyed the Moabite garrison on the west side of the Jordan, with Benjaminites and Ephraimites whom he swiftly summoned to his aid. The aim of warding off the attacks of the Moabites on the land west of the Jordan was thereby achieved, and the situation restored, which was evidently considered normal at the time, namely that the lowest part of the course of the Jordan was the Israelite-Moabite frontier; the possibility of crossing over to the eastern side of the Jordan is not envisaged at all in the story of Ehud.

Nevertheless this still implies a quite extraordinarily wide extension of Moabite territory in a north-western direction. But this situation did not last very long. At least, at the beginning of the Israelite monarchy, we already find not only a great part of the plain north of the Arnon as Israelite State territory, but it was evidently already inhabited by Israelites to some extent. This can hardly have happened all at once and will not have been possible without warlike altercations and, possibly, numerous minor battles. We are in the dark about all this, since the tradition regarding the pre-political period of the Israelites' life in Palestine mainly records such events as are linked with particular leaders. It was, at any rate, the tribe of Gad, which was able to extend its territory at the

[1] Unfortunately it is not clear from the story of Ehud where the murder of Eglon took place (whether it was west or east of the Jordan).

expense of the Moabites. Perhaps the successful conquest of the neighbouring city-state of Hesbon had so strengthened the position of this tribe that it was now able to prevail over the Moabites. Moab was a small people and the Moabite state a small state, which was unable to develop any great power and only achieved successes against Israel when, for some reason or other, the situation was particularly in its favour. To begin with, the Moabites had been able to strike out a fair way northwards beyond the Arnon when the Israelite settlement in the land east of the Jordan had still been very weak, and the tribe of Gad had been limited to a small and far from favourable area consisting for the most part of pasture land (cf. Num. xxxii, 1). But later on Gad had advanced, at any rate on the western border of the table land, right up to the Arnon, as King Mesha of Moab remarks in his inscription (Z. 10) in the middle of the 9th century B.C., that 'the men of Gad' had 'lived in the land Ataroth (the modern ʿattārūs about 12 kilometres north of the Arnon) from time immemorial; and the city of Dibon (the modern dībān, 5 kilometres north of the Arnon) is described as 'Dibon-Gad' in Num. xxxiii, 45 f., and was therefore not only incorporated in Israelite State territory later on but also inhabited by Israelites (Gadites). This advance made by the tribe of Gad certainly took place in the period before the formation of the State. We do not know how far Gad was able in the course of its expansion to seize other cities further to the east on the table land.

The Ammonites resided north-east of Moab in the region of the upper course of the Jabbok. Their centre was the city of Rabbra (also called רַבַּת בְּנֵי־עַמּוֹן after them) on the site now occupied by the capital of Jordan, ʿammān, in whose name the old name of the Ammonites survives. They too had a monarchy and formed a small State very early on, at any rate long before the Israelites. The association which they had with their northern neighbours the Aramaeans, which occasionally came into prominence later on, suggests that they were closely related to them. To begin with, they had no relations with Israel, since they lived away from Israelite territories. It was only when the ancient land of Gilead, south of the Jabbok, was colonised by Ephraimites from the west Jordan mountains of Ephraim that contacts resulted, the more so since the Ammonites had a tendency to expand to the north-west. Here lay the small fertile plain that is now called el-buḳēʿa, north of the modern cross-roads at eṣ-ṣuwēliḥ; and the Ammonites settled in this plain particularly as they had not much scope for expanding in other directions. They thereby became direct neighbours of the

Ephraimite settlers in the land of Gilead; and they were bound to come into conflict with them if they intended to advance still farther to the north-west. That they did in fact once attack the land of Gilead we learn from the story of Jephthah in Judges x, 6-12, 6[1]. According to this they one day occupied Gilead (the modern khirbet jelʿad), which was a settlement on 'mount Gilead', from which the whole district had acquired its name; and this occupation was no doubt achieved by force of arms (Judges x, 17a). To ward off this attack the Gileadites first of all looked for a leader, and as they could not find one in their own ranks they thought of one Jephthah, a son of a Gileadite of inferior status, who had been excluded from the family inheritance, and who went about in the 'land of Tob'[2] at the head of a band of adventurers and had meanwhile proved his worth in deeds of war. Jephthah gathered together the militia of the Gileadites in Gileadite Mizpah (probably somewhere in the modern rēschūni, a few kilometres north-west of Gilead), at whose shrine 'the spirit of the Lord came upon Jephthah' (Judges xi, 29) so that he now marched forth as a charismatic leader at the head of the Gileadites against the Ammonites, conquered them and drove them out of Gilead again[4], thus securing the land of Gilead for its Ephraimite inhabitants. We hear nothing of any further effort by the Ammonites to seize the land of Gilead. Admittedly, the Ammonites remained unscathed in their territory (no doubt including the buḳē ʿa). It had been a purely defensive victory. But Jephthah later occupied the office of 'judge of Israel' for six years until his death (Judges xii, 7). North of Ammon, in Israel's early period, the Aramaeans were on the point of gaining a footing on the soil of Palestine and constituting themselves in what were apparently, to begin with, anything but permanent political organisations[5]. A group of Aramaeans settled for a time south of the Jabbok immediately to the east of the land of Gilead; and it was here that the first historical encounter between Israelites and Ammonites that is known to us took place, and this was of a peaceful nature. By agreement between the two parties a stone was

[1] The passage in Judges xi, 15-26 in which Moab appears quite inappropriately as an enemy is a secondary interpolation. Judges xi, 34-40 and Judges xii, 1-6 contain separate stories.

[2] Unfortunately it is impossible to identify the situation of this 'land of Tob', which may be compared with 2 Sam. x, 6, 8. It was probably one of the districts east of Jordan which was still but sparsely inhabited at that time, most likely north of the Jabbok.

[3] Unfortunately it is impossible to identify the places mentioned in Judges xi, 33 which define the scene of the battle.

[4] Later on the Ammonites undertook another attack, under different conditions, on the Israelite possessions east of Jordan.

[5] Details in M. Noth, BBLAK, 68 (1946-1951), pp. 19 ff.

set up on 'mount Gilead' to mark the frontier which they bound themselves not to transgress with evil intent (Gen. xxxi, 44-54). In the folk-like story of this agreement Jacob represents the Israelites, that is to say in fact the Gilead Ephraimites, and Laban the Aramaeans who were their eastern neighbours. It was apparently only a temporary state of affairs, since it is unlikely that the probably small group of Aramaeans had gained a very firm footing at this place. At any rate we do not hear any more of Aramaeans south of the Jabbok. Probably the Ammonites moved forward to this place.

For the rest, in the early period the Israelite tribes had no contacts with the Aramaeans, who were later to intervene so persistently for a time in Israelite history. It was only the gradual occupation of the land north of the Jabbok, the modern region of ʿajlūn, by Manassites who came from the land west of Jordan which brought Israel into direct touch with the Aramaeans who had settled north east and north of the ʿajlūn. But this did not take place until later. For the time being the territory of the Canaanite city-states of the northern land east of Jordan began on the borders of the ʿajlūn. In contrast to the southern land east of Jordan, the city-state system had survived here even in the Middle and Late Bronze Age and right into the Iron Age. On both sides of the Jarmuk, in the land of Bashan, there were numerous urban centres on the fertile table-land west of the steeply rising basalt mountain of jebel ed-drūz. The Old Testament tradition tells of a King Og of Bashan, who resided in Ashtharoth (the modern tell ʿashtara) and Edrei (the modern der ʿa on the southern border of the Jarmuk Valley)[1], and had ruled over the many cities in Bashan (Deut. iii, 1-7; cf. Num. xxi, 33-35; Jos. xiii, 12, 30 f.). This story is, admittedly, only found in deuteronomistic and secondarily deuteronomistic passages; but there is no doubt that the deuteronomistic historian included it as an already existing tradition. It implies quite correctly that Bashan was an area with old-established cities. This was of interest to Israel when the Manassites in the land north of the Jabbok extended their settlement into the neighbourhood of this region of city-states. The figure of King Og is, however, far from clearly defined historically. That one of the city kings seized the dominion over the whole area of city-states is very curious and conceivable at most only as a passing episode of which the Israelites might have received word. But the fact that this King Og is included among the 'Rephaites', that awe-inspiring population of

[1] Originally Ashtaroth alone was regarded as the seat of Og (cf. Jos. ix, 10), and Edrei, the site of the battle, was only added later.

giants from primeval times who were associated in the northern land east of Jordan with the very numerous ancient megaliths[1], shows that at best this King Og of Bashan is a very shadowy historical figure. The Israelites encountered King Og of Bashan in stories emanating from the city-state territory of Bashan but not directly as a historical figure; and so the victory of the Israelites over Og at Edrei can scarcely be called a historical event, but merely an indirect expression of the fact that Israel claimed possession of the city-state territory in the northern land east of Jordan without ever really having possessed it. It is highly probable that no warlike conflicts with the city-states took place at all in the early period, but that a state of peaceful co-existence developed such as was customary in the other parts of Palestine; all the more so since the Manassite settlement of the ʿajlūn was hardly very dense and there was therefore no pressing necessity to extend this territory, just as the cities in the land of Bashan can hardly have had any reason to encroach on the wooded mountain country north of the Jabbok, from the fertile table-land.

On the eastern side, where their neighbours lived, and against which Israel had to assert itself in its early period, Palestine was open to invasions from the desert, aimed not at a gradual occupation of Palestinian soil but merely at plundering its produce. The danger of such invasions had existed ever since the domestication of the camel had been developed to such an extent that it became possible for fairly large groups not merely to live in the desert in comparative independence of watering-places, but also to traverse fairly large tracts without water, and to move quickly over great distances. In earlier times the camel had not been entirely unknown in the ancient Orient, but according to our literary and archaeological sources it did not play any part worth mentioning until the Late Bronze Age. It was only after the occupation of the land by the Israelites that the camel was sufficiently domesticated for that special kind of bedouin existence to develop, of which we first hear in the early Arabian period[2]. Very soon, however, the new opportunities arising from the use of the camel made their influence felt in Palestine, which was so near to the desert. This

[1] The fact that, according to Deut. iii, 11, King Og's 'bedstead of iron', probably a basalt dolmen, was shown in Ammonite Rabbath, makes the lack of uniformity in the tradition especially clear.

[2] Cf. W. F. Albright, *From the Stone Age to Christianity* ([2] 1946), pp. 120 f.; *Archaeology and the Religion of Israel* ([2] 1946), pp. 96 ff. Albright assumes, and, to the best of our knowledge, rightly, that the real domestication of the camel took place *circa* 1100 B.C.

new departure forms the background to the stories of Gideon in Judges vi-viii which tell of the invasions of the land west of the Jordan by the Midianites coming from the east[1]. The Midianites evidently constituted a large and fairly widespread association of tribes in the desert east and south of Palestine[2]. One day they began to make a deep inroad into Palestine with their camels; in fact they threatened the country right up to the coast[3], after seed-time just when the seed was coming up. They let their camels graze off the seed and took what they needed of the produce of the land and the cattle of the inhabitants—anything they had not already destroyed during their invasions. The most threatened areas were naturally such fertile plains as the plain of Jezreel (Judges vi, 33); but the Israelite possessions in the hill country were not spared either. The appearance of the Midianites, which for a time apparently occurred every year, spread wide terror in the country where these swift-moving camel nomads were obviously a complete novelty and a sinister phenomenon. The terror they aroused can still be felt in the story of Gideon, where it refers to the 'camels without number' of the Midianites (Judges vi, 5; vii, 12) and how 'because of the Midianites children of Israel made them the dens which are in the mountains, and caves, and strongholds' (Judges vi, 2).

It was the great achievement of Gideon, a Manassite of the clan of Abi-ezrites which dwelt in Ophrah, that he dared to meet the danger. In view of its nearness to the plain of Jezreel in the south the tribe of Manasseh certainly suffered from these attacks on the plain. At the head of a small band of brave comrades of the tribe (cf. the episode described in Judges vii, 2-7) Manasseh invaded the camp of the host of the Midianites, who were resting for the night beside the well of Harod (the modern ʿēn jālūd) at the north-western foot of Mount Gilboa (the modern jebel fuḳūʿa), that is, at the south-western end of the plain of Jezreel, after an evidently successful bout of plundering in the plain. This well-prepared and completely unforeseen attack terrified the Midianites so much that

[1] In Judges vi, 3, 33 the Amalekites and the 'children of the east', *i.e.* the inhabitants of the eastern desert in general, are mentioned along with the Midianites.

[2] According to Num. xxii, 4, 7 the Midianites participated in the worship of Baal-Peor (cf. above, p. 155), which is not surprising as they resided in the vicinity of the southern land east of Jordan. On the other hand, we also find them in the southern desert; for it was no doubt here that the story of Israel's encounter with the Midianites at the 'mount of God' was enacted (Exod. xviii, 1 ff.). If they were a great tribal unit this wide distribution is not surprising. The place madyan which lies on the eastern side of the gulf of el-ʿaḳaba provides evidence, dating from Roman times, that they lived there (the evidence is given, for example, in R. Kittel, *Geschichte des Volkes Israel*, I, 5, 6 [1923], p. 347, note 1); they may have originated in this remote district.

[3] In Judges vi, 4 Gaza is mentioned in this context.

they made for the open country on their camels and fled to the Jordan through the plain of the nahr jālūd and farther eastwards beyond the Jordan[1]. Gideon's victory over the Midianites appears to have put an end to the nuisance which they had been causing, or at any rate to have roused the inhabitants' determination to defend themselves, so that we hear no more about attacks by the Midianites. The terror which they had spread makes it easy to see why Gideon's victory, which broke the spell, was remembered for so long. When, in Isa. ix, 3 (4 in the English Bible) the 'day of Midian', that is, the day of the victory over the Midianites, is quoted as an example of an especially brilliant victory, the reference is no doubt to the surprising success of Gideon the Manassite.

In the early period the existence of Israel in Palestine was not really threatened fundamentally from the east, either by the small neighbouring peoples on the eastern border or the nomads who made occasional incursions. Nor were they threatened by the older Canaanite population, which no longer had any great military force at its disposal. The threat came from the elements which set foot in the land from the west about the same time as the Israelite tribes: from the Philistines and the 'maritime' elements related to them, who had established themselves as a ruling class in a series of ancient Bronze Age cities in the maritime plain. They represented the strongest force in the country and were developing great military resources, to begin with, mostly in the area of the Canaanite city-state territories. At the outset there was no large-scale military conflict with the Israelite tribes if one overlooks the fact that Sisera may have been a member of the 'maritime' ruling class. But in any case Sisera stood at the head of a group of old Canaanite city-states in the plain of Jezreel and possibly the plain of Akko as well, against which Barak won his famous victory (cf. above, p. 149 f.). Of the Philistines, in the narrower sense of the term, who ruled in their five city-states in the southern part of the maritime plain of Palestine, we hear in the stories about Samson in Judges xiii-xvi. The tribe of Dan, to which Samson is assigned, and which tried to gain a footing in the hill country in the neighbourhood of the modern ṣarʿa, lived under the pressure of the adjacent Philistines; and all that is related of Samson is that he played all kinds of tricks on the Philistines until he finally succumbed to their

[1] It is impossible to reconstruct the details of the event. The main narrative in Judges vii, 1–viii, 3 closes with aetiological elements (vii, 25); and Judges viii, 4-21 contains the end of a parallel story, which deviates in a number of points from the main narrative. It is impossible to be certain about the relationship between the two stories and the historical events.

superior might. But the tribe of Dan then had to withdraw from the hill country[1] and left behind only a few remnants in the district of ṣarʿa. For the rest, they tried to find a new territory in the far north of the country by the sources of the Jordan.

The Philistines were able—possibly in association with the other 'maritime' elements farther to the north—to set about subjugating the whole country, at any rate west of Jordan. And they began the attempt quite soon. A decisive struggle for predominance with them was in store for the Israelite tribes; and the conflict led Israel on to the path of political power which it had not trod before. It is very characteristic that the struggle for self-assertion which took place with the earlier inhabitants and neighbouring peoples after the Israelites had occupied the land was not regarded as a concern affecting Israel as a whole. The individual tribes had to guard their possessions for themselves and, where necessary or desirable, try to extend their settlement on their own. In certain cases neighbouring tribes may occasionally have combined to protect their common interests. But in this early period we hear nothing at all of joint undertakings by the whole society of the twelve tribes for the protection or extension of their property and life, and evidently nothing of the kind in fact occurred. It was only the late deuteronomistic conception of an 'age of judges' which magnified the occasional charismatic leaders of individual tribes and groups of tribes into personalities of importance to Israel as a whole, whereas we know from the traditions that survive that their role was strictly limited. They acquired this exaggerated importance by being combined with the quite different office of 'judge' of Israel (cf. above p. 101 f.) which, though it did refer to Israel as a whole, was only entrusted with internal functions.

[1] According to Judges i, 34 f. the Danites had to yield to the pressure of the 'Amorites'. That may be true; but no doubt the Philistines stood in the background.

CHAPTER II

THE TRANSITION TO THE DEVELOPMENT OF POLITICAL POWER

14. *The Episode of the Monarchy of Saul*

FROM time immemorial the Canaanite cities in Syria-Palestine had normally had city kings with a feudal ruling class. The Philistines —and probably the other 'maritime' groups in the land as well— had their 'princes'[1], who also resided in the urban centres with a heavily armed retinue of warriors, and, in addition, a following of mercenary leaders[2] who were invested with a piece of land and had to perform military service with the mercenaries they collected together[3]. They therefore represented an intensely concentrated military force. The neighbouring peoples in the southern land east of Jordan, who had settled about the same time as the Israelite tribes, had apparently succeeded in developing simple political organisations, including a monarchy, soon after their occupation of the land; and even the groups of Aramaeans on the borders of the northern land east of Jordan, who only gradually became consolidated in Palestine, were already on the point of establishing political organisations which were, to begin with, however, very unstable, with kings at their head[4].

It was only in the sacred society of the tribes of Israel that a concentration of political power and the formation of a State were not achieved until long after they had occupied and settled down in Palestine. The individual tribes were left to look after their own stability and security. Evidently there were certain impediments which hindered further political developments. An anecdote in Judges viii, 22-23 records that after his brilliant victory over the Midianites Gideon was asked by the Israelites to accept the hereditary office of 'ruler' in Israel; he replied as follows to this

[1] The Old Testament calls them specifically סְרָנִים, a term which has been connected with the word *τύραννος*, which is non-Greek in origin.

[2] Cf. as an example the description of Goliath in 1 Sam. xvii, 4 ff.

[3] David was in this position for a time; cf. 1 Sam. xxvii, 2 ff.; xxix, 1 ff.

[4] More details in M. Noth, BBLAK, 68 (1946–1951), pp. 25 ff.

request: 'I will not rule over you, neither shall my son rule over you: the Lord shall rule over you'. This brief story may have been drafted long after kings had appeared in Israel, and may therefore have been aimed indirectly against the already existing monarchy, but it fairly certainly reflects an attitude that was current among the tribes of Israel before the rise of the monarchy, since only this kind of outlook can explain the historical fact that the idea of monarchy became active so late and went so much against the general grain in Israel. The argument for rejecting the idea of hereditary monarchy which is given in this little anecdote probably reflects the attitude to the institution that was prevalent among the tribes, who were, after all, familiar with a great variety of forms of monarchy in the world around them. The sacred society of the tribes of Israel was committed exclusively to its own God and his will became a historical force in the historical manifestation of the 'particularity' of Israel.

The fact that a monarchy was finally established in Israel[1], thereby deflecting Israel from the line to which it had kept so strictly heretofore, on to the road to political power, was a result of the historical situation in Palestine, which threatened the continuity and existence of Israel as a whole. The historical background to Saul's elevation to the monarchy was the growing power of the Philistines, who were attempting to gain absolute control over the whole country. In an old story about the fate of the Sacred Ark, deriving roughly from the time of David, which is contained in 1 Sam. iv, 1b-7, 1 and 2 Sam. vi, 1-16a, 17-19[2] we learn of the first large-scale military clash between the Israelites and Philistines. This took place *circa* 1000 B.C.[3]. The Philistines gathered their forces in Aphek (probably the modern tell el-mukhmar near rās el-ʿēn[4]) on the upper course of the river which is now called nahr el-ʿōja that flows into the Mediterranean north of jafa. Aphek was right up on the northern border of their territory. It was a favourable point of departure for an attack on the mountains of Central Palestine, which rise east of Aphek, where the central Israelite tribes had established themselves. And such an attack was evidently their intention, since it was certainly the Philistines who took the

[1] Cf. on the following, above all, A. Alt, *Die Staatenbildung der Israeliten in Palästina. Verfassungsgeschichtliche Studien* (Reformationsprogramm der Universität Leipzig, 1930) = *Kleine Schriften zur Geschichte des Volkes Israel*, II (1953), pp. 1 ff.

[2] On the extent and nature of this 'story of the Ark' cf. L. Rost, *Die Überlieferung von der Thronnachfolge Davids* (BWANT, III, 6 [1926]), pp. 4 ff.

[3] Only very rough dates are possible even for this period; cf. below, p. 224.

[4] Cf. M. Noth, *Das Buch Josua* (² 1953), p. 72.

initiative. After having achieved predominance, together with the other 'maritime' groups in the land, in the maritime plain which was occupied by Canaanite city-states, they were bound, if they intended to extend this supremacy over the whole country, to subjugate the Israelite tribes. In view of the imminent danger the Israelites gathered at a place called Eben-Ezer, which is on the edge of the mountains opposite Aphek and roughly on the site of the modern mejdel jaba. It is impossible to say for certain who actually took part on the Israelite side. The main participants were probably the militia of the tribe of Ephraim which was most immediately threatened from Aphek. But some of the neighbouring tribes of the central Palestinian mountains will also have taken part, and, in view of the enormous danger, reinforcements from other tribes may also have been present. In an initial encounter the Philistines were victorious. Thereupon the amphictyonic shrine of the Ark was fetched from Shiloh to guarantee the presence of their God among the hard-pressed Israelites in a second battle. The 'story of the Ark', in which the emphasis is on the fate of the sacred Ark only, records this fact. The transporting of the Ark to the camp meant that the whole society of Israelite tribes was being deployed against the Philistines. So far as we know, it was the first time the tribes as a whole had come forward in defence of Israel, the reason being that this was in fact the first time the existence of Israel as a whole had really been threatened by the Philistines. The fact that there were two battles in succession against the Philistines probably means that, as hitherto, those parts of Israel to be affected first had resisted the Philistines' attack, and, when this defensive effort had completely failed, the whole confederacy of the tribes had been summoned, together with its central sacred relic. In the second battle too, however, the Israelites were utterly defeated by the overwhelming might of the Philistines, so thoroughly indeed that the Israelite armies were completely disintegrated and the sacred Ark captured by the victors (1 Sam. iv, 10, 11).

The results which flowed from this defeat were extraordinary. When, four centuries later, the prophet Jeremiah said that the temple in Shiloh which had housed the Ark was once destroyed and that even in his time it was still possible to see the ruins of this temple (Jer. vii, 12, 14; xxvi, 6, 9), in all probability this destruction had been carried out by the Philistines after their victory at Eben-Ezer, which gave them free access to Shiloh (sēlūn)[1]. After the Ark itself had fallen into their hands they also destroyed the

[1] The archaeological discoveries also show that Shiloh was destroyed about this time.

temple which had housed it, thus destroying the central shrine which had held the Israelite tribes together. In addition, they subjugated the Israelite tribes themselves. They installed garrisons in Israelite territories. We hear of one such 'governor' or 'garrison' (נְצִיב) in Benjaminite Gibeah (the modern tell el-fūl, 6 kilometres north of Jerusalem) in 1 Sam. x, 5; xiii, 3. We are not told where else they had such garrisons. They will, at any rate, have occupied the central mountains west of Jordan in this way. Israel was also disarmed. The Philistines attempted to prevent the manufacture of new weapons by forbidding the Israelites to work in metal, so that they were forced to go to the Philistines for the tools they needed for agricultural and other peaceful uses (1 Sam. xiii, 19-22). Naturally, they were able to enforce these prohibitions only so far as their occupation extended and the emergence of Saul suggests that their authority was not so effective in the more remote provinces. *De jure*, however, the Israelite tribes were subject to Philistine rule, and to all intents and purposes the Philistines had attained their object of dominating, at any rate, the land west of Jordan.

It is not surprising that Israel's situation encouraged other of her neighbours to expand their territory at her expense and to satisfy some of their old desires. The Ammonites now renewed the attempt which had been wrecked by Jephthah's victory. They apparently occupied the old land of Gilead south of the Jabbok, and encroached on the land north of the Jabbok. At any rate, we find them occupied at this time with an attack on the city of Jabesh[1], probably a Manassite foundation in the colonial land of the modern ʿajlūn, situated in the area of the wādi yābis, in the name of which the old name of the city survives[2]. In 1 Sam. xi, 1 ff. we read how the people of Jabesh, being too weak to resist by themselves, declared themselves ready to come to terms with Nahash, the king of the Ammonites, but were scornfully rejected, and how they asked for seven days' respite to seek for help among the Israelite tribes; this respite was apparently accorded to them in the certain expectation

[1] In the fuller name 'Jabesh in Gilead', which is mostly used, the extension of the name Gilead to the land north of the Jabbok is already presupposed. Cf. M. Noth, PJB, 37 (1941), pp. 72 ff.

[2] According to Eusebius (*Onomastikon*, 110, 12 f. in E. Klostermann's edition), Jabesh lay on the later Roman road from Pella to Gerasa, that is, on the upper course of the wādi yābis in the mountains, and, according to archaeological discoveries (cf. N. Glück, AASOR, 25-28 [1951], pp. 211 ff.) on the site of the present ruins tell el-maklūb on the northern side of the valley. N. Glück (*loc. cit.* pp. 268 ff.) and, following him, the *Westminster Historical Atlas to the Bible* (1945), place Jabesh at the lower end of the wādi yābis in the Jordan Valley and, in particular, on the tell abu kharaz, but this argument fails to weigh against the very precise reference made by Eusebius.

that they would never find the help they were seeking. Whether or not one regards the incident as likely, it does at least describe the situation in the land east of Jordan very strikingly; on the one side the aggressive activity and certainty of victory of the small people of the Ammonites and on the other the helplessness of the Ephraimite-Manassite settlers east of the Jordan who no longer had any support to fall back on in their motherland west of the Jordan, evidently because the power of the Israelite tribes had been completely paralysed by the Philistines. At the same time, it is clear that the arm of the Philistines did not extend as far as the land east of Jordan, so that it was possible for things to happen there which were beyond their control.

This situation forms the background to Saul's elevation to the monarchy. Saul, the son of Kish, was a Benjaminite from the Benjaminite village of Gibeah (the modern tell el-fūl)[1]. He evidently belonged to the stratum of the permanently established free members of the tribe, who lived very largely on agriculture. The main stages in the process by which he became king have no doubt been correctly recorded in 1 Sam. xi, but the details of the process will not bear closer historical scrutiny. According to 1 Sam. xi, Saul's first public appearance took place when the 'spirit of God' came upon him and he began to act spontaneously (verse 6). This happened when Saul heard of the hard-pressed Jabeshites' search for help to which the response had otherwise been merely one of despair and lamentation. This recalls the emergence of those charismatic leaders of tribes and groups of tribes which, summoned in the name of God or constrained by the spirit of God, had fought for the rights of the Israelites and had prevailed. In fact Saul's first undertaking belonged very nearly to this category. If the actions of the charismatic leaders had often been preceded by a call, tradition records a corresponding call in the case of Saul. In a folk-like story which preceded 1 Sam. xi in the old tradition of Saul, without being closely connected with it, there is a reference to Saul's meeting with Samuel, the 'man of God' or 'seer' at an unnamed spot in the vicinity of Gibeah, at which Samuel anointed Saul in the name of Yahweh to be nagid, that is, the ruler appointed by God (x, 1). This story is obviously very anecdotal, and even on the main point, the anointing to the office of nagid, the later kingship of Saul may have been casting its shadow ahead, since this rite far

[1] In 1922, and again for a short time in 1933, W. F. Albright made successful excavations on the tell el-fūl; cf. W. F. Albright, in AASOR, 4 (1924), and BASOR, 52 (1933), pp. 6-12.

exceeded the appointment of the charismatic leader, as it had always been enacted hitherto, inasmuch as the anointing implied the conferment of an office and the title of nagid appears to have denoted the man destined for a future office[1]. According to 1 Sam. xi, however, it must at least be doubted whether there was any thought of a future monarchy when this calling of Saul took place, and whether it was not evoked rather by the immediate emergency: this is all the more likely to have been the case since there was no tradition behind the idea of monarchy in Israel and it was bound to encounter serious misgivings. But if this is so, the story recounted in 1 Sam. ix, 1-10, 16 is correct in so far as Samuel inspired Saul to make his first public appearance in the name of the God of Israel.

When the distress of the people east of Jordan, and especially the people of Jabesh, came to his knowledge, Saul acted with spontaneous enthusiasm as their leader. He summoned the armies of the whole confederacy of the twelve tribes in the way that was probably customary at the time[2], and he assembled his followers in Beshek (the modern khirbet ibzīḳ) on the descent of the road from Shechem to Beth-Sean roughly opposite Jabesh, at a spot from which it was possible to reach the Jordan Valley directly and then advance further over into the ʿajlūn. The employment of the whole tribal society to defend their existence accorded with the need of the moment. Hitherto this had not been the custom, but if the supposition suggested on p. 166 is correct, there had been a precedent in the decisive, albeit disastrous, battle against the Philistines at Eben-Ezer. It is stated explicitly in 1 Sam. xi, 7 that the tribes followed Saul's call with reverential fear. The question may be asked how far this was possible under the rule of the Philistines and in the state of disarmament imposed by them. It may be that there was no garrison, and therefore no real enforcement of Philistine sovereignty on the eastern border of the mountains west of Jordan and in the land east of Jordan, and that disarmament had not been carried out there. It may also be that the Philistines were not interested in military conflicts of the other Palestinian peoples among themselves or even took pleasure in

[1] It may be asked, however, whether the title nagid, which only occurs in the Old Testament as a term for the king designate, did not formerly have the more general meaning of the man called by God to undertake a military action.

[2] On the dividing up of the oxen mentioned in 1 Sam. xi, 7, cf. Judges xix, 29 which may refer to a variation of the usual custom arising from a special case. The method of the summons to arms described in 1 Sam. xi, 7, with conjuration expressed in an oath, makes an impression of great originality (cf. above, p. 104, note 2).

them, since even an increase in the power of the Ammonites could hardly be welcome to them. At any rate, in spite of the pressure of the Philistines, Saul found sufficient armed followers to risk the attack on the Ammonites and the deliverance of the hard-pressed Jabeshites. And he achieved a brilliant success. Jabesh was relieved and the danger from the Ammonites in the land east of Jordan apparently eliminated. Apart from this immediate result, the victory had a great psychological effect on the hard-pressed Israelites. It was an encouragement to the Israelite tribes; and it is not surprising that they now began to come to themselves again and to act with resolution. What happened now had far-reaching consequences. There is a brief report in 1 Sam. xi[1], according to which, after the Ammonite war, Samuel summoned the Israelite tribes to the old shrine of Gilgal near Jericho (the exact spot is still unknown). As a 'man of God' and a figure commanding respect, the more so now as the spokesman of God who had called and inspired Saul to his liberating action, an authority in Israel, though bearing no office, Samuel may in fact have played an active part in the events that now took place. He chose the shrine of Gilgal for the assembly of the tribes, because after the disappearance of the former central shrine which was brought about by the loss of the Ark and the destruction of the temple of Shiloh, it was a suitable place for several reasons. It was an ancient and famous shrine on the Benjaminite-Ephraimite frontier, no doubt much frequented by the tribes of Central Palestine, and had possibly already played the part of the central Israelite shrine for a time (cf. above p. 95); its situation was relatively central for all the Israelite tribes, and yet at the same time probably outside the area directly controlled by the Philistines. Whereas the Philistines certainly kept the site of the previous federal shrine at Shiloh under constant supervision and occupied the central Palestinian mountains, the Jordan Valley, with the shrine of Gilgal was, presumably, like the land east of Jordan, not occupied by a permanent Philistine garrison, and what took place there was not immediately known to the Philistines. Here in Gilgal in the sanctuary 'the whole people' 'made Saul King before the Lord'. Though it took place in the sanctuary and was performed in an atmosphere of religious consecration, the ceremony was not really a sacred rite like the appointment of a charismatic leader, but rather a political act. Israel was acting as

[1] In addition to 1 Sam. xi we have, in the fragment of narrative in 1 Sam. x, 21bβ-27a, an old reference to Saul's election to the monarchy (cf. O. Eissfeldt, *Die Komposition der Samuelisbücher* [1931], pp. 7 f.). But the part played here by Saul's physical height is obviously anecdotal and the report certainly has no historical authenticity.

a 'people', no longer as a sacred confederacy of tribes. It was embarking, though to begin with in quite a modest way, on the road to political power and thereby making a decision which was to have a quite fundamental determining influence on the further course of its history. It is clear that the historical situation in which Israel found itself at this time, which involved a threat to its whole existence at the hand of the Philistines, was the direct reason for this new departure. The initiative that Samuel took will have been taken in view of the immediate situation, and the consent of the tribes will have been given in view of the immediate situation. It is clear that the new king, who had proved his worth in the victory over the Ammonites which had just been won, was expected to deliver Israel from this threat to its whole existence and to wage a successful war against the Philistines. A first step in the direction of employing the whole tribal federation had already been taken, inasmuch as the levies of the whole of Israel had been raised probably both in the decisive and disastrous battle against the Philistines and in the victorious struggle against the Ammonites, in contrast to earlier conflicts with the previous inhabitants and the neighbouring peoples. One swift campaign did not suffice, however, against the Philistines, as it had done against the much less formidable Ammonites; against the Philistines a permanent and stable military command seemed to be necessary and the new king was no doubt intended to act primarily as leader of the levies of Israel, and it was in such a capacity that he did in fact come forward. The Israelites easily found a model for the new institution of the monarchy in their own environment. It is true that, apart from the name, their monarchy had hardly anything in common with the Canaanite city monarchy and its knightly charioteers. And the Philistine system of government, which had proved so successful a factor in the struggle against the Israelites, could hardly be imitated overnight, based as it was on a professional army and a system of mercenaries. But the kindred neighbouring peoples in the east had a national monarchy, of whose character and functions we have no detailed information, but which took the lead and had proved its worth in warfare. This was the chief model for the new institution in Israel, all the more so since the social structure among these peoples was presumably similar to that prevailing in Israel. But the very fact that the monarchy in Israel was based on a model that had proved its worth in other societies inevitably made it a problem for Israel. Was it right for Israel to try to be a nation like other nations and to install a king on the model of foreign monarchies and, in spite of its distress, to embark on the road to political power? Modest though the first steps which it took in this direction were, it was a fundamentally new departure for Israel. The old stories of the election of Saul to the throne obviously refer to the event with unfeigned satisfaction; they see in it a work of the God of Israel[1] and they show an obvious delight in the personality and the first actions of the new king. Those who doubted the value of the new institution and its occupant are dismissed as 'good for nothing' (1 Sam. x, 27a). This suggests that the appointment did not proceed without opposition; and the question must be considered whether this opposition was really so frivolous as it was made out to be. No fundamental doubts about the value of Saul's monarchy are expressed until late in the deuteronomistic records[2], where the whole proceeding is introduced by the people's demand for a king 'like all the nations' (1 Sam. viii, 5) and this demand is interpreted to mean that the kingship of God over Israel, which should continue, was being rejected by the people. But it is likely that an attitude to monarchy as such was being expressed which was later confirmed time and again by the experiences which the people had of the institution[3]. These doubts had, however, existed from the very beginning and had made themselves felt even before the rise of the monarchy (cf. above p. 164 f.). In fact this attitude was justified. It is true that the organisation of the sacred confederacy of the twelve tribes had its counterparts in the surrounding world, but the monarchy and the development of political power was a secular and 'heathen' affair to a much more marked degree than that earlier institution which left the task of self-defence to the individual tribes and groups of tribes. For the time being, however, the emergency was so great that there was hardly time for detailed discussion, and the hope placed in the new king, who had proved his worth so brilliantly in the battle against the Ammonites, was so great that all doubts about him faded into the background. The

[1] In 1 Sam. ix, 1 ff. Yahweh's initiative is put into effect by Samuel, and, with reference to 1 Sam. xi, the affair is so described as if Saul was being called to be the future king from the very outset (cf. also 1 Sam. x, 1 f.: 'the matter of the kingdom', so that by electing Saul to be king the people was ultimately merely fulfilling the divine will). The fragment of narrative in 1 Sam. x, 21bβ-27a also says that Saul, whose height had proved him to be the king, had been 'chosen' by Yahweh.

[2] The deuteronomistic historian supplemented the old tradition of Saul by adding 1 Sam. vii, 2b-17; viii, 1-22; x, 17, 27a; xii, 1-25. Admittedly he made it easy for himself to reject the institution of the monarchy by making Samuel win the decisive victory over the Philistines (1 Sam. vii, 10b-11), thereby fundamentally misrepresenting the real historical background to the emergence of the monarchy.

[3] In the formulation of the 'royal law' in 1 Sam. viii, 11-18 the later development of the monarchy played an essential part.

situation impelled Saul to take up the struggle against the Philistines and he apparently embarked on the task without delay. In 1 Sam. xiii, 2 to xiv, 46 there is an old story about Saul's successful attack on the Philistine garrisons. It is true that the story concentrates mainly on the person of Saul and, above all, on that of his son Jonathan, and less on the conflict with the Philistines, and great emphasis is therefore laid on anecdotal details, but it does reveal the historical background of the conflict fairly clearly. According to this account of the battle, Saul immediately made the necessary preparations in Gilgal by forming a body of picked troops from the crowd assembled there and sharing the command with his eldest son Jonathan (cf. 1 Sam. xiv, 49), who appears as a particularly attractive figure. The first step that Jonathan undertook with his followers was an apparently surprise attack on the Philistine garrison in Gibeah, which led to its destruction (1 Sam. xiii, 3[1]). Apparently Saul's appointment as king and the military preparations had taken place so swiftly that the Philistines were quite unprepared for the attack. But this was only the opening of the battle. The Philistines quickly assembled their available forces, that is, the garrisons occupying the mountains west of Jordan and in the area that was especially threatened; they moved into camp near Michmash (the modern mukhmās) about 8 kilometres north-east of Gibeah and reconnoitred the surroundings from there (1 Sam. xiii, 16-18). Saul, however, who had moved with his followers into the same district of Michmash, proceeded with his son Jonathan into a camp near Geba (jebaʿ) which lay opposite Michmash to the south-west and was separated from it by the deep incision of the wādi es-suwenit, and once again a surprise attack on the Philistines was successful, and here again Jonathan is credited with the initiative. This second success gave new courage to the Israelites, who had been terrified by the overwhelming power of the Philistines at the first outbreak of hostilities (cf. 1 Sam. xiii, 6); and they evidently drove the Philistine garrisons out of this district, where they will hardly have been very strong in numbers.

To understand what happened and the results that ensued, it must be remembered that this initial success of Saul was not a victory over the assembled military might or even a considerable levy of the Philistines: the Philistine garrisons had merely been expelled from Israelite territory by superior tactics. Nevertheless,

[1] In 1 Sam. xiii, 3 the name 'Geba' which is now given there is usually corrected into 'Gibeah'. This is not absolutely certain. The similarity between the two names and the fact that they can be easily confused makes it impossible to come to a definite decision, particularly as both places are fairly close to each other.

this meant a good deal in the situation prevailing at the time, and the Israelite tribes' decision to make Saul king after he had proved his worth so brilliantly in the victory over the Ammonites, and entrust him with the battle against the Philistines, seemed to have been rapidly justified by the course of events. The Israelite tribes were able to breathe again. Admittedly, a decisive battle against the Philistines was bound to be imminent, since neither Saul nor the Israelite tribes could have any doubt that the Philistines would very soon set out with their united forces to recover their lost position, and that the real decision would then be achieved. To begin with, the conflict was limited to minor encounters on the frontier, of which we learn from a few general observations[1] and from various anecdotes[2]. They had no great influence on the course of events. But Saul had to endeavour to prepare for the impending conflict.

We hear practically nothing about the consolidation of the monarchy under Saul, and probably little of any significance occurred in this respect. He did attend to Israel's armed forces to some extent. According to 1 Sam. xiv, 52 he gathered together an army that was probably small in numbers, for the war against the Philistines, and 'when he saw any strong man, or any valiant man, he took him unto him'. His immediate entourage was confined to a few men who had an important part to play in his conduct of the war. In 1 Sam. xx, 25 there is a reference to the circle that used to gather round him daily at meal times; it included, in addition to his son Jonathan, who had already proved his worth in the opening battles against the Philistines, his cousin Abner whom he had made 'captain of his host', that is, leader of the levies of the Israelite tribes (cf. 1 Sam. xiv, 50, 56) and David, whom Saul had appointed his personal armour-bearer (cf. 1 Sam. xvi, 14-23). He resided in his native Benjaminite Gibeah (tell el-fūl); and there he had built for himself a modest citadel, the foundations of which have been uncovered by excavations on the site[3].

According to 1 Sam. xv, 1 ff. Saul also won a victory over the Amalekites, that body of nomadic tribes in the southern desert with whom the southern tribes of Israel lived in a state of more or less constant enmity (cf. Exod. xvii, 16). The account of this victory appears in a special tradition which has no clearly discernible literary or material connection with the other stories about

[1] 1 Sam. xiv, 52a; xviii, 17b, 21 a, 25, 27a.
[2] Cf. 1 Sam. xvii, 1 ff.; xviii, 6 f.; xxiii, 1 ff.
[3] Cf. W. F. Albright, BASOR, 52 (1933), pp. 7 ff.

Saul. Presumably, the Amalekites in the south had, like the Ammonites in the east, taken advantage of the weak state into which the Israelites had been brought by the Philistines, to extend their own territory; and after successfully warding off the Ammonites and achieving an initial success against the Philistines, Saul probably restored Israel's position in regard to the Amalekites.

More important, however, and of greater consequence, was the fact that after Saul had been made king it very soon appeared that, in spite of the brilliant initial successes, the institution of the monarchy was bound to come up against internal difficulties within the society of the Israelite tribes, because, though temporary charismatic leadership was compatible with the traditions of a tribal society subject to a divine law, a 'secular' monarchy was not: it was impossible to base the institution of monarchy on the sacred society of the tribes, and the combination of leadership and monarchy in the person of Saul was not a reliable foundation for a permanent institution. These internal difficulties came to light in the quarrel between Samuel and Saul which is explained in two different ways in 1 Sam. xiii, 7b-15a and 1 Sam. xv, 1-35. It is therefore impossible to establish the cause of the quarrel with any certainty, but in any case—both passages are in agreement here and it is consonant with the whole context of the quarrel—it stemmed from the fact that the relationship between the king's sacred and secular functions was ill-defined and the secular requirements of the monarchy conflicted with the ancient sacred traditions. Samuel, who had apparently played an active part in Saul's election to the monarchy, rejected the consequences which flowed inevitably from the establishment of the monarchy and made himself the spokesman of the old traditions, to which no doubt large sections of the Israelite tribes felt themselves committed. In fact, when Saul now pursued, as he was bound to do, his own way as king, Samuel retracted the call which he had previously issued to Saul and declared that Saul had been 'rejected' by God (1 Sam. xv, 23, cf. xiii, 14). The kingship of Saul, which was not yet firmly established on its own feet, thereby lost supporters and no doubt much of its authority among the tribes. And Saul himself became uncertain of himself and suspicious. 'But the Spirit of the Lord departed from Saul, and an evil spirit from the Lord troubled him' (1 Sam. xvi, 14). David, his young armour-bearer, became the special object of his suspicions. David's radiant personality had won the ready sympathies of the Israelites (cf. 1 Sam. xviii, 7) whilst Saul's reputation dwindled rapidly after his initial successes. The external emergency which had occasioned his elevation to the kingship turned out to be an insufficient basis for the establishment of a monarchy over the Israelite confederacy; and as soon as the external pressure had abated—albeit only temporarily—the problematical character of the institution emerged.

It is true that this internal conflict did not have time to come to a head since the external enemy, the Philistines, brought Saul's kingship to a violent end. The elimination of their garrisons inevitably stirred the Philistines into action. To begin with they had merely allowed themselves to be surprised, but in view of their military superiority they had every prospect of regaining the position they had lost. In spite of the fact that Israel's armies were now united under a royal command it had not really added to its power since the defeat at Eben-Ezer and it was also labouring under internal difficulties. The Philistines will scarcely have allowed much time to elapse before making their decisive counter-thrust. If, in the editorial note in 1 Sam. xiii, 1 which is probably only deuteronomistic, Saul is said to have reigned for two years over Israel, the statement is incontestable on textual grounds[1] and probably historically too, so that it must be assumed that the deuteronomist was incorporating part of a sound tradition[2]. This statement implies that, after Saul's successful surprise attack, the Philistines prepared for their counter-attack in the following year; and even if the traditional record did not state this explicitly we should be bound to assume it as a probability. The Philistines can hardly have wanted to give Saul time to consolidate his monarchy before engaging in battle with him. As it was the custom to embark on large-scale campaigns in the spring after the end of the winter rains (cf. 2 Sam. xi, 1), the Philistines no doubt chose the spring of the year following Saul's appointment as king as a suitable moment for their counter-attack.

We learn what ensued in considerable detail from the traditional account of David's rise which is contained in 1 Sam. xvi, 14 ff. Once again the Philistines gathered together their armies in Aphek

[1] The usual alteration of the text ('twenty years') is based not on textual but historical considerations. But the deuteronomist doubtless wrote 'two years', since only this figure fits into his chronological system; cf. M. Noth, *Überlieferungsgeschichtliche Studien*, I (1943), pp. 18 ff.

[2] It is difficult to believe that the deuteronomist invented this figure for the sake of his chronological system, since he could have built this up in another way to suit his scheme. The reference to the king's age on his accession which is provided for in the deuteronomistic scheme of the introduction of reigns has been omitted in 1 Sam. xiii, 1, probably because the deuteronomist had no evidence.

(1 Sam. xxix, 1)[1]. This time, however, they did not attack the Central Palestinian mountains from there directly but advanced northwards through the maritime plain and then—no doubt by the usual route or through the modern bilād er-rūḥa—into the plain of Jezreel to the city of Jezreel (the modern zerʿīn), cf. 1 Sam. xxix, 11b. This presupposes that they joined up with the other 'maritime' elements in various cities in the northern coastal plains and the plain of Jezreel. They attacked Saul at a particularly vulnerable point in his domains, where the unfinished Israelite settlements were hemmed in particularly closely by Canaanite city territories so that the Galilean tribes were only connected with the tribes in southern Palestine by a narrow bridge of Israelite territory. They thereby prevented Saul from bringing all his forces together, and in fact, according to 1 Sam. xxxi, 7 'the men of Israel that were on the other side of the valley and they that were on the other side of Jordan'[2], that is, the tribes in the Galilean hills and the land east of Jordan, did not take part in the battle against the Philistines. Saul set out against the Philistines with the armies of the central and south Palestinian tribes 'by a fountain which is in Jezreel', probably by the source of the Harod, south-east of the city of Jezreel at the foot of Mount Gilboa (the modern ʿēn jālūd), where Gideon had once undertaken his famous attack on the Midianites. The situation was hopeless from the very outset, and Saul gave up his cause for lost even before the battle had begun. A special tradition contained in 1 Sam. xxviii, 3-25 relates how before the battle he went in his despair in disguise to a necromancer in near-by Endor (the modern khirbet eṣ-ṣafṣāfe near endūr) to enquire of Samuel's ghost about his fate, and how, through the woman's arts, he was merely given the answer that his monarchy and his life were lost.

In fact, according to 1 Sam. xxxi, the Philistines' attack sufficed to break up Saul's armies straight away. They scattered and took their flight over the mountains of Gilboa, pursued by the victorious Philistines. In the course of the pursuit Saul's sons lost their lives, together with a great part of the Israelite armies. Saul committed suicide so as not to fall alive into the hands of the Philistines. The Philistines' victory was complete and Israel's situation more desperate than after the second battle of Eben-Ezer. The Philistines occupied the territory of the Israelite tribes all over again, and this

[1] Cf. above, p. 165.

[2] The usual alteration of the text in this passage is not justified on textual or material grounds; there were no Israelites in the 'cities of the plain' and there were no 'cities of the Jordan' at all.

time included Galilee and the land east of Jordan (1 Sam. xxxi, 7). They took cruel vengeance on Saul and his sons when they found their corpses on Mount Gilboa. They cut off Saul's head and carried it through their cities with his armour as a trophy. They fastened his body and that of his sons to the wall of Beth-Sean (the modern tell el-ḥöṣn near bēsān), which lay not very far from the battlefield in the lower part of the broad valley of the nahr jālūd and was at that time still the seat of a government of maritime peoples related to the Philistines[1]. Thus Saul and his sons would have been denied the last offices of burial if people from Jabesh, which was not far from Beth-Sean, who owed Saul their deliverance from the Ammonites, had not fetched their bodies secretly from the wall of Beth-Sean and buried them in Jabesh. The Philistines had now attained their goal and the question of sovereignty in Palestine appeared to have been settled in their favour once and for all. The final outcome of Saul's short reign was as hopeless as it could possibly be.

15. *David's Empire*

The situation which ensued after the end of Saul forms the background to the amazing ascent of David. With the coming of David, following the monarchy of Saul, which was a mere episode, Israel's progress to political power entered a completely new and decisive phase. Unlike Saul, David set out on the road to political power quite deliberately and consistently from the very beginning. That is why in the Old Testament a new kind of historical tradition begins with David. The tradition of David must be regarded as, for the most part, a purely historical record, a work of 'scholarship', whereas for the earlier historical periods up to and including Saul we have mainly popular stories and traditions concerning prehistorical times, based on religious confessions. The development of political power and historical action was the precondition for the beginning of historical writing. For the history of David we have at our disposal source material which allows us to discern the historical processes and, above all, their mutual relationships more clearly than was possible from the earlier purely popular stories. This also applies to David's climb to power, for which we have a connected narrative which deals with the subject of David's

[1] Cf. A. Alt, *Zur Geschichte von Beth-Sean 1500–1000 B.C.* (PJB, 22 [1926], pp. 108-120).

progress from the beginnings up to the establishment of the Judaean-Israelite State with obvious expert knowledge and a sure grasp of the underlying circumstances[1].

David[2] was a Judaean from Bethlehem (the modern bēt laḥm, 8 kilometres south of Jerusalem), the capital of the tribe of Judah. In the person of David the tribe of Judah, the most important of the southern Palestinian tribes, emerges for the first time as a factor of historical importance. David's career began when he first attracted attention as a capable and talented young man who was drawn into Saul's immediate entourage as his armour-bearer (1 Sam. xvi, 21)[3]. For a long time, however, he was not a member of Saul's entourage. Having quickly acquired popularity on account of his particularly charming nature, he became the special object of Saul's suspicions and preferred to escape from the king's growing animosity towards him. He fled to his homeland, but did not remain in Bethlehem: he retired to the southernmost part of the mountains west of Jordan and gathered together a band of adventurers, with whom he lived on all kinds of plundering expeditions (for an example see 1 Sam. xxv, 2-43), and he was now pursued all the more by Saul, who failed, however, to obtain possession of him. This period in his life had a decisive influence on his further development, for it turned him into a *condottiere*, a professional warrior, for whom warfare—at first only on a small scale—became the whole content of his life. At the same time, evidently in order to profit therefrom later on, he established good relationships with the tribes that had settled south of Judah. According to 1 Sam. xxv-xliii he married one Ahinoam from Jezreel, which was probably Kenite[4] (south-east of Hebron, though we do not know precisely where) and, according to 1 Sam. xxv, 42, one Abigail, the wife of the rich Nabal from Maon (the modern tell maʿīn about 15 kilometres south of Hebron) who had been killed at a lavish

[1] 1 Sam. xvi, 14–2 Sam. v, 25. This work was subsequently extended, particularly in its first part, by some secondary additions, but it is still possible to reconstruct its original form with fair certainty.

[2] The name David has become a problem because in the Mari-texts a word *dawidūm* often occurs with the meaning 'commander', 'troop leader' (cf. W. v. Soden, WO, I, 3 [1948], p. 197), which can hardly be separated from the name David. If it is the same, it hardly looks as though 'David' was originally a personal name at all. Perhaps David first gave himself or was given this name during the period he was a leader of mercenaries (see below) and the title may have become a pseudo-personal name and taken the place of another personal name, unknown to us, which was his origina name.

[3] The well-known story of Goliath contained in 1 Sam. xvii is secondary, both textually and materially, compared with the narrative in 1 Sam. xvi, 14-23.

[4] Cf. M. Noth, *Das Buch Josua* (²1953) on Jos. xv, 55-57a.

sheep-shearing feast by fear of an imminent visit from David and his men. This Nabal was probably also a Kenite[1].

For David and the band of men gathered around him the Philistine military system which employed mercenaries[2] as well as heavily armed hand-to-hand fighters, offered the best opportunities. One day, therefore, David offered the service of himself and his men to the Philistine ruler Achish of Gath (1 Sam. xxvii, 2 f.). Achish gave him Ziklag with the adjoining territory, in return for which he had to render military service when required. The whereabouts of Ziklag is no more certain than that of Gath; it was probably on the inner border of the southernmost part of the maritime plain. It was certainly a risky move for David to go over to the Philistines, with whom an imminent life-and-death combat awaited the Israelites. It is true that mercenary leaders are not usually very particular about whose service they enter provided they are well paid, and in any case this was David's simplest and surest way of escaping from Saul's ambushes. But to the Israelite tribes the move was bound to seem a betrayal of their cause, though David himself regarded it merely as a means to an end in his own career. In his choice of means he evidently had few inhibitions. He was playing a double game. From Ziklag he continued to develop his contacts with the south-Judaean tribes. With his men he undertook all kinds of plundering expeditions in the surrounding country and made presents of the spoil to the elders of various places in the area occupied by these southern tribes (1 Sam. xxx, 26-31). There was no need for his liege lord Achish to know that: he continued to believe that David had broken with Saul and the Israelite tribes once and for all. The Philistines did not, however, trust him absolutely. The other Philistine rulers insisted, against the wishes of his liege lord Achish, that David and his men should be excluded from taking part in the decisive battle against Saul (1 Sam. xxix, 2-11a), although he was naturally under an obligation to serve in such a great enterprise: they were afraid he might betray them. David was spared, therefore, from having to take an active part on the Philistine side in the struggle against Saul and the Israelite tribes.

The news of the disaster which had befallen Saul, that reached David in Ziklag, was evidently no surprise to him and could not be a surprise for such a shrewd man anyway. In fact it appears that

[1] Maon was situated in the same later Judaean district as Jezreel; cf. Jos. xv, 55 f.

[2] Apart from David himself we have another example of this phenomenon in the 'Gattite' Ittai with his 600 men (2 Sam. xv, 18 ff.).

he had evidently already considered and prepared what he would do if the event which he expected actually occurred. He now acted very methodically and skilfully, making first of all for the one goal that was within his immediate reach, thereby making a move forwards which he certainly did not regard as the final stage in his progress. He was skilled in the great art of waiting until things came within his grasp, and this was the way he created the great empire which represents the climax in the development of political power in Israel. In 2 Sam. ii, 1-3 we read that after Saul's terrible end David moved up to Hebron with all his followers and entourage and settled there. Calebite Hebron formed not merely the natural centre of the south Palestinian mountains but also possessed in its immediate vicinity the famous tree sanctuary of Mamre (the modern ḥaram rāmet el-khalīl) which was probably at the same time the religious centre for all the south Palestinian tribes which appear to have been united around this centre in a confederacy of six tribes forming a separate group within and alongside the great Israelite confederacy of the twelve tribes. These six tribes (Judah, Caleb, Othniel, Cain, Jerahmeel, Simeon) led a life of their own, which, though it did not isolate them from the greater Whole, did give them a special position. This fact now became historically important because David turned it to account. David was himself a Judaean; through his first marriages he was related to the Kenites; from Ziklag he had deliberately cultivated relations with the southern tribes. These relationships now inevitably bore fruit. 'The men of Judah came, and there [in Hebron or Mamre] they anointed David king over the house of Judah' (2 Sam. ii, 4a). The term 'house of Judah' is used here in contrast to the simple term 'Judah' evidently to signify the whole confederacy of the six southern tribes. Who induced the six tribes to this momentous step? The institution of monarchy, until recently quite foreign to Israel, had led to a fearful catastrophe soon after its emergence in the person of King Saul. It is hardly likely that, in these circumstances, the idea of a king in Israel can have taken such firm roots in Israel that, following the end of Saul, the election of a new king was bound to appear a matter of course and merely a question of choosing the right man. We are not given any details regarding the process by which David was elected king over the 'house of Judah' but we shall not be far wrong if we assume that David himself played a part in persuading the southern tribes to make this move. His personal influence was no doubt great. As Saul's armour-bearer he had already made himself universally popular. Moreover, for the southern tribes he was a man from their own circle, and, after his separation from Saul, David had proved himself emphatically a man of the southern tribes. If the institution of monarchy had been brought into rapid disrepute by Saul, the Benjaminite Saul was to blame for his own failure: David, the Judaean, would certainly make a better job of it. The special position of the southern tribes within the greater Whole, which had no doubt already existed for some time, played a fundamental part, and David will have exploited this situation in his own interest. Since under David's monarchy the southern tribes constituted a State on their own, 'the house of Judah', they not only thereby underlined and intensified their special character but brought about a political division within the totality of the Israelite tribes which continued in a more or less pronounced form throughout the history of Israel and had the most unfortunate effects on its outward course.

The 'anointing' of the king was a rite of consecration enacted at a shrine; and in this case it probably took place at the religious centre of Mamre. This ceremony followed the election of David to the monarchy by the 'men of Judah'[1], and the election appears to have taken place without any religious foundation such as the designation by a prophet. It was a purely political act. That is typical of David's rise to power. His own personality and connections and his military entourage were the basis of his accession to the power represented by the kingship over the house of Judah. But how could the Philistines allow all this to happen after their great victory over Israel? There can be no doubt that David still remained their vassal and that, as tenant of Ziklag, he was still obliged to render military service with his band of mercenaries. Evidently, the Philistines had no objection to the 'men of Judah' electing this vassal of theirs to the monarchy. Whether or not the Philistines trusted David, at any rate they may have thought it a gain for themselves that the establishment of a separate Judaean monarchy involved a splitting up and therefore a weakening of Israel. It eliminated the federation of the twelve tribes as a political and military unit since the southern tribes had acted regardless of the continuance of this association. For the time being, therefore, the Philistines gave at any rate their tacit consent to the course of events. They maintained the same attitude to events which took place among other tribes, since these also appeared to involve the permanent division of Israel into two parts. Saul's captain, Abner,

[1] 2 Sam. ii, 4a contains an abbreviated statement. The 'men of Judah' could only proclaim David king, whilst the anointing was no doubt performed by a priest.

had survived the disaster on Mount Gilboa and he now assumed the leadership. He took Eshbaal, Saul's sole surviving son[1], as far away as possible from the Philistines, to Mahanaim in the land east of Jordan, the capital of the Ephraimite territory in the land of Gilead south of the Jabbok (the modern tell hedd schaj) and made him king there. This was a purely arbitrary action (2 Sam. ii, 8-9). Eshbaal's kingship was entirely without religious foundation. But the beaten and bewildered Israelite tribes apparently agreed to his appointment. They knew from the other monarchies in the world around them that monarchy was hereditary and, apart from Saul's sole surviving son, no other suitable candidate was available. And although it had been anything but a success under Saul, monarchy was the only institution to hand. Since the southern tribes had gone their own way with David, Eshbaal's sovereignty covered the somewhat ill-defined territory of the tribes in the Galilean and Samaritan mountains east of Jordan, as is recorded fairly precisely in 2 Sam. ii, 9. Like Saul, Eshbaal called himself 'king of Israel' and claimed to rule over all the Israelite tribes. But as the southern tribes had branched off from the rest under Eshbaal the political concept of 'Israel' in fact only covered the major part of the tribes excluding the southern tribes, and from this time this limitation of the name 'Israel' continued in force within the political sphere in which 'Judah' and 'Israel' confronted one another. The name 'Israel' now had two different meanings: as a term covering the whole of the tribes of Israel which represented and continued to represent the traditions of the basic deeds of God in prehistoric times 'Israel' was still used in the language of the faith, but 'Israel' also signified a particular political structure which included only a section of the Israelite tribes and soon absorbed non-Israelite elements.

'Israel' and 'Judah' and Eshbaal and David were soon involved in military conflicts in the frontier region, which were presumably caused by the fact that Eshbaal, or rather, Abner, whose importance and influence continued to be greater than that of the king, made the far from promising attempt to subjugate the southern tribes by force. Naturally, David was not only a match for, but the superior of, his opponent. But these battles were only of minor importance, apart from the fact that in their course Abner slew a brother of Joab, who was a member of David's personal entourage

[1] The name Eshbaal is only preserved unchanged in 1 Chron. viii, 33; ix, 39, whilst in 2 Sam. it is distorted into the form Ishbosheth, because it contains the name of the God Baal which later became taboo.

and who was intended to play a part as the captain of his armies and was consumed with a passion for revenge against Abner which he put into effect soon afterwards (2 Sam. ii, 12–iii, 1). This happened in the following way. Eshbaal was unwise enough to fall out with Abner, because Abner had taken one of Saul's concubines. The unscrupulous Abner at once betrayed Eshbaal and got in touch with David through messengers, with the object of presenting him with the tribes under Eshbaal's rule (2 Sam. iii, 6 ff.). David was prepared to receive Abner with a view to further negotiations provided that he brought him Saul's daughter Michal to be his wife[1]. This episode is typical of David's aims and methods. Abner naturally took into account the fact that David regarded his kingship over Judah only as a beginning and that David aspired to rule over all the Israelite tribes, and Abner was obviously right. David's intended marriage with Michal was also designed to promote this end, since one day, when all of Saul's sons had gone, Saul's inheritance[2] and the succession to his throne[3] might fall to him even if Abner's plan failed. Moreover, Abner reckoned that the non-Judaean tribes would also be easily won over to the idea of making David their king; here too he was right. Since the time when he had been Saul's armour-bearer David had not been unknown to them and had enjoyed great popularity. Since he had been king of Judah he had lost no opportunity of establishing official relationships with them[4]. Nevertheless, David was wary about Abner's proposal. He knew him personally, as they had both been members of Saul's entourage. For Abner the condition that he should bring Michal with him meant the clear and final consummation of his break with Eshbaal and the transfer of his allegiance to David. Abner fulfilled the condition, negotiated with David in Hebron and came to terms with him. But the plan was not carried out, since, on his return, Abner was murdered by Joab at the gate of Hebron on the pretext of vengeance for the murder of his

[1] The later tradition made Michal become David's wife during Saul's lifetime, in the context of David's victory over Goliath (1 Sam. xviii, 27). This is historically incorrect and the reference to this tradition in 2 Sam. iii, 14 is shown by the context to be secondary. In 2 Sam. iii, 15 the context requires 'Abner' (instead of 'Ishbosheth') as the subject of the sentences.

[2] The age and distribution of the daughters' right of succession in Israelite law, in the case of no sons, are doubtful, however; cf. the late passage in Numbers xxvii, 1-11.

[3] Naturally, there was not yet any definite right of succession to the throne. But, as in the case of Eshbaal, it was easy enough to fall back on a member of the family of the previous king in the search for a successor.

[4] As an example the writer in 2 Sam. ii, 4b-7 tells of a message which David sent to the people of Jabesh, after he had learnt that they had buried Saul and his sons. His sole intention in sending this message must have been to make them think well of him.

brother, but in fact owing to jealousy and the fear that Abner's connection with David might endanger his own relations with David.

David rejected the not entirely unwarranted suspicion that he had engineered the murder of Abner, who was a power in Israel; he arranged for Abner to be buried in Hebron in his own presence. It is not likely that he wanted this murder, as it could easily have lost him the sympathy of many people who were important for the next period in his career, and in 2 Sam. iii, 37 the chronicler is able to state with satisfaction that 'all the people [probably in Hebron] and all Israel understood that day that it was not of the king to slay Abner the son of Ner'. It was not long before the Israelite tribes' confidence in, and affection for, David led to the goal which he desired. One day the weak Eshbaal, who now lacked the strong hand of Abner, was murdered in Mahanaim during his midday sleep by two professional soldiers ('captains of bands') from the originally Canaanite city of Beeroth which had been absorbed by the tribe of Benjamin, and the inhabitants of which had probably been forced to leave the city in a conflict with Saul and now took their revenge on the son of Saul (2 Sam. iv, 1 ff.). Eshbaal was not a king for long. The note in 2 Sam. ii, 10 gives him a reign of two years, from his election until an unknown day in the following year. This statement cannot be refuted on textual or material grounds. It is unlikely anyway that this weak monarchy could have survived for long without proper foundations. That Eshbaal was murdered probably suited David quite well. But that the two murderers soon appeared before him in Hebron with Eshbaal's head, in order to receive his praise and reward, could only embarrass him. If the murder of Abner had already aroused suspicions, it now seemed obvious that David was trying to make his way by murder generally. David had both the men killed at once and Eshbaal's head buried in Abner's tomb in Hebron. Again it is in fact unlikely that David tried to accelerate the almost inevitable course of events by instigating a murder instead of calmly and shrewdly awaiting the end of Eshbaal's reign as king; and once again the Israelites appear to have believed him when he claimed that he had had no share in the murder of Eshbaal.

There now remained practically only one path for the tribes of Israel to take. They had to hold fast to the institution of monarchy whether they liked it or not; after the southern tribes had founded their monarchy, the old confederacy of tribes could not be developed into a political organisation such as appeared to be necessary in the present emergency. Among their own people they evidently found no man whom they could have made king. Of Saul's male descendants the sole survivor was now a lame son of Jonathan (cf. 2 Sam. ix, 1-3) who was out of the question. Meanwhile, however, David had become Saul's son-in-law through his marriage with Michal, had established other connections and had proved his worth as king of Judah. The elders of the tribes of the State of Israel therefore came to David in Hebron and offered him the kingship over Israel too. David made a 'league' with them and they anointed him 'king over Israel' (2 Sam. v, 1-3). This again was a political move. It is true that the contract was concluded 'before Yahweh', that is, in the sanctuary; but that merely means that this agreement was placed under divine protection, as in the case of other human agreements. The anointing was a sacred act following his election to the kingship. It is true that in 2 Sam. v, 2b there is an explicit reference to the fact that the Lord had said to David: 'thou shalt be a captain (nagīd) over Israel' (cf. above, p. 000). We are not told what this statement refers to. If the voice of a prophet unknown to us had uttered these words, it hardly meant more than that the elders of the tribes were confirmed in the move which the situation demanded in any case; and the agreement concluded in Hebron was still the important thing. David was now 'king of Judah and Israel'. Two different acts at different times had made him first king over Judah and then king over Israel (in the narrower political sense of the term). Both kingships had their own legal basis and it was no longer possible to amalgamate them in a unified political structure. At any rate, David considered it right to keep to the foundations which had developed historically. The only factor uniting the two political structures was the person of the king himself: the link between them was a 'personal union'. Even after David had been elected king over Israel the juxtaposition of 'Israel' and 'Judah' continued; and the division of the Israelite tribes into two different States went on unaltered. Neither of the two States was a 'national State', in the way that Saul's kingship over the whole confederacy of Israel had been a kind of 'national monarchy'; and the functions of the tribal federation could not be continued by either of the States. Both States had been brought about by the special conditions which followed Saul's disastrous end.

The union of the two States in one hand could no longer be a matter of indifference to the Philistines. Until then they had presumably regarded David and Eshbaal as vassals under Philistine sovereignty. We are not told how far this vassal relationship worked in practice The co-existence of the two States may have suited them very well, and they do not appear to have interfered in the internal affairs of Israel so long as their sovereign rights were not affected. But the amalgamation of Judah and Israel in the person of their vassal David was bound to appear to threaten their power and authority and induce them to intervene. In fact, we read in 2 Sam. v, 17 that when they heard that David had been anointed king over Israel, all the Philistines 'came up to seek David'[1] and they occupied the valley of Rephaim (verse 18) immediately west of the city-state of Jerusalem (the modern el baḳʿa). There were good reasons for this. The territory of Jerusalem separated the areas occupied by the States of Judah and Israel from one another. By attacking at this point they had hopes of preventing David from entering on his reign over Israel or at least making it impossible to assemble the armies of the two kingdoms. For David everything was now at stake. He could only maintain the position he had achieved if he succeeded in warding off the Philistines and destroying their supremacy; for their part the Philistines could only hold their supremacy if they were able to remove David from his kingship over Judah and Israel. The question as to who was to be supreme in Palestine had to be decided now. The decision went in David's favour. David set forth against the Philistines[2] with his band of professional soldiers[3] and probably made a surprise attack near the shrine of Baal-Perazim on Mount Perazim[4]. It is impossible to identify this place exactly.

[1] In 2 Sam. v the story of David's conquest of Jerusalem takes precedence, though it took place a good time after David had united the two kingdoms (cf. below, pp. 189 f.). Historically the conflict with the Philistines no doubt preceded the conquest of Jerusalem. 2 Sam. v, 17 refers back quite correctly to 2 Sam. v, 1-3; and the only question is whether the writer of the story of David's rise to power anticipated the story of the conquest of Jerusalem because he regarded it as particularly important, and then reported at a later stage on the victories over the Philistines in 2 Sam. v, 17-25, but followed on explicitly from verse 1-3 (2 Sam. v, 4-5, 11-16 are secondary in this context from a literary point of view), or whether only a later writer introduced the anticipatory passage about Jerusalem, so that the original order—corresponding to the historical sequence of events—was 2 Sam. v, 1-3, 17-25, 6-10 (with verse 10 as the emphatic conclusion).

[2] According to verse 17 David 'went down to the hold' and, according to verse 9, this can only mean the 'fort' of Jerusalem. This can hardly be the original wording but a secondary reference to the Jerusalem story which now has precedence. 1 Chron. xiv, 8 offers instead the general statement: 'he went out against them'. That too can hardly be the original text. Probably the traditional text was no longer intact at this point and was 'improved' in various ways, so that it is now impossible to reconstruct the original text.

[3] In verse 21 there is a specific reference, quite rightly, to 'David and his men'.

[4] In Isaiah xxviii, 21 there is mention of Mount Perazim, which was no doubt well-known to the Jerusalemites and which lay in their neighbourhood, in an allusion probably to the victory that David had just won there, at which Yahweh had intervened with great power. In 2 Sam. v, 20 the name 'Perazim' is derived quite artificially from David's victory over his enemies.

It was probably on the southern border of the plain of Rephaim. David certainly came from the south, from Hebron, and will have approached the plain of Rephaim on minor roads, and therefore unnoticed[1]. He succeeded in vanquishing the Philistines completely. He beat them by using their own methods. He had been a mercenary leader under the Philistines and knew their style of warfare. He confronted them, not, like Saul, with the large, but unwieldy, armies of the tribes, but with a band of mercenaries which he may have strengthened and developed meanwhile as king of Judah and which had a professional understanding of the art of war. He beat the Philistines with the aid of this nimble instrument and with his own inimitable skill. In view of the all-important nature of the conflict, however, the Philistines made another attempt. The first time, underestimating the strength and military skill of the enemy, who was their own vassal, they had presumably not raised their full strength. The only point in making this second attempt, presumably quite soon after the failure of the first, was to enter the fray with all the military forces at their disposal. They appeared once more on the plain of Rephaim. And David beat them again, this time at a place described as 'over against the mulberry trees' (2 Sam. v, 23). This place, probably well known to the near-by inhabitants of Jerusalem, is naturally impossible to identify. Perhaps this time David came upon the Philistines with his troops from the side of the State of Israel, from the north—no doubt as suddenly as before—anyway, according to 2 Sam. v, 25, the pursuit of the utterly defeated Philistines took place north of the plain of Rephaim 'from Gibeon[2] until thou come to Gezer' (tell jezer in the maritime plain south of Lydda). Pursuing them right up to the borders of their own territory, David completed his victory over his most powerful and most important enemies.

The Philistines made no further attempt. They were forced to surrender their supremacy in the land. The period of their predominance had come to a rapid end. Henceforth they were limited to their old possessions in the southern part of the maritime plain and formed one of the small neighbouring States which gave trouble to Judah and Israel as occasion offered but were no longer able to make any decisive historical interventions. David's decisive victories over the Philistines were the fundamental and the most

[1] Cf. A. Alt, PJB (1927), pp. 15 f., where it is suggested that the sanctuary of Baal-Perazim is identical with the modern sanctuary of sitt el-bedrīye on the rounded hill-top of eshsherāfāt.

[2] Instead of the 'Geba' which is given in the text, one should read 'Gibeon', in accordance with 1 Chron. xiv, 16.

lasting successes of a life that was rich in success. They gave him freedom to develop and elaborate his political system along his own lines. No doubt one of his first measures was to give the State a centre. He still resided in Hebron, which, though it formed a natural centre for the State of Judah, was not in the long run a suitable place from which to govern the greater State of Israel as well. Hebron was not only too far from the centre to be a suitable capital for the dual monarchy, but in Hebron David was and remained primarily king of Judah, and the tribes in Israel did not want to be ruled by the king of Judah but by the David they had themselves elected king of Israel. He could not, however, make an Israelite city such as Shechem his residence, natural centre of the land though it was, else he would have hurt the feelings of the Judaeans who had been the first to make him king and would hardly have forgiven him if he had moved to the State of Israel. In view of the jealousy and bad feeling between the two States of Judah and Israel which he had to take into account and which was to lead to open conflict even during his reign, with the sure instinct of the wise statesman he chose a city on neutral soil between the territories of the two States. This was Jerusalem, which had not yet been conquered by the Israelite tribes and was still occupied by a group of earlier inhabitants of the country, the Jebusites. The territory of the State of Judah began south of Jerusalem and that of the State of Israel north of Jerusalem[1]. It was an ancient city, the first literary reference to which appears in the Egyptian 'execration texts' at the beginning of the second millennium B.C.[2]. The Amarna tablets show that it was the seat of the city ruler Abdihipa[3]. In the Amarna period it had played a certain part as a ruler's residence; but up to now it had not been one of the really important cities of the land. It lay on a hill within the hollow of a valley[4] in a firm position, but not one commanding a large area, at a height of about 800 m. on the rather inaccessible southern part of the hills west of Jordan, near the main north to south road over the hills, which followed the watershed, but lacking good communications with the east and west. It was in no sense the obvious centre of the land and its natural position did not predestine it to be the

[1] Cf. above all A. Alt, *Jerusalems Aufstieg* (ZDMG, N.F. [1925], pp. 1-19).

[2] In K. Sethe (cf. above, p. 18, note 3) e 27/28 f. 18.

[3] The Amarna letters Nos. 285-290 derive from this Abdihipa (Knudtzon).

[4] Pre-Davidian and Davidian Jerusalem lay on the so-called 'south-east hill' above the Gihon fountain and outside the residential area of the modern city; cf. *Westminster Historical Atlas to the Bible* (1945), Pl. xvii. The comprehensive work by J. Simons, *Jerusalem in the Old Testament. Researches and Theories* (1952), should now be consulted on all questions regarding the ancient topography of Jerusalem.

capital. What it became under David, and what it has meant in history right up to our own day, it owes not to nature but to the will and the insight of a man who, disregarding the natural conditions, made a decision that was right in a particular historical situation.

David took his time over this step too. According to 2 Sam. ii, 11–v, 5a he resided in Hebron for seven and a half years, of which only two coincided with the simultaneous reigns of Eshbaal and David. For a time, therefore, he ruled over both States from Hebron. Then he conquered Jebusite Jerusalem with his mercenaries (2 Sam. v, 6-9)[1] and made it his residence as 'the city of David'. It was not attached to either the State of Judah or the State of Israel but remained a city-state and David was still the city ruler of Jerusalem as legal successor to the previous Jebusite city ruler. The city was not inhabited by either Judaeans or Israelites, but was reserved for its previous inhabitants and only received the king and his entourage, his household and his mercenaries. All these made up a considerable body of people, however, corresponding to the size of the State that was now ruled from here.

David then moved into his new capital the ancient tribal relic of the Ark, which had apparently not been taken much notice of for some time or had been carefully shunned in the old Canaanite city of Kirjath-Jearim which was annexed to the tribe of Benjamin since the Philistines had captured it. By bringing it to his capital David restored it to a place of honour (2 Sam. vi, 1-15; 17-19). He wanted to give this city the dignity pertaining to this central relic of the federation of the twelve tribes and thereby make use of it for his own ends. In fact the position in world history which Jerusalem has occupied ever since is due to this very act. David presumably set up the Ark in the city shrine, which was probably on the rounded hill-top above the city where Solomon later erected his buildings. The ancient Israelite shrine now stood in a Canaanite place of worship in a Canaanite city which, though it was now David's royal city, had hitherto known no Israelite traditions of any kind. The priests who served it were royal officials (2 Sam. viii, 17a, 18b; xx, 25b, 26). Admittedly, the Ark had stood in former times in one or the other old local sanctuary and the Israelite tribes now revered the sanctuary of Jerusalem as their own religious centre. 'Mount Zion'—this was the name of the hill-top on which Jerusalem's place of worship stood—became a concept in Israel's religious vocabulary.

[1] In 2 Sam. v, 6 the writer refers correctly again to the 'king and his men', whereas 1 Chron. xi, 4 tendentiously substitutes, 'David and all Israel'.

The territories of the State of Judah and Israel were not very clearly defined owing to the contiguity of Israelites and Canaanites. This was true in particular of the State of Israel. By incorporating the hitherto independent Canaanite city-states David gave the States of Judah and Israel the territorial concentration which they had been lacking. We have no direct information about this, but it is possible to infer it indirectly. In 2 Sam. xxiv, 5-7 there is a description of the territorial frontiers of Israel and Judah. It is true that, according to the text, it was the route which David's officers took for the purpose of the census of the people which was evidently conducted with a view to a reassembly of the levies. But in fact a description of the frontiers is offered for this route. It begins in the southern land east of Jordan on the Arnon (sēl el-mōjib) with the city of Aroer (the modern khirbet ʿarāʿir) and therefore includes the whole plateau north of the Arnon with its cities in the east roughly as far as the line Aroer-Dibon (dībān) Medeba (mādeba) in David's sovereign domains, then lists the 'land of the Hittites' between the land of Gad[1] and the Ephraimite-Manassite territory of the land of Gilead on the one hand, and the city of Dan by the sources of the Jordan on the other. 'The land of the Hittites'[2] can only mean an ancient city-state territory and, according to the context, a strip of city-state territories north-east and north of the ʿajlūn must be meant, which David had also subjugated. Then there follow from the 'stronghold of Tyre'[3] onwards—this probably means the mainland base of the island city of Tyre (probably the modern tell reshēdīje) evidently in a southerly direction 'the city of the Hivites and of the Canaanites', that is, the city-states of the maritime plains north and south of the Carmel salient as far as an unnamed southern frontier which must be located roughly on the nahr el-ʿōja, beyond which the territory of the Philistine cities began in the maritime plain, which, though stripped of their power, had remained independent States. The statements contained in Judges i, 27-35, according to which the Canaanite cities which were not conquered by the tribes to begin with were rendered politically dependent, though not occupied 'when Israel was strong' must be taken as referring to this measure of David's. From this

[1] The name Jazer described the province of Gad (cf. xxxii, 1), whereas the curious הגד (with article) that precedes it, is obviously erroneous. One would expect a verbal form in its place.

[2] Verse 6 should be read thus, with a branch of the Septuagint tradition instead of the obviously distorted text. It is impossible to reconstruct the following word with any certainty.

[3] 'Zidon' in verse 6 is possibly intended to mean 'Phoenicia' quite generally. This is admittedly difficult to decide, since the preceding words are again distorted.

passage we learn in particular that the great cities on the plain of Jezreel were subjugated as well, which one would anyway have assumed to be the case in the nature of things. If, in accordance with the enumeration of the provinces of the State of Israel in Solomon's time which is given in 1 Kings iv, 7-19, Israelite tribal territories and Canaanite city territories together constituted the territory of the State of Israel, the subjugation of the Canaanite cities which this presupposes can hardly be ascribed to Solomon, of whom there is otherwise no record that he extended the area of his States, but must have been the work of David.

This means that the Israelites had achieved a final victory over the old Canaanite population and the States of Israel and Judah had received a generous accession of territory, to round off their domains. The process was most advantageous to the State of Israel, in which the settlements of the tribes or groups of tribes were far from self-contained and much divided by city territories. At the same time, whilst the State of Israel was greatly expanded, for the State of Judah it presumably merely involved the lesser acquisition of city-state territories in the adjacent hill country to the west. It is true that this accession of power and territory also meant the loss of national compactness, especially for the State of Israel and to a lesser degree for the State of Judah as well.

The Canaanite system was now incorporated in the States of Israel and Judah. The inhabitants of the cities, who were so foreign to the Israelite tribes, evidently remained substantially untouched by these annexations, and the political and social structure of their lives probably remained fundamentally the same. The place of the city kings was merely taken by the king of Israel or Judah; and where the cities had been governed aristocratically, the ruling class now had to acknowledge the sovereignty of this king. Their submission was enforced, on the whole, by the superiority of David's power which had been revealed so clearly in his victory over the Philistines. Anyway, we do not hear that warlike undertakings were required to secure their submission. In both States the Israelite tribes were the uppermost and decisive factor; but the Canaanite inhabitants were now a more-or-less important factor as well. On the basis of his authority as king of Judah and Israel, David also subjugated his neighbours. He thereby created a great empire extending far beyond the confines of the Israelite tribes, including a greater part of Palestine and Syria. Far-flung political organisations had occasionally existed on Palestinian-Syrian soil, especially in the period when Palestine and Syria had been under Egyptian rule[1]. The Egyptian model also played an apparently not insignificant part in the internal organisation of David's empire. In 2 Sam. viii, 1-14, there is an annalistic compilation of David's exploits to extend his power, presumably in chronological order; and in 2 Sam. x, 1-11, and xii, 26-31, there is a more detailed account of his conflicts with the Ammonites and Aramaeans. The list in 2 Sam. viii begins appropriately enough with the Philistines (verse 1); the note in this verse that David 'smote the Philistines and subdued them' refers presumably to David's victories over the Philistines which are recorded in 2 Sam. v, 17-25, which, whilst they did not make the Philistines permanently dependent on David politically, forced them to acknowledge his superiority and sovereignty over the major part of the land[2]. In their small province, however, they remained the only power which David did not subjugate sooner or later. In 2 Sam. viii, 2, there follows the note about the subjugation of Moab, whose territory at that time only began south of the Arnon, since David had extended the State of Israel as far as the Arnon. No mention is made of any special reason for the war with Moab. David beat Moab and after the victory he had two-thirds of the Moabite army slaughtered. It may possibly be inferred from this cruel treatment that Moab had wantonly seized on some frivolous excuse to go to war with David. David turned Moab into a vassal state and forced it to pay tribute to him; evidently the monarchy in Moab continued. After this David's wars with the Aramaeans are reported in 2 Sam. viii, 3-8. According to 2 Sam. x-xii they were caused by the rashness of the Ammonites. Completely disregarding the new situation in Israel, the Ammonites, who were probably still planning to expand at the expense of the Israelites east of Jordan, in spite of their having been conquered by Saul, treated a deputation from David, which was making a courtesy visit on the occasion of a change of sovereign, with such contempt that a war with David became inevitable. Because of their own insignificant resources the Ammonites tried to secure the help of their neighbours and relations, the Aramaeans. The latter had meanwhile established a few minor states. North of the Ammon the nearest neighbour east of the ʿajlūn on the farthest border of Palestine was the Aramaean State of Beth-Rehob (the modern riḥāb). The 'man of Tob' was probably not far from here, probably an Aramaean group with no

[1] Cf. A. Alt, *Das Grossreich Davids* (ThLZ, 75 [1950], columns 213-220).

[2] The expression מתג האמה, in verse 1b, which must certainly not be 'improved' in accordance with 1 Chron. xviii, 1, is unfortunately quite obscure. The explanation given by O. Eissfeldt in ZDPV, 66 (1943), pp. 117 f., is not really satisfactory. It is not certain that the text is in order.

very firm political organisation. Their help was also enlisted by the Ammonites. There was, in addition, the monarchy of Maacha, presumably an Aramaean domain too, which was probably situated at the southern foot of Mount Hermon. The Ammonites succeeded above all, however, in obtaining the assistance of King Hadadezer of Zobah. He ruled over the Aramaean tribes on the eastern side of the Anti-Lebanon, which were probably not yet fully established; he also governed the Aramaean tribes in the steppe as far as the Euphrates. All these Aramaeans came with a great body of men to relieve the Ammonite capital Rabba (the modern ʿammān), which David had meanwhile ordered to be attacked by the Judaean-Israelite militia under Joab. Joab succeeded in beating these Aramaeans so completely that they refused to give any further aid to the Ammonites, and most of them also desisted from any further battle with David. Only Hadadezer himself made another personal effort, with freshly assembled forces, which now included the Aramaeans from Damascus, who had evidently established an Aramaean domain in this famous old oasis city and probably ruled over some of the city-state territories to the south of Damascus as well. Once again, however, David, who appears to have been present in person this time, succeeded in obtaining a decisive victory near a place called Helam, which must have been somewhere in the northernmost land east of Jordan. As a result of this victory the Ammonites' cause was lost. In the following year David gave orders to Joab to lay waste the Ammonites' land and besiege their capital Rabba. Finally David himself hastened to be present at the capture of the city's citadel. He punished the Ammonites severely and not without good cause. He had the inhabitants of the Ammonite cities led away as slaves. He put the Ammonite crown on his own head, however; in other words he did away with the native monarchy and made himself king of Ammon. The kingdom of Ammon was added to the kingdoms of Judah and Israel and the city-state of Jerusalem. But on Aramaean territory the city-state territory of the northern land east of Jordan was organised as far as Damascus as a province of the State of David, under governors appointed by David, who resided in Damascus, and under the obligation of regular payment of tribute; the minor Aramaean domains on the borders of the northern land east of Jordan may have been annexed to this province in one form or another. In this way David extended his rule far to the north-east. As the ruler of widely scattered and far from firmly established Aramaean tribes, Hadadezer of Zobah could hardly be permanently subjugated to David's rule. After his defeat he was forced to make a payment of golden shields or quivers[1] which David took to Jerusalem as trophies, and he was thereby forced to acknowledge David's supremacy at any rate formally. He was obliged to deliver supplies of ore, but they were probably not intended to be kept up permanently. The supplies may have come from the beka' between Lebanon and Anti-Lebanon where the presence of ore deposits had been exploited even in ancient days and over which Hadadezer had extended his rule[2]. David's influence extended, therefore, indirectly at any rate, into the depths of central Syria, and it is not surprising that the king of Hamath on the Orontes in northern Syria (the modern ḥama) tried to establish good relations with him by sending him a deputation with lavish presents: the fame of his victories had reached as far as Hamath (2 Sam. viii, 9 f.)[3].

Finally David's victory over Edom is recorded in 2 Sam. viii, 13 f. In this case, too, we do not know what caused a military conflict and what was the reason for the cruel treatment meted out to the Edomites which is reported in another context in 1 Kings xi, 15-17. According to the latter account, David beat Edom—in the 'valley of salt' as it is called in 2 Sam. viii, 13[4]—and Joab rampaged for six months in Edom 'to cut off every male in Edom'. The royal house was also eliminated and only the little Prince Hadad managed to escape to Egypt through the Sinaitic desert with some of his father's faithful servants. David also organised Edom as a province under its own governors; and this province, remote though it was, was important because it made access possible to the gulf of el-'aḳaba and hence to the Red Sea and because it included the numerous ore deposits on the borders of the wādi el-'araba which had already been exploited: the possibilities which this opened up were exploited later on under Solomon.

In conclusion, David maintained peaceful and friendly relationships with King Hiram of Tyre and all the Phoenician coastal cities for which Tyre appears to have been the main centre at the time[5].

[1] It is impossible to establish the meaning of the word שֶׁלֶט.

[2] In 2 Sam. viii, 8, the two cities of Yebah (the version in the original text) and Berothai are mentioned as the sites of ore deposits. Unfortunately it is impossible to localise them exactly, as we have no certain evidence.

[3] The excavations of ḥama (cf. H. Ingholt, *Rapport préliminaire sur sept campagnes de fouilles à Hama en Syrie* [1932–1938], 1940) have shown that Hamath was resettled *circa* 1200 B.C. as a seat of government by a population which used the 'Hittite hieroglyphs' as their script (cf. WAT, p. 166 and illust. 8c). The king, who was a contemporary of David, belonged to them.

[4] This 'valley of salt' was probably east of the wādi el-'araba (cf. also 2 Kings xiv, 7) and probably not in the modern wādi el-milḥ ('valley of salt') east of Beer-Sheba.

[5] Cf. W. F. Albright, *Studies in the History of Culture* (1942), pp. 33 f.

Through him David obtained, no doubt in return for services rendered, the coveted and precious cedar wood from the Lebanon as well as expert craftsmen for the royal buildings in Jerusalem (2 Sam. v, 11)[1].

After all his victories David was king of Jerusalem, king of the States of Judah and Israel which had been generously supplemented by the annexation of Canaanite city-states, king of Ammon, ruler of the provinces of Aram (Damascus) and Edom, which were administered by governors, and sovereign over the vassal monarchy of Moab and, in name, possibly sovereign over Hadadezer of Zobah. The whole realm had become an extremely complicated political structure and had grown far beyond the confines of a purely Israelite State. It had become a Palestinian-Syrian Empire united in the person of the king and embracing numerous different peoples. David's political organisation was the first great independent power structure on Palestinian-Syrian soil of which we have knowledge[2], embracing directly or indirectly most of Palestine and Syria: a tremendous phenomenon from the point of view of world history and basically the achievement of one intelligent and uncommonly successful man. The general historical situation in the Orient had been in his favour. In Egypt and the Land of the Two Rivers there was at the time no greater power which might have encroached on Palestine and Syria and enforced a claim to rule over it. The Egypt of the 21st Dynasty was weak, disunited and restricted by the theocratic rule of the priests of Thebes[3]. In the Land of the Two Rivers Babylon had long since lost its importance as a political power after the foreign rule of the mountain people, the Cassites, which had now lasted for centuries. After the golden age of the central-Assyrian States, Assyria, the rising power of the time, had declined again around the turn of the millennium. In Asia Minor, however, there had been no power of any significance at all since the fall of the mighty Empire of the Hittites. It was therefore possible for new forces to develop in Syria-Palestine without interference from outside, and David's Empire had developed in the southern part of Syria-Palestine.

Within a short time the situation had changed completely for

[1] The note in 2 Sam. v, 11, was probably originally part of the context of 2 Sam. viii, 1-14, and was only transferred to its present position because of its reference to Jerusalem.

[2] Perhaps the Hyksos had at one time formed a great Palestinian-Syrian State, before they conquered Egypt and transferred their seat of government there.

[3] Cf. Ed. Meyer, *Gottesstaat, Militärherrschaft und Ständewesen in Ägypten. Zur Geschichte der 21. und 22. Dynastie* (Sit.-Ber. d. Preuss. Akad. d. Wiss., phil.-hist. Kl. XXVIII), 1928.

the Israelite tribes. It was not long since that they had had to be content to maintain themselves against the previous inhabitants of the country; even more recently they had had to submit to the supremacy of the Philistines. Now, however, the king they had chosen ruled over an imposing Empire and was widely esteemed and widely feared. Their external security was assured and they were sharing in an impressive historic process which was bound to increase their self-awareness and self-confidence. For the first time in their history they were taking part in a great historical movement, not as victims and sufferers but creatively. Admittedly the participants were no longer merely the Israelite tribes, and it may be asked whether, despite their admiration for David's greatness and success, the tribes did not note with some anxiety that what was taking place went far beyond the bounds of the authentic history of Israel. The Israelite tribes formed the nucleus of David's Empire only to a limited extent. They were divided among two separate political organisations and these organisations were no longer purely Israelite. David no longer waged his wars simply with the armies of the tribes of Israel. It is true, he still used the tribal militia or had it used, above all, against the neighbouring peoples east of Jordan[1] and they even took the old tribal relic of the Ark with them[2], as though David was still waging a 'holy war'. David evidently took the Ark very seriously because it represented the confederacy of the tribes. The weapon which David preferred, however, was his band of mercenaries[3] who were by no means purely Israelite but, presumably, a very motley assortment[4], and in any case they belonged to him personally and not to the Israelite tribes. He had begun his climb to power as a leader of mercenaries and he had won with them such important successes as the decisive victory over the Philistines and the conquest of the city-state of Jerusalem. Later on he will have continued to use his mercenaries in important enterprises. The political structure that arose in this period was not so much an Israelite Empire as David's Empire. All the same, the tribes still regarded him as one of their own and their central shrine was in David's royal city; and they had had at any rate a share in his ascent to great power.

The existence of David's Empire was so dependent on the strong

[1] Cf. 2 Sam. xi, 1 (Joab the captain of the host with 'all Israel' against Ammon); 1 Kings xi, 15 (Joab the captain of the host in Moab); 2 Sam. x, 17 (David with 'all Israel' against the Aramaeans).

[2] Cf. 2 Sam. xi, 11.

[3] Beside the captain of the host David had a special commander in charge of the mercenaries (2 Sam. viii, 18; xx, 23).

[4] Cf. already 'the thirty heroes of David' and K. Ellinger, PJB, 31 (1935), pp. 29-75.

personality of its founder that its survival beyond his death only seemed assured provided a successor of more or less equal stature could be found. David no doubt realised that too, and he must have realised equally well that owing to the complete lack of any traditional right of succession and the importance of his own personality for the establishment of his complicated Empire much depended on his personal decision regarding a successor. Strangely enough, David failed in this respect, because he was apparently unable to make up his mind and delayed making the decision far too long. The final period of his reign was therefore filled with all kinds of disturbances caused by various of his sons attempting to enforce their claim to succeed their father. A historical work that was probably written before the death of Solomon described these upsets with great expert knowledge and also the ultimate solution of the problem of the succession to the monarchy[1]. That one of David's numerous sons would succeed him was practically certain. If Saul's sole surviving male descendant, a son of Jonathan named Merib-baal[2], who was a cripple anyway, believed his great hour might still come when he would be offered the throne (2 Sam. xvi, 3) this merely showed how childish he was. After the terrible failure of Saul's monarchy there could hardly be many people among the Israelite tribes in favour of a continuation of this monarchy, even in Saul's own tribe of Benjamin, despite the fact that the monarchy of David the Judaean, who had taken Saul's place, still met with embittered hostility in this tribe (cf. 2 Sam. xvi, 8). The new State had so little in common with Saul's monarchy and was so much David's personal achievement that only members of David's family could be seriously considered fit to succeed him. Moreover, the 'prophet' Nathan, who evidently played a not unimportant part at David's court in Jerusalem had solemnly proclaimed in the name of his God that David's dynasty would endure beyond his death, referring to the fact that David's successful rise to power had proved that Yahweh had chosen him to be the king[3].

The practical question was therefore which of David's sons was

[1] We have this historical work in 2 Sam. vii; ix, 1-20, 22; 1 Kings i, 2; cf. L. Rost, *Die Überlieferung von der Thronnachfolge Davids* (BWANT, III, 6), 1926.

[2] The original form of the name is only contained in 1 Chron. viii, 34; ix, 40. In 2 Sam. iv, 4; ix, 6 ff. and elsewhere the name appears in the distorted form Mephibosheth.

[3] Probably the remark in 2 Sam. vii, 8, should be taken as meaning that Yahweh had called David to be nāgīd over Israel. We do not hear anything about such a call having played any part in David's rise to power (cf. above, p. 186). Possibly it was only established retrospectively that David must have been called by Yahweh to be nāgīd. 2 Sam. vi, 21, will have to be judged in the same way.

to succeed him. If a dangerous state of chaos was to be avoided when he died the question had to be settled during his lifetime. When David had asked for the hand of Saul's daughter Michal (cf. above, pp. 184f.) and had made her his wife, his idea had no doubt been that a son, possibly the eldest son of this marriage, who would have been a grandson of Saul, would become the favourite among his sons and might attract the sympathies of those who still supported the house of Saul. But as is stated explicitly in 2 Sam. vi, 23, the marriage of David and Michal remained childless ('Michal had no child until the day of her death'). The obvious possibility that a son of this marriage might be elected to succeed his father was therefore ruled out. For the rest, according to the ancient Israelite law of succession, which assigned the main share of the inheritance to the father's first-born son without regard to the mother's position among the father's wives (cf. Deut. xxi, 17), the idea that David's eldest son should succeed him was quite natural; and, as far as we know, in the house of David the monarchy did in fact usually continue to pass to the king's eldest son. In the case of David himself, the founder of the monarchy and dynasty, the eldest son 'born in the purple', that is, the first son born after David's accession to the throne, might have had special priority. David's sons themselves apparently paid no particular attention to this latter aspect but regarded themselves as the presumptive successors to the throne in the sequence of their respective ages. In 2 Sam. iii, 2-5, there is a list of the five eldest sons of David, who, if the editorial notes on this list were correct, would have been born in Hebron, during the period of David's Judaean monarchy, but, as David had had at least two wives considerably earlier (cf. 1 Sam. xxv, 42-43) some of the sons were probably somewhat older. The list given in 2 Sam. iii, 2-5, is supplemented by the enumeration of the sons of David who were born in Jerusalem, which appears in 2 Sam. v, 13-16.

In 2 Sam. iii, 2, Amnon is described explicitly as David's first-born son, his mother being the Ahinoam from South Judaean Jezreel, by marrying whom David had strengthened his ties with the South Judaean tribes. Amnon was evidently regarded by himself and by others as the future king. The writer of the story of the succession to the throne also hints at this; obviously this is the sole reason why in 2 Sam. xiii, xiv, he tells the story of the murder of Amnon by Absalom in such detail as part of the story of the succession. Amnon was unwise enough to supply Absalom with a pretext for murdering him, by raping his half-sister Tamar. In fact, Absalom thereby removed the next man ahead of him as a claimant to the throne. According to 2 Sam. iii, 3, since David's second eldest son, who is mentioned here, was omitted for some unknown reason, after the death of Amnon, Absalom, as the third oldest son, was the next candidate. It is true that, to begin with, the murder of Amnon cost him his father's good-will. But with the help of Joab, the military commander, he finally obtained David's absolute forgiveness. David probably had a weak spot for his sons in general and, at any rate, for Absalom in particular. (2 Sam xiii, 39; xiv, 1). Even in David's own lifetime Absalom tried to seize the throne by force. This led to the so-called 'rebellion of Absalom', the course of which is described in great detail in 2 Sam. xv-xix. Absalom succeeded in gaining the sympathy and support of the Israelite tribes, especially in the State of Judah, but in the State of Israel too, apparently, so that in the end he was able to take the risk of having himself proclaimed king in the ancient and royal Judaean city of Hebron (2 Sam. xv, 10). This signified the deposition of David. We do not learn exactly what had made David so unpopular in Israel in the meantime that Absalom apparently had no difficulty in setting himself up as king. In time every regime loses sympathisers and acquires enemies; and it is easy to conceive that the Israelite tribes were more and more dissatisfied with the growth of David's dominion into an empire extending far beyond the territory of the Israelite tribes. At any rate, the defection of the tribes from David became so serious that all the ageing king had left was the personal loyalty of his own mercenaries. He therefore decided to escape to Mahanaim in the land east of Jordan with his mercenaries, to avoid being surprised by Absalom and his followers in Jerusalem. Absalom was thus able to enter David's royal city and to take over the government of the city in due form. In the armed conflict that ensued, however, David's professional soldiers proved superior to the militia of the Israelite tribes that Absalom had assembled and which were no doubt far stronger numerically. The decisive battle took place somewhere in the wooded hill country in the central land east of Jordan south of the Jabbok in the 'wood of Ephraim' (2 Sam. xviii, 6). Absalom had led the militia there to attack David's position east of Jordan. He lost the battle and was killed as he was taking flight, despite David's explicit order to his soldiers that his life should be spared. There now remained nothing for the Israelite tribes in the States of Judah and Israel but to recall David as their king (2 Sam. xix, 10, 11). This led to a very remarkable sequel, which revealed the latent conflict between the States of Judah and Israel within David's political organisation and at the same time showed David making a definitely unwise move for the first time. David—while evidently still in Mahanaim—ordered the Judaean tribes to summon him to the throne of Judah as one of their own (2 Sam. xix, 12 ff.). Had he become so impatient that he could not wait for what was bound to come about in any case? When the Judaeans' representatives, following his summons, fetched the king from the Jordan and escorted him to the shrine of Gilgal near Jericho, the representatives of the tribes of the State of Israel appeared and reproached David for not getting them to come and fetch him, since they represented the majority of the tribes. The result was that under the leadership of a Benjaminite called Sheba the watchword went out to the indignant tribes of the State of Israel: 'We have no part in David, neither have we inheritance in the son of Jesse: every man to his tents, O Israel!' (2 Sam. xx, 1). And the first thing David had to do after his return to Jerusalem was to call up his mercenaries and the Jewish militia to suppress the rebellion in the State of Israel by force of arms. He soon succeeded in this (2 Sam. xx); but this quarrel between the State of Judah and Israel that erupted under David was a bad omen for the future.

In the end, therefore, David had regained his full supremacy. But the problem of the succession was still not solved. After the elimination of Absalom, Adonijah was now David's oldest son (2 Sam. iii, 4) and Adonijah proceeded to claim the throne (1 Kings i, 5). If Absalom had sought his followers among the broad masses of the Israelite tribes, Adonijah sought and found the support of a few influential men from David's entourage. He won over Joab the captain and Abiathar the priest from the royal sanctuary in Jerusalem (1 Kings i, 7). But this also meant—for this is the way things happen in the atmosphere of a royal court—that other equally influential men were ranged against Adonijah, including, no doubt not by accident, the mercenary leader Benaiah, who was Joab's rival, together with David's personal retinue, and Zadok, the other priest of the royal sanctuary, who were joined by Nathan, the court prophet (1 Kings i, 8). This opposition party succeeded in obtaining a decisive influence over king David who was now very old. They used one of the king's wives, the Bath-Sheba whom David, enchanted by her beauty, had once taken for himself adulterously, and whose husband Uriah he had had treacherously murdered (2 Sam. xi, 2 ff.). She had become David's wife and the mother of his son Solomon. At the time Nathan had remonstrated very earnestly with David on account of the crime he had committed against Uriah and Bath-Sheba (2 Sam. xii, 1 ff.). He now exploited the influence which Bath-Sheba still had. It is impossible to ascertain to what extent Bath-Sheba played an active part in what now followed and how far she was merely used by Nathan, who was clearly the leader of the party opposed to Adonijah; it is also impossible to establish how far what was said to David was the whole truth or merely a semblance of the truth. In any case, it was reported to him that Adonijah had made himself king on his own responsibility, whereas David had once promised to Bath-Sheba that her son Solomon should succeed him (1 Kings i, 11 ff.). The result which they hoped for was achieved, and David at last uttered his decision regarding the succession to his throne and appointed Solomon to reign in his stead, and had him anointed by Zadok the priest without delay, and then proclaimed him king in Jerusalem (1 Kings i, 28-40).

David's authoritative ruling had solved the problem of the succession at one blow. Adonijah at once abandoned his cause and Solomon was already king and co-regent with David. That the choice fell on Solomon can hardly have been due to his personal qualities, judging from all we hear about him. He was by no means the oldest of David's numerous sons, and he was not even the first of those 'born in the purple' (cf. 2 Sam. v, 14). What distinguished him from the others was that his mother Bath-Sheba was David's favourite wife, whether or not he had really promised her explicitly that her son Solomon should succeed him as king. In view of the priority which she enjoyed, some of the leading officials at court appear to have sided with Solomon, and, by playing a clever hand, to have finally obtained David's ruling that he should succeed him. If, despite the detailed and vivid account which is given within the framework of the tradition regarding the succession to the throne of David in 1 Kings i the background and the actual course of events are not entirely clear, it is at any rate obvious that Solomon became David's successor, in opposition to Adonijah, as a result of an intrigue at court. The successor whom David ultimately chose did not prove equal to his task: the history of his reign shows that. The only question is whether any of the other of David's surviving sons would have been any more suitable. The task which confronted David's successor was extraordinarily difficult. The extremely complicated Empire which David had built up could only be held together and consolidated by a successor who was to some extent the great king's equal in wisdom and strength; and such a man was not easily found.

16. *The Reign of Solomon*

It is noteworthy that the tradition concerning Solomon which has been preserved within the framework of the great deuteronomistic history is quite different in kind from the tradition regarding David that has come down to us. It is true that the latter does not provide a complete picture of David's reign, since it is made up, above all, of the two great narratives of the rise of David up to his accession to the kingdoms of Judah and Israel and Jerusalem and from the period of the controversy about David's succession up to the accession of Solomon; on the development of David's Empire all we have is the brief annalistic record in 2 Sam. viii, 1-14, and a few scattered details elsewhere; the two great narratives were, however, very clearly influenced by the great events of the time and attempted to include them within their scope. They do present a living and full-blooded picture of David. Concerning Solomon's reign, the traditional records merely cover a mass of details; apparently no one was stimulated to compile a connected historical account of his reign. For his section on Solomon (1 Kings iii-xi) the deuteronomist was able to make use of a 'Book of the Acts of Solomon' (1 Kings xi, 41) from which he extracted the essential details. This book evidently represented a compilation and elaboration of the material provided by the king's official records and contained a wealth of sometimes very concrete detail about a great variety of governmental measures taken in Solomon's reign[1]. The Solomonic tradition also contains a number of anecdotes about Solomon which evidently continued to circulate for a long time. The subject of these anecdotes is Solomon's wealth and wisdom. The royal household and buildings provided reason enough for the idea that he was immensely wealthy; and the fact that, rightly or wrongly, he was credited with the writing of proverbs (cf. 1 Kings v, 12-13) helped to add to his posthumous fame as a 'wise man'.

After the death of David, Solomon succeeded his father without difficulty or untoward incidents, once David had made up his mind and had him anointed king. He had, however, attained this goal as the candidate of a particular party at court and there had also been an opposition party in support of Adonijah who was, at the time, David's eldest son. At the very beginning of his reign Solomon eliminated the leaders of this opposition party, including Adonijah

[1] For further details see M. Noth, *Überlieferungsgeschichtliche Studien*, I (1943), pp. 66 f.

himself, in the most brutal fashion, as recorded in the story of David's succession to the throne in 1 Kings ii, 13-44, 46a, which only then proceeds to state that 'the kingdom was established in the hand of Solomon' (1 Kings ii, 46b). David's mercenary leader Benaiah rendered very material services to Solomon in the removal of his enemies (1 Kings ii, 25, 34, 46a) and was rewarded by being made supreme commander of the army (1 Kings ii, 35a). It may be that Solomon had reason to establish his power against strong and influential enemies in this way, and that in so doing he was to some extent following his father's advice (cf. 1 Kings ii, 5 f., 8 f.). But it is probably more than a mere accident that we do not hear of David having paved his way to power by liquidating his personal enemies in this cruel way. David was above that kind of action. Faced with the interplay of the opposing forces at the court in Jerusalem, which had meanwhile become large and influential, Solomon's personality was not apparently strong enough to absolve him from the necessity of having to watch jealously over the safety of his realm, at any rate to begin with. Solomon had entered upon a great inheritance. The prestige which the great Davidian Empire had enjoyed in the world of Palestine and Syria and even further afield in the ancient Orient continued in the main under Solomon, but he failed to add to his father's inheritance. There is nothing in the records concerning any military enterprise on the part of Solomon, and in fact he probably did not engage in war at all. At the outset the political structure bequeathed by David seemed firm and secure enough to make any further expansion of military power unnecessary. But in a situation of that kind a standstill usually means the beginning of a decline. And the decline of David's Empire did in fact begin under Solomon. According to 1 Kings xi, 14-22, and xi, 25a, b, the news of David's death and of the death of his brutal and dreaded commander Joab, whom Solomon had had killed at the outset of his reign as one of his enemies, had caused the Edomite prince Hadad, who had once escaped to Egypt (cf. above, p. 195), to return to his Edomite homeland where he made himself king over Edom. This seems to have occurred fairly early in Solomon's reign. Admittedly there can be no question of Hadad having ruled over the whole of the former territory of Edom, since Solomon apparently had unrestricted access to the gulf of el-ʿaḳaba and the port of Ezeon-Geber which he had developed and used (1 Kings ix, 26), through the wādi el-ʿaraba, that is to say, through a substantial part of the province of Edom. Hadad's rule can therefore only have extended to parts of the more inaccessible Edomite mountains east of the wādi el-ʿaraba. The emergence of Hadad does show, however, that it was not long before Solomon no longer had complete control of the province of Edom; and Solomon apparently took no measures to regain complete possession of Edom. The fact that, according to 1 Kings xi, 23-25a, an Aramaic adventurer named Rezon was able to seize the city of Damascus with a warlike band that he had collected, and made himself king there, was even worse. This, too, may not have involved the loss of the whole province of Aram. But the most important city in this province, the seat of the Davidic governors, had thereby fallen into foreign hands and, again, Solomon does not seem to have done anything to restore his power in the province of Aram. We are not told exactly when this happened but, to judge from the wording of 1 Kings xi, 25a, it was probably early in Solomon's reign. The foundations were thus laid for the Aramaic kingdom of Damascus which was soon to develop with vigour and become, for a time, the strongest power in Palestine and Syria. For Solomon the inevitable result of losing Damascus was that the influence which David had exerted on the Aramaeans in the remoter parts of Syria came to an end. Otherwise, however, Solomon was able to preserve the complicated political structure established by David. He managed to suppress a serious rebellion in the State of Israel. According to the scanty details in 1 Kings xi, 26-28, which provide no really clear picture, for reasons unknown to us, the Ephraimite Jeroboam, who had been discovered by Solomon during the building operations in Jerusalem and entrusted with an office[1] in the house of Joseph, revolted against the king. We do not know whom Jeroboam had behind him nor how widespread the revolt was. In any case, the undertaking failed; but Solomon was not able to arrest Jeroboam, who managed to escape to, and remain in, Egypt. After Solomon's death he was to play an important role once more[2].

[1] The word סֵבֶל which is used in 1 Kings xi, 28, to describe the sphere of this office is usually translated by 'compulsory labour', thus making Jeroboam an official within the Solomonic organisation of compulsory labour. But it should be noted that, although the word means something like 'bearing burdens', it is not the usual word for 'compulsory labour' (מַס, cf. under Solomon 1 Kings iv, 6; v, 27-28 [English Bible, v, 13, 14]; ix, 15, 21). Moreover, it is at least doubtful whether the 'house of Joseph' was used for compulsory labour (cf. below, p. 209). It is therefore still uncertain what the special task was with which Jeroboam was entrusted by Solomon.

[2] We do not know exactly when Jeroboam's revolt took place. Perhaps quite early in Solomon's reign, since the building activities in the city of David which first brought Jeroboam to the fore probably belong to the beginning of Solomon's reign; the only question is how long Jeroboam was one of Solomon's officials before he 'raised his hand against the King'.

Whilst menacing incidents occurred in some of the outlying provinces, which Solomon evidently did not consider necessary to counter by force of arms, he devoted himself to the internal development of the kingdom and, above all, to a comprehensive scheme of building activity intended primarily to add lustre and distinction to the royal house. The most detailed accounts of Solomon's activities, which derive from the 'Book of the Acts of Solomon', deal with the royal buildings. Above all, Solomon extended the royal city of Jerusalem. David had been very largely satisfied with the old and narrow Jebusite Jerusalem on the so-called south-eastern hill above the spring of Gihon[1], and had merely had a new royal palace built in place of the Jebusite palace or may have only had the latter extended (2 Sam. v, 11). Solomon continued to 'repair the breaches' of the 'city of David his father'. But the old 'city of David' was no longer equal to his needs. Therefore, soon after his accession[2] he began to extend Jerusalem by adding an entirely new piece of land for his extensive palace buildings. The old Jerusalem, which was limited on the eastern side by the deep incision of the valley of Kidron and on the west by the shallower valley we call the 'city valley', could only expand on the northern side where the hill on which the old city was sited ascended greater heights. Therefore, Solomon erected his buildings north of the city of David, thereby giving Jerusalem extraordinary length from north to south compared with the very narrow breadth from east to west[3] caused by the two valleys already mentioned. The buildings of Solomon's royal palace, which were enclosed by a wall of their own, towered above the old Jebusite city and took up at least as much space. Solomon worked on this great scheme for a long time[4]. The royal temple was also built within this complex and it has become the most famous of Solomon's buildings: the Temple

[1] On the natural setting and architectural history of Jerusalem cf. H. Guthe, *Bibelatlas* ([2] 1926), No. 2a, I, and No. 3, II, and also K. Galling, ZDPV, 54 (1931), pp. 85 ff., Pl. 6, and J. Simons, *Jerusalem in the Old Testament* (1952), especially pp. 60 ff.

[2] According to 1 Kings vi, 1, 37, 'Yahweh's Temple', which formed part of the whole complex of the new buildings in Jerusalem, was begun in the fourth year of Solomon's reign.

[3] Contrary to earlier assumptions, the settlement of the so-called west hill on the farther side of the 'city valley' did not take place until very much later and not at all during the age of David and Solomon (cf. Galling, *loc. cit.*). No archaeological remains of pre-Hellenistic times have been found so far on this west hill (a point that is conceded by Simons, *loc. cit.* pp. 251 f., in spite of the fact that on the whole his views are contrary to mine).

[4] There is a short report on the palace buildings as a whole in 1 Kings vii, 1-12. According to verse 1 they took altogether thirteen years. According to 1 Kings vi, 37-38, the sanctuary of the Temple which formed part of the whole complex, was begun in the fourth year and finished in the eleventh year of Solomon's reign.

of Solomon. The deuteronomist was already particularly interested in this building and therefore extracted from the 'Book of the Acts of Solomon' all the facts concerning the building of the Temple and the compiling of the inventory (1 Kings vi, 1-38; vii, 13-51). The Temple was erected on the site which is now occupied by the Islamite shrine called the 'rock Cathedral' (ḳubbet eṣ-ṣakhra); and the 'Holy of Holies', the Adyton of this temple, towered above the highest elevation of the whole palace site, and the 'sacred rock' in the middle of the Dome of the Rock is still clearly visible today[1]. This rock had presumably been a sacred spot from time immemorial, the ancient shrine on the heights of pre-Israelite Jerusalem. Solomon had so designed the whole lay-out of the palace grounds that the royal sanctuary of the Temple should stand on this ancient holy site. In any case, he could not have desecrated a traditional place of worship by covering it with palace buildings but could only develop it as a holy place within the whole design. The building itself followed the local, that is, the Canaanite traditions; a temple is an urban sanctuary and the Israelite tribes adopted their urban culture from the Canaanites who had preceded them. Furthermore, Solomon used Phoenician craftsmen for his buildings (1 Kings v, 32 [English Bible, v, 18]; vii, 13 ff.). It is also possible that the plan of the Temple in the Syrian-Palestinian style, as a long building with a raised Adyton at the rear end and an entrance hall, which was moulded by Mesopotamian influence in the second millennium, had incorporated various Egyptian elements as well, in keeping with the generally hybrid nature of Syrian-Palestinian culture[2]. As is implied by the old votive utterance in 1 Kings viii, 12, 13, the Temple was conceived as a House of God; in particular, the darkened Adyton was regarded as the place of the presence of God who 'said that he would dwell in the thick darkness' (1 Kings viii, 12). Solomon moved into this Adyton the ancient tribal relic of the Ark which David had brought to Jerusalem as a throne for the invisible divine presence and set it up in place of the image or symbol of God which normally stood in the Adyton in the local type of temple. Thus the royal sanctuary within the complex of palace buildings,

[1] Cf. H. Schmidt, *Der heilige Fels in Jerusalem* (1933).

[2] Cf. K. Möhlenbrink, *Der Tempel Salomos* (BWANT, IV, 7 [1932]), who emphasises the connections with the Assyrian method of building temples, and C. Watzinger, *Denkmäler Palästinas*, I (1933), pp. 88 ff., who rightly lays stress on the connections with pre-Israelite Syria-Palestine, and, above all, A. Alt, *Verbreitung und Herkunft des syrischen Tempeltypus* (PJB, 35 [1939], pp. 83-99, especially pp. 96 f.)=*Kleine Schriften zur Geschichte des Volkes Israel*, II (1953), pp. 100-115.

served by priests who were royal officials, became at the same time the central shrine of the Israelite tribes.

In addition, Solomon built in other cities, above all in formerly Canaanite cities which David had incorporated in the States of Judah and Israel and in which, as legal successor of the former city rulers, the king was the landowner. According to 1 Kings ix, 19, Solomon built cities for his chariots and teams of horses, that is to say, he had special grounds laid out for this purpose in existing cities. The American excavations in Megiddo (the modern tell-el-mule-sellim) have thrown remarkable light on this activity, since they have revealed the remains of a great complex of stables for which Solomon was no doubt responsible[1]. To judge from this evidence Solomon built a great complex of stables around three sides of an inner courtyard which was capable of accommodating several hundred horses in the north-eastern section of the ancient and important Canaanite city of Megiddo on the south-western border of the plain of Jezreel, which gradually declined at the end of the Late Bronze Age and was finally incorporated in the State of Israel under David, losing its political freedom[2]. Rows of stone pillars on both sides of a rough-cast central corridor separated the horse-boxes from one another. Other similar but less well-preserved and therefore less obvious buildings in various cities in Palestine may also have been stables erected by Solomon. In 1 Kings ix, 19, no names are given to the 'cities for his chariots and cities for his horsemen'; but in verse 16b and 17 there is a list of the cities which Solomon 'built', though the purpose of the building is not mentioned. Megiddo is included among these cities. It would seem, therefore, that at any rate some of the other cities mentioned may have been 'cities for his chariots and cities for his horsemen'[3]. It is clear that Solomon maintained a very considerable force of chariots which were distributed among various garrisons, following the example of the ancient Oriental monarchs of his time. David had already maintained a standing army in his contingents of mercenaries, in addition to the tribal militias. But they still fought

[1] Cf. P. L. O. Guy, *New Light from Armageddon* (Oriental Institute Communications, 9 [1931]), and C. Watzinger, *loc. cit.* pp. 87 f., and especially paragraphs 80, 81.

[2] This discovery in Megiddo represents the hitherto most important surviving remains of Solomon's copious building activities in the land.

[3] The city of Gezer is also mentioned in this context; and in fact the famous row of massebahs 'of Gezer' (cf. Gressmann, AOB², Nos. 411, 412) is probably nothing but part of the row of pillars of a Solomonian stable building. According to 1 Kings x, 26, Solomon also had chariots and horses in Jerusalem itself, *i.e.* inside his great palace grounds, which one would assume to have been the case anyway.

on foot[1]. He had not known what to do with the teams of horses and chariots[2] captured from the Aramaeans; apart from a small reserve, he had made no use of this particularly valuable booty (2 Sam. viii, 4). Solomon, however, even surpassed the simplicity of the age of David. He waged no wars and never really used his chariots at all: they merely served to add to his royal lustre[3]. Apart from the 'cities of chariots and horses', 1 Kings ix, 19, also refers to 'cities of store' built by Solomon; this must mean that he had royal warehouses built in existing cities which were probably used to store the tribute collected from the country. Solomon's building activities required an enormous labour force which the country had to raise at a time when all the basic operations still had to be done by hand. Solomon also greatly developed the institution of compulsory or statute labour. We have no details as to how the groups of forced labourers were selected or how long they were required to serve. Organised compulsory labour had already existed under David. In the latter part of his reign (2 Sam. xx, 23-26) the list of his senior officials included a 'chief of compulsory labour' (verse 24a), though it had not done so in his early period (cf. 2 Sam. viii, 16-18). David will also have employed compulsory labour on his royal buildings. The records do not contain much about David's building activities (2 Sam. v, 11) and they will, in fact, have been on a modest scale and possibly confined to Jerusalem. This state of affairs was changed under Solomon. During his reign Adoniram was still 'over the tribute' as he had been in David's reign (1 Kings iv, 6b) but his work was certainly far more extensive. The tradition of Solomon includes two contradictory statements about the use of compulsory labour. According to 1 Kings v, 27 (English Bible, v, 13), the force was raised 'out of all Israel', whereas in 1 Kings ix, 15a and 20-22, it is emphasised that only the non-Israelite population of the old Canaanite city-states, which were now incorporated in Judah and Israel, were called on to supply compulsory labour. Of these city-states, which the Israelite tribes had been unable to

[1] At this time even the king did not yet go into battle in a chariot (cf., on the other hand, for a later period, 1 Kings xxii, 34, 35, 38) but rode, when he did not go on foot, on a donkey or a mule; it is true that we do not hear that David did this, but it is reported of Absalom who was made king (2 Sam. xviii, 9).

[2] It is surprising that the Aramaean king Hadadezer of Zobah went into battle in a chariot; he must have had under his command, probably in Syria and perhaps in the northern land east of the Jordan too, old city-states which had to provide him with contingents of chariots.

[3] When they were preparing to succeed to the throne, David's elder sons had already provided themselves with chariots in the 'modern' fashion (2 Sam. xv, 1; 1 Kings i, 5); but they too had only used the chariots as tokens of royal dignity. They did not intend to go into battle with them (cf. the last note but one).

conquer in the period before the formation of the State, it is stated explicitly in Judges i, 27 ff., that later on, 'when Israel had become strong', *i.e.* when, with the advent of the monarchy, she had proceeded to develop her political power, they were forced to perform statute labour ('become tributaries') (verses 28, 30, 33-35). Probably the reference in 1 Kings ix, 15a and 20-22, is substantially correct and the statement in 1 Kings v, 27 (English Bible, v, 13), all too summary and therefore inaccurate. Whilst perhaps the free men of the Israelite tribes were legally liable for army service, they were not liable for compulsory labour and it would have been a monstrous infringement of their legal rights on the king's part to have compelled them to do compulsory labour. In the Canaanite cities, on the other hand, the king had at his disposal a slave population which had already had to perform compulsory labour for the city rulers and now had to do it for the king in Jerusalem[1].

Solomon also needed an enormous amount of material for his buildings. The stone he required could be quarried in the mountains. But the lack of forest made it necessary to import the necessary timber. From earliest times one of the main sources of timber in the ancient Orient had been Lebanon on the northern borders of Palestine. Solomon therefore concluded a treaty with King Hiram of Tyre (1 Kings v, 15-26 [English Bible, v, 1-12]), who had already sought the favour of the mighty David and had already supplied him with timber for his buildings. Hiram contracted to supply timber and to enlist expert craftsmen, of whom there was a shortage in Solomon's predominantly rural State. In return, Solomon agreed to maintain a regular supply of wheat and olive oil to the commercial State of Tyre, which had little agricultural land[2]. To keep up these quite considerable supplies Solomon had to commandeer the produce of his subjects, especially of the agricultural Israelite tribes.

Solomon's buildings in Jerusalem were the setting for a brilliant and expensive royal household; for this, too, the country had to foot the bill. In 1 Kings v, 2-3 (English Bible, iv, 22-23), there is a precise account of the court's daily requirements of grain and meat.

[1] The Israelite tribes' complaint about his reign after the death of Solomon (1 Kings xii, 4) can therefore hardly refer to compulsory labour, but to such things as taxes, etc.

[2] The brief account in 1 Kings ix, 10-13, according to which Hiram eventually had twenty cities in western Galilee ceded to him for his deliveries to Solomon, may not belong to this context since its explicit intention is an aetiological explanation of the name of the city Kabul (the modern kābūl), and it is merely based on the assumption that the district of Kabul, which was really situated in Israelite Galilee, belonged to the territory of Tyre. This could have been related subsequently and secondarily to Solomon's well-known connections with Hiram of Tyre; but cf. below, p. 212, note 2.

If one bears in mind that the consumption of meat among the primitive rural population was always limited to special events and festive occasions, it is easy to realise that life at Solomon's court, with its daily consumption of great quantities of cattle, was far removed from the everyday life of the ordinary people. To guarantee the regular arrival of supplies from the country Solomon introduced a comprehensive system of taxation. He divided the whole State of Israel[1] into districts each of which had to be responsible for supplying the royal court for one month of the year (1 Kings iv, 7). At the head of each district there was an 'overseer' (נִצָּב) who no doubt had to divide responsibility for maintaining supplies among the various landowners and to see that deliveries were made on time, collected in the 'cities of store' mentioned above, and delivered to Jerusalem in the appointed month. The head of the whole organisation was a supreme official who was called 'chief of the overseers' (עַל־הַנִּצָּבִים), whose office had not existed under David and who first appears among the leading officials in Solomon's reign (1 Kings iv, 5a). Presumably David had already been compelled to impose the duty of supplying the court with certain provisions on the State of Judah and Israel, thereby interfering with the freedom of the Israelite tribes to dispose of the produce of their agriculture and cattle-breeding in their own way; under Solomon, however, the system of payment of duty in kind was enormously extended and far more highly organised. The classification of the districts which was introduced, the details of which are given in 1 Kings iv, 8-19, provides a clear picture of the total extent and internal organisation of the State of Israel in general[2], particularly as it shows very clearly the juxtaposition and the administrative division of tribal areas and city territories within the one political system based on historically evolved groupings and boundaries. A whole series of districts was formed by Israelite tribal territories, including the districts of 'Benjamin' (verse 18),

[1] It is remarkable that we have no information about any corresponding division of the State of Judah into districts by Solomon. It is evident that the division of the State of Judah into twelve districts, on which the lists of places in Joshua xv, 18, 19, is based, derives from a considerably later period (cf. A. Alt, *Judas Gaue unter Josia* [PJB, 21 (1925), pp. 100-117]=*Kleine Schriften zur Geschichte des Volkes Israel*, II [1953], pp. 276-288) and even the basis of it is clearly post-Solomonic (cf. M. Noth, *Das Buch Josua* [[2] 1953], p. 14). It is therefore an open question whether Solomon did not impose taxation on Judah at all, possibly because this State was too small and poor, or whether it is merely an accident that there is no reference in the traditional records to a similar measure in Judah, which was later made the basis of a new division into districts in Judah.

[2] Cf. A. Alt, *Israels Gaue unter Salomo* (BWAT, 13 [1913], pp. 1 ff.)=*Kleine Schriften zur Geschichte des Volkes Israel*, II (1953), pp. 76-89.

'mount Ephraim' (verse 8) (with the tribal territories of Ephraim and Manasseh) and also the Galilean districts of Issachar (verse 17), Naphtali (verse 15) and Asher (verse 16). Issachar presumably included the territory of Zebulūn, whilst the territory of Dan certainly formed part of 'Naphtali'. Finally, in the land east of the Jordan, the districts of Mehanaim (verse 14) with the Ephraimite-Manassite colonial territory in the land of Gilead south and north of the Jabbok and 'Gad' (verse 19)[1] with the area to the south; the other five districts included city-state territories, the three districts referred to in verses 9, 10 and 11 covering the city-states in the coastal plain as far north as the Carmel, the district mentioned in verse 12 covering the city-states in the plain of Jezreel and in the adjoining plain of Beth-Sean and, finally, the district of 'Ramoth-Gilead' in verse 13, the city-states on the north-eastern border of the 'ajlūn' (cf. above, p. 191)[2]. Solomon's subdivision of the districts and his organisation of the system of tribute were maintained after his death in the State of Israel[3]. Presumably Solomon also extended the Crown lands and controlled its administration. At any rate we find among his leading officials a 'chief of the household' (1 Kings iv, 6a) who had not existed under David and who no doubt controlled all the royal properties, including not only the palace and the buildings pertaining thereto in Jerusalem but also all kinds of landed property in the country. This consisted of land inherited by the royal family and all manner of estates which devolved on the king, such as the property of criminals condemned to death[4]. It was therefore distributed through the whole country and appears to have consisted mainly of vineyards and orchards from which the royal household met its great requirements of wine and oil, which, according to 1 Kings v, 2-3 (English Bible, iv, 22-23), were not covered by the tribute of the country population[5]. To judge from all this, Solomon devoted himself most earnestly to

[1] In the text the name 'Gad' was later altered in error to 'Gilead'.

[2] It is noteworthy that the plain of Akko was not included in this division into districts. Under David it appears still to have belonged to the State of Israel (cf. above, p. 191). Had a loss of territory taken place here too under Solomon, possibly by cession to Hiram of Tyre, of which the aetiological narrative contained in 1 Kings ix, 10-13 (cf. above, p. 210, note 2), contains a no longer completely accurate memory?

[3] This is shown by the Samaritan ostraka from the period probably of Jeroboam II in the 8th century. Cf. M. Noth, PJB, 28 (1932), pp. 58 f.

[4] We have an example of this from a later period in 1 Kings xxi. The king acquires possession of the vineyard near the city of Jezreel which he covets by having the owner falsely condemned to death.

[5] This is also shown by the Samaritan ostraka. On the whole question cf. M. Noth, *Das Krongut der israelitischen Könige und seine Verwaltung* (ZDPV, 50 [1927], pp. 211-244).

the development of the royal properties and prestige, thereby striving to emulate the great kings of the ancient Orient in Egypt and the Land of the Two Rivers, as the heir of David's Empire.[1] All this occasioned great expenditure which it was difficult to raise in the territory of his own State, since it was not greatly blessed with a wealth of natural resources. Hence, Solomon tried to add to his wealth by means of a variety of profit-making undertakings, and in fact he managed to amass great riches in Jerusalem. The records refer admiringly to Solomon's immense wealth (1 Kings x, 14-22) and posterity spoke of his proverbial wealth and 'glory' (Matt. vi, 29; Luke xii, 27). The fact that he had access to the gulf of el-'aḳaba through the province of Edom, and hence to the Red Sea, caused him to undertake profitable voyages through the Red Sea with a fleet which he built himself (1 Kings ix, 26-28; x, 11, 12). These voyages were evidently a royal monopoly. Hiram of Tyre put experienced naval craftsmen and mariners at his disposal and received in return a share in the profits of these trading enterprises; having few harbours in their country, the Israelites were no seamen. These royal voyages extended as far as the land of Ophir from which gold[2], valuable timber and all kinds of exotic rarities and valuables were brought home (cf. also 1 Kings x, 11-22). The exact position of Ophir is uncertain and it is not even known for sure whether it was on the Arabian or, what is more likely, the African side of the Red Sea. Nor is it known whether Ophir was the source of the treasures which the fleet brought home or merely an emporium. We do not know what Solomon offered in exchange. Presumably he engaged in successful trading as a middleman. As the home port for his mercantile navy, Solomon built the city of Ezeon-Geber on the northern shores of the gulf of el-'aḳaba. Its remains have been re-discovered in the modern tell el-khlēfi west of el-'aḳaba[3]; and the excavations[4] undertaken on the site have

[1] A few details show that the example of the ancient oriental kingdoms, especially of the neighbouring Egyptian kingdom, was already influential in the development of the State under David. In PJB, 31 (1935], pp. 29-75, K. Elliger has shown very clearly that 'David's thirty heroes' correspond, as a royal escort, to an Egyptian institution known from the period of Ramessides; and J. Begrich, ZAW, N.F. 17 (1940–1941), pp. 1-19, has shown that it is very probable that Egyptian models were followed for the supreme offices of מַזְכִּיר and סוֹפֵר (2 Sam. viii, 16 f.; xx, 24 f.; 1 Kings iv, 3).

[2] 'Ophir gold' is mentioned in the inscription cut on a potsherd from the end of the period of the Israelite kings, which was found on the tell kasile north of jafa (cf. B. Maisler, IEJ, I [1951], pp. 209 f., Fig. 13 f., Pl. 38A). Unfortunately this brief inscription does not throw any more definite light on the term 'Ophir gold'.

[3] Cf. Fr. Frank, ZDPV, 57 (1934), p. 244.

[4] Cf. the reports by N. Glück in BASOR, 71 (1938), pp. 3-17; 75 (1939), pp. 8-22; 79 (1940), pp. 2-18.

shown that Solomon's port was based on very careful plans and had been preceded at the most by a quite meagre fishing settlement of which all traces have vanished. At the same time, they have made it clear that the city of Ezeon-Geber also served another purpose to which there is no reference in the literary records of Solomon's activities. Extensive installations were used for smelting copper and iron, by making use of the wind from the gulf of el-ʿaḳaba. Copper and iron were obtained from the mines on the borders of the wādi el-ʿaraba and manufactured in Ezeon-Geber into all kinds of hardware products, great quantities of which have been found in the tell el-khlēfi. As Ezeon-Geber was a royal establishment, presumably the mining and manufacture of metal in the province of Edom was also a royal monopoly which doubtless brought Solomon abundant profits. Finally we learn from 1 Kings x, 28-29, that Solomon engaged in a brisk and no doubt lucrative trade in chariots and horses with which 'the King's merchants' (סֹחֲרֵי הַמֶּלֶךְ), *i.e.* Solomon's agents, were occupied. The chariots and horses came from Egypt, the horses also from Cilicia[1] and they were sold to 'the kings of the Hittites' and 'the kings of Aram', meaning, probably, the kings of the small States in central and northern Syria.

Solomon therefore maintained extensive contacts and connections in the ancient oriental world and his prestige was no doubt very great. He had inherited a mighty Empire from his father, and the lustre of his monarchy will have brought him admiration and esteem from far and wide. It was entirely in keeping with his position that he had numerous foreign women in his harem. In 1 Kings xi, 1 ff., the deuteronomist criticised him for this and made out that these women induced him to forsake his god and worship idols. This latter notion is specifically deuteronomistic, but it is no doubt a fact that he had a large and motley harem. It was thought especially noteworthy that his women included an Egyptian princess (1 Kings iii, 1; ix, 16[2]); she will have been a daughter from the harem of one of the unimportant Pharaohs of the 21st Egyptian Dynasty. A particularly close relationship with Egypt

[1] In 1 Kings x, 28, the name Kue occurs twice—now in a distorted form in the text—which we know from Assyrian sources as the name of a Cilician land or State.

[2] The statement inserted between 1 Kings ix, 15 and 17, in 1 Kings ix, 16, that the Pharaoh conquered the city of Gezer as a Canaanite city and had given it to his daughter as a dowry is strange and inexplicable. How could Gezer (the modern tell deschezer near abu schusche) have maintained itself as an independent Canaanite city on the border of David's great State? And how can the Palestine campaign of a Pharaoh of the 21st Dynasty be explained? Cf., however, A. Alt, *Israel und Ägypten* (BWAT, 6 [1909]), pp. 20 ff.

need have been neither the precondition nor the result of her presence in Solomon's harem. It is understandable that the lustre of the monarchy in Solomon's State was regarded with admiration and possibly also with pride, but it is clear that the people groaned under the burdens which it imposed and, above all, its entirely secular and political set-up made an unfavourable impression on the Israelite tribes. The trend that had begun under David increased rapidly and intensely under Solomon and it is not surprising that the basic rejection of the monarchy was based henceforth on the conception created by the historical actuality of Solomon's reign[1]. In fact Solomon represented the decadent successor who has entered upon a great inheritance and administers it with an outward show of brilliance but who in reality allows it to fall into decay because he fails to acquire for himself through his own skill and efficiency what he has inherited from his fathers.

17. *Israel's Intellectual and Cultural Life under David and Solomon*

The historical events which took place in the reigns of David and Solomon occasioned extraordinary changes in the Israelites' conditions of life. A strong monarchy had relieved them of concern for self-preservation in their historical world and they enjoyed the advantages of living in a State that was not merely powerful but also well governed. We are told almost nothing of the administrative measures of David's reign, and we are merely told a few things connected with his buildings and the royal household in Solomon's reign. But there can hardly be any doubt but that David was responsible for some fundamental changes. Evidence for this is supplied by the lists of his leading senior officials (2 Sam. viii, 16-18; xx, 23-26) each of whom had to administer a particular department and was no doubt assisted by a staff of lower officials. It is clear that this organisation gradually became more elaborate. From the list contained in 2 Sam. viii, 16-18, which it is impossible to date precisely, to the list in 2 Sam. xx, 23-26, which belongs at any rate to David's later period, and to the Solomonian list in 1 Kings iv, 2-6, there is apparent a constant increase in the number of principal officials. Evidently these officers were responsible for the whole territory of David's and Solomon's kingdoms, or at any

[1] Cf., above all, the formulation of the 'royal law' in 1 Sam. viii, 11-18, on the part of the deuteronomist.

rate for the State of Judah and Israel, which were therefore united not only by the person of the king but also by these high officials[1]. The Israelite army was probably raised without regard to the distribution of the tribes among the two States of Judah and Israel. In these two States the tribes were now combined with numerous Canaanite city-states and this also brought about a change in their position. It is true that, as is shown by the division of the State of Israel into districts under Solomon, the historically evolved frontiers between tribal territories were taken into account in the administrative subdivision of the two States; but as a result of being united in the compact States of Judah and Israel, tribes and cities inevitably came into closer touch with one another and this living together with the Canaanites was bound to affect the Israelites' way of life. Even though the feeling that the Canaanites were foreigners (cf. above, pp. 142 f.) continued to prevail among them, urban ways presumably began to exert a stronger influence on them. A large and permanent political structure demands an urban foundation, not merely one urban centre—David had already created that in the royal city of Jerusalem—but urban centres throughout the country, which are necessary for efficient administration and where the specialisation of life in industry and commerce can take place which is involved in living together in a State. Hence, no doubt, urban phenomena such as a money economy[2] and the consequent development of the distinction between rich and poor[3] found their way into the life of the Israelite tribes. It is impossible to trace this process in any detail in the records that have come down to us. It was certainly not a sudden change but a process which developed from the age of David and Solomon onwards. The fact, however, that the distinctively urban way of life was still regarded as not authentically Israelite is shown by the decree according to which dwelling-houses in walled cities —one assumes that Israelites lived in such houses—were not to be subject to the jubilee regulations which applied to landed property in the rural areas.

The closer association of Israelites and Canaanites could easily have had serious consequences in the religious sphere. If, ever

[1] Here, too, the reference to Egypt is closely connected with the union of Upper and Lower Egypt under *one* monarchy with its single civil service.

[2] To begin with, weighed-off metal was used as money; as far as we know, stamped coins with an officially guaranteed weight were not introduced in the ancient Orient until the establishment of the Lydian State and the Persian Empire.

[3] The statements by later prophets (above all, Amos, Isaiah and Micah) show these matters in their full development.

since the tribes had settled in Palestine, the Israelite system of worship had lived intensely on the indigenous traditions, it is possible that the Canaanite religion may now have influenced the Israelite tribes all the more. And when, later on, the prophets refer to such peculiarly Canaanite fertility rites as so-called religious prostitution, or the sacrifice of children as having established themselves here and there in the worship of Yahweh, and the worship of Yahweh having become assimilated to the Canaanite worship of Baal[1], the incorporation of the Canaanite cities in the States of Judah and Israel, and the consequent blurring of the differences between the Israelite and Canaanite way of life, will have contributed to this result.

On the other hand, however, the formation of the State and the consequent strengthening of the roots which Israel struck in the ancient cultural traditions of the land, and the opening up of contacts with the wider world of the ancient Orient, aroused new intellectual forces in Israel. This led to the beginnings of universal education. Probably the tradition of the 'wisdom of Solomon' (1 Kings v, 9-14 [English Bible, iv, 29-34][2]) must be seen in this context. From the earliest times in the ancient Orient the 'wisdom' literature had promoted the transmission of a body of knowledge and experience within a 'cultured' stratum represented, above all, by the 'learned' scribes in the great cultures of the ancient Orient. Solomon's 'wisdom' is explicitly related to the great 'wisdom' tradition of the ancient Orient (1 Kings v, 10, 11 =iv, 30, 31 in the A.V.). The fact that he is said to have spoken of trees and animals, birds, reptiles and fishes, suggests that his 'wisdom' was connected with the lists of natural phenomena which were well known from Egypt and the Land of the Two Rivers and in which an attempt was made to be as all-inclusive as possible. The only difference is that Solomon is stated specifically to have formulated this knowledge in 'proverbs' and 'songs'. What is said with particular reference to Solomon in 1 Kings v (English Bible, chap. iv) may no doubt be applied more generally to his whole age; and it may even be that the later tradition recapitulated in the person of the king something which was true of the Israel of the age of Solomon in general, in which an educated class developed at the royal court and among the royal officials who needed not only for their work of internal administration, but also for the tasks which resulted from the world-wide importance of the Empire of David and

[1] Cf., above all, Hosea and the young Jeremiah.
[2] Cf. A. Alt, *Die Weisheit Salomos* (ThLZ, 76 [1951], cols. 139-144).

Solomon, a culture which then spread among the broader masses of the population. At any rate, new forces were awakened in the intellectual sphere in David's and, above all, in Solomon's time. This is supremely true in the field of literature. Difficult though it is to compile a real history of Israelite literature, since most of the writings incorporated in the Old Testament are anonymous and impossible to date precisely, and on the whole not extant in their original form, it is, nevertheless, possible to make one or two fairly certain statements in the present context. Writings which it is possible to describe as literature, in the sense of having been the deliberate and considered work of a professional writer, have come down to us only from the age of David and Solomon. They are historical works, describing the events of the time. In the earlier period historical memories had been recorded in the form of popular and primarily oral legends. The creative stage of the legend appears to have come to an end when the State was formed. It belonged to the phase when the clans and tribes were still free and independent. Anyway, the legendary material preserved in the Old Testament, as it is found above all in the narratives of the Pentateuch and the occupation of the land in the Book of Joshua and in the stories contained in 'Judges', are older than the formation of the State[1]; and there followed the protracted and complicated process of recording this material in writing. In the age of David and Solomon the historical chronicle took its place beside and replaced the popular legends. The great historical events of this period, in which the Israelites had an active share, and such important historical figures as David himself, who had emerged from Israel, provided sufficient incentive for recording the events of the time. Added to these incentives, however—and this is the novel and surprising thing—there was the ability to perceive the fundamental elements and underlying relationships within the events and to express them objectively and with literary skill. The result is by no means simply a mere register of historical events. Such reports were made, it is true,—and they were also an innovation at the time—in the form of official royal annals which were no doubt kept by the 'scribe' who was a leading royal official (cf. 2 Sam. viii, 17b; xx, 25a). The list of David's conflicts with neighbouring peoples in 2 Sam. viii, 1-14, was probably based on an extract from the royal annals; and under Solomon, who had two leading 'scribes' (1 Kings iv, 3a), the royal annals were probably kept with still greater thoroughness and provided the

[1] Cf. M. Noth, *Überlieferungsgeschichte des Pentateuch* (1948), pp. 47 f.

material for the 'Book of the Acts of Solomon' (1 Kings xi, 41). These historical works were, however, more than mere enumerations of individual events. Based though they were on solid first-hand knowledge, they were intended to expound the fundamental development and setting of a deliberately chosen segment of history.

The main examples of this new type of historical writing are the account of the rise of David in 1 Sam. xvi, 14–2 Sam. v, 10, and the treatment of the question of David's succession to the throne in 2 Sam. vii, 20, and 1 Kings i, 2, the former deriving in all probability from the age of David itself and the latter fairly certainly written before the death of Solomon. The anonymous writers of the two works must have been in fairly close touch with the court of David and Solomon, as is clear, in particular, from the intimate knowledge of events at court which is revealed in the story of the succession to the throne. All the same, these works were obviously not commissioned officially. It is true that the description of David's rise to power is unlimited in its admiration for the great king's successful progress, but the other narrative clearly shows the shadows in David's portrait, reporting as it does on David's adultery with Bath-Sheba, the cruel injustice towards his follower Uriah of which he was guilty, his weakness towards Absalom and his lack of resolution in the matter of the succession to the throne. The great personalities and events of the period inspired the minds of brilliant men of literary talent and led them to describe important phases of history. These writers did not, however, merely want to describe the course of events: they discerned in the happenings of the time the actions of their God. They speak of this divine activity in quite a new way, unlike the old popular narratives. They no longer see God intervening directly in the course of events with isolated mighty actions. In the foreground they see men acting with their human desires, their wisdom and successes, their follies and wickedness; and the events of their age seemed to them to be completely determined by human actions and their varied motives. Yet God still remained the Lord of history inasmuch as—often almost invisibly—He determined human actions and by means of this human activity led the course of history to the goal which He intended. The story of David's rise to power opens in 1 Sam. xvi, 14, with the remark that 'the spirit of the Lord departed from Saul', and in 1 Sam. xvi, 18, David is introduced straight away with the comment that 'the Lord was with him'. This is followed by the description of David's successful rise to power, with the implication that David himself was solely responsible for his success. At the end, however, there is the sentence in 2 Sam. v, 10, which illuminates all the previous story: 'And David went on, and grew great and the Lord God of hosts was with him'. The same thought is expressed with even greater restraint in the story of his succession to the throne. When Absalom revolted, the whole future depended on David gaining time to gather his forces and, in fact, after his entry into Jerusalem, Absalom decided, against the advice of the shrewd Ahithophel, to wait and call up the whole militia. In 2 Sam. xvii, 14b, the writer comments: 'The Lord had appointed to defeat the good counsel of Ahithophel, to the intent that the Lord might bring evil upon Absalom'. The two historical works we have mentioned represent a completely new departure[1], and they are at the same time masterpieces of their kind. They are also completely unique in the whole world of the ancient Orient; for though the Orient has bequeathed to us a wealth of sporadic historical information, mainly in the form of royal annals or other annalistic compilations, it has left no single historical work deserving the name. The fact that the god of Israel had met and still met his people primarily in historical events made Israel attentive to the interrelatedness of historical events, because in the final analysis they were the product of divine activity. And so in the age of David and Solomon historical expositions of interrelated events were produced long before there was any historical writing in Greece or anywhere else in the known world.

Other literary works from the Old Testament are less easily ascribed to the age of David and Solomon. All the same, it is probable that the oldest large-scale literary recapitulation and formulation of the extensive and originally oral material of the Pentateuch tradition, that work of the so-called Yahwist, may be attributed to this period. Whilst this work is traditional, and establishes the traditional narrative form of the basic religious themes of Israel's prehistory, it is not merely a masterpiece of the art of literary narration but also a theological work, which sets the divine influence on Israel's life within the wide framework of the whole of human history. The introduction at the beginning of primeval history, constructed from all kinds of traditional materials

[1] This may be compared with the brief account of Abimelech in Judges ix which summarises the sequence of events as follows in verses 56, 57: 'Thus God rendered the wickedness of Abimelech, which he did unto his father, in slaying his seventy brethren; And all the evil of the men of Shechem did God render upon their heads; and upon them came the curse of Jotham the son of Jerubbaal'. It is not certain, however, that Judges ix was written before the period of David.

which the Yahwist added to the older traditions, opens up a world-wide vista, and with its very grave and gloomy statements about the nature of man in this world it forms the background for an understanding of the history of Israel by means of which Yahweh desires to bestow his blessing on humanity (cf. especially Gen. xii, 1-3). This work therefore also represents a great intellectual achievement and, if the above dating proved to be correct, would be evidence of the spiritual excitement and widening horizons of the age of David and Solomon.

It may be taken for granted that the literary recording of earlier popular stories and, in particular, of series of stories, began in this period and hence the collation of oral traditions which had hitherto been widely scattered. In the nature of things, it is possible to date this process only in the rarest cases. All the same, it is possible to assign the combination of old local aetiological narratives into a description of the occupation of the land, as seen from an all-Israel point of view, which is contained in the old material of Jos. i-xii with a high degree of probability, not, admittedly, to the immediate age of David and Solomon but to the period directly following the death of Solomon[1]. The incentives which the period of David and Solomon provided to create literary work and, above all, to write historical narratives and to collect, edit and record traditional material naturally continued to operate beyond the period itself.

In all this a rationalising tendency was at work, aimed at the arrangement, collation and interpretation of the traditions which had come down from earlier ages. Whereas reference had been made in confessions of faith to the basic acts of salvation of the God of Israel, and Israel's historical experiences of God had been passed on from one generation to another in oral legends, these traditions were now recorded and interpreted theologically. Not without good reason G. v. Rad has called the Solomonic period a period of 'typical Enlightenment' and has referred to a 'Solomonic-post-Solomonic humanism'[2].

These great descriptions of episodes from the history of David[3] have also a special significance in so far as they have established once and for all the fact that the monarchy represented an institution on the soil of Israel which had emerged in history long after the Israelite tribes had settled in Palestine and consolidated their position, and that after the episode of Saul David was the first to

[1] Cf. M. Noth, *Das Buch Josua* ([2] 1953), p. 13.

[2] G. v. Rad, *Der heilige Krieg im alten Israel* (1951), pp. 39, 49.

[3] They were probably combined at a very early date with the collected and recorded stories of Saul into the great complex of the story of Saul and David.

establish and bequeath to his son the monarchies over Judah and Israel which continued to exist in history. It was therefore difficult for the idea to emerge in Israel that the institution of the monarchy as such and the actual monarchies in Judah and Israel were elements of an unalterable and everlasting world order. If it is also borne in mind that the problematical nature of monarchy in general was felt among the Israelite tribes possibly from the very beginning and with ever-increasing force as time went on (cf. above, pp. 164 f.) it will be realised that the monarchy was bound to appear in a very different light than was the case in the rest of the ancient Orient and, above all, in the ancient oriental empires where monarchy was regarded as an essential element in an everlasting, divine order of things. In Israel the monarchy was bound always to be regarded as an institution that had evolved in the process of history, and it was precisely under the influence of the historical emergence of the monarchy that the form of historical writing arose in Israel to which there is no counterpart in the world of the ancient Orient. It was the result of Israel's unique historical consciousness which was based on the special nature of its experience of God. It is therefore wrong to apply without question to the monarchy in Israel the ancient oriental ideas of a sacred divine monarchy, with the attendant religious observances.

This is not to suggest that the monarchy was considered a purely secular institution in Israel[1]. Yahweh had 'been with David' (cf. above, p. 220), that is, he had led him invisibly on his path to power and thereby not merely approved of the establishment of David's Empire but actually brought it about, just as previously he had summoned the charismatic leaders before the foundation of the State and 'been with them' (Judges vi, 16) and led them to victory by 'delivering their enemies into their hand' (Judges iii, 28; iv, 14; xi, 32). The only way it was possible to understand the great events in David's period was by assuming that Yahweh had played an active part in them. Moreover, David's monarchy contained a divine promise for the future. At the opening of the old story of the succession to the throne there is recorded a word of the 'prophet' Nathan spoken to David (2 Sam. vii, 8-16) which, though it was later revised, was no doubt formulated in the main before the death of Solomon and must therefore be regarded as historically authentic. In the name of Yahweh Nathan promises David that his monarchy

[1] This occurred at best from the point of view of the fundamental rejection of the monarchy, as it is found in the deuteronomist, who saw this institution as containing something secular and 'heathen' (cf. 1 Sam. viii, 5).

will be permanent and his dynasty endure. In fact, the relationship between Yahweh and David's heirs is described as a relationship between father and son (verse 14). Though this recalls the ancient oriental conception of divine kingship, it is characteristic that it should appear in a fundamentally different form. Possibly as a deliberate reaction to this ancient oriental conception, the formula of adoption is used to describe the relationship; the God-King relationship has no foundation in Being and the King is not divine, but he is declared to be a son when he ascends the throne—by a manifestation of the divine will. Probably when the heirs of David acceded to power the formula of adoption was solemnly pronounced (Ps. ii, 7, and perhaps also Ps. cx, 3). This means that the relationship was confirmed, on a historical basis, at each new accession: it was not regarded as having any intrinsic and absolute existence. This shows that, whilst the Davidian monarchy made just as great claims in Israel as monarchy did elsewhere in the ancient Orient, it was different in quality. Moreover, the content of Nathan's promise implied that the God of Israel desired the kingship of David and would continue to desire it because it served his purposes —about which nothing is said in this connection. The declaration by a particular group of prophets later on, that David's monarchy would play a fundamental part in God's plan of salvation, linked up with this. This conception of the significance of God's activity in history was something quite different from the idea of the intrinsically divine nature of kingship which was current in the rest of the ancient Orient.

CHAPTER III

THE COEXISTENCE OF THE MINOR STATES OF JUDAH AND ISRAEL

18. *Judah and Israel after the Death of Solomon*

SOLOMON died during the year which ran from the autumn of 926 B.C. to the autumn of 925 B.C. His death is the earliest event in the history of Israel which it is possible to date precisely, with the possible error of merely a few years. The death of Solomon was made the beginning of the uninterrupted chronological sequence of the history of the kings of Judah and Israel which the author of the deuteronomistic history was able to draw from the official annals contained in the 'Diaries of the Kings of Judah' which he used as sources. These chronological dates supply, in the first place, the duration of the reigns of the kings in both kingdoms and, then, the synchronisation between Judah and Israel in accordance with which every change of sovereign in one of the two States was dated according to the length of the king's reign in the other State. The system of relative chronology of the reigns in Judah and Israel which was arrived at in this way was linked up with the chronology of the neo-Assyrian Empire which it is possible to fix absolutely by means of astronomical calculations[1]. According to 1 Kings xi, 42, when he died Solomon had reigned for forty years, and in 2 Sam. v, 4, 5, David's reign is also stated to have lasted forty years—reckoning from his appointment as king of Judah. In both cases it is probably merely a matter of a round figure[2]; if the figure is more or less correct—and there is no reason to question that—the reigns of David and Solomon occupied roughly the first three-quarters of the 10th century B.C.

[1] Cf. the brief reference to this in WAT, pp. 211 f., and in detail in J. Begrich, *Die Chronologie der Könige von Israel und Juda* (Beiträge zur historischen Theologie, 3), 1929. In what follows I give the dates according to Begrich (cf. the summary of his results, *loc. cit.* p. 155) without going into the details. The latest attempt at a chronology of the kings of Judah and Israel, which differs in some details from that of Begrich, is by W. F. Albright, BASOR, 100 (1945), pp. 16-22.

[2] The number 40 often occurs elsewhere in the old Testament as a round number for the space of time in which a generation of grown men usually dies out.

At his death Solomon left David's Empire outwardly in a splendid condition but it was already in a state of decline owing to threats from or, at any rate, the partial loss of some of the outlying provinces and, above all, the bad feeling which had arisen among the Israelite tribes about the ostentation of Solomon's reign. His successor was therefore faced with an unusually difficult task which only a man of special strength and wisdom could master. That Rehoboam, who was probably his eldest son, was intended to succeed him does not seem to have been in doubt. And in the city-state of Jerusalem and the State of Judah Rehoboam apparently succeeded his father on the throne without any trouble. In the Canaanite city-states succession by heredity had long been the normal custom, and the fact that an heir of David again became king in the 'city of David' did not raise any problems. But at that period and thereafter the State of Judah also held fast to the Judaean dynasty of David and apparently recognised Rehoboam as the new king without any further ado[1]. In the State of Israel, however, the situation was different. We learn something about the events which took place there from the narrative of the prophet Ahijah of Shilo (1 Kings xi, 9-39; xii, 1-32; xiv, 1-18) in which it is claimed that Yahweh fulfilled the promise made to Jeroboam by Ahijah and then rejected Jeroboam after he had turned traitor[2]. After this the tribes of the State of Israel gathered in Shechem, the recognised urban centre of the Israelite tribal territories and the oldest seat of the central federal shrine. Rehoboam repaired there and the assembled tribes wanted to 'make him king', that is, they wanted to discuss the appointment with him and to make their own conditions. Their elders—and we may assume that they had gathered together in Shechem—did not recognise the automatic succession by inheritance which had occurred in the emergency which followed the fall of Saul, owing to the influence of the mighty Abner (2 Sam. ii, 8-9), and again after the death of David on the strength of his own great authority; as had already been the case when Saul was made king (1 Sam. xi, 15) and, above all, when David was chosen to be king of Israel (2 Sam. v, 3), they wanted to bestow the crown themselves and to 'make a covenant' with the new king. They gave prior consideration to Rehoboam as Solomon's oldest son, but required an assurance that the burdens which had

[1] Perhaps this took place by means of a solemn act, possibly in the ancient Judaean royal city of Hebron.

[2] In this narrative, too, God is seen as acting in human decisions. It was a 'dispensation' (סִבָּה) of Yahweh, that Rehoboam acted unwisely, because Yahweh wanted to fulfil his promise to Jeroboam (1 Kings xii, 15); cf. above, pp. 220 f.

become so oppressive under Solomon, would be relieved. No doubt they had in mind, above all, the payment of tribute in kind—and the compulsory service which was obligatory in the former Canaanite cities. Contrary to the advice of his experienced counsellors, Rehobaom gave an abruptly negative reply, being evidently completely mistaken as to the true situation; and so the elders of the State of Israel parted from the dynasty of David. Once again the watchword that had been issued in a dangerous situation in David's reign (2 Sam. xx, 1) was revived: 'we have no part in David'. It is impossible to say for sure how far the Ephraimite Jeroboam played a part in the background in the negotiations with Rehoboam. He had once 'lifted his hand against Solomon', had then escaped to Egypt (cf. above, p. 205 f.) and had now swiftly returned on hearing the news of Solomon's death. Anyway, he was now made king of Israel by the elders in Shechem in place of the Davidite. He had been designated a future king of Israel by the prophet Ahijah in the name of Yahweh, probably at the time of his revolt against Solomon[1]; and, apart from his personal ambition, this was the main reason why the elders elected Jeroboam in Shechem.

This brought David's Empire to an end. Important outposts were now inevitably lost. The Aramaean province in the north-east, in which the new independent Aramaean province of Damascus had already come into being in Solomon's reign, was now impossible to hold. With its ancient cities it became the centre of the new kingdom, which was rapidly consolidated and became a formidable enemy of the State of Israel. The rule of the Davidites in Ammon also inevitably came to an end now, that is, assuming Solomon had been able to hold it until his death. Whilst there is no first-hand evidence of the existence of an independent king of Ammon until three-quarters of a century later[2], it is nevertheless clear that the Davidites, who lost their territorial hold on Ammon owing to its detachment from the State of Israel, were no longer in a position to remain kings of Ammon. The new king of Israel had no contact of any kind with the Ammonite Kingdom which David had once assumed for himself. Only the small State of Moab still continued to pay tribute to the State of Israel for another brief century; and despite the new monarchy that had emerged in Edom, the province of Edom remained at least to some extent in connection with the State of Judah, at any rate for a time. Judah and

[1] This was at any rate the opinion of the redactor who inserted the beginning of the story of Ahijah (1 Kings xi, 29-39) between 1 Kings xi, 26-28 and xi, 40.

[2] In the monolithic inscription of King Salmanassar III of Assyria, col. II, l. 95 (cf. Gressmann, AOT[2], pp. 340 f.; TGI, p. 46).

Israel now had to establish themselves as minor Powers within the political world of Syria and Palestine. The State of Judah, which was considerably the smaller of the two, had the advantage over Israel inasmuch as it had more to build on and it therefore found it easier to set up a stable order. So long as it existed at all it held unflinchingly to the succession of the dynasty of David. As the house of David was Judaean once the 'men of Judah had anointed David king over the house of Judah' (2 Sam. ii, 4a), and the monarchy had passed by David's will to his son Solomon, the State of Judah remained faithful to the house of David even after the death of Solomon; and this had established the principle of succession by inheritance so firmly that on subsequent occasions the throne passed on the whole without difficulty to the king's eldest son. Occasionally squabbles did occur for special reasons, but they took place within the dynasty of David itself. The State of Judah had also had its royal city from the very beginning. Jerusalem as the 'City of David' remained with the Davidites after the death of Solomon and they resided there until the State of Judah came to an end. It was, however, no longer the royal city of an Empire to which it had been raised by David and brilliantly developed by Solomon; as a merely Judaean city it was bound to languish. All the same, however, it did remain *the* royal city. In the sanctuary of the royal palace it contained the ancient sacred Ark[1], and it therefore was and continued to be the real religious centre of the Israelite tribes to which the tribes in the State of Israel as well as the tribes in Judah looked as their spiritual home.

The whole situation was very different in the State of Israel. The appointment of Jeroboam as king after the death of Solomon implied a return to the earlier mode of election that had been followed in the case of Saul and which originated in the ancient charismatic leadership of the period before the formation of the State. The man designated to be the future king had been proclaimed by a prophet in the name of Yahweh; when a man had thus been designated he could expect to ascend the throne at the next opportunity. In the State of Israel, therefore, the monarchy was a most unstable institution, and it is not surprising that a man appointed to be king had every reason to remove the reigning monarch and usurp the throne by violence, and that even an ambitious man who had not been designated could easily seize the

[1] We hear of the Ark for the last time on the occasion of its transfer to the Temple by Solomon (1 Kings viii, 1 ff.); it may have remained there until the destruction of Jerusalem in the year 587 B.C.

throne. On the other hand, however, in the struggle against the system of charismatic leadership the monarchy tended to become more firmly established even in Israel and this assisted the custom of succession by inheritance. The beginnings of this tendency had been apparent in the succession of Saul-Eshbaal and David-Solomon. This recurred so often that in the end real dynasties were established. Jeroboam was followed by his son Nadab. But the latter had hardly begun his reign[1] when there emerged in the year 906–905 B.C. an Issacharite named Baasha who was designated by a prophet (cf. 1 Kings xvi, 2) and seized the throne by murdering the king Nadab who was in camp with his militia. The new kingdom of Baasha did not fare any better, however; Baasha's son Elah, who succeeded his father, was not on the throne long[2] when he was murdered in the royal palace by one of his principal officials, Zimri, the Captain of half the chariots (1 Kings xvi, 8 ff.): a case of assassination which led to the seizure of the throne by a high court official on his own responsibility. There is no reference to Zimri having been appointed by a prophet, and the omission is clearly no mere accident. The probability is that the sole reason for the murder was Zimri's personal ambition. And Zimri did not receive the recognition that would certainly have come to him if his appointment had been authorised by a decree spoken in the name of Yahweh. He was only able to hold the throne for seven days, and as apparently no one had been designated to be the future king, a struggle for the succession erupted from which, in the end, as often happens in such cases, a military leader emerged triumphant. This was Omri, the head of the whole army, who acceded to the throne in the year 878–877 B.C. These events show how a monarchy which was opposed to the formation and consolidation of a dynasty because of its basic association with the old system of charismatic leadership could easily become the plaything of ruthless and violent pretenders to the throne. After the disturbances Omri succeeded in maintaining his hold on the throne sufficiently for three of his descendants to sit on it and for the house of Omri to rule more than thirty years in the State of Israel. Omri thereby became the founder of the first, albeit a short-lived, dynasty in Israel. We know nothing about Omri's family background. That may be no mere accident. His name does not sound

[1] Two years are ascribed to his reign (1 Kings xv, 25). According to the method of reckoning which was in use at this period, which counts parts of calendar years at the beginning and end as full years, this merely means that his reign covered one change of calendar year.

[2] The official reckoning again only gives him 'two years' (1 Kings xvi, 8).

very Israelite nor does that of his son Ahab[1]. As leader of the militia Omri could quite easily have emerged from the ranks of the mercenaries, and a band of mercenaries usually contains elements of very varied origin. The dynasty of Omri was finally overthrown when a new king, appointed in the name of Yahweh, appeared once more. According to 2 Kings ix, 1 ff., Jehu, one of the officers of the militia who happened to be in the field at the time, was appointed and anointed by an emissary of the prophet Elisha[2]; and this Jehu proceeded brutally to wipe out the then reigning descendant of Omri and the whole family and to ascend the throne himself. As a result—a good three-quarters of a century after the death of Solomon—the custom of the designation of a king of Israel by a prophet became extinct, as far as we know. Jehu formed a dynasty which occupied the throne in the State of Israel for about a century. And when Jehu's last descendant had been murdered after a short reign[3] (2 Kings xv, 10) for the last twenty years of its existence the throne in Israel was for the most part in the hands of swiftly alternating usurpers who were unable to claim any kind of divine authorisation for themselves. In the name of his God the prophet Hosea could only say of them: 'They have set up kings but not by me' (viii, 4). After the death of Solomon the State of Israel still had, to begin with, no traditional royal city. In Shechem, the ancient and important urban centre of Mount Ephraim, which was favourably placed from the point of view of communications, Jeroboam had been proclaimed king, and here in Shechem he resided to begin with. According to 1 Kings xii, 25 he 'fortified Shechem', that is, he organised it as his royal city. But then he left Shechem and 'fortified' Penuel as a residence, which lay in a remote part of the land east of the Jordan in the deep valley of the Jabbok (the modern tulūl eḏ-ḏahab)[4]. This strange transfer of the residence was no doubt occasioned by some emergency, and the correct explanation is probably that Jeroboam withdrew beyond the Jordan, with his residence, in face of a warlike incursion of the

[1] The root of the name Omri is common in Arabic names, and the name Ahab can also be explained on the basis of Arabic nomenclature; cf. M. Noth, *Die israelitischen Personennamen* (BWANT, III, 10 [1928], pp. 63, 222, note 7. Was the striking prohibition contained in the deuteronomist 'royal law' against appointing a foreigner king (Deut. xvii, 15) based on the concrete case of Omri?

[2] In 1 Kings xix, 16, the anointing of Jehu is connected with the prophet Elijah, but probably on the basis of a secondary tradition.

[3] According to 2 Kings xv, 8, he only reigned for six months.

[4] According to N. Glück, *Explorations in Eastern Palestine*, III (AASOR, XVIII/XIX [1939]), pp. 232 ff., the archaeological discoveries show that of the two hills of tulūl eḏ-ḏahab, tell eḏ-ḏahab esch-scherḳi, only the eastern one can have been the site of ancient Penuel.

pharaoh Schoschenk (cf. below, pp. 237 f.). In the end he gave up Penuel again as it was in such an unsuitable spot, and returned to the land west of the Jordan when Schoschenk had moved away and no further threats were expected from that quarter. Curiously enough, he did not return to Shechem[1] but chose the city of Thirza, the precise location of which has not yet been discovered but which was somewhere on Mount Ephraim[2]. In Thirza the kings of Israel who succeeded Jeroboam continued to reside for a time. It was in Thirza that Baasha ascended the throne (1 Kings xv, 33); it was in Thirza that Elah was murdered by Zimri (1 Kings xvi, 9) and in Thirza Zimri himself lost his life (1 Kings xvi, 23). Omri then presented the State of Israel with a new royal city. Since, for some reason or other, Thirza was inadequate or unsuitable, in the process of consolidating his monarchy, Omri bought a hill on Mount Ephraim about 10 kilometres north-west of Shechem in a beautiful and dominating position overlooking a broad, fertile valley moving westwards, and here he built the royal city of Samaria (the modern sebastje) (1 Kings xvi, 24) which remained the residence of the Israelite kings for a century and a half until the State of Israel came to an end. The excavations carried out on the site[3] have disclosed the remains of the Israelite palace which was extended by various kings after Omri, and they have revealed that there was no previous urban settlement on this site and that Omri in fact established a new city for the Israelite monarchy, thereby giving the State of Israel a permanent centre, which belonged to the king in person.

It was more difficult to put the State of Israel on its own feet in the sphere of worship. The royal Judaean sanctuary in Jerusalem continued to attract the tribes living in the State of Israel with the Ark as the ancient common object of devotion, and there is hardly any doubt but that they made pilgrimages to Jerusalem. The story of Ahijah (cf. above, p. 225) shows that the religious tradition connected with Jerusalem was already so firmly established after the death of Solomon that it was possible to uphold the authority of the Temple as the central shrine of the tribes even though the

[1] It is not, apparently, to be assumed that Shechem was too greatly destroyed by Schoschenk, since Shechem was probably not mentioned at all in the hieroglyphic list of the Israelite cities conquered by Schoschenk; cf. M. Noth, ZDPV, 61 (1938), p. 289.

[2] Cf. F.-M. Abel, *Géographie de la Palestine*, II (1938), pp. 485 f., who criticises the early suggestions including the locating of Thirza on the tell el-fārʿa about 10 km. north-east of Shechem; but his own suggestion has no assured basis either.

[3] Cf. Reisner-Fisher-Lyon, *Harvard Excavations at Samaria, 1908–1910*, I/II (1924), and the report on the later continuation of the first excavation by J. W. Crowfoot, K. M. Kenyon, E. L. Sukenik, *Samaria-Sebaste Publications*, I (1943).

authority of the Davidites was rejected. That Jeroboam already regarded this as most undesirable, since it meant that there was at least an indirect point of contact between all the Israelite tribes and the dynasty of David, was only natural, and was stated in so many words in 1 Kings xii, 26 ff. Jeroboam therefore raised to the status of royal places of worship the two famous and ancient shrines of Bethel (the modern burj bētīn near bētīn) and Dan (the modern tell el-ḳāḍi) in the extreme south and north of the State of Israel, which the Israelites had doubtless been attending for a long time[1]. He provided each of them sumptuously with a so-called 'golden calf'. Later on, the residence of Samaria was no doubt given a royal shrine and probably a 'golden calf' was erected there too; at any rate the prophet Hosea mentions the 'calf of Samaria' (viii, 5-6). Admittedly these royal Israelite centres of worship were unable to compete with the Ark in Jerusalem and its unique tradition, even though the kings of Israel provided them with all the necessary equipment, with priests appointed by the king and a system of festivals which was an imitation of the one observed in Jerusalem. Later on, the deuteronomist, assuming that Jerusalem had always been the one and only authorised religious centre in the country, saw in the establishment of these royal shrines in Israel the supreme sin committed by Jeroboam and all the subsequent kings of Israel. His assumption was not strictly applicable to the period of the Israelite kings, and the 'golden calves' were not intended as 'idols'. They were intended as part of the worship of the God of Israel who had done great things for Israel and 'brought Israel up out of the land of Egypt' (1 Kings xii, 28, cf. Exod xxxii, 4); and they were probably not intended to be thought of as divine images, especially as theriomorphic images were unknown in the Near East—as opposed to Egypt. They were probably conceived as pedestals for the god who was imagined to be standing on them unseen[2]. The common folk may, however, have seen them as representations and materialisations of the deity; and even at that time it was probably clear that the Ark was the sole place where God was present for the whole of Israel: the one authentic and specifically Israelite shrine. Even in the pre-deuteronomistic narrative of the prophet Ahijah of Shiloh Jeroboam was severely castigated for erecting royal shrines in Israel (1 Kings xii, 28-32).

[1] It is not clear what legal rights the Israelite king had to take possession of ancient local sanctuaries in places inhabited by Israelites.

[2] In the Near East animals and anthropomorphically conceived deities were only connected in this way (cf. Gressmann, AOB², Nos. 331, 335, 338, 345, 354-356). For another interpretation of the 'golden calf' see O. Eissfeldt, ZAW, N.F. 17 (1940–41), pp. 199 ff.

With its official religion the Israelite monarchy was to some extent opposed to the authentic and strict Israelite tradition from the very beginning; in this respect it was at a decided disadvantage compared with the Jewish monarchy of the Davidites. To begin with, the relationship between the two States of Judah and Israel was anything but friendly. Our knowledge of the history of the two States after the death of Solomon is, admittedly, very incomplete. We have to rely very largely on the little that the deuteronomist incorporated from the 'Diaries of the Kings of Judah and Israel' and on the historical information which it is possible to gather from the various prophetic narratives which were embodied in the deuteronomistic history. In making extracts from the 'Diaries' the deuteronomist's aim was not in the least to provide a connected account of the history of the States of Judah and Israel. The 'Diaries' themselves had presumably summarised the official annals of the two States from particular points of view of which we have no information. The deuteronomist extracted, in the first place, everything concerning the succession of the kings and the chronological sequence of events; as far as the State of Israel was concerned he very largely left it at that. For the history of Judah, however, he also incorporated the details about the Temple in Jerusalem, since the house of David, with the promise given to it, and Jerusalem as the city of David and the city of Solomon's Temple, and, above all, the Temple itself as, according to deuteronomist law, the sole legitimate shrine of Israel, were matters of importance to him. He judged the kings according to their attitude to the exclusive legitimacy of the Temple in Jerusalem. From this standpoint he was bound, with only a few exceptions, to pass a negative judgement on almost all the kings. The monotonous repetition of these condemnations only shows that he had no intention of describing the individual kings as persons in their own right or in the light of their historical importance. He aimed, rather, to represent the monarchy as a fundamental cause of Israel's defection from its God. It is clear, therefore, that he was unable to offer a history of the States of Judah and Israel. It should be remembered, however, that he did not consider that his task at all. This is obvious from the fact that he refers any who are interested to know what a particular king 'had done' to the 'Diaries of the Kings of Judah and Israel' which he had used as sources himself. Nevertheless, the little that the deuteronomist does transmit from his sources affords some insight into the course of the history of Judah and Israel after the death of Solomon.

After the death of Solomon enmity prevailed for a long time between Judah and Israel. It is true that Rehoboam's attempt to seize the throne in Israel, which is mentioned in the prophetic narrative in 1 Kings xii, 21-24, was soon abandoned. And if in Judah the claim of the Davidites to the Israelite monarchy continued to be maintained for a time, it was probably soon accepted that the separation of the two States was inevitable. The dispute regarding the definition of the common frontier probably continued for a long time, however. Rehoboam succeeded in annexing for Judah part of the tribal territory of Benjamin, which had belonged to the State of Israel under Eshbaal, David and Solomon. We do not know how this came about; presumably Rehoboam was able to seize this land by force of arms and keep it for Judah[1]. This was important for him, since his royal city of Jerusalem was situated precisely midway between the State territories of Judah and Israel —that was just why David had chosen it (cf. above, p. 189). After the separation of the two States it came to be on the border of the State of Judah and in direct contact with the State of Israel. The annexation of part of Benjaminite territory and the consequent shifting of the common frontier some distance northwards away from Jerusalem meant the acquisition of a glacis for the city over against the State of Israel and a protection against sudden attacks and invasions. Evidently minor frontier warfare took place here continuously. When there is mention of constant war between Judah and Israel in the period of the kings Rehoboam and Jeroboam (1 Kings xiv, 30), and in that of the kings Asa and Baasha (1 Kings xv, 16), the reference is to this border warfare[2]. Probably Judah was able to maintain its hold on part of the Benjaminite glacis for Jerusalem against Israel which claimed, not unfairly, possession of the whole of Benjamin. The border conflicts, in which presumably both sides had some successes and reverses, probably took place entirely within the territory of Benjamin. This is suggested by the events which the deuteronomist records in greater detail because the treasures of the Temple in Jerusalem played a part in them (1 Kings xv, 17-22). According to this account, the Israelite king Baasha (906–905 to 883–882 B.C.)

[1] Retrospectively the story of the prophet Ahijah describes this so as to suggest that Yahweh assigned the government of Israel to Jeroboam with the exception of a single tribe (*i.e.* Benjamin) (1 Kings xi, 31, 32, 36). Cf. also 1 Kings xii, 20, where 'tribe of Benjamin' originally stood in the place of 'tribe of Judah'. The kingdom of Judah which the Davidites naturally retained is not discussed at all in the story of Jeroboam.

[2] The basis of the story of a war of king Ahijah of Judah with Jeroboam, which the chronicler elaborated in 2 Chron. xiii, 3-20, belongs to this context.

succeeded in occupying the city of Ramah (the modern er-rām) which lies at the centre of Benjaminite territory on the main road leading to Jerusalem from the north, 9 kilometres away from Jerusalem, and began to develop it as an Israelite stronghold. In this difficult situation the Judaean king Asa persuaded the Aramaean king of Damascus to attack the State of Israel from the north, by making him a rich present from the treasures of the Temple and Palace in Jerusalem. Baasha had therefore to withdraw from his southern border to defend his northern frontier. Asa exploited the difficulties of his Israelite enemy not only by occupying Ramah but by moving the frontier of Judah and Israel still farther northwards. By using the materials that Baasha had assembled for fortifications in Ramah, he fortified the cities of Geba and Mizpah as Judaean frontier strongholds. Geba (the modern jebaʿ) lay 3 kilometres east of Ramah, south of the deep wādi eṣ-ṣuwēnīṭ which ran south-eastwards and which became the frontier between the two States in this area; Mizpeh was probably situated on the modern tell en-naṣbe, 4 kilometres north of Ramah on the abovementioned main road[1]. The frontier that was established in this way apparently became a permanency since, under the Judaean king Josiah (639–609 B.C.) Geba still appears as the northern frontier city of Judah in the phrase 'from Geba to Beer-Sheba' (2 Kings xxiii, 8). Anyway, soon afterwards a change occurred in the relationship between Judah and Israel which brought the initial frontier disputes to an end. On the hills in the area of the main road which runs parallel with the watershed, Judah remained in possession of a considerable part of Benjaminite territory for the protection of the royal city of Jerusalem[2]. As part of a deliberate policy the Israelite kings of the dynasty of Omri buried their minor disputes with their Judaean neighbours (cf. below, p. 239) and tried to come to an understanding with them. The existing balance of power resulted in the smaller State of Judah following behind the State of Israel, which was led by able kings. The Israelite kings

[1] The situation of Mizpeh has long been, and still is, in dispute. But the results of the excavations on the tell en-nasbe (cf. C. C. McCown and J. C. Wampler, *Tell en-Nasbeh excavated under the Direction of the late William Frederic Badè*, I/II [1947]) fit in various respects so well with what we know about the history of Mizpah that it is at any rate highly probable that Mizpeh was on the tell en-nasbe. Cf. the detailed discussion of the question in A. Alt, ZDPV, 69 (1953), pp. 1 ff.

[2] A considerable shift of the frontier took place in the Jordan Valley; at any rate the territory of the old city-state of Jericho was retained by the State of Israel (cf. 1 Kings xvi, 34). But in the western hill country Judah was able to obtain some land at the expense of Israel. Rehoboam was able to develop the city of Aijalon (the modern jalo), which once belonged to one of the districts of the State of Israel (1 Kings iv, 9), into a Judaean stronghold (2 Chron. xi, 10).

were able to maintain the upper hand over their obviously less important Judaean colleagues. The prophetic narrative in 1 Kings xxii, 2-38, reveals the Judaean king as the confederate of the king of Israel[1] in a military enterprise aimed at the possession of the city of Ramoth in Gilead which was only indirectly important for the State of Israel; and in 2 Kings ix, 16 ff., we again find King Ahaziah of Judah in the entourage of the Israelite king Joram. The prophetic narrative in 2 Kings iii, 4-27, which is very obscure historically and difficult to elucidate, also refers to the Judaean king acting in unison with the Israelite king[2] in a war against Moab, which was primarily the concern of the State of Israel, since Moab was the immediate neighbour and had previously been the vassal of the State of Israel. The two royal houses were even united by marriage; the Judaean king Joram (852–851 to 845–844 B.C.) married, probably while still crown prince, Athaliah, a daughter of king Ahab of Israel (2 Kings viii, 26)[3], and this marriage naturally had a political background.

With the fall of the dynasty of Omri in Israel Judah's political tie was destroyed again. In fact, to begin with, the rule of the Omrites, which had just been eliminated in Israel, returned in Judah. After the Judaean king Ahaziah had lost his life in Jehu's rising against the house of Omri as a confederate of the last of the Omrite dynasty (2 Kings ix, 27 f.) his mother, the above-mentioned Athaliah, evidently a very tyrannical woman, with a great love of power, seized the throne and had all the surviving members of the house of David killed. She then ruled, probably very despotically, for six years (845–844 to 839–838 B.C.), but no details of her reign have come down to us. In the end she was overthrown and killed by a clever trick perpetrated by the high priest Jehoiada (cf. the detailed account in 2 Kings xi). A son of the last king Ahaziah, who was still quite a small child at the time when he was rescued from Athaliah's lust for blood, had continued to be hidden from her. This small Davidite, Jehoash by name, was now set on the throne of his fathers and the lawful succession of the Davidites was continued. Henceforth, as far as we can judge, there were no close ties between the States of Judah and Israel, nor was there any enmity between

[1] The names of these kings were not mentioned in the original form of the narrative; and it is not quite certain whether the deuteronomist's historical arrangement of the reigns of the kings Jehoshaphat and Ahab is factually correct.

[2] Here, too, the names of the kings Jehoram and Jehoshaphat obviously do not belong to the original contents of the narrative.

[3] In this passage she is called a 'daughter of Omri'. But it is clear from the following verse that this merely indicates her membership of the dynasty of Omri and that she was in fact a daughter of Ahab.

them. Only once did there occur a strange incident. According to 2 Kings xiv, 8-14, the Judaean king Amaziah (800–799 to 785–784 B.C.) one day challenged king Jehoash of Israel (802–801 to 787–786 B.C.), the grandson of Jehu, the founder of the dynasty, to a military trial of strength. The result was a battle at Beth-semes (the modern tell er rumēle near ʿēn shems) in which Amaziah was soundly beaten. As a result, the victorious Israelites were even able to occupy Jerusalem, plunder the Temple and the palace treasury (that is the reason why the deuteronomist tells the story) and pull down part of the city wall. The real background of the event is not clear, but it does not seem to have had any lasting repercussions.

The dynasty of Jehu which was, to begin with, gravely troubled by foreign enemies, was unable, in the end, to give the State of Israel a period of relative peace and security. The long reign of king Jeroboam II (787–786 to 747–746 B.C.) was a comparatively good period for Israel[1]. The equally long reign of the almost contemporary king Ussia brought a period of similar calm to Judah. This was the state of affairs shortly before new and tremendous events completely altered the situation for both Judah and Israel.

19. *Struggles with neighbouring States*

The disintegration of the Empire of David and Solomon turned Judah and Israel into minor States within the political world of Syria and Palestine. They were forced to fight for their survival in repeated conflicts with the other powers in this world. It is not surprising that the change in the situation caused the Philistines in the south-west to bestir themselves again. Admittedly the earlier power of the Philistines had been broken by David once and for all, and all that ensued now was border warfare with no far-reaching effects[2]. Rehoboam had already protected the little State Judah by means of a complete system of fortified strongholds (2 Chron. xi, 5-10) and in this system the particularly powerful fortification of

[1] The ostraka which have been found in the royal palace of Samaria throw a little light on the internal organisation of Israel. They are the oldest known written documents from Israel and probably belong to the period of Jeroboam II (cf. W. F. Albright, *Archaeology and the Religion of Israel* [[2] 1946], p. 214, note 41). They belong to the royal administration of the crown lands and were published by Reisner-Fisher-Lyon, *Harvard Excavations at Samaria* (1924), I, pp. 227-246, II, Pl. 55; cf. also WAT, p. 174 and III, 10 and TGI, p. 50.

[2] On the following, cf. O. Eissfeldt, *Israelitisch-philistäische Grenzverschiebungen von David bis auf die Assyrerzeit* (ZDPV, 66 [1943], pp. 115-128).

the western border of Judah is especially remarkable[1]. It is surprising to find the city of Gath among these fortified strongholds; this must be the famous one-time Philistine city whose king had played a leading part in David's time among the Philistine rulers and which still enjoyed political independence when Solomon came to the throne (cf. 1 Kings ii, 39, 40)[2]. We do not know when and how this most inland of the Philistine cities had come into the possession of Judah. Did Solomon really take it by force of arms? Or did Rehoboam succeed in annexing this neighbouring Philistine city in his attempt to consolidate Judah as an independent State? In any case, it is not surprising that the Philistines henceforth tried to regain Gath. According to 2 Kings xii, 18 f., however, Gath was still in the hands of Judah at the time of the Judaean king Jehoash (839–838 to 800–799 B.C.). At that time the Aramaean king Hazael —evidently as an ally of the Philistines, who were no match for Judah on their own—conquered the city of Gath and even threatened Jerusalem, so that the king of Judah had to pay dearly for Hazael's retreat by rendering tribute from the Temple and palace treasury in Jerusalem. Possibly the State of Judah lost Gath once more[3]; anyway, about a century later we find Gath in Philistine hands again. The State of Israel waged repeated border warfare with the Philistines near the city of Gibbethon. On two occasions we learn accidentally that the whole of the Israelite militia was encamped at Gibbethon (1 Kings xv, 27; xvi, 15-17). This place Gibbethon is probably identical with the modern tell el-melāt[4], and if so, it lay about 4 kilometres west of the city of Gezer (tell jezer) and also about 4 kilometres east of the Philistine city of Ekron (ʿāḳir). The real struggle was therefore obviously for one of these two cities; the only question is whether the State of Israel tried to annex the neighbouring Philistine city of Gath, or whether the Philistines threatened Gezer, which belonged to Israel. Apparently neither side was successful, and the Philistine wars had no great effect. The Philistines became dangerous for Judah and for Israel at this period only in so far as they worked hand in hand with the

[1] Cf. G. Beyer, *Das Festungssystem Rehabeams* (ZDPV, 54 [1931], pp. 113-134, and especially the sketch-map on p. 116).

[2] It is impossible to ascertain its exact position. Most probably it was on the tell eṣ-ṣāfi (as suggested most recently by K. Elliger, ZDPV, 57 [1934], pp. 148 ff., and O. Eissfeldt, *loc. cit.* p. 119). *The Westminster Historical Atlas to the Bible* (1945), p. 109, represents a different view.

[3] The note in 2 Chron. xxvi, 6, according to which the Judaean king Ussia pulled down the walls of Gath, Jabneh and Ashdod on a campaign against the Philistines, is of uncertain origin and significance.

[4] G. v. Rad has suggested and argued this in PJB, 29 (1933), pp. 38 ff.

far stronger Aramaeans of Damascus. Just as, for Judah, this probably led to the loss of Gath, it also seems, according to the supplement to 2 Kings xiii, 22, in the Septuagint, to have injured Israel. In the latter case, too, it was king Hazael of Aram who helped the Philistines to achieve their successes (cf. also Isa. ix, 11).

On one occasion a greater power from the south-west intervened for a time in the history of Israel and Judah. In the fifth year of king Rehoboam, that is, in the year 922–921 B.C., the pharaoh Shishak I, a Libyan leader of mercenaries, who had founded the 22nd Dynasty in Egypt, undertook an expedition to Palestine, evidently in order to renew the tradition of the great Pharaohs of the New Kingdom who had for a time possessed the whole of Syria and Palestine. In 1 Kings xiv, 25-28, it is recorded that Rehoboam assembled all the treasures of the Temple and palace in Jerusalem to pay tribute to the pharaoh. This was the price he had to pay in order to spare Judah and Jerusalem. This is clear, too, from the list of cities which were conquered in Palestine, which was compiled in imitation of similar lists which various pharaohs of the New Kingdom had affixed to a wall of the great Amun temple of Karnak in Upper Egypt, in commemoration of his expedition[1]. There is no mention of any Judaean cities in this list. On the other hand, however, Shishak infested not only the Negeb in the south of Palestine and the district of Edom, but, above all, he sent his troops into the plain of Jezreel and advanced from there in various directions. In Megiddo, which is mentioned explicitly as No. 27 in his list, he even left documentary evidence of his presence; during the excavations a small fragment of a stele was found which bears his name[2]. This campaign of Shishak did not have any serious consequences, however; it probably passed over quickly, and nothing of a similar nature occurred in subsequent years. It was intended as a demonstration and a plundering expedition. That is why Rehoboam's payment of tribute was sufficient for the pharaoh to desist from plundering the State of Judah. It is quite unlikely that Shishak wanted to intervene in the internal relations between the State of Judah and Israel and take sides with one or the other. The aim of his expedition was simply to plunder the land in Western Asia nearest to Egypt.

The dangers which loomed from the north-east were far more

[1] More details of this list in M. Noth, ZDPV, 61 (1938), pp. 277-304.

[2] Published in Cl. S. Fisher, *The Excavation of Armageddon* (Oriental Institute Communications, No. 4 [1929], Figs. 7 A, 7 B, 9.

menacing for Judah and, in particular, for Israel than the military embarrassments from the south-west. In the north-east the Aramaean monarchy of Damascus, which had been founded in Solomon's time, quickly became a dangerous enemy, and soon the strongest power of all, in the world of Syria and Palestine. From Damascus it dominated in the first place the ancient city-state territory of the northern land east of the Jordan and was therefore Israel's neighbour along the north-eastern border of the ʿajlūn and the eastern border of the upper Jordan Valley. It ruled over the beḳāʿ between the Lebanon and Anti-Lebanon which abounded in ore and over which the Aramaean king, Hadadezer of Zobah, had once ruled (cf. above, p. 195), and no doubt included under its rule the Aramaeans who had settled in the interior of Syria. The surprising discovery of a stele of the king Benhadad I dedicated to the Tyrian god Melkart, and containing a brief inscription in Aramaean, in the district of Aleppo in northern Syria[1] illustrates the extent and varied nature of the ramifications of the Damascus monarchy. This Benhadad, who describes himself[2] as a son of a Tabrimmon and grandson of a Hadian in the inscription which is, however, very damaged at this point, and who was therefore a member of a dynasty of 'kings of Aram' which had already reigned for several generations, must have had connections of a friendly character with the Phoenician coastal cities[3] and must, moreover, have been ruler of the Aramaeans as far as northern Syria. It is this same Benhadad I whom we meet as the first dangerous military enemy of the State of Israel. He was the Aramaean king whom King Asa of Judah persuaded to attack Israel in the reign of Baasha by making him a sumptuous present (cf. above, p. 233). He gave orders for his troops to invade the uppermost valley of the Jordan from the beḳāʿ, which was under his rule, and to occupy the Israelite cities of Ijon (the modern tell dibbīn on the merj ʿeyyūn), Dan (the modern tell el-ḳādi), Abel-beth-maacah (the modern tell ābil) and the western section of the hills of Galilee (1 Kings xv, 20). We are told nothing about the result of this undertaking which forced King Baasha to look to the defence of his northern frontier. Probably Benhadad did not seriously intend to take permanent possession of this Israelite

[1] Published by M. Dunand, *Bulletin du Musée de Beyrouth*, 8 (1941), pp. 65 ff.; cf. also W. Albright, BASOR, 87 (1942), pp. 23 ff.

[2] Cf. 1 Kings xv, 18. 'Benhadad' is the usual Hebraisation in the Old Testament of the name which appears as 'Barhadad' in Aramaic.

[3] It is impossible to ascertain the basis of Benhadad's relations to the god Melkart of Tyre, to which the inscription testifies.

territory which he had invaded, and he may have withdrawn of his own accord.

The situation was different in the land east of the Jordan which appears soon afterwards as the main battleground between Israel and Aram. Here David had incorporated part of the city-state territory north-east of the ʿajlūn in the State of Israel (cf. above, p. 191), and Solomon had then joined it to the province of Ramoth (cf. above, p. 211). The Aramaeans evidently claimed possession of these city-states, since the rest of the city-states in the northern land east of the Jordan belonged to them. At any rate, in the period that followed, the Solomonic capital of Ramoth in Gilead (the modern tell rāmīṯ 7 kilometres south of er-remṯe)[1] was repeatedly contested by Israelites and Aramaeans.

The Israelite kings of the dynasty of Omri made the warding-off of this threat the main item of their policy. They brought to an end the frontier disputes with the neighbouring State of Judah, and the Judaean kings now appear as their allies in the struggles against the Aramaeans (cf. above, p. 234). They sought to establish contacts with the Phoenician coastal cities which were beginning at this period to embark on extensive and successful colonization in the Mediterranean area[2]. The marriage of the crown prince Ahab, the son and successor of Omri, to Jezebel, the daughter of the 'king of the Zidonians', Ethbaal of Tyre[3], calls for mention in this connection. Since the Aramaean king Benhadad was also developing his connections with the Phoenician cities (see above) it is very easy to see that, through his son's marriage, Omri was trying to establish a firm bond with the rich and powerful maritime and mercantile cities. Ahab's marriage with Jezebel aroused strong opposition in Israel itself, however, and this was personified in Elisha the prophet. No doubt Jezebel, with her Tyrian retinue, practised her own Tyrian religion in a sanctuary built specially in the royal city of Samaria just as Solomon had had shrines built for the devotions of his foreign women on the Mount of Olives east of Jerusalem (cf. 2 Kings xxiii, 13). These religions were not that of

[1] Cf. N. Glück, AASOR, 25-28 (1951), pp. 96 ff.

[2] Cf. W. F. Albright in *Studies in the History of Culture* (1942), pp. 40 ff.

[3] In 1 Kings xvi, 31, there is a reference to 'Ethbaal king of the Zidonians', whereas Menander of Ephesus, the historian of the Phoenicians, speaks, according to the quotation preserved in Josephus, *Antiqu. Iud.* VIII, 13, 2, § 324 Niese, of the 'Tyrian king' 'Ιθώβαλος. To judge from this, the king's name was wrongly vocalised in the Old Testament and was really Ittobaal. The connection between 'Zidonians' and 'Tyrians' was probably that 'Zidonians' was used to describe the Phoenicians in general, and Ittobaal was a Phoenician king residing in Tyre about whose dominions we have no precise details.

the State, and Yahweh no doubt remained *the* God of Israel for king Ahab and the State of Israel[1]. But the very existence of this foreign religion and its attendant priests[2] in Samaria was resisted by the powerful and ancient tradition of the Israelite tribes, for whom the strictly exclusive service of Yahweh was an absolute requirement. A terrible drought which resulted from a complete lack of rain in one year[3] was interpreted as a divine punishment for the worship of Baal[4] in Israel[5]. The despotic impulses of king Ahab were also attributed to the influence of the foreign queen[6]. It again became clear that the monarchy was bound to follow 'secular' laws of its own and for that reason wise, strong and resolute kings—and the kings of the dynasty of Omri were among the historically most important personalities on the throne of Israel—came into conflict with the authentic tradition of Israel. The internal opposition finally brought about the downfall of the Omrites. Jehu was appointed king, with the obvious task of removing the house of Omri that had compromised itself in Samaria by its association with the worship of 'Baal'.

In foreign policy and, above all, in the conflicts with the Aramaeans the Omrites were on the whole the losers in spite of all their efforts. The increasing strength of the Aramaeans had made the situation altogether too difficult for the State of Israel. Admittedly there is little concrete information available on this matter, and it is impossible to define the course of the conflict between Israel and Aram. The deuteronomist failed to pass on any details on this matter from the 'Diaries of the Kings of Israel' and our only source

[1] Attention has rightly been drawn to the fact that all the children of Ahab known to us have names which are compounds of the divine name Yahweh.

[2] In this context the Old Testament often refers to 'the prophets of Baal' ([1 Kings xviii, 19, 40;] 2 Kings x, 19).

[3] Menander of Ephesus also reported on a great ἀβροχία at the time of the king Ittobaal of Tyre (in Josephus, *loc. cit.*) which had obviously been a great and noteworthy catastrophe for Palestine-Syria. He states that it lasted precisely *one* year. According to 1 Kings xviii, 1, the drought came to an end 'in the third year', but in fact this comes to the same thing because, in accordance with the then customary method of pre-dating, the dry summer of the previous normal year was reckoned as the first year.

[4] In the stories of Elisha the god of the foreign cultus is simply called 'Baal'; in fact this was the State god of Tyre who was named Melkart.

[5] The divine judgement on Mount Carmel (1 Kings xviii, 17-46) originally had nothing to do with the struggle that arose from the worship of Baal in Samaria, but was concerned with the taking over of a local sanctuary for the worship of Yahweh; for further details see A. Alt, *Festschrift Georg Beer* (1935), pp. 1-18=*Kleine Schriften zur Geschichte des Volkes Israel*, II (1953), pp. 135-149.

[6] Cf. the story of Naboth's vineyard in 1 Kings xxi. It takes place in the city of Jezreel (the modern zerʿīn) where the Omrites had landed property—perhaps a family estate. The last Omrite also stayed in Jezreel at the time of Jehu's rebellion and was killed there, together with the old queen Jezebel (2 Kings ix, 15 ff., 30 ff.).

of information is therefore in the narratives in 1 Kings xx and xxii and the longer narratives about Elisha in 2 Kings vi, 8–vii, 20 and xiii, xiv ff. These sources did not, however, originally refer to any definite kings by name but only to the 'king of Israel' or the 'king of Judah' and always called the king of Aram 'Benhadad', so that it is impossible to give a definite date to the narratives and provide them with a historical interpretation[1]. All that can be gathered from them is something about the situation in general. From what it is possible to infer, the battles were full of changing fortunes for both sides—sometimes the Aramaeans would take a few cities from the Israelites and vice versa; the cities in question were no doubt city-states in the northern land east of the Jordan on the border of the ʿajlūn or the jolan (1 Kings xx, 34), where the Aramaeans acquired trading rights in Samaria and then the Israelites acquired similar rights in Damascus (1 Kings xx, 34). The battles were waged for the most part in the land east of the Jordan; Aphek (the modern fīḳ east of the Lake of Tiberias) and Ramoth in Gilead (the modern tell rāmīt) are mentioned (1 Kings xx, 26, 30 [cf. 2 Kings xiii, 17] and xx, 3 ff.) as the scenes of the battles. But, on the whole, Israel appears to have suffered most of the defeats. In 1 Kings xxii, 2-38, there is a reference to a fruitless attempt to regain Ramoth in Gilead that was occupied by the Aramaeans and an annihilating defeat at Ramoth in Gilead. There is even mention of incursions by the Aramaeans in Mount Ephraim, west of the Jordan, in 2 Kings vi, 24 ff. At some time or other the city of Samaria itself was besieged by the Aramaeans. All the same, in spite of a few losses which were probably incurred on the frontiers, Israel was able to maintain her possessions in face of the Aramaeans' attacks. According to the story of the downfall of the dynasty of Omri (2 Kings ix, 10) the last Omrite had Ramoth in his hands again (ix, 14b), but had been wounded himself in the wars against the Aramaeans (ix, 15).

How difficult and troublesome the Aramaean wars had made the

[1] Cf. A. Jepsen, AfO, 14 (1942), pp. 154 ff. Jepsen presumes that the period of Jehu's dynasty forms the historical background to these stories of the prophets. I find that difficult to accept; they have therefore been dealt with above in connection with Omri's dynasty, following the deuteronomist's classification. But how unreliable the present reference to particular kings in fact is, in these stories and their classification in the books of the Kings, is clear from the fact that the story in 1 Kings xxii, 2-38, cannot be referred to King Ahab. G. Hölscher, *Eucharistion Hermann Gunkel zum 60. Geburtstag*, I (1923), p. 185, has pointed out that the annalistic note in 1 Kings xxii, 40a, assumes that Ahab died a natural death, whereas according to 1 Kings xxii, 2-38, he fell in battle (cf. Jepsen, *loc. cit.* p. 155). In fact, the name Ahab only occurs in verse 20 and the text is doubtful at this point (cf. BHK[3], *loc. cit.*) and was perhaps merely occasioned by the placing of the story in the context of the books of the Kings.

situation for Israel is shown by the fact that Moab, who had, since the reign of David, been liable to pay tribute to the State of Israel, now saw that the time had come to break these ties with Israel. According to 2 Kings iii, 4-5, king Mesha, king of Moab, ceased paying tribute to Israel after the death of Ahab. Furthermore, Moab was able to seize the fertile table-land north of the Arnon, which had been in dispute between Israel and Moab for many years, had belonged to the State of Israel under David and Solomon and had for the most part remained Israelite territory ever since. We learn this, with much detail, from the inscription on the stele of king Mesha of Moab, which was discovered in 1868 in Dibon (the modern dībān) north of the Arnon (sēl el-mōjib[1]). According to this inscription, the southernmost part of the table-land with the city of Dibon, from which king Mesha himself came, had been occupied once before by the Moabites in circumstances of which we have no knowledge. Mesha succeeded, however, in extending Moabite rule as far as the latitude of the northern end of the Dead Sea and conquering the Israelite settlements and the cities subject to Israel on the table-land in a triumphant campaign. The Mesha inscription mentions the name of king Omri, who had 'oppressed Moab for a long time' (l. 5) and speaks of his sons who had succeeded him as king and reckons 'the reign of Omri and half the reign of his sons' at 'forty years' (l. 8). This is clearly very much a round figure. But it implies that Mesha's victorious campaign came at the very end of the dynasty of Omri. Apparently the last Omrite was seriously defeated in the battles east of the Jordan.

The first serious encroachment of the new Assyrian empire on Syria-Palestine also occurred in the period of the dynasty of Omri. To begin with, though only for a time, this heralded a great change in the history of Syria-Palestine. In the 9th century B.C. the power of the Assyrians began to rise again. They advanced beyond the Euphrates to the Mediterranean coast. The Assyrian king Assurnasirpal II (884–859 B.C.) had already made a thrust into northern Syria and had reached the coast and received tribute from a number of Phoenician cities on the coast. In a number of expeditions his son and successor, Salmanassar III (859–824 B.C.) advanced farther towards central and southern Syria. The small States of Syria and Palestine were in no sense a match for this great

[1] Illustration of the stele in H. Gressmann, AOB², No. 120; the text of the inscription in Hebrew transcription in M. Lidzbarski, *Altsemitische Texte I; Canaanäische Inschriften* (1907), pp. 5-9, and in TGI, pp. 47-49; German translation of the text in H. Gressmann, AOT², pp. 440-442; on the historical interpretation of the details cf. M. Noth, ZAW, N.F. 19 (1944), pp. 42 ff.

power and could at best only try to resist the dangerous enemy by joining their combined forces and, in fact, on Salmanassar's first appearance in central Syria, they shelved their quarrels and joined together. In the 6th year of Salmanassar, in 853 B.C., a battle took place between Salmanassar and a coalition of Syrian and Palestinian rulers. Among his enemies Salmanassar mentions, in addition to Hadadezer[1] of Damascus and king Irhuleni of Hamath[2], 'the Israelite Ahab' (ʿa-ha-ab-bu mat sir-ʾ-la-ai) who participated with 2000 chariots and 10,000 soldiers[3]. The battle took place near the city of Karkar in the province of Hamath (the modern khirbet ḳerḳūr in the valley of the Orontes east of the Nosairian mountains) in northern Syria, where the allies had met Salmanassar[4]. Salmanassar boasted of a great victory. But, as far as one can see, the victory led to no tangible results, and, in the following years, his 10th, 11th and 14th year, Salmanassar attacked Syria again to fight 'the 12 kings of the land of Hatti' among whom kings Hadadezer of Damascus and Irhuleni of Hamath were still mentioned as the most important. By their combined efforts the allies in Syria and Palestine still succeeded in resisting the Assyrian, and at any rate delaying his advance. The battle of Karkar took place at the end of Ahab's reign (871–870 to 852–851 B.C.). He took part in it as the ally of the king of Aramaea. In view of the great impending danger, the disputes between Israelites and Aramaeans, which, compared with the problem of resisting the

[1] The name which is given in cuneiform script as ᵈAdad-idri can only be the well-known Aramaic king's name Hadadezer which is familiar from 2 Sam. viii, 3 ff. and elsewhere. Usually this ᵈAdad-idri is identified with the Benhadad who is often mentioned in the Old Testament. But there is no sufficient reason for this, particularly as the prophetic narratives containing the name Benhadad are impossible to date precisely (cf. Jepsen, *loc. cit.* pp. 155, 158 f.). If, according to an inscription of Salmanassar (cf. below, p. 246) this ᵈAdad-idri was murdered by Hazael, whilst in 2 Kings viii, 7-15 the king murdered by Hazael is called Benhadad, this is not important since the name Benhadad in 2 Kings viii, 7, 9, is probably an addition to the original expression 'the king of Aram'. In the later transmission of the prophetic narratives Benhadad was regarded as denoting an Aramaic king in general. The Benhadad I who is known from the stele of Aleppo and from the annalistic record in 1 Kings xv, 18, 20, had died meanwhile, and Hadadezer (ᵈAdad-idri) was king of Aram *circa* the middle of the 9th century B.C.

[2] Hamath (the modern ḥama) was at that time the centre of a fairly large political organisation in northern Syria.

[3] This is stated in Salmanassar's annalistic report in his monolithic inscription, col. II, ll. 87 ff. (German translation in H. Gressmann, AOT², pp. 340 f., and also TGI, pp. 45 f.). According to this, Israel represented, with Damascus and Hamath, the largest contingent in the combined force. The other confederates were represented by much smaller contingents; the Israelite chariot force was far and away the largest, even compared with that of Damascus and Hamath.

[4] Cf. the passage mentioned in the previous note. In other inscriptions, too, Salmanassar refers to the battle of Karkar, without enumerating the confederate enemies in detail (apart from Hadadezer of Damascus and occasionally Irhuleni of Hamath).

Assyrian, were at bottom merely border disputes, were put on one side, though they revived no doubt once Salmanassar had withdrawn again. We are not told to what extent Ahab's successors took part in the combined resistance to Salmanassar's subsequent Syrian expeditions[1]. It is conceivable that Ahab was magnanimous enough to shelve the internal disputes in Syria and Palestine and join the king of Aram against Salmanassar, but that his successors turned their entire attention to holding their position *vis-à-vis* their immediate neighbours.

During an interval between Salmanassar's various campaigns and a war with the Aramaeans, the house of Omri finally came to a somewhat inglorious end with the emergence of Jehu who had been designated king (845–844 B.C.).

Jehu rebelled against the house of Omri and its worship of Baal in Samaria in the name of the ancient Israelite tradition. He acted as champion of the unsullied worship of Yahweh. According to 2 Kings x, 15 ff., he was in league with Jonadab the leader of the Order of Rechabites who personified the 'nomadic ideal' in his way of life (cf. Jer. xxxv, 1-19), thereby protesting against life in Palestine with its foreign religious influences. He thought Israel's task was to maintain its original, authentic way of life. In his 'zeal for the Lord' (2 Kings x, 16) Jehu destroyed the shrine of Baal in Samaria (2 Kings x, 18-28). In spite of all this, however, Jehu's monarchy was also a secular institution and he, too, had to act in accordance with secular policies. For all his 'zeal for the Lord' Jehu had usurped the monarchy, and a century later the prophet Hosea declared that Jehu's extermination of the house of Omri had laden the dynasty of Jehu with a guilt which Yahweh would yet avenge (Hos. i, 4). In accordance with the watchword with which Jehu had emerged, he was bound to abandon the political line of the Omri era. He gave up the connections with the Phoenician cities which had led to the worship of Baal in Samaria. He also dropped the special relationship with the State of Judah, since the State of Israel was now no longer strong enough to hold Judah in a state of vassalage. Apparently he gave up all foreign involvements whatsoever. When in his 18th year (841 B.C.) Salmanassar appeared in Syria for the fourth time, Jehu evidently made no attempt at resistance but paid tribute to the Assyrian monarch like the Phoenician cities.

[1] If Salmanassar constantly speaks in a stereotyped manner of 'twelve' Syrian-Palestinian kings, this is a conventional expression and does not prove that he was always confronted in every campaign with the same coalition of enemies.

On the basalt obelisk of Salmanassar (the so-called black obelisk)[1] which was discovered in the Royal Assyrian city of Kalah (the modern tell nimrūd) the payment of Jehu's tribute is portrayed, and in the description his name is mentioned explicitly (ia-u-a mâr ḫu-um-ri-i)[2].

Israel's isolation exposed it all the more to the Aramaeans; and in Damascus Hazael, who soon became a particularly dangerous enemy of Israel, sat on the king's throne. At the outset he was still preoccupied with the necessity of resisting the Assyrians. Salmanassar mentions ᵈAdad-idri[3] for the last time in his 14th year (845 B.C.) and Haza-ilu (Hazael) for the first time in his 18th year (841 B.C.)[4]. Jehu and Hazael may therefore have come to the throne about the same time, both of them as usurpers[5]. According to 2 Kings viii, 7-15, Hazael murdered the 'king of Syria' in Damascus and set himself on the throne; Salmanassar also provides the information in the inscription on his great basalt statue[6] which was found in the city of Assur, that ᵈAdad-idri was murdered and 'Hazael, the son of a nobody'[7] had set himself on the throne (front ll. 25-27)[8]. Salmanassar's Syrian campaigns, which took place in his 18th and 21st year (841 and 838 B.C.), were aimed primarily against Damascus. In 841 B.C. Salmanassar advanced on the city of Damascus itself, and encircled it for a time, though he did not conquer it. He then moved on through the city-state territory of the northern land east of the Jordan as far as the Hauran mountains (šadū ^{māt}ḫa-ú-ra-ni), the modern jebel ed-drūz, that is, through the heart of the State of Aramaea. He then proceeded to the mountain of Ba'lira'si 'which lies on the shore of the sea'[9]. These are the

[1] Cf. the illustrations in H. Gressmann, AOB², Nos. 121-125.

[2] This means literally 'Jehu of the house of Omri'. By 'house of Omri' Salmanassar means the State of Israel, since Israel had opposed him for the first time (853 B.C.) under the Omri dynasty. The Assyrians apparently did not know that Jehu had overthrown the house of Omri and founded a new dynasty. An annalistic extract of Salmanassar's also mentioned Jehu's tribute in Salmanassar's 18th year (cf. Gressmann, AOT², p. 343, and TGI, p. 47).

[3] Bull, inscription of Salmanassar's l. 100 (Gressmann, *loc. cit.* p. 342).

[4] Obelisk inscription ll. 97 f. amongst others (Gressmann, *loc. cit.* p. 343).

[5] Hazael and Jehu are thus described side by side and parallel with one another in 1 Kings xix, 15-17.

[6] Cf. the publication of this inscription by E. Michel, WO, I, 2 (1947), pp. 57-63.

[7] This expression is intended to mean that he was a usurper, perhaps even by descent a slave. According to 2 Kings viii, 13, the prophet Elisha had promised him his future kingdom in the name of Yahweh (in 1 Kings xix, 15, the task was entrusted to Elijah) and thereby induced him to murder his predecessor.

[8] There is a German translation of the relevant section from the inscription of the basalt statue in H. Gressmann, AOT², p. 344.

[9] Cf. the annalistic extract for the 18th year of Salmanassar (E. Michel, WO, 14 [1949], pp. 265 ff.; Gressmann, *loc. cit.* p. 343), ll. 14-23.

foothills on the nahr el-kelb north-east of bērūt; and here he set up alongside the old pictures of the pharaoh Ramses II his own portrait in relief on the rock above the coast-road, which can still be seen today, as a token of the growing power of Assyria, which now claimed possession of Syria and Palestine, of which the pharaohs of the New Kingdom had once been so proud[1]. The pressure which Salmanassar put on king Hazael in the opening years of Jehu's reign undoubtedly resulted in a slackening of the strain applied by the Aramaeans. And from this time on the situation in Syria and Palestine was very largely determined by the Assyrians.

As far as we know, Salmanassar proceeded against Syria for the last time in the year 838 B.C. and captured several cities in the 'land of Damascus'[2]. He then withdrew from all further interference with Syria without having really gained any serious footing in central and southern Syria. After him, Assyria did not intervene actively in Syria again. This made it possible for Hazael to consolidate and extend the power of Aram again and to bring home to the State of Israel the superior might of Aram. The age of the first kings of the house of Jehu seems to have involved Israel in the most serious difficulties with the Aramaeans. In the traditional records of the Old Testament Hazael is considered a particularly dangerous, dreaded and successful enemy (cf. 2 Kings viii, 11-12). Unfortunately no details about these battles have been preserved[3]. When, however, the prophet Amos mentions that the Aramaeans cruelly devastated the land of Gilead, that is, the Ephraimite-Manassitic settlement east of the Jordan (Amos i, 3), he can only be thinking of this last third of the 9th century B.C. The Aramaeans' successes encouraged other enemies to renewed attacks. Hazael supported the Philistines in their conflicts with the States of Israel and Judah (cf. above, p. 236). Amos's allusions to military successes of the Philistines (Amos i, 6) also probably refer to the period of Hazael. The Ammonites also took advantage of Israel's difficulties to invade the land of Gilead. According to Amos i, 13, they perpetrated some extremely brutal murders among the population. The land in question will have been the Gilead south of the Jabbok

[1] Cf. the illustrations in H. Gressmann, AOB², Nos. 146, 147. The Assyrian king on the relief of the nahr el-kelb is probably not Assarhaddon, as was formerly assumed, but Salmanassar, who states explicitly, *loc. cit.*, that he had set up a royal portrait of himself on the mountain of Ba'lira'si.

[2] Cf. obelisk inscription ll. 102 ff. (Gressmann, *loc. cit.* p. 343).

[3] Unless some of the prophetic narratives originally referred to this period (cf. above, p. 242, note 1). In 2 Kings x, 32, 33; xiii, 3 ff. the deuteronomist only makes a few general observations.

to which they had laid claim from an early period and in which they now wanted to 'enlarge their border' (Amos i, 13). A change in this situation was finally brought about by the Assyrians. In his 5th year (800 B.C.) the Assyrian king Adadnirari III marched against Damascus, thus reviving the tradition established by Salmanassar III. He encircled the king of Aram[1] in Damascus and forced him to submit and to pay tribute[2]. This attack appears to have broken the power of the State of Aram. In central Syria we note in the 8th century B.C. a more intense development of the power of the monarchy of Hamath (ḥama) at the expense of the authority of Damascus[3]; and there now came a period of revival for the State of Israel[4]. The decline of Damascus was the inevitable precondition for the successes of Jeroboam II (787–786 to 747–746 B.C.) of whom it is briefly recorded in 2 Kings xiv, 25, that he 'restored the frontier of Israel from the pass of Hamath as far as the sea of the plain' (=the Dead Sea). This is a reference to the restoration of the whole length of the Israelites' eastern frontier from north to south. As a result of this Jeroboam II was probably able to enforce again the Israelites' territorial claims on the Aramaeans and renew the frontier as it was in the age of David and Solomon, which included a strip of the city-state territory in the northern land east of the Jordan with Ramoth in Gilead. Perhaps he was also able to turn back the Ammonites to their frontiers, if they had gained a footing in the land of Gilead. It is not clear what is meant by the expression, 'the sea of the plain', in 2 Kings xiv, 25. In this context the reference is to the frontier with Moab. Was Jeroboam able to revive the Israelite-Moabite frontier as it was in the age of Mesha in the longitude of the northern end of the Dead Sea[5] even if the Moabites exploited Israel's difficult position in order to make further annexations? Or did he even succeed in re-occupying the land as far as the Arnon? Since the Assyrians, once they had broken the power of Damascus, made no further inroads of any consequence for the time being, the State of Israel enjoyed a kind of Golden Age in the first half of the 8th century B.C. in

[1] Adadnirari calls this king ma-ri-'; this is, however, probably not a name but the Aramaic word 'lord' which was used to address the king. It is doubtful if Hazael was still king at this time.

[2] Cf. the inscription on a relief stele of Adadnirari III, of which there is a German translation in Gressmann, *loc. cit.* p. 345.

[3] Cf. M. Noth, PJB, 33 (1937), pp. 47 ff.

[4] There is a reference to this turn of affairs in 2 Kings xiii, 22-25 (cf. 2 Kings xiii, 4, 5); it is only connected here, however, with the transfer of the monarchy from Hazael to his son (the latter took the traditional Aramaic royal name Benhadad and was, as far as we know, the second with this name).

[5] The wording of 2 Kings xiv, 25 supports this assumption perhaps.

which the State of Judah also shared. In the last resort they owed this Golden Age to the intervention of the Assyrians against Damascus. The great power of Assyria loomed sinisterly in the background, even though Israel and Judah rejoiced at the change of fortune which occurred in their affairs *circa* 800 B.C. and believed they were living in a period of renewed prosperity.

PART THREE

ISRAEL UNDER THE RULE OF THE GREAT POWERS OF THE ANCIENT ORIENT

CHAPTER I

THE AGE OF ASSYRIAN AND NEO-BABYLONIAN POWER

20. *The New Situation and its Meaning for Israel*

IN the year 745 B.C., at the time when the long and happy reigns of Kings Ussia and Jeroboam II came to an end in Judah and Israel with the death of these monarchs[1], Tiglat-pileser III came to the throne in Assyria. He was not only himself an indefatigable and successful commander and conqueror, but he was the first of an uninterrupted series of great soldiers on the throne of Assyria who quickly brought the Neo-Assyrian Empire to the zenith of its power and created an empire in the ancient Orient which for the first time united almost the whole of the ancient Orient under Assyrian rule. To be assured of the possession of Syria and Palestine was an essential condition for success, since, for a power in the Land of the Two Rivers, Syria and Palestine was not only a valuable object in itself because of its wealth in timber and ores, which were so rare in the Orient, and its long coast-line to the Mediterranean and its rich commerce, but at the same time it was the gateway to south-east Asia Minor on the one hand and to Egypt on the other. Thus Tiglat-pileser immediately took firm steps to incorporate substantial parts of Syria and Palestine in the Assyrian Empire and to establish Assyrian sovereignty over the whole of Syria and Palestine. In so doing he went substantially further than the Assyrian kings in the 9th century who were, in the main, content with the payment of tribute by the Syrian and Palestinian kings they conquered. The Assyrians entered the land from the north, and thus northern Syria was the first to be affected. But the conquerors rapidly moved farther southwards into Syria-Palestine, which, from the Assyrians' point of view, was of no great size, and Tiglat-pileser even included central and southern Syria-Palestine in his campaigns. The whole of Syria and Palestine suffered a

[1] According to Begrich, *loc. cit.* p. 155, both kings died in the year 747–746 B.C. It is not certain that this was the exact year, but it is correct within a few years.

fundamentally similar fate. A great power without had all the threads of destiny in its hands, and once the Assyrians had taken possession of the land, its history was henceforth determined very largely by the interplay of alternating, mutually hostile and alternatingly victorious, foreign powers; these powers were too overwhelming for resistance to be feasible anywhere in Syria and Palestine for any length of time.

Israel in both the States of Judah and Israel was also affected, particularly as the formation of the State had implicated Israel in the history of the small States of Syria-Palestine in the most intimate way. Israel's period of political independence now came to an end; and to the very end of its history Israel remained dependent on foreign powers—except for one brief interlude. Fundamentally the situation was not a new one at all, for Israel's previous history had been determined all the time by the general historical situation and had been constantly and completely dependent on the historical conditions prevailing over a wide area. Nevertheless Israel had gone its own way, and in the age of David and Solomon had attained a zenith of intrinsic importance. Even though it had become entangled in the conflicts raging in Syria-Palestine in which other, and to some extent more powerful, forces were victorious, it had still been possible for the States which had arisen on Israel's soil to hold their own with more or less success. Now, however, Israel was the victim of an overwhelming process which made all attempts at resistance hopeless, and the scale of which was so great that the whole of Syria-Palestine was forced to submit to it. In fact, the whole of the ancient Orient was affected by it and it soon proved to be not a mere passing storm but a historical turning-point of lasting significance. Along with the other States of Syria-Palestine Israel now came to know the meaning of world history—within its own limited horizons—and all it could do was to yield to its pressure. But this very endurance was instrumental in giving Israel an experience of the nature of world history. The naïve idea that world history is simply an extension on a vast scale of a nation's own history and revolves around that history now became inconceivable. In concrete and extremely brutal events world history proved to be a movement that exceeds the range of a people's own life and an overwhelming process in which a people's life represents but a tiny force.

One has to try and realise what that meant for Israel's faith in God. It was an old idea that the God of Israel displayed His power in the guidance and preservation of His people. He had once caused the tribes to settle in Palestine with His active aid and had stood by them in their struggles to hold their own. He had been 'with David' in his establishment of a brilliant Empire and had promised that his monarchy and dynasty would endure. It had long since been declared that He created and rules over the whole world and that He had special plans for Israel[1] within the world of nations, the far-reaching ramifications of which it had been possible to form some idea since the age of David and Solomon. According to this traditional and widespread conception the only possible interpretation of the process that was now beginning was that, like the gods of neighbouring peoples and States, the God of Israel was now succumbing to the gods of the victorious Assyrians who appeared to be proving themselves even stronger and at whose behest the conquering Assyrian kings, as they solemnly aver in their inscriptions, were taking the field. There will have been many people in Israel who expected that their God must still 'save' them by a miracle[2], and who were disillusioned again and again by the actual course of events.

In this situation there arose one voice in Israel that gave a different interpretation of these events. We refer to the unique historical phenomenon of the so-called 'classical prophecy' of the Old Testament which began about the middle of the 8th century B.C., just at the time when this change in the history and whole world of Israel was taking place, and which pronounced judgement on the historical events. Like the Hebrew word נביא which was applied to begin with to ecstatics, and then to men of God endowed with 'power', who were also a common phenomenon, the term 'prophet', which in Greek means one who proclaims divine oracles (a common type in the history of religion), merely serves as a makeshift to describe the manifestation of classical 'prophecy'. They were men who came forward as messengers of God[3] and claimed a hearing as preachers of a divine message which they presented in the form of axioms and sayings. The content of their message was that the historical events that were now occurring and which would continue, were a divine judgement, a judgement of the very God in whose name they spoke, the God of Israel. Inasmuch as Israel was

[1] This is more or less what the Yahwist (cf. above, p. 220) had said.

[2] Such expectations have also come down to us in the Old Testament; cf. Jer. xxviii, 1 ff., and elsewhere.

[3] The figure of a messenger of God who has to convey divine instructions appears in the sphere of the Mari texts (cf. above, p. 18) (cf. M. Noth, *Geschichte und Gotteswort im Alten Testament* [Bonner Akademische Reden, 3 (1949)], pp. 9 ff.; W. v. Soden, WO, I, 5 [1950], pp. 397 ff.); but the content of these divine messages was not concerned with the great events of history.

being forced to endure these events the God of Israel was proving Himself to be the god not of a tribal confederacy or a single people or State, beside whom the gods of other tribal societies could and must exist, but the Lord of the world, standing above the whole of human history. From this standpoint history appeared no longer merely as the history of a single nation or State but of the whole world in which God acts, no matter how far the world extends in a particular time and situation. The prophets were the first to interpret the events of their time from this universal and divine point of view, not explaining the past retrospectively or making a vague forecast of the general trend of future events, but discerning in the events of their own age the beginnings of the operation of a divine plan.

There is no real parallel to this manifestation of 'prophecy' anywhere else in human history. Above all, we can find nothing resembling it among Israel's neighbours, though the events in question affected the whole world of Syria and Palestine and led to the same results, as the 'prophets' themselves said more than once (cf. Amos i, 3 ff., and elsewhere). The voice of the prophets was heard only in Israel. It was heard in the middle of the 8th century B.C. and thereafter in every time of great historical movements and changes. Moreover, the 'prophets' explained quite clearly that everything that was happening was aimed in the first place at little Israel; they proclaimed this in Israel that Israel might know where it stood. It was God's purpose to execute an annihilating judgement on the present substance of this people because of its unforgivable faithlessness and disobedience. The prophets dared to declare that God was using the whole history of the ancient Orient for this one purpose. For this end the mighty king of Assyria became an instrument in the hand of God (Isa. x, 5), and later on the neo-Babylonian king Nebuchadnezzar became a 'servant' of God (Jer. xxvii, 6) and the Persian king Cyrus an 'anointed' of God (Isa. xlv, 1). They dared to declare that, despite its historical insignificance, Israel was nevertheless the centre of world history in the events of their age, not, it is true, in the role of a leading power, but as the object of God's judgement, of a God who is the Lord of the world, not the visible pivot of historical movements but the secret centre of events. The 'unhistorical' was working in the midst of human history. They were able to say all this solely on the basis of the hypothesis that God had from time immemorial encountered Israel in history and that Israel's duty was to serve God in the future too in the realisation of His universal purpose. In the period that followed, what the 'prophets' had been proclaiming from the middle of the 8th century B.C., that Israel's traditional substance was to be shattered by historical events, was soon translated into reality.

21. *Subjection to the Assyrians*

For Tiglat-pileser (Assyrian: Tukulti-apil-Esarra) III, who reigned in Assyria from 745–727 B.C., the subjugation of Syria and Palestine was one of his principal aims. Unfortunately the annals of this king are defective and incomplete so that it is impossible to get a clear view of all the details of his campaigns. But we know the main events. In the year 740 B.C. he began with the conquest of northern Syria and the establishment of Assyrian provinces on Syrian soil. In the year 738 B.C. he subjugated the northern and central Syrian State of Hamath (ḥama) which had increased its power since the decline of Damascus; he turned great parts of it into Assyrian provinces and left only a remnant as a small dependent State. At this time most of the other Syrian States, including various Phoenician coastal cities and a number of States in Asia Minor, paid tribute to him as a result of his victory[1]. Among the tribute-paying kings he mentions 'Rezon of Damascus' (Raṣunu mātDimaskai)[2] and 'Menahem of Samaria' (Minihimme alu-Samerinai)[3]. In the State of Israel the dynasty had meanwhile been overthrown. After the murder of the last king of the house of Jehu (2 Kings xv, 10) disturbances had occurred in connection with the succession to the throne, from which Menahem finally emerged as a usurper, and he was able to hold the throne of the State of Israel for a number of years. There is a reference to his payment of tribute to Tiglat-pileser in 2 Kings xv, 19 f.[4].

[1] *Annalen*, ll. 150 ff., German in H. Gressmann, AOT², p. 346; for an English translation of the relevant sections of the Assyrian royal inscriptions see ANET, pp. 282 ff.

[2] This is the Rezin mentioned in 2 Kings xv, 37; xvi, 5 f.; Isa. vii, 1 ff. and elsewhere, whose name is not quite correctly vocalised in the Old Testament. The correct reading Rezon is also presupposed in the Septuagint.

[3] The State of Judah appears to have still held aloof from events. All the same, Tiglat-pileser reports in *Annals*, ll. 103 ff., that in 738 B.C. he subjugated an *Azrijau* of *Jaudi* and forced him to pay tribute. The annalistic text, which is very fragmentary at this point, seems to indicate that this Azrijau was at the time the heart and soul of the opposition to Tiglat-pileser. It is difficult not to identify this Azrijau of Jaudi with Asarja = Azariah of Judah. It is stated explicitly in 2 Kings xv, 17, 23 that (against the chronology of Begrich) Azariah of Judah was still contemporary with Menahem of Israel. It is admittedly very difficult to explain historically how small Judah, lying wholly in the south, could have played such a part in the events of 738 B.C.

[4] Tiglat-pileser III is referred to here by his Babylonian throne name of Phul.

According to this he paid a thousand talents of silver and collected this sum from the free landowners in his State who were liable to military service.[1] According to verse 19b he promised himself, as a result of this payment, a consolidation of the monarchy which he had usurped and which he was no doubt only able to maintain with difficulty in this age of regicide and disputes about the succession; Tiglat-pileser may indeed have desired that the kings who had surrendered to him of their own will should remain on their thrones. But Tiglat-pileser did not rest content for long with the success he had achieved in 738 B.C. For the year 734 B.C. the Assyrian register of Eponyms[2] records as the most important event of the year an expedition 'to Philistea'[3]. Tiglat-pileser had therefore advanced as far as the remotest south-west corner of Syria-Palestine. We learn a few details about this campaign from a fragment of the Annals of Tiglat-pileser which has recently been discovered during the excavations in the royal Assyrian city of Kalaḫ (tell nimrūd)[4]. According to this, the Assyrian king, after he had secured a victory on the coast of central Syria, first of all forced his way through the territory of the State of Israel, the western parts of which extended as far as the coastal plain of Palestine, through which the Assyrians moved to the south. In view of its importance for communications they may have, in fact, occupied this part of the State of Israel[5]; he then effected the subjugation of the Philistine State of Gaza, which is dealt with in Tiglat-pileser's 'Small Inscription' No. 1[6] in line 8 ff., after King Hanun had escaped to Gaza to avoid having to surrender, and had abandoned his city to the Assyrians. Finally he established a base on the 'brook of Egypt' (the modern wādi el-ʿarīsh), that is, on the extreme south-western border of Asia. In this way he intended to make it quite impossible for the small States in Syria-Palestine to have any connection with Egypt. Probably the small States in the southern part of Syria-Palestine which were not yet directly affected by these

[1] The figures mentioned here add up to a total of 60,000 such landowners in Israel.

[2] This list, which has been preserved in innumerable parts and copies, enumerates the high officials of the Empire in chronological order, after whom it was customary to name the years within each reign, and from the middle of the 9th century it makes brief catchword-like comments on the campaigns and other events of the individual years; cf. A. Ungnad, *Eponymen* (Reallexicon der Assyriologie, II [1938], pp. 412 ff.).

[3] Cf. A. Ungnad, *loc. cit.* p. 431 and D. D. Luckenbill, *Ancient Records of Assyria and Babylonia*, II (1927), pp. 427 ff., especially p. 436.

[4] Published by D. J. Wiseman, *Iraq*, 13 (1951), pp. 21 ff., Pl. xi.

[5] On this interpretation of the badly preserved lines 10 ff. of the fragment cf. A. Alt, *Tiglathpilesers III erster Feldzug nach Palästina* (*Kleine Schriften zur Geschichte des Volkes Israel*, II [1953], pp. 150-162).

[6] In German translation in Gressmann, *loc. cit.* pp. 347 f.; TGI, pp. 52 f.

events—and these must have included the State of Judah—had to recognise Assyrian sovereignty by the payment of tribute. Within a few years, therefore, Tiglat-pileser had invaded the whole of Syria-Palestine, had spread fear of Assyria's overwhelming power everywhere, and where he did not convert the conquered territories into Assyrian provinces he had made the kings pay tribute to him. To counter these triumphs another attempt at combined resistance seems to have been planned for the following year, 733 B.C., in central and southern Syria-Palestine; and for the last time Damascus played a leading part. Probably the so-called Syrian-Ephraimite war[1] of which we hear in the Old Testament came about in this connection. According to 2 Kings xv, 37; xvi, 5 and Isa. vii, 1 ff., Jerusalem was attacked by the combined forces of the Aramaean State of Damascus and the State of Israel and subjected to the beginnings of a siege; according to Isa. vii, 6 the object of this undertaking was to overthrow the dynasty of David in Jerusalem and to install a king over the State of Judah in its place, who, to judge from the name of his father, mentioned in Isa. vii, 6, was an Aramaean. The Davidic king affected was King Ahaz, a grandson of the King Ussia, who had meanwhile ascended the throne of David after the brief reign of his father Jotham[2]. In the State of Israel a usurper named Pekah, son of Remaliah[3] had lately occupied the throne. The background of this Syrian-Ephraimite war was obviously the fact that Aram and Israel wanted to take the risk of resisting Tiglat-pileser but King Ahaz of Judah, frightened perhaps by Tiglat-pileser's campaign against near-by Philistea in the previous year, refused to join in. The two others intended to depose him, therefore, and replace him with an Aramaean who would bring the State of Judah into the anti-Assyrian coalition. The attack by the two superior enemies on Jerusalem made good progress to begin with (cf. Hos. v, 8-11)[4] and Ahaz was extremely hard-pressed and fearful in Jerusalem (cf. Isa. vii, 2). In this situation Ahaz decided—against the urgent insistence of the prophet Isaiah that he should trust quietly in his God (Isa. vii,

[1] This traditional description is due to the fact that Luther, as well as the English Bible, always renders the name Aram as 'Syria' and that the State of Israel was often called 'Ephraim' by the contemporary prophets (especially Isa. vii, 1 ff.) after its central district.

[2] The chronology of the Judaean kings is very uncertain in this period; probably Ahaz had only been king for a short time (this is contrary to Begrich's view).

[3] In Isa. vii, 4 ff. he is disdainfully called 'the son of Remaliah', without his own name, to denote his non-royal descent.

[4] Cf. the historical interpretation of this word of the prophet by A. Alt, *Hosea v, 8–vi, 6* (NKZ, 30 [1919], pp. 537 568=*Kleine Schriften zur Geschichte des Volkes Israel*, II [1953], pp. 163-187).

1-17)—to enlist the aid of the mighty and he sent a 'present' from the Temple and the palace treasury in Jerusalem to no less a personage than Tiglat-pileser himself, with an offer of surrender and a request for help against his enemies Aram and Israel (2 Kings xvi, 7-9). Unfortunately we are not told where Tiglat-pileser was at this time. Probably he was already with his army somewhere in Syria. Apparently events now moved rapidly. Thanks to the immediate intervention of the Assyrians Ahaz was freed from his tight corner even before Jerusalem fell into the hands of the attacking Aramaeans and Israelites; and so the Syrian-Ephraimite war came to a premature end. It is clear that Tiglat-pileser had not needed Ahaz's request for help as an incentive for his campaigns in Syria-Palestine. At that period his aim anyway was the complete subjugation of Syria-Palestine. He had already appeared in Philistea in 734 B.C. and after Hamath had been finished with in 738 B.C. he found that the Aramaean State of Damascus and the State of Israel were the more considerable powers in Syria-Palestine. For the years 733 and 732 B.C. the above-mentioned list of Eponyms has the note 'to Damascus'. On the other hand, he does seem to have crushed the State of Israel first of all in the year 733 B.C., probably in order to isolate Damascus and keep in check the small states of southern Palestine. At any rate, he notes in his Annals, after he has discussed the conquest of Damascus in detail, that he had already settled accounts with Israel in an 'earlier campaign' (ll. 227 ff.)[1]. According to 2 Kings xv, 29 he invaded the uppermost part of the Jordan Valley in 733 B.C.—coming through the beḳāʿ between the Lebanon and Anti-Lebanon, and from there he conquered Gilead on the one hand and Galilee on the other, and in the Annals ll. 227 ff. he himself recorded that he had annexed 'all the cities' of the land and only left Samaria (Samerina). It follows from the lists of Assyrian provinces that have been preserved, that Tiglat-pileser only left king Pekah of Israel Mount Ephraim with the royal city of Samaria but, for the rest, incorporated the territory of the State of Israel in the Assyrian system of provinces. He divided it among three different provinces, which, according to the Assyrian custom, were usually named after the provincial capitals. Galilee was amalgamated with the adjacent plain of Jezreel in the province of 'Megiddo'. The province of 'Dor' (the city of Dor is the modern el-burj near eṭ-ṭanṭūra)

[1] A German translation of the—unfortunately again very fragmentary—section of the annals on the events of 733–732 B.C. will be found in Gressmann, *loc. cit.* pp. 346 f., TGI, pp. 51 f.

included the Israelite portion of the coastal plain of Palestine from Carmel in the north to roughly the nahr el-ʿōja in the south. The Israelite land east of the Jordan became the province of 'Gilead'[1]. Whilst the indigenous Israelite peasant population in the new provinces was generally left where they were as a subject people, in accordance with a custom that had arisen in the neo-Assyrian Empire, the urban upper class was deported 'to Assyria' as is stated, rather vaguely, in 2 Kings xv, 29. They were sent, that is to say, to some province or other in the Land of the Two Rivers or farther to the east of the Assyrian Empire. In exchange for them, Assyrian governors and officials and a new upper class from other parts of the Empire were sent to the new provinces. King Pekah (Assyrian Pa-ḳa-ha), however, was overthrown by his own people after his defeat (Ann. l. 228; Small Inscription No. 1, l. 17) and according to 2 Kings xv, 30 he was murdered by a certain Hoshea who now made himself king over what little remained of Israel, and paid tribute to Tiglat-pileser and was then confirmed by Tiglat-pileser as a dependent vassal-king (Small Inscription No. 1, l. 17 f.)[2] After Tiglat-pileser had conquered Damascus in the year 732 B.C. and terribly laid waste the State territory of Damascus and turned the whole of it into a series of Assyrian provinces, he was able to consider most of Syria-Palestine subject to his rule, since even the kings who still existed outside the Assyrian provinces administered by Assyrian governors were tribute-paying vassals [3]. And so the situation continued until his death in 727 B.C.

Some years later king Hoshea of Israel was unwise enough to cease paying tribute to the Assyrian Emperor—after the death of Tiglat-pileser the new emperor was Salmanassar V—and to establish relations with Egypt, evidently with the object of escaping from Assyrian sovereignty (2 Kings xvii, 4). It is not to be assumed that the tiny remnant of the State of Israel was acting independently and on its own in this matter. Several States in southern Palestine will have co-operated, but we have no details. This was in the year 724 B.C. An Assyrian force succeeded in seizing king Hoshea in some way or other and occupying the land. Only the strong city of Samaria was able to resist for another three years. Salmanassar

[1] For the details see E. Forrer, *Die Provinzeinteilung des assyrischen Reiches* (1921), pp. 59 ff., 69 and above all A. Alt, *Das System der assyrischen Provinzen auf dem Boden des Reiches Israel* (ZDPV, 52 [1929], pp. 220-242= *Kleine Schriften zur Geschichte des Volkes Israel,* II [1953], pp. 188-205).

[2] Tiglat-pileser says in this passage that he had appointed Hoshea (A-u-si); he means that he confirmed the usurper.

[3] Cf. the list of the vassals in Gressmann, *loc. cit.* p. 348.

will scarcely have employed all his forces to besiege Samaria. Samaria finally fell in the year 722–721 B.C. at the beginning of the reign of the Assyrian king Sargon, Salmanassar V having died a short time previously[1]. And now even the remnant of the State of Israel was abolished and turned into the Assyrian province of 'Samaria' (Assyrian: Samerina). The State of Israel thereby ceased to exist, once and for all. Once again the upper class was deported, this time to Mesopotamia and Media, as is stated in 2 Kings xvii, 6; and there it no doubt suffered the fate of most of the deported upper classes, of being gradually absorbed into the numerically much greater indigenous population. A foreign upper class was introduced into the new province of Samaria, which, according to 2 Kings xvii, 24, came partly from Babylon, from the city of Babylon itself and the Babylonian city of Cuthah, and partly from Hamath in northern Syria[2], partly from places unknown to us. These foreign elements brought their own way of life and above all their own religions with them (cf. 2 Kings xvii, 29-31), but in time they too were absorbed by the Israelite population.

To begin with, we hear little about the further fate of the four Assyrian provinces which arose on the territory of the State of Israel. In the year 720 B.C. risings took place in Syria-Palestine in which the inhabitants of various provinces, including Damascus and Samaria, participated. The residue State of Hamath rebelled against the Assyrians, but the rising was suppressed and the State was turned into the Assyrian province of 'Hamath'. In addition, king Hanun of Gaza bestirred himself again at this period in combination with the rather vague figure of the Sib'u, the 'supreme commander' of the land of Egypt[3], or, at any rate, with Egyptian help. A battle between Assyrians on the one hand and Hanun and Sib'u on the other took place near Rapiḫu (the modern refaḥ) on the extreme south-western border of Palestine, about 25 kilometres south-west of Gaza, in which Hanun fell into the hands of the Assyrians and Sib'u was forced to withdraw into Egypt. This not especially important encounter, which brought the State of Gaza back into dependence on the Assyrians, is noteworthy as the first hostile encounter of the Assyrians, who had achieved supremacy in Syria-Palestine, with Egypt, the power that was henceforth to

[1] Sargon often makes a brief reference in his texts to the conquest of Samaria; cf. Gressmann, *loc. cit.* pp. 348 f.; TGI, pp. 53 f.

[2] Probably these Hamathesians only came after the elimination of the remnant of the State of Hamath in the year 720 B.C. See below.

[3] This Sib'u is no doubt identical with the 'king of Egypt' with whom king Hoshea of Israel established relations, when he ceased paying tribute to the Assyrians in 724 B.C.

be behind all the anti-Assyrian undertakings in Syria-Palestine. The seditious risings in the provinces were doubtless crushed with no great difficulty.[1] For the subsequent century there is only very scanty information available about the provinces in the former State of Israel. A number of governors of the provinces of Samaria and Megiddo appear as Assyrian Eponyms in the course of the 7th century B.C.[2]. A few cuneiform documents from the province of Samaria throw some light on life in the provinces. The governors themselves, and presumably their immediate subordinates, were also no doubt Assyrians. A cuneiform text found in the ruins of the city of Samaria informs us of the title of one such official: the 'rab alāni', the 'head of the cities', who presumably had charge of the cities in the province and, above all, the crown properties, which were given to the members of the new upper class which had been transplanted to the provinces[3]. The personal names which occur in two cuneiform legal documents from the middle of the 7th century B.C. which were found during the excavations in Gezer (tell jezer) throw some light on the ethnic structure of the foreign upper class; they entirely confirm the information about their origins which is contained in 2 Kings xvii, 24[4]. It is worth noting that in one of the documents of Gezer the 'mayor' of this city appears with an Egyptian name. He was evidently the head of the old-established population in which, since Gezer was formerly a Canaanite city, Egyptian names may have occurred from early times. For the rest, it is not surprising that we hardly hear anything of the indigenous Israelite, and to some extent Canaanite, subject population in the provinces[5]. If the State of Israel had been completely eliminated because of its anti-Assyrian activities in 733 and 722 B.C., for the time being the State of Judah continued to exist as a dependent vassal State. King Ahaz had submitted of his own free will to Tiglat-pileser in 733 B.C. (cf. above p. 260). He continued to pay tribute to the Assyrian Emperor. He is mentioned by Tiglat-pileser in a list of the tributary vassal kings[6]. He appears

[1] Cf. especially the annals of Sargon on the second year of his reign (ll. 23-31), in German in Gressmann, *loc. cit.* pp. 348 f., and also the Sargon texts, *loc. cit.* pp. 349 f. (cf. TGI, pp. 54 f.).

[2] Cf. Forrer, *loc. cit.* p. 69 and above all, A. Alt, ZDPV, 52 (1929), p. 226, note 3; p. 229, note 1.

[3] More details will be found in A. Alt, PJB, 37 (1941), pp. 102-104.

[4] The details in K. Galling, PJB, 31 (1935), pp. 81 ff.

[5] It is possible that in the Galilean province the city of Akko (the modern 'akka) replaced Megiddo as the provincial capital already in the Assyrian period, cf. A. Alt, PJB, 33 (1937), pp. 67 ff.= *Kleine Schriften zur Geschichte des Volkes Israel*, II (1953), pp. 376 ff.

[6] Gressmann, *loc. cit.* p. 348. King Ahaz is mentioned here with the full form of his name Jauhazi=Joahas.

to have continued to resist the temptation of taking part in the attempts at rebellion in Syria-Palestine. At least, we do not hear that Judah was implicated in the defection of king Hoshea of Israel and the movement of the year 720 B.C. which took hold of the neighbouring province of Samaria in the north and near-by Gaza in the south-west. Unfortunately, we do not know for certain if Ahaz was still king at this period, since there is no authentic record of the year of his death[1]. He was followed by his son Hezekiah; and under Hezekiah anti-Assyrian activities took place in Judah too. It need not be assumed that Hezekiah's attitude to Assyria was fundamentally different from his father's. But in his time favourable opportunities seemed to offer for getting rid of Assyrian suzerainty. In the years 713–711 B.C. anti-Assyrian risings started in the Philistine State of Ashdod. Sargon reports on them in various inscriptions, though the information cannot be accepted as entirely historical evidence, since the temporal sequence of events is not stated. It is possible, all the same, to discern the main course of events. According to a prismal fragment of Sargon[2] a revolt against Assyria took place in the ninth year of his reign (713 B.C.) arising from disturbances concerning the succession to the throne in Ashdod, in which Sargon had intervened after a cessation of tributary payments. The neighbours were also drawn into this revolt. Sargon reports that, in addition to the Philistines, the 'land of Judah' (^{māt}ja-u-di), the land of Edom and the land of Moab took part in the fighting, and that a combined effort was made to secure the aid of the 'Pharaoh, the King of the land of Egypt' (pi-ir-'-u sar ^{māt}mu-uṣri). In Egypt, probably in 714 B.C., the 25th Ethiopian dynasty had come to power with the accession of the pharaoh Shabaka; and Shabaka seems to have taken an immediate interest in this activity in southern Palestine. At any rate various negotiations took place and Hezekiah of Judah also participated in them. According to Isa. xviii, 1-6, it was at this period that the foreign-looking Ethiopian legates of the Ethiopian pharaoh appeared in Jerusalem. Sargon, who was preoccupied in the north and north-west at the time[3], did not intervene with armed force until the third year[4]. He then sent the Assyrian supreme com-

[1] Begrich, *loc. cit.*, places the death of Ahaz in the year 725–724 B.C. According to 2 Kings xviii, 1 it took place even earlier. According to the dates of the reigns of the Judaean kings given in the Old Testament and according to 2 Kings xviii, 13, it seems likely that it took place later, however; W. F. Albright, BASOR, 100 (1945), p. 22, note 28, suggests the year 715 B.C.

[2] Gressmann, *loc. cit.* p. 351.

[3] Cf. the annals of Sargon on the years 9-11 of his reign.

[4] He reports on this in his annals for the eleventh year of his reign (ll. 215 ff.) and also in the so-called display inscription ll. 90 ff. (Gressmann, *loc. cit.* pp. 350 f.; TGI, pp. 55 f.).

mander, the turtanu, to Ashdod with an army.[1] During these three years the prophet Isaiah warned against trusting in Egyptian-Ethiopian help by means of a sensational and symbolical action in Jerusalem (Isa. xx, 1-6). And in fact the help did not come, when in the 11th year of Sargon's reign (711 B.C.) the rising in Ashdod was put down by the Assyrians. In fact the Pharaoh even handed over to the Assyrians the seditious king of Ashdod who had escaped to Egypt from the Assyrians. The territory of Ashdod, which included the former Philistine city of Gath at this period[2], which had then become Judaean and was later lost to the State of Judah (cf. above p. 000 f.) was turned into an Assyrian province. Its neighbours in southern Palestine including the State of Israel, seem to have withdrawn from the undertaking in good time and to have paid their tribute to Sargon. At any rate they seem to have escaped with impunity.

The anti-Assyrian risings which were occasioned by the death of King Sargon in 705 B.C. were on a larger scale. In the first years of his reign, his successor, Sanherib, was preoccupied in various parts of his great Empire, in enforcing his rule in the face of various rebellions. The South Palestinian States also used the opportunity to throw off Assyrian suzerainty, and this time Judah under Hezekiah did not play a purely marginal role, but was very active and took the lead. Payment of tribute was stopped, and the relationship of dependence on the Emperor thereby abandoned, and all the tokens of foreign suzerainty removed. The so-called religious reforms of king Hezekiah to which a brief reference is made in 2 Kings xviii, 4, and for which Hezekiah was praised unreservedly by the deuteronomist (2 Kings xviii, 3) arose in this context. In the ancient Orient a political régime required the adoption of the official State religion, not in place of, but alongside, the native hereditary religions. In the Assyrian provinces the Assyrian cultus was no doubt introduced in the provincial capitals and practised by the governors; and in the provinces too, on the territory of the former State of Israel, there existed alongside the traditional religion of the local Israelite population, which naturally persisted (cf. also 2 Kings xvii, 25-28, 32-34), not only the religions which the foreign upper class had brought with them from their own land, so long as they maintained their own character (2 Kings xvii, 29-31),

[1] Sargon worded his reports to suggest that he himself went to Ashdod. But Isa. x, 1 contains the obviously more accurate statement that he sent Tartan. Sargon was only able to deal with the south Palestinian rising incidentally. Even in his 11th year he was busy in the north-west of Asia Minor.

[2] Sargon's texts give the name of Gath in the form *Gimtu*.

but also the official Assyrian religion, especially that of the imperial god Assur. This was also true of the dependent vassal States. When king Ahaz of Judah surrendered to Tiglat-pileser, he had to make room for the Assyrian religion in the official sanctuary in Jerusalem. 2 Kings xvi, 10-18 contains a detailed report of how Ahaz had to appear before Tiglat-pileser in Damascus—after the fall of Damascus in 732 B.C.—and had an altar erected in Jerusalem by the priest Urijah, in place of Solomon's old burnt-offering altar, in a central position in front of the Temple building, modelled no doubt on an Assyrian altar which stood in the new provincial capital of Damascus. The previous burnt offering altar was set aside and other furnishings of the traditional religion were modified; above all, the special 'king's entry' into the shrine—a symbol of royal authority over the sanctuary—was removed, and all this was done 'for the king of Assyria' (verse 18). So long as Judah was a tributary Assyrian vassal, that is to say, far into the reign of king Hezekiah, the official Assyrian religion had a place alongside the traditional worship of Yahweh in the State sanctuary in Jerusalem. When Hezekiah abandoned his dependence on Assyria in 705 B.C., he quite consistently abolished this Assyrian religion and thereby 're-formed' public worship in Jerusalem[1]. Hezekiah had allies in his activities, above all among the neighbouring Philistines. It is true that the Philistine States of Gaza and Ashdod[2], which had rebelled against Assyria in 734 and 720 or 713–711 B.C. and had been severely punished, did not join in this time but king Ṣidḳa of Askalon probably co-operated as did the people of Ekron[3] and their king Padi, who remained loyal to Assyria, was delivered by them in chains to Hezekiah of Judah. Judging from this, Hezekiah was evidently playing a leading part at this time in southern Palestine. Egyptian aid was also obtained again—the Ethiopian Shabaka was still on the throne of the Pharaohs—and help was promised. At this time, too, the prophet Isaiah often warned against trusting in the power of Egypt (Isa. xxx, 1-5; xxxi, 1-3 etc.); he alludes to the fact that envoys, no doubt Jewish envoys, 'went down

[1] Incidentally, non-Assyrian elements also fell victim to this 'Reform', such as the old brazen serpent of Nehushtan (2 Kings xviii, 4) which had probably stood in the Temple, since Hezekiah's measures will have referred specifically to the State sanctuary.

[2] A king of Ashdod again appears before Sennacherib, although Ashdod had become an Assyrian province in 711 B.C. We do not know whether a native king was left under the governor or whether the province had been given up again for unknown reasons.

[3] Sennacherib calls the name of this city Amkarruna; its real name was therefore ʿAkkaron. The traditional form of the name is based on a secondary erroneous vocalisation.

into Egypt' to negotiate for military aid[1]. Hezekiah's connections extended as far as the Land of the Two Rivers. After Sargon's death Babylon had renounced Assyrian suzerainty under Merodach-baladan (Babylonic: Marduk-apla-iddin), and one of the Isaiah narratives (2 Kings xx, 12-19) records that this Merodach-baladan sent envoys to Hezekiah with letters and gifts, and that these envoys were shown the treasures, and, above all, the armoury in Jerusalem; this suggests that the main purpose of the mission was to discuss joint military action against Assyria. The defection from Assyria had spread so far that for a time it was possible to hope that at last the effort to destroy the suzerainty of the emperor would be successful. And in fact Sennacherib did require a number of years to suppress all the risings. First of all, he enforced his rule in the Land of the Two Rivers and in the east of his kingdom, subjugating Babylon again and banishing Merodach-baladan. It was not until 701 B.C., four years after his accession, that he undertook the famous campaign against Syria-Palestine to restore the old order there as well[2]. He himself reported on the campaign at length. He had no difficulty in marching through northern and central Syria-Palestine, to restore the old order there as well; these provinces had apparently remained calm. Then he marched along the Phoenician coast, where his only task was to crush king Luli of Sidon[3], whilst the other coastal towns hastened to pay tribute to him as swiftly as the king of Ashdod and the kings of Ammon, Moab and Edom. He then turned his attention to the subjugation of the seditious Philistine States of Askalon and Ekron. Whilst he was engaged on this, an Egyptian force appeared in south-western Palestine. Near Altaḳū, that is, the Eltekeh mentioned in Joshua xix, 44 (the modern khirbet el-muḳanna'), a clash occurred between Assyrians and Egyptians which ended with a victory for the Assyrians. It is not likely that the Egyptians will have used a very formidable force. Sennacherib describes his opponents as 'the kings of Egypt', that is, city rulers probably from the Delta, and also the archers and charioteers of the 'King of Ethiopia', that is, of the Ethiopian

[1] There is no doubt that the formulations in xxx, 2; xxxi, 1 must be understood thus. It is uncertain whether xxx, 4 also refers to Judaean legates.

[2] This report is on two clay prisms, the so-called 'Taylor-cylinder' (German translation of the relevant section, II, 34-III, 41 in Gressmann, *loc. cit.* pp. 352 ff. and TGI, pp. 56 ff.) and a clay cylinder now in Chicago (cf. D. D. Luckenbill, *The Annals of Sennacherib*, Oriental Institute Publications, II [1924] and ANET, pp. 287 f.). On Sennacherib's campaign cf. W. Rudolph, PJB, 25 (1929), pp. 59-80; H. Haag, RB, 58 (1951), pp. 348-359.

[3] This Luli is identical with the 'Ελουλαῖος on whom Menander of Ephesus reports in a quotation to be found in Josephus, *Antiqu. Iud.* IX, 14, 2, §§ 284-287 Niese.

Pharaoh. The reference in one of the Isaiah narratives to the intervention of 'King Tirhakah of Ethiopia' against Sennacherib (2 Kings xix, 9) is evidently a mistake, since in the year 701 B.C. Shabaka was still Pharaoh and Tirhakah, his nephew, did not ascend the throne of the Pharaohs as his second successor until 689 B.C. After the defeat of Altaḳū the remnants of the Egyptians withdrew from the scene and the rebellious States in south-western Palestine were now completely at the mercy of the overwhelming forces of the Assyrian Emperor, who quickly vanquished the Philistines. At the same time he had the land of Judah occupied by his troops. 'Forty-six of the fortified walled cities and the small towns were occupied.' In other words, the whole land fell into the hands of the Assyrians. Hezekiah was only able to hold out in Jerusalem, which was encircled by the Assyrian troops[1]. One or two of the strongholds on the western frontier also continued to offer resistance, including, for example, the city of Lachish (the modern tell ed-duwēr), which was besieged by Sennacherib himself[2]. In this situation there was nothing for king Hezekiah to do but submit to the emperor and pay him a weighty tribute. And he did so, as is recorded in 2 Kings xviii, 13-16, in accordance with the Royal Annals of Judah, and also in Sennacherib's report[3]. Sennacherib accepted this surrender and allowed Hezekiah to stay on his throne once again as a tributary vassal. Admittedly, he inflicted a severe punishment on him. He restricted his authority to the small city-state of Jerusalem, the city of David, and took the whole land of Judah away from him and gave it to the loyal Philistine kings, king Mitinti of Ashdod, king Silbēl of Gaza and king Padi of Ekron who was restored to his old throne[4].

Later on the land of Judah was restored to the Davidites for some reason and on some occasion unknown to us. Possibly this took place under Hezekiah or his son and heir Manasseh. But from 701 B.C. for about three-quarters of a century until the downfall of the Assyrian Empire the Davidites continued to be politically dependent on the Assyrian emperor. No doubt Hezekiah had

[1] This situation presupposes the prophet's sayings in Isa. i, 4-9.

[2] Sennacherib had his siege and conquest of Lachish represented on relief pictures in Niniveh (cf. Gressmann, AOB², Nos. 138, 140, 141). According to 2 Kings xix, 8 he had to besiege the city of Libnah (probably= tell Cornāṭ) as well as Lachish. He did not appear outside Jerusalem but, according to 2 Kings xviii, 17, sent his commander-in-chief (turtanu).

[3] From the fact that thereafter Jerusalem did not have to be conquered again by force, the later Isaiah narratives in 2 Kings xviii, 17–xix, 9a; 36, 37 and 2 Kings xix, 9b-35 derived the idea of the city's miraculous deliverance.

[4] Further details on this in A. Alt, PJB, 25 (1929)= *Kleine Schriften zur Geschichte des Volkes Israel*, II (1953), pp. 242-249.

once again, to make room for the official Assyrian State religion in the Royal sanctuary in Jerusalem, thereby opening the door to foreign modes of religion, for the practice of which his son Manasseh, who reigned for such an astonishingly long period, was severely criticised in the traditional records (2 Kings xxi, 1-18). Probably, in the course of time, all kinds of other foreign religious customs infiltrated into Jerusalem and other parts of Judah with the foreign State religion (cf. Zeph. i, 4-6, 8, 9; 2 Kings xxiii, 4 ff.). All this was the result of political dependence.

The great events in the last third of the 8th century had deprived Israel of the possibility of the free and independent development of her own historical life. The greater part of Israel now lived in a state of subjection in a number of Assyrian provinces, robbed of its upper class which had been deported to other parts of the Empire; and the smaller parts lived in the politically dependent vassal State of Judah. From 701 B.C. there was neither the opportunity nor the desire for political activity. The great events of world history, above all the Assyrian conquest of a great part of Egypt under Sennacherib's son Assarhaddon, which brought the neo-Assyrian Empire to the zenith of its power, took place near at hand but no longer had a direct influence on Israel.

22. *The End of Assyria and the Restoration under Josiah*

The great and dreaded supremacy of the neo-Assyrian Empire collapsed with surprising speed, only a short time after it had attained the summit of its power. The strength of the great Empire suddenly flagged, it seems, and fell a prey to various new enemies. King Assarhaddon had been succeeded by his son Assurbanipal in 669 B.C.; and Assurbanipal did not pursue any warlike activities. His interests were mostly of a different kind; the library of cuneiform tablets which he assembled in his residence at Niniveh and for which he had the works of Accadic literature copied, is famous. In the years 650–648 B.C. his authority was seriously disturbed by internal troubles. The brother of the king, who was called Šamaš-šum-ukin and was appointed viceroy in Babylon, rebelled against Assurbanipal. Assurbanipal managed to suppress this revolt, but, thereafter, the power of the neo-Assyrian Empire declined rapidly. We have scarcely any information about the last years of Assurbanipal's reign. But when Assurbanipal died in about 632 B.C. and left the Assyrian throne first to his son Aššur-etil-ilani and later to the latter's brother Sin-šar-iškun, the Empire was already in decline. Babylon made itself independent under a monarchy of its own as early as 625 B.C. Meanwhile Chaldean tribes whose home had been on the borders of Palestine in the land south of the mouth of the Euphrates, had established themselves and seized the reins of government. A Chaldean named Nabopolassar (Nabu-apal-uṣur) now made himself king of Babylon and became the founder of the neo-Babylonian monarchy. And his monarchy was sustained by the ancient enmity of the Babylonians towards the Assyrians. From the Iranian mountains the Medes began to thrust forward westwards towards the land of the Tigris and threatened the very centre of Assyrian power; under a king whose foreign-sounding name is rendered as Umakistar in Accadish and Kyaxares in Greek, they became an important power and began to play an active part in the history of the ancient Orient. Finally, there appeared at this very same moment the bands of Umman-manda, evidently a Scythian and aggressive people from the steppes of southern Russia, apparently with no definite aim in view, but constituting a danger, nevertheless, on the borders of the Land of the Two Rivers and driving the Assyrians into a tight corner. To these three powers Assyria succumbed.

A fragment of the so-called 'Babylonian chronicle' in which the most important events of the years 616–609 B.C. are briefly summarised from the Babylonian angle, throws some light on the way in which Assur came to his end[1]. The document illuminates the eventful conflicts of those years. By 616 B.C. the battles were already taking place, chiefly around the central land of Assyria and Mesopotamia which adjoined it on the west; the other parts of the Empire that had known such greatness until recently no longer played any part at all. These battles led to the royal Assyrian city of Niniveh falling into the joint hands of the Babylonians, Medes and Umman-manda in 612 B.C. The king Sin-šar-iškun lost his life in the process. Thereupon, a certain Aššur-uballiṭ made himself 'king of Assyria' in the city of Harran in western Mesopotamia, to maintain a residue of the old Empire. But in 610 B.C. the Babylonians and Umman-manda also conquered Harran and expelled Aššur-uballiṭ; an attempt which Aššur-uballiṭ made in the following year to seize the city of Harran back from Syria with Egyptian help, was a failure. This was the end of the Assyrian

[1] This piece was discovered by G. J. Gadd in the British Museum and published in 1923 under the title *The Fall of Nineveh*. German translation in H. Gressmann, AOT², pp. 362-365 and TGI, pp. 59-63.

Empire. Even with Egyptian help it was no longer possible to save it. Egypt, which two generations ago had been the last great target of Assyrian conquest, was now Assyria's sole ally in its death-agony. Meanwhile, in Egypt from 663 B.C. onwards, the 26 Saitic Dynasty had regained its independence and consolidated its position. Though it had emerged in opposition to the Assyrian invaders, in the end it may have thought it worth while to preserve a weakened and reduced Assyria as a protection against the dangerous powers in the east, which were now threatening Assyria in the first place, but might soon encroach on the whole of the ancient Orient. So, at the very outset of his reign (609–593 B.C.) the Pharaoh Nechoh hastened to the aid of Aššur-uballiṭ, albeit in vain. Still, he had to march through the whole of Syria-Palestine, thus laying his hands on this land after Assyrian rule had come to an end.

As a result of these stirring and revolutionary events, the history of Israel also took a new turn. It is not surprising that the peoples subjugated and enslaved by the Assyrians in their far-flung Empire began to stir when they saw that the dreaded power was showing signs of decline. In Israel, too, the fall of the tyrant who, according to the 8th-century prophets, had been the instrument of divine judgement on the people of Israel, was awaited with the utmost yearning[1]. In the political field too, however, the new situation was assessed quite realistically. In the four provinces on the soil of the former State of Israel there was, for the time being, as far as we know, no reaction. Presumably the Assyrian administrative machine continued to function automatically for a time, even without the power of the Empire behind it. The situation was different in the vassal State of Judah. Here king Josiah drew the fitting conclusion from the changed position. King Manasseh, who had sat on the throne of David for more than half a century as the faithful vassal of the Assyrians[2], had been succeeded by his son, who, after quite a short reign, succumbed to a conspiracy in his palace by members of his entourage[3]. The conspirators do not, however, appear to have achieved their aim; the old-established inhabitants of Judah rose against them straight away[4], killed the conspirators and installed the eight-year-old son of the murdered

[1] This expectation is given lively expression above all by the prophet Nahum shortly before the fall of Niniveh.

[2] In an enumeration of his vassals in the west of the Empire, Assarhaddon also mentioned king Manasseh of Judah (Gressmann *loc. cit.* pp. 357 f.).

[3] It is possible that עַבְדֵי אָמוֹן mean above all supreme royal officials.

[4] This is what is meant by עַם־הָאָרֶץ.

king, Josiah, to preserve the traditional succession in the House of David (2 Kings xxi, 23, 24; xx, 1). We are not told why the conspirators murdered Amon. It is possible that it was simply an act of personal vengeance or due to a court intrigue. But it is not impossible—it took place in the year 639–638 B.C.—that the decline of Assyria was one of the reasons and that the conflict between a pro-Assyrian and an anti-Assyrian attitude was partly responsible. It is not possible to be certain about this. The new king Josiah soon followed a line quite consistent with the general historical situation. During the first years of his reign, when he was still under age[1], nothing of decisive significance took place. But as soon as the time for independent action was ripe, he succeeded by degrees in breaking his dependence on Assyria. In 2 Kings xxiii, 4-20 there is an extract, in chronological order, from the Royal Annals which concentrates on the king's activities in the sphere of public worship, but these also throw some light on the king's political line. As part of his so-called 'reform of public worship' he first of all removed the elements of the Assyrian State religion from the royal sanctuary (this is clearly implied in 2 Kings xxiii, 4). This meant the complete revocation of the vassal relationship, and it may be assumed that he also ceased the payment of tribute. Assyria did not take any counter-measures, for it obviously no longer had the power to enforce its sovereignty among its refractory vassals. We do not know exactly when Josiah took this step; it may well have been during the last years of Assurbanipal. Josiah continued to remove from the city-state of Jerusalem all the other Assyrian forms of worship which had infiltrated, especially the worship of astral deities (2 Kings xxiii, 5).

The decline of Assyrian power caused him to envisage as a further goal the restoration of the rule of the house of David in the former State of Israel, which was now divided among four Assyrian provinces. In the absence of a king in Israel, the way was clear for an attempt to enforce the old claim of the house of David to rule once more over the State of Israel and thereby to restore the former dual monarchy of David and Solomon in Judah and Israel. No serious opposition was to be feared from the Assyrians, since the Assyrian provinces in Syria-Palestine were more or less autonomous. Josiah pursued this goal only very gradually. To begin with, he seized the adjacent southern part of the province of

[1] We do not know precisely at what age a king could begin to reign independently and whether a particular age was laid down. From Zeph. i, 8, where the 'king's sons' are mentioned alongside the supreme officials, but not the king, it is usually inferred that Josiah was under age at this time, and not yet personally responsible.

'Samaria'. According to 2 Kings xxiii, 15, he demolished the ancient and famous shrine of Bethel which had formerly belonged to the Israelite kings. This presupposes that he had meanwhile brought under his rule Bethel, which was in the province of Samaria (cf. 2 Kings xvii, 28) and the whole of the southern part of this province. This stage of affairs is recorded in a document to be found in Jos. xv, 18, 19. On closer examination the list of places contained in these chapters turns out to be a list of the twelve districts of the State of Judah, the present form of which can only derive from the period of king Josiah[1]. The twelfth of these districts (Jos. xv, 61b, 62a; xviii, 21b-24a), which originally embraced the eastern part of Benjaminite territory, in so far as it had fallen to the State of Judah after the death of Solomon, included, according to this list, Bethel and Ophrah in the hills west of the Jordan (the modern eṭ-ṭaiyibe north-east of Bethel) and the city of Jericho in the Jordan Valley, that is, what was formerly Israelite State territory and then an Assyrian province. The same list also shows that the fifth district, which had originally embraced only the most northerly part of the hill country west of Jerusalem, was astonishingly wide in extent (Jos. xv, 45 and xix, 41-46).

The formerly Philistine city of Ekron and at least part of its territory as far as the hinterland of the port of Japho (the modern Jaffa)[2] now formed part of this district. Josiah had therefore already widened his sphere of influence considerably to the north-west and even occupied Philistine territory which had not even belonged to the State of David and Solomon. In addition, Jos. xiii also contains a list of places in a new, thirteenth district[3] which shows that in the southern land east of the Jordan too, Josiah began by seizing the territory of the former State of Israel which had presumably fallen meanwhile to the Assyrian province of 'Gilead', in so far as the neighbouring Moabites or Ammonites had not acquired the land south of the Jabbok when the State of Israel fell. Josiah stretched out his hand, therefore, in various directions, towards the territory of the former State of Israel; it is clear that he was making a systematic attempt to bring this area under his control. He aspired to restore the Empire of David. At the same time, however, it is evident that he pursued this goal with all possible care and caution and only advanced towards it by degrees as far as the means at his command allowed him. Presumably, the

[1] Cf. A. Alt, *Judas Gaue unter Josia* (PJB, 21 [1925], pp. 100-116= *Kleine Schriften zur Geschichte des Volkes Israel*, II [1953], pp. 276-288).

[2] Cf. the sketch map in M. Noth, *Das Buch Josua* (² 1953), p. 91 and the description on pp. 92 ff.

[3] Cf. most recently, M. Noth, ZAW, N.F. 19 (1944), pp. 49 ff.

governors of the provinces affected put up as much resistance as they could, with the help of the newly established foreign upper classes. The list of the districts of Judah under Josiah illuminates the initial stage in Josiah's undertaking which lingered on for sufficient time for a new demarcation of the northern districts to be undertaken.

That this was merely an entirely provisional situation is shown by the fact that the accession of territory was added, to begin with, to the State of Judah which was divided into districts and not sufficient to form the basic constituent of the State of Israel which still awaited reconstruction. Later on, Josiah went far beyond this early provisional stage. According to 2 Kings xxiii, 19, he later enforced his religious policy in 'all the cities of Samaria'—this is the first time the name 'Samaria' appears in the Old Testament no longer as the name of a city but, in accordance with the Assyrian practice, the name of a province or country—so he now possessed the whole territory of the Assyrian province of Samaria and therefore the central district of the old State of Israel. Finally, he even encroached on the province of Galilee. In 2 Kings xxiii, 29, we hear of him with his army at Megiddo, the previous capital of this Assyrian province. He had already come fairly near his goal of reviving the State of Israel under his rule. In Megiddo, however, his life and reign came to a sudden end before he had attained his goal. Josiah attempted to restore the old order in internal as well as external affairs as understood in the light of his own age. In reality, he did not merely return to an old order but, as usually happens in such endeavours, created something new. In the 18th year of his reign (621–620 B.C.) a 'Book of the Law' was discovered during building operations in the State sanctuary in Jerusalem and was laid before the king by the high priest (2 Kings xxii, 3-23, 3). This 'Book of the Law' proved to be what was apparently an ancient formulation of the divine law which claimed authority for itself and the ordinances of which were being very largely flouted at this time. The king decided to enforce this 'Book of the Law'. The gradual elimination of the Assyrian State religion from the royal sanctuary was probably already under way as part of the process of breaking Assyrian sovereignty, when the 'Book of the Law' was discovered; Josiah now incorporated in his religious programme the observance of the ordinances of the 'Book of the Law'. He solemnly accorded official recognition to it, not by bestowing on it the status of a State law by dint of his royal authority, but by assembling the elders of Judah and Jerusalem in the Temple, and, reverting to the old tradition of Sinai, causing a covenant to be made in which the partners were Yahweh on the one side and the people, represented by the elders, on the other, whilst he himself, by virtue of his secular position as the ruler of the sanctuary in Jerusalem, which still ranked as the central shrine of the tribes of Israel, took part by conducting the ceremony. This led to a vague amalgamation of the religious order and the State which determined the future course of events[1].

In all probability, this 'Book of the Law' was identical with the original form of the deuteronomist law as preserved in the Old Testament. It was presumably compiled in the course of the 7th century B.C. and was based on various older collections of laws, interspersed with homiletic commentaries, the intention of the compilation being to reformulate the ancient divine law for the present age and to gain recognition for it[2]. It was presented as an interpretation of the law deriving from Moses and, because of this law and the literature arising from it, Moses became traditionally the specific mediator of the law. In fact it contains not merely very ancient statutes but its whole tendency of underlining the purity of the Israelite worship of God as against the local Canaanite religion, was based on an ancient Israelite attitude of mind; and whilst the initial demand for a single place of worship represents a new element and something not required in this way before, it does link up with the old system of the one central place of worship for the sacred federation of the Israelite tribes. We do not know exactly in what circles in the 7th century this 'Book of the Law' was written on the basis of an ancient tradition; nor do we know how it came to the Temple in Jerusalem and remained unnoticed to begin with[3]. Its historical influence only began when it was discovered in the reign of Josiah.

The king was not only responsible for the covenant but used his royal authority to enforce the statutes of the 'Book of the Law'. In this way, though with the best of intentions, he again exceeded his authority by allowing the power of the State to encroach on the realm of the ancient religious and pre-political orders. As far as it was a matter of purifying the worship of God from foreign elements in the royal sanctuary in Jerusalem he had authority to enforce the law and was even committed to doing so according to the covenant for which he was responsible, simply as a member of the Israelite

[1] Cf. M. Noth, *Die Gesetze im Pentateuch* (1940), pp. 34 ff.

[2] Cf. G. v. Rad, *Deuteronomium-Studien* (1947), pp. 11 ff.

[3] The formerly widely accepted idea, that only a 'pious deception' on the part of the Jerusalem priests had staged the alleged discovery, is hardly tenable.

people. But he went further. He singled out the requirement for a unified place of worship and defiled and abolished the local places of sacrifice in the land (2 Kings xxiii, 8a) which had been held sacred from very early times and had then been taken over by the Israelite tribes. He abolished them all in favour of the shrine in Jerusalem which was in fact intended by the law to be the one lawful place of worship within his sphere of government; in the areas which he subjugated anew during the course of his reign he also proceeded to destroy the local places of worship (2 Kings xxiii, 15-19). He no doubt did so on his own royal authority although his secular powers did not entitle him to. The only obligation he had assumed as a member of Israel and as a result of the covenant was to share in the enforcement of the statutes of the 'Book of the Law'. The abolition of the local sanctuaries was an exceedingly violent infringement of the traditional religious life of the people. The limitation of all religious activity to the one and only holy place in Jerusalem reduced the number of religious observances to an extraordinary degree and inevitably brought about a separation between everyday life and religious activity. Hitherto there had been a close bond between them. A particular problem was what was to become of the priests who had been serving the shrines which were now abolished. The 'Book of the Law' in which this question had been carefully considered, had decreed that the priests were to be entitled to sacrifice in Jerusalem and perform their priestly functions there (Deut. xviii, 7). It was not possible, however, to realize this entirely (2 Kings xxiii, 9), probably owing to the opposition of the priests already in Jerusalem. There now came into being, therefore, a second-grade class of country priests, who received the traditional share of religious taxes to which they were entitled but who were not allowed to sacrifice. It was only later that the position of this inferior class of priests was defined and established more precisely (cf. below p. 337).

Josiah's religious policy had a powerful influence in the following period, since the 'Book of the Law' on which it was based, continued to be recognised as authoritative. The centralisation of the place of worship was quickly realised and was soon taken so much for granted that it was no longer necessary to enforce it specifically. The fate which befell the king's political enterprises and successes was different. The restoration of the independence of the throne of David and the initially successful attempt to revive the old State of Israel alongside the State of Judah were possible only thanks to the decline of the Assyrian Empire which, to begin with, left Syria-Palestine to itself, just as David's development of an Empire had been based on the fact that in the 10th century none of the powers of the ancient Orient had been in a position to lay their hands on Syria-Palestine. At the end of the 7th century, however, the revival of Israel was merely a brief episode which only lasted until power relationships in the Near East had settled into a new pattern after the exciting collapse of Assyrian power, and a new great power had appeared in place of the old. In the middle of the 8th century there came upon the ancient Orient the ascendancy of alternating great powers, one power declining only because another was ready to take its place. The great Assyrian Empire had succumbed in this way to powers which were now making ready to take over the reins of power. The age of Josiah, which appeared to open up the prospect of a restoration of the old order, was bound to remain a mere episode; and after Josiah had enjoyed a free hand for a time he was finally drawn once more into the interplay of the great powers which led to the end of his monarchy and his work.

In the year 609 B.C. a conflict occurred between Josiah and the Pharaoh Nechoh. At the time Nechoh was on the way to bring back the Assyrian king Aššur-uballiṭ to Harran (cf. above p. 270) hoping in this way to save at any rate a residue of Assyrian power[1] and at the same time to regain possession of that part of Syria-Palestine that had once been controlled by Egypt and which he hardly intended to give back to Assyria. By this action he became the absolute enemy of Josiah. Josiah's work was based on his disengagement from Assyria and therefore on an anti-Assyrian policy; in fact Josiah was on the side of the powers who were preparing the way for Assyria's downfall, and hence, on the opposite side to Nechoh. At the same time, he was bound to be opposed to the Egyptian seizure of Syria-Palestine, since the independence of Syria-Palestine was necessary for the achievement of his aims and

[1] From the 'Gadd Chronicle' (cf. above, p. 270, note 1) it is clear that the statement about Nechoh in 2 Kings xxiii, 29 is materially incorrect. It is stated in this passage that Nechoh had 'gone up *against* the king of Assyria'. Possibly the preposition was later altered accidentally or—owing to a misconception—intentionally (על instead of אל; it would also be better to read על instead of the following אל). The chronistic parallel report is worded with striking differences and in much more general terms (2 Chron. xxxv, 20: 'came up to fight against Charchemish by Euphrates') and does not thereby contradict what actually took place, probably, however, not as a result of better knowledge of the facts, but in reference to Jer. xlvi, 2, though it is not certain that this passage relates to the events of 609 B.C. A correct tradition has been preserved, however, alongside 2 Kings xxiii, 29 (or is it perhaps based on an earlier version of 2 Kings xxiii, 29?); in *Ant. Iud.* X, 5, 1, § Niese Josephus states the Pharaoh's goal quite correctly in the words: Μήδους πολεμήσων καὶ τοὺς Βαβυλωνίους, οἳ τὴν 'Ασσυρίων κατέλυσαν ἀρχήν· τῆς γὰρ 'Ασίας βασιλεῦσαι πόθον εἶχεν.

he could have no desire to see Assyrian sovereignty being replaced by Egyptian, just as, on the other hand, Nechoh could not allow a stronger power to arise in Palestine if he intended to subjugate Syria-Palestine. It therefore came about that Josiah resisted Nechoh when the latter invaded Syria-Palestine to bring Aššur-uballiṭ back across the Euphrates. The clash occurred near Megiddo (2 Kings xxiii, 29) where the great road through Syria-Palestine which Nechoh evidently used, struck out from the coastal plain of Palestine into the plain of Jezreel after traversing the hill country in the rear of Mount Carmel, to lead them to northern Syria by way of Damascus. At the time Josiah was apparently already in possession of a part of the province of Galilee to which Megiddo belonged, and at this strategically favourable spot[1] he tried to hold up the Pharaoh. The attempt was a failure. In 2 Kings xxiii, 29 there is a remarkably brief reference to the event: 'He [the Pharaoh] slew him at Megiddo, when he had seen him'. We may conclude from this that a battle between the two sides did not in fact take place at Meggido[2] but that Nechoh succeeded in some way or other in seizing the person of Josiah and that the Israelite forces gave up the fight after the king had been killed. And so Josiah's political work was destroyed, not so much because it had been too much bound up with the personality of this obviously very shrewd and energetic monarch, who found a successor of equal quality, but because the victorious Nechoh used his superior power to destroy the political structure that Josiah had built up. After his success at Megiddo, Nechoh moved on first of all to northern Syria to make a vain attempt to help Assyria, which was already in a state of collapse. Meanwhile the body of Josiah was taken to Jerusalem and Jehoahaz, who was presumably his eldest son, was raised to the throne of David in his stead, by the free inhabitants of the land of Judah which, once again, championed the traditional system of hereditary succession in the House of David (2 Kings xxiii, 30). Jehoahaz, however, was only king for three months (2 Kings xxiii, 31), that is, only so long as Nechoh was preoccupied in the north. According to the Babylonian chronicle, ll. 66 ff. the battles around Harran, in which the Egyptians took part, lasted from the month of Du'uz (June/July) to the month of Ulul (August/September). Then Nechoh returned across the Euphrates

[1] The issue of the great road into the plain near Megiddo had already played a part in a similar way on one occasion under Thutmose III (cf. A. Alt, PJB, 10 [1914], pp. 53 ff.).

[2] The chronicler was the first to think of a battle and to describe one (2 Chron. xxxv, 23 f.).

without having achieved his purpose and acted as if he was master of Syria and Palestine. He pitched his headquarters in Ribla (the modern rable in the northern part of the beḳāʿ south of the Lake of ḥömṣ). He ordered Jehoahaz to come there and punished him severely (2 Kings xxiii, 33 f.). He not only deposed him, but had him imprisoned and later taken to Egypt, where he died. Probably Jehoahaz had begun to continue his father's policy; Nechoh would not tolerate this but considered it a rebellion against himself as ruler of Syria-Palestine. He imposed a heavy fine on the country, which, 'according to the commandment of Pharaoh' the inhabitants had to pay each according to his income (2 Kings xxiii, 35). Of his own accord Nechoh made another son of Josiah, named Eliakim, king, changing his name to Jehoiakim. This change of name was no doubt intended to show that the new king was subject to Pharaoh. There can be no doubt but that Nechoh reduced the dominions of the Davidites to the frontiers of the pre-Josiah period, limiting them to the city-state of Jerusalem and the old State of Judah. He demanded recognition of his sovereignty and had the provinces on the territory of the former State of Israel administered as Egyptian provinces. He will have proceeded similarly in the rest of Syria-Palestine. Thus, Syria-Palestine was relegated to its former state of dependence on an Empire; and the prospects which the decline of Assyrian power had seemed to open up, were gone.

23. *Nebuchadnezzar and the End of the State of Judah*

Egyptian rule did not last long. After the fall of Assyria the victorious Medes and Babylonians—the Ummanmanda had now disappeared from the scene—shared the Assyrian booty. The Medes took possession of the north-west and north of the Empire, that is, the Assyrian mother country and the Iranian-Armenian hill country as far as eastern Asia Minor, whilst the new Babylonian government seized the rest of the Land of the Two Rivers and also claimed Syria-Palestine. To gain control of Syria-Palestine, it still had to contend with Egypt, which had meanwhile seized this part of the Assyrian Empire. A battle ensued quite soon. Unfortunately we have hardly any reliable information about this event, the important results of which are so evident. Unlike their Assyrian predecessors, the neo-Babylonian kings, from whom one would expect to have had some information, left behind no annalistic inscriptions and referred to their historical actions only in general terms in inscriptions on their buildings. We are therefore dependent on the information in Jer. xlvi, 2 and the extract from the 3rd Book of Χαλδαϊκά of Berossus[1] which has survived in Josephus, *Ant. Iud.* X, 11, 1, §§ 219 ff. Niese. According to Jer. xlvi, 2, the Egyptian Pharaoh Nechoh, was slain by the 'king' Nebuchadnezzar[2] of Babylon in the fourth year of the Judaean king Jehoiakim—*i.e.* in 605 B.C. Berossus stated more precisely that Nebuchadnezzar was not yet king at that time, that he was entrusted with the command of the Babylonian forces by his father Nabopolassar, who was already a sick man, and he was therefore still only crown prince when he obtained his victory over Nechoh which had such an important influence on the consolidation of the neo-Babylonian Empire. He had to return quickly to Babylon after the victory and the subsequent subjugation of Syria-Palestine, to succeed his father who had died meanwhile (in 604 B.C.). According to Jer. xlvi, 2, a battle took place on the Euphrates near Carchemish (the modern jerāblus which lies at an important crossing of the Euphrates from Mesopotamia to northern Syria); on the face of it, it is not unlikely that a battle ensued at the spot where the two former powers had abutted on one another. It has been doubted, however, whether the reference to Carchemish in Jer. xlvi, 2[3] was originally part of the report on the defeat of Nechoh[4]; and so the question as to the exact site of the battle must be left undecided. Of greater importance is the fact that the neo-Babylonian power obtained possession of Syria-Palestine as a result of its victory over Egypt. This is stated explicitly in 2 Kings xxiv, 7 in the words: 'And the king of Egypt came not again any more out of his land: for the king of Babylon had taken from the river of Egypt (wādi el-'arīsh) unto the river Euphrates all that pertained to the king of Egypt'. And so Syria-Palestine had a new overlord once again, this time apparently without any further incident: at least we do not hear of any. The still existing independent political organisations, especially in southern Palestine, including the State of Judah had to recognise the sovereignty of Nebuchadnezzar. Unfortunately, we

[1] In the 3rd century B.C. Berossus compiled a history of Babylon with the materials available to him in his Χαλδαικά.

[2] We use this form of the name which has become conventional and which derives from the inaccurate rendering in many passages in the Old Testament (especially in the Book of Daniel). The form Nebukadressar, which occurs above all in the book of Jeremiah is better (in Babylonian the name is Nabu-kudurri-usur).

[3] Josephus, *Ant. Iud.* X, 6, 1, § 84 ff. Niese, already connects it with the statement about Nebuchadnezzar's victory.

[4] Cf. B. Alfrink, *Biblica*, 8 (1927), pp. 395 ff.; W. Rudolph, *Jeremia* (HAT, I, 12, 1947), p. 231.

have no details about how the subject and dependent peoples were treated in the short-lived neo-Babylonian Empire in which the most important of the kings was Nebuchadnezzar (604–562 B.C.). It is therefore uncertain whether King Jehoiakim of Judah—like the other vassal kings—now had to provide a space for the Babylonian State religion in the royal sanctuary in Jerusalem. No doubt, the vassals had to pay regular tribute to Babylon. For the rest, the Old Testament passes a very unfavourable judgement on Jehoiakim. According to 2 Kings xxiv, 4, he was a tyrant who shed much blood in Jerusalem, and the prophet Jeremiah also describes him as an unjust and brutal despot whose chief interest was in the sumptuous enlargement of the royal palace in Jerusalem (Jer. xxii, 13-19). He was not a worthy successor of his father Josiah[1]. Moreover, Jehoiakim was unwise enough to try and escape from Babylonian sovereignty. According to 2 Kings xxiv, 1 he only remained loyal to Nebuchadnezzar for three years[2]; when he rebelled, Nebuchadnezzar sent Babylonian troops against him and also gave orders for troops from the neighbouring states of 'Edom', Moab and Ammon to proceed against him. According to the period mentioned in 2 Kings xxiv, 1 this must have occurred around 602 B.C. Either Jehoiakim was able to withstand this not particularly strong attack for a time, or he reverted to his former acknowledgment of neo-Babylonian sovereignty, only to secede again after three or four years. At any rate it was not until the year 598 B.C. that Nebuchadnezzar punished Jehoiakim with any force, by besieging Jerusalem[3]. It is true that the punishment no longer affected Jehoiakim personally, since he died in that year and left the State of Judah and the royal city of Jerusalem to his son and successor, Jehoiachin, in an extremely precarious position. According to 2 Kings xxiv, 8, Jehoiachin, who was only 18 years old at the time, was only king for three months and it is possible that he came to the throne when Jerusalem was already being besieged and unable to hold on much longer. The city was occupied[4] and the king was deported with his family and retinue to Babylon. The treasures

[1] In Jer. xxvi and xxxvi Jehoiakim appears as a scorner of the prophet's words.

[2] The statement in Dan. i, 1 that in the third year of the reign of Jehoiakim Nebuchadnezzar besieged and captured Jerusalem is derived from this chronological reference, the beginning of which must be the neo-Babylonian occupation of Syria-Palestine or Nebuchadnezzar's accession, and from a faulty combination of 2 Kings xxiv, 1 f. with 2 Kings xxiv, 10 (but cf. Alfrink, *loc. cit.* pp. 396 ff.).

[3] Probably he was not present himself. In 2 Kings xxiv, 10 ff. the subject is partly the 'subordinate (officers)', partly Nebuchadnezzar himself (verse 11 tries to smooth out this inconsistency).

[4] The reference to the year in 2 Kings xxiv, 12b ('eighth year of' Nebuchadnezzar's reign) is not entirely correct.

of the Temple and the Palace and other precious things in Jerusalem were seized as booty. The artisans in Jerusalem and the military ruling class who had probably been called up to defend the royal city were removed to Babylon (2 Kings xxiv, 12-16). Jehoiachin continued to live for a long time in Babylon. Four cuneiform documents found in Babylon from the period of Nebuchadnezzar mention his name (Ja-'-u-kīnu or Ja-ku-ú-ki-nu) and even describe him as 'King of (the land of) Juda' (Ja-ú-du or Ja-a-hu-du or Ja-ku-du); they mention that certain quantities of sesame oil were given to him and 'the five sons of the King of Judah'—as Jehoiachin was very young when he was deported to Babylon, this probably refers to princes of the royal house in the wider sense, and to 'eight people of the land of Judah'. These documents were discovered in the royal palace of Babylon. It appears from this that Jehoiachin lived in this palace as a deposed king with members of his family and retinue in a household of his own[1]. The Judaeans who were deported to Babylon dated their years from 'the captivity of King Jehoiachin' (Ezek. i, 2)[2] and probably regarded Jehoiachin as the last and rightful king of Judah and hoped for his return and reinstatement (cf. Jer. xxviii, 1 ff.)[3]. When, after the death of Nebuchadnezzar in the year 562 B.C., Amel-Marduk (in the Old Testament his name appears in the form Evil-Merodach) became king of the neo-Babylonian Empire, Jehoiachin was probably brought to the royal court and treated with honour as part of an act of amnesty (2 Kings xxv, 27-30); this did not, admittedly, imply a restoration of his royal prerogatives but was simply a friendly, purely personal gesture.

After the conquest of Jerusalem Nebuchadnezzar had things reorganised in Judah. He allowed Judah to continue as a vassal State under its own king and still refrained from making it a Babylonian province. As king he installed an uncle of Jehoiachin, a younger son of Josiah (cf. 1 Chron. iii, 15) named Mattaniah, and he changed his name to Zedekiah (2 Kings xxiv, 17), probably, again, to mark the fact that the king and his kingdom were subject to him. In addition, he probably reduced the territory of the State of Judah. Anyway, the word of the prophet in Jer. xiii, 18-19,

[1] Cf. E. F. Weidner in *Mélanges syriens offerts à R. Dussaud*, II (1939). During the excavations on the tell bet mirsim in Palestine the seal of a certain 'Eliakim, servant of Jwkn' was found, that probably belonged to a vassal of the deported king Jehoiakim; cf. W. F. Albright, JBL, 51 (1932), pp. 77 ff.

[2] The Book of Ezekiel continues to date events from this era.

[3] Cf. A. Malamat, *Journal of Near Eastern Studies*, 9 (1950), pp. 223 f.; *Palestine Exploration Quarterly*, 83 (1951), pp. 81 ff.; M. Noth, *Revue d'histoire et de philosophie religieuses*, 33 (1953), pp. 81 ff.

referring to the catastrophe of the year 598 B.C., notes that 'the cities of the South shall be shut up, and none shall open them'. It may be inferred from this[1] that the Negeb was lost to the State of Judah at this time and the southern frontier running north to the latitude of Hebron established, which is well known to us as the southern frontier of the later province of Judah from Persian times. The southern part of the territory of the State of Judah which was separated off in this way was presumably left to the Edomites, who had long since encroached on the southern borders of the land west of the Jordan from their original home, having come westwards across the wādi el-ʿaraba, and were advancing in a northerly direction towards the hills west of the Jordan. The defeat of the State of Judah in 598 B.C. was an important success for them.

In the reduced vassal State of Judah the people found it difficult to acquiesce in the new situation. In spite of the historical experiences forced on them in the last hundred and fifty years there were still voices among them proclaiming the early restoration of what had been lost (cf. Jer. xxviii, 1-4). They were able to gain a hearing and to stir up the people, and they tried with success to influence the obviously weak and undecided king Zedekiah. At this period the prophet Jeremiah issued urgent and repeated warnings and demanded obedience to the sovereign will of Nebuchadnezzar as to the will of God who had for the time being put world supremacy into his hands (Jer. xxvii-xxix). But the people were loath to listen to the prophet and distrusted him as a traitor (cf. Jer. xxxvii, 11-16). It is true that the king himself, who owed his throne to the Babylonian overlord, was not, in his perplexity, entirely unreceptive to the prophet's warnings. To the very end he sometimes summoned him in secret—for fear of public opinion—and asked him for his advice (Jer. xxxvii, 17-21; xxxviii, 14-27). In the end, however, he allowed himself to be persuaded by his leading officials and the clamour of the people to take the insane step of renouncing his allegiance to Nebuchadnezzar. As a consequence, in the 9th year of his reign (589 B.C.) a Babylonian army appeared in his land (2 Kings xxv, 1). His defection will therefore have occurred shortly before this. Probably Zedekiah did not make his move entirely without some preparation. It is true that we hear nothing of one or other of the vassal States in southern Palestine joining in the enterprise, but we have to remember that neo-Babylonian sources contain nothing about events in Judah in the years 589–587 B.C. and that the extracts from the royal Judaean annals concentrate specifically on the fate

[1] Cf. A. Alt, PJB, 21 (1925), p. 108.

of the city of Jerusalem. It may be inferred, however, from the course of events that Zedekiah attempted to establish contact with Egypt at any rate and probably received a promise of aid from that quarter. Anyhow, the State of Judah was, to begin with, apparently, at the mercy of the neo-Babylonian attack and there was no question of Egyptian help. Almost the whole territory of the State of Judah probably fell quite rapidly into the hands of the neo-Babylonian troops and only a few strongholds were able to hold out against them. In Jer. xxxiv, 7 there is a reference to a situation in which, except for Jerusalem, only the two fortresses of Lachish (the modern tell ed-duwēr) and Asekah (the modern tell ez-zakarīye) in the hill country on the western border of the State of Judah, held out, whilst all the other strongholds and, naturally, all the open land had already fallen to the enemy. This may have taken place in the course of the year 588 B.C. The so-called Ostraka of Lachish, inscribed potsherds which were found during excavations on the tell ed-duwēr on the site of the great gateway to this city[1], contain brief reports in letter form, obviously addressed to the commander of the fortress of Lachish. They come from various outposts which maintained communications between the besieged cities in enemy-occupied territory. At the same time they record all kinds of observations. The ostraka reveal very clearly the desperate situation of the State of Judah. They probably include a reference to the fall of the fortress of Asekah which took place at the time. At any rate, in IV, 10 ff. it is stated that 'we give heed to the signals of Lachish . . . we can no longer see the (signals) of Asekah'. On the situation in Jerusalem it is recorded that there were people there 'who weaken the hands of the land and the city' (VI, 6 ff.). According to Jer. xxxviii, 4, this reproach was made in the same words to the king by the supreme officials in Jerusalem in reference to Jeremiah; and if the comment of the writer of the ostrakon does not expressly mention the prophet Jeremiah, it does refer to the influence which proceeded from him and from those who shared his views. The statement in III, 13 ff., according to which the leader of the Jewish militia named Kebaryahu, the supreme commander, 'went down to Egypt', and supplied himself with provisions *en route*, is of great historical importance. The encirclement of Jerusalem where Kebaryahu must, after all, have had his real headquarters, and the enemy occupation of the land, do not seem

[1] Cf. H. Torczyner, *The Lachish Letters* (Lachish, I), 1938. The text of these ostraka is also given in J. Hempel, ZAW, N.F. 15 (1938), pp. 126 ff., and the text of the six most important ostraka in TGI, pp. 63-65.

to have been too severe to make that impossible. In any case we do not learn what commission Kebaryahu had in Egypt, but it must have been concerned with obtaining Egyptian help.

In fact an Egyptian army did appear in the land at this time and forced the Babylonians to suspend the siege of Jerusalem for a time (Jer. xxxvii, 5; cf. Jer. xxxiv, 21). To begin with, the Babylonians had to ward off the Egyptian attack. They probably managed to do that very quickly; the Egyptian army will not have been very strong. Jeremiah proved to be right with his prophecy (Jer. xxxvii, 7-9) that the Egyptians would return to their country and the Babylonians would renew the siege of Jerusalem. Once again the faith in Egyptian help was disappointed; and the fate of the State of Judah was thereby sealed once and for all. After Asekah, the fortress of Lachish also fell and was burned to ashes by the conquerors, as the excavations have shown. And, finally, Jerusalem was overtaken by its fate.

2 Kings xxv only contains a description of the fate of Jerusalem at and after its fall, on the basis of the details contained in Jer. xxxix. This is the only episode in the whole final struggle of the State of Judah which is mentioned. According to this source Jerusalem was besieged from 10th month of the 9th year of Zedekiah to 4th month of the 11th year. With the short interruption caused by the Egyptian attack, the city defied the enemy for well over one and a half years. By then it was starved out and on that 9th day of the 4th month, that is, in the August of the year 587 B.C., the besiegers succeeded in making a breach in the city wall and entering in through it. King Zedekiah tried to escape with his retinue to the east through the 'wilderness of Judah' and then into the land east of the Jordan, but was captured by Babylonian troops as he crossed the Jordan Valley near Jericho and was taken captive to Nebuchadnezzar. Nebuchadnezzar himself was not present at the conquest of Jerusalem, but had his headquarters in Ribla in central Syria like the Pharaoh Nechoh in the year 609 B.C. It might be inferred from this that at the time he was having to enforce his authority elsewhere in Syria-Palestine and that Zedekiah's defection took place in connection with other attempts at rebellion in Syria-Palestine. But we have no definite information on this point[1]. In Ribla he inflicted a stern punishment on the faithless Zedekiah. Zedekiah had to watch his sons being 'slaughtered'; he was then blinded

[1] An inscription of Nebuchadnezzar from the wādi brīsa (translated in AOT[2], p. 365 f.) reports on battles waged by Nebuchadnezzar in the region of the Lebanon. Unfortunately we are not told when these took place.

himself and led off to Babylon in chains, where he probably died soon after. We hear nothing more of him. But conquered Jerusalem was plundered by the conquerors and set on fire, with the royal palace and Temple. According to 2 Kings xxv, 8 this took place on the 7th day of the 5th month of that same year, about a month after the occupation and probably on the express instructions of Nebuchadnezzar, who had first to be fetched from his headquarters in Ribla. The Temple of Solomon went up in flames, and with it presumably the ancient tribal relic of the Ark, about which tradition is silent after the news of its transfer to the Temple built by Solomon and which had since stood in the adyton of this Temple as a reverently guarded traditional object of worship though it may not have played any considerable part in public worship[1]. As we know of no earlier plundering of the Temple to which it might have fallen victim, it was probably destroyed after 587 B.C. with the rest of the Temple, since the Babylonians are reported to have taken the treasures of the Temple in 598 B.C. but not to have taken or destroyed the Ark (2 Kings xxiv, 13). The city wall of Jerusalem was pulled down and the population were no doubt subjected to cruel treatment.

Nebuchadnezzar now made an end of Judaean autonomy. The neo-Babylonians were apparently more hesitant in introducing new political systems than the Assyrians. But Nebuchadnezzar now did what he had failed to do in the year 598 B.C.; he incorporated Judah in the provincial organisation of the Neo-Babylonian Empire and eliminated the Davidian monarchy which had ruled in Jerusalem for about four centuries. Following the Assyrian custom, he turned out the leading upper class. A few men from king Zedekiah's immediate entourage as well as a number of especially prominent people in Jerusalem and the land of Judah who had not been taken prisoner with the king, were now arrested in Jerusalem and taken to Nebuchadnezzar's headquarters in Ribla, where they were put to death (2 Kings xxv, 18-21). For the rest, after the old upper class in Jerusalem and Judah had been taken away in 598 B.C., the urban population of Jerusalem was deported, presumably to Babylon[2]. The peasant population, on the other hand, remained where they were. Inasmuch as he did not

[1] From all kinds of allusions in devotional psalms it is assumed that the Ark was fetched from its adyton on the occasion of particular devotional festivals during the period of the kings and carried around in public processions (cf. Gunkel-Begrich, *Einleitung in die Psalmen* [1933], pp. 411 f.), but there is no absolute proof.

[2] Probably the prophet Ezekiel was not deported until this time (cf.—though with differences on certain details—Bertholet, *Hezekiel* [1936], pp. xiii ff.), and deported to Babylon.

transplant any foreign upper class to Judah and did not set up any new independent organisation in the little territory, Nebuchadnezzar left the reorganisation of the population unfinished. In this respect the situation in Judah was quite different from that in the provinces established by the Assyrians on the territory of the former State of Israel; and this was important for the future course of events. It also shows that the Babylonians acted less consistently than the Assyrians had done before them. Subjugated Judah was even given a Judaean as its supreme administrator. He was a certain Gedaliah, the son of a high Judaean official who is well known from the period of the kings Josiah (2 Kings xxii, 12, 14) and Jehoiakim (Jer. xxvi, 24). We do not know why Nebuchadnezzar chose him for the new post. To begin with, his official residence was not in Jerusalem. The reason for this was probably not so much the intention of degrading the seditious city since the Assyrians had also had no scruples about installing their governors in the conquered royal cities. The reason was probably rather that Jerusalem had been destroyed so thoroughly that for the time being it was impossible to use it as an administrative centre. Gedaliah resided in Mizpeh (probably the modern tell en-naṣbe). which was situated rather eccentrically on the northern border of Judah. Perhaps the reason why this city was chosen was that it had not suffered so badly as other Judaean cities in the battles of the years 589–587[1].

Gedaliah's period of office was not very long. He was soon murdered by a few Judaean officials or officers who had escaped from the catastrophe and fled to the Ammonites in the land east of the Jordan The motive behind their action is unknown and is not made any clearer by the statement in Jer. xl, 14 that they acted on behalf of the king of the Ammonites. The only reason why we have any details about these events is that the prophet Jeremiah was involved in them because Gedaliah's murderers and many other Judaeans in Mizpeh and elsewhere decided to flee to Egypt for fear of Nebuchadnezzar's vengeance for the murder of his agent, and took the prophet with them against his will. We lose sight of him once he has arrived in Egypt. We have the fairly detailed report in Jer. xl, 7-43, (there is an extract from it in 2 Kings xxv, 22-26), but we have no information at all concerning the further course of

[1] The archaeological findings on the tell en-naṣbe which should throw a more exact light on this, are not entirely clear (cf. Tell en-Naṣbeh, I [1947], pp. 50 ff.); but they do show that the settlement on this site lasted beyond the beginning of the 6th century until the Persian period; and traces of a great catastrophe in the year 587 B.C. have apparently not been found.

events. It is possible that Judaeans were appointed as administrative officials even after the murder of Gedaliah. Tiny Judah was probably not established at all as an independent province; it was probably incorporated in the neighbouring province of Samaria, so that the Judaean at its head was only a subordinate of the governor of Samaria, a deputy-governor with limited rights; this might explain the situation which we find very much later in the middle of the 5th century B.C.[1]. In time Mizpeh was also abandoned as an administrative centre, and, in the Persian period, the deputy-governor resided in Jerusalem again. The frontiers of the administrative area of Judah were identical with the area of the State in its last period, if the separation of the southern part of Judah had taken place already in 598 B.C. (cf. above, p. 283). It embraced the ancient and authentic tribal territory of Judah in the hills west of the Jordan, which only began north of the city of Hebron, and also the former city-state territory of Jerusalem with the larger southern part of the old tribal territory of Benjamin.

24. *The Situation after the Fall of Jerusalem*

What happened in the year 587 B.C. was merely the conclusion of a long historical process, which had already begun in the middle of the 8th century B.C. It did not signify in any way a sudden change in the historical situation for Israel. The overwhelming intervention of a foreign great power in Israel's history had long been a fact or which had constantly to be reckoned with. But it is obvious that the destruction of Jerusalem first revealed the whole truth about its historical situation to Israel and that Israel regarded this event as a great and decisive turning-point in its history. Under the impact of this event the deuteronomistic historian described the history of his people, on the basis of the sources available to him, as a history of constantly repeated and increasing disobedience, leading to this culminating event[2]. The threatening prophecy of the 8th and 7th century seemed to be fulfilled in this event; the divine judgement that had been foretold had now come to pass.

In fact, whilst the end of the State of Judah was no epoch-making event of world-historical importance—in Nebuchadnezzar's inscriptions it is not even considered worth mentioning at all—it

[1] Cf. A. Alt in *Festschrift Otto Procksch* (1934), pp. 5 ff.= *Kleine Schriften zur Geschichte des Volkes Israel*, II (1953), pp. 316 ff.

[2] Cf. M. Noth, *Überlieferungsgeschichtliche Studien*, I (1943), pp. 100 f.

was important for Israel from several points of view. It meant the end of the last remnant of political independence on the soil of Israel. Admittedly, for one and a half centuries, apart from a few brief intervals, Judah had merely been a dependent vassal State within the dominions of alternating oriental powers, and it had included only a small part of the Israelite tribes. But it had at any rate had its own king and its own administrative system, and therefore an albeit somewhat restricted political life of its own; with various opportunities of cultivating and safeguarding its life and substance with its own resources. It was still possible to hope that this small and limited residue of independence might some time become the basis of a restoration of Israelite independence; and the successes of king Josiah not so long ago had shown that the hope was not entirely groundless. In Jerusalem this hope had now vanished completely. Above all, the Davidian monarchy had now disappeared in Jerusalem, with the promise and the hope that had been attached to it. It is true that the deported Davidite Jehoiachin lived for a time, though only as a prisoner of the Emperor in Babylon; and it is highly probable that all kinds of hopes of revival were connected with his person, both among the Israelites remaining in the old Palestinian homeland and among the scattered deportees. But in the end Jehoiachin died, as the deuteronomist reports at the end of his work (2 Kings xxv, 27-30), without any of the hopes that had been placed in him having been fulfilled. The Israelite tribes now merely formed a subject population in various provinces, which were governed by the king's representatives; and even though the deputy-governor of the province of Judah may have continued to be a Judaean, he was, all the same, an official of the emperor and as such responsible in every respect to the emperor.

The institution of the monarchy had now come to an end on the soil of Israel. Viewed from the standpoint of the whole of Israel's history it had merely been an episode. It had only emerged when the Israelite tribes had already lived united in a sacred federation for more than two hundred years on the soil of Palestine; and as an independent institution it had not lasted longer than a mere two and a half centuries in the two States of Judah and Israel; for one and a half centuries all that remained was the vassal monarchy in the State of Judah. For more than four centuries Israel then continued without a king and without a political life of its own. After its rapid and extraordinary rise in the age of David and Solomon, the monarchy had soon become an element of decay and had involved Israel in the quarrels of the minor States of Syria and

Palestine and drawn her into mostly unhappy altercations with the intervening great powers. Its disappearance did not mean the end of Israel, just as its emergence had not represented the beginning of the history of Israel. But a return to the state of affairs before the formation of the State was no longer possible in Israel.

It is true that the Israelite tribes continued together on the soil of Palestine with their basic stock and substance. But they were no longer free tribes, as they once had been with the task and chance of self-assertion in their own hands. They had become absorbed in the great and motley company of subjects of a foreign power. What held them together and marked them off from others was their faith which they evidently still had the opportunity of practising in religious observances. Admittedly, the ancient tribal relic of the Ark, which had formed the sacred centre of the tribal federation, had been destroyed. But the Ark had probably long since receded into the background in public worship and become merely a relic guarded in the sanctuary. Meanwhile, the holy place in Jerusalem which the Ark had made the religious centre of the tribes, and which had meanwhile acquired an importance of its own, had become more significant. It had become the place where 'the Lord of hosts dwelt' (Isa. viii, 18) where Yahweh 'caused his name to dwell' (Deut. xii, 11 and elsewhere). It is true that the Temple which Solomon had built on this site had gone up in flames. But the sacredness of the place was not tied to the Temple building. As a ruin it still remained a holy place, it still remained the, 'house of Yahweh'. According to Jer. xli, 5, even after the destruction of Jerusalem by the Babylonians, people came from Shechem and Samaria, in other words, from the territory of the tribes that had never belonged to the State of Judah, but which, without regard to the political frontiers, made their pilgrimage to the sanctuary in Jerusalem as the central sanctuary of the tribes, to make their sacrifice to the 'house of Yahweh'; and religious ceremonies no doubt continued to take place in Jerusalem's holy place, and the tribes remained in touch with this place.

The tribes had not, however, remained completely intact. Their upper classes had been deported by the victors. Even though these upper classes had only formed a tiny part of the tribal stock numerically, they had provided the political and intellectual leaders; and that was the very reason why the victors wanted to take them and uproot them. A foreign upper class had been introduced in the four provinces on the soil of the former State of Israel which had brought with it its own intellectual and religious traditions. It is true that in time it became assimilated to the indigenous country population, just as the inhabitants of the Canaanite city-states which had been incorporated in the States of Israel and Judah under David had been absorbed by the local population. This meant, however, that the greater part of the Israelite tribes became mixed with a foreign element, and only the tribes in the area of the former State of Judah continued with this foreign element of a new upper class. Their own leading groups had been taken off to more or less remote parts of the Empire. Those who had been deported by the Assyrians in the 8th century had long since vanished completely; and only the recently deported upper class lived together in Babylon and probably kept up the connection with those who remained behind in their own homeland; and the same will have applied to the Judaeans who had migrated to neighbouring Lower Egypt after the murder of Gedaliah.

Although the old way of life and the old traditions were maintained to some extent both in Babylon and Lower Egypt, nevertheless the tribes left behind in the old country continued to be the centre of Israelite history and Israelite life. For them the events of 587 B.C. did not in any way signify the end. The links with Israel's past were preserved as was the worship in the holy place in Jerusalem. Probably the deuteronomistic history was written in Palestine[1], where all the sources for the history of Israel contained in literary notes, which the author used in his work, were available. Here, above all, the deuteronomic law continued to be known and applied. The tribes had committed themselves to it in the covenant established by king Josiah and it played an important part in the deuteronomist's work as the authoritative formulation of the divine will. It is true that we have no direct information about the Israelite tribes in Palestine for the half century following the fall of Jerusalem, either concerning the outward circumstances and the course of its life or its spiritual situation. This is a painful gap in our knowledge; for no doubt the reorganisation which took place at the beginning of the Persian period was based on the situation as it had developed in the interim. Source material on this topic is completely lacking. The only continuous source which we have for the history of Israel up to the end of the monarchs is the deuteronomistic history with the traditions which it used. But this work comes to an end with the fall of Jerusalem; and the very much later chronicle which provides a continuation of the deuteronomistic history in a certain direction in its final section (Ezra/Nehemiah),

[1] Cf. M. Noth, *loc. cit.* p. 110 note 1.

was able to make use of a few sources for the Persian period but completely ignored the final fifty years of neo-Babylonian rule for lack of knowledge and lack of interest. There are no sources outside the Old Testament available for the period in question, not only because the neo-Babylonian monarchy, which was ruling in Syria-Palestine at the time, left behind very few historical records anyway, but also because hardly any events of any importance or any substantial changes took place in the western provinces of the Empire which could have had any significance for the Empire as a whole. The only question is whether the vassal States of southern Palestine, which were neighbours of the former State of Judah, did not themselves lose their political independence in the neo-Babylonian period, so that, except for a few Phoenician towns on the coast, the whole of Syria-Palestine was incorporated in the provincial organisation of the Empire. Round about the time of the fall of Jerusalem the States of Ammon, Moab and Edom were still in existence. According to Jer. xl, 14, the then king of Ammon had had a hand in the murder of the Judaean agent Gedaliah; and Jer. xxvii, 3 provides evidence of the existence of kings in Ammon, Moab and Edom alongside the kings of the Phoenician cities of Tyre and Sidon, at any rate in the 4th year of Zedekiah[1]. These eastern States were evidently not affected by the catastrophe which fell upon the State of Judah; in the first place we do not hear of anything to this effect and, secondly, it is expressly stated in Jer. xl, 11 that in the year 587 B.C. many Judaeans fled to Moab, Ammon and Edom, no doubt because there they were able to escape from the direct clutches of the Babylonians. In the course of time, however, these States too were brought to an end[2]. Unfortunately we have no details at all. All the same, a statement by Josephus deserves attention in this connection, according to which, five years after the conquest of Jerusalem (582 B.C.) and in the 23rd year of his reign, Nebuchadnezzar made war on and subjugated the Ammonites and Moabites during a campaign against Koile-Syria[3], following this up with a campaign against Egypt. It is quite impossible to check this information and place it historically. But we must regard it as probably accurate and it may mean that the independence of these States was destroyed presumably because of a revolt against Babylonian sovereignty.

[1] The date given in the present text of Jer. xxvii, 1 has been misrepresented and should be altered in accordance with the original text of xxviii, 1.

[2] *Antiq. Iud.* X, 9, 7, §§ 181 f. Niese.

[3] The inscription of Nebuchadnezzar from the wādi brīsa mentioned above on p. 285, note 1 may perhaps be regarded as confirming this.

In this case only the final fate of the Edomite kingdom remains completely shrouded in darkness. For Israel these events in Ammon, Moab, and possibly in Edom too, meant that she was completely encircled by the dominions of the foreign Empire, that Israel now lived in the world of Syria and Palestine inside a completely uninterrupted provincial system, and that any attempt to change their political situation was unthinkable until such time as the existing order was overthrown by great historical events.

Important though the tribes living in Palestine continued to be for the history of Israel, the fact that parts of Israel were living in other lands far from the homeland also acquired significance. The lands in question were above all Egypt and Babylon; self-contained groups lived there, sticking together and keeping to the old traditions. Stray individuals who had emigrated for one reason or another or had been driven somewhere or other by the revolutionary historical events, soon became lost; and all the time individuals were no doubt leaving the larger self-contained groups and soon becoming absorbed in the foreign environment. For obvious reasons we rarely hear any more of them[1]. As far as Egypt is concerned, we know hardly anything about the life and fate in the immediately following period of those who migrated to Lower Egypt in connection with the catastrophe in Judah. The Lower Egyptian group does not emerge as an important and significant factor until the hellenistic period[2]. The only reason we refer to them at all in this context is that they had their origin in that migration of a numerically far from large band of Judaeans who did probably keep together. On the other hand, we are comparatively well-informed about the so-called 'Judaean military colony' of Elephantine owing to the discovery of papyrus from the island of Elephantine at the lower end of the first cataract of the Nile. The colony consisted of Israelites who had been settled on this island on the Nile by the Pharaohs, with their families, and who were maintained there as a border force to guard the southern frontier of Egypt. Contrary to the deuteronomist requirement of a

[1] In cuneiform documents, especially of the 5th century B.C. (cf. above all *The Babylonian Expedition of the University of Pennsylvania*, Ser. A. Cuneiform Texts, ed. by H. V. Hilprecht, Vols. IX, X, and the University of Pennsylvania, The Museum, *Publications of the Babylonian Section*, Vol. II), we meet numerous Judaean names, particularly in the documents of the great business house of the 'sons of Marasu'. These Judaeans had evidently become absorbed in Babylonian life and felt they were part of the Babylonian world.

[2] Edition of the text and (English) translation in A. E. Cowley, *Aramaic Papyri of the Fifth Century B.C.* (1923). German translation of a few important pieces in AOT[2], pp. 450 ff.

single place of worship, they had a temple in Elephantine in which two other deities were worshipped besides Jahu, evidently a female deity and apparently a young god, in other words, a triad of Gods, like other similar groups of deities in the ancient Near East[1]. The colonists practised a considerably paganised cult of Yahweh, but celebrated the festivals of the ancient Israelite tradition[2] and maintained their connection with Jerusalem[3]. The papyri of Elephantine derive from the 5th century B.C., that is, from the period of Persian rule. But the colony originated in a considerably earlier period, at least as far back as the neo-Babylonian period. In one of the papyri the colonists say explicitly that their fathers built the temple in Elephantine and that the Persian king Cambyses found this temple already completed when he came to Egypt and subjugated the land to Persian rule[4]. Unfortunately it has not been possible to ascertain the exact date and the circumstances of the foundation of this military colony, and the origin of the curious cult of the three gods, which certainly did not begin in Egypt, but was introduced from somewhere in Syria-Palestine, is still somewhat obscure. Anyhow, in the neo-Babylonian, and also the Persian period, the military colony of Elephantine was one of the self-contained groups which lived as Israelite outposts far from the homeland, and that is why we have mentioned it in this context. Unlike the Lower Egyptian group about which we know so little, this Upper Egyptian colony did not apparently last very long. We hear nothing more about it after the 5th century. Probably it was scattered and dispersed in the end[5] and disappeared.

The Judaeans who were deported in 598 and 587 B.C. lived in Babylon; and this Babylonian group played a not unimportant role at the beginning of the Persian era. As was probably also the case in Lower Egypt, the group kept together and maintained the traditions of their own past, except for a few individuals who became absorbed in the new environment. We have all kinds of information about the Babylonian groups which shows that they cultivated and continued the traditions of their fathers. Admittedly,

[1] Cf. especially the *Pap. Cowley*, No. 22, which provides a list of the taxes for the temple of Elephantine for the year 419 B.C. (brief extract from this in AOT², pp. 453 f.). The three deities are named here as יהו, ענתביתאל and אשמביתאל.

[2] According to *Pap. Cowley*, No. 21 (AOT², p. 453; TIG, p. 73) at any rate the feast of Passover and unleavened bread was celebrated from the 14th (15th) to the 21st of the month of Nisan.

[3] Cf. above all the letter sent by the colony to the governor of Judah in Jerusalem in the year 408 B.C. (*Pap. Cowley*, No. 30 [AOT², pp. 450 ff.]).

[4] Thus *Pap. Cowley*, No. 30, ll. 13 f. (AOT², p. 451).

[5] *Pap. Cowley*, No. 30, ll. 4 ff., already reports on the attacks by the neighbouring Egyptians on the colony and the destruction of its temple.

the importance of this group must not be exaggerated. Basing himself on a conception of legitimacy which is understandable in the context of his own age and in very marked antithesis to the Samaritan schism[1], the writer of the historical chronicle so portrayed the course of events as to suggest that the real history of Israel after the fall of Jerusalem may be traced by way of the 'Babylonian exile' of the Judaeans and the later return of these 'exulants' to the province of Judah. This view of things, which has become traditional under the influence of the chronicler, is one-sided. Certain though it is that very important developments in life and thought took place among those deported to Babylon, which were to influence the whole later history of Israel, nevertheless even the Babylonian group represented a mere outpost, whereas Palestine was and remained the central arena of Israel's history, and the descendants of the old tribes who remained in the land, with the holy place of Jerusalem, constituted not only numerically the great mass but also the real nucleus of Israel.

There is some information about the life of the deportees in Babylon in the early period in the book of Ezekiel. Even though, contrary to the later tradition, the prophet's warnings from the period before the fall of Jerusalem were probably spoken in Jerusalem, he was presumably one of those deported to Babylon in 587 B.C. In any case, the book of Ezekiel was edited in Babylon from the standpoint of conditions there; and so it is a source of information on the mode of life of the deportees. It shows very clearly that the deportees were not 'prisoners' but represented a compulsorily transplanted subject population who were able to move about freely in their daily life, but were presumably compelled to render compulsory labour service. The deportees had villages where they 'dwelt' (Ezek. iii, 15); they were able to build houses and plant gardens there and enjoy their produce. They were able to marry and give in marriage (Jer. xxix, 5 f.). According to the Book of Ezekiel the main centre of the deportees was in the region of the 'river Chebar' (Ezek. i, 1-3 and elsewhere), the naru kabaru, one of the canals which traversed the deep alluvial land of the lower Euphrates and Tigris and irrigated its fertile soil[2]. One of the places inhabited by the deportees was Tel-Abib (Ezek. iii, 15)[3]; a few other names of deportee settlements in Babylon are

[1] Cf. M. Noth, *Überlieferungsgeschichtliche Studien*, I (1943), pp. 174 ff.

[2] These are the 'waters of Babylon' which are referred to in Ps. cxxxvii, 1 as a typical feature of the Babylonian landscape.

[3] The name Tel-Abib is probably a native place-name which the deportees altered to suit their own pronunciation.

mentioned in Ezra ii, 59 = Neh. vii, 61. The deportees were able to meet together, and they gladly met whenever someone wanted to sing or speak to them (cf. Ezek. xxxiii, 30-33). They felt strangers in this new land. For them it was a 'strange land' (Ps. cxxxvii, 4), an 'impure' land (cf. Ezek. iv, 13), in other words, a land where it was impossible for them to worship. Their religion was bound up with their old homeland and, according to the deuteronomist requirement, linked specifically with the holy place of Jerusalem; and so they yearned for Jerusalem which they could not forget (Ps. cxxxvii, 5 f.).

The result of this separation from religious observances was that certain traditional customs acquired importance as tokens of their unity with their own past and with the tribes in the old homeland and at the same time as signs of their own unity. These customs were not necessarily connected with real religious observances and had been practised hitherto without having any particular weight attached to them. First of all there was the custom of Sabbath rest on every seventh day, a very old custom, the origin and original meaning of which are lost in obscurity. Among the deportees the observance of the Sabbath now became an expression of the old faith and a mark of separation from the foreign environment; fundamentally the Sabbath was not a religious festival but a kind of 'tabu day' which could be observed without religious ceremonial. The Book of Ezekiel refers repeatedly to the 'sabbaths of Yahweh' as a 'sign (of unity) between Yahweh and his faithful' which is to be 'kept holy' and not 'profaned' (xx, 12 ff.; xxii, 8, 26; xxiii, 38). Presumably the custom of circumcision acquired a similar importance in the same situation. On the other hand, it is not mentioned in the Book of Ezekiel and it may therefore only have become important later on. It had been generally practised in the Syrian-Palestinian world in which Israel had lived hitherto, as much as it was in Egypt. Only the 'uncircumcised' Philistines had seemed foreigners among Israel's neighbours. It could not therefore be a distinguishing mark in this region. The Land of the Two Rivers, however, had apparently never known this custom and in this *milieu* it could and was bound to become a 'sign', a 'token of the covenant betwixt me (God) and you' (Gen. xvii, 11). It is therefore probable, though it is impossible to prove, that the custom of circumcision which was not religious in the narrower sense and was not in any case tied to one particular place of worship, acquired the significance among the deportees in Babylon which it later assumed beyond their immediate sphere. In the course of time the influence of this group became important inasmuch as the customs which had become significant in their special situation acquired great weight for the whole of Israel. The latest stratum of the great Pentateuch tradition, the so-called Priestly Code connects the Sabbath with the creation of the world (Gen. ii, 3) and makes circumcision a 'token' of the 'covenant' between God and Abraham which was fundamental for the history of Israel (Gen. xvii, 11). It is hardly possible to prove, or even merely to suggest, that the Priestly Code was written in the midst of the deportees in Babylon. The strong emphasis on the observances of the Sabbath and circumcision presupposes that these customs had acquired fundamental importance throughout Israel; and, on the other hand, owing to the Priestly Code and the Pentateuch which was based on it, they assumed great prominence throughout Israel.

Altogether Israel's situation had become more and more difficult in every respect since the intervention of the Assyrians in the middle of the 8th century B.C.; and after the loss of the last remnant of political independence in the year 587 B.C. the external situation was well nigh hopeless. Israel was now completely at the mercy of world historical events, bereft of almost all chance of independent action in the maintenance and safeguarding of its life; and this was true of the tribes remaining in Palestine as well as the groups living in Egypt and Babylon. Fundamentally, Israel now lived on the traditions of the past. The backward glance to its previous history and traditions filled its whole life; it held on to whatever it was possible to hold on to, and these things now assumed particular significance. These traditions were so rich in content that they were able to survive and keep the separated parts connected with the whole. Israel had shared the fate of losing its political independence, and the partial dispersal and deportation of the upper class with all the peoples in Syria-Palestine. But so far as we know, none of these peoples was able to preserve the idiosyncrasy of its character and way of life as did Israel, whose uniqueness now led to this historically concrete result. The traditions to which Israel looked back also contained a reference to the future. In the midst of the annihilating events of the past one and half a centuries the prophets of the 8th and 7th centuries had not only spoken their warning of the imminent judgement of God, which was already in operation, but at the same time they had occasionally spoken of God's further plans for Israel. It may be that, under the immediate impact of the final catastrophe, it was difficult to keep alive any hope in a future restoration and that very many were unable to believe in it any longer. And yet this hope did not die even when outward circumstances were most oppressive. Perhaps these very circumstances revived it more and more. And the hope in a new future, which had been promised, no doubt helped to keep Israel together and maintain its awareness of its particularity among the many peoples of the great World Empire. It only needed the reasoned prospect of a fundamental change in the world historical situation to fan the glimmering fire of hope into life again.

CHAPTER II

THE RULE OF THE PERSIANS AND MACEDONIANS

25. *The Re-establishment of the Sanctuary and the Cultus in Jerusalem*

THE neo-Babylonian Empire did not last long. It declined rapidly after the death of Nebuchadnezzar in the year 562 B.C. Its last king Nabonidus (Nabu-na'id), who came to the throne in 555 B.C., was a quaint character who allowed the political organisation to decay, and fell out with the priests of the imperial god Marduk in Babel. But meanwhile events were taking place in the near-by Iranian highlands which were soon to have a decisive influence on the history of the whole ancient Orient. The Medes had contributed in a decisive manner to the collapse of the Assyrian Empire, and acquired as an addition to their Median motherland the northern part of the Assyrian realm as the fruit of their victory, and extended their rule over Armenia and the mountains of Asia Minor westwards as far as Halys. In the south-east they had subjugated the Persian rulers of the house of Akhaemenides, who ruled over ancient Elam[1]. The latter were responsible for the fall of the Medes about the middle of the 6th century B.C. In alliance with the neo-Babylonian king Nabonidus, who feared the military strength of the Medan Empire in his vicinity, the Akhaemenide Cyrus overthrew the Medan king Astyages, with the support of certain circles among the Medan nobility who rebelled against the despotic rule of their own king. Cyrus allowed himself to be made king of the Medes and Persians by the Medan and Persian nobility and assumed the government of the great Iranian kingdom in the Medan capital of Ekbatana. Babylon now saw the still more dangerous Persian monarchy arising in its vicinity in place of the dreaded Medan monarchy. To begin with, however, Cyrus extended his power farther to the west and east. His western neighbour was the Lydian kingdom in the western part of Asia

[1] Cf. P. J. Junge, *Dareios I, König der Perser* (1944), pp. 14 ff.

Minor which arose at the beginning of the 7th century B.C., the first power of any size to emerge on the soil of Asia Minor since the collapse of the Hittite Empire. The proverbially rich king Croesus of Lydia was a contemporary of Cyrus. When the overthrow of the Medan monarchy at the hands of Cyrus upset the stability of Iran, Croesus attacked the kingdom of the Medes and Persians, but was utterly beaten by Cyrus in 546 B.C. and lost his kingdom to the king of the Persians, whose power extended henceforward as far as the western coast of Asia Minor. When Cyrus had subjugated the broad territories to the east of Iran he held an extraordinary wealth of power in his hands.

It was inevitable that these events should be followed with very great anxiety in the neo-Babylonian Empire. But the subject peoples had good reason to hope for the imminent collapse of neo-Babylonian power. The Judaeans who had been deported to Babylon looked with great expectation to the victorious and powerful Cyrus. It is therefore not surprising that the prophet with the unknown name who is called 'Deutero-Isaiah' (Isa. xl-lv), who at this time foretold a new and imminent intervention of the God of Israel as the one divine Lord of all history, continuing the older prophecy of the 8th and 7th century, incorporated Cyrus in his prophecy as the king empowered with government by God as his instrument, and even occasionally mentioned him by name (Isa. xliv, 28 xlv, 1), and that he foretold the imminent fall of Babel quite plainly (Isa. xlvii). It is unfortunately impossible to decide whether Deutero-Isaiah, who was no doubt one of those deported to Babylon, based his prophetic words on the historical events in near-by Iran or whether, on the basis of the prophetic tradition, he proceeded from eschatological expectations of the coming of the kingdom of God and a revival of Israel and then incorporated the person of the victorious Cyrus in these expectations[1]. It may be taken for granted, anyway, that his words were gladly listened to by the deportees in Babylon and powerfully kindled their hopes for a change in their affairs.

In fact Cyrus's expected attack on the neo-Babylonian Empire followed quite soon. After Cyrus had extended his power in various directions to the limits of his horizon, the only power left for him to subjugate was the neo-Babylonian Empire with its dominion over the Land of the Two Rivers and over Syria-Palestine. And he no doubt knew that he was far superior to this power and that he only needed to attack it to quickly overthrow it. He turned against

[1] Cf. J. Begrich, *Studien zu Deuterojesaja* (1938).

Nabonidus in the year 539 B.C. He gave orders to one of his high officials, Gobryas, to attack him. Nabonidus was defeated in a pitched battle, and soon after the victors occupied the city of Babylon, which Nebuchadnezzar had developed in a brilliant and generous fashion as the royal seat of the neo-Babylonian Empire. Cyrus then entered into the ancient and famous city, welcomed as liberator by the priests of Marduk and by many Babylonians who were dissatisfied with the government of Nabonidus. The neo-Babylonian Empire thereby devolved upon him. The Land of the Two Rivers will have submitted to him without difficulty and Syria-Palestine will also have recognised the mighty victor without any further ado, even though, as far as we know, he did not appear there with his army. After his son and successor, Cambyses, had subjugated Egypt to Persian rule in the year 525 B.C., the whole area of the ancient Orient was combined in one Empire, which far exceeded the size of even the neo-Assyrian Empire, which at the time of its greatest power in the first half of the 7th century had represented the hitherto most far-reaching power in the whole history of the ancient Orient. And the whole of Israel, the part which remained in the old homeland, as well as the groups living far away from home, was now in the hands of one emperor.

But the foundation of the Persian Empire signified more than a mere change of sovereign and a further concentration of power. In contrast to their Assyrian and Babylonian predecessors, the Persian kings—and this was to become important for Israel too—adopted a fundamentally different policy in their treatment of the numerous subject-peoples in the Empire. Whilst their predecessors had tried to secure their authority as far as possible by uprooting and putting under tutelage the indigenous peoples in the subjugated areas, and forming a uniform mass of subjects by deporting the upper classes, and introducing the official religion—at any rate in the provincial capitals—alongside the local religions, which they continued, however, to tolerate, the Persian kings respected the traditions and character of the subject-peoples. Certainly not out of benevolent tolerance. Needless to say, they kept the real power in their own hands. It remained concentrated in the person of the king; and the leading officials of the Empire—since the distribution of satraps, introduced by Darius I, they were satraps with great authority—were Persians in every part of the far-flung Empire. Nevertheless, it was a principle of official Persian policy, adopted no doubt in their own interest, not only to allow but even to command their subjects to develop their own life within the limits of political necessity. This is shown by the official regulation of the language question in the Empire which embraced so many peoples. The great monumental inscriptions of the first Akhaemenide kings which have survived, are in three languages; they are written in a Babylonian version as well as an ancient Persian and an Elamic version[1], and all three are in the cuneiform script which derives from the Land of the Two Rivers[2]. Hitherto the emperors of the ancient Orient had only had their inscriptions written in their own language, the language of the nation in power at the time. The fact that the Akhaemenide inscriptions were in three languages put the subjugated peoples on a level with the victors, at any rate in this respect. In official correspondence in the Empire, however, even more official languages were permitted according to local conditions, and these were also used in correspondence with the central government. Thus Aramaic was regarded as the official language throughout Syria-Palestine and in Egypt. This Aramaic, which had been fairly widespread as a spoken language in central and northern Syria, and along the middle course of the Euphrates, since the Aramaic tribes had occupied the land towards the end of the 2nd millennium B.C., and had come to be written more and more in the alphabetic script deriving from the Canaanite world, had, in the final period of the neo-Assyrian Empire, penetrated into originally non-Aramaic regions in Mesopotamia and Syria-Palestine and Egypt as a commercial language, not, to begin with, as a spoken vernacular, but at any rate as an international language which was understood by royal officials and scribes and merchants, and which could be written and read by reason of the simple alphabetic script[3]. By the very nature of things it was the only

[1] Elam had been subject to their dominion even before the great rise of Persian power.

[2] Cf. F. H. Weissbach, *Die Keilinschriften der Achameniden* (1911).

[3] Cf. above all 2 Kings xviii, 26, according to which already at the end of the 8th century B.C.—provided that the prophetic legend in question has not anachronistically in mind the conditions of a period about a century later—whilst the people in Jerusalem could not yet speak Aramaic, the ministers of the Judaean kings as well as the high Assyrian officer and official who was besieging Jerusalem at the time were able to. As far as the latter is concerned, we may leave it aside—the narrative presupposes somewhat naïvely that he was also able to speak 'Judaean'—but this passage is certainly typical of the situation in Syria-Palestine towards the end of the Assyrian period. In this connection the letter of a south Palestinian ruler found in sakkara in Egypt in 1942—his name and the name of his residence have unfortunately not been preserved in the fragmentary text—is very significant. It is addressed to the Egyptian Pharaoh in the period of neo-Babylonian rule, and is written in Aramaic, which was not the mother-tongue of either the writer or, still less, of the addressee. (The text in H. L. Ginsberg, BASOR, 111 [1948], p. 25.) Aramaic written in letter script was used at this period for international correspondence, like the Babylonian which was written in cuneiform script in the Amarna period.

language that could be used as an official language in a major part of the Persian Empire and Syria-Palestine and Egypt because it was already so widespread. The official use of Aramaic in the south-western parts of the Persian Empire had an important influence on the development of this language. It not only promoted the further advance of Aramaic as a spoken vernacular, but at the same time a particular form of language was developed in official correspondence, and a particular orthography, the so-called 'Imperial Aramaic'[1] which was the basis of the further development of the Aramaic dialects.

Even more important, however, than this consideration for the linguistic independence of the many peoples living in the Empire was the attitude of the Persian government to traditional local religions. This was a sphere which the subject peoples inevitably felt to be particularly closely bound up with their very being, and the importance of which was only enhanced by their political tutelage. The Persian kings treated this matter with particular care, no doubt with the intention of thereby reconciling their subjects to their sovereignty. By means of this wise policy they strove, certainly not without success, to strengthen their Empire. We have some remarkable evidence from various sources on this point. After his entry into Babylon, Cyrus revived the local religions in the Land of the Two Rivers, restoring to their traditional places the divine images which the last neo-Babylonian king Nabonidus had arbitrarily moved to the city of Babylon, thereby presenting himself in marked contrast to Nabonidus, as the protector of the ancient religious traditions[2]. Cambyses too, the son and successor of Cyrus (529–522 B.C.) who succeeded in bringing Egypt into subjection to Persian rule, and who made himself hated on account of his despotic and brutal nature, followed the same line; and from Egypt itself, the conquest of which was accompanied by all kinds of cruelty and senseless destruction, we have evidence that Cambyses respected the religious traditions, and, where necessary, restored them. He not only added an Egyptian throne name to his own, in accordance with the traditions of the land; he also turned his attention to the ancient cult of the goddess Neith in the Delta city of Sais—which had been the home of the last Egyptian dynasty which he had abolished—and which he probably considered the capital. According

[1] On this concept cf. H. H. Schaeder, *Iranische Beiträge*, I (Schriften der Königsberger Gelehrten Gesellschaft, geisteswiss. Kl. VI, 5 [1930]), pp. 27 ff.; the same, *Esra der Schreiber* (1930), p. 41.

[2] Cf. the so-called Cyrus-cylinder (Weissbach, *loc. cit.* pp. 2 ff.; AOT[2], pp. 368 ff.; TGI, pp. 70 ff.: ANET, pp. 315 f.), ll. 33 ff.

to the inscription of Uzahor[1], in response to the latter's representations he removed the foreign elements which had meanwhile infiltrated into the shrine of Neith, saw 'that the Temple was purified', 'that the divine property was given to the great mother of God, Neith, and to the great gods in Sais, as of old', and 'that all festivals and processions were celebrated as of old'. The Israelite colonists on the isle of Elephantine reported, however, that when Cambyses entered into Egypt not the slightest damage was done to their temple, whereas the temples of the Egyptian gods were pulled down[2]. Darius endeavoured all the more to preserve and promote the religious traditions of the subject-peoples. The most important evidence of this is the decree which he issued to the Persian administrator of crown lands, Gadatas, in the district of Magnesia on the Meander in western Asia Minor, which was cut in stone in Roman times and has therefore come down to us[3]. It is written in Greek, which was probably the official language of the Persian administration in western Asia Minor. This decree is important above all because it speaks of the royal 'attitude to the gods' thereby explicitly characterising the content of the decree as the result of a fundamental attitude to religious institutions and customs. It declares that this attitude had been handed down by the royal 'forefathers'. Gadatas is threatened with the king's wrath if he does not cease forthwith to disregard the king's attitude by imposing a tax on the 'sacred gardeners of Apollo' and forcing them to do statute labour, in other words, violating the evidently traditional privileges of certain persons connected with the cultus. For the later Akhaemenides we only have the evidence of the Passover ordinance of Darius II of the year 419 B.C. which has been found among the papyri of Elephantine[4]. The text, which is unfortunately in a bad state of preservation, contains a decree by the king which was sent to the Persian satraps from Egypt, and orders that the feast of the Passover and unleavened bread shall be celebrated in Elephantine in exact conformity with current regulations. Unfortunately it is not known what occasioned this decree. It is difficult to believe that the Persian government bothered itself with all the details of the innumerable religions in its great Empire. Wherever—as in this latter case and the case of the decree sent to Gadatas—definite abuses were brought to its knowledge in reports or complaints, it will have intervened with

[1] Cf. the translation in R. Kittel, *Geschichte des Volkes Israel*, III (1927/29), p. 291, note 1.

[2] *Pap. Cowley*, No. 30 (AOT², pp. 450 ff.), ll. 13 f.

[3] The Greek text in Ed. Meyer, *Die Entstehung des Judentums* (1896), pp. 19 f.

[4] *Pap. Cowley*, No. 21; cf. AOT², p. 453 and TGI, p. 73.

very definite official regulations designed to preserve or restore ancient local religious institutions.

The important and momentous decree of Cyrus concerning the rebuilding of the Temple also arose in this wide context. The official Imperial Aramaic text of this decree has come down to us in Ezra vi, 3-5, as part of an official correspondence between the satrap of the great satrapy of 'Transeuphrates' which embraced most of Syria-Palestine[1]—this satrap may have resided in Damascus—and the royal court, which derives from the time of Darius I. This correspondence, which is concerned with the question of permission to rebuild the Temple in Jerusalem, consists of the satrap's question as to whether the rebuilding is permissible and a reply in which Cyrus's basic decree is referred to and quoted verbatim (Ezra v, 6–vi, 12). This correspondence, which was so eminently important for the religious community in Jerusalem, became known in Jerusalem and a copy of it was preserved there. Considerably later it was put, with another correspondence referring to the rebuilding of the city of Jerusalem, in a collection of Aramaic documents, provided with a commentary, which is now to be found in Ezra iv, 6–vi, 18, and was available to the writer of the chronistic work as the main source of his exposition in Ezra i-vi[2]. Cyrus's decree dates from the 'first year of King Cyrus'—meaning the first year of his rule over the formerly neo-Babylonian kingdom, in other words, the year 538 B.C.—and ordains that 'house of God be [re-]built in the place where it is the custom to kill the sacrifices and offer "fire sacrifices"', that is, on the site of the former sanctuary where religious ceremonies had continued to be maintained. The expenditure for the reconstruction was to be met 'from the King's house', that is, from public funds. Finally, the decree ordains the surrender and return to the new Temple of the valuable fittings of the former royal sanctuary which Nebuchadnezzar had seized as booty and which were evidently still in Babylon, Cyrus's decree therefore represents an act of reparation, and clearly arose from the policy of restoring old religious institutions pursued by the Persian kings.

It may be asked how Cyrus came to bother himself about what

[1] The official Aramaic description of the satrapy was 'beyond the (Euphrates) river' (as seen from the Land of the Two Rivers).

[2] The authenticity of these documents, which has often been doubted and still is occasionally doubted even today, has been substantiated in detail and illuminatingly, above all by Ed. Meyer, *Die Entstehung des Judentums* (1896), pp. 8 ff. On the problem of the literary origins of the Aramaic section Ezra iv, (6), 7–vi, 18 and its parts cf. M. Noth, *Überlieferungsgeschichtliche Studien*, I (1943), pp. 151 ff.

he can scarcely have regarded as a very significant local religion on the very confines of his great Empire so soon after his assumption of the neo-Babylonian dominions in a land which, though it came to him as part of the neo-Babylonian Empire, he never even entered himself. The action was certainly not due to his own initiative. But it is easily conceivable that some of the Judaeans who had been deported to Babylon and who watched Cyrus's restoration of the ancient religions in the Land of the Two Rivers, drew the attention of the Persian court to the fact that a neo-Babylonian ruler had also destroyed a sanctuary in Jerusalem which ought now to be restored and that, to prove this, it should still be possible to find the booty which was stolen from this holy shrine. It was not difficult to discover this evidence in Babylon. But for the deportees, as well as the tribes who had remained in the land and for other scattered groups from Israel, the restoration of the Temple was a matter of basic importance, since the central federal religion which had been located in Jerusalem for so long was still the centre of an Israel which held fast to its traditions. It is true that the fact that Cyrus did give official instructions for the restoration of the Temple in Jerusalem did not, by any means, signify the fulfilment of the expectations which Deutero-Isaiah had linked to the person of Cyrus as the divine instrument who was to effect the final decisive change in history, but it showed, nevertheless, that the hope for a fundamental change and improvement in the situation which had been connected with the emergence and approach of Cyrus had not been unwarranted. Some have found it particularly difficult to believe that Cyrus made available State funds for the rebuilding of the Temple, and have used this as an argument against the authenticity of the decree quoted in Ezra vi, 3-5. But it was in line with the policy of promoting the local religions to give State financial aid where necessary. And in the present case there was a special reason to do so; Nebuchadnezzar had destroyed and robbed the Temple, and so Cyrus, as the heir of the neo-Babylonian government, who was deliberately adopting a different policy in religious matters, had cause to make amends for the wrong done by Nebuchadnezzar, and, in addition, the Temple was formerly a royal sanctuary, the care of which now devolved on the Persian Emperor as the legal successor of the former Judaean kings. But if Cyrus made himself responsible for the cost of restoring the Temple, it was only fitting that he should also give some general directives on the style of the new building (Ezra vi, 4a).

Cyrus's decree refers exclusively to the restoration of the sanctuary. Later on, in his story of the new beginning after the 'exile', the chronicler gave a paraphrase of his own in Hebrew (Ezra i, 2-4), on the basis of the text with which he was familiar, connecting the release of the deportees with the order for the restoration of the Temple. As he thought of the ancient homeland, and, in particular, the city of Jerusalem as an almost uninhabited ruin, he was probably bound to conclude that Cyrus made available the forces needed for the restoration work and allowed those deportees to return home who offered their services for the work. His view was that only a tiny residue of country folk (cf. 2 Kings xxv, 12) had stayed in Palestine and that only the foreign upper class had remained in the provinces of the former State of Israel. According to him, however, none of these elements took part in the sacred work of rebuilding the Temple. For him the legitimate line of Israel's history was represented by the Judaeans who had been deported to Babylon, many of whom had to return to the homeland if the restoration of the Temple was to be feasible. He therefore supplemented the original text of Cyrus's decree in the way that seemed to him objectively necessary and historically correct. In fact there is no mention in Cyrus's decree of a repatriation of the deportees. It was not necessitated by the rebuilding of the Temple, since the main body of the tribes had remained in the land and had continued to hold religious services in the holy place even after Nebuchadnezzar's destruction of the Temple. They could now undertake the restoration. It may be that some of the deportees did return to Jerusalem and the land of Judah and that the Persians did not put any obstacles in their way; but the number who returned was presumably not very large, particularly as conditions in the land, with so many towns and villages destroyed and the city of Jerusalem itself still very largely in ruins, can hardly have been very inviting[1].

How far from encouraging the situation actually was, in spite of Cyrus's decree, is shown by the pathetically slow progress of the work itself. Cyrus had to issue a special order to get his decree enforced. According to the information of the elders in Jerusalem and Judah, which was used in the above-mentioned communication from the satrap of 'Transeuphrates' to Darius I, Cyrus had

[1] In Ezra ii, 1-67 (69) = Neh. vii, 6-69 (71) we have a great list, of which it is uncertain whether the chronicler used it as traditional source material or whether it was inserted at a later date. It is introduced as a list of home-returning deportees; but it is impossible to decide whether that is what it really represents or when the return of the people listed took place. On this list cf. now K. Galling, JBL, 70 (1951), pp. 149 ff.

commissioned a certain Sheshbazzar[1] to take the stolen treasures of the Temple back to Jerusalem and to take charge of the rebuilding, and this Sheshbazzar had at any rate caused the foundations of the new building to be laid (Ezra v, 14-16). Sheshbazzar is described as a 'governor'[2] installed by Cyrus (Ezra v, 14). All the same, it is not easy to say what official position he held. Was he governor of the province of Judah, which now continued as an independent province or had been reconstituted; or was he deputy-governor of the special district of Judah which came under the administration of Samaria? Or was he perhaps not a real governor at all, but merely a special agent charged with returning the Temple fittings and the restoration of the Temple[3] in accordance with the instructions described in Ezra v, 15? It is impossible to give a decisive answer. All that is known for certain is that Cyrus in fact gave a definite commission for the execution of his decree. Nor do we know who Sheshbazzar was. His Babylonian name shows that he was not a Persian official. As it is not clear why a Babylonian should have been given the commission, one wonders if he was a deported Judaean who, like others of his kind in Babylon, had been given a Babylonian name[4] and for some reason or other seemed to the Persian government to be a suitable person for this task. It is idle to attempt to identify him with any other known personality[5], such as the Shenazar mentioned in 1 Chron. iii, 18, who appears fourth in the list of sons of the Judaean king Jehoiakim[6]. Conceivable though it is that a Davidite was entrusted by the Persians with the execution of the royal decree concerning the rebuilding of the Temple, there is no real case for identifying Sheshbazzar with Shenazar[7]. It is better to accept the fact that all we know about the person of Sheshbazzar is the little contained in Ezra v, 14-16.

[1] This form (English Bible: Sheshbazzar) reproduces the Babylonian name Samas-apla-usur. The chronicler mentioned Sheshbazzar in Ezra i, 7-11 in connection with the list—authentic or feigned—of the restored treasures of the Temple which he includes (cf. on Ezra i, 7-11 K. Galling, ZDPV, 60 [1937], pp. 177-183) and of his own accord he gave him the title 'Prince of Judah'.

[2] The Hebrew-Aramaic פחה is not entirely clear, and could describe a Persian satrap or a provincial governor.

[3] In the latter sense see Galling, *loc. cit.* p. 179.

[4] Cf. for example Zerubbabel who will be mentioned later, and also Dan. i, 7, and also M. Noth, *Die israelitischen Personennamen* (1928), p. 63.

[5] The chronicler does not appear to distinguish him from Zerubbabel, since he tacitly has Sheshbazzar's instructions carried out by Zerubbabel (Ezra iii, 1 ff.).

[6] Thus, above all, Ed. Meyer, *loc. cit.* pp. 75 ff., and latterly E. Sellin, *Geschichte des israelitisch-jüdischen Volkes*, II (1932), pp. 83 f.

[7] If manuscripts of the Septuagint seem to suggest the likelihood of this identity of names, what has happened is either that the names have inadvertently been distorted or, possibly, the two names have been intentionally approximated to one another.

The foundations of the new Temple were laid without delay. But then the work came to a standstill. The reasons may be inferred from the prophetic sayings in Hag. i, 1-11. The situation in Jerusalem and in the surrounding country was so bad, and therefore so discouraging, that no one could muster any enthusiasm for the work of rebuilding the sanctuary, and even the royal ordinance that the work was to be paid for out of State funds did not suffice as an incentive to start operations. It was said: 'The time is not come, the time that the Lord's house should be built' (Hag. i, 2). People were still far too preoccupied with their own troubles and worries and 'every man ran unto his own house' (Hag. i, 9). There were, it is true, people who were already living in 'ceiled houses' (Hag. i, 4), but probably they were few in number and Jerusalem was still very largely a ruined city where many people were pitifully housed, and in the countryside things were no better. On top of all this there was a drought (Hag. i, 10 f.) and in its train bad harvests (Hag. i, 6) to make the inhabitants concentrate all the more on their own personal afflictions. Thus the foundations remained untouched and the work presumably soon came to a complete standstill.

A new impulse was needed to bring about a change. It was provided once again from great historical events. Sixteen years after the Cyrus decree and after the first start at rebuilding the Temple the Persian king Cambyses died (522 B.C.) without leaving a son to succeed him. The monarchy thereby devolved on another line of the house of Akhaemenides, on Darius, the son of Hystaspes, who had been a member of Cambyses' immediate entourage until the latter's death in Syria. But before Darius was able to take over, he had first of all to overcome numerous dangerous risings which broke out in many parts of the Empire after the death of Cambyses. Cambyses had had a younger brother named Bardija, who, unlike Cambyses, had not been born until after Cyrus's accession and enjoyed wide esteem. Before embarking on the conquest of Egypt, Cambyses had secretly had this brother killed as a dangerous rival. After the death of Cambyses a man called Gaumata passed himself off as this brother, who had allegedly not been killed at all, assumed the name Bardija and usurped the Persian throne. He found many supporters, above all in the central parts of the Empire, in Media-Persia as well as in the Land of the Two Rivers, and at the same time various parts of the Empire took the opportunity of regaining their former independence. For a whole year Darius overcame his enemies in unremitting, intense, but on the whole successful, battles and subjugated the seditious areas, until in the end, towards the end of the year 521 B.C., he was able to regard his monarchy as fundamentally secure[1].

In Israel the shock that went through the great Empire in that year revived the expectation of the last decisive crisis in history which the prophets had foretold. Even though Syria-Palestine was not directly involved in the disturbances of the time, the course of events was watched with excitement, and the excitement had an after-effect when the situation in the Persian Empire had become consolidated again. In the second half of the year 520 B.C. the prophet Haggai spoke in Jerusalem, and at the beginning of the year 519 B.C. the prophet Zechariah had the nocturnal visions recorded in Zech. i, 7–vi, 15.[2] Both prophets were awaiting the coming of God's reign which was heralded by the historical confusions of the time. For both of them it was important in this connection that the Temple in Jerusalem should at last be rebuilt and completed in view of the impending events. Unlike the earlier prophets of the 8th and 7th centuries, they were unable to conceive the presence of God except in relation to a holy place. Therefore Haggai urged the resumption of work on the Temple. The difficulties of the time—he argued, as against the general opinion—did not in any way prohibit the work of restoration: on the contrary, these very troubles were themselves the divine punishment for the delay in resuming the work (Hag. i, 1-11). And if the shabbiness of the new building—compared with the splendour of the former royal shrine of David, which old people in Jerusalem had seen with their own eyes in their youth—took all pleasure from the work of reconstruction, it should be remembered that every nation would soon be bringing its treasures to this house of God, once the Kingdom of God had dawned (Hag. i, 15b–ii, 1-9). In fact, by his insistence Haggai brought about the resumption of work on the Temple towards the end of the year 520 B.C. (Hag. i, 12-14). In one of his visions Zechariah saw the high priest being purged and dedicated to the service of the new sanctuary (Zech. iii, 1 ff.).

At the time the Davidite Zerubbabel was 'governor' in Jerusalem. He was a grandson of the king Jojachin, a son of the latter's first-born son Shealtiel[3]. He was appointed as a Persian official and

[1] Cf. now P. J. Junge, *Dareios I König der Perser* (1944), pp. 43 ff., which is based on the great Darius inscription on the rock of Behistun (illustrated in the *Westminster Historical Atlas to the Bible* [1945], p. 9).

[2] For a different chronological estimate and historical interpretation of Zechariah's night-visions see now K. Galling, *Vetus Testamentum* ([2]1952), pp. 18-36.

[3] In Haggai (and also in Ezra) Shealtiel is always referred to as father. This is probably correct in view of the statement in 1 Chron. i, 19, according to which Zerubbabel was the son of a younger son of Jehoiachin. The name Zerubbabel is Babylonian (Zēr-Bābili).

acted as provincial governor in Judah or deputy governor under the governor or of the province of Samaria. According to Hag. i, 1 ff. his attention was drawn to the work of rebuilding the Temple by the prophet, and according to Hag. i, 12 he did in fact take an interest in the work. But very much more far-reaching hopes were associated with him. Should he, the scion of the House of David, presumably even in the line of the first-born, and at the moment the leading man in Jerusalem and Judah, albeit for the time being only an official of the Empire, not be the future king in a renewed Davidian Empire as occasionally foretold by the prophets of the 8th and 7th century? In fact Haggai and Zechariah saw the figure of Zerubbabel more or less clearly in this light. In face of the imminent convulsing of the whole world, Haggai addresses him as the signet chosen by Yahweh (ii, 20-23) meaning probably that in the Kingdom of God Zerubbabel would be God's representative on earth. In vi, 9-14, however, Zechariah speaks of a divine commission which came to him to prepare a crown and to set it on the head of Zerubbabel as the future king[1]. This is a unique case of prophets referring the expectation of a future 'Messiah' to an already existing historical figure, and it is clear from this with what feverish excitement men were looking for an impending, imminent and final change in the historical situation. We do not learn the extent of the influence exerted by the prophetic vision expressed by Haggai and Zechariah and the hope reposed in Zerubbabel, but it is easy to imagine that the impatience and excitement were great in Jerusalem itself and probably among the tribes in the countryside too.

We know nothing about the outcome of this affair. When Haggai and Zechariah were speaking, Darius I had the Empire firmly in his hands again; and it was soon bound to become clear that the disturbances that followed the death of Cambyses had not been 'the beginnings of sorrows' (Mark xiii, 8) of the eschatological end of time, but only a temporary crisis, that the Empire was again rapidly consolidated in the hands of a strong and shrewd ruler and that the course of history resumed its progress on the same line as before. And so the hopes that had moved men's minds for a time soon had to be abandoned as false. Outwardly this movement probably did not make much impact or find expression in concrete action. It is possible that the Persian authorities did not have to intervene. There had been no open revolt against their

[1] Subsequently the name Zerubbabel was replaced by the name of the priest Josiah in Zech. vi, 11 in view of the historical outcome.

sovereignty. Possibly, too, nothing further happened to Zerubbabel in spite of the hopes that had been reposed in him. At any rate, we do not hear of anything happening to him, though it must be remembered that, apart from the fairly late commentary on the Aramaic documents in the Book of Ezra, there is no Old Testament tradition from which one might have expected any information on the matter. Perhaps Zerubbabel continued as governor or deputy governor in Judah.

Perhaps, on the other hand, if the internal happenings in Jerusalem and Judah had become known to the governor of Samaria and the satrap of Transeuphrates and the Persian court, he was recalled as a somewhat dangerous official and replaced with a successor. Evidently the whole affair was of no great importance to the Persian authorities.

This is clear from the fact that Darius gave express permission for work on the completion of the Temple in Jerusalem to be continued. The most important historical result of the eschatological hopes of the first years of Darius's reign had been the resumption of work on the rebuilding of the sanctuary. Admittedly it was contested by the satrap of Transeuphrates, though this was the only thing he did object to; he had enquiries made in Jerusalem and sent in a report to Darius with a request for further instructions and he received a reply from the Persian court. This official correspondence has been preserved in Ezra v, 6–vi, 12. Unfortunately it is not precisely dated, but it undoubtedly derives from the period after the appearance of the prophets Haggai and Zechariah described in the later commentary in Ezra v, 1-5. After all, it was these prophets who succeeded in getting work on the Temple resumed; and the satrap could not have obtained a report on it until it had been resumed. It is striking that in his report the satrap only passes on the information given by the elders in Jerusalem, in which reference was made above all to Cyrus's decree about the rebuilding of the Temple without any mention of the movement which proceeded from Haggai and Zechariah and the figure of the governor, Zerubbabel. The Persian authorities took no official cognisance at all of the movement and possibly they never even heard of it. But Darius's reply explicitly confirmed Cyrus's decree on the basis of official statements, and repeated the instruction contained in the decree that the costs of rebuilding were to be borne by the State, and that even the requirements of the sacrificial rites in the former royal sanctuary, which had formerly been the concern of the Judaean king, were to be provided from State resources (Ezra vi,

8, 9), and that, in return, prayers were to be offered in the new sanctuary 'for the life of the King' (Ezra vi, 10). The old character of the building as a State shrine—the elders in Jerusalem had expressly mentioned that 'a great king of Israel' had built the Temple (Ezra v, 11)—was therefore to that extent preserved; and this was entirely in line with the policy of restoring the ancient religious customs, the only difference being that the rights and duties of the earlier kings of the now subject peoples had now been transferred to the Persian monarchy and its great administrative machine.

The impulse that had proceeded from Haggai and Zechariah continued, even though the eschatological hopes behind it inevitably died away for the time being; and so, after Darius had confirmed the Cyrus decree, within a few years the rebuilding of the Temple was completed. According to a statement in Ezra vi, 15 which, belonging to the framework of the Aramaic documents, may be regarded as quite reliable and based on a firm tradition, the rebuilt sanctuary was solemnly consecrated on the third day of the month Adar in the 6th year of Darius's reign, *i.e.* in the spring of the year 515 B.C. Israel again had a religious centre where the traditions of Solomon's Temple could be resumed, and the event was of decisive importance for Israel's future life precisely because it had lost its political independence and many of its people were living away from the homeland. Even if the old sacred federation of the twelve tribes had continued to exist, not merely as an idea but also as a reality, even during the period of the Kings, with Jerusalem, the place of the sacred Ark, as its religious centre[1], nevertheless, as an outward form of Israel's life, it had inevitably been pushed into the background by the various and varied political organisations; and in this period the central sanctuary had been in the first place a royal sanctuary. Political independence and the institution of an independent monarchy had now fallen to the ground and the Temple, whose character as a State sanctuary was now only apparent in the fact that its restoration had been ordained in a decree issued by the far-off Persian Emperor and that in it prayers were offered for this Emperor, and that the requirements above all of sacrificial animals for the official rites were met from public resources, had again become the real centre of Israelite life. Israel was now the great religious communion centred on this shrine. Among the many peoples embraced by the Empire which extended over most of the known world, Israel was

[1] Cf. M. Noth, *Die Gesetze im Pentateuch* (1940), pp. 23 ff.

marked out and held together by the tradition of the deeds which God had performed on its behalf, by a number of special customs, and, above all, by a common allegiance to the Temple in Jerusalem. This did not mean a return to the former amphictyonic organisation. The tribal system had been, at any rate, greatly relaxed. It is true that substantial parts of the old tribes still lived in their old tribal areas. But in addition to them there were now strong and important groups in Babylon and Lower Egypt, among whom membership of a particular tribe ceased to have any real meaning; and to these groups were added, in the course of time, further larger and smaller groups of scattered Israelites in the wide realms of the Persian Empire and even beyond its frontiers. It was impossible to revive the functions of a tribal confederation, which, already limited in many respects since the formation of the State, were bound gradually to decay as a result of the events which took place after the middle of the 8th century. The tribal relic of the Ark no longer existed; all that remained was the holy place which it had formerly occupied and which retained its unique significance as a place of worship. Israel remained gathered round it as a religious community, in the narrower circle of those who had remained or had returned to the homeland and in the wider circle of the Diaspora.

This led to the priestly element in Israel acquiring an importance which it had not had hitherto. The first priest of the Temple in Jerusalem now became the head of all Israel: he became the 'High Priest'. Israel had not had a priestly hierarchy before. We do not know whether the former tribal federation had maintained an amphictyonic priesthood at the central sanctuary. In any case, numerous local sanctuaries had existed alongside the central place of worship, and these, or at any rate the more important of them, had had their own bodies of priests. And so it had continued in the age of the kings, when the priests at the central sanctuary in Jerusalem had been royal officials of the house of David, whose authority only extended, however, to this central sanctuary, and who were quite unconnected with the other priests in the country. It was king Josiah's fulfilment of the deuteronomist requirement of a single place of worship that had made the High Priest of Jerusalem the priestly head of all Israel. But he still remained a royal official. The end of the house of David effected a change. We do not know who saw to the continuance of worship on the site of the ruined Temple of Solomon. The rebuilding of the Temple which resulted from Cyrus's decree, and the reorganisation of public worship in Jerusalem which this made possible, also led to a reorganisation of the priesthood in this sanctuary. As royal officials and members of the upper class in Jerusalem the Zadokites, who had held priestly office in Jerusalem by heredity since the reign of David and Solomon, had been deported by Nebuchadnezzar. It may be that members of the Zadokite family had remained behind in Jerusalem, that they continued to act as priests and that they formed the basis of the reorganisation of the priesthood. It may also be that, as a result of Cyrus's decree, some deported Zadokites returned to Jerusalem[1]. In any case it is highly probable that the Zadokites formed the priesthood in the new sanctuary, with a new and far more important role at the head of Israel. In Haggai and Zechariah, and thereafter in the commentary on the Aramaic collection of documents and in the chronistic narrative, in Ezra i-vi we meet Jeshua the son of Jozadak as 'High Priest'. He is the first holder known to us, and presumably the first anyway of this office, which played such a great part from now until the end of Israel's history. After the decline of the old amphictyonic organisation and the elimination of the independent State as the basic vehicles of Israelite life, the cultus and priesthood came into the foreground.

26. *The Reorganisation of Life under Persian Influence*

For the next half-century after the dedication of the new Temple we have practically no information about the history of Israel. The restoration of the sanctuary and the reorganisation of the priesthood did not lead to the complete renewal of the decayed organisations of the old Israel or their replacement by new organisations. There was a plan for reorganisation, which probably arose among the deportees in Babylon, since it was appended to the book of the prophet Ezekiel which was compiled in this circle (Ezek. xl-xlviii). This plan reckons, however, with an eschatological order of things and disregards historical facts. It was therefore only of limited use as the basis of a practical order which was bound to take into account the actual historical situation.

Thus life in Israel continued for the time being without a new organisation. In principle the deuteronomist law continued to be

[1] In this case the statement in 1 Chron. v, 41 may be historically correct. According to this the father of the Joshua who is mentioned immediately afterwards was a Zadokite deported by Nebuchadnezzar.

valid; it had not been introduced as a State law, so that it did not necessarily cease to have validity when the State organisation was dissolved. As it had received its authority from a covenant between God and People it was not dependent on political changes. In fact the deuteronomist requirement of a unified place of worship appears to have been strictly adhered to; and, so far as we know, no other sanctuaries, such as had flourished a generation previously, emerged again, even in the period when the sanctuary in Jerusalem was in ruins. After its restoration, however, the Temple of Jerusalem was regarded all the more as the only legitimate shrine. In other respects, however, the deuteronomist law which Josiah had already regarded merely from the point of view of its demand for unity in worship, was probably given scant attention. How far from satisfactory conditions were after the restoration of the Temple is shown by the collection of prophetic words which has been preserved under the unauthentic name 'Malachi' and which is usually assigned, probably correctly, to the period between the completion of the Temple and the emergence of Ezra and Nehemiah. In this collection there is a reference to the carelessness with which the priests carried out their functions, inasmuch as they disregarded the regulation that the animals intended for sacrifice should be blameless, and neglected their duty of religious teaching (i, 6–ii, 9). There is also mention of their dishonesty in the delivery of tithes for the sanctuary (iii, 6-12), of their failure to take the worship of God and the fear of God seriously enough (iii, 13-21), of their frivolity in dissolving marriages (ii, 10-16). Marriages were often made with foreign women from neighbouring peoples, and such foreign marriages even occurred in the families of the priests themselves (cf. Neh. xiii, 23-28). Strict observance of the Sabbath was no longer carried out (cf. Neh. xiii, 15-22).

The impulse for a new order of life proceeded in the end from the deportees in Babylon, who probably kept more strictly to their fathers' traditions and ordinances in their foreign environment than did the tribes who had remained in Palestine. They managed to interest the Persian government in the need for reorganisation in Palestine. Certainly the Persians themselves had no personal knowledge of the nature of the organisations which were important for Israel. But they were probably able to understand the importance of consolidating the situation in Palestine and particularly in the land of Judah. It is true that this was only a small and peripheral part of their great Empire, but it was of some importance. The rebellion of the satrap Megabyzos of Transeuphrates about the middle of the 5th century B.C. made Syria-Palestine a delicate spot for them, and they were inevitably concerned to create as calm an atmosphere as possible in this area; the more so as in the second half of the 5th century Persian rule had to be enforced in Egypt against all kinds of attempts at independence. But the land of Judah was near the marching route to Egypt, not far from the final halting-places on Near Eastern soil before the passage through the Sinaitic desert into the land of the Nile. The grounds of a warehouse form the 5th-4th century have been found near the province of Judah, south of the frontier stronghold of Gaza, in the ruin of tell jemme which lies on the wādi ghazze. This store was evidently intended for the supply of the Persian troops who were sent to Egypt[1]; still further south on the wādi ghazze the tomb of a Persian from the last third of the 5th century has been discovered, evidently that of a Persian officer who was stationed there[2]. In a word, it is clear that the Persians were interested in restoring stability in the land of Judah and in Palestine in general and that they were therefore open to suggestions which seemed likely to appease the population in this area, especially if these proposals seemed likely to result in the restoration of the traditions of one of the subject peoples, which they had always promoted. This is the wider context in which the sending of Ezra and Nehemiah to Jerusalem is to be understood.

It is not easy to unravel the traditional records concerning Ezra and Nehemiah, nor is it easy to assign precise dates to them. We hear of both of them only within the framework of the great chronistic history which was not written till very much later, though in this section it was able to turn to account certain literary sources. The tradition concerning Nehemiah is, however, much more certain and fruitful than that concerning Ezra. For Nehemiah the chronicler had at his disposal Nehemiah's own statement, the so-called 'Memoirs of Nehemiah', and he incorporated this statement verbatim and perhaps in its entirety. According to Neh. i, 1; ii, 1 Nehemiah was sent to Jerusalem for the first time in the 20th year of Artaxerxes. This must refer to Artaxerxes I Longimanus, since in a papyrus of Elephantine of the year 408 B.C. there is mention of the sons of the governor Sanballat of Samaria[3], who is no doubt identical with the Sanballat whom Nehemiah repeatedly refers to as his enemy. This rules out all possibility of a later

[1] Cf. Fl. Petrie, *Gerar* (1928), Pl. xiii.

[2] Cf. Fl. Petrie, *Beth-Pelet*, I (1930), Pls. xliv-xlvi and also J. H. Iliffe, *Quart. of the Departm. of Antiqu. in Palestine*, 4 (1935), pp. 182 ff.

[3] *Pap. Cowley*, No. 30, l. 29 (cf. AOT², p. 452).

Artaxerxes having been Nehemiah's royal master. Nehemiah therefore went to Jerusalem for the first time in the year 445 B.C. The traditional sources regarding Ezra are very much more meagre. The chronicler had at his disposal the official document commissioning Ezra, of which he gave the Imperial Aramaic text in Ezra vii, 12-26. Everything else that is told about Ezra is contained in the late chronicler's own account as is proved by a linguistic scrutiny of the whole story of Ezra[1]. The content of the Ezra narrative is based entirely on the information in the above-mentioned document and the chronicler's own combination of Ezra and Nehemiah[2]. Now this document also mentions an Artaxerxes as having commissioned Ezra (vii, 12). That this is also a reference to Artaxerxes I is to begin with merely the opinion of the chronicler, whose work was probably only composed in the course of the 3rd century B.C. and of which it is impossible to be certain that he had at his disposal a trustworthy tradition of the Ezra-Nehemiah period based on oral transmission. He described the story of Ezra and Nehemiah on the assumption that their activities were more or less contemporaneous and very largely interlocked. The authentic sources, the Ezra document and the Nehemiah memoirs, make no reference to any such co-operation. All the same, it is probable that Ezra's Artaxerxes was also Artaxerxes I Longimanus (465–424) and not Artaxerxes II Mnemon (404–358)[3] or even Artaxerxes III Ochus (358–337), since the reorganisation of life in the religious community in Jerusalem with which both Ezra and Nehemiah were particularly concerned, emerged as an urgent problem about the middle of the 5th century and was also recognised as such by the Persians. All the same, the assignment of Ezra to the reign of Artaxerxes I is merely very probable, not absolutely certain; and even then the exact dating of Ezra is problematical. It is true that it is stated in Ezra vii, 7-9 that Ezra was sent to Jerusalem in the 7th year of Artaxerxes—the year 458 B.C. if one accepts that this was Artaxerxes I. But not only is Ezra vii, 7 a post-chronistic addition, but presumably the passage Ezra vii, 8, 9 was only subsequently inserted in the chronicler's work[4], since it plainly interrupts the flow of the narrative. It is

[1] Cf. A. S. Kapelrud, *The Question of Authorship in the Ezra-Narrative* (1944). There is not sufficient evidence for the opinion expressed here that at any rate an oral Ezra-tradition was transmitted in 'chronistic circles', until it was finally fixed in writing.

[2] Cf. M. Noth, *Überlieferungsgeschichtliche Studien*, I (1943), pp. 145 ff.

[3] The thesis that Ezra did not come to Jerusalem until after Nehemiah and under Artaxerxes II was first argued in detail by A. van Hoonacker, *Néhémie et Esdras, une nouvelle hypothèse sur la chronologie de l'époque de la restauration* (Le Muséon, 9 [1890], pp. 151-184; 317-351; 389-401.

[4] Cf. M. Noth, *loc. cit.* pp. 125 ff.

not known why Ezra's mission was later placed in the 7th year of Artaxerxes' reign. But if the Aramaic Ezra document and the chronistic work places Ezra in the age of Artaxerxes (I) only in a general way, the question of his chronological relationship to Nehemiah still remains unsolved. It is true that we have the chronicler's opinion that Ezra came to Jerusalem before Nehemiah; but again it can hardly be assumed that this opinion was based on a real tradition. It might well be the case that the chronicler only put Ezra first and made him work simultaneously with Nehemiah because Ezra's special task seemed to him more urgent and important. The question would then be whether it is possible to reach some conclusion on objective grounds about the chronological relationship between Ezra and Nehemiah. It might be said that Nehemiah found cause in Jerusalem and the land of Judah, to create order in the chaotic situation in religious and everyday affairs, and this would not suggest that Ezra had already brought to Jerusalem that law whose task was to provide the foundation for a binding organisation of the whole of life[1]. For this reason Nehemiah will be put before Ezra in what follows here, and it will be assumed that Ezra only came to Jerusalem in the latter years of Artaxerxes' reign[2]. It must be stressed, however, that it is impossible to reach an absolutely firm decision on this point because there is a lack of reliable and unambiguous evidence, and that all we can hope to attain is a limited degree of probability.

Nehemiah was descended from the group of deportees in Babylon. He had reached the position of a royal cup-bearer in Shushan, one of the Persian royal cities. This gave him the opportunity of direct access to the king's person. He is the sole concrete example known to us of the way in which it was possible to obtain the Persian king's interest in Jerusalem's affairs. He was perhaps not the only deportee to obtain some kind of post at court. At the outset of his own account of himself (Neh. i, 1–ii, 8) he tells how once some people who had to come to Shushan from Judah reported to him on the hopeless conditions that still prevailed in Jerusalem, with its walls and gates and a good part of its houses in

[1] The chronicler's account makes Ezra wait for the appearance of Nehemiah before proclaiming and enforcing his law. This is highly unlikely to have been the case (Neh. viii, 9). Nehemiah is then said to have carried through various reforms without any reference to this law (Neh. xiii, 4 ff.).

[2] W. F. Albright also places Ezra chronologically after Nehemiah in the final period of Artaxerxes I (*The Biblical Archaeologist*, 9 [1946], p. 13); cf. also H. H. Rowley, *The Chronological Order of Ezra and Nehemiah* (Ignace Goldziher Memorial Volume, I [1948]), pp. 117 ff.

ruins. He used the good-will which he evidently enjoyed with his king to have himself sent on an official mission to Jerusalem to restore the walls of Jerusalem. To safeguard his journey he was given official letters to the provincial governors of the satrapy of Transeuphrates and also instructions to a keeper of the king's forest—his official district is unfortunately not mentioned—to provide the timber necessary for the building in view of Palestine's lack of timber. He finally arrived in Jerusalem with a military escort of horsemen and their officers (Neh. ii, 9). He appeared in Jerusalem not only with a special mission, but also with an official position which the king had conferred on him. He became governor of the province of Judah (Neh. v, 14)[1], and he remained in Jerusalem long after his special mission of building the walls had been fulfilled. According to Neh. v, 14 he was in Jerusalem from the 20th to the 32nd years of Artaxerxes' reign (445-433) and, according to Neh. xiii, 6 f., he had himself sent to Jerusalem again, no doubt with the same position. Nehemiah's appointment as governor, which brought him the king's good-will, probably signified at the same time the constitution of Judah as an independent province. If Judah had hitherto been merely a district of the old province of Samaria, it was now separated from Samaria and raised to the status of an independent province[2]. Not surprisingly, this brought Nehemiah the enmity of the governor Sanballat of Samaria from the very outset[3]. Sanballat was associated in this enmity with 'Tobiah, the servant, the Ammonite'—as Nehemiah likes to call him—who was probably the governor of the neighbouring province east of the Jordan (Neh. ii, 10). Nehemiah had presumably made the king agree to the restoration of Judah's independence because it was a necessary condition for the proposed work of rebuilding the walls of Jerusalem.

This work had had a previous history in which officials of the province of Samaria had played a part. A correspondence about the rebuilding of the city of Jerusalem and its walls which derives from the period of Artaxerxes has been preserved in the framework of the collection of Aramaic documents in the book of Ezra (Ezra iv, 7-22). Later on it was wrongly put together with the correspondence about the building of the Temple by the narrative frame of the

[1] The word התרשתא, which is ued to describe Nehemiah in Neh. (viii, 9), x, 2, seems to be a (Persian) title; cf. Ed. Meyer, *loc. cit.* p. 194.

[2] Cf. A. Alt, *Festschrift Otto Procksch* (1934), pp. 5 ff.

[3] That Sanballat was governor of Samaria we learn explicitly for the first time from the Papyri of Elephantine (*Pap. Cowley*, No. 30, l. 29; AOT[2], p. 452); Nehemiah himself disdained to call him by his official title.

documents, but the text of the documents shows quite plainly that the matter under discussion in this correspondence is the rebuilding of the city, which was quite separate from the restoration of the sanctuary. The Artaxerxes who is named as the recipient of the first document can only have been Artaxerxes I. The correspondence must have taken place in the period before Nehemiah's mission which finally settled the question of the rebuilding of the walls. The documents in question do not bear any more exact date; all we can say is that they come from some time during the first twenty years of Artaxerxes I's reign. They show that officials of the provincial government of Samaria[1] in Jerusalem, which was presumably still subject to the governor of Samaria, along with the district of Judah, ascertained that it was intended to rebuild the city and its walls and that a start had already been made; and they sent a report on the matter to the king, probably through official channels via the satrap of Transeuphrates[2], pointing out that Jerusalem which, as they say, had been a rebellious city from of old, would become a menace to the security and safety of the Empire once it felt safe again within the protection of its walls. In this connection we hear for the first time from an authentic traditional record that Judaeans had come to Jerusalem from Babylon (iv, 12). Meanwhile an assortment of deportees had in fact returned to the homeland, probably not in one big movement, but in smaller groups; and they may have provided the initial impulse that led to the restoration of the ruined city. The people who had remained in the country had hardly been able to summon up enough strength for the task of even merely building the sanctuary, and had left the city lying in ruins, so that the returning deportees were the first to take on the task of reviving the city of which they had thought with such longing in far-away Babylon (cf. Ps. cxxxvii, 5-6). In Samaria, the governor's residence, however, and the former royal city of Israel, the revival of the ancient royal Judaean city was looked on with disfavour. Because of its sanctuary it played a special part among the Israelite tribes anyway, and once it was rebuilt it could become an undesirable rival. As a result of the report which was sent to Artaxerxes, further work on the rebuilding of Jerusalem

[1] Apart from the two provincial officials mentioned by name who conducted the correspondence, a whole series of Persian official titles, some of which are unintelligible, and various ancestral titles are listed in iv, 9. All these probably refer to members of the foreign upper class which was deported to Samaria.

[2] The rather obscure introductory formulae in iv, 7, 8 may perhaps be understood in this sense. The satrapy 'Transeuphrates' is mentioned in the introductions to the report and the king's answer (iv, 10, 17).

was expressly prohibited until further notice (iv, 21) in a decree which the king sent to Samaria (iv, 17-22).

Nehemiah's appearance on the scene was probably more or less closely connected with this incident. Some time after the issue of the prohibition the deportees who had returned home used their connection with the deportees in the Land of the Two Rivers to secure the king's permission to continue the rebuilding. Nehemiah's position in the king's personal entourage offered a welcome opportunity for an approach to the king. Resistance to the rebuilding had started in Samaria. If the restoration was to succeed, Jerusalem and Judah would have to become as independent as possible of this province and its government. Nehemiah knew this, or the people from Judah told him so. He therefore obtained the king's sanction for the separation of Judah from the province of Samaria, and the restoration of its independence. As governor of the newly constituted province of Judah he was in a position to embark on the restoration of Jerusalem without having to consult officially with the province of Samaria.

Nevertheless, after his arrival in Jerusalem, Nehemiah had to proceed with all the caution and shrewdness at his command to attain his goal. It was only to be expected that the governor Sanballat of Samaria would do all he could to hinder the rebuilding of Jerusalem. To begin with, Nehemiah kept his plans secret and three days after his arrival he inspected the whole extent of the walls by night, on horseback and with only a few men with him (Neh. ii, 11-15)[1]. Only then did he announce his plans and he found willing hearers. It was now a matter of acting as swiftly as possible before the neighbours could hinder the work. Nehemiah therefore divided the whole wall into sections, all of which were taken in hand simultaneously; and at the same time, as the population of Jerusalem was still fairly small, he summoned labourers from the whole province, bringing in the heads of the districts into which the province was divided, with their people. The families in Jerusalem, and these district administrators, were each allotted a section of the wall to rebuild (Neh. iii, 1-32). To begin with, this somewhat improvised undertaking merely aroused the scorn of the neighbours in Samaria and the east Jordan province of Ammon (Neh. iii, 33 ff. [English Bible, iv, 1 ff.]). But when the wall had already been half built and the workers were working with enthusiasm and joy, the

[1] On the topography of this nocturnal ride along the city wall cf. A. Alt, PJB, 24 (1928), pp. 91 ff. For a different account see J. Simons, *Jerusalem in the Old Testament* (1952), pp. 437 ff.

neighbours attempted to destroy the work by force (Neh. iv, 1 ff. [English Bible, v, 7 ff.]). The governors of Samaria and Ammon gave orders for an attack on Jerusalem—no doubt unofficially, in the background—in which people from the south and west also took part[1]. The plot did not remain secret, however. People living on the borders of the province brought the news to Jerusalem so that Nehemiah was able to take defensive measures in time. When this became known, the attack which was intended to be a surprise, was called off. All the same, the incident showed that it was necessary to be on guard in Jerusalem. Nehemiah therefore organised a permanent watch and made arrangements for rapid warning to be given to all the workers on the wall. The work now had to be done under these disturbing conditions; but nevertheless the wall was finally completed. It is true that Nehemiah's enemies[2] still tried to intimidate him by imputing seditious intentions to him, or to seize his person by cunning, in order to remove him (Neh. vi, 1-14). But Nehemiah was wise enough not to meddle with anything, and so in spite of all opposition he finally attained his goal. The work was completed in the astonishingly short period of 52 days (Neh. vi, 15). Nehemiah made arrangements for the newly walled city to be carefully guarded under a 'captain of the fortress' and for the opening of the city gates in the morning and their closure at night (Neh. vii, 1-3). Thus the province of Judah again had a safe and sure centre and seat of government. But the city which was laid in ruins and unprotected for so long was still only sparsely inhabited. Nehemiah therefore filled it up with a 'Synoikismos' by resettling in Jerusalem a tenth part of the inhabitants from all the provinces who were chosen by lots (Neh. vii, 4, 5a and xi, 1, 2)[3]. When this had been carried through, the solemn dedication of the new city wall took place (Neh. xii, 27 ff.). It is clear that, to begin with, this new Jerusalem had no greater need of space than David's city. If the Jerusalem of the kings had managed with the old Jebusite and Davidian city on the small 'south-east hill' in the Kedron Valley above the spring of Gihon, and the city of Solomon immediately to the north, had

[1] In Neh. iv, 1 [English Bible, v, 7] Arabians and Ashdodites are mentioned in addition to Ammonites. The Ashdodites were no doubt people from the neighbouring province in the west which was officially called Ashdod, whereas the Arabians were probably neighbours in the south who had introduced themselves into the west Jordan part of the province from the southern desert.

[2] Among them there appears in this context as well as Sanballat and Tobiah, the Arabian Geshem (Neh. ii, 19; vi, 1 ff.), who may have been no more than a tribal chieftain.

[3] This connected passage in the Nehemiah memoirs was subsequently interrupted by the chronistic insertion of Nehemiah (vii) viii-x.

managed with the site of the royal palace, and had only been increased on the western side of Solomon's city by a not very extensive 'new city' (2 Kings xxii, 14; Zeph. i, 10). Nehemiah's Jerusalem was confined to these narrow limits, and, in the ensuing period, the city hardly needed any expansion. This accords with the fact that archaeological research has produced not a trace of evidence that Jerusalem extended to the broad hill in the west in pre-Hellenistic times. It was only Hellenistic Jerusalem's need for more space that extended the city beyond its former narrow limits.

After the completion of the wall Nehemiah continued as governor to attend to the ordering of life in Jerusalem and in the province of Judah wherever opportunity offered. This was no doubt part of the mission with which he had been entrusted when he was sent to Jerusalem. He found the province divided into a number of districts. We learn this from the reference to the allotment of the various sections of the wall to the heads of these districts and their people in Neh. iii, 1-32. We do not know what period this division of the province into districts dates from. As the districts are described by the Accadian word pilku>pelek, they may have already been instituted in the neo-Babylonian period. These districts were named after their seat of government, though there were some twin districts which shared a capital because of the lack of cities in the country[1]. So we have a twin district of Jerusalem, a twin district of Beth-Zur (the modern khirbet eṭ-ṭubēḳa) in the southern part of the province as well as a double district of Keilah (the modern khirbet ḳīla) in the hill country extending to the west of the Judaean mountains. The district of Beth-Haccerem was probably west of Jerusalem, if this place is identical with the modern ʿēn kārim. The district of Mizpeh (the modern tell en-naṣbe) occupied the northern part of the province. From these positions we can obtain a rough idea of the total extent of the province, which had apparently not been extended since Nebuchadnezzar's institution of the district of Judah. A few details contained in the report on the building of the wall in Neh. iii about isolated communities which took part in the building as special groups, round off the picture. The province extended in the mountains southwards to a line between Beth-Zur and Hebron, which already, since the occupation of the land, had formed the boundary between the authentically Judaean tribal area and the areas of the Calebites, and other small tribes that had settled in the most southerly parts of the mountains. The land south of this line had probably been

[1] Cf. the cartographical description in H. Guthe, *Bibelatlas* ([2] 1926), No. 7 III.

separated from the State of Judah as early as 598 B.C. and been ceded to the Edomites, and had meanwhile become part of the province of Edom which lay on both sides of the Dead Sea and the wādi el-ʿaraba. With its extension into the western hill country the province reached, north of the latitude of Beth-Zur, approximately the western frontier which the State of Judah had normally had. The same applies, generally speaking, to the northern border, which ran north of Mizpeh. The only striking feature is the extension of the province to the north-east as far as the lowest part of the Jordan Valley with Jericho. According to Neh. iii, 2, 22, the 'men of Jericho' and the 'men of the (Jordan) plain' took part in the building of the wall. The western half of the lowest part of the Jordan Valley had once been Israelite State territory and then belonged to the province of Samaria. Apparently a small part of Josiah's annexations continued here (cf. above p. 273), since this area presumably remained in the State of Judah even after the collapse of Josiah's work, and then belonged first of all to the sub-province and finally to the independent province of Judah.

As governor, Nehemiah introduced one or two innovations in this very small province which had an important stabilising influence. In his memoirs, in the midst of his description of the building of the wall, he reports on a general remission of debts which he ordered. As the memoirs are obviously arranged chronologically, this remission of debts was probably one of Nehemiah's first measures. (Neh. v, 1-13). It was occasioned by an obvious abuse. After the Judaean upper class had been abducted by Nebuchadnezzar, a new antithesis, which had already characterised the economic and social situation in the latter period of the kings, had come into being between rich and poor within the population that remained behind. It is impossible to say how far this had been promoted by the return of the deportees who claimed their family property again. In any case Nehemiah was confronted with an impoverished and debt-ridden population which had in the end to sell its property and became enslaved to debt. This restless and rebellious element constituted a danger. Nehemiah therefore made the creditors solemnly promise in the sanctuary to agree to a general remission and to restore mortgaged or alienated property. How poor the province was as a whole, is clear from the fact that Nehemiah voluntarily forewent the revenues due to the governor which were normally raised by the province, and contented himself with modest taxes in kind (Neh. v, 14-19).

At the end of his statement (Neh. xiii) Nehemiah mentions

various regulations which he made to introduce order into the situation in the province, and above all, in Jerusalem. It is clear from Neh. xiii, 6 f. that these regulations were made partly or perhaps even entirely in the second part of his governorship, when, after twelve years in office, he had returned to Babylon in the 32nd year of Artaxerxes' reign (433 B.C.) and then returned to Jerusalem as governor after more or less considerable absence. We are not told the reason for his return. It may be that new abuses in the province called him back and that the regulations listed in Neh. xiii were intended to redress them. In particular, the behaviour of the high priest Eliashib, who had taken part in the building of the wall (Neh. iii, 1), gave cause for the intervention of a restraining hand. He had taken advantage of Nehemiah's departure from Jerusalem to follow his own political line, which was based on maintaining good connections with the governors and upper classes of the neighbouring provinces, whereas Nehemiah—following tendencies which were active, above all, among the deportees in the Land of the Two Rivers—had worked for the independence and isolation of the province of Judah. This is the first evidence we have of the high-priestly Zadokites adopting that friendly attitude to the neighbouring, and partly foreign, surrounding provinces which they showed repeatedly in later periods. It is also the first sign of that contrast between an open-minded approach to the surrounding world and an attitude of strict isolationism, which permeated the whole spiritual history of Israel after the loss of political independence. The fact was that Eliashib, one of whose grandsons was the son-in-law of the Samaritan governor Sanballat (Neh. xiii, 28), had for some unknown purpose given the 'Ammonite Tobiah' a space in the Temple in Jerusalem, which was really intended to serve the religious needs of the sanctuary (Neh. xiii, 4 ff.), because he was related in some unspecified way to this Tobiah[1]. After his return to Jerusalem Nehemiah put a stop to this abuse of the Temple in no uncertain manner. Furthermore—before or after this—he proceeded against the numerous marriages between Judaeans and members of foreign neighbouring peoples, not actually dissolving them, however—at any rate there is no explicit statement to that effect—but making the Judaeans swear not to allow their children to contract such marriages (Neh. xiii, 23 ff.)[2].

[1] It is not certain that the priest Eliashib who was given the 'oversight of the chamber of the house of our God' (Neh. xiii, 4 ff.) was identical with the high priest Eliashib Neh. iii, 1; xiii, 28); but he was at any rate a member of the priestly Zadokite family.

[2] The reference to the 'law of strangers' of Deut. xxiii, 4-6 in Neh. xiii, 1-3 is a later addition.

Nehemiah then took action against the negligence in the delivery of the tithes due to the sanctuary which was already complained of in the book of 'Malachi'. He pledged the 'rulers' of the people[1] to see that the payment of the tithes was punctually fulfilled and appointed reliable inspectors in the sanctuary to check the incoming tithes (Neh. xiii, 10 ff.). He also regulated the delivery to the sanctuary of the timber that was needed for the sacrifical fires (Neh. xiii, 31). The fact that these measures were necessary shows how much public worship had been neglected, even in Jerusalem, almost a century after the rebuilding of the Temple by people in the province of Judah, and the Israelite tribes who remained loyal to the sanctuary in Jerusalem. Finally, Nehemiah had to take measures to see that the Sabbath was properly observed. On this matter Nehemiah probably championed the strict views of the Babylonian deportees. It is true that the Sabbath had already been observed in the age of the Judaean-Israelite kings as a day when work in the fields (2 Kings iv, 23), and buying and selling in the cities (Amos viii, 5), had to cease. Among the deportees, however, the observance of the Sabbath had acquired a special importance (cf. above, p. 295), whereas in Jerusalem and elsewhere in the land it was grossly neglected. In Jerusalem, the chief market of the land, people came in from the countryside on the Sabbath with their donkeys, to offer their produce for sale; and the Tyrian merchants who had settled in Jerusalem to sell the fish caught on the Mediterranean coast and other goods, took no notice whatsoever of the Sabbath. In view of these conditions Nehemiah enforced the keeping of the Sabbath, at any rate in Jerusalem, by closing the market and keeping the city gates shut throughout the Sabbath (Neh. xiii, 15 ff.).

A document preserved in Neh. x is related in a strikingly direct fashion to Nehemiah's measures as reported in Neh. xiii. It contains an 'agreement' in which, in the form of a solemn declaration in the first person plural, the obligation is undertaken conscientiously to fulfil certain requirements, in fact more or less the above-mentioned instructions issued by Nehemiah. According to verse 1 the agreement was deposited in a document signed by representatives of the whole community and attested with their seals[2]. This

[1] These 'rulers' are mentioned fairly often in the Nehemiah memoirs and described with an Accadian word as סגנים. Their functions appear to have corresponded roughly to those of the earlier 'elders' of the tribal associations that had meanwhile decayed; they may have been the heads of the local associations. Cf. also Ed. Meyer, *loc. cit.* pp. 132 ff.

[2] The list of signatories inserted in Neh. x, 2-28 is certainly apocryphal and was only later inserted in this inappropriate position.

document was obviously not included in Nehemiah's Memoirs; it forms part of the great chronistic interpolation in the Nehemiah Memoirs. The chronicler appended it to the story of Ezra's proclamation of the law, because for him Ezra was primarily responsible for the introduction of the law; but in fact it obviously has nothing to do with Ezra. If it is an authentic document—and there is no good reason to doubt that—it may be regarded as a traditional document that came down to the chronicler but which he classified wrongly. Its connections with Neh. xiii would suggest that Nehemiah ultimately pledged the responsible men in the province of Judah to carry out his instructions by means of a written declaration; and this declaration was preserved in Jerusalem and finally came to the notice of the late chronicler.

Nehemiah's work had been concentrated in the main on the external organisation of the province of Judah; no doubt the wording of the instructions he received from the Persian government was along these lines. He had rebuilt and repopulated the urban centre and seat of government; he had rectified certain abuses in public worship at the central sanctuary, which had been restored on official instructions and out of public resources, and introduced the most urgent social reforms in the province. In addition, however, he had taken a personal interest in some special concerns of the Babylonian group of deportees, such as the separation of the population in the provinces from the neighbouring peoples, and the strict observance of the Sabbath. Apart from these particularly obvious matters he had not concerned himself with the inner life of the religious community in Jerusalem. The conditions that he found when he arrived showed, however, that reform was urgently needed in this sphere too. Nehemiah had worked in the main with political methods and from a political standpoint, and he regarded public worship in Jerusalem as one of the province's public institutions. If the 'agreement' recorded in Neh. x is based on a genuine tradition and if it was really due to Nehemiah's initiative, it provides us with a very typical example of Nehemiah's methods. It represented a legal act, the signing of a binding document by the responsible representatives of the whole community, and there is no mention of the act being solemnly consecrated. The content of the 'agreement' ensued from the abuses which it was intended to rectify, and from a number of special concerns which probably derived from the Babylonian group of deportees. There is an occasional reference to 'the Law'; and if the 'law' in question is one that has come down to us, it appears to refer most probably to the deuteronomist law which had continued to be in force since the making of the covenant under Josiah, and the introductory formula of the 'agreement' (verse 30) does suggest a markedly deuteronomist style.

The time now seemed to have come to give the religious community in Jerusalem, which was not in the least identical with the population of the province of Judah, a new and binding organisation, since the old tribal federation and its organisations had dissolved, and its place had been taken by an 'Israel' that was to some extent dispersed in the Diaspora, which maintained the old traditions in various ways and still found its unity in the worship in Jerusalem, but which had not yet really found a new form. This is obviously where Ezra's mission came in. We are much less well-informed about Ezra's than about Nehemiah's work, as the only authentic traditional material we have about him is his official instructions which are recorded in Ezra vii, 12-26. For the rest, it is impossible to use the story of Ezra as the work of the chronicler, since it can hardly be assumed that the chronicler was able to draw on a direct oral tradition concerning Ezra. On the other hand, we learn from these official instructions that Ezra had in his hand 'a law of the God of heaven'—in the Persian period this was the normal official term for the God of Israel—which it was evidently his task to enforce. Such a mission would fit into the period directly following Nehemiah very well, however, so let us assume that the possibility we considered above on p. 318, that Ezra appeared in the latter years of Artaxerxes I, is correct.

Ezra was a priest (Ezra vii, 12); and as he was sent to Jerusalem from the 'province of Babylon' (Ezra vii, 16) and evidently came from the Babylonian group of deportees, he will probably have belonged to a family of the Zadokites who were deported from Jerusalem. His official mission may have been instigated by himself or by influential people in his circle. In view of the confused situation in Jerusalem and Judah and the opposition to be expected, it was important for him to arrive with official instructions from the Persian government. If Artaxerxes had already agreed to instal Nehemiah as governor of the newly independent province of Judah, and he will now have agreed to give Ezra instructions, the content and range of which were no doubt suggested to him by members of the group of deportees. Perhaps Ezra's mission can and must be connected with Nehemiah's second mission. Both episodes must have been very close chronologically if Ezra really followed Nehemiah, yet still went to Jerusalem, during the reign of Artaxerxes;

only the last nine years of Artaxerxes' reign were available for Nehemiah's return to Babylon, his second mission and Ezra's mission. What probably happened was that the news of the unsettled conditions in Jerusalem and Judah which made Nehemiah ask for his second appointment as governor, induced the deportees in Babylon to think beyond the possibilities open to Nehemiah, who could, in his position, merely remove a few crying abuses, and to prepare a comprehensive plan of reform and to urge that Ezra should be entrusted with the execution of the plan, the political importance of which they were probably able to explain to the Persian authorities. At any rate Ezra ultimately received a special commission, which did not burden him with the administration of a particular office, like Nehemiah, but merely assigned him with a special and single mission. This is clear even from the official title which, according to Ezra vii, 12, he received for the fulfilment of his task. Apart from the description of 'priest' which concerned his position in the religious community of Jerusalem, he also bore the official title of 'a scribe of the law of the God of heaven'. The chronicler later tried to paraphrase this title in Hebrew in Ezra vii, 6 in the words 'a ready scribe in the law of Moses, which the Lord God of Israel had given', and also in Ezra vii, 11; in Neh. viii, 1 ff., however, he chose the abbreviation, 'Ezra the scribe'[1]. The development in the meaning of the word šōfer then led to the idea of 'Ezra the scribe'. In reality, however, Ezra's official title was a technical term in the Imperial Aramaic official language of the Persian Empire, which was not intended to describe Ezra either as the writer of the 'law of the God of heaven', or a learned expert in or interpreter of this 'law'. In this official language the Aramaic word 'scribe' was rather a common expression for an official with a particular official sphere which was described with the dependent genitive. Ezra was therefore an 'official for the law of the God of Heaven' or—as his mission was not to be repeated—'State commissioner for the law of the God of Heaven'[2].

To judge from this title his mission to Jerusalem inevitably included the task of enforcing a particularly sacred law. There is no explicit mention of this, however, in the official instructions to him recorded in Ezra vii, 12-26; it was taken for granted that that was the real purpose of his mission. Only at the end, in verse 25 f.,

[1] The passage Ezra vii, 11b looks like an addition to vii, 11a; in the latter verse the Aramaic title is rendered with the circumlocution 'a scribe of the words of the commandments of the Lord and of his statutes to Israel'.

[2] On the meaning of the word šāfar/šōfer cf., above all, H. H. Schaeder, *Esra der Schreiber* (1930), pp. 39 ff.

is it ordained that in the area of the satrapy Transeuphrates 'the people'—which can only mean 'Israel', which lived not only in the province of Judah but as a compact group in several provinces of this satrapy, and also dispersed in other parts as well[1]—was to be judged according to the new law which, as a sacred law, necessarily embraced certain spheres of everyday life as well—and that the law was to be made known to and binding on the whole 'people'. This could hardly mean that all the surviving descendants of ancient Israel were to be forcibly subjected to the law of Ezra, since it would hardly have accorded with the Persian habit to apply compulsion in this way. But it probably was intended to mean that all those who still desired to be considered members of the community of 'Israel' and to belong to the religious community in Jerusalem, had to submit to this law. For them Ezra was to appoint judges, who were to judge according to the new law. It may seem surprising that a Persian ordinance should have gone so far in support of a strict legal reform in Israel, but it must be remembered that it is possible that the influence of the Babylonian deportees of Artaxerxes was so great that he gave his official consent to a proposal put to him from this quarter—perhaps the whole text of Ezra's official instructions was drafted by deportees—and gave the 'divine law' submitted to him the binding force of a 'royal law', so that it was possible to mention the 'divine law' and the 'royal law' in one and the same breath (verse 26).

The enforcement of the 'law of God' throughout Israel with the support of Persian authority had a far-reaching effect. Submission to this law became the decisive token of membership of Israel and the religious community in Jerusalem. The organic unity of the old Israel was replaced by the group of those who acknowledged the law; and this group was, on the one hand, more confined than the descendants of the Israel of old, since many of the scattered Israelites were no doubt constantly leaving the old community, and, on the other hand, it was wider, since in principle and in practice there was nothing to stop non-Israelites joining the ranks of those who acknowledged the law and therefore entering the religious community. All the same, on the whole the group no doubt continued to consist of descendants of the former tribes who had remained in the old homeland, and the scattered Israelites who held fast to the old traditions. In this way, however, after the dissolution of the old

[1] 'Scattered' Israel also existed outside this satrapy, above all in the Land of the Two Rivers and in Egypt. This fact is not taken into account, since Ezra's mission was limited to the satrapy of Transeuphrates.

tribal federation and after the interim period of a formless gathering around the old traditions and the Temple worship in Jerusalem, Israel found a new form authorised by the State, as a community subject to a special law of God, for which this law was binding, but which had at the same time a claim, recognised by the State, to be judged according to this law. It is obvious that the meaning which the divine law thereby acquired for Israel was bound to become extraordinarily important, not only for its outward but also for its spiritual life.

We have no certain information as to how Ezra carried out his task. On the occasion of his mission to Jerusalem he obtained a few extra rights which are listed in his official instructions. As he was inevitably concerned to strengthen the influence of the Babylonian group of deportees, who stood behind his mission, he was anxious to take with him a group of repatriates from this group; and so the king gave permission for any who wished voluntarily to return home to do so (verse 13), and Ezra will probably have recruited volunteers in Babylon. No doubt he did go to Jerusalem with a body of repatriates. Then, in view of the difficult economic conditions in the impoverished province of Judah, as they are clearly described in the Nehemiah Memoirs, he wanted to take money with him to Jerusalem. He therefore obtained from the king and his leading advisers a special oblation for 'the God of Israel, whose habitation is in Jerusalem' (verse 15), as well as permission to collect free-will offerings in the province of Babylon (verse 16), which were intended in the first place for the purposes of public worship in Jerusalem, and also to receive gifts in kind for the sanctuary in Jerusalem (verse 19). In addition he obtained the renewal of the privilege already given by Darius by which the needs of the sanctuary in Jerusalem were to be partly met from public funds, within limits which were now exactly defined (verses 20-22). Finally he secured official confirmation of the general exemption from taxation for the whole staff of the sanctuary, which it is possible already existed (verse 24). With these official concessions Ezra finally went to Jerusalem with his attendants.

On Ezra's activities in Jerusalem all we have is the chronicler's account. According to him, the first matter which Ezra tackled on his arrival in Jerusalem was the question of mixed marriages (Ezra ix, x). He knew from the Nehemiah memoirs that there had been numerous marriages between Israelites and members of neighbouring peoples at that period, and could probably not help, concluding that Ezra, whom he placed before Nehemiah chronologically, was bound to have removed this, in his eyes, particularly serious stumbling-block. According to his account it was only considerably later, after Nehemiah had arrived in Jerusalem, that Ezra proclaimed the law he had brought with him in a solemn assembly, that it was explained by the Levites, and that a Feast of Tabernacles was celebrated in exact conformity with the ordinances of the law (Neh. viii). It is impossible to say whether Ezra had reason to concern himself with the question of mixed marriages after Nehemiah, who presumably preceded him, had dealt with it. In any case he did not, as the chronicler would have it, wait for years before fulfilling his main task, the proclamation of the law. There is no authentic record of the manner in which this took place. No doubt it can only have occurred within the framework of a sacred act. Probably a covenant was concluded in accordance with the Israelite traditions which Josiah had followed when he introduced the deuteronomist law. This act of covenant committed the whole of 'Israel' to the new law. It was not a matter of concluding a new covenant between God and the people. On the contrary, even after the dissolution of the old tribal federation—and in spite of the threats of the prophets of the 8th and 7th century—the conviction was upheld that the covenant still continued in force. Just as in former times the 'renewal of the covenant' had been celebrated (cf. Deut. xxxi, 10-13) and Josiah had instigated a reform of the covenant by means of the deuteronomist law, so now once again the law between God and the 'people' was re-defined by means of a new law, the only difference being that now the relationship increasingly became merely an element in an old tradition, which was now affirmed again in an act of covenant-making organised by Ezra, though for the rest the law now emerged as an absolute revelation of the divine will[1].

There still remains the important and difficult question as to where this 'law of the God of heaven', which 'was in the hand of Ezra' had come from, and what were its contents. There is no reference to this either in Ezra's official instructions or in the later chronistic narrative. In all probability this law had been compiled or elaborated among the Babylonian group of deportees and was then made binding on the whole of Israel with the authority of the Persian State. Apart from the prophecy of Deutero-Isaiah, this was the most important and momentous example of the influence of the Babylonian group on the life of Israel as a whole. If Ezra's law gave the Israel of the religious community in Jerusalem its

[1] Cf. M. Noth, *Die Gesetze im Pentateuch* (1940), pp. 70 ff.

permanent form after the interim period following the loss of political independence—and we have every reason to assume that this was so—as we hear of no other occasion which could have given rise to the reform which can be clearly discerned in the following period—the law must necessarily have come down to us as part of the Old Testament tradition, the canonising of which began not so long after Ezra. In the past it has occasionally been assumed that it was the Priestly Code stratum of the Pentateuch narrative (P) that Ezra brought to Jerusalem and introduced as the 'law'. This is not very likely since P was a narrative work, and much more exclusively so than was thought when numerous legal sections were assigned to it which in fact did not belong to it originally or even secondarily[1]. P was no 'law' and could hardly be described as such even unauthentically. It might more easily be thought of as an assortment of regulations which were subsequently incorporated in the great Pentateuch narrative as such, for example the corpus of the so-called law of holiness in Lev. xvii-xxvi or certain collections of religious regulations such as may now be found in Lev. i-vii and Lev. xi-xv, or perhaps as a collation of various pieces of that kind. This possibility must be taken seriously into account, though it would still be difficult to define the extent and content of Ezra's law. Probably the most widespread idea is that it was the more or less completed Pentateuch that Ezra brought with him to Jerusalem[2]. In that case Ezra's 'Law' would have rested on a broad narrative foundation and would have been presented within the framework of the whole tradition of Israel's prehistory which was basically very old. The reformation of religious life in Jerusalem would then have proceeded in the closest connection with a renewed remembrance of the great historical acts of God which had befallen Israel, and given it its special position among the nations. It is clear that it would have been very important if this remembrance had been behind the reform of life in the religious community in Jerusalem. Unfortunately the thesis that Ezra brought with him the whole of the Pentateuch and made it a binding document of the 'law' for the religious community in Jerusalem, cannot be proved. It is not even probably correct since there are important reasons against its acceptance. Above all, there is no cogent reason why the Pentateuch should have been compiled in Babylon rather than Palestine. Even the Priestly Code was more

[1] Cf. M. Noth, *Überlieferungsgeschichte des Pentateuch* (1948), pp. 7 ff.

[2] Thus J. Wellhausen, *Geschichte Israels*, I (1878), p. 421, and, in recent times, H. H. Schaeder, *loc. cit.* pp. 63 f., O Eissfeldt, *Einleitung in das A.T.* (1934), p. 621, and probably also A. Weiser, *Einleitung in das A.T.* ([2] 1949), p. 247.

likely written in Palestine and the older sources of the narrative arose and were transmitted in Palestine in any case. It is therefore highly unlikely that the whole of the Pentateuch was brought to Jerusalem from Babylon and that it was 'the law in the hand of Ezra'; and that it was not rather compiled in Palestine itself. Admittedly, this must have taken place very soon after Ezra, unless the Pentateuch *narrative* existed before Ezra, since about a century later the Samaritan community who parted from Jerusalem retained the complete Pentateuch as a holy book that had already been firmly accepted. In this case, however, 'the law' of Ezra is probably embedded in the legal sections that were subsequently interpolated in the Pentateuch narrative, since it became, at any rate, part of the document of the Pentateuch that was soon canonised as the valid basis of the life of the religious community in Jerusalem. Unfortunately it is quite impossible to define this law of Ezra exactly.

With the consolidation of the province of Judah, which resulted from Nehemiah's governorship, and the reform of the life of the religious community in Jerusalem which resulted from Ezra's special mission, presumably some degree of stability was established after the collapse of the old order, producing conditions in which Israel was able to live.

27. *The Life of the Religious Community in the Persian Period*

For two centuries Israel lived under Persian rule with the whole of the Near East. Apart from what we learn from the traditional records about the reform of public worship in Jerusalem resulting from Cyrus's decree, and about Nehemiah's governorship in the province of Judah in the third quarter of the 5th century, and finally about Ezra's mission in the period immediately after Nehemiah, we know almost nothing about the history of Israel in this long period. And even what we do know is, generally speaking, limited to the narrow confines of the small province of Judah with Jerusalem its centre. But Israel extended far beyond the province of Judah, apart from the members who were scattered in the Diaspora. In the neighbouring provinces of Samaria and Akko—assuming that was the name of the Galilean province at the time (cf. above p. 263, note 5)—and to some extent also in the provinces of Ammon and Ashdod there lived descendants of the old Israelite tribes who, as is evident from the history of the following period, still regarded themselves as belonging to the community of Israel and the religious community in Jerusalem, and took part in public worship in Jerusalem. Ezra's introduction of the law naturally had them in mind too (cf. above p. 330); Ezra's work was not merely a Judaean concern but referred to 'Israel' as a whole, and Ezra carried out his task in Jerusalem not as the capital of the province of Judah but as the centre of the Israelite religion. But we know practically nothing about the history of the Israelites in the other Palestinian provinces during the Persian period. Israel was excluded from taking independent historical action at this time and as long as Persian rule persisted, historical events such as the constantly recurring struggles to maintain Persian sovereignty in Egypt, which were waged with varying success, or the military conflicts with rebellious Phoenician coastal cities which were waged repeatedly during the 4th century, passed Israel by on the whole, and did not affect it very materially, despite their proximity.

We know even less about the fate in this period of the more important groups in the Diaspora, not to mention the smaller groups of scattered Israelites. From the story of Nehemiah and Ezra we learn a little of the Babylonian groups' interest in public worship in Jerusalem and the whole organisation of the religious community and how they managed from time to time to influence the Persian court; but these are only isolated details in the history of this group which it is impossible to set in a wider context. We have no knowledge at all of the life of the Lower Egyptian group in this period. This is the more regrettable, as this group played quite an important part in the subsequent Hellenistic period, and there can therefore hardly be any doubt that it was already an important factor in the Persian period. On the other hand, the above-mentioned papyri of Elephantine from the 5th century B.C. throw some light on the life of the Israelite military colony on the Upper Egyptian border; but although they still occasionally turned with their problems to the governor in Jerusalem[1], in the course of time these colonists no doubt abandoned their connection with the religious community in Jerusalem as they had a strange Temple worship of their own, and in this way they were lost to Israel; after the 5th century all trace of them is lost.

The period of Persian rule was, however, of quite fundamental importance for Israel inasmuch as reforms took place in the most varied spheres which had a decisive influence on its later history.

[1] Cf. *Pap. Cowley*, No. 30 (AOT², pp. 450 ff.).

Whilst it is possible to discern, at any rate the main outlines of the new shape of things, lack of source-material makes it impossible to trace the development of the reforms, except where particular details came to light, more or less accidentally, during Nehemiah's governorship and are therefore mentioned in his report on his activities.

It was during the Persian period that the Jerusalem cultus acquired the form which persisted in its essentials until the end of its existence. After Cyrus had given instructions for the rebuilding of the sanctuary, Jerusalem became the religious centre not only for the Israelites in the vicinity but throughout the world; and any local religion that still survived or was brought into being was therefore branded as illegal and heterodox. In Jerusalem there ruled a priestly hierarchy with the 'High Priest' at its head and a self-contained body of priests who derived from the Zadokite families of the Davidian period and now traced their origin to Moses' brother Aaron, who was now assigned great prominence in the tradition[1]. The connection with the Zadokites of the period of the kings certainly existed, although after the rather long and chaotic transition period some families' claim to membership of this family was doubtful and disputed[2] and the precise delimitation of the 'Zadokite' priesthood was only achieved after all kinds of internal conflicts. In the course of the Persian period the *clerus minor* of the now so-called 'Levites' developed alongside this priesthood in what was presumably a fairly long process. In the programme for the future in the Book of Ezekiel the priests of the local sanctuaries that had been abolished by Josiah, to whom the deuteronomist law had granted sacerdotal rights in Jerusalem (Deut. xviii, 6 f.) but who had presumably been excluded by the Jerusalem priests from the right to sacrifice, were considered eligible to carry out inferior services in the sanctuary and above all to prepare the sacrificial rites (Ezek. xliv, 9-14) from which the lay element was now wholly excluded. In fact a staff of 'Levites' was formed after the restoration of the sanctuary. The element of the priestly families from the former local sanctuaries may have been included on the staff from Josiah's time onwards[3]; but in time they were joined by all kinds of groups of non-priestly

[1] Cf., above all, the description of the Priestly Code in Lev. viii, 9 and also the list in 1 Chron. v, 27-41.

[2] Cf. Ezra ii, 61-63= Neh. vii, 63-65. Disputes about the rights of the priests have also been recorded in a few later sections of the Pentateuch narrative such as Num. xvi, P.

[3] Cf. the lists of Levites in P (Num. iii, 5 ff. and elsewhere) and K. Möhlenbrink, ZAW, N.F. 11 (1934), pp. 184 ff.

personnel, all of whom were finally embraced by the consolidating body of 'Levites'.[1]

Not surprisingly, priests and Levites were concentrated in Jerusalem around the sanctuary; but they also lived outside Jerusalem and only came to the sanctuary at their strictly appointed hours of service (cf. Luke i, 39 f.). The far-reaching organisation of the religious staff, particularly on the level of the 'Levites', made precise distribution of the various official functions essential. This took place no doubt step by step over a fairly long period. But its foundations were certainly laid in the Persian period.

Public worship itself also assumed new forms during the Persian period. The Temple in Jerusalem was no longer, as in the Davidian period, a royal shrine, in which the king arranged for sacrifices to be offered by his official priests according to the customs traditional in the land and the place, and for the other usual religious rites to be observed. In the programme for the future in the Book of Ezekiel the king's empty place is occupied by the person of a 'prince' who, in essentials, merely has to carry out the former king's religious functions (Ezek. xlv, 7 ff.)[2]. But the 'prince' which Ezekiel envisaged failed to become a historical reality. On the contrary, after the restoration of the Temple, and, above all, after the reform which Ezra presumably introduced, the whole religious community became responsible for public worship in Jerusalem. The old institution of the State sanctuary only survived in so far as the Persian kings met the cost of part of the materials needed for sacrifice and caused prayers to be made in the sanctuary 'for their life' (cf. above p. 313). But they can hardly have exerted any direct influence on the actual conduct of public worship. They probably left it to the congregation itself to organise its worship in accordance with tradition. The Jerusalem congregation naturally stuck to the form of worship traditional in Jerusalem; but the change in the situation led inevitably to all kinds of innovations. Whilst the three traditional pilgrim feasts, which were originally harvest festivals rooted in Palestinian tradition, but had meanwhile become to some extent festivals of remembrance of the great fundamental acts of God, continued to be celebrated, but there was now in addition a particularly important 'day of atonement' which was observed five days before the beginning of the great autumn

[1] Especially the chronistic work contains in its secondary additions numerous lists of various groups of Levites, and mentions, above all, Levite Temple singers (cf. especially 1 Chron. xxiii [2b], 3–xxvii, 34).

[2] Cf. the maintenance of the king's religious functions in other respects after the removal of the monarchy, *e.g.* the ἄχρων βασιλεύς in Athens.

festival on the 10th day of the 7th month (Lev. xxiii, 27-32), and this now took the place of the autumn festival as the real beginning of the religious year (cf. Lev. xxv, 9 f.). An earlier ritual of the atonement of the sanctuary was further developed (Lev. xvi). This introduction of the 'day of atonement' was connected with the increasing importance that was now attached to expiation in general in public worship; the divine judgement and its influence on the present situation had aroused great fear of transgressing the divine commandments and a demand for repeated purification. The worship itself was increasingly based on the punctilious fulfilment of existing regulations—the 'law of the God of Heaven' which Ezra had brought with him had no doubt included an order for public worship—and it thereby lost something of the unselfconscious 'rejoicing before Yahweh' of which the deuteronomist law had still spoken stereotypically.

Above all, however, the Persian period was important because it saw the beginnings of the canonisation of a particular literature It is certain that it was in this period that the Pentateuch not only acquired its definitive form but also became a holy book which was binding on the whole religious community in Jerusalem. It is true that the literary history of this great work goes much further back. But the older constituents had never played as great a part as was now played by the whole work. It had provided brief creed-like summaries of the basic acts of God, which it was the custom to recite on certain religious occasions; and the wealth of narrative material which had gathered around the individual themes of these creeds had been established in theological works which were read and passed on, without apparently having acquired any official sanction. Probably the concentrated formulations of the divine law had been binding on the old tribal society, and these may have been set down in writing at quite an early period. It is impossible to trace their history in any detail. We are better informed about the fate of the deuteronomist law which represents, however, in its paranetically diffuse form, a comparatively late stage in the formulation of the law, and included and developed earlier compilations[1]. This deuteronomist law was made binding on the tribal society, which still existed at least in theory, by the covenant instigated by Josiah. This was, as far as we know, the first time that a more extensive document was recognised as valid for the whole of 'Israel'; and whilst it contained at its centre a collection of ordinances of the divine law, it constantly referred to the historical basis

[1] Cf. G. v. Rad, *Deuteronomium-Studien* (1947), pp. 7 ff.

of God's special relationship to Israel in the homiletic elements with which it was interspersed. In Josiah's time there still existed at least the remnants of Israel's old traditional institutions. But with the loss of independence they soon collapsed completely, and, despite the fact that it now lacked the background of an existing institution, the document of the deuteronomist law now acquired a special weight as a record of traditional observances. The further development which took place in the Persian period followed on from this point. Though the deuteronomist law had still continued in force, Ezra had ultimately secured recognition for the 'law of the god of Heaven' which he had brought with him probably by means similar to those used to enforce the deuteronomist law. Once again a document, a book, had become the foundation of life and action. Even if this 'law' of Ezra's was a compilation of ordinances of which we have no detailed knowledge and not the complete Pentateuch itself (cf. p. 334 f.) it was soon followed by the final redaction of the great Pentateuch which pursued the same line and included Ezra's 'law'. It represented the culmination of a fairly long process of editing, and summarised all the basic traditions concerning Israel's pre-history with the most important earlier and later formulations of divine law[1]; and this great work was no doubt quickly acknowledged as authoritative, perhaps even without a special ceremony to give it official status. Thereafter it became the canonic holy book of the Jerusalem congregation, and as such it became the basis of the collection of writings now included in the Old Testament. The reading and knowledge of this holy book which, characteristically, was later simply called 'the law', in spite of its narrative foundations, thereby became a basic task of the religious community and the religious individual; and this provided the impulse for a particular form of divine service alongside the central sacrificial rite, which it was possible to cultivate outside Jerusalem as well, above all in the Diaspora and which consisted in the reading aloud and interpretation of sections of 'the law'. It also led to the development of a technique of expounding this holy book, every detail of which was becoming important and which was not always immediately intelligible owing to its complicated background. Synagogical worship and exegesis do not emerge into the clear light of history until the later Hellenistic period. The beginnings of

[1] Only the deuteronomic law was not contained in the Pentateuch to begin with. But the combination of the Pentateuch with the deuteronomistic history which finally incorporated the deuteronomist law in the Pentateuch (cf. M. Noth, *Überlieferungsgeschichtliche Studien*, I [1943], pp. 211 ff.) certainly took place during the Persian period.

this important process are obscure. We cannot be certain that it was already developing in the Persian period. But the colonising of the Pentateuch was the first step that was bound to lead to the synagogue and the scholarly interpretation of the holy book.

The traditional records of the prophets' sayings also continued to be read and collected in the Persian period. Once the Pentateuch had conferred importance on the study and collection of the literary records of the past, this study was extended to the prophetic writings which contained the threats which had been confirmed so clearly by the judgement of God, and the promises which directed men's eyes away from the afflictions of the present to hope in what God might do in the future. The existing collections of words of the prophets were supplemented with various re-formulations of the promises from the standpoint of these contemporary hopes for the future. It is almost certain that a fairly large part of the secondary material in the books of the prophets that have come down to us derives from the Persian period, though it is naturally impossible to trace this process in detail. It continued into the subsequent Hellenistic period, until the tradition of the prophets finally became consolidated some time in the course of the first century of the Hellenistic period, and further development was brought to an end by combining the existing books of the prophets with the main part of the deuteronomistic history, which was now regarded as prophetic, to form the prophetic canon as the second part of the authoritative holy writings. A number of other writings which were finally included in the third part of the Old Testament canon doubtless came into being in the Persian period, though it is impossible to be certain about the details.

The Persian period clearly had, in many respects, a decisive influence on the later course of Israelite history and Israelite life. After the decline and fall of the old order in the historical events of the Assyrian and neo-Babylonian period, a new beginning and a reformation took place in the religious life of Jerusalem as a consequence of the instructions for the reconstruction of the sanctuary in Jerusalem which Cyrus issued in his very first year, and, as a result of the pressure which was repeatedly brought to bear on the Persian State authorities by the Babylonian group of deportees, who obviously played a not unimportant part at this time. The things that were developed and prepared in this period had an important effect on the whole further course of Israel's history right up to its very end.

We have no continuous historical record of this period, as we have for the period of the Judaean-Israelite kings. The sporadic traditional records do, however, illuminate one or two important events. There is only a little information available outside the Old Testament. As a subject-people forming part of a large empire, Israel had even less influence on the outward course of history in the Near East than hitherto. It is not surprising, therefore, that archaeological excavation had yielded remarkably little from this period of Israel's history. The miserable and oppressive conditions under which the Israelite tribes lived in Palestine at the time made it difficult for them to develop their gifts in the fields of building and the crafts generally. The only noteworthy building of this period of which there is literary evidence, the new sanctuary in Jerusalem, which was built with difficulty over a fairly long period, cannot be studied archaeologically since the site is still occupied by a famous Muslim shrine and is not available to archaeological research. Hitherto, therefore, there have been hardly any results worth mentioning in this field of research[1]. The only thing of note is that coins have been found from the Persian period with the inscription jhd = 'Judah'. Coins, the value of which was officially guaranteed by having their denomination stamped on them were not in circulation throughout the ancient Orient until the Persian period, though they had been previously introduced in the Lydian State. These coins with the inscription jhd[2] show that in this sphere too the province of Judah was granted autonomy by the Persians; and it may be that this was done in consideration for the religious community in Jerusalem which the Persians promoted and which had its centre in the province of Judah, just as other important sanctuaries were given the right to mint their own coins by the Persians[3]. The jhd coins appear to have come on the scene in the course of the 4th century. Numerous pitcher handles stamped with the letters jhd or jršlm have also been found (in Jerusalem). The clay vessels which had their handles stamped in this way were presumably used in the cultic taxation system. The most remarkable point is that the coins, which were made of silver, were minted on the model of Attic drachms, partly with the image of Zeus, partly with a picture of the Athenian owl[4]. The ceramics of this period also included all kinds of Greek-Ageaian ware. This Greek influence and these imports, which also made their appearance outside the province of Judah a

[1] The section on this period in W. F. Albright, *The Archaeology of Palestine* (1949), pp. 142-145, is characteristically brief and deals mainly with things which do not appertain directly to the history of Israel but only to Israel's neighbours.

[2] Cf. K. Galling, PJB, 34 (1938), pp. 57 ff.

[3] Cf. Albright, *loc. cit.* p. 143.

[4] Cf. the ill. 4 and 5 in Galling, *loc. cit.* p. 77.

long time before the Macedonian conquest of the Orient, came through the Phoenician coastal cities, which enjoyed considerable independence under Persian rule and were developing their maritime trade on a large scale. The description of the Mediterranean coasts which goes under the name of Skylax, an Admiral of the time of Darius I, and which was probably written in the last years of the Persian era, shows that substantial parts of the coastal plain of Palestine were subject to various of these Phoenician cities at this time[1]. Phoenician maritime trade had many contacts with Greek commerce; and the Attic drachm had been current since the time of the Attic maritime alliance and through the influence of the Phoenicians it came into, and was imitated in, Syria-Palestine, and with it there came other products of the Greek world. Such indirect contacts with this world will, however, scarcely have had much influence on the inner life of the religious community in Jerusalem.

Persian rule has left some archaeological traces at least in the immediate vicinity of the province of Judah. Apart from the Persian installations in the extreme south-west of Palestine, on the border of the Sinaitic desert, already mentioned on p. 317, a remarkable legacy of this period has been found on the tell ed-duwēr, the site of ancient Lachish: the remains of an imposing Persian palace from the end of the 5th or the beginning of the 4th century[2]. This suggests that Lachish must have been an important centre of Persian government; it is conceivable that this was the seat of the Persian governor of the province of Edom, which embraced the district on both sides of the southern end of the Dead Sea[3] and was the Province of Judah's southerly neighbour. If the centre of the provincial government was in fact Lachish, the peripheral situation far to north-west was probably due to the fact that the main approach to the province was from the north-west. Here was the area from which the road led to always uncertain Egypt, and which was important for the Persian rulers. In Gezer (tell jezer), not so far north of this area, which occupied the south-west corner of the province of Samaria and was quite close to the north-west frontier of the province of Judah, tombs have been discovered belonging to the Persian period[4], in which, in all probability, Persians, or at any rate officials in Persian employ, were

[1] The details will be found in K. Galling, ZDPV, 61 (1938), pp. 66 ff., especially p. 78 ff.

[2] For the ground-plan of this palace see Albright, *loc. cit.* p. 144, fig. 47.

[3] Cf. M. Noth, ZDPV, 67 (1944–1945), pp. 62 f.

[4] On the condition and correct dating of this, tombs which were originally thought to be 'Philistine', cf. K. Galling, PJB, 31 (1935), pp. 88 ff.

buried. This also suggests that here was a minor centre of Persian government.

We have now mentioned all the important archaeological finds which the soil of Palestine has yielded from the Persian period.

28. *The Macedonian Conquest of the Orient and the Samaritan Schism*

After his victory over Darius III Codomannus at Issus in the year 333 B.C., Syria-Palestine fell into the hands of Alexander the Great after he had conquered Asia Minor. In 332 B.C. he moved from the north—Issus was situated near the modern North Syrian harbour of Alexandretta—southwards along the coast of Syria-Palestine, to reach and occupy Egypt as quickly as possible. For seven months he was forced to stay outside the ancient island stronghold of Tyrus, which he finally overcame with the aid of a dam leading from the near-by mainland to the island, and he had to spend another two months besieging the city of Gaza in south-west Palestine, until he was finally able to reach Egypt through the Sinaitic desert and occupy this rich land. He could not spare the time to conquer the interior of Syria-Palestine; he left it to his commander-in-chief, Parmenio, who gained control of the land without difficulty. In Palestine the only place that had to be conquered by force was the governor's seat in the province of Samaria, the former Israelite royal city of Samaria; thereupon a Macedonian colony was established there by the Macedonian Perdikkas. Like the other Palestinian provinces inhabited by Israelites, Jerusalem and the province of Judah yielded without resistance to the new power that appeared so suddenly and with such great military strength; and apart from the city of Samaria itself the Macedonians probably met little resistance in the province of Samaria. In the year 331 B.C. Alexander proceeded once again from Egypt through Palestine-Syria into the Land of the Two Rivers, where he dealt the decisive blow at the Persian Empire in the great battle of Gaugamela and Arbela, and set about building his Greek-Oriental Empire. These were events of world-historical proportions which brought the history of the ancient Orient to an end and marked the beginning of the Hellenistic period in the eastern Mediterranean world. The progress of Alexander's campaign in 332–331 B.C. brought the main Macedonian force in direct proximity to the area inhabited by the Israelite tribes and must have made a powerful impression on them. Nevertheless there is no definite reference to the event in the Old Testament. The historical writings in the Old Testament do not go any further than the end of the old States of Israel and Judah and—in the chronistic narrative—the reform in the Persian period; and the later historical writings (Maccabeans, Josephus) do not go back so far with any definite information. Perhaps one might expect some references to the age of Alexander in very late parts of the prophetic canon, which was only concluded in the course of the 3rd century. Attempts have in fact been made to see in Alexander's campaign the historical background of the prophet's words in the Book Habakkuk (Hab. i, 2) in which a tyrannical and audacious conqueror is threatened with the judgement of God[1]; this is not improbable, but we have no certain proof; and the words of the prophet in Zech. ix, 1-8 have also been thought to refer to Alexander's march through Syria-Palestine in the year 332 B.C.[2]. But these are mere possibilities that call for consideration; apart from the impression made by Alexander's overwhelming and rapid incursion, the passages we have mentioned throw no detailed light on the fate of the religious community of Jerusalem in this period. Presumably the transition from one sovereign power to another did not make any great impact on it.

The struggles of the Diadochs for power after the death of Alexander in the year 323 B.C. again took place partly in Syria-Palestine, the centre of so many traffic routes, and occasionally in direct proximity to the religious community in Jerusalem. First of all Ptolemy, Alexander's governor in Egypt, had near-by Palestine and Phoenicia occupied from Egypt. In the battles against Antigonus and his son Demetrios Poliorketes, who claimed the inheritance of Alexander and therefore had most of Alexander's other governors against them, Demetrios Poliorketes was beaten in 312 B.C. in a battle at Gaza, and Ptolemy proceeded to take renewed possession of Palestine and Phoenicia. After Antigonus had lost the battle and his life at Ipsus in Phrygia in 301 B.C. the dominions of the Diadochs, who had meanwhile adopted the style of King, were gradually consolidated. Egypt formed the nucleus of the Ptolemian State with the 'City of Alexander' in the western delta of the Nile (Alexandria) as the royal seat. The centre of gravity of the Seleucid State lay in northern and central Syria. This State acquired its royal centre in the new foundation of Antioch on the

[1] Thus, above all, B. Duhm, *Das Buch Habakuk* (1906).
[2] Thus in recent times K. Elliger, *Das Alte Testament Deutsch*, 25 (1950), pp. 135 ff. and ZAW, 62 (1949–1950), pp. 63-115.

lower Orontes and to the east it embraced the Land of the Two Rivers. To begin with, the Ptolemeans were able to hold Palestine and Phoenicia against the Seleucids who, not surprisingly, were interested in acquiring this neighbouring country. The central area of the religious community of Jerusalem therefore belonged for the time being to the Ptolemeans.

We know very little about the fate of the religious community of Jerusalem in the period of Ptolemean rule. It is hardly likely that this new power intervened in its personal life, and the change of government that took place after the collapse of the Persian Empire may have, to begin with, not had much effect on it. We learn a little about the Ptolemean period in Palestine from the Zenon papyri which were found in 1915 in the ruins of the military colony of Philadelpheia in the oasis of faijum, south-west of the delta of the Nile[1]. These papyri contain the correspondence of a certain Zenon who was the land agent of the Ptolemean minister of finance Apollonius (261–246 B.C.). Apollonius owned all kinds of estates in Palestine including the land east of the Jordan which he had probably received in fief from his king Ptolemy II Philadelphos. These estates were presumably old and, possibly, very old crown lands. The kings of Israel and Judah had already had their crown lands (cf. above, p. 212); and after the abolition of the independent State this crown land had passed into the direct ownership of the reigning power, which was able to use it for the benefit of its officials and military organisations. We have no detailed information about the extent and contents of this crown land. But parts of it no doubt appeared in Apollonius's property in Palestine. The Ptolemeans certainly will not have encroached on the property rights of the Israelites any more than did the Persians before them.

A considerable group of members of the religious community of Jerusalem probably gathered in the Ptolemean royal city of Alexandria in the 3rd century, some of whom were descendants of those who had migrated to Lower Egypt and some others of whom were new-comers attracted by the flourishing city. This group adopted the Greek language which prevailed in Alexandria instead of the Aramaic language; and Alexandria soon became one of the most important spots in a Greek-speaking Hellenistic Diaspora which also appeared in other Hellenistic cities in the eastern Mediterranean. Earlier groups of scattered Israelites were joined by a variety of new elements who were attracted by the worship and faith of the religious community of Jerusalem and submitted to its

[1] Cf. J. Herz, PJB, 24 (1928), pp. 105 ff. (here, too, p. 106, note 1 ff. bibliography).

'law'; they were called Proselytes (προσήλυτοι), *i.e.* 'converts'. In these groups, which no longer understood or did not understand at all the Hebrew of the Old Testament and the Aramaic vernacular of the Israelites resident in Palestine, there arose the need for a Greek translation of the holy book of the religious community of Jerusalem, which for the time being consisted merely in 'the Law' (Pentateuch). And so, in the course of the 3rd century, the section of the 'Law' which was appointed to be read aloud and interpreted, was translated into Greek, to begin with probably orally in the synagogue service, and from this there developed in Alexandria, and possibly elsewhere as well, a Greek translation of the Pentateuch, which lacked uniformity to begin with, but was later followed by translations of the parts of the Old Testament which were canonised[1]. This was a very important step. In the Greek-speaking Diaspora the holy book of the religious community of Jerusalem was distinct from the original Hebrew, which even then was restricted to public worship and exegesis, and thereby became exposed to the possibility of the influence of Greek thought which exerted an influence on this translation through the Greek language and mode of expression itself. All this followed inevitably from the process which had started with Alexander's emergence in the Orient, though one does not have to assume that, as the rulers of Palestine and Phoenicia, the Ptolemeans instigated the Hellenisation of the religious community in Jerusalem during the 3rd century or helped to shift its centre to the Hellenistic or Hellenised Diaspora. They no doubt allowed the traditional religious rites to continue unimpeded in Palestine and Phoenicia as they did in Egypt.

In the end, however, the Ptolemeans lost Palestine and Phoenicia to the Seleucids. In the Seleucid State the reign of Antiochus III (223–187 B.C.) marked the zenith of its power. In combination with Philip of Macedonia it was able to extend its rule into Asia Minor and make its influence felt as far as Greece. Before it came into conflict with the Romans on this account, it was able to realise the old claim of the Seleucids to Phoenicia and Palestine. It is true that

[1] The so-called pseudepigraphical Aristeas-letter which has been preserved in numerous manuscripts (German translation in E. Kautzsch, *Die Apokryphen und Pseudepigraphen des A.T.s* [1900], II, pp. 1 ff.) provides a legend describing the translation of the 'law' into Greek at the instigation of Ptolemy II Philadelphos (285–246 B.C.). It was not written until the end of the 2nd century B.C. and was intended to proclaim as possessing exclusive authority a particular translation of the Old Testament into Greek which existed in Alexandria at the time (cf. P. Kahle, *The Cairo Genize* [1947], pp. 132 ff.). It claims that this translation was prepared in the 3rd century by seventy-two scholars (hence the name 'Septuagint') on official instructions. Probably there is truth in this legend in so far as it places the beginnings of the Greek translation in 3rd century Alexandria.

a first attempt failed. In the year 217 B.C. the Seleucids were beaten by Ptolemy IV Philopator in a battle at Raphu (the modern refah) in the extreme south-western corner of Palestine on the coast road to Egypt, and had to give up Palestine and Phoenicia which they had conquered. But in 198 B.C. they finally succeeded in defeating Ptolemy V Epiphanes—who had meanwhile come to the throne—so decisively in the district of the sources of the Jordan near the city of Paneas (the modern bānyās), that they obtained possession of Phoenicia and Palestine once and for all, and Ptolemy was forced to make peace with them on this basis. Once again, therefore, the Israelites in Jerusalem and Palestine had a change of sovereign. They do not appear to have disliked the change. At any rate we learn from a document which we are about to discuss that, evidently after the battle of Paneas, they captured the Ptolemean occupation forces in Jerusalem and gave a 'splendid' welcome to the Seleucid troops with their elephants and provided them with abundant supplies. Perhaps all that was behind this was the discontent which a foreign power always evokes among its subjects in the end and the understandable intention of commending themselves to the new sovereign once he had clearly shown himself as such. For his part, Antiochus at once showed his good-will to the religious community in Jerusalem in order to win them over to his side, which he regarded as important, especially in view of the far-reaching connections they had as a result of their widespread Diaspora. In *Ant. Iud.* XII, 3, 3 (§ 138-144 Niese) Josephus has recorded the text of a decree issued by Antiochus III to a certain Ptolemy, who may have been the State commissioner for the newly conquered regions. This decree contains a number of regulations benefiting Jerusalem and the religious community of Jerusalem, and, as a document preserved in Jerusalem, it may presumably be considered authentic[1]. By this decree the city of Jerusalem was granted the return of the inhabitants who had been dispersed in the course of the wars of the preceding period and the release of those who had been enslaved as well as a general exemption from taxation and the reduction of tithes by a third for the duration of three years (§ 138, 139, 143, 144). All this was intended as a reward for the city's behaviour

[1] The authenticity of this decree has often been doubted (cf. most recently H. Willrich, *Urkundenfälschung in der hellenistisch-jüdischen Literatur* [1924], pp. 21 f.). For its authenticity cf. Ed. Meyer, *Ursprung und Anfänge des Christentums*, II (1921), pp. 126 f., and latterly E. Bickermann, *Revue des études juives*, 100 (1935), pp. 4-35 (with detailed historical interpretation) and A. Alt, ZAW, N.F. 16 (1939), pp. 283 ff. (here there is an analysis of the complicated structure of this decree). For the Greek text of the decree see TGI, pp. 76 f.

during the change of government from the Ptolemeans to the Seleucids (cf. above). In this connection we learn incidentally that Jerusalem had probably suffered considerably in the fighting between the Ptolemeans and the Seleucids; few details about these battles have come down to us. At any rate, the new power tried to repair the damage that had been caused. Furthermore, Antiochus's decree granted certain privileges to the sanctuary in Jerusalem; above all, the supply of sacrificial materials and other religious requirements up to a certain limit from State resources, probably from the produce of the crown lands, and also the right to live in accordance with 'the laws handed down by their fathers', and finally permanent exemption from taxation for the staff of the Temple (§ 140-142). These privileges had already existed in the Persian period (cf. above, p. 332) and may not have been infringed by Alexander and the Ptolemeans, so that Antiochus, as the new sovereign, may merely have been confirming the old rights rather than giving fresh permission. Some of the details may have been extended, however. For example, State aid was promised for the extension of the sanctuary (§ 141) and the supply of wood for the sacrificial fires which Nehemiah had had to pledge the members of the religious community to supply themselves (Neh. x, 35), was made duty-free (§ 141). Finally, the exemption from taxation accorded to the staff of the Temple was extended to the 'council of elders' (*γερουσία*) and the 'scribes' (*γραμματεῖς*), who here make their first appearance in history.

The friendly relationship between the new power and the religious community in Jerusalem which this created did not last for long. Antiochus III was soon involved in conflicts with the Romans, who encroached on the eastern Mediterranean world immediately after the Second Punic War, because the power of Antiochus III, who was allied with Philip of Macedonia and to whom Hannibal had fled after his defeat, seemed to them to be becoming dangerous. In the battle of Magnesia on the Meander in Asia Minor, Antiochus was defeated by the Romans in 190 B.C. and was forced to agree to the humiliating Peace of Apamea. This was the beginning of the decline of Seleucid power; and in the course of this decline the great conflict with the religious community in Jerusalem took place under Antiochus IV Epiphanes, which initiated a new phase in Israelite history.

Meanwhile, however, an event which had an important effect on the inner history of this community had taken place, namely the separation of the Samaritan congregation from Jerusalem and the establishment of an independent Samaritan cultus on the ancient holy mountain of Gerizim near Shechem. It is impossible to assign an exact date to the achievement of this separation; but it merely meant the consummation of a long development, the beginnings of which went back a long way. The process had its ultimate roots in the age-long division between the southern group of tribes and the rest of the tribes, which had their main representatives in the Central Palestinian group. David had brought the southern tribes into prominence historically, and after the death of Solomon the southern State of Judah had kept within its sphere of influence the ancient tribal relic of the Ark which formed the religious centre of the whole tribal federation. This relic, no doubt, continued to be visited by members of all the Israelite tribes. But the kings of Israel tried to compete with the Jerusalem shrine with State shrines of their own (cf. 1 Kings xii, 26 ff.); and Jerusalem as the central shrine will hardly have been acknowledged wholeheartedly among the tribes of the State of Israel, particularly as they still remembered that the new dignity of Jerusalem was due to the Judaean David and that it entirely lacked the authority of age, whilst the Ark and the religious centre had previously always been set among the central group of tribes, first in Shechem, then possibly for a time in Bethel and Gilgal and finally in Shiloh, and religious observances had continued to take place on the ancient sacred site of Shechem, which pointed to Shechem's original role as a central place of worship. In view of the tenacity with which religious institutions and ideas are usually preserved, this memory will hardly have faded completely when the State of Israel came to an end and its State shrines lost their previous importance and a foreign ruling class came into the country with its own religions. It is unlikely that these foreign systems of religion had any considerable influence on those parts of the tribes that stayed behind in the former State of Israel or on their religious traditions. Then came Josiah, who abolished the local places of worship even in the province of Samaria which he had annexed, including the ancient and celebrated shrine of Bethel, and who centralised the whole religious system in Jerusalem on the basis of the deuteronomist demand for unity of worship; for a time the old local shrines may have continued among the Galilean and East Jordanic tribes, *i.e.* in the Assyrian provinces of Megiddo and Gilead, which Josiah had not yet subjugated when he met his sudden death[1]; we have no definite

[1] Josiah only seems to have been able to gain control of the small southern part of the land east of the Jordan (cf. above, p. 273).

information on this point, however, and Jerusalem may have quickly established itself as the one authorised place of worship attended by members of all the tribes that had remained in the land. This probably continued to be the case after the Temple had been destroyed in the year 587 B.C. and only the holy place as such remained. It was now no longer a royal Judaean shrine and could therefore be recognised more readily as the one central shrine common to all. But the old antithesis between north and south still continued below the surface and broke out again when plans were made for the rebuilding of the sanctuary in Jerusalem following Cyrus's decree. This time the resistance came from the Judaean side. The inhabitants of the land of Judah regarded the Temple as their own sanctuary and its rebuilding as their task, and did not want the Israelites from the neighbouring provinces to take part, who not unjustly claimed a share in the work of restoration since the building in question was the ancient central shrine. The inhabitants of the neighbouring provinces, in which the foreign upper classes had been gradually absorbed or were on the point of being absorbed by the local Israelite population, were regarded by the Judaeans, who had had no foreign upper class imposed on them, as religiously contaminated. At any rate this is how the prophet Haggai appears to have looked at the matter, if the symbolical action of questioning the priests about the effect of 'clean' and 'unclean' which is reported in Hag. ii, 10-14, and which implies that 'this people and this nation' were infected with contaminating religious uncleanness, referred to the inhabitants of the neighbouring provinces who were not to be allowed to defile the purity of the work of restoring the Temple[1]. It may be that the Judaeans who were deported to Babylon, and who influenced the course of events in Judah in this period by dint of their access to the Persian court, also wanted to have the restoration of the cultus in Jerusalem regarded as a purely Judaean concern.

Perhaps the old political conflict between Judaeans and Israelites still played a part at this period, though the religious and devotional approach appears to have been more to the fore, the more so since Judah was probably still subject to the governor of Samaria and the restoration of the Temple came under the jurisdiction of the Samarian government.

[1] Thus W. Rothstein, *Juden und Samaritaner* (1908). Later on in Ezra iv, 1-5 the chronicler assumed that there was a conflict between the repatriated deportees and the population that had remained in the homeland over the rebuilding of the Temple and thereby introduced a slightly false emphasis. At the time of the rebuilding of the Temple hardly any of the deportees had returned home.

The situation changed when Judah was constituted as an independent province under Nehemiah and a marked antithesis arose again between Samaria and Jerusalem, to which Nehemiah refers repeatedly in his Memoirs[1]. This political rivalry, in which the old claim of the Central Palestinian tribes to represent the heart of Israel was revived in a new form, inevitably had an effect in the religious sphere. It was only with reluctance that the Israelites in the province of Samaria—the Galileans and East Jordanians were no doubt less interested in this political antithesis—recognised Jerusalem as the only authorised centre of worship. But, to begin with, they apparently acquiesced in the situation as it had evolved, particularly as the Jerusalem sanctuary was the object of Persian interest and receiving all kinds of privileges from them. But they were moving towards separation from the sanctuary in Jerusalem and towards the establishment of their own cultus based on the age-old religious traditions of their area; the only question is when the time arrived for them to realise this intention.

In *Ant. Iud.* XI, 8, 3-7 Josephus tells of Alexander the Great's progress through Syria-Palestine, and in this connection he makes the high priest in Jerusalem defy Alexander out of loyalty to the Persian Emperor, whilst, according to him, the governor of the province of Samaria submitted straight away to the conqueror and asked for permission to erect a shrine of his own, which permission Alexander granted at once (§ 321-324 Niese). The whole story is full of legendary details and introduces all kinds of figures, such as the Samaritan governor Sanballat, who do not belong to this historical context. The story of how Alexander finally came to Jerusalem himself, and how, in spite of the initial attitude of the High Priest, the city was saved in a miraculous fashion (§ 325-339 Niese), is obviously completely lacking in any real foundation. But it is possible that the story of the difference between the attitude to Alexander's emergence which was adopted in Jerusalem and Samaria does contain an accurate tradition. It is so likely historically that the appearance of a new sovereign was welcomed in Samaria, as opposed to Jerusalem which had obtained so many privileges from the Persians, and that the change of government was used by the Samaritans to realise the desire of establishing a cultus of their own and one independent of Jerusalem, that one might be inclined, even without Josephus's story, to place the

[1] This conflict appears to have remained hidden from the colonists in Elephantine; as late as 408 B.C. they wrote on one and the same matter simultaneously to the governor Bagohi in Jerusalem and to the sons of the governor Sanballat of Samaria (*Pap. Cowley*, No. 30; cf. AOT[2], pp. 450 ff.).

establishment of the Samaritan cultus on the Gerizim at the beginning of the Hellenistic period. It is not very likely that the goal was attained during the Persian period in Samaria. The Persian attitude to the Jerusalem cultus militated against the attainment of this end. And it was also necessary for the Pentateuch to have become so firmly accepted as the holy book in the Jerusalem community as to leave the Samaritans no option but to adopt it as the foundation of their cultus too. This would bring us, at the earliest, to the end of the Persian period. On the other hand, however, it would be wrong to go too far into the Hellenistic period. It is true that the first explicit evidence of the existence of the Samaritan sanctuary on the Gerizim dates from the period of Antiochus IV Epiphanes (2 Macc. vi. 2); but it here appears alongside Jerusalem as an important shrine, already distinguished presumably, by a certain tradition. Needless to say, Josephus's story of Alexander's having given immediate permission for the erection of a Samaritan sanctuary on his first arrival in Syria-Palestine can lay no claim to historical truth; but it is probable, nevertheless, that during the period of Alexander's rule, or during the conflicts with the Diadochs, Samaria had an opportunity of obtaining official permission to establish the cultus of her own for which she had striven for so long.

Leaving out of account the less important Israelites who were still living in Galilee and the land east of the Jordan, the cultus on the Gerizim was no doubt intended for the whole population of the province of Samaria, who were thereby to be given their own religious centre, just as the Province of Judah had for so long had its centre in the city of Jerusalem. This goal was not, it is true, completely achieved. The new cultus no doubt attracted most of the Samaritans. But the old tradition of Jerusalem which had been for so long the religious centre for the inhabitants of the province of Samaria as well, maintained its hold on many of them. At any rate the Israelites in the southern districts of the province of Samaria apparently maintained a fairly solid attachment to Jerusalem owing to their proximity to Judah and Jerusalem, and this ultimately led, about the middle of the 2nd century B.C., to the separation of these districts from the province of Samaria and their assignment to the province of Judah[1].

Not surprisingly, people in Jerusalem always regarded the cultus on the Gerizim as unauthorised. The Samaritans were considered apostates and religiously unclean. The whole chronistic history was

[1] Cf. below, p. 377, and the detailed remarks by A. Alt in PJB, 31 (1935), pp. 94 ff., especially pp. 100 ff.

compiled—about 300 B.C.—with the purpose of proving the unique authority of the Jerusalem tradition historically, as opposed to the Samaritan cultus. With this in view, David and his God-pleasing work of preparing the building of the Temple was given prominence from the very outset, then the history of the kings of Judah was traced as the real history of Israel, and finally, as the bearers of the authentic tradition, the group of deported and later repatriated Judaeans were connected with the work of restoring the Temple and the reorganisation of the religious community[1]. We have no information about how the Samaritans regarded things. Probably they answered the question whether men 'ought to worship in this mountain (*i.e.* on the Gerizim) or in Jerusalem' (John iv, 20), by pointing out that Shechem had an older tradition as an Israelite shrine, and that the transfer of the Ark into the royal Judaean city of Jerusalem by the Judaean David was an unauthorised act of despotism.

The religious community of Samaria managed to survive through the ups and downs of history. Adopting the Judaean point of view, Josephus criticises the Samaritans for a contemptible lack of principle, as a result of which they had tacked their way through the twists and turns of history, stressing, as seemed most opportune at the time, either their relationship to the whole of Israel and their connection with the Jerusalemites, or their separateness and special position (*loc. cit.* 340 ff.). At bottom the Samaritans shared the fate of all those who, though appealing perhaps to age-old traditions, rebel against a situation that has evolved over a long period of time, and try to base their life on historical conditions which have long since disappeared. They gradually degenerated and became almost completely uncreative. Today there is a tiny remnant of Samaritans in the city of nāblus (Shechem)[2]; they celebrate their Passover on the Gerizim[3] but have otherwise become a mere historical curiosity.

[1] Cf. M. Noth, *Überlieferungsgeschichtliche Studien*, I (1943), pp. 174 ff.

[2] P. Kahle gives a survey of the Samaritan population in the year 1909 in PJB, 26 (1930), pp. 89 ff.

[3] Cf. J. Jeremias, *Die Passahfeier der Samaritaner* (1932).

PART FOUR

RESTORATION, DECLINE AND FALL

CHAPTER I

THE MACCABEAN RISING AND THE REVIVAL OF THE MONARCHY

29. *The Conflict under Antiochus IV and its Consequences*

THE Seleucid dominion in Palestine did not last very long. After only one generation there broke out the great conflict between this power and the religious community in Jerusalem which was ultimately related to the process of the decline and fall of the Seleucid State, and which finally led to the emancipation of the religious community from political domination, and to the establishment of its own monarchy. About the events of this period we are comparatively well informed, thanks to the literary records, and, above all, to the two Books of Maccabees, which were included in the Greek form of the Old Testament, the Septuagint, and thus preserved. The First Book of Maccabees, which was probably originally written in Hebrew, but which only survives in Greek translation, relates the events of the period from 175 to 134 B.C. and is a valuable historical source in which it is possible that notes made at the time were used. It portrays things from the point of view of a strict reverence for the law and attempts, above all, to emphasise the merits of the Maccabean-Hasmonaic leaders. The Second Book of Maccabees only deals with the period from 175 to 161 B.C. and forms, in accordance with its own statement (2 Macc. ii, 23 ff.), an extract from the history of one Jason of Cyrene, who is otherwise quite unknown to us, but who evidently wrote a work on the history of the period in five books which the writer of the Second Book of Maccabees made it his task to summarise in one book. Jason of Cyrene evidently came from the Hellenistic Diaspora and probably wrote in Greek, and so Greek is the original language of the Second Book of Maccabees. The Second Book of Maccabees provides more detailed information on the prehistory and beginnings of the Maccabean rebellion than the First Book of Maccabees, but does not equal the latter in historical value, since the obviously legendary element is represented more strongly in it. There are all kinds of discrepancies between the two books in their description of events; and one is inclined to give more credence to the first Book in such cases, though it should be remembered that this First Book also sees and summarises events from its own special and subjective point of view[1].

The conflict broke out because the Seleucid authorities made serious encroachments on the property, rights and organisation of the sanctuary in Jerusalem and the religious community of Jerusalem. The reason for these infringements is not quite clear. They did not accord with the fundamental attitude of the Hellenistic rulers to subject peoples and their religions. The fact that Antiochus III had explicitly confirmed the privileges of the religious community in Jerusalem, after the conquest of Palestine, and had also shown his good-will in other ways, had been nothing out of the ordinary. In the interim, however, the situation of the Seleucid State had considerably deteriorated. Antiochus III had already succumbed to the Romans and had been forced to conclude the Peace of Apamea with them in 189 B.C. He had been followed after his death in 187 B.C. by his son Seleucus IV Philipator, whose brother Antiochus had to live in Rome as a hostage. Seleucus managed to secure his return by sending his own son Demetrios to Rome as a hostage in his stead. When Seleucus was murdered by his minister Heliodor in 175 B.C., this brother of his, Antiochus, seized power as Antiochus IV Epiphanes by passing over the real heir to the throne, Demetrius, who was living in Rome. This initiated the period of disputes about the throne in the Seleucid dynasty which prevented the State from attaining any calm and stability, and which contributed to its decline. In addition the Romans were reaching out more and more powerfully into the eastern Mediterranean world and when things became serious the Seleucid State was no match for them. Danger also threatened from Ptolemean Egypt, which had until quite recently been in possession of Palestine and Phoenicia, and the danger was the greater since at this period Rome was supporting the Ptolemeans against the Seleucids; Antiochus IV was compelled to fight several campaigns against Ptolemy VI Philometor. In a word, the power of the Seleucids had become very shaky, and they became increasingly touchy about the independence of, and any

[1] The question not merely of the relationship between the contents of the two books of Maccabees but of their literary relationship is very complicated. There are grounds for presuming that they both drew from a common source, but the nature and origin of this common source still remain an open question, cf. W. Kolbe, *Beiträge zur syrischen und jüdischen Geschichte* (1926), pp. 124 ff., who assumes that Jason of Cyrene was also the source of the first book of Maccabees, and, on the other side, F.-M. Abel, *Les Livres des Maccabées* (1949), pp. xxxviii ff., who disputes the existence of any common literary source at all.

signs of unrest among the subject peoples. The disastrous wars, and their new military tasks, also landed them in great financial straits which made them covet the possessions of the subject peoples[1].

On the other hand, conflicts had also arisen in the bosom of the religious community in Jerusalem which could not be welcome to the Seleucid State and which gave it reason to intervene. And this was the real source of the conflicts which broke out under Antiochus IV. In the first place it was a question of the antithesis between the traditional character of the Jerusalem community and the Hellenistic character. The Hellenisation of the Orient which was initiated by the Macedonian conquest of the whole of the Persian Empire, was bound to have an effect on the religious community of Jerusalem, especially as this community had itself a Greek-speaking Diaspora in the Eastern Mediterranean world which, though not perhaps very large numerically, had many ramifications. For the sake of the Diaspora, part at least of its holy book had already been translated into the Hellenistic vernacular from the venerable original Hebrew. No doubt the central place of worship in Jerusalem was regularly visited by members of the Diaspora, who thus made Jerusalem familiar with Hellenistic ways. Hellenistic life had, however, entered into Palestine itself and hence into the immediate vicinity of the centre of the religious community in Jerusalem, even in the period of Ptolemean government. The centres of this life were in Hellenistic cities which were founded in place of earlier urban settlements and which were no longer crowded, unplanned agglomerations of dwellings within a city wall, but more spacious, well-planned sites based on the so-called Hippodamic system, which was named after the architect Hippodamos[2]. In the Alexandrian period Perdikkas had replaced the former Israelite royal city of Samaria with a Macedonian military colony. Under the Ptolemean government there arose Hellenistic cities which their very names sometimes prove to have been Ptolemean foundations, like Philadelphia, which was named after Ptolemy II Philadelphos and which was built on the site of the ancient Ammonite capital of Rabbath-bene-Ammon (the modern ʿammān), and Ptolemais (the modern ʿakka) which was laid out on the site of the former city of Akko (the modern ʿakka), and Philoteria (the modern khirbet

[1] On the whole complex of problems cf. H. L. Jansen, *Die Politik Antiochos' des IV* (1943), especially pp. 17 ff.

[2] Cf. C. Watzinger, *Denkmäler Palästinas*, II (1933), p. 11. Only slight archaeological traces have survived of these Hellenistic cities, since they were usually extended in Roman and Byzantine times and the Hellenistic stratum has disappeared under the later strata.

el-kerak) which was situated at the southern end of Lake Tiberias. In the Ptolemean or at the beginning of the Seleucid period there arose the Hellenistic city of Nysa-Skythopolis (the modern bēsān) which took the place of the former city of Beth-Sean[1]. It was inevitable that the Hellenistic life that developed in these cities, with its freedom and glamour, should make an impression on the Israelites and stimulate them to copy it. And no doubt very many were attracted by it. The establishment, recorded in 2 Macc. iv, 12 ff. *circa* 175 B.C. by a high priest in Jerusalem of a 'Gymnasion' to form the centre of a community living in the Hellenistic style within the ancient holy city, where discus throwing and the like was carried on and attracted enthusiastic spectators, was not the peculiar idea of one particular scoundrel, but the result of a movement among Israelite people who, as participants or spectators, fervently joined in the activities of the new 'Gymnasion'; 2 Macc. iv, 14 f. notes explicitly that even some of the priests in Jerusalem were carried away by the attractions of this new way of life. On the other hand, there were no doubt many people who rejected the foreign ways more or less vigorously and consistently for the sake of their own venerable traditions, and who saw in the departure from ancestral customs an act of disloyalty to the traditional faith in God, and nothing less than disguised or even open idolatry. In so far as there was in fact an ancient and intimate connection between the Greek-Hellenistic games and the Greek worship of the gods, they had good reason for their view. The conflict first becomes evident in the Books of the Maccabees for the period *circa* 175 B.C.; there can be no doubt that it did not suddenly appear at that time, but had gradually developed, perhaps more or less latently, in the course of the 3rd century, as part of the process of the advancing Hellenisation of the Orient under the rule of the Diadochs. It confronted the religious community of Jerusalem with the serious and fundamental question as to what its attitude should and must be to the foreign Hellenistic customs and ways of life. The solution of this question could only reach maturity over a period of time, but the problem threatened, unless a solution was achieved in time, to result in a violent explosion in view of the increasing force and bitterness of the conflict. It only needed some incident to touch off an explosion. At the beginning of the 2nd century B.C. the internal situation of the religious community of Jerusalem was certainly very strained, and the unrest that this might lead to in Palestine in

[1] On these Hellenistic urban foundations cf. A. H. M. Jones, *The Cities of the Eastern Roman Provinces* (1937), pp. 238 ff., 447 ff.

the vicinity of a hostile Egypt was bound to be a source of worry to the Seleucid government, and to stimulate it to try and force a decision and as far as possible a stabilisation of conditions.

Another cause of disturbance in Jerusalem about this time were all kinds of struggles for the office of high priest. The conflict between the traditional and the Hellenistic way of life only played an incidental part in these contentions. Fundamentally, the priests appear to have welcomed Hellenism, and at any rate they tried to establish good relations with the Seleucid ruler. But various priestly families and persons were probably contending for the political power of the supreme priestly office. We have no information about the early history of these disputes, as there are no reliable records about the history of the office of high priest in the 3rd century and the beginning of the 2nd century. Under Seleucus IV we meet a high priest named Onias; he was regarded by the circle who remained faithful to the law as a pious and worthy representative of the office (2 Macc. iii, 1 ff.; iv, 1 ff.), but he had enemies among his fellow priests who tried to get him removed by conveying slanderous reports on him to the king (2 Macc. iii, 4 ff.; iv, 1 ff.). Seleucus, who, according to 2 Macc. iii, 3, once more explicitly confirmed the privileges of the religious community of Jerusalem, does not seem to have yielded to their demands. But when Antiochus IV seized power in 175 B.C. after the murder of Seleucus, a certain Jason, who, according to 2 Macc. iv, 7, was the brother of Onias, succeeded in getting Onias removed from office by royal command and having himself made high priest by promising the king rich gifts of money and a vigorous promotion of Hellenisation in Jerusalem (2 Macc. iv, 7 ff.)[1]. This was a monstrous intervention of the royal power in an internal concern of the religious community of Jerusalem, but it was not due to the king's own initiative. It was brought about by certain of the Jerusalem priests themselves, who tried to obtain the king's support in their struggle for power, thereby inciting the king to intervene now and in the future in the appointment of the high priest and in the affairs of the religious community of Jerusalem in general. And this is what happened henceforward. When, three years later, one Menelaus[2] offered the king still larger sums, Jason was removed by command of the king and Menelaus appointed high priest in his stead (2 Macc. iv, 23 ff.). When, in the year 169 B.C., the rumour

[1] According to Josephus, *Ant. Iud.* XII, 5, 1, § 239 Niese, this Jason's original name was Josua, but characteristically he assumed the Greek name of Jason.

[2] According to Josephus, *loc. cit.*, Menelaus's original name was Onias, which he too exchanged for a Greek name.

spread that Antiochus had lost his life in a campaign in Egypt, Jason seized the city of Jerusalem and the office of high priest again by force of arms and banished Menelaus and his supporters, who went to Antiochus. The latter restored Menelaus by force, so that Jason had to flee once more to the land east of the Jordan, where he had retired after his first deposition (2 Macc. v, 5 ff.).

These events, which involved Antiochus in the quarrels in Jerusalem, made him take a further step. His financial anxieties made him covetous, anyway, for the treasures and valuables of the shrines within his sphere of government. Polybius comments on one occasion (XXX, 26 fin. Büttner-Wobst) that Antiochus IV had 'robbed most of the sanctuaries', though it is not clear from the context whether this remark was intended to be taken generally or referred to a particular district. Moreover, we know from a brief note in Granus Licianus[1], that he plundered the Temple of 'Diana' in Hierapolis and robbed it of its treasures, and Polybius (XXX, 19 Büttner-Wobst) reports that immediately before his death he made a vain attempt to acquire the riches of a temple of 'Artemis' in the country of Elymais (Elam), where he had come on a campaign against the Parthians. These are pieces of information that happen to have survived and it is not unlikely that to get money Antiochus pursued this path elsewhere. It is not surprising that the sanctuary in Jerusalem, in whose affairs he was repeatedly involved, should also have interested him from this point of view. It is reported in 2 Macc. iii, 6 ff. that Seleucus IV had already had his attention drawn to the riches of the Temple by a Jerusalemite enemy of the then high priest Onias, and had tried to seize these treasures through the agency of his minister Heliodor, but, by a miracle, the attempt had failed. The whole story may be legendary, but it does show that the hankering of the Seleucid rulers of that period after the treasures of the sanctuaries had to be taken into account. Thus Antiochus IV also took advantage of the restoration of Menelaus to the office of High Priest in 169 B.C. to take with him the valuable inventory of the Temple in Jerusalem and to this end he even entered the Temple himself (1 Macc. i, 17-28; 2 Macc v, 15 ff.). This violation of their sanctuary naturally made the strict law-abiding Israelites extremely angry. They were now compelled to regard Antiochus as a determined enemy of their faith, in so far as the king's interference in the appointment of the high priest had not already made them see him in this light. It was now hardly possible to conceal a feeling of hostility towards the king.

[1] Cf. Jansen, *loc. cit.* p. 34.

Perhaps the incident even led to a regular insurrection in Jerusalem which would help to explain the measures which the king proceeded to take[1]. When on a renewed campaign against Egypt in the year 168 B.C., Antiochus had been forced by a decree of the Roman Senate, delivered by Popilius Laenas, to leave Egypt and to abandon all his designs on Egypt, he gave orders for his leading tax-official—according to 2 Macc. v, 24 this was the 'Mysarch' called Apollonius—to make a surprise attack on Jerusalem, and for the city to be pillaged and burnt down and its houses, and above all, its walls pulled down; many inhabitants of Jerusalem lost their lives. Women and children were taken as slaves and Jerusalem was treated as an enemy city (1 Macc. i, 29 ff.). Above all, the fortified position was created which is often referred to by the Greek name of 'Akra' in the First Book of Maccabees and by Josephus, and which played a considerable part in the history of the following years. According to 1 Macc. i, 33 ff. 'godless people' were established inside these grounds which were protected by a strong circular wall furnished with towers. These 'godless people' were probably primarily the Hellenistically minded section of the Jerusalem population. The law-abiding Jerusalemites fled from the city in great numbers. Weapons and provisions were stored in these grounds to make them immune against attack; and they were occupied by Seleucid troops. This 'Akra' therefore took the place of the former city of Jerusalem which was now robbed of its enclosing wall and partially depopulated, the new community probably being organised on Hellenistic lines. It is impossible to define its position exactly. It has been located on the so-called 'West hill' of the city territory of Jerusalem, in the west opposite the sanctuary and separated from it by the so-called 'city valley'[2]. But, as it is stated in 1 Macc. i, 33 that it was built on the site of the 'city of David', and as the author of 1 Macc. may, unlike Josephus, who came later, have known the exact position of the historical 'city of David', the probability, which is supported by archaeological and topographical discoveries, is that the 'Akra' was situated on the south-east hill, *i.e.*, on the mountain-ridge south of the sanctuary[3].

This interference with the status of the city of Jerusalem was extraordinarily violent. But Antiochus IV soon took a further

[1] Cf. on the following above all E. Bickermann, *Der Gott der Makkabäer* (1937), pp. 69 ff.

[2] Thus most recently F.-M. Abel, *Histoire de la Palestine*, I (1952), p. 122.

[3] Cf. most recently, with detailed evidence, J. Simons, *Jerusalem in the Old Testament* (1952), pp. 144 ff.

decisive step. As part of his hostile policy he decided to eliminate the, in his eyes, rebellious religious community of Jerusalem altogether. In a decree (1 Macc. i, 41) he prohibited all important religious observances; he forbade the presentation of the traditional sacrifices, he forbade the observance of the Sabbath, he forbade the custom of circumcision, he had the holy books destroyed. He made the breaking of these prohibitions punishable by death. He even introduced a foreign system of worship in the sanctuary in Jerusalem and dealt with the Samaritan sanctuary on the Gerizim in the same way[1]. According to 2 Macc. vi, 2 a cult of Zeus Olympius was established in Jerusalem and a cult of Zeus Xenius on the Gerizim; and the king required everyone to take part in these new cults. The king's officials had to try to enforce the king's instructions throughout the land. On the 15th day of the month Kislew in the 145th year of the Seleucid era (1 Macc. i, 54) *i.e.* in the December of the year 167 B.C., the 'abomination of desolation' was set up in the Temple in Jerusalem. This probably means that the new cult was begun. In the provinces altars were set up at which everyone now had to sacrifice. The privileges which had been granted to the religious community in Jerusalem from the beginning of the Persian period by the reigning Emperors, and which had been repeatedly confirmed right up to the reigns of Antiochus III and Seleucus IV, and which guaranteed the community the right to live according to its own religious laws, were thereby abolished.

Antiochus may have thought that the religious community in Jerusalem would submit to these ordinances, even though under protest, just as many other subject peoples under his rule had in time accepted Hellenistic or Hellenising cults. But this was impossible for the religious community of Jerusalem; they served a God who could not be compared with the traditional deities of the surrounding peoples. On this soil a bitter war of religion against the secular power was inevitable. The most prominent part in this religious war was taken by those resolute people who had always rejected the Hellenistic way of life, who had perhaps not hitherto played a very active part, but for whom the moment had now come to defend their faith. The Hellenising elements were paralysed because they had already taken a step in the new direction; and some of them had already departed so far from the old traditions

[1] We do not hear anything about the Samaritans' attitude to Antiochus; presumably they kept as far away as possible from the disputes which took place in Jerusalem, but were treated by Antiochus, who probably saw no fundamental difference between them, in a similar way to the Jerusalemites.

that they did not want to offer any resistance at all. The High Priest Menelaus who was appointed by Antiochus probably aquiesced, and with him a great many of the Hellenistically inclined priests. Many others, who were horrified by the things that were happening, submitted out of fear and joined in the pagan sacrifices when the worst came to the worst. The little band of those who 'would rather have been killed than be desecrated by unclean foods and profane the sacred covenant' (1 Macc. i, 63), was probably not very large to begin with. Many of them will no doubt have escaped persecution by fleeing from their homes. For the immediate future action depended on the resolution of the determined minority, and for them the fight against the king's violent measures became at the same time a fight against the Hellenistic way of life in general.

The struggle was aided by the situation of the Seleucid State which was burdened with all manner of internal difficulties and conflicts in the royal house. But it would, all the same, hardly have attained its goal if it had not soon found determined and resolute leaders. In the small town of Modein (the modern el-midye) on the western border of the mountains east of Lydda there lived a priestly family which traced its descent from the priestly house of Joiarib (Neh. xii, 6, 19; 1 Chron. xxiv, 7) (1 Macc. ii, 1). Its more recent ancestor was a certain Hasmon (Josephus, *Bell. Iud.* 1, 3, § 36; *Ant. Iud.* XII, 6, 1, § 265 Niese[1]), and they called themselves 'Hasmonaeans' after him. At this time the senior member of the family was Mattathias, who had a number of sons. When a Seleucid official appeared in Modein, to require the pagan sacrifice from all the people there, Mattathias not only refused to comply with the order, but he killed with his own hand an Israelite who made the required sacrifice, and the royal official as well (1 Macc. ii, 15-28). This was the signal for open resistance and the news of Mattathias's action was no doubt swiftly spread abroad. It was impossible for Mattathias to stay with his family in Modein. He called on his fellow-inhabitants to follow him and escape with him and went with his supporters to the mountains in the inaccessible wilderness of Judah. There, in the course of time, like-minded followers gathered around him. All this took place in the course of the year 166 B.C. To begin with, it merely led to minor engagements between this steadfast band and the Israelites who had submitted to the royal commands, and who for the sake of their own peace

[1] Josephus gives the name in the form Ἀσαμων(αῖος), the later Judaean tradition probably in the form (י)חשמונ; cf. G. Dalman, *Aramäisch-neuhebräisches Handwörterbuch*[2] (1938), p. 163.

and security wanted to avoid having an insurrection in the land. Mattathias's supporters made surprise attacks, destroyed pagan altars, killed apostates who agreed to take part in the pagan sacrifices, used force to circumcise children who had, in accordance with the royal command, failed to be circumcised. They attacked their enemies in their hiding-places and tried to eliminate them; they took advantage of the pious observance of the Sabbath which made resistance on the holy day impossible (1 Macc. ii, 29-48). The aged Mattathias died during these minor conflicts, probably in the course of the year 166 B.C. His place was taken by his third oldest son Judas. According to 1 Macc. ii, 4 he was nicknamed Μακκαβαῖος[1], *i.e.* 'the hammer', or better perhaps, 'the hammer-like man'; this nickname, which was intended to mark him out as a dreaded and ready warrior, was given to him no doubt because of his military achievements. We call the struggles of the faithful in which Judas won the decisive victories, the 'Maccabean' rising and the period which it marked, the 'Maccabean' period, after his nickname. Judas was indeed a bold warrior, 'resembling the lion in his deeds and like a young lion pouncing with a roar on its prey' (1 Macc. iii, 4). But above all he was a bold, far-sighted leader, who took events beyond the stage of minor battles and sudden attacks, and envisaged a general conflict between law-abiding Israel and the enemy forces. To that extent the episode is rightly called by his nickname; and it is not surprising that he acquired numerous new supporters, especially after he had won his first clear-cut victories.

Under his leadership the first conflicts with the Seleucid power took place. The Seleucids could not look on idly at events in Palestine for long but were bound to take up arms against the rioters. According to 1 Macc. iii, 10-12, Judas succeeded, first of all, in defeating a Seleucid division under the leadership of a certain Apollonius[2] at an unspecified place, and Apollonius was killed in this engagement. After this he defeated Seron, the military commander of 'Syria'[3], at Beth-Horon (the modern bēt'ūr), in the north-west of the province of Judah, where an army division approaching the coastal plain from the north first reached the province of Judah, and he pursued the defeated enemy to the

[1] The basis is an Aramaic מַקָּבָא or מַקָּבִי (cf. Hebrew מַקֶּבֶת).

[2] This was perhaps the same Apollonius who, according to 2 Macc. v, 24, had carried out the conquest and pillaging of the city of Jerusalem in the year 168 B.C. on behalf of Antiochus (in 1 Macc. i, 29 the name of this 'supreme tax official' is unfortunately not mentioned).

[3] 'Syria' is obviously not intended to mean the whole Seleucid State but only a part of it, possibly the so-called 'Koile-Syria' which probably embraced the southern part of the land of Syria.

coastal plain (1 Macc. iii, 13 ff.). Thereupon the king Antiochus was forced to take more drastic measures. As he was himself having to fight the Parthians in the east he left the fighting in Palestine to Lysias, who had been left behind as regent, and the latter sent out the three generals Ptolemy, Nikanor and Gorgias with a considerable army against Judas and his followers in the 147th year of the Seleucid era (in the summer of 165 B.C.). A battle took place at Emmaus (the modern ʿamwās) on the western border of the mountains south of Beth-Horon in which Judas was able, by skilful manœuvring, to defeat his enemies once again (1 Macc. iii, 27-4, 25). Lysias now took charge himself. This time he approached Judaea, not from the west, but from the south through the province of Idumaea, and a battle took place on the southern frontier of the province of Judah near Beth-Zur (the modern khirbet eṭ-ṭubēḳa). Judas was able to secure a victory in this case too (1 Macc. iv, 26-35). These amazing successes led to Judas with his supporters becoming the ruler of the province of Judah, except for the 'Akra' in Jerusalem with its Seleucid garrison. It may be asked how these victories were possible. No doubt the Seleucid State, which was involved in fighting the Parthians in the east, was unable to muster any very large armies against Judas[1]. All the same, their forces were certainly superior in numbers and equipment. On the other hand, Judas and his supporters had the advantage of detailed local knowledge of their own homeland, the mountainous character of which provided them with all kinds of opportunities for skilful operations, but above all they had the conviction that they were waging an urgent war for the cause of their own faith, and the readiness to stake everything for this cause regardless of their personal safety.

The successes which they had achieved encouraged the faithful to hope that their cause would triumph in spite of the forces opposed to it; and they no doubt brought Judas many new followers and fellow-combatants, who had previously held back for fear. But these successes also made it plain to the devout that God was on their side, since only his help against the secular power could have made the victories possible. In fact it appeared that the final issue between the rule of God and the secular rule of man was being decided in these battles, which were concerned to save the foundations of the faith. It was during the period of these successes that the visions recorded in the second half of the Book of Daniel were

[1] The numbers of the enemy armies mentioned in the books of the Maccabees are probably exaggerated, as was often the case in old traditional records.

written in their final form (Dan. vii-xii). In them the events of the time were interpreted as the ultimate phase of history before the imminent irruption of the rule of God on earth which would be realised in the 'royal power of the saints of the most High' (Dan. vii, 18). The brutal and bloody suppression of the religious community of Jerusalem by Antiochus IV, which was without precedent in Israelite history, and the life and death struggle which its loyal adherents were forced to wage against this abolition of privileges which had existed for centuries, and against the violations which followed, awakened the conviction that an ultimate and final decision was now at hand. Following up a series of stories which had arisen in the course of the 3rd century, and which were intended to demonstrate by examples God's help for the faithful who held out against the pressure of the world (Dan. i-vi), the visions of Daniel interpreted the events of the time as the beginning of the end of the worldly power which had appeared in the course of time in a series of successive world empires, and as the preparation for the coming of the rule of God, for which the successes of Judas and his followers could only be a provisional 'little help' (Dan. xi, 34), and which would be rather a mighty act of God. And so there developed in the midst of the troubles and excitements of the time the so-called Apocalyptic, which, continuing the prophecy of the earlier period, explained the world and its history as leading to an end brought about by God. It is probable that this vision gave Judas and his struggle a great stimulus and brought him supporters. Judas himself and many of his fellow-combatants will, however, presumably not have entirely shared the conception of the apocalyptic visions of Daniel, and will not have thought of their actions as merely a 'little help', but will have seen the waging of this war against the power of the State as an important and fundamental task. When it is stated in Dan. xi, 34 that 'many shall cleave' to the fighters for freedom 'with flatteries', what the writer had in mind was possibly the expectation of winning a secular victory by force of arms, instead of expecting everything to come from the acts of God himself. This is the first evidence of a dissension at the heart of the Maccabean rebellion which was soon to come into the open.

The task which Judas envisaged after his initial successes was the liberation of Jerusalem and the restoration of the sanctuary. After the desecration of the Temple in 167 B.C. the faithful had erected a kind of substitute in Mizpeh (tell en-naṣbe) north of Jerusalem. In accordance with the law it was not permissible to offer sacrifices there; but meetings were held there, and the tithes required by the law were brought there, and such of the priestly garments and the holy books as it had been possible to save were taken there (1 Macc. iii, 46-49). But violated Jerusalem, which was now Judas's goal, still remained the real holy place. In the second half of the year 164 B.C. Judas and his followers came to Jerusalem. He had the Seleucid garrison and the disloyal population locked up in the 'Akra' to prevent them causing any trouble; and he then turned his attention to the restoration of the sanctuary. He appointed priests who had remained loyal to the ancestral traditions; he had the elements of the worship of Zeus Olympius removed and the burnt-offering altar, which had been desecrated by the foreign cultus, pulled down, and a new one built in its place and a new list made of necessary equipment. On the 25th Kislew of the 148th Seleucid year, *i.e.* in the December of the year 164 B.C., that is three years after its desecration, the Temple was restored to its rightful service by an eight-day festival with sacrifices, prayer and singing. To ensure its safety the area in which it stood was fortified and garrisoned, just as Beth-Zur on the southern border of the province of Judah was fortified and garrisoned (1 Macc. iv, 36-61).

A most important step had thus been taken. In the following spring the arch-enemy Antiochus IV Epiphanes died during a campaign against the Parthians, and he was succeeded by his eight-year-old son Antiochus V Eupator, who was entirely dependent on his guardian, the regent Lysias. But the urgent struggle was not yet ended. The 'Akra' with its garrison still existed alongside the site of the Temple in Jerusalem and the ordinances of Antiochus IV, which had prohibited the whole worship of the religious community in Jerusalem, had not yet been rescinded, and outside the province of Judah Seleucid dominion was undisputed and its representatives were able to insist on the members of the religious community of Jerusalem, who lived outside the province of Judah, carrying out these orders. And so in the year 163 B.C. Judas undertook campaigns which led far beyond the frontiers of the province of Judah, above all to Galilee and into the land east of the Jordan inhabited by Israelites who were faithful to the religious community of Jerusalem. They were in a difficult position, since they were living away from Jerusalem on the periphery in districts with a mixed population and in the vicinity of foreign peoples and Hellenistic cities. They were sore oppressed in the period of persecution by Antiochus IV. So Judas sent his next eldest brother Simon, who now appears in history for the first time, to Galilee, and he himself went to 'Gilead', *i.e.* into the land east of the Jordan, with his youngest brother Jonathan. Both of them had military successes; but as their power was not great enough to maintain these old Israelite areas permanently, they took the whole of the Israelite population that wanted to remain members of the religious community of Jerusalem with them to Judaea. Judas then undertook another expedition to Idumaea, where he besieged and destroyed Hebron, and to Philistaea, where he made a surprise attack on Ashdod, probably only to inspire the neighbour of the province of Judah with fear and respect (1 Macc. v, 1-68)[1]. Then Judas began to besiege the 'Akra' in Jerusalem with its garrison. The garrison appealed for help to Antiochus V, and other pro-Hellenistic Israelites also took the opportunity of trying once again to persuade the king to intervene on their behalf. And this time Antiochus V, with Lysias, did make a serious effort to crush the rebels (163–162 B.C.). An attack with a strong force was made from the south. Beth-Zur, which Judas had fortified, was hard pressed and Judas withdrew from this fortress to the north. Afterwards Beth-Zur was forced to surrender to the aggressors. But meanwhile the Seleucid's main force pursued Judas northwards. A battle took place near Beth-Zacharia (the modern bet iskārye), about 10 kilometres south-west of Bethlehem, in which the Syrians, who had to use elephants, were victorious, so that it was now possible to besiege the fortified sanctuary of Jerusalem to which Judas and his men had returned and to reduce it to the direst straits by starvation (1 Macc. vi, 17-54). The cause of Judas and his supporters now seemed lost. But unexpectedly an internal dissension in the Seleucid State came to their aid; and as a result of the rapidly advancing degeneration and decay of the Seleucid monarchy one of the surprising changes took place which were often to occur in the following period. A rival of the regent Lysias, whom Antiochus IV had appointed guardian of his young son and heir before his death on the Parthian campaign, was preparing to seize power, so that Lysias suddenly found it urgently necessary to bring the campaign in Judaea to a rapid end. He therefore induced the young king to offer peace to the besieged, on the basis of an assurance of freedom to worship in accordance with the traditional law. When this assurance was confirmed by an oath, Judas accepted the offer and surrendered the fortified area of the Temple. It is true that, contrary to the agreement, the fortifications of the Temple area were subsequently demolished; but the Syrian army withdrew, and above all, the orders issued by Antiochus IV in the year 167 B.C.,

[1] On these military campaigns of 163 B.C., cf. K. Galling, PJB, 36 (1940), pp. 43 ff.

which had led to the outbreak of the military conflict, were now officially rescinded and the religious community of Jerusalem was thereby restored to its old position.

The goal of the Maccabean rising thereby seemed to have been attained; and there was no apparent reason for continuing the struggle, particularly as the Seleucids now evidently had peaceful intentions too. In the year 162 B.C. Demetrius, the son of Seleucus IV who had been the real heir to the throne after his father's death but had been living as a hostage in Rome at the time, had appeared in Antioch, and, after he had instigated the murder of Antiochus V and Lysias at the hands of the military, he had ascended the throne as Demetrios I Soter. In Jerusalem, after the last high priest Menelaus had been removed by Antiochus V, probably in connection with the newly conceded organisation of the cultus (cf. 2 Macc. xiii, 1-8), a certain Alcimus[1], who appears to have been a legitimate member of the high-priestly family (1 Macc. vii, 14), was officially appointed high priest. The evident purpose of this appointment was to serve the cause of peace within the religious community of Jerusalem, and a message was sent to Judas and his followers inviting them to come to terms. At the time many of the devout in Israel, including those who had taken part in the urgent struggle against violence and oppression, believed that the time had come to rest content with what had been achieved; the right to conduct public worship and daily life in accordance with the traditional law had been officially recognised, and a legitimate High Priest was once again in office, and even though there was still a Seleucid garrison in the 'Akra' in Jerusalem and Seleucid officials and troops were still present in the land, this was merely due to the fact that the land was under the sway of a foreign power and the religious community of Jerusalem had lived for centuries under a foreign power. But Judas and his followers were of a different mind and their view is clearly expressed in the description of the events and personalities we have just mentioned, which is given in 1 Macc. vii, 1-25. They had no confidence in the peace. In fact they considered it obnoxious that, for all his legitimacy, the new High Priest had been appointed by the king with the aid of political and military resources in the same way as his immediate predecessors had been appointed by enemy kings. The events that followed also showed that there was some justification for fearing that further attempts would be made to interfere in the internal affairs of the religious community of Jerusalem. But, above all, Judas and his

[1] His name is probably a Greek form of the original name Eliakim.

followers were aiming at complete political independence and the complete elimination of the foreign power. This purpose now emerged quite clearly. If the struggle had begun as a fight against the king's destructive acts of despotism and a fight for freedom, in time the leaders of the struggle came to envisage a goal leading far beyond the restoration of the previous state of affairs. But this led to a disastrous and momentous cleavage in the ranks of those who had hitherto worked together. On the one side were the 'Hasmonaeans' with their followers, who were forced by this cleavage more and more on to the purely political line, and on the other side were those groups who were mainly concerned with the freedom to practise their religion unhindered and with the right to live strictly in accordance with the law. These latter formed a group on their own and simply called themselves 'the devout'[1]. There were, in addition, Hellenising groups, particularly, it seems, among the priestly families, the 'Sadducees'[2], and the High Priest Alcimus probably tended in this direction too.

The uncompromising attitude of Judas and his followers made the intended peace impossible. According to 1 Macc. viii, 1-32, Judas had tried to establish contact with Rome by sending a deputation there and in this way he had made his fight for freedom a part of the great historical conflicts of the time, another indication that his aims were now primarily political. Alcimus, who had been brought to Jerusalem with a military escort, was unable to maintain his position. He soon had to ask Demetrius for help. The latter sent Nikanor to Jerusalem with an army to quell the rebels. The attempt to induce Judas into submission by negotiation came to nothing; hostilities therefore broke out. Judas was victorious in an engagement at Kaphar-Salama, which may have been identical with the modern khirbet selma, 1 kilometre north-west of ej-jīb, that is, about 10 kilometres north-west of Jerusalem. After Nikanor had summoned further reinforcements, a battle ensued on the 13th Adar, *i.e.* in the March of the year 161, near Adasa (the modern khirbet ʿadāse), 7 kilometres north of Jerusalem. Nikanor was defeated and lost his life in the battle; Judas was able to pursue the

[1] In Hebrew they described themselves as חֲסִידִים, and from that was derived the Greek 'Ἀσιδαῖοι (1 Macc. vii, 3 and elsewhere). Later on the term 'the separatists', ★פְּרִישִׁים, Φαρισαῖοι, 'Pharisees', emerged for the same circles (cf. Josephus, *Ant. Iud.* XIII, 5, 9, §§ 171 f. Niese and elsewhere).

[2] According to an interpretation by A. Geiger (*Urschrift und Übersetzungen der Bibel* [1857], p. 102), which has been vigorously contested but is still not unlikely, the 'Sadducees' were the 'Zadokites', *i.e.* members of the old family of priests in Jerusalem which was still the legitimate family of priests. It became a party in the conflicts of the 2nd century.

defeated enemy right down into the coastal plain (1 Macc. vii, 26-50). Thereupon Demetrius entrusted Bacchides, who occupied the high position of a 'friend of the king', with the task of crushing the rebels. His retinue included the high priest Alcimus, who had evidently made representations to the king again. This time, in the first month of the 152nd Seleucid year, *i.e.* in the April of 160 B.C., a very imposing force was evidently summoned to obtain the desired victory once and for all. As it is unfortunately impossible to interpret the references to places in 1 Macc. ix, 2 ff., we have no exact information about Bacchides's marching-route and it is also impossible to locate the place called Elasa, which is mentioned as the scene of the decisive battle. Confronted with such overwhelming forces Judas was in a very difficult position, particularly as many of his supporters refused to venture on the seemingly hopeless engagement. Nevertheless Judas plunged into the battle with a small band of faithful followers. He was defeated and fell in the battle himself (1 Macc. ix, 1-12). Bacchides now tried, with the help of the high priest, to restore peace and order in the land. Freedom of worship and the validity of the law were not restricted; but wherever it was possible to get hold of them, Judas's adherents were removed. Some of them were able to save their lives only by escaping to hide-outs in the desert of Judah. They were now in a similar position to the one in which Mattathias and his followers had found themselves at the beginning of the Maccabean rising. In the place of Judas they chose his youngest brother Jonathan to be their leader. They now seemed to have hardly any prospect of success, for the majority of those who were faithful to the law now acquiesced in the new situation and refused to have anything more to do with these unswerving fighters. Bacchides had established a number of strongholds and occupied them with garrisons to secure the Seleucid regime. All that Jonathan could do with his followers was repeatedly to harass the land. If occasional collisions with royal troops such as the engagement on the Jordan recorded in 1 Macc. ix, 43-49, or the struggle for Beth-Bassi (probably the modern khirbet bēt baṣṣa) east-south-east of Bethlehem on the edge of the desert of Judah, which Jonathan had lightly fortified (1 Macc. ix, 62-69), turned out successfully, they were only minor engagements and the results were unimportant; they had little effect on the general situation. Nor did the connection which Jonathan sought to establish with the Nabataeans who had settled on the eastern side of the Dead Sea and were the natural enemies of Seleucid rule in neighbouring Palestine, have any important consequences. Johannes, the oldest brother of Jonathan, had been killed on a mission to the Nabataeans (I Macc. ix, 35 ff.); and probably the attempt to establish contact with the Nabataeans was abandoned after that.

Once again internal difficulties in the Seleucid State unexpectedly came to the aid of Jonathan's purposes. This is the only possible explanation of the fact that after the engagement at Beth-Bassi Bacchides suddenly agreed to negotiate with Jonathan. At Jonathan's request he handed over the prisoners and the booty and waived further hostilities. Obviously, as a result of an understanding with Bacchides, Jonathan now established his residence in Michmas (the modern mukhmās), 12 kilometres north-north-east of Jerusalem, and from there he 'judged' 'the people' as if he was one of the old 'judges of Israel' (I Macc. ix, 70-73). This was in the year 157 B.C. For the present the war now really had come to an end. The high priest Alcimus had died two years previously (I Macc. ix, 54-56) and his position had not yet been filled again. But in Jerusalem the 'Sadducean' priesthood held sway and for the time being Jonathan evidently refused to have any dealings with them. He therefore ruled from Michmas. Subsequently Jonathan turned the disputes about the throne in the Seleucid house very cleverly, but also most unscrupulously, to his own account, in order to come nearer his goal, which was fairly obviously political, secular power. In the year 153 B.C. a certain Alexander Balas, who passed himself off as a son of Antiochus IV Epiphanes, and as such claimed the Seleucid throne, rebelled against the king Demetrius. Under these circumstances Demetrius considered it a good thing to have friends, and he therefore tried, by offering amazing concessions, to win over Jonathan. He gave him official permission to maintain an armed unit and to obtain other military equipment; he also handed over the hostages who had been held in the 'Akra' in Jerusalem. Armed with these concessions, Jonathan moved to Jerusalem, refortified the area of the Temple and kept the anxious garrison and staff of the 'Akra' in check. The only other garrison which the Seleucids still maintained was the one in the fortress of Beth-Zur (I Macc. x, 1-14). But at the same time the pretender Alexander Balas was also seeking Jonathan's favour, and Jonathan accepted his benefactions too without the slightest hesitation. Alexander entrusted him with the office of high priest which had been vacant since the death of Alcimus; and Jonathan solemnly entered upon this office at the great autumn festival in the year 152 B.C. And so the supreme and leading office in the religious community of

Jerusalem had been conferred in due form—by a sovereign act of the foreign Seleucid king—on a member of the non-'Zadokite', non-'Aaronite', family of the Hasmonaeans; and Hasmonaeans occupied this office until the reign of Herod. Alexander even sent Jonathan a purple mantle and a golden crown, the tokens of secular power, and thus Jonathan was given the position of a deputy king under the Seleucid government (1 Macc. x, 15-21). All these things were the gifts of a pretender to the throne, who made himself out to be the son of the former arch-enemy Antiochus IV Epiphanes! For a time Jonathan will have, as far as possible, steered a middle course between Demetrius and Alexander. But in the end he declined as insincere a further offer by Demetrius, which included universal exemption from taxation and rich donations to the religious community in Jerusalem, as well as the inclusion of a contingent of Judaean troops in the Seleucid army (1 Macc. x, 22 ff.). Jonathan went over to Alexander's side. And he was fortunate, for in time Alexander made his way against Demetrius and, finally, in the year 150 B.C., Demetrius was killed in a battle against Alexander. Jonathan was rewarded for his support. He was invited to Ptolemais (Akko) where Alexander Balas celebrated his marriage with Cleopatra, the daughter of Ptolemy VI Philometor, and Alexander honoured him highly and made him a 'general' and 'joint-ruler' in the Seleucid State (1 Macc. x, 59-66). It is not surprising that, under these circumstances, Jonathan's position in the province of Judah became more and more uncontested. His old adherents had triumphed with him and no doubt new followers rallied round the successful leader, whilst his enemies were forced to be silent (cf. 1 Macc. x, 61-64).

Alexander Balas continued to need Jonathan's support, since, in the year 147 B.C., the son of Demetrius I, who was also called Demetrius, rebelled against his monarchy. To begin with, Jonathan stood by Alexander and undertook a few expeditions in the region of the Philistine cities against the troops of the young Demetrius, and as a reward he received the city of Ekron (the modern 'āḳir) and its adjoining territory. But, for the rest, he took advantage of the disturbances of the time, in which Ptolemy VI also intervened, to besiege the Seleucid garrison in the 'Akra' of Jerusalem. Alexander Balas was finally defeated in the year 145 B.C. and, shortly after, Ptolemy VI died on his Palestinian-Syrian campaign. The young Demetrius was therefore able to ascend the throne as Demetrius II Nicator (1 Macc. x, 67-xi, 19). The new king immediately summoned Jonathan to Ptolemais to call him to account. Jonathan succeeded in assuaging the king's wrath and even winning his favour by the offer of rich presents; and instead of being punished for his behaviour he returned to Jerusalem with new concessions from the king. Demetrius not only explicitly confirmed him in his offices and also confirmed the privileges of the religious community of Jerusalem but, in return for a rich present, he handed over to him the three southern districts of the province of Samaria, whose inhabitants had remained loyal to the cultus of near-by Jerusalem and did not take part in the Samaritan cultus on the Gerizim (cf. above, p. 354) and turned them over to the province of Judah. The districts in question were Aphairema (the modern eṭ-ṭaiyibe north-east of Bethel) on the eastern slope of the mountain, Ramathaim (the modern rentīs, about 25 kilometres east of yāfa) on the western side of the mountain and Lydda (the modern lidd) on the inner border of the coastal plain. In this way the province of Judah was enlarged by a wide strip of land northwards and north-westwards. Demetrius also granted exemption from taxes to this enlarged province (1 Macc. x, 20-37).

In the end, however, Jonathan's political manœuvrability became his own downfall. Demetrius II was not prepared to make further concessions—Jonathan wanted the withdrawal of the Seleucid garrison from the 'Akra' in Jerusalem and from Beth-Zur —not even after Jonathan had sent troops to help him to suppress a rebellion in Antioch (1 Macc. xi, 41-53). And so Jonathan parted from Demetrius. When a certain Diodotus Tryphon appeared in the year 145 B.C. to win the Seleucid throne for the son of Alexander Balas, who was called Antiochus and still under age, he joined forces with this agitator and was, with his brother, given the task of subjugating the whole of the southern part of Syria-Palestine 'from the Tyrian ladder to the Egyptian frontier' (1 Macc. xi, 59) for the young aspirant to the throne. Jonathan and Simon undertook this task in a series of successful campaigns which extended from the southern coastal plain as far as Galilee and the region of Damascus (1 Macc. xi, 60-74; xii, 24-38). But this made Jonathan's position dangerously strong. Once again he established contact with Rome and also with Sparta (1 Macc. xii, 1-23). Furthermore, he built strongholds in the province of Judah, strengthened and raised the wall of Jerusalem and built a high wall between the Syrian occupied 'Akra' of Jerusalem and the rest of the city to make encroachments from the 'Akra' impossible. Diodotus Tryphon, who had merely used the young Antiochus as a pretext and was striving after the throne himself, could not let this go unpunished. He lured Jonathan with only a small retinue to Ptolemais and had him imprisoned there. In Jerusalem his brother Simon, Mattathias's second oldest son, was put in Jonathan's place. Simon was able successfully to defend the province of Judah which Tryphon tried to attack from various sides. Tryphon took the captive Jonathan with him on his expeditions and finally had him killed in the land east of the Jordan at a place called Baskam which it is now impossible to locate (1 Macc. xii, 39–xiii, 32). This happened in the year 143 B.C.

After the connection with Tryphon had had such evil consequences, Simon now turned to Demetrius II who, since he was having difficulty in maintaining his throne against Tryphon, was very anxious to come to a good understanding with Simon and was prepared to make concessions to this end. He granted the Judaeans freedom from tithe duty and also an amnesty, and later sanctioned the fortifications which Simon had meanwhile taken in hand in the province of Judah. Simon behaved more and more as an independent ruler and at this period the Seleucid State was hardly in a position to enforce its authority. With the consent of the people Simon gave himself the official title of 'great high priest, general and leader of the Judaeans' (1 Macc. xiii, 42), and made the first year of his reign the beginning of a new era; he reckoned the 170th Seleucid year (142–141 B.C.) as his '1st year' (1 Macc. xiii, 41 f.). He kept up the connections with Rome and Sparta which Jonathan had begun (1 Macc. xiv, 16-24). Above all, he succeeded in forcing the 'Akra' of Jerusalem to surrender, and its inhabitants to withdraw, by laying siege to it, and the king was unable to intervene. The traditional records have assigned a precise date to this important event; on the 23/II of the 171st Seleucid year, that is, in the middle of the year 141 B.C., there was celebrated in Jerusalem the entry into the 'Akra' which had for so long been occupied by a disloyal population and protected by a foreign garrison, and once again Simon strengthened the defences of the Temple precincts (1 Macc. xiii, 49-52). He had the site of the former 'Akra' settled with '(faithful) Judaeans' and probably had it included within the city wall which he had improved (1 Macc. xiv, 37). He also extended the territory of the province of Judah as a result of a number of successful campaigns, and once again the king was unable to check him. He conquered the city of Gazara, the ancient Gezer (the modern tell jezer) on the coastal plain south-east of yāfa; he annexed it for the province of Judah and assigned Gazara as a garrison to his son Johannes, whom he had made commander of the military forces in the province. But, above all, he conquered the port of Joppe (yāfa) and thereby acquired direct access to the Mediterranean for the province (1 Macc. xiv, 5). The fact that in 1 Macc. xiv, 6, it is stated in this connection that he 'extended the frontiers for the people' suggests that he may also have been responsible for the extension of Judaea to the north-east at the expense of the province of Samaria, which is first documented by Josephus[1] and Pliny[2], but which had no doubt taken place considerably earlier. This extension covered, in addition to the three Samaritan areas of Aphairema, Ramathaim and Lydda which had been made over to Jonathan in 145 B.C., the farther district of 'Akrabattene', *i.e.* the district of Akraba (the modern 'aḳrabe) about 12 kilometres south-east of nāblus (Shechem)[3] which had also previously belonged to Samaria. As a result of this expansion the province of Judah extended north of the district of Aphairema on the heights and the eastern side of the Samarian mountains fairly near to Shechem, the ancient metropolis of the Central Palestinian mountains; and on the north to south road on the mountain heights between Jerusalem and Shechem the place called Anuath Borkaios now became, as Josephus noted later[4], the boundary between the provinces of Judah and Samaria. Its name survives in the name of the spring 'ēn berḳīt which is only about 15 kilometres from Shechem, but over 35 kilometres north of Jerusalem. And so Simon was able to round off and secure his territories and reign fairly undisturbed in the province of Judah. Simon is described as a just and benevolent regent, and, after the troubles that had preceded it, his reign was regarded as a time of peace and prosperity (1 Macc. xiv, 4, 8 ff.). On the whole, Simon was able to consider his achievements complete and secure, and in a great assembly of the people it was resolved, at his instigation, to record his *res gestae* and publish them on bronze tablets on the Temple Mount in Jerusalem; his father and his brothers, above all Jonathan, were briefly commemorated too, but the main reference was to his own successes and services (1 Macc. xiv, 25-49).

Finally Simon was affected once again by the conflicts in the Seleucid house; but his position was no longer seriously endangered by them. Probably in 140 B.C. Demetrius II Nicator undertook an expedition against the Parthians in the east, on which he was taken prisoner by the Parthians. Thereupon his brother, Antiochus VII Sidetes, set himself on the throne in Antioch. The latter took up the

[1] *Bell. Iud.* III, 3, 4, 5, §§ 48, 55 Niese.
[2] *Hist. Nat.* V, 14, 70.
[3] Cf. A. Alt, PJB, 31 (1935), pp. 97 f.
[4] *Bell. Iud.* III, 3, 5, § 51 Niese.

struggle against Diodotus Tryphon, who was still alive, and for this reason he was anxious for a good understanding with Simon (1 Macc. v, 1-14). But he soon managed to overcome Tryphon who finally gave up the struggle and took his own life, and he now attempted to proceed against Simon's very independent position. He called on Simon to surrender the conquered territories, above all Gazara, Joppe and the 'Akra' of Jerusalem. When Simon refused, he sent his general Cendebaeus against the province of Judah (1 Macc. xv, 25-41). Simon instructed his two sons Judas and John to ward off the attack of the enemy, who had already begun to lay waste parts of the province of Judah from Jamnia (the modern yebna). In the vicinity of Modein, the ancient home of their family, the two sons succeeded in defeating Cendebaeus and pursuing the enemy troops far out into the plain (1 Macc. xvi, 1-10). Thus the safety of the province of Judah was again assured, and apparently no further effort against Simon was undertaken.

At the beginning of the year 134 B.C. Simon, now stricken in years, succumbed to an attempt on his life by his son-in-law Ptolemy. The latter was commander in the district of Jericho and had a residence called Dok by the spring which is still called ʿen duk, west-north-west of Jericho. On a visit to Dok, Simon with his two sons Mattathias and Judas were treacherously murdered by Ptolemy, who was striving for power himself. Ptolemy now sought to establish relations with the king and to obtain his support, and meanwhile he prepared to occupy the whole province with his troops and, above all, to remove Simon's son John, whom Simon had installed in Gazara and who resided there. John was warned in time, however, and was able to meet the attack and, before Ptolemy was really under way, he had himself installed in his father's offices in Jerusalem (1 Macc. xvi, 11-22). As a grandson of Mattathias and son of Simon he probably soon received the approbation and support of the Judaeans. He locked up the murderer Ptolemy in his residence Dok, but did not dare to attack him in any strength, since his mother was in Ptolemy's hands. In the end he gave up the siege, but Ptolemy murdered his mother all the same and escaped[1].

[1] Josephus, *Ant. Iud.* XIII, 8, 1, §§ 230 ff.; *Bell. Iud.* I, 2, 3, 4, §§ 54 ff. The first book of Maccabees closes with the story of the murder of Simon. From that point onwards we are primarily dependent on Josephus, who only provides scanty information on the following period to begin with, but with more and more detail as time proceeds, very largely on the basis of the tradition of, for example, Nicolaus of Damascus, who lived at the court of Herod and had also written history himself. In the introduction to the *Bellum Iudaicum* Josephus made a fairly brief summary of his data—beginning with Antiochus Epiphanes—for the period up to the intervention of the Romans. He

As John Hyrcanus I, John then reigned in the province of Judah in the offices and with the titles of his father. In his very first year, however, he landed into most serious trouble. After the defeat of his general Cendebaeus, Antiochus VII Sidetes made a renewed attempt to destroy the independence of the province of Judah. This time he succeeded in occupying the province and locking up John Hyrcanus in Jerusalem and besieging the city, which in time came into the direst straits owing to starvation. In the end, however, an agreement was reached. In view of the general state of affairs in his State, Antiochus was probably unable to afford to spend a long time on the siege of Jerusalem and had presumably hoped to finish it off more quickly. John had to make a considerable payment for the districts conquered by his father, above all Joppe; but its membership of the province was now at any rate officially recognised. He had to hand over his weapons and furnish hostages (*Ant. Iud.* XIII, 8, 2, 3, §§ 236 ff.). Finally Antiochus VII undertook a campaign against the Parthians and met his death on this campaign in the year 128 B.C. During the campaign Demetrius II had been released by the Parthians, and, as the rival of his brother Antiochus, he ascended the throne again, attacking his brother in the rear. After the death of Antiochus, Demetrius became king again for a few years. But from now on quarrels about the succession to the throne went on all the time among unimportant and weak members of the Seleucid house, and to all intents and purposes this meant independence for the province of Judah. In the year 128 B.C. the long and difficult conflict of the religious community of Jerusalem with the Seleucid power, which had entered a critical stage with the violent interference of Antiochus IV Epiphanes with the Temple worship in Jerusalem, came to an end.

30. *The Rise and Fall of the Hasmonaean Monarchy*

After the Maccabean rising had achieved freedom of worship for the religious community of Jerusalem in quite a short time, the sons of the priest Mattathias strove more and more clearly and confidently for the political independence of, to begin with, the province of Judah. Judas already envisaged this goal and Jonathan and Simon even more so, and Simon's son John Hyrcanus went

reports in greater detail on this period in the *Antiquates Iudaicae*, a work which was written later, and which will therefore be the main source of our subsequent quotations.

further in the same direction. This striving after secular independence and power did not meet with the undivided approval of the religious community in Jerusalem. Many of the 'devout' rejected it or, at any rate, reserved judgement. They were satisfied with the assurance of freedom of worship and freedom to lead a life in accordance with the law, and for the rest they awaited liberation from the troubles and afflictions of the time, not from human actions but from a future glorious act of God which would remove the powers of this world. Nor will the 'devout' have approved of the not always particularly straight paths which the Maccabean leaders, especially Jonathan, took to approach their goal in these tumultuous times and amidst the quarrels of this world. On the other side there were the friends of the Hellenists, probably including some of the 'Sadducean' priesthood, who could hardly have any inclination to fight the Hellenistic power. All the same, the Maccabean leaders must have had a great band of supporters which increased with their successes, otherwise they would not have been able constantly to hold their position through all the ups and downs of events and in spite of what were, to begin with, great difficulties. In these circles their actions were felt to be of historical importance; and, in fact, after centuries of dependence on one Empire after another, the Maccabean rising signified a renewal of Israel's active intervention in the development of its own history. It is therefore not surprising that the deeds of Mattathias and his descendants found historians ready to record them. David had stimulated the writing of the first important Israelite history, and now historians described the way trodden by Mattathias and his descendants as right and pleasing to God. So far as we can tell from the traditional records that have survived, this was the first time since the age of David and Solomon that historical writing was composed under the more or less immediate impact of the events and persons described. The oldest document of which we have certain evidence is the 'Diary of the Office of High Priest' by John Hyrcanus mentioned in I Macc. xvi, 24, which was probably finished soon after his death, *circa* 100 B.C. As it has not survived, it is impossible to say whether it was already an authentic historical work or not rather simply an annalistic compilation. The First Book of Maccabees, which quotes from this 'Diary', was probably written soon afterwards. No doubt on the basis of traditional records, it gives a connected account of the deeds of the 'Maccabeans' up to Simon with a marked bias to their side. The five-volume work of Jason of Cyrene on 'the Maccabean Judas and his brothers' (2 Macc. ii, 19), which was subsequently summarised in the Second Book of Maccabees, adopted a similar attitude. Unfortunately it is impossible to fix the time and place of its origin. The events of the 2nd century also gave a new stimulus to other literary activity[1]. We have already mentioned the Book of Daniel (cf. above, p. 000), the only one of these literary productions to be included in the Hebrew canon of the Old Testament. According to the preface to the Greek translation of the Book of Jesus Sirach, the original Hebrew version of this beautiful and weighty book of wisdom must have been written about the beginning of the Maccabean period. The revival of the Hebrew language for literary works instead of the everyday Aramaic—except among the Greek-speaking and writing Hellenistic Diaspora—was a sign of the newly awakened interest in the venerable traditions and values of the past. Whilst the Daniel narratives (Dan. i-vi) had been written down in Aramaic in the 3rd century in the period of persecution between 167 and 164 B.C., the vision of Daniel was still composed in Aramaic, but Hebrew was used for the later visions. As is stated in the Preface to the Greek edition, and explicitly confirmed by the original text, which has been discovered, the Book of Wisdom of Jesus Sirach was written in the Hebrew language. Probably the First Book of Maccabees, of which only the Greek translation is extant, was originally written in Hebrew rather than Aramaic.

In spite of everything, the events which took place in connection with the Maccabean rising could not lead to a real rebirth of Israel and the ultimate revival of the monarchy. The restoration of political independence cannot really be compared with the emergence of the monarchy under Saul and David. The foundations of the Hasmonaean monarchy were shaky from the very beginning. Only favourable circumstances, the fact that the Seleucid State was in a condition of increasing decline but still sufficiently powerful to prevent other powers laying hands directly on its territory, led to adroit leaders on the periphery of this State in southern Palestine founding a State of their own which was really independent though it had not broken away formally from Seleucid sovereignty. This state of affairs did not last very long. As soon as

[1] Apparently at this time people again studied the subjects of the old Pentateuch tradition in the groups of the Hellenistic Diaspora in which the traditional stories were reinterpreted mythologically and rationalistically in a clearly derivative manner. The adaptations of the traditional narratives by Artapanus and Eupolemus, of which we have only indirect and quite fragmentary knowledge, may have originated about the beginning of the 1st century B.C.; cf. A. Schlatter, *Geschichte Israels von Alexander dem Grossen bis Hadrian* ([3] 1925), pp. 187 ff.

a stronger hand seized the Seleucid State the independence of the Hasmonaean monarchy came to an end, since it was lacking in real substance. David's monarchy had been sustained by the consent of the free Israelite tribes in the two States of Judah and Israel, whereas, to begin with, the Hasmonaean monarchy relied very largely on the support of a particular party in the province of Judah; and even though it did reach out beyond these narrow confines, the substance of the people on which it was inevitably based had become far too undermined after centuries of foreign rule and many ups and downs of fate to form the basis of a permanent political structure. The religious community of Jerusalem had become something different from what the ancient people of Israel had been. With their supporters the Hasmonaeans established and maintained their power primarily by military means. From the outset they had to reckon on numerous, albeit not over-active, enemies among the Israelites and they were, therefore, never able to attain a healthy, organic political system. I am not suggesting that they were mere adventurers. The goal they had in mind was a monarchy over Israel and David's formation of a State will have served as their model. Judas had already concerned himself with the Israelites in Galilee and the land east of the Jordan, and later on the Hasmonaeans were able to extend their rule over roughly the whole territory of the old Israelite tribes. But the conditions needed for a restoration of the Davidian monarchy never really existed in their time.

The Hasmonaeans left few visible traces of their rule behind. We know a little about the building activities of the Hasmonaean rulers more from literary records than archaeological discoveries. They helped to change the face of the royal city of Jerusalem. According to Josephus (*Bell. Iud.* V, 4, 1, § 139) the Hasmonaeans levelled the site of the one-time 'Akra'[1], thereby probably beginning the end of the settlement on the 'south-eastern hill' of Jerusalem which to this day has never been inhabited as a self-contained unit again. On the other hand, they built a royal palace in Jerusalem, though unfortunately no information about the building has come down to us; but Josephus, who mentions a 'Hasmonaean house' in Jerusalem (*Bell. Iud.* II, 16, 3, § 344) and a 'royal fort' in Jerusalem which derived from the Hasmonaeans (*Ant. Iud.* XX, 8, 11, § 189 f.), testifies to its existence. This Hasmonaean palace was located on a part of the west hill of Jerusalem which projects

[1] Later on, Josephus specifically attributed this work to Simon (*Ant. Iud.* XIII, 6, 7, §§ 215 ff.) but probably in error.

opposite the southern part of the Temple area[1]. In addition to this, the Hasmonaeans also established on a hill north-west of the Temple area a fortress which was evidently intended to dominate the sanctuary and which was called 'Baris' (*Ant. Iud.* XV, 11, 4, § 403). As a result, the centre of gravity of the city of Jerusalem was gradually shifted westwards and northwards. Herod's later building activities intensified this tendency still more. The Hasmonaean rulers also erected forts in the country outside Jerusalem. To judge from its name, the fort of Hyrcania was established by John Hyrcanus; it lay east-south-east of Jerusalem in the Sinaitic desert on the site of the modern khirbet mird, and more than once played an important part in times to come. The fort of Alexandreion which lay on the summit of the ḳarn ṣarṭabe which jutted out into the lower valley of the Jordan from the west Jordan hills, and which derived its name from Alexander Jannaeus, played an important part in the fighting of the late Hasmonaean period. The same Alexander Jannaeus also extended the fort of Machaerus in the southern land east of the Jordan (the modern khirbet el-mkāwer). However, all these Hasmonaean installations were put in the shade by the later buildings of Herod.

After the death of Antiochus VII Sidetes in the year 128 B.C. had given him more or less a free hand, John Hyrcanus I, as high priest and ethnarch, extended his power in various directions as a result of military campaigns. For this purpose he used primarily mercenaries which he had recruited, just as David had done. But whereas David, who had himself been a professional soldier, used this method because it was part and parcel of the strategy with which he was familiar, with John Hyrcanus it was a sign of his lack of popular support. With these mercenaries he marched into the southern land east of the Jordan, and after a six months' siege he captured the city of Medeba and then a few other places, laying his hands on the country of el-belḳa which under David had been part of the State of Israel. He also undertook a campaign against the province of Samaria, seized the city of Shechem, occupied Mount Gerizim and destroyed the Samaritan Temple built on it. Furthermore, he invaded the province of Idumaea ('Edom') which adjoined Judaea in the south and the territory of which had been Judaean until the year 598 B.C., seized the cities of Adora (dūra) west-south-west of Hebron and Marissa (tell sandaḥanne) near the modern bet jibrīn, and forced the inhabitants of Idumaea to accept the custom of circumcision and the whole law of the religious

[1] Cf. J. Simons, *Jerusalem in the Old Testament* (1952), pp. 152 f.

community of Jerusalem, and incorporated them by force in this religious community (*Ant. Iud.* XIII, 9, 1, §§ 254 ff.). Later on he attacked the province of Samaria once again, including the provincial capital of Samaria itself. It had to be besieged for a long time and John Hyrcanus left this task to his two sons Aristobulus and Antigonus[1]. As the inhabitants summoned Seleucid help in their affliction, for a time the besiegers were in serious difficulties. They finally succeeded in capturing the city in the year 107 B.C. after besieging it for about a year. The city was completely destroyed (*Ant. Iud.* XIII, 10, 2, 3, §§ 275 ff.).

John Hyrcanus's successes were great. Nevertheless he had internal difficulties. In *Ant. Iud.* XIII, 10, 5, 6, §§ 288 ff., Josephus tells anecdote-fashion, but probably with a basis of truth, of a disagreement between him and the Pharisees, who can indeed scarcely have approved of his political and military activities. This led to Mattathias's grandson approaching the Sadducees, who, with their pro-Hellenistic attitude, found it easier to reconcile themselves to his activities. For the rest he behaved like an independent ruler. He had coins minted with the inscription: 'The High Priest Johannes and the community of the Judaeans' or 'The High Priest Johannes, the Head of the community of the Judaeans'. On these coins double cornucopias appear as on Seleucid copper coins and also a poppyhead, symbols of fertility, which were no doubt intended to refer to the benefactions of the government of John Hyrcanus[2].

In the year 104 B.C. John Hyrcanus died. He intended his wife to succeed him. But his eldest son, Aristobulus, seized power, had his mother taken to prison and starved. He also imprisoned three of his brothers and allowed only his brother Antigonus to share the government with him. Intrigues were now started against the latter by members of Aristobulus's entourage, which made the latter distrust his brother and finally have him treacherously murdered (*Ant. Iud.* III, ii, 1, 2, § 301 ff.). This fratricide clearly reveals the degeneration of the Hasmonaean dynasty which was soon to assume even worse forms. Aristobulus drew the logical conclusion from the actual situation and assumed the title of king and conferred a diadem on himself. On the coins which derive from him, however, he does not bear the title of king. Their inscription

[1] The Greek names (or nicknames) of the two are noteworthy.

[2] Cf. C. Watzinger, *Denkmäler Palästinas*, II (1933), p. 23; A. Reifenberg, *Ancient Jewish Coins* (2 1947), pp. 13 f., 40 f., Pl. II. A coin found during the excavations at Beth-Zur with the name probably of a high priest probably comes from the pre-Maccabean Hellenistic period (cf. W. F. Albright, BASOR, 53 [1934], p. 22).

runs: 'High Priest Judas[1] and the community of the Judaeans'[2]. According to Josephus, *Ant. Iud.* XIII, 2, 3, §§ 318 f., he waged war in the extreme north of the country and forced the Ituraeans in the north of Galilee to introduce circumcision and accept the law of the religious community of Jerusalem. He therefore appears to have at any rate partly subjugated Galilee. He died in the year 103 B.C. after he had reigned only for a year.

Aristobulus's wife, Salome[3] Alexandra, now released the three imprisoned brothers of the dead king from prison and appointed one of them king. His real name was Johannes but he was called by his pet name Jannai and only used his real name as a surname to a Greek name, so that he became known as Alexander Jannaeus[4]. The degeneration of the Hasmonaean dynasty was clearly revealed in him, the grandson of Mattathias. It is no longer possible to decide how far the Salome Alexandra who put him on the throne, contributed to this. At any rate, she married him[5] and took on the government after his death; this suggests that she will already have had a strong influence during his lifetime. Of his two surviving brothers he had one murdered—evidently to safeguard his own authority—but the other one, who had no political ambitions, he left alone (*Ant. Iud.* XIII, 12, 1, §§ 323). For the rest, he constantly made war, with changing fortune, but with the result, nevertheless, that in the end he controlled practically the whole of Palestine. An attack on the port of Ptolemais (Akko) at the beginning of his reign involved him in an armed conflict with Ptolemaeus Lathyrus who, banished from Egypt, was ruling in Cyprus at this time and had been called to their aid by the inhabitants of Ptolemaeus. Ptolemaeus Lathyrus invaded the land and defeated Alexander Jannaeus so thoroughly in a battle on the middle Jordan near Asaphon[6] that he was able to regard himself as master in the land. Only the opposition which Ptolemaeus Lathyrus encountered from Egypt, especially from his mother Cleopatra, forced him to with-

[1] According to Josephus, *Ant. Iud.* XX, 10, 3, § 240, Judas was the original name and Aristobulus the Greek nickname.

[2] Cf. A. Reifenberg, *loc. cit.* pp. 14, 41, Pl. ii.

[3] In *Ant. Iud.* XIII, 12, 1, § 320 this name is distorted to Salina.

[4] On his coins (cf. also C. Watzinger, *loc. cit.* p. 23; A. Reifenberg, *loc. cit.* pp. 14 f., 41, Pl. ii) so far as they followed the previous type of high priest coins, he referred to his original name in the inscription: 'The high priest Jonathan and the community of the Judaeans'. In addition he then had new royal coins minted with the bi-lingual inscription: 'The King Jonathan (Hebrew)—King Alexander (Greek)'.

[5] There is no explicit evidence of this event; but probably Salome Alexandra was nevertheless always one and the same person at this period.

[6] On the precise situation of Asaphon or Asophon cf. F. V. Filson, BASOR, 91 (1943), pp. 27 f., and, on the other hand, N. Glück, AASOR, 25/28 (1951), pp. 354 f.

draw to Cyprus and free Alexander Jannaeus from his distress. (*Ant. Iud.* XIII, 12, 2-13, 2, §§ 324 ff.). Once he had a free hand again, Alexander Jannaeus marched first of all into the land east of the Jordan, captured, after a long siege, the city of Gadara (the modern umkēs) which lay on the south side of the Jarmuk, and then the city of Amathus (the modern ʿammata) on the eastern border of the central valley of the Jordan, thereby laying his hands on the central land east of the Jordan. He then turned his attention to the southern coastal plain and occupied the cities of Rapẖu (the modern refaḥ) and Anthedon (north-west of Gaza) and finally overcame the important city of Gaza by treachery, and had it sacked and set on fire (*Ant. Iud.* XIII, 13, 3, §§ 356 ff.). Later on he invaded the land east of the Jordan again, subjugated the inhabitants of Moabitis and Galaaditis, *i.e.* of the southern and central land east of the Jordan again and captured the city of Amathus once again; his rule, which was based on purely military resources —he too waged his wars with mercenaries—was nowhere very permanent and always began to crumble once he was making war in another area. After the conquest of Amathus he penetrated as far as Gaulanitis, the present region of jōlān north of the Jarmuk. An engagement took place here with Obedas, the 'King of the Arabs', *i.e.* Obodath, the king of the Nabataeans, who was preparing to subjugate the land east of the Jordan as far as Damascus. He fell into an ambush and only just managed to save his life, escape and flee to Jerusalem. The episode showed how strong the opposition to him was among his own people. They tried to rid themselves of his rule and even appealed for the help of the Seleucid Demetrius III Eukairos who was in control of part of Syria *circa* 90 B.C. And at Shechem his forces did in fact defeat Alexander Jannaeus, who was already in a very tight corner anyway. He had to flee to somewhere in the mountains. In this situation enough supporters who did not want their own monarchy to be defeated rallied around him, however, and, according to Josephus, he was joined by 6000 Judaeans; and with them Alexander Jannaeus was able to establish his rule again. Demetrius III withdrew and Alexander Jannaeus took a terrible and cruel vengeance on his Judaean enemies (*Ant. Iud.* XIII, 13, 5-14, 2, § 372 ff.). He maintained authority by terror and thereby succeeded in ridding himself henceforth of all internal difficulties. But he still had to go through struggles with his external enemies, above all with the Nabataeans, whose growing power and lust for expansion was endangering near-by Palestine. From their ancient dwellings in the mountains south-east of the Dead Sea they not only pressed forward to the far north on the eastern border of the land east of the Jordan, but they also tried to reach the Mediterranean by way of the wādi el-ʿaraba on the southern border of Palestine; and everywhere their nearest important neighbour was the land ruled by Alexander Jannaeus. And so the latter was involved in the struggles between the Seleucid State and the Nabataeans. When one of the last of the Seleucids, Antiochus XII Dionysus, a younger brother of the above-mentioned Demetrius, tried to proceed against the Nabataeans through the coastal plain of Palestine and hence through Alexander Jannaeus's territory, the latter attempted to block the Seleucid's way by means of a ditch and a wall which he set up between Kapharsaba (the modern kefr sāba) and Joppe (yāfa); the Seleucid burnt and destroyed this work, but soon afterwards he was killed on the Nabataean campaign (*Ant. Iud.* XIII, 15, 1, §§ 387 ff.).

This was followed by direct and serious conflicts between the Nabataeans and Alexander Jannaeus. Aretas, who had meanwhile become king of the Nabataeans, advanced far into Judaea, and at Adida (probably el-ḥadīle east of Lydda) he inflicted a severe defeat on Alexander Jannaeus, so that he was forced to make concessions to obtain the withdrawal of the enemy (*Ant. Iud.* XIII, 15, 2, § 392). Finally, he carried out a number of successful expeditions in the land east of the Jordan. He occupied the cities of Pella (the modern khirbet fahil) on the eastern border of the central valley of the Jordan and Gerasa (jerash) in the ʿajlūn, and also north of the Jarmuk, the cities of Golan, the capital of the Gaulanitis (exact position unknown)[1], and Seleukeia (the modern selūḳye) and Dia (the modern tell ashʿari) as well as the citadel of Gamala[2]. In the land east of the Jordan his life came to an end. Weakened by a dissolute life, he died in his 51st year during the siege of the citadel of Ragaba (the modern rājib) in the southern ʿajlūn. Besides many military successes he had also suffered a number of serious defeats. Apart from ancient Judaea he had also inherited Samaria and Galilee from his predecessors and made conquests himself in the southern coastal plain and then, above all, he extended his dominion in the land east of the Jordan and managed to maintain his power to some extent against the increasingly powerful Nabataeans. In *Ant. Iud.* XIII, 15, 4, §§ 395-397 Josephus

[1] This city is often identified with the modern sahem ed-jolan.

[2] The names given in *Ant. Iud.* XIII, 15, 3, §§ 393 f. and *Bell. Iud.* I, 4, 8, §§ 104 f. differ somewhat. Both lists have been collated with one another above.

describes the dominions of the 'Judaeans' towards the end of the reign of Alexander Jannaeus; according to this, they more or less embraced the territories of the old States of Judah and Israel which David and Solomon had ruled over, and also the former land of the Philistines and the coast road to Egypt as far as and including Bhinokorura (el-ʿarīsh). Though his successes did bring him some supporters, he had had to contend with the enmity of the 'devout' and the 'Pharisees' who hated this secular and already intensely degenerate monarchy. Josephus relates in *Ant. Iud.* XIII, 15, 5, §§ 399 ff. that before his death he advised his wife, Salome Alexandra, to allow the Pharisees a certain influence in the future, *i.e.* to try to reconcile them to the Hasmonaean monarchy, which could not stand this internal discord in the long run.

After the death of Alexander Jannaeus in the year 76 B.C. his energetic and shrewd wife, Salome Alexandra, reigned for nine years. She presumably seized the throne on her own responsibility, particularly as her elder son, Hyrcanus (II), who should have succeeded his father, was very indolent and irresolute. She allowed him to succeed his father in the office of high priest which the existing law prevented her from assuming, but kept the monarchy for herself. She held back her younger son, Aristobulus (II) who, unlike his brother, was very bold and enterprising. Above all she now established contact with the Pharisees and complied to a very large extent with their wishes and demands. Hence her reign was regarded as a satisfying period. There was also the fact that she managed, without waging wars, to keep the Hasmonaean State together and steer it through all kinds of difficulties (*Ant. Iud.* XIII, 16, 1-6, § 405 ff.). The only person she failed to manage was her son Aristobulus. The Sadducee priesthood had more reason for dissatisfaction than anyone else because of the influence which the Pharisees had suddenly acquired. This discontent was turned to account by the restlessly ambitious Aristobulus, who had been kept under and who was striving for power. But before it came to open rebellion the queen died in the year 67 B.C. at the age of 73 and left the Hasmonaean dominions to the dissensions of her two sons.

To begin with, Hyrcanus II, who was entitled to the throne as the elder of the brothers, did in fact take up the royal office; he had already been High Priest since the beginning of his mother's reign. But Aristobulus, who was the stronger character, refused to acquiesce in this state of affairs. With his followers he defeated Hyrcanus's forces at Jericho and hosts of the latter went over to the enemy. He then locked up Hyrcanus in the fortress[1] of Jerusalem and forced him to surrender. Hyrcanus ceded his office as king and high priest to his brother and in return he was promised a guaranteed income (*Ant. Iud.* XIV, 1, 2, § 4 ff.). This appeared to have brought the dispute to an end. But a new figure now appeared on the scene, who was soon to play a great part in the history of Israel. Under Alexander Jannaeus and Salome Alexandra a certain Antipater (Antipas for short) had been governor in Idumaea[2]. His son of the same name, whose official position is not definitely known, but who may also have been governor in Idumaea, now espoused the cause of the defeated Hyrcanus. Probably he did not much like the government of the ambitious and energetic Aristobulus. He assembled followers in Judaea and also got in touch with the Nabataean king Aretas and managed to persuade Hyrcanus to leave Jerusalem for security reasons and put himself under the protection of the Nabataean king. Hyrcanus left the city by night with Antipater and went to the royal Nabataean city of Petra. The Nabataean king promised to take him back to Jerusalem with a military escort and install him as king there in return for the surrender of a number of cities on the eastern side of the Dead Sea, in the old land of the Moabites, which Alexander Jannaeus had taken away from the Nabataeans; and Hyrcanus promised to fulfil this condition (*Ant. Iud.* XIV, 1, 3, 4, §§ 8 ff.). Thereupon Aretas proceeded to Judaea with an army and defeated Aristobulus's forces in a battle, the place of which is not mentioned by Josephus. The result was that a major part of Aristobulus's troops went over to the victor and Aristobulus, who was thus left in the lurch, was forced to withdraw to Jerusalem to defend himself in the fortified Temple area, where the priests still stood by him. But Aretas besieged him in the sanctuary, and the people in Jerusalem and probably elsewhere as well supported the party that was for the moment in the ascendant. The prospects for Aristobulus were far from favourable and it appears that Hyrcanus might soon have attained the goal desired by Antipater if another and much stronger power had not intervened at this moment, which gave the course of events a completely new twist. The situation in which this happened revealed once again the whole wretchedness to which the Hasmonaean monarchy had sunk. Two brothers were quarrelling

[1] This fort was not the former 'Akra' which had played such a great part in the Maccabean fighting, but the fortification laid out by the Hasmonaeans on an elevation north-west of the Temple enclosure which was called 'Baris' at the time.

[2] That Antipater was himself an 'Idumaean' is stated by Josephus, *Ant. Iud.* XIV, 1, 3, § 8 and elsewhere.

about the throne. The driving force behind the dispute was a leading royal official, possibly the governor of Idumaea, who wanted to see the king who was functioning at the moment removed. The dispute was conducted with the military aid of the Nabataean king whom this official had enlisted for the purpose. The price which had to be paid to the foreign king, who was a natural enemy of the Hasmonaean State, considered in the surrender of a large area which had been acquired in the process of restoring the Israelite kingdom, more or less, on the model of David's kingdom. And now this foreign king, who had been summoned to help by the Judaeans themselves, was encamped with his troops outside the sanctuary in Jerusalem which was being used as a fortress; and the Judaean troops and the people were on his side because he was the superior and obviously victorious party. It was clear that the Hasmonaean monarchy had already lost the historical game. Forty years had not yet passed since a Hasmonaean had first called himself 'king' and already the complete decay of this institution was evident.

31. *Israel's Inner Life in the Hellenistic Period*

The struggles that began in the Maccabean period not only greatly agitated the religious community of Jerusalem externally, but also stirred up its internal life intensely. The traditional records about this period reveal very varied religious and intellectual tendencies. Needless to say, this differentiation of the community's inner life was not brought about in the first place by the conflict with the Seleucid powers; it merely became very intensified in the process of these events; it had its roots in earlier periods about which we are unfortunately much less well-informed. We have to reckon with the fact that life in Israel had been becoming more and more individualised for a long time. Even though the old Israel of the twelve tribes, living as a self-contained unit in its homeland, was certainly not a shapeless collectivity in which the individual was no more than a mere member of a greater Whole, and even though such a thing as 'Salomonic-post-Salomonic humanism' (cf. above, p. 221) had existed, nevertheless it was inevitable that the gradual undermining of the organism of the original Israel, resulting from the catastrophes of the divine judgement which destroyed Israel's political independence, should lead to a further dissolution of traditional ties and an ever-increasing prominence being given to the individual with his personal inclinations and decisions. It is true that the events of the Persian period had reunited Israel as a great community gathered around the Temple worship in Jerusalem with its long traditions, and had given all Israelites a binding rule for daily life in the 'law of the god of heaven'; but this very law had confronted the individual with the question of his personal recognition and therefore membership of 'Israel' and also made it possible for individual non-Israelites to share this recognition. It may be assumed that the process of individualisation was further promoted by involvement in the intellectual atmosphere of the Hellenistic world, though it is impossible to prove the point in detail. Above all, in the widespread Diaspora the individual was dependent on his own resources in a foreign environment and had, if necessary, to prove his loyalty to the traditions of Israel on his own responsibility. The Daniel narratives in Dan. i-vi which probably originated and were put together in the course of the first century, reveal the typical situation of the Diaspora Israelite who could easily find himself forced to maintain his obedience to God and his law by his own strength of faith. And in view of the constant intercourse between the Diaspora and the homeland, the situation in the Diaspora no doubt had a lasting effect on the intellectual outlook of the Israelites who were still living together in Palestine. Even before the outbreak of the Maccabean conflicts, Israel's life will therefore have been full of individuality; and it is not surprising that the reaction which the events of the period of Antiochus IV Epiphanes evoked in the religious community of Jerusalem was by no means uniform. The crisis that occurred in this period did, however, no doubt elucidate and clarify the existing differences and bring about particular groupings within the religious community of Jerusalem which continued to be of great importance right into the Roman period.

There were certain pro-Hellenistic circles which, in so far as they were not simply absorbed by the pagan world, and thereby withdrawn from the history of Israel, but adhered more or less deliberately to their membership of the religious community of Jerusalem, were devoted to the Hellenistic life which surrounded this community on every side in the homeland and in the Diaspora, especially the Egyptian Diaspora. These groups began to play an important part under Antiochus IV and probably had a considerable share in the outbreak of the conflict in Jerusalem (cf. above, p. 359 f.). No doubt they evolved an intellectual life of their own both before this, and also afterwards, in which an attempt was made to combine Israel's traditions with Hellenistic thought in some way or other. But hardly any evidence of this intellectual life has survived. The fact is that these groups succumbed in the fighting of the 2nd century, at least in Palestine; and when, after the end of Israel, the synagogue withdrew into itself and rejected all seemingly foreign elements, works which had arisen in these circles, even if they were still read in the Diaspora of the Mediterranean world, were no longer handed down to the next generation. All that we possess of this Israelite-Hellenistic literature are the meagre fragments which found a place in the works of early Christian writers by way of the great collector Alexander Polyhistor (first half of the 1st century B.C.) or by other routes. All the same, these fragments do show that this type of literature existed. Thus, about the middle of the 2nd century, the philosopher Aristobulus in Alexandra attempted to show that the basic content of the Old Testament law coincides with the various schools of Greek philosophy, in fact that Greek philosophy, had from of old, drawn on the Mosaic law[1]. This was an attempt to interpret and justify the traditions of Israel before the forum of the Hellenistic thought. The method used was that of allegorical exegesis. Philosophers of the type of Aristobulus were joined, as mentioned above on p. 382, note 1, by historians such as Artapanus and Eupolemus[2]. Later on we find the same approach in the allegorical and mystical philosophy of Philo of Alexandria on the one hand and the historical writing of Josephus on the other, as far as the latter is a description of Israel's ancient history for the Hellenistic and Roman world, and not contemporary history.

In the Maccabean-Hasmonaean period the Sadducees sympathised with this Hellenising tendency. They were the group of priests in Jerusalem, and, as such, the representatives of a legitimist approach in public worship, though only in a predominantly formal sense, so that they were not averse in principle to the adoption of Hellenistic modes of life. Thanks to the inertia of religious traditions they were able to endure the whole crisis of the conflict with Hellenism and survive right up to the end of Israel's history.

Admittedly, the anti-Hellenistic forces won the victory in the struggles of the 2nd century. The division which occurred in their midst and which we have discussed above on p. 372, came about

[1] A German translation of the fragments of Aristobulus will be found in P. Riessler, *Altjüdisches Schrifttum ausserhalb der Bibel* (1928), pp. 179 ff. Cf. also on Aristobulus A. Schlatter, *Geschichte Israels* (³ 1925), pp. 81 ff.

[2] For the fragments of Artapanus and Eupolemus see Riessler, *loc. cit.* pp. 186 ff., 328 ff.

when the leaders of the struggle against the Seleucid encroachments set out for and attained the goal of political independence and secular power, to find their ultimate successors in the rebels against Roman supremacy, who helped to bring about the end of Israel's history. Even in an early stage of the struggles against the Seleucids the 'devout' who had, to begin with, contributed to the movement of resistance against the encroachments on the substance of the religious community of Jerusalem, but later no longer approved of continuing the line of military and political action, parted company with these political activists. The important thing for them was the unhindered continuation of the Jerusalem cultus and the freedom to live their lives in accordance with their ancestral traditions. They formed themselves into the group of Pharisees, and as such they continued to exert a determining influence on the inner life of the religious community of Jerusalem to the very end of Israel's history, and even after its end they left a decisive mark on the face of the Jewry that then arose. The most important evidence of their attitude from the 2nd century is the series of visions of Daniel in Dan. vii-xii. These visions are based on a very clearly pronounced conception of world history as a succession of world powers which will one day be brought to an end by the irruption of the rule of God. This conception of the process of history had an even earlier beginning. The collection of Daniel narratives in Dan. i-vi already contained that vision (Dan. ii, 29 ff.) which, using extra-Israelite theories of the ages of the world and patterns of world history, had formulated the antithesis of secular and divine government in the sense of a succession in time, no doubt on the basis of earlier prophetic announcements in the Old Testament of an expected Kingdom of God. In the period of persecution by Antiochus IV this vision of history was actualised in the conviction that the age of world powers had run its course and the coming of the rule of God was imminent (cf. especially Dan. vii). World history is conceived here as a great unity, not only in the sense that it can be represented simply as a succession of empires but also that it has emerged from the ungodly chaos (cf. Dan. vii, 2b, 3a) and must be regarded as fundamentally anti-God. This conception prepared the way for a dualistic view of the world, which, in spite of all their recognition of the human presumption and guilt which govern history, was not yet held by the Old Testament prophets. It is possible that this dualistic tendency had its source in a rationalisation of the content of faith which went hand in hand with individualisation, and that it was not uninfluenced by the Iranian dualism with which this kind of rationalisation was much in line. The centuries-long life of the religious community of Jerusalem within various Empires, whose protection it enjoyed and whose magnanimity in the allotment of privileges to the Jerusalem cultus it experienced, but to whose dominion and power and, in some cases, tyranny, it was exposed, and which followed a system of worship which the religious community of Jerusalem condemned as 'pagan', was the experience behind the rationalising historical view of history of the visions of Daniel. But at the same time the hope for an end of the historical process which had been determined by the godless world-powers was still alive. It was a development of the Messianic announcements of the pre-Exilian prophets and the eschatological expectations of the post-Exilian period, which looked for a gathering together and a liberation, and also a glorification of the people of God now under oppression. There was also a rational element in this hope in so far as it was considered possible to determine and even to calculate the moment of the great change over from secular to divine government. The conviction that the period of persecution under Antiochus IV represented the ultimate stage of the present course of the world, had probably developed spontaneously to begin with under the impact of extreme and unprecedented affliction; but an attempt was made to prove the accuracy of this conviction, not only by believing man was living in the fourth age of world power, in accordance with the traditional schema, and hence the final and irrevocable stage, but also trying to estimate by a complicated reckoning in 'year weeks', as put forward in Dan. ix, 24-27, how short the time would be until the coming of the rule of God.

The Apocalypse which was to play a great part among the 'devout' arose with the visions of Daniel, on the basis of a comprehensive view of history and the expectation of a final and imminent change, and on the assumption that it was possible to calculate the position of the present age within the flow of events. The expectation was that everything would come from an act of God, who would make an end to the hitherto existing course of history without human assistance. The sole concern of the religious community of Jerusalem was to remain faithful to their God in obedience to the 'Covenant' (cf. Dan. ix, 27) in order to receive a share of the blessings of the coming reign of God. How far the 'Israel' which was living in the form of the religious community would occupy a special position in the future kingdom of God was a question that was answered differently according to circumstances. If 'the saints of the most High' who, according to Dan. vii, 18, are to be given the government after the end of world history, originally meant, as seems likely, heavenly beings, who will reign on God's behalf, nevertheless they were interpreted as referring to the Israelites from a very early period, in fact even in the secondary additions to the visions of Daniel (cf. Dan. vii, 21). They will not bring about the rule of God but receive the gift of 'power' from God, though no precise indications are given of the character and scope of this 'power'. Those already dead may also share in the life of this future time. In Dan. xii, 2, 3 there is a reference to the 'awakening' of those who 'sleep in the dust of the earth', *i.e.* in the world of the dead, of an awakening either 'to everlasting life' or 'to everlasting contempt'. 'Many' of the dead, it is said, will share this awakening and receive a different fate, evidently as a reward or punishment for their deeds in the time of their earthly life. It is possible that these 'many', who can obviously only represent a part of the total number of the dead, refer primarily to those who fell or lost their lives in other ways in the Maccabean fighting, and who according as to whether they stood for obedience or disobedience to the ancestral traditions, have to expect divine reward or punishment even after death. In any case this is the first explicit and general reference to a resurrection of the dead and a divine judgement after this resurrection, though there had already been expressions, within the Old Testament faith, of the conviction that even the death of the body would not bring union with God to an end (cf. Ps. lxxiii, 24). Individual expectation of a life after the death of the body thus took its place alongside the expectation of the ending of history by the coming of the Kingdom of God, though for the time being no attempt was made to establish a closer connection between them.

In the following period a fairly richly developed apocalyptic literature was added to these beginnings[1]. Its productions were not included in the selection of 'canonic' writings made by the Synagogue after the fall of Jerusalem at the end of the 1st century A.D. In so far as they did not vanish altogether, they only survived for a time in various forms of the Greek translation of the Old Testament used in the early Christian Church, and from there they reached the Oriental national churches, where they were included in various Oriental translations of the Old Testament[2]. It is there-

[1] Cf. P. Volz, *Die Eschatalogie der jüdischen Gemeinde im neutestamentlichen Zeitalter* ([2] 1934).

[2] In German translation in E. Kautzsch, *Die Apokryphen und Pseudepigraphen des Alten Testaments*, II (1900).

fore difficult to ascertain their original Hebrew-Aramaic form and the time when they were written. In general, however, they derive from the 2nd/1st century B.C. They add to the element of eschatological expectation for the individual, for Israel and for humanity and angelology, of which the beginnings already emerge in the Book of Daniel, as well as a strong cosmological interest. Alongside the development of apocalyptic literature there was a further preoccupation with the old narrative tradition of the Old Testament. The 'Book of Jubilees' in which the material of the Book of Genesis is presented in a new priestly-Pharisean version, probably derives from the 2nd century B.C. This book was also not included in the Old Testament canon, although it was certainly composed in Hebrew (or Aramaic) in Palestine.

The fact that they were not included in the canon later stamped these literary works deriving from the 'devout' of the 2nd/1st century as illegitimate, apocryphal and sectarian. Originally this blemish was certainly not attached to them amidst the various religious and intellectual movements of this period. It may be asked, however, whether, once the 'Pharisees' had taken the path of 'separation' (cf. above, p. 372, note 1) from the tendencies prevailing at the time of their emergence, though they later became a very influential group within the religious community of Jerusalem, the tendency to this kind of separation did not soon extend beyond the Pharisees, in the direction of an absorption in apocalyptic-gnostic speculations, and above all in the direction of a rigorism surpassing the legalism of the Pharisees in matters of ritual purity and ascetic abstinence. This latter tendency was bound to lead to the formation of conventicles and sects. The later Rabbinist tradition and Josephus and Philo have made us familiar with baptising sects and, above all, with the 'Essenes' in the 1st century B.C. and especially the 1st century A.D.[1]. The concept of the 'Essenes', whom Josephus places as a third group alongside the Sadducees and Pharisees, probably embraces a whole wealth of slightly differing sectarian organisations. It is highly probable that these separatist movements originated in the internal and external upheavals of the 2nd century. They are at the same time an indication that the inner life of the religious community of Jerusalem had become sterile. The persecution under Antiochus IV had once again aroused lively and vigorous forces of resistance in an atmosphere which was perhaps not, generally speaking, unfavourable to Hellenism. But the victory of these forces had not given any

[1] Cf. above all A. Schlatter, *Geschichte Israels* ([3] 1925), pp. 170 ff., 173 ff.

really new content to the community as a whole. The victors pursued the path of outward power; those, such as the Pharisees, that did not go this way, turned increasingly to a legalistic moralism, which led to an increasingly subtle casuistry of the traditional laws of God, and even the apocalyptic expectations of the end, as they had been expressed in the visions of the Book of Daniel, receded into the background. It is not surprising that many sought the fulfilment of their hopes in small groups, some of which united their members by means of a common life. It is not unlikely that the community which has become known as a result of the discovery of its writings in some caves in the neighbourhood of the khirbet ḳumrān on the north-western border of the Dead Sea[1], originated in the 2nd century B.C. According to the evidence of the archaeological discoveries on the khirbet ḳumrān this community lived in the first century A.D. until the great rebellion of the years A.D. 66–70 in a monastery-like settlement in the otherwise almost uninhabited area on the Dead Sea south of Jericho, and probably carefully preserved its writings in these caves to prevent their destruction in the chaos of the insurrection, and was later unable to retrieve them from this hiding-place. It is very difficult to date the manuscripts palaeographically; they may have been in use for a good time before they were put in the caves. In so far as they are not Biblical books such as the Book of Isaiah, which is extant in two copies, the writings themselves contain compilations of regulations for the life of the community, liturgical pieces and apocalyptical material, the latter also in the form of the interpretation of a traditional book of the Old Testament ('Commentary on Habakkuk'). It is not yet possible to assign an exact date to these writings which contain various allusions to contemporary history; some of the contents suggest the period when the Seleucid Empire was still in existence, *i.e.* the century following Antiochus IV[2]. It is also possible that the various writings were composed at different times. However this question is ultimately solved, it remains probable at any rate that the community of khirbet ḳumrān derived from the separatist tendencies of the agitated period of the 2nd century; and the manuscript discoveries by the Dead Sea throw a surprising light on the conventicles and sectarian organisations in the bosom of the religious

[1] On this sensational manuscript discovery which was made in the spring of 1947 see a brief report in WAT, pp. 246 ff.

[2] Cf. H. H. Rowley, *The Zadokite Fragments and the Dead Sea Scrolls* (1952)—which includes a detailed account of the scholarly investigations into the meaning of the manuscripts that have been made so far and a complete bibliography of the literature that has appeared on them up to 1952.

community of Jerusalem of which no trace can be found in earlier times, and which, as far as we can see, only developed from the Maccabean period onwards. Even if they did not play a very important part in the foreground of historical events, they did have an important influence on Israel's internal life in the final phase of its history.

CHAPTER II

THE ROMAN PERIOD

32. *The Intervention of the Roman Power*

IN the year 65 B.C. the Roman power appeared in Syria-Palestine. Israelite history thereby acquired a new background. From now on its course was decisively affected by this new power. It thereby entered into its final phase. It is true that, indirectly, Rome had already influenced it for a long time; the decline and decay of the Seleucid State which had made possible the events of the Maccabean-Hasmonaean period had, since the defeat of Antiochus III at Magnesia in 190 B.C., been an indirect result of the expansion of Roman power in the eastern Mediterranean; and the Maccabeans had already established relations with Rome from time to time. But, practically speaking, this had meant little; hitherto Rome had remained afar, whereas now the military might of Rome appeared in Syria-Palestine itself.

After Pompey had conquered the Pontic kingdom of Mithradates and the Armenian king Tigranes had agreed to surrender, under the impact of the Roman victories, Pompey prepared to impose a new order in the Roman style on western Asia and to liquidate the Seleucid State, which was already in a state of complete decay. In this connection he sent his legate M. Aemilius Scaurus to Syria in 65 B.C. The latter heard in Damascus of the conflict in Judaea and went there straight away. Not surprisingly, both the hard-pressed Aristobulus in Jerusalem and the successful Hyrcanus turned to him. Both offered him an equally expensive gift to obtain his favour and support. Scaurus decided to help Aristobulus because, despite his present position, he thought his chances better from a long-term point of view. By means of threats he forced Aretas to raise the siege and to withdraw, and he confirmed Aristobulus in his previous offices (*Ant. Iud.* XIV, 2, 3, §§ 29 ff.). Thus the situation came about in which the course of events was determined by the judgement or the arbitrariness of Roman decisions. Henceforth, to be successful it was necessary to obtain the good-will of whatever Roman authority happened to be most important in the particular situation; and this gave rise to the undignified striving for the favour of Roman overlords, which played an important part in the following period. How varied this was to make the course of events was to be shown very quickly in the present case. At this time Rome was entering the period of great internal conflicts and civil wars; and the commotions of this period were bound constantly to affect the history of Israel.

Pompey himself soon appeared in Syria, where he spent the winter of 64/63 B.C. in winter quarters. In the spring he moved on to Damascus where deputations from all parts of the country appeared very soon with requests and entreaties. Aristobulus had already tried to influence him with an expensive present. He had also sent his legate to Pompey, whilst at the same time Antipater appeared before Pompey as Hyrcanus's representative, as did envoys of the people, evidently from Pharisean circles, who wanted to see Hasmonaean rule completely abolished and the former position of the priesthood restored. Aristobulus and Hyrcanus appeared in Damascus in person. Pompey took Aristobulus's brutal manner amiss, but postponed a definite decision and promised to reorganise Judaean affairs once he had completed the intended campaign against the Nabataeans (*Ant. Iud.* XIV, 3, 1-3, §§ 34 ff.). As Aristobulus refused to wait, and quickly returned to Judaea, probably to take measures to safeguard his power, Pompey deferred the Nabataean campaign and also went with his army to Judaea. He went via Pella (khirbet faḥil) and Skythopolis (bēsān) to Koreae (the modern ḳarāwe in the lower wādi fārʿa), where the territory of the real province of Judah, with its four extensions into south and south-east Samaria, began. In the vicinity, west of the issue of the wadi farʿa into the Jordan Valley on the impressive rounded mountain top dominating the Jordan Valley, which now bears the name ḳarn ṣarṭabe was the fort Alexandreion which Alexander Jannaeus had extended (cf. above, p. 384). Aristobulus had proceeded to this fort. After some hesitation Aristobulus surrendered the fort on Pompey's orders, but then went in haste to Jerusalem to organise resistance against Pompey. Pompey followed him through Jericho into the vicinity of Jerusalem. But then Aristobulus gave up his cause for lost. He went to Pompey's camp and promised to hand over the city of Jerusalem. Pompey held on to him and sent Gabinius to Jerusalem with troops. The inhabitants refused to admit him into the city, however. Enraged by this, Pompey had Aristobulus locked up and moved on Jerusalem with the whole of his armed forces. Most of the inhabitants gave up the fight and opened the gates of the city to the Romans; only a minority, who were determined to continue to defend the city at all costs, went on resisting fiercely in the fortified area of the Temple. Pompey was forced to proceed to a regular siege with battering-engines and took three months to make a breach in the wall and occupy the area of the Temple. The defenders were terribly massacred. Pompey himself and other Romans entered the Temple and even the Holy of Holies to see it for themselves: an action which outraged the faithful. The Temple was not plundered, however, and on the following day Pompey gave orders for the resumption of the traditional sacrificial rites. Hyrcanus was re-installed as high priest (*Ant. Iud.* XIV, 4, 1-4, §§ 54 ff.). Aristobulus was taken to Rome as a prisoner and likewise his two sons Alexander and Antigonus, though the first of them escaped. When Pompey celebrated his triumph in Rome in the year 61 B.C. the Hasmonaean king Aristobulus was forced to show himself to the Roman people in the triumphal procession along with the other prisoners, whilst his brother was, by Roman dispensation, high priest in Jerusalem.

In 63 B.C., after the end of Seleucid rule, Pompey introduced a fundamental reorganisation in Syria, also rearranging the territorial dispositions of the previous Hasmonaean State. Syria-Palestine, *i.e.* the western part of the former Seleucid State, became the Roman province of Syria and M. Aemilius Scaurus its first governor. New political organisations were created in this province under the hand of its governor. In Palestine the Hasmonaean conquests were for the most part separated from Judaea again. The coastal cities were constituted as independent urban communities and placed directly under the province. The same thing happened with a number of cities in the central and northern land east of the Jordan, including Pella and Skythopolis in the Jordan Valley, which combined to form the community of the 'ten cities' ('Decapolis'). These were for the most part Hellenistic foundations or re-established cities which had then been subjugated by the Hasmonaeans. They were now 're-liberated' and rightly regarded this liberation as the beginning of a new chapter in their history, counting their years henceforth from the beginning of the 'Pompeian' era. Samaria was also re-separated from Judaea. The city of Samaria, formerly a Macedonian military colony, was constituted as an independent urban community, but for the rest the land of Samaria was put directly under the province of Syria, as the Samaritan religious community's own area, like the area of the religious community of Jerusalem. If the cultus on the Gerizim had been stopped under Hasmonaean rule, a point about which we have no definite information, it was at any rate reopened now. The territory of the religious community of Jerusalem under the high priest, who was subject to the provincial governor, was now restricted once again to the old province of Judah, with the addition of Peraea and Galilee. Judaea retained the four south and south-east Samaritan areas, which Jonathan and probably Simon had acquired, and also Idumaea which had been conquered by John Hyrcanus I, but was now separated again from the sea coast by the 'liberated' coastal cities. A strip of the southern and central land east of the Jordan connected with Judaea, remained under the control of the high priest; this strip was now called 'Peraea' and was bordered in its southern half by the still independent State of the Nabataeans and in its northern half by the territories of the cities of the 'Decapolis'. The Galilean interior was also left to the religious community of Jerusalem under the high priest but was now separated spatially from Judaea and Peraea. On the whole, Pompey appears to have placed those areas under the high priest whose inhabitants took part in the Jerusalem cultus more or less as a solid body; these were the old Israelite territories in Judaea including Idumaea, in the western part of the southern and central land east of the Jordan and in the interior of Galilee. With the establishment of a cultus of its own on the Gerizim Samaria had parted from Jerusalem and was accordingly granted independence within the framework of the Syrian province. One is bound to admit that the arrangement introduced by Pompey was a fitting one and on the whole took into account the actual membership of the religious community of Jerusalem. The Hasmonaean State and its conquests was thereby liquidated and once again there remained the authentic religious community of Jerusalem with its high priest at the head and with the people who actually took part in the Jerusalem cultus. The Hasmonaean family only continued to play a part in the person of the high priest Hyrcanus.

In the year 57 B.C. the Syrian governor A. Gabinius reorganised the affairs of the religious community of Jerusalem once again. As proconsul and Pompey's favourite he had been entrusted in 57 B.C. with the administration of the province of Syria, which was important on account of its position on the eastern frontier. After Pompey had deprived Hyrcanus of the title of king, he took away from him all the political authority which he had had as head of the areas of Palestine which belonged to the religious community of Jerusalem, and confined him entirely to his religious office. He divided the territory of the 'people' who made up the religious community of Jerusalem, into five independent districts, which were placed directly under the provincial governor. The real Judaea was thereby broken up into the districts of Jerusalem, Gazara[1] and Jericho. The district of Jerusalem will have embraced the Judaean-Idumaean mountains, the district of Gazara will have covered parts of the western hill country and the district of Jericho the eastern slope of the mountain with Aphairema and the Akrabattene, whilst Peraea was constituted as the district of Amathus (ʽammata) and the interior of Galilee as the district of Sepphoris (the modern ṣaffūrye) (*Ant. Iud.* XIV, 8, 5, §§ 169 f.)[2].

The arrangements introduced by Pompey and Gabinius should have settled the conflicts in Palestine and above all stabilised the position of the religious community of Jerusalem and brought peace to the country. But the passions of the antagonists were still so inflamed that they continued to create unrest, and the situation in Rome was so unstable that affairs in the Syrian province were constantly being influenced by the great political movements of the time. There now ensued a very unpleasant drama of disputes and intrigues in which Aristobulus, who was still imprisoned in Rome with his son Antigonus, and also his son Alexander, who had escaped from the Romans, as well as Antipater and his increasingly prominent sons Phasael and Herod, and finally, in the background, Pompey and Caesar, Antonius and Octavian and the Roman governors and generals in Syria all played their part. Josephus gave a detailed account of these events in *Ant. Iud.* XIV, 5-16, and *Bell. Iud.* I, 8-18. It is not worth while going into them in detail and it will suffice briefly to mention the driving forces.

First of all, Aristobulus and his two sons Alexander and Antigonus tried to regain the position of which they had been deprived by Pompey, at the expense of Hyrcanus who had been installed by the Romans. In this they were widely supported by members of the religious community of Jerusalem itself, who were dissatisfied with the weak Hyrcanus and with the reorganisation of their affairs. To begin with, only Aristobulus's elder son Alexander was free to act, as he had succeeded in escaping from Pompey and had not been taken to Rome. Soon after Pompey had departed he tried to proceed against his uncle Hyrcanus by force of arms. When A. Gabinius

[1] In *Ant. Iud.* and *Bell. Iud.* the manuscripts give, in error, Gadara instead of Gazara.
[2] Cf. H. Guthe, *Bibelatlas* ([2] 1926), No. 10.

came to Syria in the year 57 B.C. he forced Alexander to surrender in the fortress of Alexandreion (ḳarn ṣarṭabe) which was his base. Soon afterwards Aristobulus himself succeeded in escaping from Rome with his younger son Antigonus. They arrived in the land and took up arms against Hyrcanus with their supporters but were seized by Gabinius in the fortress of Machaerus on the southern border of Peraea on the eastern side of the Dead Sea (the modern khirbet el-mkāwer) and taken to Rome again. Gabinius had hardly embarked on an expedition to Egypt when Alexander took up arms again. But as soon as Gabinius returned to Syria, Alexander was soundly beaten by him in the region of Mount Tabor on the southern border of Galilee. Gabinius, who was defending the order established by Pompey, now thought it his duty to strengthen the position of the high priest Hyrcanus against which the machinations of Aristobulus and his son had been directed. He therefore cancelled the division of the territory of the religious community of Jerusalem into five independent districts that he himself had introduced in 57 B.C. and placed the whole area under the high priest again. In the year 54 B.C. M. Licinius Crassus, one of the triumvirs of the year 60 B.C., took over the province of Syria to conduct the war against the Parthians. He pillaged the province very thoroughly and also plundered the treasures and valuables of the Temple in Jerusalem. In the following year he was attacked and murdered by Parthian soldiers after an ill-starred campaign against the Parthians. The province was now administered from 53 to 51 B.C. by his quaestor C. Cassius Longinus. The latter was again forced to suppress a revolt against the existing organisation of the religious community of Jerusalem.

In the year 49 B.C. Caesar crossed the Rubicon and Pompey and the Pompeans retired to the eastern half of the Empire. Caesar wanted to send Aristobulus, who was still a captive in Rome, to Syria to fight Pompey's partisans. Since it was Pompey who had deprived Aristobulus of his offices of king and high priest in Jerusalem he will have gladly accepted this task. Before he departed, however, he was poisoned in Rome by Pompeans, and as he had presumably been involved in his father's intended mission, his son Alexander was murdered soon afterwards in Antioch on Pompey's instructions. No doubt Hyrcanus and Antipater continued on Pompey's side for the time being. But when Pompey was defeated at Pharsalus on 9 Aug. 48 and soon afterwards murdered on the coast of the Egyptian Delta, Hyrcanus and Antipater quickly attempted to win the favour of the victorious Caesar. When Caesar was faced with difficulties in Alexandria Antipater obliged him by sending him auxiliary troops which, together with those sent by Mithradates of Pergamon, conquered the important frontier-fortress of Pelusium on the eastern side of the Delta for Caesar and performed other services for him in Egypt; and Hyrcanus, as high priest, persuaded the members of the religious community of Jerusalem in Egypt to side with Caesar. In the following year, 47 B.C., Caesar came to Syria. Antigonus, Aristobulus's surviving son, did, it is true, try to plead his allegedly better right to the office of high priest with Caesar and to put his right hand, Antipater, in the wrong. But Caesar obviously did not really trust Antigonus, although only a short while previously he himself had tried to use Aristobulus and his sons against the Pompeans in Syria. He bestowed his favours more on Hyrcanus and Antipater. He not only left them in their old positions and thereby rejected Antigonus's claims; Antipater and his master, Hyrcanus, had succeeded so well in taking sides with the victors and obtaining Caesar's good-will that Caesar richly rewarded them both for their assistance. Hyrcanus was expressly confirmed in the hereditary office of high priest, and he was also appointed to the hereditary office of 'ethnarch'. The religious community of Jerusalem was granted the power of jurisdiction in its own affairs. Hyrcanus, with his descendants, was declared the 'confederate' of the Romans and his territory exempted from military contributions and from the duty of billeting Roman troops in the winter. Permission was also given for Jerusalem to be fortified again. Roman citizenship was conferred on Antipater, however, and he was appointed Roman procurator (principal administrative official) of Judaea. The territory of Judaea was extended. Above all, the important port of Joppe (yāfa) was restored to Judaea and also the villages on the great plain, *i.e.* the plain of Jezreel, evidently the area outside the already existing city territories[1]. Elsewhere in the Diaspora, in the region of the eastern Mediterranean, Caesar also granted privileges o the members of the religious community of Jerusalem and promised them, above all, freedom to conduct their worship with all its attendant rites[2]. These were astonishing concessions, which it is impossible to explain merely as a reward for the military help in Egypt. Caesar, who was deeply interested in the eastern parts

[1] These important regulations are given in *Ant. Iud.* XIV, 8, 5, §§ 177 ff. They were apparently subsequently confirmed by decree of the Senate. Cf. the collection of documents in *Ant. Iud.* XIV, 10.

[2] Cf. the documents in *Ant. Iud.* XIV, 10, of which the authenticity is admittedly not uncontested.

of the great Empire, wanted to conciliate the subject peoples in order to give his power a firm foundation.

Caesar's ordinances had greatly strengthened the position of Antipater, who now brought his two sons Phasael and Herod to the fore. The elder son Phasael was given the administration of Judaea and Peraea and the younger son Herod that of Galilee, both with the title of 'strategos'. It is not surprising that the power of Antipater and his sons aroused the displeasure of many members of the religious community of Jerusalem, above all of the priesthood and the aristocracy. They tried to act on the weak Hyrcanus and to incite him to take action against Antipater and his sons. Under their pressure Hyrcanus did in fact make an effort to rouse himself into action. In Galilee Herod had put an end to the banditry that flourished there and had the leader of a band of robbers and many of his followers executed. This gave his enemies an opportunity to sue him since he had thereby forestalled the jurisdiction of the Sanhedrim, the 'Supreme Council', the assembly in which the priestly aristocracy and the pharisaic scribes dealt with the fundamental internal affairs of the religious community of Jerusalem; and Hyrcanus dared to summons Herod to appear before the Sanhedrim. Herod, who had a strong rear cover in the then Syrian governor Sextus Caesar, put on such a dictatorial air that the Sanhedrin did not dare to sentence him. Herod departed secretly from Jerusalem and soon appeared outside the city again with troops. This was too much even for his father Antipater. With difficulty he restrained Herod, who wanted to take a bloody vengeance on the Sanhedrim, from brute violence and Herod returned again to Galilee after he had at any rate shown what he was made of.

In the year 44 B.C., on the Ides of March, Caesar was murdered. The murderers then made for the eastern parts of the Empire; and one of them, C. Cassius Longinus, who had already administered the province of Syria in the years 53–51 B.C. for the Crassus who had been murdered by the Parthians, became governor of Syria from 44 to 42 B.C. He exploited the province intensively and thereby made himself very unpopular. Antipater, however, who always tried to be on good terms with whoever was in power, served him untiringly. This could only damage his reputation still further in the eyes of the religious community of Jerusalem. In the end he fell victim to a conspiracy in which purely personal antagonism played a part. Hyrcanus was also drawn into the plot. Antipater was poisoned. But it was already too late. The position of his sons

Phasael and above all Herod was already too strong for the murder of Antipater to make any essential difference to the situation. Herod had the real instigator of his father's murder, an Arab named Malichus, who was himself attempting to attain an influential position in Judaea, treacherously murdered, thereby intimidating Antipater's enemies. In addition, the power of the governor Cassius was behind Phasael and Herod.

Antigonus, the son of Aristobulus, now bestirred himself again. He invaded Galilee with his army but was defeated by Herod and expelled from Galilee. This victory even brought Herod the goodwill of Hyrcanus, who mistrusted the superior power of Antipater and his sons, although they were responsible for keeping him in his position. All the same, his nephew Antigonus was his real enemy since he coveted his position and Hyrcanus was therefore grateful to Herod for driving Antigonus away and persuaded him to become engaged to his grand-niece Mariamne[1], a Hasmonaean, a grand-daughter of his brother Aristobulus and a daughter of the latter's son Alexander. Antigonus then sought for further opportunities to realise his intentions. When in the year 42 B.C. Caesar's murderers had been defeated by M. Antony and C. Julius Caesar Octavianus in the Battle of Philippi, the government of the east devolved on Antony. Various deputations from the religious community of Jerusalem tried to prejudice him against the brothers Phasael and Herod but without success, although the attempt was made to play off Hyrcanus against the two of them. By appearing before him in person Herod was able to win over Antony; and when Hyrcanus himself also visited Antony, when he came to Antioch, and declared himself for Phasael and Herod, their position was again secure for the time being, particularly as Antony had been the guest of their father Antipater during his earlier stay in Syria under A. Gabinius[2]. For the moment, therefore, Antigonus had no prospects of success. It is true that Antony made himself very unpopular in Syria owing to the great sums which he extorted in taxation, but nothing could be done to shift him. Finally, however, Antigonus reached his goal owing to a quite unforeseen event. When Antony was staying with queen Cleopatra in Alexandria and also very much preoccupied with events in Italy, the Parthians invaded the Roman provinces in the Near East and also occupied Syria. This was in the year 40 B.C. By making them substantial

[1] Strangely enough Josephus does not mention this name in *Ant. Iud.* XIV, 12, 1, § 300, but in the parallel passage in *Bell. Iud.* I, 12, 3, § 241.

[2] Phasael and Herod were appointed tetrarchs and entrusted with political leadership and Hyrcanus was thereby relegated again to his office of high priest.

promises Antigonus succeeded in enlisting their support. While the Parthians were still in northern Syria he hastened to Judaea, collected supporters and invaded Jerusalem, where he became involved in fighting with Phasael and Herod. The Parthian forces then came to Jerusalem, and, under pretext of wanting to settle the quarrel, they summoned Phasael to the Parthian headquarters in Ekdippa (the modern ez-zīb north of Akko). In spite of the warnings of his brother Herod, who saw through the deceit, Phasael went with Hyrcanus and both were immediately imprisoned. The Parthians then installed Antigonus as king and high priest in Jerusalem and for three years he attained his heart's desire. A small Parthian garrison stayed behind in Jerusalem; Hyrcanus and Phasael were handed over to Antigonus by the Parthians. Phasael killed himself; Antigonus had Hyrcanus's ears cut off, thereby incapacitating him for the office of high priest, and then handed him back to the Parthians, who took him with them to Babylon as a prisoner. There are in existence coins from the reign of Antigonus (40–37 B.C.) which, like the coins of Alexander Jannaeus, bear a Hebrew-Greek inscription and also refer to the original name of Antigonus, Mattathias, whom otherwise we know only by his Greek name; the inscription reads: 'The High Priest Mattathias (Hebrew)—King Antigonus (Greek)'[1]. Otherwise we know nothing about his reign.

The only opponent of Antigonus who was left now was Herod. When Hyrcanus and Phasael were captured by the Parthians, he rescued his family and that of his brothers and took them to the almost inaccessible steep rock of Masada on the western shore of the Dead Sea (the modern es-sebbe) and left them in the care of his younger brother Joseph. He himself wanted to go to Petra to secure the help of the Nabataean king but he was not allowed in. He therefore decided to try and obtain the strongest possible force for his undertaking and went on an adventurous journey to Rome. It was clear anyway that Rome did not approve of the monarchy of Antigonus who had been installed by the Parthians and that Antigonus would not be left in office after the expected reconquest of Syria; and Rome would welcome assistance in the reconquest of Syria from one who was nevertheless acting in his own interest. By skilful negotiation and presents Herod succeeded in winning over Antony in Rome, and, through Antony, Octavian was also won over. At the end of the year 40 B.C. the Senate decided to appoint Herod king of Judaea. Admittedly, Herod had first to conquer his

[1] Cf. A. Reifenberg, *Ancient Jewish Coins* ([2] 1947), pp. 17 f., 42, Pl. III.

kingdom. He went straight from Rome to Syria and landed in Ptolemais. In Syria the Roman governor P. Ventidius had meanwhile driven out the Parthians. It is true that they made another attack in the year 38 B.C. but this time they were repelled once and for all by P. Ventidius. For the time being Ventidius had left Antigonus undisturbed in Jerusalem. With the support of the Roman governor, Herod made his first progress in 39 B.C. He occupied Joppe and was able to relieve the members of his family who had been besieged in Masada on instructions from Antigonus. But then there began to be difficulties. A siege of Jerusalem was a failure since the Roman general who was second in command did not support him or, possibly, was unable to support him owing to opposition among his troops. Herod therefore went to Galilee. In the year 38 B.C. the Romans had to deal with the renewed invasion by the Parthians. Herod therefore made little progress. At the time Antony was occupied with the siege of Samosata on the upper Euphrates. Herod took the opportunity of calling on him and reassuring himself of Roman support. During his absence with Antony, his brother Joseph, who was acting as his deputy in Judaea, was defeated by Antigonus and fell in the battle himself. When Herod returned, he embarked anew on the conquest of his kingdom —this time with the real support of the new Syrian governor C. Sosius. First of all he obtained possession of Galilee; then, still in the year 37 B.C., the rest of the territory except for Jerusalem accrued to him in various successful battles against Antigonus and his forces. In the year 37 B.C. Jerusalem was also occupied by Sosius and the Roman troops after a fairly long siege and assault. The Roman victors wrought great havoc in the fallen city so that Herod had to persuade Sosius to withdraw the Roman troops, by offering him presents. Herod was now able to take up his royal office in Jerusalem. Antigonus was taken away as a prisoner by the Romans and, at Herod's request, executed in Antioch.

33. *The Reign of Herod and his Descendants*

From 37 B.C. onwards Herod was in uncontested possession of his kingdom. For this he had entirely to thank the Romans with whom his father Antipater had been constantly in touch and with whom he himself sought the closest possible relations. He was obviously unusually clever and successful in getting the support of the most important men of the time. He spared no pains in securing a personal audience with them at the right moments and he achieved a good deal in this way. On one further occasion his position was gravely threatened. Since the battle of Philippi his patron had been Antony. When the inevitable conflict between Antony and Octavian broke out and Antony was defeated by Octavian in the decisive battle of Actium on the 2nd September 31 B.C. and took his own life soon afterwards in Alexandria, as Antony's supporter Herod was threatened with the victor's vengeance. In the year 30 B.C. Herod—and this was typical of his whole mode of behaviour—went to see Octavian in person while the latter was staying in Rhodes and with a theatrical gesture he voluntarily laid his crown at Octavian's feet. His action did not fail to have the desired effect; he received his crown back from Octavian and was rewarded with an extension of his territory. For the rest of his life in his own interest, he remained deliberately subservient to Octavian-Augustus.

We have detailed information about the reign of Herod (37–4 B.C.), above all from Josephus, who describes it in great detail in *Ant. Iud.* XV, 1-XVII, 8, and in *Bell. Iud.* I, 18-33, drawing mainly on the history of Nicolaus of Damascus who himself lived at the court of Herod. Imposing remains of Herod's numerous buildings have also survived, and even today they convey an impression of the outward splendour and luxury of this monarchy[1].

Herod held the position of a 'confederate king' within the Roman system of government. As such he did not come under the governor of the province of Syria, but was directly responsible to the princeps and received from him or the Senate all important directives on foreign policy. He had to provide auxiliary troops and to protect the Imperial frontier in his area, which was bounded on the east and south by the kingdom of the Nabataeans with Petra as its capital. In the internal administration of his State Herod was independent and did not have to pay tribute.

Herod was able to round off the frontiers of his kingdom under very favourable conditions. When he entered office in the year 37 B.C. the territory he had under him was more or less the area that Pompey had left to the religious community of Jerusalem after the elimination of the Hasmonaean State, in other words, Judaea with Idumaea, and also Peraea and the interior of Galilee. To these had been added the port of Joppe and the villages of the Jezreel Plain which Caesar had ceded to Hyrcanus. To begin with,

[1] On Herod and his descendants, cf. W. Otto, *Herodes*, 1913 (separate publication of the articles on the subject in Pauly-Wissowa's *Realencyklopädie*).

this territory was threatened by the ambitious and tyrannical queen Cleopatra who was friendly with Antony, and wanted to see the old Ptolemean claim to Palestine and Phoenicia fulfilled by Antony who was ruling in the east at this period. In fact Antony gave her all the coastal cities of Palestine, which meant that Herod lost Joppe again, and he also gave her the area of the tropically fertile oasis of Jericho (34 B.C.). Probably Cleopatra, who once visited Jerusalem herself, wanted still more. Her own death and that of Antony left her wishes unfulfilled. When in 30 B.C. Herod had obtained the favour of Octavian and visited him once again in Alexandria after the death of Antony and Cleopatra, the Palestinian areas which had been presented to Cleopatra were transferred to him, so that Herod now became master of the whole of the coastal plain of Palestine, and he was also given the city and province of Samaria as well as the cities of Gadara (umkēs) and Hioppos (ḳalʿat el-ḥöṣn) in the northern land east of the Jordan. Finally Herod was given the country of Trachonitis, Batanaia and Auranitis in the land east of the Jordan north of the Jarmuk, eastwards as far as the great mountain of jebel ed-drūz (23 B.C.). Herod thereby came into possession of practically the whole of Palestine with the exception of the territories of the free cities of the 'Decapolis'; and he ruled over all this territory until his death.

Herod honoured Augustus most zealously. Even before his visit to Rhodes he took part in fighting Antony's supporters in Syria to make his change of position immediately clear. When Augustus marched through Syria on the way to Egypt in 30 B.C. he received him with ceremony in Ptolemais; and after he had paid a visit to Augustus in Alexandria after the death of Antony and Cleopatra, he accompanied him on his return journey through Syria as far as Antioch. When Augustus came to Syria again in the year 20 B.C. he gave Herod a few more districts in the uppermost part of the Jordan Valley. In the year 12 B.C. Herod himself travelled to Italy and met Augustus in Aquileia, to get him to settle a quarrel with two of his sons; and soon afterwards he was in Italy and Rome once again. Only once, about the year 9 B.C., Herod temporarily incurred the Emperor's displeasure on account of his methods of fighting the Nabataeans; but the good understanding between Augustus and Herod was restored through the mediation of Nicolaus of Damascus. Herod also tried to be on the best of terms with the Emperor's influential friend, M. Vipsanius Agrippa. About the year 22 B.C. he visited Agrippa in Mytilene on Lesbos, and in the year 15 B.C. Agrippa himself came to Jerusalem at

Herod's invitation and was received with great pomp and ceremony. Herod showed him his magnificent buildings all over the country. Later on Herod visited Agrippa again in Asia Minor. Herod honoured Augustus by naming his rebuilt cities after him. The first work of this kind was the extension of the old city of Samaria. Gabinius had already begun to build a city in the Hellenistic-Roman style on the beautiful hill in the mountains of central Palestine which had borne the royal city of the former State of Israel and which afforded the space for a more extensive city[1]. Herod, who had received Samaria from Augustus in the year 30 B.C., began a few years later sumptuously to extend this city and to erect an imposing Augustan temple, the outside staircase of which is still in existence *in situ* today To this city which he made into a strong fortress with a city wall and embattled gateways, he gave the name 'Sebaste'[2] in honour of Augustus. Herod's greatest achievement in city building was the new port on the Mediterranean coast. About 35 kilometres south of the summit of the Carmel there was a fairly old and rather small place called 'Straton's-Tower'. This place had been made over to Herod in the year 30 B.C. with the whole coastal area. On its site Herod had a magnificent city built at great expense over a period of twelve years, with artificial harbour installations and with all the public buildings such as a theatre, amphitheatre and hippodrome which formed part of a Hellenistic-Roman city. In the year 10 B.C. it was ceremoniously opened with magnificent games for which Augustus and Livia gave a considerable sum. And again, it was given a name in honour of the Emperor: Herod called the city 'Caesarea' (the modern ḳēṣārye) and its harbour 'Sebastos-harbour'.

Apart from these urban foundations in honour of Augustus Herod did an extraordinary amount of other building in the land[3]. No period in the history of the country ever saw so many splendid buildings arise in such a short time as the period of Herod. He changed the face of the royal city of Jerusalem with the massive buildings he had erected. In the north-western corner of the city, in the area of the modern Gate of Jaffa, he had a new royal fort built with massive towers. In the year 20 B.C. he began work on the renewal of the Temple building. By means of great embankments and an imposing outer wall, wide stretches of which can still be

[1] Cf. C. Watzinger, *Denkmäler Palästinas*, II (1933), pp. 25 f.

[2] The Greek translation of the word 'augustus' is σεβαστός; hence the settlement on the site of the old city of Samaria is still called sebaṣṭye.

[3] The best detailed description of Herod's building activities, on the basis of the archaeological findings, is in C. Watzinger, *loc. cit.* pp. 31 ff.

seen today and at a considerable height, for example by the so-called 'Wailing Wall', he extended the area of the Temple and thereby created that great holy area which is still by far the most impressive memorial of the old city of Jerusalem. He had gates and market-halls built in the Temple district and began to rebuild the real sanctuary on the model of the Salomonic Temple. In the north-west corner of the Temple square he had already had a citadel built on the site of the Hasmonaean 'Baris' (cf. above, p. 384), which had been named 'Antonia' after his friend of that period. He surrounded the site of the tombs of the patriarchs in Hebron with a tremendous outer wall—like the outer-wall of the Temple in Jerusalem—and he likewise enclosed the venerable shrine of Abraham of Mamre north of Hebron (the modern ḥaram rāmet el-khalīl) in a rectangular wall. On the other hand, he also provided the shrine of the pagan god Pan at the source of the Jordan right up in the north near the modern bānyās, with a temple for the worship of Augustus.

For himself he built a series of fortresses, above all in the inaccessible areas of the wilderness of Juda and the Dead Sea. The development of the enormously high and steep rock of Masada (the modern es-sebbe) on the western edge of the Dead Sea roughly opposite the peninsula of el-lisān was particularly praiseworthy. On the flat surface of this rock he had a great palace and extensive storerooms built[1]. North-east of this, on the other side of the Dead Sea, was the castle of Machaerus, which had already been fortified by Alexander Jannaeus and which Herod rebuilt on a bigger scale as a strong fortress. Five kilometres south-east of Bethlehem, on the edge of the desert of Juda, he built on a mountain, the summit of which he had levelled down for the purpose, a great castle with a settlement at the foot of the mountain and he called this castle, in which he had his own tomb built, 'Herodeion' (the modern jebel ferdēs). Above Jericho he built a castle which he called 'Kypros' after his mother's name[2]. In building these castles he was concerned to provide refuges for his family where they could find safety in an emergency.

Apart from the great cities of Sebaste and Caesarea which we have already mentioned, he had other places built or developed in the Hellenistic-Roman style. South of the ancient site of Jericho

[1] Cf. on the basis of detailed archaeological investigations A. Schulten, *Masada. Die Burg des Herodes und die römischen Lager* (ZDPV, 56 [1933], pp. i ff.; with numerous illustrations and plans).

[2] Cf. A. Alt, PJB, 21 (1925), pp. 23 f., who locates this citadel on the modern tell el-akabe.

the existing remains still testify to Herod's building activities which gave a new appearance to this oasis settlement[1]. To the south, below the Hasmonaean fortress of Alexandreion (ḳarn ṣarṭabe), which was probably also further developed by Herod, he built a new settlement in the Jordan Valley and called it Phasaelis (the modern khirbet faṣāʿil) after his dead elder brother Phasael after whom he had also named one of the massive towers of the royal fort in Jerusalem. He named the city of Antipatris which he either founded or revived on the inner edge of the coastal plain near the sources of the nahr el-ʿōja, which reaches the Mediterranean north of Jaffa, after his father.

The great number and the, for Palestine, unusual size of all these buildings, clearly shows what an imperious ruler Herod was. It is obvious that all this building required an enormous amount of money and labour which had to be supplied by the far from large realm over which he ruled. Outside his own land, too, he presented Hellenistic cities with gifts and buildings to increase his fame and prestige, thus imitating the great and rich Hellenistic kings. That he was able to extract all this from a country that had been exhausted by the almost endless wars and conflicts of the last one and a half centuries, shows what a forceful ruler he was. On the other hand, however, he also succeeded in increasing the prosperity of his land in the peaceful period which began with his accession. Admittedly he used cruelty and brutality to overcome his real or supposed enemies. His path to the power which he finally obtained had already been marked by cunning and violence; and as king he continued on this path. In love and hate, particularly in the latter, he apparently brooked no restraints. The outstanding qualities of his character were passion, egotism and suspicion. As king he was a cruel tyrant, above all in his own house. The details of these domestic incidents which are reported in details by Josephus need not detain us. The best known of them is the execution of his second wife, the Hasmonaean Mariamne, against whom his jealousy had been aroused by slander, and the later execution of the two sons of his marriage with Mariamne, Alexander and Aristobulus. For a time his son Antipater played a great part. He was a product of his father's first marriage with the Jerusalemite

[1] On the recently begun American excavations on the site of Herodian Jericho which now bears the name tell abu el-ʿalāyiḳ and on which traces of Hellenistic building have been found among the Herodian remains, on which, therefore, the Hasmonaeans had evidently erected some building or other, apparently at least a fortified tower, cf. the preliminary accounts in J. L. Kelse, BASOR, 120 (1950), pp. 11-22 and J. B. Pritchard, BASOR, 123 (1951), pp. 8-17.

Doris and was Herod's first-born son. It was he above all who had instigated the removal of his two half-brothers Alexander and Aristobulus. In his first will his father had appointed him his successor. But in the end he fell victim to his own cunning, and only a few days before his own death Herod had him executed.

It is not surprising that the rule of Herod was abominated by very many members of the religious community of Jerusalem. Perhaps there was less concern here about the quarrels and intrigues in the royal house. They were merely a symptom of the objectionableness of this monarchy in general. Above all, Herod was rightly regarded as a friend of Rome and was unpopular as such, since the Roman authorities had already repeatedly interfered high-handedly in the affairs of the religious community of Jerusalem and, in spite of all the occasional favours that they had bestowed, through Caesar for example, they were felt increasingly to represent an oppressive foreign dictatorship. And whatever his descent may in fact have been, Herod himself was considered a foreigner. Neither his splendid rebuilding of the sanctuary in Jerusalem nor his interest in the patriarchal sites in Hebron was able to reconcile the religious community of Jerusalem to his rule. In spite of his formal membership of the religious community of Jerusalem Herod was in fact fundamentally a Hellenistic pagan ruler, who was far more interested in the building of large-scale cities in the Hellenistic-Roman style and the erection of places of worship for his imperial master Augustus than in the concerns of the religious community of Jerusalem and its law. Under his wilful rule the Sadducee priesthood in Jerusalem was unable to play any part and his character and actions were even more an abomination to the devout and especially to the strict Pharisees. He used the office of high priest in the most improper ways and made it the object of political moves. At the beginning of his reign he had appointed a certain Ananel as high priest, since, not being of priestly descent himself, he could hardly combine the office with the monarchy, as the members of the old priestly family of the Hasmonaeans had been able to do. Ananel had come from Babylon and from a priestly family. It is true that the old Hyrcanus, who had been high priest until 40 B.C., had meanwhile returned from Babylon. But the mutilation that Antigonus had inflicted on him made it impossible for him to take the office on again. In the year 30 B.C. Herod found a pretext to have him executed, at the age of 80, as a possible rival. But the ambitious Alexandra, a daughter of Hyrcanus and wife of her cousin Alexander, who had been put to death by order of Pompey (cf. above, p. 406) agitated against Ananel. She was the mother of Mariamne and therefore Herod's mother-in-law. She demanded the office of high priest for her son Aristobulus, who was Herod's brother-in-law, and, in her view, the rightful hereditary successor. This was the period when Antony and Cleopatra were still ruling in the east; and Alexandra was in touch with Cleopatra. Under these circumstances Herod thought it advisable not to annoy the two dangerous women, and he therefore deposed Ananel again and made Aristobulus high priest. After one year, however, he found an excuse to have the high priest drowned whilst bathing in Jericho, as a result of treacherous intrigues (35 B.C.); and after he had come to an understanding with Cleopatra he also had Alexandra imprisoned and later had her killed. This treatment of the high priest's office, which went as far as the murder by the king of a high priest while in office, inevitably aroused the utmost displeasure of the religious community of Jerusalem, among the Sadducee priests as well as the strictly legalistic Pharisees.

Herod's rule was founded on terror and violence; and he managed to remain in undisputed possession of the monarchy. His position was never seriously threatened during his reign, and the main reason was that he succeeded in keeping in with the great Roman power. Outwardly his monarchy was brilliant, and in this respect a final climax in the history of Israel; and after the long period of endless armed conflicts, it was certainly a blessing for the land to be without internal warlike disputes and serious battles for a generation and more. This was also a result of Augustus's pacification of the Roman world. Nevertheless this monarchy could not possibly endure for long. If the Hasmonaean monarchy, in spite of the fact that it had resulted from a lively reaction to oppression by a foreign power, had had no firm foundation, as it was impossible for the religious community of Jerusalem even in the parts that still existed in Palestine to be a nation, Herod's Roman-supported tyranny was all the more lacking in healthy organic substance. It was only to be expected that it would not last long after his death. Revolts had occasionally occurred even during his lifetime, but he had managed to crush them quickly and ruthlessly; but they showed that he would not be able to leave his monarchy in a very compact state, particularly as, owing to the continuous troubles in his own house, he had not been able to solve the problem of the succession clearly or for very far ahead.

In the year 4 B.C. he died in Jericho after a long and painful illness, from which he had sought healing or relief at the thermal springs of Callirrhoe on the eastern shore of the Dead Sea. His death was scarcely lamented. His body was brought from Jericho to the Herodeion in a magnificent funeral procession and buried there. Shortly before his death he had made a new will. In it he had made provision for his younger sons, the two sons from his marriage with the Samaritan Malthake, Archelaus and (Herod) Antipas, and the son from his marriage with the Jerusalemite Cleopatra, Phillipus. Archelaus was to inherit the actual monarchy, whilst Antipas and Phillipus were to become more or less independent tetrarchs of Galilee and Peraea, or the most northerly area of the land east of the Jordan This will had to be confirmed by Augustus, and so Archelaus and Antipas went one after the other to Rome to press their claims and to get as much as they could for themselves. In accordance with an earlier will his father had made, Antipas wanted the whole succession for himself. Other members of Herod's family also went to Rome to plead their cause; and the leading circles of the religious community of Jerusalem also sent a deputation to Augustus to ask to him put an end to the rule of the Herodians altogether and to restore the former independence of the religious community of Jerusalem. Faced with these various requests, Augustus made his decision in the main according to Herod's last will. Archelaus was given Judaea with Idumaea and Samaria, though without the title of king, but with the title of ethnarch. He also had to give up the city of Gaza as well as the Decapolis cities of Gadara and Hippos which Augustus had made over to Herod; they were placed directly under the province of Syria as self-governing urban communities. In accordance with the terms of the will, Herod's sister Salome was given the cities of Ashdod and Jamnia in the southern coastal plain as well as a palace in Askalon and also the new Herodian foundation of Phasaelis in the Jordan Valley. Antipas and Phillipus both became tetrarchs; the first was given the geographically separated territories of Galilee and Peraea and the latter the Trachonitis, Batanaia and Auranitis with a part of the uppermost valley of the Jordan (*Ant. Iud.* XVII, 9-12; *Bell. Iud.* II, 1-6). The result was that Herod's State was shattered; and that was probably what the Emperor had intended.

The history of these states ruled by Herod's descendants was anything but glorious. Once again Josephus has recorded the details in *Ant. Iud.* XVII, 13– XIX, 9 and *Bell. Iud.* II, 7-12. Immediately after the death of Herod, and all the more during the absence of the aspirants to the throne in Rome, riots had broken out in various parts of the country which were directed against the rule of the Herodians but also against the Roman power. P. Quintilius Varus, well known for his later unfortunate campaign in Germania, who was governor of the province of Syria from 6 to 4 B.C. had to intervene, as did the procurator Sabinus whom Augustus had sent to Palestine to settle the question of the succession to the throne. Varus occupied Jerusalem by force of arms and had the rebels sought out and punished throughout the country. The severity with which the Roman troops proceeded could not help but increase the anti-Roman feeling. When Herod's successors returned, the country remained unsettled. The power of Archelaus, on whom had devolved the greatest part of his father's inheritance, was the quickest to come to an end. His severe and despotic government soon made him so hated that a deputation of his subjects went to Augustus to complain about him; and Augustus found cause to depose him and to banish him to Vienna in Gaul (A.D. 6). Barely ten years after the death of Herod the land governed by Archelaus, that is, the central and southern part of the land west of the Jordan, was deprived of its independence and constituted as a procuratorial province. This situation was only interrupted in the years A.D. 41–44. As a minor province of inferior status[1] this territory was given a special administration under a procurator (governor) who resided in the port of Caesarea founded by Herod. This procurator had military command over the troops which were raised from the land itself. Garrisons were maintained in various places, including the fortress of Antonia in Jerusalem. The procurator also exercised the supreme judicial powers. The jurisdiction exercised by the Sanhedrim was recognised, but the procurator reserved the right to pass sentence of death. The procurator was responsible for gathering in the taxes which were collected by the local authorities. The territory under the procurator was divided, for administrative purposes, into eleven so-called toparchies, on the basis of older divisions. The toparchies were Jerusalem, Gophna (the modern jīfna) north of Jerusalem, Akrabeta (the modern ʿaḳrabe) north-east of Gophna, Thamna (the modern tibne) west of Gophna, Lydda (the modern lidd), Emmaus (the modern ʿamwās), south-east of Lydda, Bethleptepha (the modern bēt nettīf) south of Emmaus, Idumaea (embracing the southern part of the mountains and the hill country), Engaddai (the modern ʿēn jidi on the western

[1] On the legal status and the organisation of such procuratorial provinces, of which there were several in the Roman Empire at this time, cf. F.-M. Abel, *Histoire de la Palestine*, I (1952), pp. 424 ff.

edge of the Dead Sea), Herodeion (the modern jebel ferdēs) on the border of the desert of Judah south of Jerusalem, and, finally, Jericho in the lower Jordan Valley[1]. The particularities of the religious community of Jerusalem were respected as far as possible. It is true that they were required to take the oath of allegiance to the Emperor but not to take part in worship of the Emperor. The Roman garrison on the Antonia in the immediate vicinity of the Temple also supervised the proceedings in the Temple, but as a rule the troops did not bring their pictures of the Emperor with them to Jerusalem.

In spite of all the careful consideration which the Romans showed, opposition to the appearance of Roman power in the land was strong. In the period of the first procurator the governor of the Syrian province, P. Sulpicius Quirinius, carried out the Roman census in 'Judaea'—that was the official name of the territory under the procurator's jurisdiction—in order to reorganise the system of taxation. This measure caused great excitement and led to the rise of a radically anti-Roman movement which was soon to make itself felt with calamitous effect. To begin with, there was some outward acquiescence in the strong Roman government. The procurators did not, in many cases, behave very carefully, and often gave cause for not unjustified indignation. The best known of them was Pontius Pilate, who held the office of procurator from A.D. 26–36. He had scant regard for the scruples of the religious community of Jerusalem and also acted cruelly towards the Samaritans. In the end he was deposed at the suggestion of the Syrian governor, L. Vitellius, who treated the Jerusalem cultus with particular respect.

Whilst Jerusalem and the whole of the central and southern part of the land west of the Jordan was already under direct Roman administration, Herod Antipas ruled as tetrarch under Roman suzerainty in Galilee and Peraea in a fairly long reign (4 B.C.–A.D. 39). To begin with, the capital of his territory was Sepphoris (the modern ṣaffūrye) in the hills of Lower Galilee, which Gabinius had made the centre of the district and which Antipas now raised to the status of a city. Later on, *circa* A.D. 20, Antipas built himself a magnificent new residence on the western shore of Lake Genezareth, calling it Tiberias after the Emperor Tiberius. To the present day it has remained the most important settlement on the shores of the lake. He had a royal palace built there. Previously he had

[1] Cf. the list in *Bell. Iud.* 3, 5, §§ 54 f. On Bethleptepha cf. *Bell. Iud.* IV, 8, 1, § 445 (the other passage gives instead, probably inadvertently, the name 'Pelle').

already developed Betharamptha (the modern tell er-rāme) in Peraea in the Jordan Valley north-east of the northern end of the Dead Sea, as a fortress over against the neighbouring Nabataeans and gave it the name of Julias or, later, Livias. These names show how deliberately he courted the favour of the Roman Imperial house. It is true that Antipas was somewhat more careful than his elder brother Archelaus, and was therefore able to continue longer in power; but in his personal life he was probably not much less uninhibited than his father. The story of his marriage to the ambitious Herodias, a daughter of the Aristobulus who resulted from Herod's marriage to the Hasmonaean Mariamne, is well known. He himself had first been married to the daughter of the Nabataean king, and Herodias had had as husband an otherwise undistinguished son of Herod who was also called Herod and a stepbrother of Antipas. Herodias thought she would be able to attain greater distinction at the side of the tetrarch Antipas. At Herodias's instigation Antipas therefore cast off the Nabataean and married Herodias. This marriage produced a daughter, Salome[1], who, with her mother, played a part in the beheading of John the Baptist. John had appeared in Peraea on the Jordan in Antipas's territory and Antipas had had the inconvenient and dreaded preacher of penitence arrested and imprisoned in the fortress of Machaerus[2], and finally had him executed. The marriage to Herodias only brought disaster to Antipas. The repudiation of the Nabataean woman, which had taken place at her instigation, involved him in a war with his Nabataean neighbour in which he was defeated (A.D. 36) so that the Emperor Tiberias had to send the governor L. Vitellius of Syria against the Nabataeans. The restlessly ambitious Herodias also persuaded Antipas to apply to the Emperor—he was now C. Caligula—for the title of king. This was his final ruin, for he thereby incurred the opposition of the Herodian Agrippa of whom we shall be speaking in a moment. He had Antipas charged before the Emperor, and in A.D. 39 Caligula deposed him after a long reign and banished him to Lugdunum in Gaul.

After Herod's death in A.D. 4 his son Phillipus had inherited the territories in the most northerly part of the land east of the Jordan as tetrarch. Josephus praises him as a good ruler. Admittedly, we know little about his period of office. In the year 2/1 B.C. he

[1] We only know this name from Josephus, *Ant. Iud.* XVIII, 5, 4, §§ 136 ff.

[2] Josephus only mentions Machaerus as the place of imprisonment in his section on John the Baptist, *Ant. Iud.* XVIII, 5, 2, §§ 116 ff.

established a Residence for himself in the vicinity of the shrine of Pan by the easternmost source of the Jordan at the south-western foot of Mount Hermon, and called it Caesarea (Caesarea Philippi) in honour of the Emperor. Lake Genezareth and the course of the Jordan north of this lake formed the boundary between the tetrarchies of Antipas and Phillipus. In the borderland east of the Jordan, near its discharge into Lake Genezareth, Phillipus attempted to raise Beth-Saida to the status of a city called Julias, but apparently he abandoned the attempt[1]. He finally married Salome, the daughter of Antipas and Herodias, but died childless in the year A.D. 34. Thereupon his territory was added to the province of Syria.

Eventually a Herodian once again had the chance of ruling over almost the whole of Herod's dominion for a short time as king. He was a son of Herod's son Aristobulus, whose mother was the Hasmonaean Mariamne, and who was therefore a full brother of Herodias. He was called Agrippa, so named after M. Vipsanius Agrippa, the friend of Augustus. This Agrippa lived in Rome and had succeeded in obtaining the favour of the Emperor C. Caligula, even before the latter ascended the throne. Immediately on his accession Caligula gave his favourite the tetrarchy of Phillipus, which had fallen three years previously to the province of Syria, as his own domain, and at the same time he conferred on him the title of king. He also gave him the Abilene, *i.e.* the district of Abila (the modern sūḳ wādi barada) north-west of Damascus in the region of the Anti-Lebanon, which had hitherto formed a separate tetrarchy adjoining Phillipus's tetrarchy in the north. This was the success which had given his sister Herodias no peace. When Agrippa, who had, to begin with, remained for a time in Rome, arrived in Palestine during the year A.D. 38 and came forward as king, she persuaded her husband Antipas to ask the Emperor to give him the royal title too. But, as the Emperor's favourite, Agrippa managed to get Antipas deposed instead and himself assigned the Antipas's tetrarchy, in other words, Galilee and Peraea. (A.D. 39). Eventually, Agrippa, who had returned to Rome in the year A.D. 40, was also given Judaea with Idumaea and Samaria. Meanwhile very grave incidents had taken place there. When, in the year A.D. 38, Agrippa had been in Alexandria on his journey from Rome to Palestine, the sight of the king had given rise to serious excesses against the members of the religious community of Jerusalem in that place. Soon after his accession, Caligula, who considered

[1] Cf. A. Alt, PJB, 33 (1937), p. 85, note 4.

himself a god, had proceeded to require his subjects throughout the Empire to participate in the worship of the Emperor. The demand was fulfilled with more or less zeal. Only the members of the religious community of Jerusalem would not and could not take part in the worship of the Emperor. For adopting this attitude they were hated by the others. Not only was King Agrippa publicly derided in Alexandria, but the Alexandrines also demanded that pictures of the Emperor should be placed in the synagogues of the city; and the Roman governor of Egypt, A. Avilius Flaccus, to whom Caligula was not very favourably inclined, and who therefore strove in every way to obtain the Emperor's good-will, complied with the Alexandrines' demands without the slightest resistance. The synagogues in Alexandria were partly desecrated by the setting up of pictures of the Emperor and partly they were destroyed altogether, and intense and bloody persecution befell the members of the religious community of Jerusalem in Alexandria. It is true that Flaccus was recalled in the autumn of the year A.D. 38, but there was, to begin with, no fundamental change under his successor. In the year A.D. 40 a deputation from both of the contending parties went to Rome from Alexandria to see the Emperor, and the leader of the synagogical deputation was the well-known writer Philo. The Emperor treated the synagogical deputation very ill-humouredly and with marked discourtesy and conceded nothing at all[1]. It was not until the following year that the Emperor Claudius put an end to the persecution in Alexandria shortly after his accession by restoring the privileges of the religious community of Jerusalem and promising it unhampered freedom of worship. But meanwhile the incidents had spread to Palestine. Probably during the year A.D. 39 the pagan inhabitants of the city of Jamnia (the modern yebna) had set up an imperial altar, which was destroyed by members of the religious community of Jerusalem. When this was reported to the Emperor, he commanded his picture to be set up in the Temple in Jerusalem; and the Syrian governor, P. Petronius, whose duty was to enforce the Emperor's intentions in Jerusalem, was given instructions to carry out this monstrous order. Petronius was prudent enough to desist from the use of force for the time being. First of all he sent for the heads of the community while he was in Sidon, where he was staying on his march from Antioch and tried to persuade them to comply; needless to say, in vain. The news of these menacing proceedings led to enormous excitement in the religious community of Jerusalem. When

[1] Cf. the treatise of Philo, *Legatio ad Gaium*.

Petronius had moved on to Ptolemais he was stormed by a great crowd of people who besought him not to carry out the order. He thereupon wrote to the Emperor to ask him to postpone the order; but in vain. He then went to Tiberias, and once again he was surrounded for forty days by a great crowd imploring him not to carry out the order. He then decided on his own responsibility not to fulfil his commission; he took his troops back to Antioch and wrote to the Emperor to ask him to cancel his instructions. At the same time King Agrippa tried to get his friend the Emperor to revoke his order. But the Emperor now refused to yield to him, although in response to a letter from Agrippa he did make one concession, but he rescinded it straight away. The sudden murder of the Emperor Caligula in January A.D. 41 saved the religious community of Jerusalem from the threat of further violent persecution and the governor Petronius from the punishment intended for his disobedience. Fortunately the Emperor's letter which commanded him to take his own life did not reach him until after the news of the Emperor's murder. The new Emperor Claudius desisted, however, from enforcing the worship of the Emperor in the religious community of Jerusalem.

Agrippa, who was still in Rome, had supported the accession of Claudius, whom the soldiers had chosen as their leader after the murder of Caligula. To thank him for this service, Claudius gave him, in addition to the areas which he had already received by favour of Caligula, the parts of Judaea (*i.e.* the real Judaea with Idumaea and Samaria) which had previously been administered by procurators. Agrippa now combined under his royal sceptre the whole territory ruled by his grandfather Herod with the exception of the south-western coastal plain around Gaza and the territories of the cities of Gadara and Hippos in the northern land east of the Jordan; furthermore, in the far north he possessed Abilene in the Anti-Lebanon. Soon after his success in Rome Agrippa returned to Palestine (A.D. 41). He was then about 50 years old. He had already led a stirring and frivolous life, had often been for long periods in Rome since his childhood and had there acquired a thorough knowledge of, and himself practised, the gambling life of adventure and intrigue. Fortunate circumstances had now played an imposing kingdom into his hands. There is little to be said in praise of his short reign. He passed himself off in Jerusalem as a man of exemplary devoutness, apparently observed the ordinances of the legalistic Pharisees, spent money on the Jerusalem cultus, gave a golden chain, which had been presented to him by the

Emperor Caligula, to the Temple treasury and championed the interests of the religious community of Jerusalem. This attitude was based on political motives, not on personal conviction. In Caesarea he organised games, and outside his own dominions he acted like a rich Hellenistic ruler, made great donations, for example, to the city of Berytos (bērūt), arranged for gladiatorial games to be held there and made a great display of his wealth. His conduct in Jerusalem—and this was his intention—attracted much sympathy from the religious community of Jerusalem, whereas the Hellenistic cities such as Sebaste which came under his rule were less satisfied with his regime. All the same, the country enjoyed some years of peace under him. He tried to extend and re-fortify the city of Jerusalem. On the north side of the city he began, north of the previous wall, the building of a very strong section of wall with towers, which was intended to give the city more space on this side. It is the so-called 'third wall'[1]. This work was not finished, however, not merely because the king's short reign was not sufficient but also because the Syrian governor, C. Vibius, was instructed by the Emperor to protest against its continuance. In other ways, too, he occasionally behaved like an independent ruler with great political plans. He invited to Tiberias five other Roman vassal rulers from Syria and Asia Minor. It is difficult to say what the intention of this meeting was. It was probably more in the nature of a boastful undertaking on the part of Agrippa. The meeting actually took place, but no sooner had it started than the Syrian governor Marsus appeared and the gathering was dispersed.

Agrippa was not important: even if he had lived longer, his reign would probably not have acquired any significance. He died suddenly in the year A.D. 44 in Caesarea during festive games that were being held there in honour of the Emperor, after he had appeared in public with great regal ostentation and the people had greeted him as an incarnate god. Shortly after, he was attacked with violent pains, had to be carried away, and within a few days he was dead (cf. Acts xii, 21-24). Apart from a few daughters, he left a son aged 17, who was also called Agrippa. The Emperor

[1] Whether this 'third wall' of Agrippa (Josephus, *Bell. Iud.* V, 4, 2, §§ 147 ff.) is to be identified with the stretch of wall in the northern outer district of modern Jerusalem, impressive remains of which have been preserved and rediscovered (cf. E. L. Sukenik and L. A. Mayer, *The Third Wall of Jerusalem* [1930], or whether it was not rather on the line of the later Turkish north wall, which still shuts off the old city of Jerusalem on the northern side (cf. J. Simons, *Jerusalem in the Old Testament* [1952], p. 459), is a question that has not yet been solved.

Claudius did not, however, allow this son to succeed his father, but turned the whole territory into a Roman province and put it under procurators who again resided in Caesarea. The whole of the territory under these procurators was officially called Judaea. The legal and actual position in this Judaea was now the same as in that smaller Judaea which had been formed after the deposition of Archelaus in the year A.D. 6 and which had lasted until A.D. 41. The tensions between the Roman power and administration and the religious community of Jerusalem soon emerged again; and the agitation among wide circles of the religious community of Jerusalem became more and more menacing.

34. *The Rejection of Christ*

Whilst people in Jerusalem and elsewhere in the country resented the Roman power and complained about the behaviour of the Roman procurators who still resided in Caesarea, and whilst the anything but worthy Antipas was ruling as tetrarch in Galilee and Peraea, events of decisive importance were taking place within the bosom of the religious community of Jerusalem. Jesus of Nazareth was living and working at this period. World history took no notice of him at the time. Not even Josephus, who records so many details about the movements and forces of the period, found cause to devote one word to his appearance[1]. Only when his followers had emerged as a historically concrete fact did his name begin to be mentioned[2]. In the history of Israel the important concerns of the time seemed to be the self-assertion of the religious community of Jerusalem against the constantly threatening encroachments of superior secular forces, the safeguarding of the threatened freedom of worship, the preservation of the right to live in accordance with the strict requirements of the traditional law. They did not include the attitude to be adopted to an itinerant preacher who had gathered a band of followers around him and finally appeared in Jerusalem with high-flown pretensions He seemed an insignificant figure in the history of Israel, which was so full of striking or strange personalities. For a brief moment his appearance had caused a flutter of excitement in Jerusalem; then the episode belonged to

[1] It is generally agreed that a section on Jesus in *Ant. Iud.* XVIII, 3, 3, §§ 63 f. is a later Christian insertion.

[2] Josephus also finally mentioned 'Jesus the so-called Christ' in *Ant. Iud.* XX, 9, 1, § 200. Cf. the well-known statements by Suetonius, *Claudius*, ch. 25 and Tacitus, *Ann.* XV, 44.

the past and there were more important-seeming affairs to worry about. And yet an ultimate and final decision had been made in the history of Israel.

The story of Jesus's human life had been, in the first instance, simple and straightforward. He had worked among the still surviving Israelite tribes in the interior of Galilee[1]. Nazareth (the modern en-nasira), his home, was a village in the hills of Lower Galilee north of the plain of Jezreel of which there are no records from earlier times and which was perhaps still a recent settlement in Jesus's time. It is true that it was only six kilometres south of Sepphoris (ṣaffūrye), Antipas's first Residence, which he had made a city, but it did not belong to the territory of this Hellenistic-Roman city, but to a group of villages in the old territory of the tribe Zebulon and was no doubt inhabited by Israelites. Jesus had gone from there to the north-western shores of Lake Genezareth, not to the magnificent royal city of Tiberias which had just been re-established by Antipas, but into the region of the no doubt Israelite villages such as Capernaum (the modern tell ḥūm) and Chorazin (the modern khirbet kerāze) north-east of Tiberias. This area was near the frontier which divided the tetrarchies of Antipas and Phillipus. A few kilometres north-east of Capernaum the Jordan flowed into Lake Genezareth and on the other side of the Jordan the village of Beth-Saida was already inside the tetrarchy of Phillipus. But a basically Israelite population lived on both sides of the Jordan and the fishermen on the lake plied freely from one shore to the other in spite of the tetrarchical boundary in between. All the same, there were custom-houses and also a Roman garrison in this frontier area. It was here that Jesus preached among the simple Israelite people around the lake and found men who followed him and crowds who listened attentively to his words. Travels farther afield occasionally took him as far as the area of Caesarea Phillipi, the tetrarchical residence which had been newly established by Phillipus (the modern bānyās) right up in the north of the old Israelite settlement, or into the Tyrian-Sidonian area, *i.e.* probably to the territory of the city of Tyre, which extended through the whole of Upper Galilee to the western border of the uppermost Jordan Valley and therefore also included part of the territory settled by the ancient Israelites. This itinerary and preaching therefore took place in the first instance on the periphery of the Palestinian domains of the religious community of Jerusalem

[1] On the following, cf. above all A. Alt, *Die Stätten des Wirkens Jesu in Galiläa territorialgeschichtlich betrachtet* (BBLAK, 68, 1 [1949], pp. 51 ff.).

and will hardly have been noticed in Jerusalem where people were more concerned about the central sanctuary and its integrity. We learn all this only from the stories which were passed on orally, to begin with, among Jesus's followers.

Finally, however—and this is, too, only recorded in the early Christian tradition itself—Jesus went to Jerusalem to bring about a decision between his claim to be the revelation of the living God and the traditions of the religious community of Jerusalem. It is not possible to ascertain the exact year in which that took place. It was shortly before the day of the Passover. Jesus entered into the city of Jerusalem as Messiah, riding on a donkey; and then he appeared in the holy precincts of the Temple, preaching with authority. On his entry he had been hailed by an enthusiastic crowd as the long-awaited Messianic king, and they gathered round to hear him. But the official leaders of the religious community of Jerusalem did not submit to his claim; and they used their influence to turn the crowd against him. They could not see the promised Messiah in this Jesus of Nazareth from Galilee. In the long period of foreign rule the old Judaean prophets' expectation of a future Messianic king had developed into the hope for a political liberator; and the more incensed people had become with the Roman regime the more the idea of a Messianic victor over the odious foreign power had become an obsession. In the light of this conception Jesus of Nazareth could not be the expected Messiah. And this dichotomy gave the leading men in Jerusalem a welcome reason for rejecting Jesus's claim. The human guardians of a sacred tradition are always inclined to defend the tradition against a vital innovation. But if Jesus of Nazareth was not the Messiah, the 'Christ', then he must be a seducer and a deceiver. And if he was a dangerous seducer and deceiver then he must be removed for the sake of the safety and peace of the religious community of Jerusalem. Therefore the sanhedrim which was responsible for the religious community took action against Jesus. One night he was arrested by trickery and immediately brought before the sanhedrim, the supreme court in the internal affairs of the religious community of Jerusalem. The fact that Jesus acknowledged that he was the Messiah and therefore, in accordance with Old Testament statements, the Son of God, sufficed to condemn him to death for notorious blasphemy. According to the existing law, this sentence needed to be confirmed and carried out by the Roman procurator. At the time this office was held by Pontius Pilate (A.D. 26–36) who was hated on account of his infringements of the laws of the religious community of Jerusalem. He had just come up to Jerusalem from Caesarea for the impending Feast of the Passover, to supervise in person the proceedings which would be attended by a great multitude of people, and he resided, presumably, in the royal palace in the north-west of the city built by Herod. The captive Jesus was presented to him by the men of the sanhedrim and at the same time a crowd was raised in order noisily to demand the death sentence from the procurator. And the procurator agreed, after pains had been taken to explain to him the danger to the State the prisoner was alleged to constitute. He had practically no idea what the case was really about, but it gave him an opportunity to do the people of Jerusalem a favour which he could make up for later by further infringements of their rights. In Judaea the *ius gladii* belonged to the procurator alone; and he therefore arranged for Roman soldiers to carry out the sentence of death on Jesus of Nazareth. At this time the Romans often used the infamous and agonising method of execution by crucifixion, above all for rebellious subjects in the provinces. It was chosen this time, especially as the accusing multitude had expressly clamoured for this method. Outside the walled-in city Jesus was crucified with a few other prisoners by soldiers appointed for the task. A small band of followers stayed together in Jerusalem and soon began to spread the gospel by their preaching. Their enterprise did not appear to have much significance. But it was frowned on by the leaders of the religious community of Jerusalem who had intended the condemnation of Jesus of Nazareth to settle the whole affair. As occasion offered, therefore, attempts were made to suppress Jesus's followers and their activities. King Agrippa in Jerusalem with his ostentatious Pharisaean piety, also tried to make himself popular by persecuting Jesus's followers. He had one of the leaders of this band, James by name, killed for some unknown reason, and another, Simon Peter, he had put in prison (Acts xii, 1 ff.). Later on, a high priest took advantage of a short vacancy in the procuratorial office, the new procurator not yet having arrived, and, exceeding his authority, since executions could only be authorised by the procurator, had a brother of Jesus who was also called James, stoned with a few other followers of Jesus (A.D. 62)[1]. For the rest, however, Jesus's followers, who sent out representatives into the country and began to preach in the Greek-speaking Diaspora and in the whole Mediterranean world, did not attract much attention

[1] Cf. Josephus, *Ant. Iud.* XX, 9, I, §§ 200 ff.; in this connection Josephus mentions the name of 'Jesus the so-called Christ'.

to begin with. This is roughly how things must have appeared to the religious community of Jerusalem. Jesus himself, with his words and his work, no longer formed part of the history of Israel. In him the history of Israel had come, rather, to its real end. What did belong to the history of Israel was the process of his rejection and condemnation by the religious community of Jerusalem. It had not discerned in him the goal to which the history of Israel had secretly been leading; it rejected him as the promised Messiah. Only a few had joined him, and from them something new proceeded. The religious community of Jerusalem imagined it had more important concerns, and kept aloof from this new movement. Hereafter the history of Israel hastened quickly to its end.

35. *The Insurrections against Rome and the End of Israel*

Dangerous conflicts soon occurred in the procuratorial province of Judaea which had been newly constituted in the year A.D. 44. A touchy and irritated attitude towards the Roman government became ever stronger. Already after the removal of Archelaus, when Roman procurators had been brought in for the central and southern part of west Jordan, a party had been formed whose aim was resistance to, and the abolition of, foreign rule. These people called themselves 'Zealots'. They drew concrete political conclusions from the demand that the one God should be worshipped exclusively, and interpreted the traditional promises from a national point of view. They refused to pay taxes to a foreign power and intended to fight for the freedom of the people of God with weapons in their own hands, just as Mattathias had done with his sons and followers under the Seleucid regime. The Pharisees, from whose ranks the movement had proceeded, considered it inconsistent and weak because, in spite of their faithful adherence to tradition and the law, they put up with the foreign power as a necessary evil; and the attitude of the Sadducees, who had always been inclined to live on good terms with the ruling secular power, was, in their sight, even more reprehensible. Using violence not, to begin with, on a large scale but in innumerable minor engagements, they kept the land in a state of constant commotion. The more the Roman procurators indulged in provocative or merely careless encroachments on the religious community of Jerusalem, the more their band of followers naturally increased, though the great mass of the population no doubt kept aloof from these radical elements. No major incidents occurred in the first third of the century, and the situation remained fairly calm on the whole. But the excesses of the year A.D. 39 and the Emperor Caligula's threatened interference with the Jerusalem cultus seemed likely to lead to a serious crisis; and only the good sense of the Syrian governor, Petronius, prevented the worst from happening (cf. above, p 423 f.). The three years of the reign of King Agrippa (A.D. 41–44), who, though he owed his kingship to the Emperor's favour, did exert a power of his own and behaved towards the religious community of Jerusalem as if he was one of their own, brought a brief period of appeasement. But after his death the previous situation recurred.

Josephus has recorded the details of what followed in *Bell. Iud.* from the second book onwards. He is our main source for this period too. The land was administered by the Roman procurators from Caesarea. The younger Agrippa, the son of King Agrippa, occupied a curious position. To begin with, he lived, as his father had done, in Rome. After his father's death the Emperor Claudius had not given him his father's kingdom, on the pretext that he was too young. But as he had good connections in Rome he was ultimately compensated for this loss. In the year A.D. 50 he received the small kingdom of Chalcis (the modern ʿanjar) in the beka between Lebanon and Anti-Lebanon after the death of his uncle, Herod, a brother of his father, who had previously held this kingdom. Soon afterwards this small territory was exchanged for a rather larger kingdom, which embraced Phillipus's former tetrarchy in the northernmost land east of the Jordan and the Abilene in the Anti-Lebanon north-west of Damascus. Above all, however, with the kingdom of Chalcis he had received the right to supervise the Temple in Jerusalem and to appoint the high priest in Jerusalem; and he exercised this right up to the outbreak of the insurrection in the year A.D. 66. This represented a final remnant of independent royal suzerainty within the religious community of Jerusalem, and the Emperor no doubt intended the arrangement as a concession to the community which would prevent the Roman procurator from meddling with the sanctuary in Jerusalem. The younger Agrippa also championed the interests of the religious community of Jerusalem on various occasions. The legalistically minded could not, however, really reconcile themselves to a Herodian deposing and appointing high priests at his own discretion. Nor was he a particularly worthy steward of the Temple. At any rate his cohabitation with his sister Berenice (cf

Acts xxv, 13), the widow of his uncle Herod of Chalcis, gave rise to the most defamatory gossip.

The first two procurators after A.D. 44 still managed to treat the religious community of Jerusalem with the necessary discretion, and their period of office was therefore comparatively peaceful. It is true that they were unable to prevent a variety of agitators in the religious community of Jerusalem stirring up trouble. Under the third procurator, Ventidius Cumanus (A.D. 48–52), however, very serious incidents occurred. The mocking of the crowd which had assembled for the feast of the Passover by a Roman soldier led justifiably to great indignation, against which the procurator proceeded with armed force. Above all, a band of Galilean pilgrims to the festival were attacked and murdered by Samaritans on their journey through Samaria; since the procurator, who had been bribed by the Samaritans, did not intervene, a group of Zealots undertook a cruel campaign of vengeance against Samaria, and the procurator used military force against the Zealots. The waves of excitement in the religious community of Jerusalem, which seemed likely to have the direst consequences, were assuaged only because the younger Agrippa, who happened to be in Rome at the time, succeeded in persuading the Emperor Claudius to have the leading Samaritans executed and the procurator Cumanus deposed. His successor was Antonius Felix (cf. Acts xxiii, 24 ff.) one of the Emperor's favourites, who was in office from A.D. 52–60. He quickly made himself hated. His personal life was obnoxious; he was married three times, among others, to a sister of the younger Agrippa named Drusilla (cf. Acts xxiv, 24) whom he had adulterously fastened to himself. In the exercise of his office he indulged in every possible form of despotism. Anti-Roman agitation therefore increased enormously under him. Groups of so-called Sicarians were formed, who made a habit of carrying a dagger (*sica*) hidden on their persons, and who filled the land with murders. Porcius Festus, a fair and just man (cf. Acts xxiv, 27 ff.) was unable to alter this situation in his short term of office (A.D. 60–62) not least because he was followed by the shamelessly corrupt Albinus (A.D. 62–64) under whom the general corruption and maladministration in the land only increased still more. If further deterioration in the situation was possible, it was brought about by the next procurator Gessius Florus (A.D. 64–66). He plundered the land quite openly and freely, and wherever there was a chance of deriving personal advantage from it he gave full scope to disorder and robbery.

Things were moving towards an open outbreak of hostilities

between the Roman power and the people, and only some small incident or other was needed to kindle the flame of a great and general insurrection. The Roman procurators with their corrupt and violent administration no doubt bore an abundant measure of responsibility for this development. But it must be remembered that we owe our knowledge of these events very largely to Josephus, who, particularly as he himself played an active part in the insurrection, was concerned to show that the representatives of the Roman power were primarily to blame for the outbreak of hostilities, and selected his details accordingly. All the same, it is also evident from his statements that the struggle against Roman power had already been in progress in the religious community of Jerusalem for some long time, on grounds of principle and not merely as a reaction to Roman interference. And the Zealots had been using violence for a long time and in a minor way had kept the country in a state of constant unrest. There is no doubt at all that they had constantly been challenging and attacking the Roman representatives and giving them cause for counter-measures and reprisals. The conflict, therefore, became more and more critical, and it was brought to a head in the end by a further act of despotism on the part of the Roman procurators. The religious community of Jerusalem which had lived comparatively peacefully for centuries under one secular power after another, had proceeded, after resisting the persecution which it suffered at the hands of Antiochus IV Epiphanes and which had struck at its very substance, to seek the way of political and national freedom for Israel. This way had led to the fragile Hasmonaean monarchy and then to the hated regime of Herod, the protégé of Rome. The stalwarts now provoked a struggle against the superior power of Rome. This was the logical culmination of the path they had been treading, and the struggle led to the end of Israel.

A prelude to the great struggle took place in Caesarea during the year A.D. 66. In this outwardly brilliant foundation of Herod's, in which the Roman procurators resided, there had always been friction between the pagan sections of the population and the members of the religious community of Jerusalem who lived there. In the end, the latter were only able to escape from public molestation and derision by leaving the city with their holy books. This incident inevitably added a powerful stimulus to the agitation which was already intense. Soon afterwards, in the May of A.D. 66, the procurator Florus in Jerusalem ventured on an act of violation which brought the insurrection to explosion point. He had seventeen talents taken away from the Temple treasury; to this the people in Jerusalem replied with public derision of the procurator. Thereupon, in great wrath, Florus allowed his soldiers freely to pillage a part of the city, and in spite of the expostulations of queen Berenice who happened to be in Jerusalem, the Roman troops raged with the utmost brutality. Florus then ordered the population to go out and give a ceremonial welcome to two Roman cohorts which were marching in from Caesarea. The high priest, who, with many other prudent members of the community, was trying to preserve the peace, tried to persuade the people to comply; and once again he managed to get the people to accept the humiliation required of them. But when the Roman soldiers did not return the people's greetings, the people gave vent to their displeasure in abuse of the procurator and the soldiers took up arms. The enraged Jerusalemites occupied the area of the Temple and pulled down the colonnades between the Temple area and the fortress of Antonia which was in Roman hands, to break the link between them. At the moment Florus was not strong enough to overcome the rebellious mob; he therefore withdrew to Caesarea and only left one cohort behind in Jerusalem. Meanwhile, king Agrippa had arrived in Jerusalem, and, in a public speech, he tried to persuade the people to abandon their, from a long-term point of view, hopeless resistance. The people would have been prepared to make some concessions; but they were no longer willing to obey the procurator Florus, and so Agrippa left the city without having achieved his purpose. The rebels were now masters of the situation; at their head stood Eleasar, a son of the high priest. They had succeeded in overcoming the Herodian fortress of Masada (es-sebbe) on the Dead Sea, and in Jerusalem, at the instigation of Eleasar, they decided to stop the daily sacrifices for the emperor and not to accept any further sacrifices from foreigners. This meant a complete break with the Roman power, over and above all the more or less serious conflicts in the country, and all that remained now was a struggle to the death. It is true that the high priest made another attempt, with the majority of the other priests and the more level-headed leaders of the Pharisees, to overcome the rebellious mob, this time by force. At his request Agrippa sent 3000 troopers to occupy part of the city. But even this force proved too weak. After long and bitter struggles in the city and around the Temple enclosure which was the rebels' main base, they had to retire to Herod's palace, and in the end they had to be content to make a free and honourable withdrawal. The rebels even succeeded in occupying the fortress of Antonia. The Roman cohort took refuge in the three fortified towers on the north side of Herod's palace; in the end they too were allowed to withdraw, but were then treacherously slaughtered. The high priest was murdered, his palace and also the Hasmonaean palace which Agrippa and Berenice had latterly used as a residence, had already been set on fire, and also a part of Herod's palace. The rebels were now in sole charge of Jerusalem. Bloody battles had also taken place in many other parts of the country, the results of which were determined by the relative local strength of the pagan population and the rebels. The procurator Florus was no longer able to control the situation. In the autumn of the year A.D. 66 the governor of the province of Syria, C. Cestius Gallus, approached from Antioch with a Roman legion and numerous auxiliary troops to suppress the rebellion. He marched by way of Ptolemais and Caesarea on the coastal plain southwards as far as Lydda, then went up the mountains and approached the city of Jerusalem from the north. He pitched his camp on the so-called Scopos, a hill on the northern edge of the hollow of Jerusalem across which the main road from the north enters into this hollow (the modern rās el-mshārif). He occupied the northern suburb of Jerusalem, but an attack on the area of the Temple failed. As Cestius realised that Jerusalem was being defended with enormous determination, and that his forces were not sufficient to overcome the city, he beat a retreat. As he was climbing down the mountain on the old road of Beth-Heron (the modern bēt ʿūr) he was suddenly attacked on all sides by the rebels; his troops suffered serious losses and lost most of their baggage and arms to the rebels, and Cestius had to consider himself lucky to escape with a nucleus of his troops and return to Antioch. The rebels had won the day and were now masters of the situation throughout the land. Jerusalem was jubilant.

All this had, however, only been a beginning. As so often, the rebellion that had been started with fresh enthusiasm had met with an initial success, before the enemy had had a chance to gather his forces. It was only now that preparations for a real war began to be made. The leaders of the rebels in Jerusalem, who refused to brook any opposition to their attitude, particularly as it was now impossible to turn back, tried to organise resistance to the expected counter-attack throughout the land. Complete success in forming a serviceable army from the entirely heterogeneous population, whose discipline had been undermined by the activities of the Zealots, was unthinkable. Besides, there was a complete lack of experience and the necessary war materials The land was divided into districts, each of which was allotted a military commander. Apart from Jerusalem, Galilee was bound to become an important battle area, since it had a relatively compact population which still belonged to the religious community of Jerusalem. Joseph, the son of Matthias, was sent there as commander-in-chief. He was the later historian, Josephus. He belonged to the moderate wing which did not want to carry things to extremes and still hoped for an eventful agreement with the Roman power. He was therefore opposed by the Zealots in Galilee, whose stronghold was Gischala in Upper Galilee (the modern ej-jish), and who were led by a certain John of Gischala. This John distrusted Josephus as a traitor in the struggle against Rome, made several attempts to remove him, and Josephus only barely escaped being murdered. This quarrel was symptomatic of the internal situation in the religious community of Jerusalem. The rebels were not united among themselves—and this was soon to become evident in Jerusalem too. The rather more cautious people still had the leadership in their hands; but they had behind them the utterly impetuous elements of the Zealot party, who, as was only natural, were to get the upper hand as the difficulties and failures increased. Recognising perfectly correctly that his forces would not be a match for the Roman legions in the open field, Josephus quickly had the most important cities in Galilee fortified, and formed a not inconsiderable army which he quickly had trained as a makeshift force. He also set up a special administrative organisation for Galilee, so that in an emergency Galilee would have been able to live in tolerable order independently of, and separated from, Jerusalem. Similar preparations were made in Jerusalem and the other districts inhabited by the religious community of Jerusalem.

Meanwhile, however, the Emperor Nero had commissioned one of his best-tried generals, T. Flavius Vespasianus, to suppress the rebellion, seeing that the Syrian governor had failed so badly and, incidentally, had died soon after. Vespasianus made his preparations in the winter of A.D. 66–67; he gathered a great army of Roman troops and numerous auxiliary troops in Antioch, and immediately sent his son Titus to Alexandria to fetch further Roman troops from there. The combined forces were to meet in Ptolemais. When Vespasianus arrived there in the spring of A.D. 67 he at once received from the city of Sepphoris, (ṣaffūrye) which, as a foundation of Antipas's, had a predominantly non-Israelite population, a request for a Roman garrison, and Vespasianus was

Finally, in June A.D. 69, Vespasianus prepared anew to attack Jerusalem now the situation in Rome seemed to have been clarified. In Rome, Galba had ascended the Imperial throne after the death of Nero, but had been murdered on the 15th January 69. Otho, who now seemed to have the supreme power in his hands, had become Emperor. The Judaean undertaking was then delayed once again by events in Rome. The Germanic legions had proclaimed the governor of Lower Germania, A. Vitellius, anti-emperor. Otho had taken his own life and Vitellius had marched into Rome. When news of this reached the Orient, the legions stationed in the Orient also thought it incumbent on them to act. On the 1st July A.D. 69 Vespasianus was proclaimed Emperor in Egypt and shortly afterwards in Palestine and Syria too, and within a short time he was acknowledged as such throughout the Orient. Vespasianus, whose cause finally triumphed in Rome too, and who, after Vitellius had been murdered in Rome on the 20th December 69, finally went to Rome himself in the summer of A.D. 70, was preoccupied with the Imperial matter. He left the continuation and completion of the fight against the rebels in Palestine to his son Titus. But the year A.D. 69 passed without any further action.

Titus opened his attack on Jerusalem in the spring of A.D. 70. He had at his disposal no less than four legions and numerous auxiliary troops. Apart from his father's three legions, the 5th, 10th and 15th, he also had the 12th under him. The 5th legion came up from Emmaus ('amwas), the 10th from Jericho. He himself moved up with the 12th and 15th legions from Caesarea and appeared outside the city shortly before the Passover, approaching from the north. He set up his headquarters on the Scopos hill north of Jerusalem. The northern side of the city was the best to attack from, as the city walls towered above the more or less steep slopes of the valley on all the other sides. The northern side was nevertheless particularly strongly fortified by no less than three walls, about which Josephus gives some information. One wall ran westwards from the particularly well fortified Temple precincts in the north-eastern corner, north of which the fort of Antonia extended, to the palace of Herod; it may have originated in the Hasmonaean period and been built after the residential part of the city had spread from the narrow eastern hill south of the Temple enclosure to the more spacious western hill. In front of it there extended a second wall which adjoined the fort Antonia and ran from there to a point in the first-mentioned northern wall which it is no longer possible to define exactly; it is not known for certain when it was built. Still farther to the north there followed the great wall which king Agrippa I had begun to build but had left unfinished; it enclosed the new, most northerly part of the city, and had been quickly fitted up for defence purposes in the emergency. In spite of his strong army Titus was therefore faced with a difficult task. It is true that, confronted with the approach of the Roman troops, during the Passover bloody conflicts had broken out in the city between the various parties. But when the Roman attack began, all the parties decided to combine in defence of the city. On the northern front the defence was led by Simon bar Giora, on the western sector and in the eastern sector near the Temple precincts and fort Antonia by John of Gischala. The city was defended with all possible gallantry and determination. The call for voluntary surrender was flatly rejected; and, to begin with, the Romans suffered some painful reverses in sudden sallies of the enemy. But then the real assault on the city began with all the technical resources which the Romans had at their disposal as a result of long experience in siege warfare. They were forced, nevertheless, to overcome one wall and occupy one part of the city at a time. They managed comparatively quickly to make a breach in the most northerly wall and to invade the most northerly part of the city; and soon afterwards, after one set-back, the second wall was taken and finally held. But then the struggle for the real city with fort Antonia and the Temple enclosure began in earnest and the aggressors now failed to maintain their progress. Both sides fought with great tenacity. In spite of starvation and epidemics the leaders in the city refused to contemplate surrender, and they ruled the inhabitants, whose numbers had been increased by the pilgrims to the Passover, who had just arrived when the attack began, with harshness and severity. Titus had the city surrounded with a solid siege-rampart (*circumvallatio*), making all connection between the city and the outside world impossible. He had deserters mutilated or crucified in sight of the city. He now began an assault on the strong fortress of Antonia, by having dykes built against it. After a few untoward incidents, he finally succeeded in penetrating and occupying Antonia in July of the year A.D. 70. He had the fortifications of the fort demolished and now stood on the very edge of the Temple enclosure. He intended to spare the Temple itself, where the daily sacrifice now had to be stopped; but an invitation to surrender it without a fight was rejected. Titus therefore had to begin an assault on the sacred buildings. When the first attempts failed owing to the strong fortifications, Titus set fire to the gates.

Contrary to his intention, this led to the immediate surroundings of the Temple catching fire. In the wild excitement that followed, the Roman soldiers invaded the holy places and wrought a frightful massacre. Titus himself quickly entered the famous place of worship and the holy of holies; then the building that Herod had erected went up in flames. This occurred in August of the year A.D. 70. With the destruction of its central sanctuary the religious community of Jerusalem lost its headquarters. The Romans set up their ensigns and sacrificed before them. The whole city was not yet conquered however. John of Gischala was able to escape with a band of Zealots from the Temple enclosure into the part of the city on the western hill, the so-called 'Upper City'. The last defenders took refuge in Herod's palace with its strong towers, and here Titus had to lay another regular siege. When the Romans had finally broken through the walls by the use of their special technique and had penetrated into this last bulwark, resistance came to an absolute end (September A.D. 70). The last defenders tried to escape or go into hiding. The victors murdered and plundered in the city which had withstood them so tenaciously. The city was thoroughly destroyed. Only a part of the city wall in the west by Herod's palace and the three strong towers of Herod's palace were left standing. The Roman garrison took up its quarters there. The lives of the leaders, John of Gischala and Simon bar Giora, who had fallen into the victors' hands as prisoners, were spared, and they were taken to Rome for the triumphal procession, together with a group of other specially chosen prisoners. In the following year Titus, as Imperator, displayed the greatness of his victory over Jerusalem to the Romans in a triumphal procession. The Titus arch in Rome still testifies to his pride in having conquered Jerusalem. From the illustrations of this arch[1] it is clear that he had fetched the precious implements for the holy service from the burning Temple to display them as the victor's spoils.

With the conquest of Jerusalem the issue was decided, but the insurrection had not been completely overcome. Three strongholds were still in the rebels' hands: the Herodian forts of Herodeion (jebel ferdēs), Masada (es-sebbe) and Machaerus (khirbet el-mkāwer.) Titus left them to be dealt with by the governor of Judaea, who had been left the 10th legion as garrison troops. During the struggle for Jerusalem the governor had been the commander of the 5th legion, S. Vettulenus Cerialis. After the fall of Jerusalem he was followed by Lucilius Bassus. He undertook the conquest of

[1] Cf. the illustrations, AOB,[2] No. 509.

the still existing strongholds. The Herodeion appears to have fallen into his hands without any fighting worth mentioning. He had to lay siege for a time to the fort of Machaerus east of the Dead Sea in the southern part of Peraea; in the end the defenders surrendered when assured that they would be allowed to make the free withdrawal, which was in fact granted to them. There remained Masada. This lofty fort built on a rock had been occupied at the very beginning of the rebellion in A.D. 66 by a group of Zealots under the leadership of a Galilean named Eleasar, who from there made marauding expeditions in the surrounding countryside. Masada was the most difficult fort to overcome. Lucilius Bassus, who probably died in the year A.D. 72, failed to occupy it as he had planned to do. The task devolved on his successor in the governorship, L. Flavius Silva, who had to employ all the resources of Roman skill in siege warfare to overcome the precipitous stronghold. He surrounded it with a complete *circumvallatio*. He then had a gigantic dam built to enable the battering-engines to be brought to the circular wall high up on the rock. The remains of these products of the Roman art of siege warfare have been preserved in very good condition to the present day in the uninhabited district of Masada on the southern shore of the Dead Sea. The stone wall of the *circumvallatio* can still be followed almost continuously, and the enclosures and stone foundations of the internal structures of the eight Roman camps around the *circumvallatio* are still in existence over a wide area, two big camps for every half legion and six small camps for various auxiliary troops; and the astonishing construction of the great dam can still be clearly discerned[1]. The planning of these installations needed a considerable time. Silva seems to have begun the attack on Masada in the summer of A.D. 72; but it was only in the spring of A.D. 73 that it was possible to shift the battering-engines to the wall with the aid of the dam. Meanwhile, the defenders had had time to erect a second wall on the site of the dam behind the original wall; and when the original wall had yielded to the blows of the battering-ram, the second wall was able to resist. The besiegers then succeeded in setting fire to it. The attack on the fort was to follow the next day. When the defenders realised from the sight of their burning wall that they were lost, they all killed one another in Herod's palace in the fort, after setting fire to the palace. Only two

[1] All these remains have been accurately recorded by A. Schulten, *Masada, die Burg des Herodes und die römischen Lager* (ZDPV, 56 [1933], pp. 1-185 with Plates 1-14 and Plans I-XXVIII).

women with five small children had hidden themselves and survived this gruesome tragedy. When the Roman soldiers penetrated the fort the next day they met with no resistance but only a mass of corpses in the ruins of the once proud palace of King Herod. That was the end of a revolt against Roman suzerainty which had been carried on for many years.

Vespasianus had already reorganised things in the country. Nero had transferred the procuratorial province of Judaea to him and Vespasianus now had it administered as an Imperial province under the official name of Judaea, which was retained. As before, the procurators resided in Caesarea and were simultaneously commanders (legates) of the Legio X Fretensis, which stayed in the land as a garrison and was stationed among the ruins of Jerusalem and in its surroundings. Remnants of the old population lived alongside the Roman soldiers in the shattered city. In time new inhabitants will have joined them, including, presumably, Jewish Christian groups. In place of the old Schechem a Roman colony with the Imperial name of Flavia Neapolis (the modern nāblus) was established which had a predominantly pagan population. In Emmaus (ʻamwās) Vespasianus settled 800 veterans with landed property. The members of the religious community of Jerusalem now had to pay the previous Temple tax to the *fiscus Judaicus* for the benefit of the Jupiter Capitolinus.

For the rest, there was no substantial official interference in the internal affairs of the religious community of Jerusalem. It continued to enjoy the protection of a *religio licita* in the Roman Empire. What had taken place, however, was in fact of ultimate and decisive significance. The central sanctuary had been destroyed and the possibility of rebuilding it was out of the question. The holy place had been desecrated, and no sacrificial rite could take place there any more. The priestly office could no longer be exercised. Even in the motherland it was impossible to conduct public worship and cultivate the traditions of the past except on the limited scale in which it had still been possible in the Diaspora. All the same, this much was still possible; for a long time now certain forms of synagogical worship and observance of the law had been developed in the Diaspora, and also in the motherland, apart from and independently of the central sanctuary which it was possible to preserve, even after the loss of the Temple in Jerusalem. For a long time there had been a certain antithesis between the legalistic piety of the Pharisees and the religion of Sadducee priesthood which was bound up with the sanctuary. Leadership now devolved on the Pharisees and after the great catastrophe they gathered the remnants of the religious community of Jerusalem around the Law in the motherland as well. The city of Jamnia (the modern yebna) on the coastal plain south of yāfa took the place of Jerusalem as a meeting-place. A new supreme council was formed there. The former Sanhedrim in Jerusalem, in which the priestly aristocracy and, later on, leading Pharisees had been represented, had still given something of a lead in political affairs. That was ended now. The supreme council in Jamnia consisted of 72 'Elders', who were Pharisean scribes. Its task was the authoritative interpretation and application of the Law. It also acted as a court of law and made decisions in internal matters and probably passed sentence in criminal cases. The Roman power apparently left this court of law alone; and the court will have taken care not to encroach on the judicial powers of the Roman officials. The reputation of this supreme council grew rapidly and its decisions were also accepted in the Diaspora. Its chairman bore the title of 'ruler'[1], which had come down from the Old Testament, especially from the programme for the future in the Book Ezekiel (Ezek. xl-xlviii). He soon enjoyed great prestige. Thus began the learned Rabbinical tradition which came to be represented in the course of time by a number of famous and influential men. The first name is that of Jochanan ben Sakkai; after the catastrophe in Jerusalem he had a decisive influence on the new development. He was soon followed by other celebrated rabbis, especially Gamiliel II.

After the cessation of the cultus in Jerusalem, the traditional holy scripture became the exclusive foundation of worship even more than previously. The rabbis devoted their main work to it. The synagogical canon was now established definitively in its traditional three parts, everything that was not considered genuine and authoritative being rejected. Special care was devoted to the meticulous conservation and study of the established text of the canonic scriptures. For the Greek-speaking Diaspora new Greek translations were made to replace the older Greek translation of the Septuagint, which the Christians in the Greek-Roman world used as their holy book, and which did not accord either in its extent or its text with the strict requirements of the rabbis. These new translations sometimes followed the authoritative Hebrew canon slavishly. The rabbis' exegetical work, which was based on tradition and also on new decisions, was recorded in new, great collections.

[1] Hebrew נשיא.

There is no need to do more than hint at all this here, since it no longer forms part of the history of Israel. These happenings constituted a new manifestation of Judaism, which was no doubt a continuation of developments that had already begun long since in the Diaspora, but which acquired a special and permanent form of its own in the new situation. The religious community of Jerusalem had ceased to exist. It had originated as the form in which Israel continued to live after the loss of political independence. In the first instance it had united those parts of the Israelite tribes that had remained behind in the homeland. Scattered groups had existed on the periphery which gave rise in time to the increasingly important Diaspora. But the old Israel in Palestine had continued to form the real heart of this religious community. This nucleus was, it is true, undermined more and more intensely. But Israel still existed and the city of David had been its centre. Anyone who had wantonly violated the sanctuary had been resisted throughout the territory of the ancient Israelite tribes. Antiochus IV Epiphanes had learnt that to his cost; and the Hasmonaean monarchy, that had evolved from opposition to Antiochus, had been able to make at least an attempt, albeit in an unsatisfactory manner and without permanent success, to lead Israel to political independence after the model of the period of the Kings. Even in the insurrection of A.D. 66–70, though in a tremendously distorted form, this same Israel had once again appeared, fighting for its sanctuary after it had been violated by the Roman procurator. Jerusalem was now the garrison of a Roman legion; and there was no further point in taking up arms for it. A centre in the old sense no longer existed. Jamnia with its supreme council could not really take the place of Jerusalem. The supreme council might just as well have met anywhere else. Its authority was not tied to a particular place, but only to the weight of the personalities, who as rabbis made the necessary decisions. Thus the difference between the motherland and the Diaspora, which had hitherto turned on Jerusalem, fell to the ground. To all intents and purposes life in Palestine had already been lived to a large extent 'in dispersal', and this was all the more so after the terrible losses of life that occurred in the years A.D. 66–70 (73). Even Jerusalem had now ceased to be the vital symbol of the 'homeland'. The Diaspora was everywhere, and even in the motherland life could only be lived as it had been lived hitherto in the Diaspora. Israel thereby ceased to exist and the history of Israel came to an end.

All the same, it was some time before all those involved came to realise this. It is not surprising that the hope for a 'restoration of Israel' remained alive. Had not the situation after the catastrophe of 587 B.C. been similar? And had not the Temple been rebuilt, and had not the religious community of Jerusalem reassembled round it? Was it not permissible to hope that this might happen again? Did not the Old Testament contain promises of God's final and glorious intervention, which would bring the power of this world to an end? There is no doubt that at the time the prophecies were interpreted in the sense of just such a restoration of the historical Israel. Though decimated and dispersed, there were still enough descendants of members of the former religious community of Jerusalem to form the basis of a restoration. A sequel did in fact take place which was concerned with a restoration of this kind; and this sequel therefore forms an appendix to the history of Israel, which had really already come to an end[1].

There are only a few details available about the events which took place after the year A.D. 73, because Josephus's account, which is the main source up to that year, stops at that point. The Roman emperors concerned themselves at various times with the Judaism which had already become a notable factor in their Empire. In general the Flavians were not amicably disposed to Judaism, which is not surprising in view of the great insurrection in Judaea which had cost so many Roman lives. We have no definite information, however, about the details. Presumably the Emperor Trajan (A.D. 98–117) also made various moves against Judaism; at any rate, great Jewish insurrections broke out under him, above all in the Diaspora[2]. When, towards the end of his reign in A.D. 115, he had set out for the east to wage war against the Parthians in Mesopotamia, the Jews in Cyrene and Egypt, in Cyprus and even behind the front in Mesopotamia rebelled against him. Especially in Cyprus the Jews wrought cruel havoc for a time among the heathen population, and a great deal of blood was shed in Cyprus too. Trajan overcame these risings by the use of brute force. In this connection the most interesting question is whether there were not simultaneous disturbances in Palestine which might be regarded as a prelude to what happened soon afterwards under Hadrian. This possibility is suggested by the fact that Trajan appointed his

[1] On the following cf. H. Bietenhard, *Die Freiheitskriege der Juden unter den Kaisern Trajan und Hadrian und der messianische Tempelbau* (Judaica, 4 [1948], pp. 57-77, 81-108, 161-185).

[2] All that we know about this is the little contained in Cassius Dio (LXVIII, 32) and, later, Eusebius (*Hist. eccl.* IV, 2), apart from the scattered allusions in the Rabbinistic literature.

general, Lusius Quietus, a Mauretanian cavalry leader, governor of Judaea as soon as he had ruthlessly suppressed the Jewish rebels in Mesopotamia, perhaps in order to restore order in Judaea too. But we have no definite information on this point[1].

A last great rising took place under Hadrian (A.D. 117—138). From all that can be ascertained, this was an episode on a scale comparable to that of the events of A.D. 66–70. But whereas Josephus has left a detailed account of the latter, all that we have about the rising under Hadrian are the rather laconic statements in Cassius Dio (LXIX, 12-14) and Eusebius (*Hist. eccl.* LV, 6), and a few other sporadic details. The sources even differ about the cause of this tremendous insurrection, which spread very widely and went on for several years, so we cannot be certain why it broke out[2]. Cassius Dio says that the foundation of the Roman city of Aelia Capitolina on the site of the ruins of Jerusalem, and the erection of a shrine of Jupiter on the site of the former Temple, made the Jews, who now saw heathen life and even heathen worship arising on the site that was still holy to them, so intensely furious that they took up arms. According to Cassius Dio, the foundation of Aelia Capitolina was connected with the journey to the Orient which the Emperor Hadrian set out on in the year A.D. 129. Hadrian was first of all in Syria and the province of Arabia, which had been reorganised under Trajan in the year A.D. 106; he then went to Egypt for the winter of 130–131 and came back to Syria in the year 131. So long as the Emperor was in their own country or in its vicinity the Jews had kept their peace and only made preparations; but then the storm had broken. A statement made by Spartianus (*Hadr.* 14), however, implies that the Jews had become rebellious because of a prohibition of circumcision issued by the emperor. This may be connected with the fact that Hadrian did renew and intensify a prohibition of castration already issued by Domitian, and that he evidently regarded circumcision the same as castration, which may be inferred from the fact that a decree of the Emperor Antoninus Pius (A.D. 138–161) which allowed the Jews to practise circumcision again, implies that Jewish circumcision was to be excepted from the general prohibition of castration which was still in force[3]. The problem is how to

[1] On the Rabbinistic allusions to a 'Quietus war' which may well have taken place in Palestine, cf. E. Schürer, *Geschichte des jüdischen Volkes*, I (4, 3 1901), pp. 667 f.; H. Bietenhard, *loc. cit.* pp. 69 ff.

[2] Cf. the detailed discussions in H. Bietenhard, *loc. cit.* pp. 85 ff., and also F.-M. Abel, *Histoire de la Palestine*, II (1952), pp. 83 ff.

[3] The text of this decree is given in Schürer, *loc. cit.* p. 677, note 80.

assess these differing accounts. Some scholars have taken the view that they cannot both be right, since the measures taken by the emperor can only be understood as arising from the struggle against the rebellious Jews, or as a punishment for their revolt[1]. In that case, the real cause of the revolt, in which the Jews' political-national expectations were to be realised once again, must remain unknown. The prohibition of circumcision is difficult to understand as a special measure against the Jews, particularly as it was merely considered a special case of castration, since circumcision was practised by many other peoples in the Rome-dominated Orient. It is likely, therefore, that the prohibition was a general one, but that it met with particularly stubborn resistance from the Jews, because they had long attached special importance to it as an act of acknowledgement of the ancestral traditions. Unfortunately it is quite unknown when this prohibition of castration and circumcision was issued; and it is therefore uncertain whether it played a part in the beginnings of the Jewish insurrection. On the other hand, it is not unlikely that the plan for establishing a Roman-pagan city with a shrine of Jupiter on the site of the old Jerusalem originated in the period immediately preceding the rebellion. It fits in very intelligibly, as Cassius Dio makes plain, with the emperor's oriental journey in the years A.D. 130–131, since Hadria gave instructions on other journeys for the establishment of many new cities and monumental buildings. There is also evidence to this effect in the Orient. We do not know whether Hadrian visited Jerusalem himself. In the spring of A.D. 130 he was, at all events, in the city of Gerasa (the modern jerash) in the land east of the Jordan[2]; and it is not unlikely that he took the opportunity of inspecting the garrison of the Legio X Fretensis. But even if that was not the case, it is easy to imagine that his attention was drawn to the city of Jerusalem, with its famous past, and that he then gave orders for the ruined site of Jerusalem to be rebuilt as a Roman city. And whatever may be the truth about the prohibition of circumcision, it is probable that this intention to establish a new city on the site of Jerusalem, even if nothing was done to realise it at first, drove the still unsettled, and still expectant Jews, to a desperate use of force. Furthermore, according to

[1] Thus A. Schlatter, *Geschichte Israels von Alexander dem Grossen bis Hadrian* (³ 1925), pp. 373 f.

[2] Cf. the dedicatory inscription of the triumphal arch in Gerasa erected on the occasion of the Emperor's visit, dated the 192nd year of the Pompean era of the city, which was found in 1934, and is reproduced in W. F. Stinespring, BASOR, 56 (1934), pp. 15 f.

Cassius Dio's credible report, the Jews in the Diaspora took a lively interest in what was happening in Palestine; they did all they could to support the rising in Palestine, and partly in secret and partly in the open they also rebelled against the Roman authorities; indeed the movement spread to other dissatisfied elements in the Roman Empire too.

It is impossible to trace the course of events in detail. A man named Simeon became the leader of the rising. According to Christian writers, he was given the honorary name of 'Bar-Kochba', 'son of the stars'; the famous scribe Rabbi Akiba is said, according to Rabbinical sources, to have suggested this name for Simeon as a Messianic description based on Num. xxiv, 17, and therefore to have conceived its bearer as the embodiment of the Messianic hope. Rabbinical sources give the name in the form Bar-Koziba, which was interpreted, after the failure of the enterprise, as meaning 'son of lies'. Probably Ben-Kosba'[1] was originally a term denoting descent which had its meaning changed and reinterpreted. The real revolt will have broken out in the year A.D. 132 after the emperor's return from the Orient. As the Romans failed at first to give the event the necessary attention, to begin with the rebels were able to attain their goal. 'Israel', with Simeon at its head, achieved its independence; Jerusalem was 'liberated' and Simeon ruled the country no doubt from Jerusalem. Evidence for this is provided by the so-called 'Insurrection Coins'[2]. Special coins were minted with Hebrew inscriptions. The years were re-numbered on these coins on the assumption that a new era had begun. Coins with the 'year 1' and the 'year 2' have survived. To judge from this, the rebels did, in fact, rule for a considerable time. These coins bear the inscription 'Simeon, the Prince of Israel'. The coins also celebrate the 'liberation of Israel'; the new era is dated from the 'liberation of Israel'. There are also coins

[1] A sensational discovery made very recently appears to throw light on the question of the name. In the winter of 1951–52 the fragments of numerous documents were found near the Dead Sea about 25 km. south-east of Jerusalem in a very inaccessible cave on the wādi mrabbaʿāt. They include a proclamation and two letters from a 'Simeon ben Koseba', whom one is greatly tempted to identify with the leader of the Jewish insurrection under Hadrian, particularly as the cave yielded other discoveries from the same period (*e.g.* so-called insurrection coins). In this case we should have not only original documents in the hand of this 'Messianic' leader but also evidence of the authentic form of his name; his name would then be 'Simeon ben Kos(e)ba (with ס), and if this is the case the later Rabbinistic 'Bar Koziba' (with ז) was a deliberate distortion of the name ('son of lies'). On the discovery, cf. the note by L. Rost, ThLZ, 77, (1952), coll. 317 ff., and the preliminary report by G. L. Harding, *Palestine Exploration Quarterly*, 84 (1952), pp. 105-109. A facsimile reproduction of one of the two letters of Simeon will be found in RB, 60 (1953), Pl. xiv and *Biblica*, 34 (1953), opposite p. 420.

[2] Cf. A. Reifenberg, *Ancient Jewish Coins* (² 1947), pp. 33 ff., Pll. xii-xv.

bearing the name of the city of Jerusalem or which refer to the 'liberation of Jerusalem'. It is unfortunate that we have no more exact knowledge about what took place in Jerusalem at this time. No doubt the cultus was revived. There are coins from the year 1 of the new era which bear the inscription 'the priest Eleasar'[1]. Apparently, therefore, the priesthood resumed its functions; and that can only mean that sacrifices were begun again. One would like to suppose that a beginning was made with the rebuilding of the Temple but there are no definite records on this point. Anyway, an amazing revival took place and it is easy to imagine that for a time enthusiasm and hope were intense. It seemed that 'Israel' was to rise again as a religious community and also as an independent people.

Once again, however, whilst the revolt was successful to begin with, it was crushed in the end by the superiority of the Roman forces. When the revolt began, Tineius Rufus was the Roman governor of Judaea. He did not overcome the rising. The rebels avoided an open encounter with Roman troops. They concentrated their forces on many strongholds and in inaccessible areas and waged a constant guerrilla warfare which wore the enemy down. Even when the governor of the neighbouring province of Syria, Publicius Marcellus, was ordered to Judaea to help suppress the revolt, the Romans still did not obtain a decisive victory. How unsuccessful the Romans' efforts were to begin with is shown above all by the fact that the rebels were able to remain in power for a considerable time, not only in remote recesses, but even in Jerusalem. In the end, Hadrian commissioned one of his most efficient generals, Julius Severus, who had already proved his worth in Britannia and was governor of Britannia at the time, to lead the war against the Jews; and with the help of an unusually big levy of Roman legions and auxiliary troops he succeeded in suppressing the revolt. Bearing in mind the desperate courage of the rebels, he did not proceed to open battles but chose, as Cassius Dio records, the more protracted but less costly method of starving them into surrender, *i.e.* he had to encircle innumerable bases and hiding-places until they were ready to surrender. There is no specific record of the fact, but Jerusalem probably fell in the same way. It was therefore a slow and agonising death in which the newly revived 'Israel' perished. The last act of the tragedy was again the

[1] The relationship of this priest with his own coins to the 'prince Simeon' is not very clear. As no priest coins from the 2nd year have come to light so far, it may be assumed that internal tensions and disputes were finally resolved in favour of the 'prince'.

struggle for a fortified position, in which the 'prince' Simeon was offering ultimately hopeless resistance with the surviving remnants of the rebel forces. High above the southern border of the valley through which the railway now runs from Jaffa to Jerusalem, there lies a dominating rounded hill-top called khirbet el-yehūd ('ruin of the Jews'), about ten kilometres west of Jerusalem near the present-day village of bittīr. In ancient times this hill-top was the site of Beth-Ter[1], the name of which has survived in that of the present village. Simeon entrenched himself here with his few surviving followers, probably after escaping from Jerusalem when it was occupied by the Romans[2]; and here he and his followers put up a last stubborn fight. Julius Severus was forced to lay a regular siege to the place. The surviving remains of the Roman *circumvallatio* which can still be seen on the site provide tangible evidence of this final struggle[3]. In the end the rebels were defeated, either by hunger and thirst—the only spring in the neighbourhood of the present village of bittīr had been taken by the besiegers—or by the ultimately successful use of the normal methods of assault. Here too Julius Severus had had to use a powerful force. An inscription found in the village of bittīr which will derive from the time of the siege refers to detachments of the Legio V Macedonia and the Legio XI Claudia which were employed at the time. Simeon Bar-Kochba lost his life in the struggle, but we are not told exactly how this happened. This was the end of the insurrection that had been intended to 'liberate Israel'. It probably took place in the year A.D. 135.

During the stubborn and protracted fighting the country had been terribly laid waste. Innumerable people had lost their lives. The captured rebels were sold in the market by Abraham's terebinth in Mamre or deported to Egypt. The number of these prisoners, men and women, old and young, was so great that they could only be sold for the lowest prices. The remnants of the old Israelite population which had already suffered innumerable losses in the rising of A.D. 66–70 were frightfully decimated once again. The land now became more than ever a Roman province. On the site of Jerusalem there arose the Roman colony with the official

[1] The Old Testament mentions it in Joshua xv, 59 LXX. It is doubtful whether it still existed on this site in the 2nd century A.D.

[2] Eusebius reports on this final struggle for Beth-Ter (*Hist. eccl.* IV, 6).

[3] On the archaeological discoveries cf. A. Alt, PJB, 23 (1927), pp. 10 ff. (with sketch map) and also A. Schulten, ZDPV, 56 (1933), pp. 180 ff. For the story of the struggle for Beth-Ter and the whole Bar-Kochba insurrection see H. Strathmann, PJB, 23 (1927), pp. 92 ff.

name of Colonia Aelia Capitolina, so called in honour of the victorious emperor. The plan for this new foundation, which had presumably given rise to the rebellion, was now executed magnificently as a token of the victory. The city was given a temple of Jupiter Capitolinus on the site of its holy place and an equestrian statue of the emperor Hadrian, and also a temple of Venus, roughly on the site of the later church of the Holy Sepulchre. As a Roman provincial city it was given a well-designed system of roads and adorned with the usual representative buildings[1]. The Jews were forbidden to enter it under pain of death; it was inhabited by a heathen populace. The Jews were therefore excluded from their own ancient holy city, which had for so long formed the centre of their ancestors' lives. But the province now probably exchanged its former name of Judaea for the new name of Palestine, which it bore henceforth and which derived from the older description of the maritime country as 'Philistine land'; it was not intended that the province's name should even suggest that it was still a 'land of the Jews'[2]. And so the descendants of the Israel of old had become strangers in their own former homeland as they had been in the Diaspora; and their holy city was barred from them. Thus ended the ghastly epilogue of Israel's history.

[1] On the archaeological remains of the Hadrian Aelia Capitolina cf. C. Watzinger, *Denkmäler Palästinas*, II (1935), pp. 79 ff. and also F.-M. Abel, *loc. cit.* pp. 98 ff.
[2] For the details see M. Noth, ZDPV, 62 (1939), pp. 125 ff.

BIBLIOGRAPHY

ABEL, F.-M., Géographie de la Palestine, I (1933), II (1938).
Histoire de la Palestine depuis la conquête d'Alexandre jusqu'à l'invasion arabe, I, II (1952).
ALBRIGHT, W. F., The Archaeology of Palestine and the Bible (³ 1935).
From the Stone Age to Christianity (² 1946).
Archaeology and the Religion of Israel (² 1946).
The Archaeology of Palestine (² 1951).
ALT, A., Israel und Ägypten (BWAT, 6) (1909).
Die Landnahme der Israeliten in Palästina (Reformationsprogramm der Universität Leipzig 1925).
Die Staatenbildung der Israeliten in Palästina (Reformationsprogramm der Universität Leipzig 1930).
Der Gott der Väter (BWANT, III, 12) (1929).
Die Ursprünge des israelitischen Rechts (Berichte üb. d. Verh. d. Sächs. Ak. d. Wiss. zu Leipzig, phil.-hist. Kl. 86, 1 [1934]).
Israels Gaue unter Salomo (BWAT, 13, pp. 1–19) (1913).
Judas Gaue unter Josia (PJB, 21 [1925], pp. 100–117).
Das System der Stammesgrenzen im Buche Josua (Sellin-Festschrift [1927], pp. 13–24).
Die Rolle Samarias bei der Entstehung des Judentums (Festschrift Otto Procksch [1934], pp. 5–28).
Kleine Schriften zur Geschichte des Volkes Israel, I, II (1953).
AMARNA-TAFELN : J. A. Knudtzon, Die El-Amarna-Tafeln (Vorderasiatische Bibliothek, 2) (1915).
AUERBACH, E., Wüste und Gelobtes Land, I (1932), II (1936).
BEGRICH, J., Die Chronologie der Könige von Israel und Juda (1929).
BERTHOLET, A., Kulturgeschichte Israels (1919).
BICKERMANN, E., Der Gott der Makkabäer. Untersuchungen über Sinn und Ursprung der makkabäischen Erhebung (1937).
BREASTED, J. H., Ancient Records of Egypt, I–V (1906/7).
CASPARI, W., Die Gottesgemeinde vom Sinai und das nachmalige Volk Israel (1922).
CHABAS, M., Mélanges Égyptologiennes, I (1862).
DALMAN, G., Arbeit und Sitte in Palästina, I–VII (1928–1942).
Aramäisch-neuhebräisches Handwörterbuch (³ 1938).
DUSSAUD, R., Les Origines cananéennes du sacrifice israélite (² 1941).
EIFSSELDT, O., Einleitung in das Alte Testament (1934).
Baal Zaphon, Zeus Kasios und der Durchzug der Israeliten durchs Meer (Beiträge zur Religionsgeschichte des Altertums, Heft 1) (1932).
EUSEBIUS, Historia ecclesiastica : Eusebius Kirchengeschichte hrsg. von E. Schwartz. Kleine Ausgabe (² 1914).
Das Onomastikon ed. E. Klostermann. Die griechischen christlichen Schriftsteller : Eusebius' Werke, III, 1 (1904).
FISHER, CL. S., The Excavation of Armageddon (The University of Chicago Oriental Institute Communications No. 4) (1929).

FORRER, E., Die Provinzeinteilung des Assyrischen Reiches (1921).
GADD, G. J., The Fall of Niniveh (1923).
GALLING, K., Biblisches Reallexikon (HAT, I, 1) (1937).
Textbuch zur Geschichte Israels (1950).
GLUECK, N., Explorations in Eastern Palestine I, II, III, IV (AASOR, XIV, XV, XVIII/XIX, XXV/XXVIII) (1934, 1935, 1939, 1951).
GRESSMANN, H., Altorientalische Texte und Bilder zum Alten Testament ([2] 1926/27).
GUTHE, H., Geschichte des Volkes Israel ([3] 1914).
Bibelatlas ([2] 1926).
Palästina (Monographien zur Erdkunde, 21) ([2] 1927).
GUY, P. L. O., New Light from Armageddon (The University of Chicago Oriental Institute Communications, No. 9) (1931).
INGHOLT, H., Rapport préliminaire sur sept campagnes de fouilles à Hama en Syrie 1932–1938 (1940).
JANSEN, H. L., Die Politik Antiochos' des IV (1943).
JEPSEN, A., Untersuchungen zum Bundesbuch (BWANT, III, 5) (1927).
JEREMIAS, J., Die Passahfeier der Samaritaner (BZAW, 59) (1932).
JIRKU, A., Geschichte des Volkes Israel (1931).
Die Wanderungen der Hebräer im 3. und 2. Jahrtausend v. Chr. (AO, 24, 2) (1924).
JOSEPHUS : Flavii Josephi opera recogn. B. Niese, I–VI (1888–1895).
JUNGE, P. J., Dareios I König der Perser (1944).
KAPELRUD, A. S., The Question of Authorship in the Ezra-Narrative (1944).
KITTEL, R., Geschichte des Volkes Israel, I ([5, 6] 1923), II ([6] 1925), III 1/2 (1927/1929).
KLOSTERMANN, A., Der Pentateuch (1893). Neue Folge (1907).
KOLBE, W., Beiträge zur syrischen und jüdischen Geschichte (BWANT, II, 10) (1926).
LIDZBARSKI, M., Altsemitische Texte I : Kanaanäische Inschriften (1907).
LODS, A., Israël des origines au milieu du VIIIe siècle (1930).
LUCKENBILL, D. D., Ancient Records of Assyria and Babylonia I/II (1927).
McCOWN, C. C., and J. C. WAMPLER, Tell en-Naṣbeh, I/II (1947).
MARI-TEXTE : Archives royales de Mari I–V (Musée du Louvre. Département des Antiquités Orientales. Textes cunéiformes XXII–XXVI (1946, 1941, 1948, 1951) et Archives royales de Mari publiées sous la direction de A. Parrot et G. Dossin, I–V (1950–1952).
MEYER, E., Die Entstehung des Judentums (1896).
Die Israeliten und ihre Nachbarstämme (1906).
Ursprung und Anfänge des Christentums, II (1921).
Geschichte des Altertums, II, 1 ([2] 1928), II, 2 ([2] 1931).
MÖHLENBRINK, K., Der Tempel Salomos (BWANT, IV, 7) (1932).
MORITZ, B., Der Sinaikult in heidnischer Zeit (Abh. d. Gött. Ges. d. Wiss., N.F. 16, 2) (1916).
MÜLLER, M. W., Die Palästinaliste Thutmosis' III (MVAG, XII, 1) (1907).
NOTH, M., Das System der zwölf Stämme Israels (BWANT, III, 10) (1930).
Das Buch Josua (HAT, I, 7) ([2] 1953).
Die Gesetze im Pentateuch (Schriften d. Königsb. Gel. Ges., geisteswiss. Kl. XVII, 2) (1940).

Die Welt des Alten Testaments ([2] 1953).
Überlieferungsgeschichtliche Studien, I (Schriften d. Königsb. Gel. Ges., geisteswiss. Kl. XVIII, 2) (1943).
Überlieferungsgeschichte des Pentateuch (1948).
OPPENHEIM, M. v., Die Beduinen, I/II/III (1939/43/52).
OTTLI, S., Geschichte Israels bis auf Alexander den Grossen (1905).
OTTO, W., Herodes (1913).
PETRIE, FL., Researches in Sinai (1906).
POSENER, G., Princes et pays d'Asie et de Nubie. Textes hiératiques sur des figurines d'envoûtement du Moyen Empire (1940).
PRITCHARD, J. B. (editor), Ancient Near Eastern Texts Relating to the Old Testament (1950).
RAD, G. v., Das formgeschichtliche Problem des Hexateuchs (BWANT, IV, 26) (1938).
RAS-SCHAMRA-TEXTE : C. H. Gordon, Ugaritic Literature. A comprehensive Translation of the poetic and prose Texts (1949).
REISNER-FISHER-LYON, Harvard Excavations at Samaria 1908–1910, I/II (1924).
ROBINSON, TH. H., and W. O. E. OESTERLEY, A History of Israel, I/II (1932).
ROST, L., Die Überlieferung von der Thronnachfolge Davids (BWANT, III, 6) (1926).
ROTHSTEIN, J. W., Juden und Samaritaner (BWAT, 3) (1908).
SCHAEDER, H. H., Esra der Schreiber (1930).
SCHLATTER, A., Geschichte Israels von Alexander dem Grossen bis Hadrian ([3] 1925).
SCHÜRER, E., Geschichte des jüdischen Volkes im Zeitalter Jesu Christi, I ([3, 4] 1901), II ([4] 1907), III ([4] 1909).
SELLIN, E., Geschichte des israelitisch-jüdischen Volkes, I (1924), II (1932).
SETHE, K., Die Ächtung feindlicher Fürsten, Völker und Dinge auf altägyptischen Tongefässscherben des Mittleren Reiches (Abh. d. Preuss. Ak. d. Wiss., phil.-hist. Kl. 1926, Nr. 5).
SIMONS, J., Jerusalem in the Old Testament. Researches and Theories (1952).
STURM, J., Der Hettiterkrieg Ramses' II (Beihefte zur Wiener Zeitschrift für die Kunde des Morgenlandes, 4) (1939).
THOMSEN, P., Die Palästina-Literatur. Eine internationale Bibliographie, I (1908), II (1911), III (1916), IV (1927), V (1938), VI (1954).
Palästina und seine Kultur in fünf Jahrtausenden (AO, 30) ([3] 1932).
TORCZYNER, H., Lachish I : The Lachish Letters (1938).
UNGNAD, Eponymen (Reallexikon der Assyriologie, II [1938], pp. 412–457).
WATZINGER, C., Denkmäler Palästinas. Eine Einführung in die Archäologie des Heiligen Landes, I (1933), II (1935).
WEBER, W., Das antike Judentum (Gesammelte Aufsätze zur Religionssoziologie, III) (1923).
WEISER, A., Einleitung in das Alte Testament ([2] 1949).
WELLHAUSEN, J., Geschichte Israels, I (1878).
WILLRICH, H., Urkundenfälschung in der hellenistisch-jüdischen Literatur (Forsch. z. Rel. u. Lit. d. A. und N. Test., N.F. 21) (1924).
WRIGHT, G. E., and F. V. FILSON, The Westminster Historical Atlas to the Bible (1945).

INDEX OF BIBLICAL REFERENCES

INDEX OF NAMES AND SUBJECTS